THE ROUTLEDGE COMPANION TO AESTHETICS

ROUTLEDGE COMPANIONS TO PHILOSOPHY

Routledge Companions to Philosophy offer thorough, high quality surveys of all the major topics in philosophy. Covering the key problems, themes and thinkers in each topic, all entries are specially commissioned for each volume and written by leading scholars in the field. Clear, accessible and carefully edited and organised, *Routledge Companions to Philosophy* are indispensable for anyone coming to a major topic in philosophy for the first time as well as the more advanced reader.

THE ROUTLEDGE COMPANION TO AESTHETICS

*Edited by Berys Gaut
and Dominic McIver Lopes*

London and New York

First published 2001
by Routledge
11 New Fetter Lane, London EC4P 4EE

Simultaneously published in the USA and Canada
by Routledge
29 West 35th Street, New York, NY 10001

Routledge is an imprint of the Taylor & Francis Group

Typeset in Sabon by
Curran Publishing Services Ltd, Norwich
Printed and bound in Great Britain by
TJ International Ltd, Padstow, Cornwall

British Library Cataloguing in Publication Data
A catalogue record for this book is available from the British Library.

Library of Congress Cataloging-in-Publication Data
A catalog record for this book has been requested.

ISBN 0-415-20737-1

CONTENTS

CONTENTS

CONTENTS

FIGURES

CONTRIBUTORS

Ruben Berrios is currently completing a doctorate on Nietzsche's aesthetics at the University of Southampton.

Allen Carlson is Professor of Philosophy at the University of Alberta, Edmonton, Canada. His research interests include aesthetics, environmental philosophy, and especially environmental and landscape aesthetics. In this area, he has published a number of articles and co-edited two collections of essays.

Noël Carroll is Monroe C. Beardsley Professor of Philosophy at the University of Wisconsin, USA. He is the author of several books and articles in aesthetics, including, most recently *A Philosophy of Mass Art* and an *Introduction to Aesthetics*.

Curtis L. Carter is Director of the Haggerty Museum of Art and Professor of Aesthetics at Marquette University, Wisconsin, USA. His publications include catalogues and essays on the visual arts, the museum and dance. He has contributed to the *Encyclopedia of Aesthetics* and the *International Encyclopedia of Dance*.

Ted Cohen is Professor of Philosophy at the University of Chicago, USA, and past president of the American Society for Aesthetics. He is a co-editor of *Essays in Kant's Aesthetics* and his most recent book is *Jokes: Philosophical Thoughts on Joking Matters*.

Donald W. Crawford is Professor of Philosophy at the University of California, Santa Barbara, USA. He is the author of *Kant's Aesthetic Theory* and numerous articles on Kant and aesthetics. He is also a past editor of the *Journal of Aesthetics and Art Criticism*.

Gregory Currie is Professor of Philosophy at the University of Nottingham, England. His most recent book is *Image and Mind: Philosophy, Film and Cognitive Science*. He is currently working on a book on the imagination.

David Davies is Associate Professor of Philosophy at McGill University, Canada. In addition to his work in aesthetics, he works in the philosophies of mind and language, and analytic metaphysics. He is completing a manuscript on the ontological status of the work of art.

Stephen Davies, a member of Department of Philosophy, University of Auckland, New Zealand is the author of *Definitions of Art* and *Musical Meaning and Expression*, and the editor of *Art and its Messages*. He has also published many articles on the philosophy of art.

Mark DeBellis is Associate Professor of Music at Columbia University, USA. His interests include the philosophy of music perception and cognition, the relationship of analysis to listening, and Verdi. He is the author of *Music and Conceptualization*.

Denis Dutton teaches philosophy of art at the University of Canterbury, New Zealand. He edits *Philosophy and Literature* and the *Arts and Letters Daily* website. He has lived in India and studied the sitar under Pandarung Parate, and has done fieldwork on wood carvers of the Sepik River region of New Guinea.

John A. Fisher is Professor of Philosophy at the University of Colorado at Boulder. He is the author of *Reflecting on Art* and articles on various aesthetic themes, including rock music, the ontology of recordings, technology's effect on appreciation and the aesthetics of nature.

Berys Gaut teaches in the Department of Moral Philosophy, University of St Andrews, Scotland. He is the author of many articles on aesthetics, film theory, moral philosophy, and Kant. He is currently working on a book on art and ethics.

Simon Glendinning is Lecturer in Philosophy at the University of Reading, England. He is the author of *On Being with Others: Heidegger – Derrida – Wittgenstein* and General Editor of *The Edinburgh Encyclopedia of Continental Philosophy*. He has written on Heidegger's conception of animal life and of the end of philosophy.

Alan Goldman is Professor of Philosophy at the University of Miami, USA. He is the author of five books, including *Aesthetic Value*, *Moral Knowledge* and *Empirical Knowledge*, and of articles on aesthetics, ethics and epistemology.

Gordon Graham is Regius Professor of Moral Philosophy at the University of Aberdeen, Scotland, and a Fellow of the Royal Society of Edinburgh. He has written extensively on topics in aesthetics and is the author of *Philosophy of the Arts*.

Garry L. Hagberg is Professor of Philosophy at Bard College, and the author of *Meaning and Interpretation: Wittgenstein, Henry James and Literary Knowledge*, *Art as Language: Wittgenstein, Meaning and Aesthetic Theory*, and numerous essays and reviews.

James R. Hamilton teaches philosophy at Kansas State University, USA. He has published essays on theater and other performing arts in the *Journal of Aesthetics and Art Criticism*, the *Journal of Dramatic Theory and Criticism*, and the *British Journal of Aesthetics*.

Michael Inwood is Fellow and Tutor in Philosophy at Trinity College, Oxford, England. In addition to several publications on Hegel, he is also the author of *Heidegger* and *A Heidegger Dictionary*.

Christopher Janaway is Reader in Philosophy at Birkbeck College, University of London, England. His publications include *Images of Excellence: Plato's Critique of the Arts, Self and World in Schopenhauer's Philosophy, Schopenhauer* and a number of articles on aesthetics.

Eileen John is Associate Professor of Philosophy at the University of Louisville, Kentucky, USA. Her research concerns learning experiences with fiction. Her work has appeared in the *Journal of Aesthetics and Art Criticism, Philosophy and Literature*, and the *Henry James Review*.

Matthew Kieran is Lecturer in the School of Philosophy of the University of Leeds, England. He has published articles on aesthetics, ethics and social philosophy as well as a monograph and an edited collection on media ethics.

Carolyn Korsmeyer is Professor of Philosophy at the State University of New York at Buffalo, USA. She has published several books on aesthetics, including *Making Sense of Taste: Food and Philosophy*.

Peter Lamarque is Ferens Professor of Philosophy at the University of Hull, England. He is co-author, with Stein Haugom Olsen, of *Truth, Fiction, and Literature: A Philosophical Perspective*, author of *Fictional Points of View* and editor of *Philosophy and Fiction: Essays in Literary Aesthetics*. He also edits the *British Journal of Aesthetics*.

Paisley Livingston is Senior Lecturer in Philosophy at the University of Aarhus, Denmark. He has published various papers and books in aesthetics, literary theory, and cinema studies, including *Literary Knowledge: Humanistic Inquiry and the Philosophy of Science* and *Literature and Rationality: Ideas of Agency in Theory and Fiction*.

Dominic McIver Lopes is Associate Professor of Philosophy at the University of

British Colombia, Canada. He is the author of *Understanding Pictures* and of articles on aesthetics and philosophy of mind. He is now working on a book entitled *Life Drawing: Pictures, Perception and Value.*

Colin Lyas is Senior Lecturer in Philosophy at the University of Lancaster, England. He has held the Cowling Professorship at Carleton College and the Visiting Research Professorship at the Bolton Institute.

Joseph Margolis is Laura E. Carnell Professor of Philosophy at Temple University, Philadelphia, USA. He has been president of the American Society for Aesthetics and honorary president of the International Association for Aesthetics. His most recent publication is *What After All is a Work of Art?*

Derek Matravers teaches philosophy at the Open University, UK. He is the author of *Art and Emotion* and of numerous articles on aesthetics. He is currently working on philosophy and the visual avant-garde.

Patrick Maynard, Professor of Philosophy at the University of Western Ontario, Canada, is the author of *The Engine of Visualization: Thinking Through Photography* and co-editor of *Aesthetics* in the Oxford Readings in Philosophy series.

Graham McFee is Professor of Philosophy at the University of Brighton, England. His principal interests are aesthetics, especially the aesthetics of dance, and the philosophy of Wittgenstein. He has extensive publications in both fields, including *Understanding Dance.*

Jennifer Anne McMahon teaches at the University of Canberra, Australia. She has published articles on aesthetics and perception (cognitive science). She is author of *Aesthetics and Cognition in Visual Beauty: Towards a Unified Theory of Beauty.*

Alex Neill is a Senior Lecturer in the Department of Philosophy at the University of Southampton. He writes mainly on issues at the intersection of philosophical aesthetics and the philosophy of mind.

David Novitz is Reader in Philosophy at the University of Canterbury, New Zealand. He is author of *Pictures and Their Use in Communication, Knowledge, Fiction, and Imagination* and *The Boundaries of Art*, as well as many articles in the philosophy of art.

Nickolas Pappas is Associate Professor of Philosophy at the City College of New York/CUNY and the CUNY Graduate Center, USA. He is the author of the *Routledge Guidebook to Plato and the Republic*, and articles on ancient and contemporary aesthetics.

Aaron Ridley is a Senior Lecturer in Philosophy and an Associate Director of the Centre for Post-Analytic Philosophy at the University of Southampton, England. His books include *Music, Value and the Passions* and *Nietzsche's Conscience: Six Character Studies from the Genealogy*.

Mark Rollins is Associate Professor in the Department of Philosophy and the Philosophy-Neuroscience-Psychology program, as well as Associate Dean of the University College, at Washington University, St Louis, USA. He is the author of *Mental Imagery: On the Limits of Cognitive Science* and *Minding the Brain: Perceptual Strategies and Mental Content* (forthcoming) and editor of *Danto and His Critics*.

Roger Seamon teaches English at the University of British Columbia, Canada. He is on the Editorial Board of the *Journal of Aesthetics and Art Criticism* and has published on narrative theory, photography, the theory of art, and the history of academic literary criticism.

James Shelley is Assistant Professor of Philosophy at Auburn University. He writes on aesthetics and epistemology, and is currently working on a book on Hume's theory of taste.

Richard Shusterman is Professor and Chair of Philosophy at Temple University. His books include *Analytic Aesthetics*, *The Object of Literary Criticism*, *T. S. Eliot and the Philosophy of Criticism*, *Sous l'interpretation*, *Practicing Philosophy*, and *Pragmatist Aesthetics*.

Murray Smith is Senior Lecturer and Chair of Film Studies at the University of Kent, England. He is author of *Engaging Characters: Fiction, Emotion, and the Cinema*, and co-editor of *Film Theory and Philosophy* and *Contemporary Hollywood Cinema*, as well as the author of numerous journal articles on film and aesthetics.

Nan Stalnaker has taught writing at Harvard University and philosophy at Connecticut College, USA. She is currently writing a book about the philosophical issues implicated in several of Manet's most puzzling paintings.

Robert Stecker is Professor of Philosophy at Central Michigan University, USA. He is the author of *Artworks: Definition, Meaning, Value* and many papers on aesthetics, the philosophy of mind, and the history of modern philosophy.

Robert Wicks is Senior Lecturer in Philosophy at the University of Auckland, New Zealand. He writes in the areas of aesthetics, German and French philosophy, and his main interest is in the existential and psychological dimensions of philosophical theories.

Edward Winters is Director of the Centre for Art and Critical Study and Senior Lecturer in Aesthetics in the Department of Architecture, University of Westminster, England. As well as writing in aesthetics, he is an art critic and a practising painter.

Sarah Worth is Assistant Professor of Philosophy at Furman University in Greenville, South Carolina, USA. Her publications focus on aesthetic theory, especially music aesthetics and fiction theory. She has published in the *British Journal of Aesthetics* and the *Journal of Aesthetic Education*.

James O. Young is Professor of Philosophy at the University of Victoria, British Colombia, Canada. He is the author of essays on philosophy of language and aesthetics as well as *Global Anti-Realism*. He is at work on another book, *The Epistemology of Art*.

PREFACE

Philosophical aesthetics today is a vibrant field. Twenty or thirty years ago it was not uncommon for philosophers to claim that there was nothing much of philosophical interest to be said about the arts. Non-philosophers interested in the arts used to complain that contemporary philosophers had indeed said nothing of interest to them. As the painter Barnett Newman quipped, "aesthetics is for artists like ornithology is for the birds." Even at the time, this unhappy convergence of views was badly grounded. Today it is entirely without justification. Philosophy has rediscovered aesthetics, and this volume bears the fruits of philosophers' new-found interest in art.

Partly this has arisen from philosophers' increased attention to the practice, history and criticism of the individual arts – including literature, music, painting, architecture and film – and from an awareness that philosophical problems are thrown up by the particularities of the individual art media. Understanding art as a whole depends on an appreciation of the arts individually and what makes each of them unique. Some philosophers have begun to write about individual novels, poems, symphonies and films with an attention to detail and a level of insight equaling that of literary critics, musicologists, art critics and film critics.

Renewed philosophical interest in aesthetics is also in part to be traced to the recognition that many topics of general philosophical importance – the nature of representation, imagination, emotion and expression, to name a few – cannot adequately be understood unless their roles in the arts and artistic appreciation are examined, for here they find some of their most interesting and complex applications. Also renewed interest in aesthetics partly derives from an increased pluralism within analytic philosophy itself, which has advanced outwards from its heartlands of the philosophy of language and science to conquer new areas, such as applied ethics, political philosophy, cognitive science and aesthetics.

The present volume is broadly within the tradition of analytic philosophy and shares that tradition's commitment to clarity of expression and precision of argument. It also shares, and aspires to advance, the increasing pluralism of the analytic approach, and it attends to thinkers outside the analytical tradition, showing what analytic aesthetics can learn from them.

Its purpose is to provide an introduction to many of the most important topics and thinkers in philosophical aesthetics. As such, it should prove its worth as a textbook for university courses in philosophy of art, and should also interest non-philosophers who want to learn what philosophers have to say about the arts. It also represents some of the best work being done in aesthetics today. Numbered among its authors are both distinguished senior scholars and also outstanding young researchers. We have asked them not just to provide a survey of the area, but also to communicate something of their own views. The results will be of interest not just to newcomers to aesthetics, but also to specialists in the area.

The volume is structured into four parts. The first is historical, covering many of the classic writers on aesthetics as well as some more recent and influential thinkers from within the analytic and continental traditions. Our criterion for inclusion within this section is that the body of work of the writer should be substantially complete. (A partial exception is the discussion of post-modernist theory.) Major figures who are still developing their views are discussed elsewhere in the volume, in the chapters dealing with the subjects on which they have written. The second part covers central concepts and theories within aesthetics, dealing with basic issues such as the definition of 'art,' the nature of the aesthetic, and the standards of correct interpretation. The third part covers more specific issues, such as art and knowledge and art and emotion, and also examines challenges to traditional aesthetics posed by feminism, environmental aesthetics and the role of popular art. The final part addresses the individual arts of music, painting, photography, film, literature, theater, dance, architecture and sculpture. The volume will thus work well as a companion to aesthetics courses in any of the ways in which they are standardly taught: historically, by focusing on theories of art and the aesthetic, by centering on issues in aesthetics, or by examining the individual arts.

While the *Companion* gives a wide-ranging and up-to-date overview of the field, it obviously cannot within the compass of a single volume cover everything of interest and importance in aesthetics. Each reader is likely to have his or her own view on what might usefully have been included, and we would probably agree with many of these suggestions, particularly within the historical section, where there is an overwhelming embarrassment of riches. Nevertheless, the reader should obtain from the volume a good sense of the sheer diversity, liveliness and interest of current aesthetics. Instead of short dictionary-style entries, we have asked our authors to produce chapters of around 5,000 words each: long enough to explore the debates about their topic in some detail, but short enough to be read at one sitting, and to allow for a wide range of articles within a relatively compact volume. Each chapter has cross-references to other chapters which are germane to the topic, a list of references to works discussed, and where the author thought it useful, suggestions for further reading. The reader will thus find plenty of scope for following up points of interest in any of the topics covered. The *Companion* might well be viewed as an invitation to aesthetics.

Finally, we should acknowledge the many debts which we have acquired in editing this volume. First, to our contributors, for their enthusiasm and for their ability to produce work of high quality within tight deadlines and word-limits. Second, to the many scholars we consulted in the course of planning the volume, including those who told us not to do it (we enjoy being stubborn). Third, to Tony Bruce and his team at Routledge, for their unstinting enthusiasm and support for the volume. Our final debt is perhaps less obvious, but no less important. This volume was jointly edited in Scotland and the United States, and written in the USA, Canada, the UK, Denmark, Australia and New Zealand, and almost all of this global communication was by means of the Internet. Although the *Companion* is entirely about art, it is in its own way also a testimony to the power of technology and to the existence of the world-wide community of scholars which that technology has made possible.

Berys Gaut
Dominic McIver Lopes

Part 1

HISTORY OF
AESTHETICS

1
PLATO

Christopher Janaway

Plato's writings about the arts play a foundation role in the history of aesthetics, not simply because they are the earliest substantial contribution to the subject. The close integration of Plato's philosophy of art with his metaphysics and ethics, his antagonism towards the arts, and the mastery of writing styles that makes him "of all philosophers . . . the most poetical" (Sidney 1973: 107) also contribute to his enduring influence. From a modern point of view it is striking that Plato refuses to grant autonomous value to what we call art. For him there is a metaphysical and ethical order to the world which it is philosophy's task to discover by means of rational thought, and the arts can have true worth only if they correctly represent this order or help in aligning us with it. These principles of evaluation are at their clearest in the *Republic* whose overall question is, What is justice? Plato constructs a picture of the ideally just individual and the ideally just city-state, and gives an account of the nature of knowledge and education, culminating in the proposal that the rulers of the ideal state would be philosophers, those uniquely in possession of methods for attaining knowledge of the eternally existing Forms that constitute absolute values in Plato's universe.

The arts in *Republic* 2 and 3

Plato first considers the role of the arts in education. The young, especially those who will be the Guardians responsible for the city's well-being, must receive an education that properly forms their characters. Since the young soul is impressionable and will be molded by any material that comes its way, the productive arts and crafts will be regulated so that they pursue

> what is fine and graceful in their work, so that our young people will live
> in a healthy place and be benefited on all sides, and so that something of
> those fine works will strike their eyes and ears like a breeze that brings

3

health from a good place, leading them unwittingly, from childhood on, to resemblance, friendship, and harmony with the beauty of reason.

(*Republic* 401c–d)

Much of Books 2 and 3 concerns the scenes and characters which poetry contains. Plato assumes that fictional tales and poetic representations will play a dominant role in education: a conventional assumption, as we see from remarks in the dialogue *Protagoras*:

they are given the works of good poets to read at their desks and have to learn them by heart, works that contain numerous exhortations, many passages describing in glowing terms good men of old, so that the child is inspired to imitate them and become like them.

(*Protagoras* 325–326a)

It is not sufficient, however, that the young read the works of 'good poets'. While Plato consistently praises Homer as a fine poet, in the *Republic* he proposes ruthless censorship of Homer's works. Gods and heroes must not be represented as cowardly, despairing, deceitful, ruled by their appetites, or committing crimes: hence the excision of many well-known scenes from the *Iliad* and *Odyssey*. A good fiction is one which (though false or invented) correctly represents reality and impresses a good character on its audience. Plato seems untroubled by the thought that an accurate representation of the way human beings behave in battle or in love could fail to impress the best character on its recipients. Is truthful representation or ethical effect the higher criterion? At one point Plato suggests it is the latter: some violent mythical tales are not true, and should not be told to the young even if they were (*Republic* 378a).

The other main topic for discussion is mimesis, which here should be taken as impersonation or dramatic characterization. There are two modes of poetic discourse: one where the poet "speaks in his own voice," the other (mimesis) where he "hides himself," "makes his language as like as possible to that of whatever person he has told us is about to speak," and – at the beginning of the *Iliad* – "tries . . . to make us think that the speaker is not Homer, but the priest, an old man" (393a–c). Hiding oneself behind a pretend character is implicitly deceitful and dubious, but Plato's objection to mimesis is more sophisticated. He claims that to enact a dramatic part by making oneself resemble some character causes one to become like such a person in real life. Given a prior argument that all members of the ideal community, and *a fortiori* its Guardians, should be specialists who exercise only one role, it follows that the city will produce better Guardians if it restricts the extent to which they indulge in dramatic enactment. Those whose dominant aim is the production of mimesis are ingenious and versatile individuals, but the ideal state will not tolerate them. The Guardians should use mimesis as little as possible, and be restricted to enacting the parts of noble, self-controlled and virtuous individuals, thus assimilating themselves to the kind of human being the state requires them to become.

The arts in *Republic* 10

Republic Book 10 contains Plato's most prominent criticisms of the arts. Mimesis is the chief topic, but now we must understand this term in a different sense, as image-making: making something that is not a real thing, but merely an image of a thing. Both poets and visual artists are practitioners of mimesis in this sense, but the aim of this passage is to justify the banishment of mimetic poetry from the ideal city. The grounds are that mimesis is far removed from truth, though easy to mistake for the work of someone with knowledge, and that mimetic poetry appeals to an inferior part of the soul and thereby helps to subvert the rule of intellect and reason. While promising cognitive gain, poetry delivers only psychological and ethical damage to individual and community.

Plato uses his theory of Forms to explain the nature of mimesis as such. Whereas an ordinary object, such as a bed, is an 'imitation' of the single and ultimately real Form of Bed, a painted picture of a bed is an 'imitation' merely of the way some bed would appear from a certain angle. The use of the theory of Forms here is in some respects anomalous. Plato has a god bring Forms into existence, though elsewhere they exist eternally and no one creates them. Earlier in the *Republic* it seemed that philosophers alone have knowledge of Forms; here the ordinary craftsman 'looks to the Form' for guidance in constructing a physical bed.

Plato disparages mimesis in the visual arts by comparing it with holding up a mirror in which the world mechanically reproduces itself. The point of the comparison is arguably that the painter makes no real thing, only an image. His product, when compared with the bed and the Form of Bed, is thus at two moves from reality. To make such an image requires no genuine knowledge: no knowledge of the real things of which one makes an image. By a slightly strained analogy, Plato argues that a poet makes only images and is distant from knowledge: "all poetic imitators, beginning with Homer, imitate images of virtue and all the other things they write about and have no grasp of the truth" (*Republic* 600e). They produce only images of human life, and to do so requires no knowledge of the truth about what is good and bad in life. There is moreover no evidence, Plato suggests, of any good poet's manifesting ethical or political competence.

Why does it matter that poetic image-making entails no genuine knowledge? Because there are people who hold the opposite view: "they say that if a good poet produces fine poetry, he must have knowledge of the things he writes about, or else he wouldn't be able to produce it at all," on which grounds they claim "poets know all crafts, all human affairs concerned with virtue and vice, and all about the gods as well" (*Republic* 598d-e). Plato aims to refute these claims. Fine poetry consists of image-making, and as such is compatible with the poet's ignorance of truths about what is real.

Plato also undertakes to show to which part of the human psyche mimetic poetry appeals. The higher part of the soul uses reasoning and considers what is for the overall good, but the images of mimetic poetry are gratifying to a distinct 'inferior' part, which is childish, unruly and emotional, and reacts in an unmeasured fashion to events in real life and in fiction. For example, when someone close to us dies, part of us considers what is for the best and desires restraint in feeling and outward behavior. At the same time another part tends towards indulgence in unbounded lamentation. There is a conflict of attitudes towards the same object, analogous to the phenomenon of visual illusion, where part of the mind calculates that a stick in water is straight, while another part persists in seeing it as bent. Poetry affects us emotionally below the level of rational desire and judgement. The kinds of event that provide the most successful content for mimetic poetry (and tragedy especially) involve extreme emotions and actions driven by emotion. So mimetic poetry naturally addresses and gratifies the inferior, lamenting part of us and fosters it at the expense of the rational and good-seeking part that should rule in a healthy soul.

Plato's 'most serious charge' against mimetic poetry also concerns its effects on the psyche. It is that "with a few rare exceptions it is able to corrupt even decent people" (*Republic* 605c). Even the individual who attains the Platonic ideal and is governed by the noble, rational, good-seeking part of the soul, is powerfully affected by the experience of

> one of the heroes sorrowing and making a long lamenting speech or singing and beating his breast . . . we enjoy it, give ourselves up to following it, sympathize with the hero, take his sufferings seriously, and praise as a good poet the one who affects us most in this way.
>
> (*Republic* 605c)

The distancing provided by the artistic context insidiously lulls us into a positive evaluation of responses which we should avoid in real life. We relax our guard and allow the rule of the rational part of ourselves to lapse:

> only a few are able to figure out that enjoyment of other people's sufferings is necessarily transferred to our own and that the pitying part, if it is nourished and strengthened on the sufferings of others, won't be easily held in check when we ourselves suffer.
>
> (*Republic* 606b)

The positive evaluation of our sympathetic feelings for the hero's sufferings rests on the fact that to see them brings us pleasure. So instead of regarding as valuable that which we judge to be best, we begin to value responses that happen to please us, and, Plato argues, this habit can corrode our attachment to the rational and the good in real life.

Plato makes many assumptions here, but perhaps most notable is one that has featured in recent debates about the psychological effects of television and films: that if we enjoy seeing the image of something enacted in a dramatic narrative, this causes in us an increased disposition to act or react similarly in real life. It is as if mimesis is transparent in a particular way: to enjoy or approve of a poetic image of X is not really different from enjoying or approving of X itself. Aristotle's remark in the *Poetics* that the enjoyment of mimesis is natural for human beings is the beginning of a reply to this assumption (Aristotle 1987: 34).

On the grounds that it falsely masquerades as knowledge and is detrimental to the human mind, Plato banishes poetry from his ideal city. We may wonder how much of poetry this affects. At the beginning of the discussion 'poetry that is mimetic' is to be excluded, but by the end it appears that all poetry is meant, and the intervening argument seems to tell us that all poetry is indeed mimetic, although Homer and the tragic poets (seen as a single tradition) provide the most focused target. Plato proposes to retain some poetry, namely "hymns to the gods and eulogies to good people" (*Republic* 607a). Given the earlier comments about beauty and grace, these works need not be dull and worthy, but clearly Plato prefers them because they will present a correct ethical view of the world and be a means to instill the right character in the citizens.

In his concluding remarks Plato mentions an "ancient quarrel between poetry and philosophy" (*Republic* 607b). Poetry (of the kind excluded) aims at pleasure and mimesis, but if it can satisfy philosophy by producing an argument that it is beneficial to the community and to human life, then it can reclaim its place. If philosophers hear no such a justification, they will use the argument of *Republic* Book 10 "like an incantation so as to preserve ourselves from slipping back into that childish passion for poetry" (ibid.: 608a). It is like keeping oneself away from a person with whom one is in love, but with whom an association is not beneficial. This image, and the accompanying invitation to poetry to defend itself, reveal Plato as less authoritarian than he often appears in the *Republic*. He recognizes the power of poetry over the human soul and intimates that he has full appreciation of its pleasures. It is not through insensitivity that Plato rejects pursuit of the pleasures of poetic image-making. It is because he has an argument that shows we should resist these pleasures unless poetry or its lovers perform on philosophy's home ground and present a good counter-argument.

Beauty

According to Iris Murdoch, "Plato wants to cut art off from beauty, because he regards beauty as too serious a matter to be commandeered by art" (Murdoch 1977: 17). This may be difficult for modern aestheticians to grasp, given widespread assumptions about their discipline (such as Hegel's view that its subject matter is 'artistic beauty' (Hegel 1993: 3)). Some commentators on Plato have thought, mistakenly, that a positive philosophy of art is implicit in Plato's inspirational passages on the love of beauty as an absolute value.

Plato's concept of beauty is arguably quite different from the modern aesthetic concept, whatever exactly that is. We translate Plato's word *kalon* as 'beautiful,' but a preferable translation in many contexts is 'fine.' Definitions and examples from the Platonic dialogue *Hippias Major* illuminate the broad application of *kalon*: a fine girl is fine, so is anything made of gold, so is living a rich and healthy life and giving your parents a decent burial. Here even the first two may not be cases of beauty in what we might call a purely aesthetic sense: desirability and exchange value play a part in their fineness. Another aspect of fineness is 'what is pleasing through hearing and sight': "men, when they're fine anyway – and everything decorative, pictures and sculptures – these all delight us when we see them, if they're fine. Fine sounds and music altogether, and speeches and storytelling have the same effect" (*Hippias Major* 298a). This looks like a rudimentary definition of the aesthetically pleasing. But it neither embraces the whole range of *kalon* nor lends the arts a value that rescues them from the critique of the *Republic*.

Beauty finds its most significant treatment in the dialogue *Symposium*, in the speech by Socrates, which he presents as the teaching of the wise woman, Diotima. Despite this double-nesting of narrators, the speech is usually seen as revealing Plato's own philosophical views. The whole dialogue concerns the nature of love. In Socrates' account beauty is love's highest object. To grasp this, we must make a Platonic metaphysical distinction between on the one hand the beauty of things and properties as they occur in the sensible world, and on the other, The Beautiful itself – as Plato calls the eternal, unchanging and divine Form of Beauty, accessible not to the senses, but only to the intellect (*Symposium* 211d). Instances of beauty in the sensible world exhibit variability or relativity: something is beautiful at one time, not at another; in one respect or relation, not in another; to one observer, not to another. The Beautiful itself lacks all such variability, it "always is and neither comes to be nor passes away, neither waxes nor wanes" (ibid.: 211a). This passage may be taken to imply that the Form of Beauty is itself beautiful. That reading seems to make best sense of Beauty's being an object of love on a continuum with other such objects, though whether Plato thinks of Beauty as 'being beautiful' in the same way as a boy or girl is beautiful is a matter of debate.

Elsewhere Plato describes non-philosophers as unable to grasp that there is a single unvarying Form of Beauty. The sophist Hippias equates beauty with a beautiful girl and then with the property of being made of gold. But a girl is beautiful in one relation (to other girls), not in another (to goddesses), and being made of gold makes some things beautiful, but not others: the eyes of a statue, for instance, would be repulsive if fashioned from gold. So it looks to Plato as if no object or property accessible to the senses can be what constitutes beauty as such. A similar distinction occurs in the *Republic*, where Plato disparages "lovers of sights and sounds" (*Republic* 475d-476b) who eagerly attend arts festivals, but think there are "many beautifuls" rather than the single Form of The Beautiful that the philosopher recognizes.

In the *Symposium* the ideal lover is portrayed as ascending through a hierarchy of love-objects – first the beautiful body of a particular human beloved, then all beautiful bodies equally, then the beauty of souls, then that of laws, customs, and ideas – and ending as a lover of wisdom or philosopher. At the culmination of his progress the philosophical lover will "catch sight of something wonderfully beautiful in nature . . . the reason for all his earlier labors" (*Symposium* 210e), namely the Form of Beauty itself. ('Fineness' here will hardly convey the requisite fervor.) All love desires some kind of offspring. The highest form of love catches hold of a superior object and produces a superior offspring:

> if someone got to see the Beautiful, absolute, pure, unmixed, not polluted by human flesh or colors or any other great nonsense of mortality . . . only then will it become possible for him to give birth not to images of virtue (because he's in touch with no images), but to true virtue (because he is in touch with the true beauty).
>
> (*Symposium* 211e–212a)

If we recall that in the *Republic* Plato applies the phrase 'images of virtue' to poets, a contrast suggests itself. While the poet makes only images, and understands only images, the philosopher, who strives for and encounters the eternal unchanging Beauty, can bring genuine goods into the world because he understands what virtue is. This contrast can be hard to accept for the modern reader, because Plato's own literary genius is fully manifest in this extraordinary and moving passage, and because we imagine that he must find a place for something like art in his hierarchy of beauties, or at least think that art enables its author to produce something immortal and universal. "Strangely enough," one noted historian of aesthetics has written, "Diotima and Socrates do not assign a role to the arts in this process of reawakening to Beauty, though it takes but a short step to do so" (Beardsley 1966: 41). But this is an anachronistic reaction. Plato's next step comprises the arguments of the *Republic*, probably written shortly afterwards.

Inspiration

In the short early dialogue *Ion* Plato has Socrates say that poets are divinely inspired to produce their fine works. The character Ion is a rhapsode, a professional reciter of poetry and a critic or expert on Homer. Socrates undertakes a demolition of Ion's claim that he succeeds as performer and critic because he has knowledge. An important concept in this dialogue is *technê*. The word has been translated as 'craft', 'skill', or 'expert knowledge.' Plato regards doctors, generals, and mathematicians as possessing a *technê*, meaning that they are knowledgeable about a specific subject matter, can transmit their knowledge in teaching, understand general principles or rules that apply across all instances within their field, and can give a rational account of why their practice succeeds. A further criterion of *technê*, offered in the dialogue *Gorgias*, is that it aims at the good and is based in knowledge of the good (*Gorgias* 463a–465a).

An antique translation for *technê* is 'art,' but examination of this concept will not yield Plato's 'philosophy of art,' chiefly because practices we regard as 'artistic' tend to be denied the status of *technê*. In the *Gorgias* persuasive rhetoric, tragedy, and musical performances by choruses or instrumentalists all fail to be cases of *technê*, because their aim is not to make their audiences better, but to gratify them. Plato argues that there are no principles concerning what pleases a mass audience, and that it is by guesswork that these practices succeed, rather than by rational principle or knowledge. The *Ion* takes a similar line: the rhapsode discerns what is fine and pleasing in Homer's poetry, but in so doing he works to no generalizable principles. There is no subject matter on which he is an expert solely by virtue of being a rhapsode and being familiar with Homer's fine work. Ion's preposterous claim to be an expert on 'everything,' because Homer writes finely of everything, prefigures the superficially more plausible claim, rejected in the *Republic*, about the knowledge of the poet himself.

How is it then that Ion succeeds in discerning the fineness in Homer's poetry and performing it so brilliantly as to delight his audiences? Socrates' answer is itself poetic, or perhaps mock-poetic:

> the poets tell us that they gather songs at honey-flowing springs, from glades and gardens of the Muses, and that they bear songs to us as bees carry honey, flying like bees. And what they say is true. For a poet is an airy thing, winged and holy, and he is not able to make poetry until he becomes inspired and goes out of his mind and his intellect is no longer with him.
>
> (*Ion* 534a–b)

The power of poetry is divine: the Muse attracts the poet, who is then a mouthpiece through which the divine speaks. The performer succumbs to the same attraction and transmits it to the audience. At no stage does rational thought or expert competence account for the success of the proceedings. There seems to be a mixed message here: Ion is admirable and even (if ironically) 'divine.' But he deserves no credit for his artistic success, because he is 'out of his mind.' Not only can he give no rational account of why he succeeds; he is also, Plato assumes, irrational in responding emotionally to the dramatic scene he performs, despite that scene's unreality.

The *Ion* may surprise us because although it locates features regarded in the modern era as characterizing the 'artistic,' it rates them disparagingly, or at best equivocally. The later work *Phaedrus*, a literary masterpiece which explores the nature of rhetoric, writing, love, beauty, Forms, and the philosophical life, promises a more openly positive account of the inspiration of poets. Here Socrates praises 'madness,' explicitly including the state of mind in which good poets compose, 'a Bacchic frenzy' without which there is no true poetry:

> if anyone comes to the gates of poetry and expects to become an adequate poet by acquiring expert knowledge [*technê*] . . . he will fail, and his self-controlled verses will be eclipsed by poetry of men who have been driven out of their minds.
>
> (*Phaedrus* 245a)

It has been claimed that the *Phaedrus* marks Plato's recantation of the hard-line condemnation of poetry in the *Republic* (Nussbaum 1986: 200–33), but a more sober verdict is perhaps better supported. Part of the extravagant myth Socrates enunciates concerns the fate of re-incarnated souls, who are placed in rank order. The highest, most worthy soul is that of "a lover of wisdom or of beauty... cultivated in the arts [*mousikos*] and prone to erotic love" (*Phaedrus* 248d). Sixth in rank, lower than generals, statesmen, gymnasts, doctors and prophets, is "a poet or some other life from among those concerned with mimesis" (ibid.: 248e). The contrast tests the modern reader's intuitions. Surely the prime rank must go to the genuine artist, while some poor uninspired dabbler is relegated to the sixth? Yet there is no word for 'art' here, as Nehamas reminds us: "the 'musical' . . . is not the artist, but the gentleman who patronizes the artists and knows what to take from them" (Nehamas 1982: 60). The first-ranking soul is rather that of the cultured philosopher and lover, with whom poets, all mimetic poets, including the great Homer, cannot compete. The comparative evaluation of the *Republic* is echoed in a very different tone of voice, but it is not reversed.

Philosophy and art

When Arthur Danto writes that "from the perspective of philosophy art is a danger and aesthetics the agency for dealing with it" (Danto 1986: 13), he is implicitly treating Plato as the founder of philosophical aesthetics and generalizing Plato's strategy to the whole subsequent discipline. The story is akin to that in Nietzsche's influential *The Birth of Tragedy*, where the cultural force embodied in Socrates, the 'theoretical man' and antithesis of the artist, destroys the artistic spirit that once dwelt in tragedy but has remained lost to the modern world (Nietzsche 1968: 81–98).

There is something in the thought that Plato's endeavor is to establish philosophy in opposition to the prevailing culture that not only prizes the arts but adopts certain ill-thought-out theoretical views concerning their value. It is a culture of sophists, rhetoricians, performers, and connoisseurs who advocate the educational value of poetry, but who lack a genuine conception of knowledge and any proper grasp on the distinction between what is fine because it brings pleasure and what is genuinely good or beneficial. Without the rigor of philosophical thinking, this culture lacks the critical distance required to assess the true value of the arts. Yet Plato's response is not merely that of head-on dialectical confrontation. He realizes that the art-loving, pleasure-seeking soul in all of us must be charmed and enticed towards the philosophical life. To supplant tragedy and Homer he uses rhetoric, myth, word-play, poetic metaphor, and dramatic characterization. Socrates in the dialogues is an image or invention of Plato's, who enacts for us the life and style of the ideal philosophical thinker. So if Plato is the most poetical of philosophers, it is in the service of leading us, by poetry's means of persuasion, to philosophy proper, a place from which we may begin to understand and evaluate poetry and all the arts.

That the quarrel between philosophy and poetry plays itself out within Plato is one source of the belief that he himself provides the material for a defense of art. In the history of aesthetics there have been numerous attempts to answer Plato on his own ground by claiming that art puts us in touch with the eternal and the absolute, or that it provides a privileged form of knowledge. Others have sought to reject Plato's criteria of evaluation as misguided, and have looked to aesthetic responses of various kinds to secure an autonomous value for art. Some have even combined both approaches (see Schopenhauer 1969: 169–267). But Plato's writings themselves offer none of these resolutions, and for that reason continue to be a unique stimulus to profound questioning about art, philosophy, and the relations between them.

See also Aristotle, Medieval aesthetics, Beauty, Art and emotion, Art and ethics, Art and knowledge, Pictorial representation, Tragedy, Value of art.

References

Aristotle (1987) *Poetics*, trans. S. Halliwell, Chapel Hill: University of North Carolina Press.

Beardsley, M. C. (1966) *Aesthetics from Classical Greece to the Present*, Birmingham: University of Alabama Press.

Danto, A. C. (1986) *The Philosophical Disenfranchisement of Art*, New York: Columbia University Press.

Hegel, G. W. F. (1993) *Introductory Lectures on Aesthetics*, trans. B. Bosanquet, ed. M. Inwood, London: Penguin.

Murdoch, I. (1977) *The Fire and the Sun: Why Plato Banished the Artists*, Oxford: Oxford University Press.

Nehamas, A. (1982) "Plato on Imitation and Poetry in *Republic* 10," in J. Moravcsik and P. Temko (eds), *Plato on Beauty, Wisdom and the Arts*, Lanham, Md.: Rowman and Littlefield.

Nietzsche, F. (1968) *The Birth of Tragedy* in *Basic Writings of Nietzsche*, trans. W. Kaufmann, New York: Random House.

Nussbaum, M. C. (1986) *The Fragility of Goodness: Luck and Ethics in Greek Tragedy and Philosophy*, Cambridge: Cambridge University Press.

Plato (1997) *Complete Works*, ed. J. M. Cooper, Indianapolis: Hackett.

Schopenhauer, A. (1969) *The World as Will and Representation*, trans. E. F. J. Payne, New York: Dover.

Sidney, P. (1973) "A Defense of Poetry," in K. Duncan-Jones and J. van Dorsten (eds), *Miscellaneous Prose of Sir Philip Sidney*, Oxford: Oxford University Press.

Further reading

Ferrari, G. R. F. (1989) "Plato and Poetry," in *The Cambridge History of Literary Criticism*, ed. G. A. Kennedy, Cambridge: Cambridge University Press. (A comprehensive, succinct account of Plato's relationship to poetry.)

Halliwell, S. (1991) "The Importance of Plato and Aristotle for Aesthetics," *Proceedings of the Boston Area Colloquium on Ancient Philosophy* 5: 321–48. (Relates Plato's refusal of autonomy for art to modern aesthetics.)

Havelock, E. A., (1963) *Preface to Plato*, Cambridge, Mass.: Harvard University Press. (Places Plato in the context of Greek culture and education.)

Janaway, C. (1995) *Images of Excellence: Plato's Critique of the Arts*, Oxford: Oxford University Press. (Philosophical commentary on all major discussions of the arts in Plato's dialogues.)

Keuls, E. (1978) *Plato and Greek Painting*, Leiden: E. J. Brill. (On painting of the period and Plato's knowledge of it.)

Moravcsik, J. (1986) "On Correcting the Poets," *Oxford Studies in Ancient Philosophy* 4: 35–47. (On Plato's ethical criticisms of poetry.)

Moravcsik, J. and P. Temko (eds) (1982) *Plato on Beauty, Wisdom, and the Arts*, Lanham, Md. Rowman and Littlefield. (A valuable collection of pieces by different authors.)

Nehamas, A. (1988) "Plato and the Mass Media," *Monist* 71: 214–33. (Explores links between Plato's criticisms and modern debates about film and television.)

Plato (1988) *Republic 10*, trans. S. Halliwell, Warminster: Aris and Phillips. (Greek and English texts, with detailed commentary.)

2
ARISTOTLE
Nickolas Pappas

Whether or not we classify any of Aristotle's writings as aesthetics proper, he certainly produced the first extended philosophical studies of an art form. Most of his works on poetry have long disappeared, leaving the *Poetics* as our only souvenir of Aristotle's theory of art. For more than 600 years that work has therefore enjoyed an unmatched cultural influence, as writers followed Aristotle's rules for composing poetry, and critics followed his rules for evaluating those writers. Even when both sides distorted the *Poetics*, they learned from its fundamental principles and passed them along, and our idea of art owes that little book a great debt.

Within the history of philosophy, the *Poetics* is noteworthy as a reply to Plato's condemnation of poetry. It makes a textbook case of Aristotle's anti-Platonism: while sharing a number of assumptions with Plato, he finds crucial points at which to oppose him, and builds those points into a decisively new theory. This article will focus on the anti-Platonic argument, for at many turns in the *Poetics* we can understand what Aristotle asserts only after determining which Platonic position he means to deny.

The value of the *Poetics*, however, goes beyond its historical significance. It is both impressive and instructive to watch Aristotle pause from his argument and ruminate on what poetry is, why it exists, and how it works. He moves back and forth between criticism and theory. He writes as a philosopher and as a fan. Above all, Aristotle lets actual dramas teach him about drama. His unhurried dissections of tragedy are one more manifestation of his biologist's observant mind, and set a standard for subsequent aesthetics.

Summary

Aristotle (384–322 BC) wrote the *Poetics* in or after 335. The extant *Poetics* amounts to the first half, or Book I, of the work that Aristotle wrote, a discussion of tragedy and epic he followed with Book II (now lost) on comedy.

Like all of Aristotle's surviving writings, the *Poetics* had been his lecture notes, and contains the ellipses and digressions that suit oral presentation but confuse readers. Poor preservation has left the *Poetics* even more confusing than the rest of the corpus. Only two medieval manuscripts exist that contain the Greek text, together with two translations into Arabic and Latin. These manuscripts were the result of many stages of recopying by hand, errors creeping into every copy; possessing only two versions makes it harder to guess which variations came into the manuscript later and which ones were in the original.

So the *Poetics* can bewilder a new reader. But it is not mystical or incoherent, nor one of those ancient oddities stuffed with isolated insights. It has a structure and a line of thought, and it makes good argumentative sense as long as the reader remains focused on a few guiding questions. What is poetry? What kind of poetry is tragedy? What are tragedy's essential elements? This general set of topics subsumes the details of Aristotle's argument within his overall plan to explain the literature of his day, and its audience's experience of it.

The explanation Aristotle provides is also a commendation: tragedy not only works but works well. Tragedy begins with a poet's knowledge, delivers universal statements, and offers the virtuous adult further moral education. For all these reasons, it belongs in the city. Plato had wanted to ban it, but then Plato had advanced a number of charges against poetry that these Aristotelian claims are intended to refute: that no knowledge undergirds poetry, as poets are ignorant (Plato, *Apology* 22b–c, *Ion* 534a) and reliant on inspiration (*Ion* 534b–e, *Phaedrus* 245a), and poetry propagates falsehoods (*Republic* 337–391); that poetry cannot deliver a universal statement, given that it expresses the poet's private mind (*Protagoras* 347c–e) or represents individual dramatic characters (*Republic* 605); that poetry's inherent idiosyncrasy makes it irrational (*Republic* 605c).

The elements of Aristotle's argument appear in condensed form in his definition of tragedy, which comes near the start of the *Poetics*: "Tragedy is the mimesis of a serious and complete action of some magnitude; in language embellished in various ways in its different parts; in dramatic, not narrative form; achieving, through pity and fear, the catharsis of such passions" (*Poetics* 1449b24–28). Four of the terms in this definition carry special weight, for Aristotle will use them to establish the worth of tragedy: catharsis, mimesis, action, seriousness. The four join together to produce the argument of the *Poetics*.

Catharsis of pity and fear

Aristotle gives nothing like a theory of catharsis: the word occurs twice in what survives of the *Poetics*, once enigmatically in the definition of tragedy and once in an irrelevant context (1455b15). But that is no reason to slight the topic. Aristotle puts catharsis at the end of his definition, and that closing clause is his customary place for stating the purpose or goal of a thing. Moreover, in *Politics* VIII he speaks of the catharsis that music and poetry bring, with the promise to say more in his work on poetry (presumably the *Poetics*). And – speaking pragmatically – the reader cannot ignore the quantity of commentary that catharsis has already inspired. Interpreters of the *Poetics* have traditionally argued for one view of catharsis or another; the new reader must at least know what the issue is.

The definition of tragedy refers to the catharsis "of such passions [*pathêmata*]," namely pity and fear and similar emotions. While that does not tell us much (and we shall see that even a claim this broad has been contested), Aristotle says enough about pity and fear to add at least a prologue to the story. Pity and fear are aroused by exactly the right presentation of characters and their adventures, which whips those emotions up to the highest pitch they can reach (*Poetics* 1453a10). This is why heroes must be decent enough to win a spectator's pity, but not so splendid that misfortune falls on them undeserved (ibid.: 1452b34–36). That would disgust the audience, and moral disgust distracts from pure fear and pity.

Aristotle appears to equate the subsequent catharsis with the essential tragic pleasure that pity and fear induce (*Poetics* 1453b11). But here the text lends itself to more than one reading, for *katharsis* was used in several different contexts before Aristotle, and those contexts slanted the word's central meaning of a 'cleaning.' A medical catharsis, for example, was a *purgation*, like a laxative or enema that cleaned out the digestive system. Catharsis in a more neutral context meant simply a clean-up or *clarification*. There are other senses as well, but these two provide the dominant modern paradigms for understanding catharsis.

Since the mid-nineteenth century, Aristotelian catharsis has tended to receive a medical reading. Tragedy flushes out unruly and undesirable passions by letting them flow freely until we return to an unemotional state. The terror aroused by a well-made tragedy lets us release the thousand little terrors we normally swallow back down.

This interpretation has ancient origins (e.g. Proclus, *Commentary on Plato's Republic*). In the modern era it ensconced itself in commentaries on the *Poetics*, until it became the received view (Lear 1988). Its appeal is plain enough, for this is an attitude toward emotions encountered in the psychologizing of everyday life. "You can't keep it bottled up inside." But Aristotle does not take emotions to come in quantities that either get released or remain suppressed. On his view, the expression of an emotion helps to strengthen that emotion: thus people who regularly give vent to their anger become more irascible, not less (*Nicomachean Ethics* II.1103b18). Moreover, the purgation reading presumes that everyone needs to be liberated from passion, but Aristotle's ethics calls for neither the celebration of passions nor their expurgation but their regular and well-regulated expression (ibid.: II.1109a25–29).

Finally, the purgation reading contradicts the spirit of something more profound that Aristotle says about *mousikê* (music and poetry) in *Politics* VIII. *Mousikê* helps educate our emotions, for songs contain accurate images of anger, courage, and other traits (*Politics* 1340a19–21). These images rouse us to emotion (1340a13); delight over the whole experience trains the soul to enjoy the sight of real-world virtue (ibid.: 1340a22–27). This arousal of the audience's emotions recalls what the *Poetics* says about pity and fear. If *their* arousal leads to catharsis (plus delight over the passions' excitement), and *this* arousal brings ethical habituation, then catharsis just is training or habituation. (See *Politics* 1339a18–23 on habituation.)

Training emotions has nothing to do with releasing them. Training presupposes that the emotions are here to stay, and need to be calibrated to fit the real-world situations that call them forth. On this view catharsis is a *clarification* of emotions (Golden 1976, Janko 1987, Nussbaum 1986). By rousing powerful emotions with a simpler train of events than life provides, tragedy teaches how fear and pity feel and where they are appropriate. That understanding forms part of the groundwork for ethical behavior, since Aristotle's ethics connects ethical behavior to well-trained emotions. Thus the clarification view helps harmonize Aristotle's aesthetics with his ethics.

The view also plays its part in an anti-Platonic argument. The emotions that Plato deplored are granted to exist in tragedy, but they benefit ethical action instead of subverting it. Where Plato gloomily rushed to the conclusion that tragedy's emotions overpower our capacity to reason, Aristotle presumes us able to reason about our emotions, and to make them more reasonable.

It is no objection to this view to say it implies that even virtuous adults need or profit from an ethical education. Aristotle expects adults to undergo a lifelong process of improvement in feeling and judgment. Still, a few obstacles remain for clarification. There is another passage in the *Politics* that speaks of poetic catharsis so as to make it resemble purgation. Aristotle there calls catharsis a "relief," something that makes the soul "settle down" (*Politics* 1342a7–15), and the passage is hard to explain away or reconcile with the clarification reading.

While the clarification reading is laudably cognitive in its goals, it may not be cognitive enough. If clarification is a kind of enlightenment, this reading fulfills the promise to show how poetry brings the pleasure of understanding (*Politics* 1448b13). But clarification remains enlightenment about the emotions; and the clarification reading thereby falls short of defending poetry against Plato's attacks. A rebuttal to Plato cannot rest with justifying the passions that tragedy arouses, because Plato does not rest with condemning them. Only one strand of Plato's attack on poetry concerns its incendiary effects. Several of his dialogues (*Apology*, *Ion*, *Protagoras*) accuse poetry of error or fatal obscurity without mentioning emotions. Even *Republic* 10 mainly vilifies mimetic poetry as the imitation of appearance; pathological emotions merely compound that effect. So while clarification is the best account of a psychological catharsis, any emotionally centered interpretation is apt to limit catharsis to one part of the story of the knowledge in tragedy.

Some interpreters have consequently taken catharsis out of the emotional arena altogether. When Aristotle's definition of tragedy mentions the catharsis "of such *pathêmata*," they say, that Greek word refers not to passions but to the *incidents in the drama*. Catharsis still means the cleaning of *pathêmata*, only that process is not psychological but narratological: the incidents get tidied up by being resolved in a logical denouement to the play (Else 1957, Nehamas 1992). Coherent and significant plot structure is the goal of tragedy.

This view of catharsis remains a minority position. Nevertheless it possesses the advantage of looking in the *Poetics* for an argument about what literature knows and how it says it. And it challenges the reader who rejects it to construct some other argument for poetic knowledge that Plato would recognize as such.

Mimesis

The *Poetics* raises the question of knowledge right at the start, when speaking of mimesis. Aristotle says bluntly, "[Mimesis] is natural to people from childhood" (*Poetics* 1448b6). For Plato, image-making, imitation, and every sort of copying resemble perversions (*Sophist* 228c with 267c); Aristotle sees them as natural propensities. Then he goes further. Mimesis is natural and pleasant because it is a way of learning (*Poetics* 1448b13; cf. 1448b8), and human beings love to learn (*Metaphysics* I.1). Not content with the weaker point that still blocks aesthetic Platonism, Aristotle stakes his position to the intellectual merit of poetry.

Aristotelian mimesis captures something about acting and drawing, and in general the works that produce resemblances to be discovered. A line drawing can show a thing's contours better than the thing itself; an impersonated Boston accent is often easier to learn to detect than the real accent would be. (In this respect Henry James's story "The Real Thing" makes an Aristotelian point about art.) Mimesis brings knowledge by both getting a thing right and simplifying it.

Plato would not accept such instruction. He wants knowledge to come in the form of universal statements, the highest sort of learning. He would not deny that the audience undergoes some process of recognition; he only laments its particularity. The painter's rendition of a bed (*Republic* 597d–598c) does not fail because the painter captured nothing about the bed, but because he captured only the look of this one bed. The imitator lacks what the user and maker have (ibid.: 601c–602a), knowledge of the properties of beds in general. Thus Plato locates the irrationality of poetry in its devotion to particulars, as he also does in the *Ion* (536), where poets seduce their fans away from abstract knowledge.

So far Aristotle has provided only the basis for an answer. Plato can reply: "This just proves that mimesis need not represent particulars, not that (in fact) it does not." Aristotle has to explain why poetry is, often enough to matter, the mimesis of general properties of things. His prefatory remarks about mimesis will not generate that argument, principally because mimesis by itself does not account for all the properties of tragedy. The definition of tragedy has shown it to be one specific type of mimesis; something about poetic mimesis, rather than about mimesis *simpliciter*, will provide the ingredient that makes poetry "more philosophical than history" (*Poetics* 1451b6f).

Mimesis of action

That additional element is Aristotle's proviso that tragedy be the mimesis of an action (*Poetics* 1449b25, 36; 1450a15, b3). He insists on this claim more than on anything else in the *Poetics*; and though his arguments supply aesthetic (ibid.: 1450a24–29, 35–39) and ethical (ibid.: 1450a16–23) justifications for the primacy of action, his real motive is the argument against Plato that mimesis communicates knowledge.

Aristotle's premise, precisely put, is that tragedy represents events and not passions, somewhat as painting is more a matter of line than of color (ibid.: 1450b2–3). Plot, not character, is the soul of tragedy. Aristotle builds an argument about causal generalizations, or in other words, general empirically grounded statements of human behavior:

1 The mimesis of action amounts to plot.
2 A good plot therefore clearly represents an action: it restricts itself to a unified action, even if that means slighting characters and character development (*Poetics* 1450b24, 1451a31–35).
3 This unity consists in the right connections among the parts of a plot. Lest the spectator be put off by implausible scenes, each event must follow the other "either by necessity or probably" (*Poetics* 1451a13, 38; 1452a20). A well-made plot is consciously arranged around such causal principles (ibid.: 1455b1–3).
4 Hence a tragedy that represents action contains a general truth.

How can the unobjectionable premises (1 to 3) add up to such an un-Platonic conclusion (4)? Indeed, what must Plato's argument have been, that this unadorned reasoning could hope to unseat it? On one view (Eden 1982, Halliwell 1986), Aristotle's argument rests on a new conception of mimesis as an active process of selective presentation. Mimesis came off as shabbily as it did in Plato because he imagined it to be something passive: just as some people today think of photography as too easy to be an art, Plato reduced all mimesis to automatic mimicry, even comparing it to the act of holding a mirror up to objects (*Republic* 596d). Aristotle brings the effort back into poetry, as in his remark about plot: "A poet must be a composer of plots rather than of verses, insofar as he is a poet according to representation, and represents actions" (*Poetics* 1451b27–29; Janko translation). The words "composer" and "poet" in this passage are both translations of the Greek word *poiêtês*, "maker," and Aristotle half-puns on this literal meaning to tell poets to make their plots. Later he explicitly enjoins poets to build a play's outline (ibid.: 1455a34–b15). Throughout the *Poetics* he speaks of the "construction" (*sustasis*) of a plot. On the basis of such remarks one may argue that Aristotle emphasizes plot as he does in order to give the poet something to do. A plot is an object that perforce gets constructed. Hence mimesis is active.

For this argument to accomplish anything against Plato, the Platonic mimesis must happen automatically. But Plato does not quite say that it does. The *Republic's* analogy to a mirror is meant to capture the superficiality of mimesis; but superficiality and automaticity or ease are different things. Indeed, the same passage damns poets precisely for misusing their intelligence (*sophia*, *Republic* 605a), with a description of poetic composition that does not sound automatic at all (cf. *Sophist* 234a on the imitator's skill). Plato knows about the selection and arrangement that go into mimesis; far from respecting poetry for this activity, he sees the work as more proof of poetry's perversity, that so many can do so much to produce so little. Already the account of mimetic activity seems to have misplaced Aristotle's argument.

It further weakens that account that Aristotle himself does not take the poet's mimetic activity to suffice for the presentation of general truths. He says that tragic poets typically do *not* invent their plots (*Poetics* 1451b15): thus the merits of good plots must derive from some source besides their having been consciously worked up. We are also told that too much plot-making busy-work can lead to unbelievable and inferior plays (ibid.: 1454b1), so plot-construction does not invariably yield aesthetic virtue. Then again, Aristotle says that poets are not at liberty to change too many details of a traditional story (ibid.: 1453b22). Here too, the poet's activity becomes a secondary matter in the presentation of a good story, and the story itself rises to eclipse it.

This – not a more complex description of poetic activity – is what Plato had overlooked. Simply calling tragedy the mimesis *of an action* establishes the possibility of its cognitive value, because Plato took dramatic poetry to be the mimesis of persons (*Republic* 393b–c, 395c–d, 396c; 605a, c–d). Dramatic characters are partial, biased perspectives on the drama's action, so Plato's assumption makes it easier to condemn the whole mimetic enterprise as an obsession with particulars. By turning his attention to plot, Aristotle deprives Plato of his crucial anti-dramatic premise. The *Poetics'* insistence on plot's supremacy over character therefore sets the stage for a defense of poetry that Plato had not imagined, against which Plato's critique has no purchase.

Some commentators reject this emphasis on plot as the element that makes tragedy wise, on the grounds that Aristotelian mimesis is not the mimesis of universals. The object of mimesis will not, by itself, turn representation into something philosophical, since the action depicted is still an individual thing.

It is true that Aristotle does not make poetry the mimesis of a universal. But even where the objects of mimesis are not universals, they can still bring about a mimesis that presents universals. All that matters is that the mimesis of an action yields a general statement as the mimesis of a person does not, thanks to the causal principles implied by an action. An inquisitive man (such as Oedipus) hears conflicting tales of his childhood and demands to talk to more witnesses until he knows the truth: this makes sense to spectators because inquisitive people do respond with curiosity to contradictory stories, especially about important things. The causal principle makes the story plausible, and contains the tragedy's general statement. The nature of action is thus the ground for the universal statement in the mimesis; and Aristotle's insistence that mimesis takes action as its object underwrites his conclusion that tragedy communicates authentically philosophical knowledge.

Seriousness

When Aristotle calls the tragic action serious (*spoudaia*), he is partly harking back to his requirement that tragic characters must be *spoudaioi* (good, serious, superior) people (*Poetics* 1448a2, 1454a17). These characters' dignity and standing ensure the importance of what they undertake and undergo.

Seriousness also means something about the type of action that can appropriately unfold in tragedy, however. The action must possess moral significance. This is not a matter of its having a moral. Some popularizations of Aristotle still go on about tragic flaws and heroes' falls, but Aristotle has no such thoughts about tragedy. Poetic justice of that variety would ruin the catharsis, since if tragic characters found their misfortunes because of morally blameworthy traits, we might fear the same thing's happening to us, but we would not feel the pity we reserve for victims of undeserved misfortune.

Moral significance means instead that Aristotle does not want tragedy to present meaningless suffering. He calls that variety of the tragic effect disgusting (*miaron*, *Poetics* 1452b36), while the appearance of purpose or order strikes him as "fine" (ibid.: 1452a6–10). So a tragedy has to make decent people's bad luck the right and fitting consequence of what they have done, and yet not a punishment for their misdeeds.

Aristotle resolves this apparent contradiction by linking the bad consequences to a character's *hamartia* (*Poetics* 1453a10). In the New Testament that troublesome word came to mean 'sin'; in Aristotle's time it embraced a variety of meanings and intensities, from mistake to error of judgment, from folly to self-deception, but not "tragic flaw" (Sherman, in Rorty 1992). A significant mistake (about who one's parents are, in Oedipus's case; in Jason's case, about the damage Medea was capable of) sets off a train of events that end in misfortune. Of course tragedy avoids the mild manifestations of *hamartia*, for it would count as a repellent display of suffering if a minor error led to such misery. Minor errors belong to comedy (*Poetics* 1449a34), while tragedy pivots on mistakes about momentous facts. But these mistakes do not have to be shards of evil in a character's heart.

Now we see another reason why tragic plots need to be fastened together with strong causal connections. A responsible moral agent ought to know that disasters can have ordinary beginnings, and to know how one mistake leads to another. The right tragic plot imparts that knowledge at the same time that it trains its audience's moral sentiments.

Seriousness of action also means that luck plays a role in tragedy, for most people's lives never contain the possibility that error will landslide into catastrophe. Really important trains of events are rare. So the tragic hero gets something wrong in a way that ordinary life does not punish. We fortunately do not always face the consequences of our actions. The unfortunate tragic hero does.

By comparison, the gravity of the tragic *characters* plays only a subsidiary role in the argument. It is true that having *spoudaioi* characters defends tragedy against the accusation of triviality. But that was not Plato's charge. He knew that tragedy represented fine men and women: this is what he deplored, the sight of such people reduced to shameless misery. That criticism only gets answered by Aristotle's accounts of mimesis and catharsis; given these accounts, he can find value in the seriousness of tragedy.

Aristotle and aesthetics

There is one final vague but important question: does Aristotle's account of poetry belong in aesthetics, or is that label anachronistic? Two features of the

Poetics seem to set it at a distance from modern aesthetics. First, Aristotle openly justifies poetry by appeal to its ethical and pedagogical effects. A good tragedy hones the emotions, details the nature of life-destroying error, shows how people insist on acting. To a formalist aesthetics, these external grounds for artistic success distract from a work's intrinsically aesthetic properties.

Austere formalism does not, however, speak for all aesthetics. A milder position is more common, that works may gain aesthetic value by producing ethical or otherwise external results, as long as the works' status as art is one of the causes of those results. A painting may appropriately lead its viewers to hate slavery, as long as its aesthetic properties help to bring that effect about. In this sense Aristotle does acknowledge the status of art works. The transmission of general truths in tragedy presupposes the process of artistic mimesis. Catharsis requires that pity and fear are aroused under shielded circumstances. The ethical effects of tragedy follow from its artistic effects, and art's artfulness has not been overlooked.

In any case, this objection to the *Poetics'* status used to sound more compelling than it does now. The last twenty years have seen renewed interest in such topics as the role of art in moral education, the ethical and political content of tragedy, and other very Aristotelian matters. Modern aesthetics has changed enough to make Aristotle's concerns less old-fashioned again.

The second cause for hesitation about "aesthetics" is Aristotle's elusive reference to beauty. He uses the word "beautiful" (*kalos*) often enough in the *Poetics* – nineteen times, as a compliment for tragic plots, language, and characters – to lead one interpreter to call beauty "the master-concept of the *Poetics*" (Else 1938). And yet this master-concept goes unexplained. Only once does Aristotle make beauty a defining criterion for tragedies, when he says they must be neither too long to surpass what the memory can hold, nor too short to count as serious (*Poetics* 1451a4–15).

This passage appears to assume a definition of beauty in terms of size and proportion (and see *Metaphysics* 1078a31–b5, *Politics* 1284b8–10). So beauty is a real property of things (cf. *Metaphysics* 1072b32–35). Aristotle says much the same thing in *De Motu Animalium* (700b26–35), when distinguishing what is beautiful in itself from what is merely perceived as desirable. However, the resemblance to Hutcheson's unity-in-variety theory does not go as far as it promises. Early modern discussions of beauty mostly took it to be a univocal property, capable of being taken in without reflection. Thus Kant distinguished between the beautiful and the good on the grounds that the former is perceived directly, while 'good' always means 'good *for*' something, and must be evaluated relative to a goal.

Plato could agree with Hutcheson and Kant that beauty has a single nature in every instantiation (*Hippias Major* 294b, *Symposium* 211a–b); Aristotle's beauty is real but equivocal. Its meaning derives from the nature of the beautiful thing in question. Aristotle tends to speak only in passing of beauty itself, but the evidence adds up to a context-dependent conception of beauty. The *Poetics* calls magnitude a necessary condition for beauty, but we know that magnitude is relative to a thing's nature (*Categories* 5b15–29); the same surely holds for order and proportion.

More explicitly, the *Rhetoric* holds that a man's beauty changes its meaning as a man ages and has different functions. The beautiful young man is one who competes athletically; the beautiful man of middle age can frighten enemies in a battle; the beautiful old man holds up against the insults of age (*Rhetoric* 1361b7–14). And in a telling passage in *Parts of Animals*, Aristotle urges his readers not to bring their prejudices about beauty to the study of zoology. All living things boast a design suited to the purpose of their sustenance and reproduction, and that is what beauty comes to (*Parts of Animals* 645a23–25).

Because beauty is a real property, Aristotle feels free to refer to it in his assessments of tragedies. But because beauty's meaning varies with the thing in question, the concept of beauty generates no conclusions about tragedy; instead one must put off using the concept until one knows what tragedy is and does. Finally, the connection between beauty and function implies that while beauty belongs in talk about poetry, it does not belong only there, or even especially there. And because beauty has nothing of its modern subjectivity, Aristotle sidesteps the stock problems of validating or defending aesthetic judgments, writing the *Poetics* as though these assessments could be made orderly and definite.

Even if Aristotle develops a philosophy of art independently of beauty, he does not belong among puritans wary of aesthetic experiences. On the contrary, his theory of tragedy grows out of such experiences, sensitively noted and respectfully analyzed. Beauty may not be an initiating concept in his theory, but in dramatic practice it will stand as the final proof that a tragedy accomplished what it set out to do.

See also Plato, Tragedy, Beauty.

References

Aristotle (1987) *The Poetics of Aristotle*, trans. S. Halliwell, Chapel Hill: University of North Carolina Press. (The recommended translation of the *Poetics*.)

Aristotle (1987) *Aristotle: Poetics*, trans. R. Janko, Bloomington: University of Indiana Press. (A good translation of the *Poetics*.)

Eden, K. (1982) "Poetry and Equity: Aristotle's Defense of Fiction," *Traditio* 38: 17–43.

Else, G. F. (1938) "Aristotle on the Beauty of Tragedy," *Harvard Studies in Classical Philology* 49: 179–204.

—— (1957) *Aristotle's Poetics: The Argument*, Cambridge, Mass.: Harvard University Press.

Golden, L. (1976) "The Clarification Theory of *Katharsis*," *Hermes* 104: 437–52.

Halliwell, S. (1986) *Aristotle's Poetics*, Chapel Hill: University of North Carolina Press.

Hutcheson, F. (1973) *An Inquiry Concerning Beauty, Order, Harmony, Design*, ed. P. Kivy, The Hague: Martinus Nijoff.

Kant, I. (1987) *Critique of Judgement*, trans. W. S. Pluhar, Indianapolis: Hackett.

Lear, J. (1988) "Katharsis," *Phronesis* 33: 297–326.

Nehamas, A. (1992) "Pity and Fear in the *Rhetoric* and the *Poetics*," in A. Rorty (ed.), *Essays on Aristotle's Poetics*, Princeton: Princeton University Press.

Nussbaum, M. C. (1986) *The Fragility of Goodness: Luck and Ethics in Greek Tragedy and Philosophy*, Cambridge: Cambridge University Press.

Proclus (1899) Commentary on Plato's *Republic*, in W. Kroll (ed.), *Platonis Rem Publicam Commentarii*, Leipzig: Teubneri.

Rorty, A. (ed.) (1992) *Essays on Aristotle's Poetics*, Princeton: Princeton University Press.

Further reading

Ackrill, J. (1966) "Aristotle and the Best Kind of Tragedy," *Classical Quarterly* N.S. 16: 78–102. (A deeper discussion of plot in the *Poetics*.)

Barnes, J., Schofield, M. and Sorabji, R. (eds) (1977, 1979) *Articles on Aristotle*, vols 2 and 4, London: Duckworth. (A wide range of articles relevant to Aristotelian aesthetics.)

Belfiore, E. (1992) *Tragic Pleasures: Aristotle on Plot and Emotion*, Princeton: Princeton University Press.

Devereux, G. (1970) "The Structure of Tragedy and the Structure of the *Psychê* in Aristotle's *Poetics*," in C. Hanly and M. Lazerowitz (eds), *Psychoanalysis and Philosophy: Essays in Memory of Ernest Jones*, International Universities Press. (On the connections between literary and ethical values in Aristotle.)

Golden, L. (1965) "Is Tragedy the Imitation of a Serious Action?" *Greek, Roman and Byzantine Studies* 6: 284–9. (A different analysis of mimesis and action.)

—— (1973) "The Purgation Theory of Catharsis," *Journal of Aesthetics and Art Criticism* 31: 473–9. (Vital to any discussion of catharsis.)

Halliwell, S. (1984) "Plato and Aristotle on the Denial of Tragedy," *Proceedings of the Cambridge Philological Society* 30: 49–71. (A discussion of Aristotle's anti–Platonism.)

——(1990) "Aristotelian Mimêsis Reevaluated," *Journal of the History of Philosophy* 28: 487–510. (Mimesis as poetic activity.)

House, H. (1956) *Aristotle's Poetics*, Hart-Davis. (An older but still very useful treatment of the *Poetics*), London.

Janko, R. (1984) *Aristotle on Comedy. Towards a Reconstruction of Poetics* II, Berkeley: University of California Press. (A controversial proposal about the lost sections of the *Poetics* that also sheds light on what the extant sections mean.)

Nehamas, A. (1987) "Dangerous Pleasures," *Times Literary Supplement* 4371: 27–8. (An indispensable review of Halliwell's book on the *Poetics*.)

Packer, M. (1984) "The Conditions of Aesthetic Feeling in Aristotle's *Poetics*," *British Journal of Aesthetics* 24: 138–48. (Another approach to tragedy and emotion.)

Sörbom, G. (1966) *Mimesis and Art*, Svenska Bokforlaget, Stockholm. (The classic discussion of pre-Platonic uses of "mimesis" and the word's later vicissitudes.)

3

MEDIEVAL AESTHETICS

Joseph Margolis

To speak of medieval aesthetics will strike many as contrived, partly because aesthetics, regarded as a distinct discipline, is usually dated approximately from the appearance in 1790 of Immanuel Kant's *Critique of Judgement* (1928), which may itself be thought contrived inasmuch as Kant has remarkably little to say about the appreciation and interpretive criticism of the arts, and proposes a formal definition of the 'aesthetic' (or of aesthetic judgment) which serious contributors to the topic admit to be too narrow or too artificial. Of course the analogy between the moral and the aesthetic, and the paedeutic use of the aesthetic, redeem Kant's standing as the initiator of philosophical aesthetics, and a similar retrospective reading of medieval texts justifies the selective reconstruction of so-called medieval aesthetics. As Paul Kristeller (1951) has compellingly shown, the very idea of the system of the 'fine arts' is a late development in western thought, by virtue of which ancient, medieval, and even early modern views of the arts are tolerably but anachronistically treated as contributing to a relatively straightforward conceptual history of aesthetics.

Viewed thus, medieval aesthetics, much like medieval philosophy, remains peculiarly problematic and historically unavoidable as a consequence of its overriding concern with the conceptual relationship between Creator and Creation. The two leading figures of western Christian aesthetics, collected in a wide sense of 'medieval,' are Augustine and Thomas Aquinas. Augustine is often viewed as the most original and influential philosopher of the early Church, and Aquinas the most magisterial voice of the high Middle Ages.

Augustine

Augustine offers the most ramified melding of Neoplatonist philosophy and Christian doctrine that the western Church achieved, and Aquinas the most ramified and authoritative melding of Aristotelian philosophy and Christian doctrine. This division of labor is not unimportant, because although the puzzle regarding the continuity and discontinuity between the natural world and God's creative act remains fundamentally the same through the whole of medieval philosophy, the conceptual relationship between categories properly applied only to nature and categories (if we may call them such) properly applied only to God becomes more controversial following the full recovery of Aristotle's texts in the thirteenth century. Aquinas produced a very bold version of the idiom of Creation and Creator that was intended to override the palpable disjunction between nature and the 'supernatural' (or, better, what is prior to and altogether different from nature). The Augustinian alternative appears to muffle the discontinuity in a more intuitive way.

There are at least two reasons why the disjunction between nature and Creator appears less problematic in Augustine than in Aquinas. For one, Neoplatonism, on which Augustine draws with great conviction, had the use of the ingenious doctrine of 'emanations' from Absolute Being or Absolute Beauty developed by Plotinus (1966) and ultimately fashioned from the central image of Plato's *Symposium* (1961). For another, Augustine had been, in his pre-Christian career, so much drawn to Stoic and Ciceronian treatments of rhetoric, the arts, and beauty that he continued such studies in terms confined to the natural world, even after his conversion.

The Neoplatonist theme appears to have been formulated in a perspicuous, but singularly abstract, way by a younger, anonymous contemporary of Augustine's known as the Pseudo-Dionysius (a fifth century Christian). In the latter's texts, notably *De Divinis Nominibus*, Beauty is identified as one of God's attributes, inseparably conjoined with Good (Tatarkiewicz 1970). The Pseudo-Dionysius's texts are said to belong more nearly to the older patristic tradition but to be distinguished from its characteristic teachings in assigning Beauty primarily to God rather than to the created order.

In any case, there is in the Pseudo-Dionysius no pointed attention to the close study of the pleasing and the beautiful in the particular arts or in our experience of the arts, that compares favorably with Augustine's empirical aesthetics, early or late, or with Plotinus's. Here for instance is a sample of *De Divinis Nominibus*:

> one should distinguish between beauty and beautifulness as the cause embracing at once all beauty. For, having made this distinction in all being between participation and things participating, we call beautiful the thing which participates in beautifulness, because from it is imparted to all reality the beauty appropriate to every thing, and also because it is the cause of proportion and brilliance.
>
> (Tatarkiewicz 1970: 33)

The problem Augustine shares with the Pseudo-Dionysius concerns the adequacy of our conceptual apparatus for making attributions to nature (*a fortiori*, to art) intelligible in terms of the prior attributes of the Creator. Viewed retrospectively, the puzzle begins with Plato's distinction between physical and spiritual beauty, mounts to Plotinus's treatment of physical beauty as (no more than) an emanation from Absolute Being (which utterly transcends the whole of sensible nature but remains continuous with it in the sense of conceding the reality and intelligibility of what emanates from it), and mounts even higher in the Pseudo-Dionysius's indissoluble conjunction of Beauty and the Good as an attribute of God: which is of course conflated with the Neoplatonist Absolute. The puzzle reaches its most baffling limit wherever Aquinas appears to emphasize the breach between Creation and Creator without benefit of Neoplatonism.

The fact remains that the Neoplatonist account requires a continuum of Being, while the Biblical account insists (or is construed as insisting) on an absolute disjunction. Clearly, creation *ex nihilo* must be made to serve the purpose of the linkage, but its adequacy is not altogether convincing. There would be an important conceptual advantage if it worked: the proportion, measure and harmonious relationship among the parts of any complex natural whole that yielded beauty or the pleasing perception of beauty could then be said to be derived altogether from the simple or unified or completely non-relational, indivisible, inherent Beauty of God.

The maneuver brings Augustine and the Pseudo-Dionysius very close to Plotinus's original solution, which, however, is entirely alien to the Biblical story. Whatever Augustine's skill in empirical studies of rhetoric and the arts, this early contribution to medieval aesthetics may be judged incapable of offering more than an armature for interpreting art and nature (God's art) as what is legible in God's Creation. This parallels Roger Bacon's *Opus Majus* (1928) which treats the pictorial function of painting, like the literal function of the sciences, as occupied with what is legible in, and of, God's Creation. This is also the upshot of Augustine's *City of God* (1972) and *Confessions* (1960) – which is to say, the upshot not only of the interpretation of the arts but of human history and personal life.

We need to be aware of these doctrines in order to grasp the import of Christian art, but to proceed thus is to treat the doctrine as a matter of partisan faith, rather than as compelling philosophy. Thus, for instance, a version of the Christian Neoplatonist thesis arose at Chartres, distinctly influenced by the theme of Plato's *Timaeus*, so that God came to be viewed by Alan of Lille, who was associated with the school of Chartres, as "an elegant architect of the world, like a goldsmith in his workshop" (Alan of Lille 1980). This makes sense in terms of Neoplatonism, but not of Biblical thought, unless creation *ex nihilo* is permitted to be read along Neoplatonist (or even Platonic) lines. The Cathedral at Chartres, the first of the great Gothic cathedrals, was constructed with some such conception in mind, which facilitates interpreting the function and harmonious proportion of the parts of Chartres as legible symbols of God's supreme art.

Augustine was quite clear that God's Creation was utterly unlike human art, in the sense that God's art proceeds *ex nihilo*. But though he was influenced by Platonic and Roman notions of mimesis, he construed the significative import of human art as symbolic of the higher meaning of God's art: that is, as exceeding mimesis. This is perhaps clearest in the *City of God* (1972) and the *Confessions* (1960), though it is not in any way narrowly deployed in aesthetic terms.

It also provides the meaning of Augustine's question and answer, "Is a thing beautiful because it pleases or does it please because it is beautiful?" Clearly, "it pleases because it is beautiful." But in that answer, Augustine opposes, or at least subordinates, the ancient mimetic doctrine to a higher analogical function. Augustine's constant rule is to bring literal meaning into accord with spiritual meaning, so as to save the higher (revealed) truth. That is, Christian doctrine's seeming falsity is always figurative. In this way, Augustine adumbrates the classic doctrine of the allegorical import of literal texts.

In accord with this commitment, his early studies of the complexity of meaning, even prior to his conversion, are thought to be notably wide-ranging and original. But the entire account contributes more to the practice of a Christian hermeneutic than to a satisfactory defense of a Christian metaphysics of art, nature and meaning. (The famous fourfold division of the literal and allegorical readings of a literary text is summarized, as a matter of course, in Dante's *Convivio* [1990].)

The whole idea that the beauty of natural phenomena is rightly informed by God's Beauty – that is, that the beauty of complex particular things is informed by the indivisible Beauty of God – is rather a pretty notion. But it has its conceptual drawbacks, two in particular of which are seemingly insurmountable. One has already been bruited, namely, that there is no legible way of explicating the mimetic beauty of art and nature by way of the singular enabling Beauty of God, except interpretively, in doctrinally acknowledged terms that cannot and need not be legitimated in any philosophically independent way. The other is entirely obvious, namely, that what counts as beautiful in art (or nature, for that matter) is contingently linked to prevailing tastes and the history of aesthetic and moral norms, and that what (as in modern and contemporary art) once passed for beauty in an earlier age no longer commands our highest regard or interest. An illuminating piece of evidence along these lines may be suggested by paintings like James Ensor's *Christ Entering Brussels in Triumph* and by other of his grotesques, which deliberately violate the canons of beauty in the proportioning of color and space and image favored by 'well-made' medieval and Renaissance images, but are now neither merely ugly nor formulaically beautiful.

The Augustinian treatment of symbolic beauty, like the interpretation of the sack of Rome in the *City of God* (1972), is certainly an expression of an impressive piety. But Augustine's interpretive rule is committed to grasping the ahistorical – indeed, the transcendent – truth of historical work and deeds; and that can hardly be compelling, even among Christians, in a world in which the corrective grasp of God's Beauty (or Goodness or Truth) is not entirely transparent. The difficulty is a philosophical one, however compelling (among the faithful) the hermeneutics may be.

Aquinas

Given the intractable puzzle regarding the continuity and discontinuity between Creation and Creator, it was more than improbable that Aquinas could have reclaimed the general purpose of the Christian conception of art and beauty without drawing on Augustine's Neoplatonist theme. Aquinas integrates in an original way (that was not possible before the thirteenth century) the main lines of Augustine's use of Neoplatonist and Aristotelian philosophical resources in his well-known union of faith and reason, *Summa Theologiae* (1942).

The essential question in understanding Aquinas's philosophical originality centers on his adaptation of the Aristotelian conception of the 'forms' of particular things, which account for their existing as things of the kinds they are. The forms, which ultimately depend on God (on the Creationist view), hold the key to the Being of things, their unity, their truth, their goodness: that is, the key to their possessing, derivatively, attributes that answer to the informing transcendental attributes of God. Here Aquinas construes beauty and goodness in a way very close to the doctrine favored by the Pseudo-Dionysius, distinguishing beauty and goodness primarily in terms of the different interests we take in viewing different aspects of the same things, without treating Beauty as a transcendental attribute distinct from Goodness.

In fact, Aquinas repeats Augustine's solution of the riddle of the priority of the beautiful over the pleasing. The question of the transcendental standing of the Beautiful was taken as a pointedly central theme in the work of a leading modern Thomist aesthetician, Jacques Maritain, in his early book, *Art and Scholasticism* (Maritain 1974). Aquinas's 'aesthetics' must, of course, be pieced together from his systematic texts. Maritain views Aquinas's doctrine as entirely straightforward. But the fact is, Aquinas was not familiar with Aristotle's *Poetics*; correspondingly, Maritain's proposal represents a respectful extension of Aquinas's actual system. The theme developed, which may be culled from

Aristotle's then-known texts, regards art (in the sense of the production of things) as the imposition of an intelligible form on natural materials (which lack that form) by the work of practical reason. But in the opinion of some – notably, Meyer Schapiro (1947) – Aquinas's aesthetics of beauty and theory of art have almost nothing in common with the aesthetics of our detailed interests in the fine arts, for instance the interpretation of the Gothic cathedral.

The problem of the transcendentals comes to this: whatever, bearing on the nature of existent things, renders those things intelligible – their Being, unity, truth, and goodness – appears in the created order in a necessarily 'oppositional' sense. That is, the instantiated attributes of existing things exhibit some joint gradation of their positive and negative manifestations (as with hot/cold, wet/dry and so on). But as far as God's putative 'nature' is concerned, the transcendentals are utterly unlike their oppositional counterparts, in that the would-be contraries lack any possible application to the Creator. In the order of understanding, it looks as if the categories answering to the transcendentals are generated 'bottom-up,' but, in the order of Being, they obtain 'top-down.'

The trick is to explain how it is that the oppositional use of the relevant categories applies in a way that argues the continuum of being linking Creator and Creation, in spite of the fact that their transcendental use necessarily lacks the oppositional structure inhering in their earthly application. Clearly, this affects the treatment of beauty in art and nature. But equally clearly, the resolution seems unable to exceed the resources of Neoplatonism.

The distinction of Aquinas's treatment of beauty, read in these terms, lies with the conditions for contemplating the determinate forms of things (that might also have been considered, for the purposes of science and morality, say, in altogether different ways). At any rate, this is thought to be a plausible reconstruction of Aquinas's aesthetics. The Neoplatonist theme has the advantage of contrasting the eternal and immutable with what is generated and decays, without involving (at that point) the problem of accounting for a separate Creator whose own 'nature' could not possibly be accounted for in terms of any prior or independent categories of the Neoplatonist sort. Aquinas is obliged to derive the resources of the Neoplatonist theme from the prior Being of the Creator.

The Eastern Church was able to defend iconoclasm (regarding would-be images of God) along broadly Neoplatonist lines, although of course images of the Divine could also be defended sympathetically on a different application of the same conception. In Aquinas's case, the question remains whether anything can truthfully be said of God. For example, are even the affirmations of negative theology meaningful with respect to God's 'nature' (Aquinas 1924)? This is a troublesome question that, in all candor, may not have been answered satisfactorily by Aquinas himself. On its resolution depends the standing of the whole of Thomistic aesthetics (and more), viewed as taking precedence over the Neoplatonist themes in Augustine. As has already been remarked, however, the concept of a Christian hermeneutics need not be affected adversely.

In general, Aquinas's treatment of the beautiful follows the lead of the Pseudo-Dionysius and Augustine and tends toward the Neoplatonist conception, whereas his treatment of art, in the productive sense (notably not keyed to the fine arts) tends to favor Aristotle's discussion of *technê*. On the first, Aquinas appears to distinguish between the good and the beautiful, not *in re* but contingently, in terms of what pleases; hence, posteriorly. Read this way, the familiar characterization of the beautiful as that which pleases in being beheld (Aquinas 1942), made famous by Stephen Daedalus's reflections in James Joyce's fiction, cannot capture more than a small part of Aquinas's comprehensive view.

Aquinas apparently intends the distinction to hold in two further regards. One accords with the transcendental identity of the Good and the Beautiful, which is then construed appetitively in terms of the soul's natural aspiration (with obvious affinities for both the Neoplatonist and Aristotelian themes). In the other, one may be moved to pleasure without recognizing that one is pleased by the intelligible form of the thing that pleases, hence in a way that is cognitive when fully realized (this is again closer to Aquinas's use of the Aristotelian model than to the Neoplatonist).

On his treatment of 'form,' with respect to both beauty and art, Aquinas was influenced by the recovery by Albertus Magnus, his teacher, of Aristotle's philosophy in the original Greek, and Albert's lectures on what we may call his aesthetics. Here are some remarks of Albert's which confirm the similarity of his thesis to Aquinas's conception: "among things existing at present, there is none which does not have a share in beauty and good;" "good is that which all desire; and moral good is good which attracts the desire by its strength and authority; and finally, beauty is the good which, in addition to this, possesses lustre and clarity;" "the essence of beauty in general consists in the resplendence of form over proportionally arranged parts of matter or over various capabilities and actions" (quoted in Tatarkiewicz 1970).

Aquinas's originality seems to lie in his emphasis on the contemplative pleasure immediately occasioned by 'beholding' some integrated and well-proportioned complex natural or manufactured thing. ('Sight' is meant metonymically to stand in for the other senses – hearing, chiefly – as well as for the perception of spiritual beauty.) Albert's theme favors attributes, not necessarily those restricted only to relations among parts. Aquinas's formula is particularly well suited to natural and created things, but with a distinctly Aristotelian emphasis on pleasure, though not pointedly in application to the fine arts. The novelty of his view may be glimpsed by contrasting it with the influential, very early view advanced by Basil, who favors both a Stoic (or Ciceronian) emphasis on the harmoniously proportioned parts of complex things and the Neoplatonist emphasis on the indivisible Beauty of the Absolute (or God), which Basil finds analogously in the simple beauty of gold. Basil treats the two accounts as fully compatible.

By distinguishing the good and the beautiful, as between the appetitive and the cognitive (or what is pleasurable when perceived), Aquinas is able to treat the discrimination of the aesthetic as unique to man: "only Man delights in the beauty of sensuous things as such" (Aquinas 1942). But he catches up Albert's emphasis on objective beauty and notes, in addition, the mixing, say, of non-aesthetic pleasures, as of odors (perfumes), with the pleasure of perceived beauty, as of women.

Aquinas makes a considerable number of 'empirical' distinctions regarding kinds of 'proportion' bearing on the objective beauty of things in the created order, in a manner akin to Aristotle's. Furthermore, in accord with his general adoption of Aristotle's approach, he fixes the condition of objective beauty by reference to the perceivable or cognizable form of the things in question. The impression persists, though, that Aquinas is thinking more about nature than about art, or more about 'art' in the way of production or manufacture than of the creation of fine things usually said to be contemplated for their own sake.

In any case, beauty and its perception and the pleasure taken in the thing perceived (or in the perceiving of it) are keyed to the formal essence of the things in question. This helps to explain his remark that:

> beauty demands the fulfilment of three conditions: the first is *integrity*, or *perfection*, of the thing, for what is defective is, in consequence, ugly; the second is proper *proportion*, or *harmony*; and the third is *clarity* – thus things which have glowing color are said to be beautiful.
>
> (Aquinas 1942)

More usually, as in the commentary on the Pseudo-Dionysius, Aquinas features only the two conditions of proportion and clarity. But both accounts tend to confirm the primacy of the beautiful in nature; or, in any case, the linkage between the perception of beauty and the manifestation of essential form.

In this sense, Aquinas emphasizes that 'art' – the productive arts construed as generously as you please – is mimetic with regard to nature, not primarily in the way of imitating the appearance of natural things (the representational among the arts) but more in the way of imitating nature's own productive capacity. In this sense, Aquinas makes room for the fine arts and, in particular, the representational in painting and sculpture. But the representational is not confined to anything like the fine arts. You may claim to have a fair sense of Aquinas's restrictions on art if you combine his tolerance of entertainment and pleasure with his conviction that art cannot create new forms. In this respect, his view is entirely unsympathetic to modern conceptions of the fine arts.

Later developments

There is widespread agreement that aesthetics in the fourteenth and fifteenth centuries tends to dwindle in importance and originality, as newer energies came to favor incipient currents that were to mature in the Renaissance. Certainly Dante, who is of the generation that follows Aquinas, readily adopts Aquinas's doctrines and other conventional views, with the notable exception of his own theme of the motive power of love in composing poetry. This appears to be a heterodox view, not clearly reconciled with the rational and cognitive bent of Aquinas's scheme. The contributions of Duns Scotus and William of Ockham are noticeably spare and hardly more than occasional. They are largely credited with reviewing (to the extent they concern themselves at all with aesthetic issues) the unexplained ambiguities and complexities of familiar formulations.

By and large, the decline in the influence and importance of medieval aesthetics, apart from its permanent place in our understanding of the hermeneutics of Christian art and thought, rests with the general absence of any commitment to the theologized metaphysics of Creator and Creation in the evolution of the post-medieval western world. It is abetted, of course, by an increasing decline in the eminence of the theory of beauty itself and in the waning of the theory of natural essences. The theory of beauty, however it is imagined to be grounded in the biological dispositions of humankind, has effectively been detached from any essentialism and increasingly wedded to the contingencies of cultural history, with the consequence that beauty itself, in the classical and medieval sense, is now largely of minor importance in the discussion of the arts.

Doubtless there will always be a need to return to the implications of the Creator/Creation relationship, insofar as Christianity (or Judaism or Islam) continues to have an effective role in the direction of the life of some part of the human family. But the fact remains that Neoplatonism has no reason to expect a revival, and the Biblical notion of a Creator appears incapable of improving on the Neoplatonist solution.

Finally, it must be said that the theory of beauty in medieval aesthetics has been pressed into service, somewhat artificially, as a surrogate for specifically 'aesthetic' concerns. But in modern aesthetics, there is almost unanimous agreement that there is no sufficient uniformity in the range of what passes for the 'aesthetic' that would justify treating what falls under that blunderbuss as conceptually uniform in any notably instructive sense. The recovery of medieval aesthetics as part of a general ethos cannot but be adversely affected by these and similar changes, though there is every reason to believe that Augustine and Aquinas belong to a small company of gifted discussants whose work may be recovered again and again by some ingenious detachment from their own particular age and the inventive reclamation of what they say in the context of historically novel questions.

See also Plato, Aristotle, Beauty.

References

Alan of Lille (1980) *The Plaint of Nature*, trans. J. J. Sheridan, Toronto: Pontifical Institute of Medieval Studies.

Aquinas, T. (1924) *Summa Contra Gentiles*, trans. English Dominican Fathers, London: Burns, Oates and Washbourne.

—— (1942) *Summa Theologiae*, trans. Fathers of the English Dominican Province, London: Burns, Oates and Washbourne.

Augustine (1960) *Confessions of Saint Augustine*, trans. J. K. Ryan, New York: Doubleday.

—— (1972) *City of God*, trans. H. Bettenson, Harmondsworth: Penguin.

Bacon, R. (1928) *Opus Majus of Roger Bacon*, trans. R. B. Burke, Philadelphia: University of Pennsylvania Press.

Basil (1950) *Writings*, New York, Fathers of the Church.

Dante (1990) *Convivio*, trans. R. H. Lansing, New York: Garland.

Kant, I. (1928) *Critique of Judgement*, trans. J. C. Meredith, Oxford: Oxford University Press.

Kristeller, P. O. (1950) "The Modern System of the Arts: A Study in the History of Aesthetics" *Journal of the History of Ideas* 12: 496–527 and 13: 17–46.

Maritain, J. (1974) *Art and Scholasticism*, trans. J. W. Evans, Notre Dame, Ill.: University of Notre Dame Press.

Plato (1961) *Collected Dialogues of Plato*, ed. E. Hamilton and H. Cairns, Princeton: Princeton University Press.

Plotinus (1966) *Enneads*, trans A. H. Armstrong, Cambridge, Mass.: Harvard University Press.

Pseudo-Dionysius (1990) *Corpus Dionysiarum*, Berlin: de Gruyter.

Schapiro, M. (1947) "On the Aesthetic Attitude in Romanesque Art," in K. B. Iyer (ed.), *Art and Thought*, London: Luzac.

Tatarkiewicz, W. (1970) *Medieval Aesthetics*, trans. R. M. Montgomery, The Hague: Mouton.

4

EMPIRICISM

Hutcheson and Hume

James Shelley

If philosophical disciplines can be said to define themselves in terms of the central terms they attempt to define, then modern aesthetics is that discipline that attempts to define 'art' and 'aesthetic.' The concepts governing both of these terms derive from the eighteenth century. It is true that the term 'art' was long in use before then, but it was not until the eighteenth century that the artforms now included in what Paul Oskar Kristeller famously calls "the modern system of the arts" began to be grouped together, and that the term thus became linked with the concept that now governs it (Kristeller 1951). The reverse is true of the concept of the aesthetic: though it was not until the nineteenth century that the term began to be linked, in the English-speaking world at least, with the concept that now governs it, that concept first took on recognizable shape early in the eighteenth century (Stolnitz 1961: 142–3). It is with justice, therefore, that we regard the eighteenth century as the formative period of modern philosophical aesthetics, since it was only then that its defining concepts assumed recognizable form, and only then, therefore, that the modern discipline itself assumed recognizable form.

The writings of eighteenth-century aestheticians thus make a particularly strong claim on the attention of contemporary aestheticians: their study promises us the kind of self-understanding that only a study of our origins can provide. In particular, a study of the philosophical forces that forged our central concepts promises both to reveal where they are necessary and where arbitrary, and generally to sharpen understanding of them in something like the way that a study of etymologies sharpens understanding of the meanings of words. One caveat must be kept in mind: to say that our central concepts can be recognized in the writings of eighteenth-century aestheticians is not to say that those concepts, and their attendant perplexities, have not undergone change during the past 200 years. Nothing, it seems, impedes our understanding of eighteenth-century aesthetics more than the tendency to read twentieth-century aesthetics into it. We thus find ourselves in a seemingly paradoxical position with respect to our eighteenth-century predecessors: we will not succeed in understanding ourselves without remembering them, but will not succeed in remembering them without first forgetting ourselves.

We owe our concept of the aesthetic particularly to the British aestheticians of the eighteenth century: their theories of taste are the direct forebears of our aesthetic theories. John Locke and the third earl of Shaftesbury stand as their immediate influences. Locke, who took no interest in matters of taste himself, provided the empiricist framework within which they worked out their theories; Shaftesbury convinced them of the philosophical interest of the concept of taste, though the vein he worked in was perhaps as Neoplatonic as empiricist (Townsend 1991: 350). We may therefore say that eighteenth-century British aestheticians placed Shaftesbury's interest within Locke's framework (Kivy 1976: 23). Their most important works include: Joseph Addison's papers on "Good Taste" and "The Pleasures of the Imagination" from *the Spectator* (1712), Francis Hutcheson's *An Inquiry Concerning Beauty, Order, Harmony, Design* (1973 [1725]), David Hume's "Of the Standard of Taste" (1985 [1757]), Edmund Burke's *A Philosophical Enquiry into the Origin of Our Ideas of the Sublime and Beautiful* (1757/1759), Alexander Gerard's *An Essay on Taste* (1759), Lord Kames's *Elements of Criticism* (1762), and Archibald Alison's *Essay on the Nature and Principles of Taste* (1790) (Townsend 1999). Because a summary of the entire period is not possible here, attention will be confined to the two works that exert the greatest contemporary influence: Hutcheson's *Inquiry* and Hume's essay. The latter is universally regarded as the masterpiece of the period: it stands with Kant's third Critique as a foundational text of modern aesthetic theory.

Hutcheson

Despite the untidy appearance it presents on a first reading, Hutcheson's *An Inquiry Concerning Beauty, Order, Harmony, Design* (the first of the two treatises constituting his *Inquiry into the Original of Our Ideas of Beauty and Virtue* (Hutcheson 1973)) can be viewed as a reasonably unified response to a single question: What is the source of the pleasure we take in beauty? It is among Hutcheson's chief merits to have grasped that this question will remain unanswered so long as our focus remains fixed on objects, as it had in rival rationalist accounts of beauty. For the source of the pleasure of beauty, it seems, lies in us as well as in objects, and Hutcheson, accordingly, treats the question as a compound of two simpler questions. First, what is the source of the pleasure of beauty in us? And second, what is its source in objects?

Hutcheson's answer to the first question is that it is in virtue of our possession of an 'internal sense' that we take pleasure in objects of beauty; his answer to the second is that it is in virtue of their possession of 'uniformity amidst variety' that objects of beauty give pleasure to us. Though both answers continue to be sources of inspiration in the twentieth and early twenty-first centuries, the first is of considerably greater historical moment. For in carving out a category of internally sensible pleasure, of which the pleasure of beauty is but one; a corresponding category of internally sensible properties, of which the property of beauty is but one; and a corresponding category of internally sensible objects, encompassing both art works and natural phenomena, Hutcheson fashions the first philosophically sophisticated incarnations of our categories of aesthetic pleasure, aesthetic properties, aesthetic objects, and so on. In short, and with important modifications, what was 'internally sensible' for Hutcheson has become 'aesthetic' for us, and it is on this basis that Hutcheson lays claim to the title of founder of modern philosophical aesthetics.

Hutcheson opens his *Inquiry* with the complaint that there are but two acknowledged categories of pleasures. One is the category of 'sensible pleasures,' which comprises those pleasures that arise solely from external sources, namely the five bodily senses, and which includes the pleasures we take in colors and in simple sounds. The other is the category of 'rational pleasures,' which comprises the pleasures that arise only with the additional involvement of reason (the only acknowledged internal source), and which is apparently exhausted by the self-interested pleasures we take in acquiring things we believe to be personally advantageous and the disinterested pleasures we take in making intellectual discoveries (Hutcheson 1973: *Inquiry* Preface). To establish that the pleasure of beauty falls under neither category, Hutcheson argues both, one, that the pleasure of beauty cannot arise with the involvement of reason, and therefore must have its source solely in the senses, and two, that the pleasure of beauty cannot arise solely from external sources, and therefore can arise only with the involvement of some internal source (or sources). By establishing these two points, Hutcheson forces the acknowledgment of a new category of pleasures: to the (externally) sensible and the (internally) rational, we must add the internally sensible, a category consisting of those pleasures that arise only with the involvement of some internal sense, which includes the pleasure of beauty.

That the pleasure of beauty arises without the involvement of reason, and is therefore purely sensible, follows, Hutcheson maintains, from the fact that such pleasure arises 'naturally,' 'necessarily,' 'immediately,' and without 'increase of knowledge.' The precise meaning he assigns to each element of this description is a matter of some debate. But what is obviously true of the final element appears equally true of the rest: each ascribes a kind of independence to the arising of the pleasure of beauty. To say that such pleasure arises 'naturally' is to say that it arises independently of "custom, education, and example" (Hutchinson 1973, *Inquiry* sect. VII, art. I). To say that such pleasure arises 'necessarily' is to say that it arises independently of mere acts of will: no mere "resolution of our own [can] vary the beauty of any object" (ibid.: sect. I, art. XIII), which means that we can "procure" the pleasure of beauty only by subjecting ourselves to beautiful objects (ibid.: Preface). To say that such pleasure arises 'immediately' is to say, in effect, that it arises independently of self-interest, since the determination of what is or is not in one's interest may require "long deductions of reason" (ibid.: Preface). And to say, finally, that such pleasure arises without 'increase of knowledge' is to say that it arises independently of the kind of disinterested knowledge that we find exemplified in "knowledge of principles, proportions, and causes" (ibid.: sect. I, art. XII). (It is worth noting that acquisition of the same knowledge may give rise either to self-interested or to disinterested pleasure: the pleasure I take in acquiring the knowledge that $e=mc^2$, for example, will be disinterested if it arises merely and immediately from the discovery itself, though self-interested to the degree that it arises from the further realization that I can use this discovery to make atomic weapons which I can use to destroy my enemies.)

Hutcheson never explains how this fourfold description eliminates reason as a source of the pleasure of beauty. But to interpret him as maintaining that each facet of the description suffices individually to eliminate reason is to do him injustice, for he must be aware that no single facet will. Hutcheson concedes that all pleasures, sensible and rational, arise necessarily (ibid.: Preface). Moreover, he concedes that some rational pleasures – the self-interested ones, specifically – do not arise from "increase of [disinterested] knowledge," and that other rational pleasures – those that arise, for example, from the discovery of "principles, proportions, and causes" – are disinterested, and therefore presumably immediate (ibid.: sect. I, art. XIV). And, finally, unless he holds the odd view that human beings must be taught to take pleasure in acquiring objects or knowledge that they believe will serve their interests, and must additionally be taught to take pleasure in intellectual discovery, he must also concede that some rational pleasures arise naturally.

Hutcheson, therefore, would appear to hold the following: while some rational pleasures arise naturally, some immediately, some without increase of disinterested knowledge, and all necessarily, no single rational pleasure arises at once naturally, immediately, without disinterested knowledge, and necessarily. That no rational pleasure does so arise, in fact, follows from the impossibility of any rational pleasure arising both immediately and without increase of disinterested knowledge: for all rational pleasures arise from some kind of knowledge, and all knowledge is either interested or disinterested. Therefore, given that the pleasure of beauty arises immediately and without increase of disinterested knowledge (as well as necessarily and naturally), it follows that reason cannot be a source of the pleasure of beauty. Moreover, that the pleasure of beauty arises in each of the four ways is consistent with – in fact, suggestive of – its arising from thoroughly sensible sources. The pleasure of beauty, therefore, must be purely sensible.

To establish that the pleasure of beauty is *internal* is simple by comparison. Hutcheson adduces two basic arguments for the conclusion that the external senses are by themselves insufficient to account for the pleasure we take in beauty. One is that some people possess all five external senses, each in perfect working condition, and are yet incapable of taking pleasure in acknowledged objects of beauty (Hutcheson 1973, *Inquiry* sect. I, art. X). The other is that not all objects of beauty are objects of external sense: Hutcheson observes, for example, that we sometimes report being struck by the beauty of certain particularly economical yet powerful "theorems" or "demonstrated universal truths," such as the propositions of Euclid's geometry or Newton's gravitational principle. (ibid.: sect. I, art. XI; sect III, arts. I, II, V). To the premise that the source of pleasure is thoroughly sensible, then, we add the premise that it arises only with the involvement of some internal source. From these considerations Hutcheson's conclusion then follows inescapably: the pleasure of beauty arises only with the involvement of an internal sense, or equivalently, the pleasure of beauty is internally sensible.

The equivalence of these two ways of putting Hutcheson's conclusion may be puzzling. The thesis that the pleasure of beauty is internally sensible, where Hutcheson's 'internally sensible' means *something* like our 'aesthetic,' may strike us as uninformative. But this is merely an artifact of the ultimate success of Hutcheson's project in fashioning a new category to house the pleasure of beauty. The equivalent thesis that the pleasure of beauty arises via an internal sense, by contrast, may strike us as far-fetched, for it may seem to imply the existence of some as yet undiscovered internal, possibly physical, organ. But 'sense' carries no such implication in Hutcheson's *Inquiry*, where it refers merely to the 'power of receiving ideas' in response to the 'action' of objects upon us ('idea,' following Locke's usage, refers to any mental entity that can be the object of consciousness) (ibid.: sect. I, arts. I and IX). That some senses depend on (physical) organs for the reception of their ideas is therefore incidental to their classification as senses. To possess the sense of hearing is simply to be capable of receiving the set of ideas we call 'sounds' in response to the action of objects suited to give such ideas; to possess the sense of beauty is simply to be capable of receiving the idea we call 'the pleasure of beauty' in response to the action of objects suited to give such pleasure.

This characterization of the sense of beauty prompts the question what quality (or complex of qualities) suits an object to give us the pleasure of beauty: the question, in other words, of the source of the pleasure of beauty in objects. The answer may seem obvious: it may seem that it is in virtue of their possession of the quality of beauty that objects give rise to the pleasure of beauty. Hutcheson rejects this answer not because it is uninformative, but because it is, strictly speaking, false. Following Locke, Hutcheson thinks of the idea of beauty as an idea of a secondary quality, which means that beauty exists as an idea merely, and not as a quality that inheres in objects (Hutcheson 1973, *Inquiry* sect. I, art. XVI). Thus Hutcheson's quest for the objective source of beauty can only terminate in the discovery of a quality (or complex of qualities) that causes the idea of beauty, and that is not (strictly speaking) the quality of beauty.

The terminus of Hutcheson's quest, as has been noted, is the discovery of the quality of 'uniformity amidst variety,' a 'compound' of the qualities of uniformity and variety (ibid.: sect. II, art. III). Hutcheson's view, contrary to what this may appear to suggest, is not that the pleasure of beauty arises from the proper balance of the opposing qualities of uniformity and variety. It is, rather that the pleasure of beauty arises from the simple presence of these two non-opposing, independently variable qualities. The stronger the concentration of each, the stronger the resulting pleasure (ibid.: sect. II, art. III). Hutcheson's notions of uniformity and variety, therefore, are somewhat non-standard: for 'uniformity' he sometimes substitutes 'order' and 'regularity' and he seems generally to regard 'variety' as synonymous with 'complexity' (ibid.: e.g. sect. VI, arts V–IX). Thus Hutcheson's thesis, roughly speaking, is that objects give rise to the pleasure of beauty to the degree they possess complex order. His chief method of establishing this empirical thesis is to assemble a diverse body of beautiful objects – natural scenes (ibid.: sect. II, art. V), animal bodies (ibid.: sect. II, arts. VI–X), music (ibid.: sect. II, art. XIII), architecture (ibid.: sect. III, art. VII), gardens (ibid.: sect. III, art. VII), theorems (ibid.: sect. III, arts. I–V), and the imitative arts of painting, sculpture, and literary description (ibid.: sect. IV, arts. I–II) – observing of each that it possesses both uniformity and variety in high degree (ibid.: sect. II, art. III).

Hutcheson's attribution of uniformity amidst variety to theorems and imitative arts calls for clarification and comment. The uniformity amidst variety of an imitative work consists, he claims, in the unification, via resemblance, of original and copy (Hutcheson 1973, *Inquiry*: sect. VI: art. I); the uniformity amidst variety of a theorem (a demonstrated universal truth) consists, he maintains, in the unification of "an infinite multitude" of particulars under a single principle (ibid.: sect. III: art. I). The classification of theorems as objects of beauty yields the pleasing result that Hutcheson's own theorem is itself beautiful, unifying, as it does, the most diverse specimens of beauty under the single principle of uniformity amidst variety. But difficulties ensue. Hutcheson's earlier conclusion that the pleasure of beauty is sensible depends crucially, as noted, on the premise that such pleasure does not arise from 'increase of knowledge.' To preserve this conclusion, Hutcheson later claims that the arising of the pleasure of beauty no more depends on the knowledge that the 'beautiful' object possesses uniformity amidst variety than the arising of the idea of sweetness depends on the knowledge that the 'sweet' object possesses the quality (or complex of qualities) responsible for the arising of that idea (ibid.: sect. II, art. XIV). But it is difficult to see how Hutcheson can maintain this line with respect to theorems. For what could it mean to take pleasure in the contemplation of a theorem (as theorem) that does not depend on the knowledge that the theorem unifies various particulars under a single principle? That a parallel problem arises involving imitative art works is of greater concern, given their status as paradigms of beauty. For what could it mean to take pleasure in an imitation (as imitation) that does not depend on the knowledge that the imitation imitates the original (Kivy 1995: 352–5)?

In answering his second question, then, Hutcheson appears to undermine his answer to the first. The conclusion that knowledge, and therefore reason, plays no role in the taking of aesthetic pleasure proves difficult to sustain once inquiry descends to the particulars of the objects that provoke it. It is significant that Hutcheson's *Inquiry* should embody precisely this tension: perhaps none is more characteristic of the tradition it inaugurates.

Hume

Hutcheson's influence is difficult to perceive in the deceptively difficult "Of the Standard of Taste," Hume's primary contribution to aesthetic theory. This should not be surprising considering that Hume addresses neither of Hutcheson's questions other than to dismiss, without argument, both of Hutcheson's answers: Hume takes the pleasure of beauty to arise with the involvement of both senses and reason, and to have not one but irreducibly many causes in objects. But both points are incidental to Hume's larger project: the seemingly hopeless search for a standard of taste.

Hume attributes the seeming hopelessness of his project to its apparent incompatibility with the Lockean thesis that "beauty is no quality in things themselves," but merely a 'sentiment' in "the mind that contemplates them" (Hume 1985: 229–30). If beauty were a quality in objects, judgements concerning their beauty would "have a reference to something beyond themselves," namely to "real matter of fact," that is, to the objects themselves, and would therefore be true or false according to presence or absence of beauty in those objects (ibid.: 230). Objects themselves would then provide a standard for judging individual tastes: good taste would consist in the ability to perceive beauty in, and only in, objects possessing it. Given, however, that beauty is merely a 'sentiment' of pleasure excited by the perception of objects, judgements concerning their beauty have "a reference to nothing beyond [themselves]," and are true or false (if either) according merely to the presence or absence of pleasure in the mind that perceives them. It thus appears that there can be no standard of taste, for assuming that we are capable of detecting the presence or absence of pleasure in our own minds, all judgements of beauty will be true, and all tastes therefore equally sound (ibid.: 230).

Hume's strategy is not to dispute the Lockean thesis, but to argue that its truth does not preclude the existence of a standard of taste. At the basis of Hume's argument is a partition of what might be called 'the mechanism of taste' into two stages: a perceptual stage, in which we perceive qualities in objects, and an affective stage, in which we feel the pleasurable sentiments of beauty, or the displeasurable sentiments of 'deformity,' that arise from our perceptions of those qualities. Because we pass through both stages in arriving at judgements of taste, differences in such judgements will divide into two categories: those arising merely at the latter stage, and which are therefore purely affective, and those arising in the former stage, and which are therefore perceptual in origin. Insofar as differences in taste are purely affective, insofar as they are *merely* differences in taste, Hume concedes that there is simply "no room to give the one the preference above the other" (ibid.: 244). But insofar as differences in taste arise from differences in perception, Hume believes that we have a standard for preferring some tastes above others because we have a standard for preferring some perceptions above others. Since we regard perceptions as accurate or inaccurate as they represent or fail to represent the nuances of the objects to which they refer, we may regard sentiments as 'right' or (presumably) 'wrong' as they arise from accurate or inaccurate perceptions (ibid.: 230). The questions whether and when there is a standard of taste thus reduce to the questions whether and when differences in taste result from differences in perception. When differences in taste do result from differences in perception, the former fall heir to the standard of the latter, and so end up having the very standard the Lockean thesis seemed to have deprived them of: "real matter of fact."

Hume opens his essay by conceding what is "too obvious not to have fallen under every one's observation": that a "great variety of Taste . . . prevails in the world" (Hume 1985: 226). Amidst that great variety, however, Hume remarks conspicuous instances of uniformity: the "same HOMER," for example, "who pleased at ATHENS and ROME two thousand years ago, is still admired at PARIS and at LONDON" (ibid.: 233). That the works of Homer, Virgil, Terence, and Cicero, among presumably many others, have pleased minds in such diverse places and times indicates that they possess qualities that the mind, by its nature, takes pleasure in perceiving (ibid.: 233, 243). That the mind naturally takes pleasure in the perception of certain properties – and displeasure, he presumes, in the perception of certain others – means that it operates according to what Hume calls 'principles of taste' or 'rules of art:' principles stating simply that the perception of certain properties of objects always gives rise to pleasurable sentiments of beauty, or to displeasurable sentiments of 'deformity,' in the human mind (ibid.: 231–4). Hume's interest in positing principles of taste – principles asserting universal causal links between the two stages of the mechanism of taste – is perhaps clear: insofar as the mind operates according to them, differences in taste can only be perceptual in origin, for insofar as uniform perceptions of objects lead inevitably to uniform affective responses, divergent affective responses lead inevitably back to divergent perceptions. It therefore follows that when, for example, we fail to take pleasure in works possessing properties "fitted by nature" (ibid.: 235) to please us, the blame falls neither on works, nor on principles, but on us. "Some particular forms or qualities, from the original structure of the internal fabric, are calculated to please," Hume writes, "and if they fail of their effect in any particular instance, it is from some apparent defect or imperfection in the organ" (ibid.: 233).

Hume devotes considerable attention to cataloging and describing the defects that prevent our taking pleasure in works 'fitted by nature' to please us. His catalogue includes five items: one, lack of 'delicacy,' two, lack of 'good sense,' three, failure to have practiced, four, failure to have formed comparisons, and five, prejudice. Delicacy is the ability to perceive each of the 'ingredients', or aesthetically relevant properties, of works perceivable by the senses, particularly those that are difficult to detect because they are overshadowed by other properties or present only in small degree (Hume 1985: 234–7). Good sense is the ability to perceive each of the ingredients or properties of works perceivable by reason, such as "the mutual relation and correspondence" of a work's parts, or the suitability of a work to achieve the particular end for which it was designed (ibid.: 240). To possess both delicacy and good sense is presumably to possess the ability to perceive all the aesthetically relevant properties of works. Hume recommends practice, it appears, merely as the best method to acquire both delicacy and good sense (ibid.: 237–8). The formation of comparisons "between the several species and degrees of excellence" enables one to assign the proper comparative weight to each pleasure occasioned by the perception of each ingredient (ibid.: 238). To be prejudiced with respect to a work is to allow pleasures or displeasures arising from extraneous factors, such as biases for or against the artist's person or culture, to distort one's response to the work (ibid.: 239–40). We may summarize, then, by saying that persons free from each of these five defects are persons whose affective response to art works arises from the properly weighted perceptions of only and all the aesthetically relevant properties of those works. We may simplify still further, perhaps, by saying that persons free from the five defects are persons whose affective response to art works arises from the ideal perception of those works. Hume refers to persons free from the five defects as 'true judges,' and concludes that "the joint verdict of such, wherever they are to be found, is the true standard of taste and beauty" (ibid.: 241).

Understanding the basis of Hume's conclusion requires a grasp of the somewhat elusive relation between principles of taste and true judges. This may best be illustrated by example. Suppose that my verdict with respect to some particular art work differs from the verdict of a true judge: the true judge responds with a balance of pleasure over displeasure and I do not. Suppose, further, that universal principles of taste govern both responses: we are both disposed, given the common nature of our minds, to take the same pleasures and displeasures in the perception of the aesthetically relevant properties of the work. In such a case, the divergence in affective response can be explained only by a divergence in perception, presumably from the true judge's success and my failure to have perceived certain of the work's aesthetically relevant properties. The only way I can now avoid conceding that the true judge's response is superior to mine, and not merely different from it, is to maintain that the true judge's perception is not superior to mine, but merely different from it. But I cannot maintain this: "the sentiments of all mankind are agreed" in acknowledging it "to be the perfection of every sense or faculty to perceive with exactness its most minute objects, and allow nothing to escape its notice and observation" (Hume 1985: 236). It follows, therefore, that where there exist universal principles linking the perception of the properties of a work to the arousal of sentiments of pleasure and displeasure in the mind, where, in other words, we would all respond uniformly to a work if we only ideally perceived it, the response of the true judge is the ideal response because the perception of the true judge is ideal perception.

Hume acknowledges, however, the existence of cases in which principles of taste do not fully govern our affective responses: cases, in other words, in which differences in affective response do not result entirely from differences in perception. He notes, near the essay's end, that in addition to the five mainly perceptual defects under which "the generality of men labour" (Hume 1985: 241), there exist two additional sources of diversity of taste: "the different humours of particular men" and "the particular manners and opinions of our age and country" (ibid.: 243). Such constitutional and cultural differences, Hume maintains, will bring about divergent affective responses to the perception of certain properties of art works, which means that no principles of taste will specify those properties, and that uniform perceptions of works possessing them will not necessarily issue in uniform affective responses. When differences in taste with respect to such works arise without perceptual basis, then they are mere differences in taste, and "we seek in vain for a standard, by which to reconcile the contrary sentiments" (ibid.: 244). It is because of the possibility of such 'blameless' differences in taste that Hume maintains that we have a standard of taste only when true judges render a *joint* verdict. To say that a verdict of true judges is joint is to say that is the verdict that any ideal perceiver would give, regardless of particular constitution or cultural background: a verdict jointly rendered by true judges, it turns out, just is a verdict governed by principles of taste. There is a sense in which such verdicts belong to us all. They are fully expressive of our own affective dispositions; they are fully expressive, we might say, of our own tastes. They are the verdicts we would all give, if only we perceived better: the verdicts of our perceptually better selves.

One element of Hume's account has not aged well. In asserting that a property that pleases in one art work will please equally in all, Hume ignores a crucial role that context is now recognized to play in the value of art works: no property of art works, we now realize, is everywhere a merit. But it is far from clear that a more nuanced account of principles cannot calm contextualist worries while accomplishing what Hume's theory asks of it. Moreover, there is nothing in Hume's theory that drives his particular account of principles: it should be possible to substitute a sophisticated version with little violence to the rest of the theory. The rest is worth saving. In distinguishing mere differences of taste from perceptually based differences of taste, and in then arguing that the latter must have a standard in "real matter of fact," Hume provides a basis for understanding aesthetic norms that is as promising as any our discipline has seen.

See also The aesthetic, Aesthetic universals, Taste, Beauty, Value of art, Kant, Sibley.

References

Hume, D. (1985) "Of the Standard of Taste," *Essays Moral, Political and Literary*, ed. E. Miller, Indianapolis: Liberty Classics.

Hutcheson, F. (1973) *An Inquiry Concerning Beauty, Order, Harmony, Design*, ed. P. Kivy, The Hague: Martinus Nijhoff.

Kivy, P. (1976) *The Seventh Sense: A Study of Francis Hutcheson's Aesthetics and Its Influence in Eighteenth Century Britain*, New York: Burt Franklin.

—— (1995) "The 'Sense' of Beauty and the Sense of 'Art': Hutcheson's Place in the History and Practice of Aesthetics," *Journal of Aesthetics and Art Criticism* 20: 349–57.

Kristeller, P. O. (1951) "The Modern System of the Arts: A Study in the History of Aesthetics," *Journal of the History of Ideas* 12: 496–527 and 13: 17–46.

Locke, J. (1975) *An Essay Concerning Human Understanding*, ed. P. H. Hidditch, Oxford: Oxford University Press.

Stolnitz, J. (1961) "On the Origins of 'Aesthetic Disinterestedness'," *Journal of Aesthetics and Art Criticism* 20: 131–44.

Townsend, D. (1991) "Lockean Aesthetics," *Journal of Aesthetics and Art Criticism* 49: 349–61.

Further readings

Carroll, N. (1984) "Hume's Standard of Taste," *Journal of Aesthetics and Art Criticism* 43: 181–94. (A critical interpretation of "Of the Standard of Taste" that questions the necessity of true judges.)

Cohen, T. (1994) "Partial Enchantments of the Quixote Story in Hume's Essay on Taste," in R. Yanal (ed.), *Institutions of Art*, University Park: Pennsylvania State University Press. (A reading of Hume's essay that focuses on Hume's use of the parable of Sancho's kinsmen from *Don Quixote*.)

Dickie, G. (1996) *The Century of Taste*, Oxford: Oxford University Press. (A comparative study of the aesthetic theories of Hutcheson, Hume, Alison, Gerard, and Kant.)

Gracyk, T. (1994) "Rethinking Hume's Standard of Taste," *Journal of Aesthetics and Art Criticism* 52: 168–82. (An attempt to bridge apparent gaps in the argument of "Of the Standard of Taste" by appeal to other of Hume's literary essays.)

Jones, P. (1993) "Hume's Literary and Aesthetic Theory," in D. Norton (ed.), *Cambridge Companion to Hume*, Cambridge: Cambridge University Press. (A broad historical treatment of Hume's various writings on literary and aesthetic matters.)

Kivy, P. (1967) "Hume's Standard of Taste: Breaking the Circle," *British Journal of Aesthetics* 7: 57–66. (A discussion of the apparent circularity of Hume's definition of the standard of taste.)

—— (1989) "Recent Scholarship and the British Tradition: A Logic of Taste – The First Fifty Years," in G. Dickie, R. Sclafani and R. Roblin (eds), *Aesthetics: A Critical Anthology*, New York: St. Martin's Press. (An essay-length discussion of the major thinkers and themes of eighteenth-century British aesthetics.)

——(1995) "The 'Sense' of Beauty and the Sense of 'Art': Hutcheson's Place in the History and Practice of Aesthetics," *Journal of Aesthetics and Art Criticism* 20: 349–57. (An assessment of Hutcheson's importance in the history of modern aesthetics.)

Korsmeyer, C. (1995) "Gendered Concepts and Hume's Standard of Taste," in P. Z. Brand and C. Korsmeyer (eds), *Feminism and Tradition in Aesthetics*, University Park: Pennsylvania State University Press. (A critical investigation of the purportedly gender-neutral status of Hume's standard.)

Matthews, P. (1998) "Hutcheson on the Idea of Beauty," *Journal of the History of*

Philosophy 36: 233–60. (A discussion of exegetical issues raised by Hutcheson's seemingly contradictory remarks concerning the idea of beauty.)

Mothersill, M. (1989) "Hume and the Paradox of Taste," in G. Dickie, R. Sclafani and R. Roblin (eds) *Aesthetics: A Critical Anthology*, New York: St Martin's Press (An interpretation of Hume's "Of the Standard of Taste" that proposes a subtext denying principles of taste.)

Shelley, J. (1998) "Hume and the Nature of Taste," *Journal of Aesthetics and Art Criticism* 56: 29–38. (An examination of the roles of human nature and perception in the argument of "Of the Standard of Taste".)

Shiner, R. (1996) "Hume and the Causal Theory of Taste," *Journal of Aesthetics and Art Criticism* 54: 237–49. (An attempt to refute causal theories of taste, as exemplified by Hume's.)

Shusterman, R. (1989) "Of the Scandal of Taste: Social Privilege as Nature in the Aesthetic Theories of Hume and Kant," *Philosophical Forum* 20: 211–29. (A critical examination of the political presuppositions of the aesthetic theories of Hume and Kant.)

Townsend, D. (ed.) (1999) *Eighteenth-Century British Aesthetics*, Amityville, N.Y.: Baywood. (A comprehensive collection of writings of eighteenth-century aestheticians, including Hume's essay and an abridged version of Hutcheson's *Inquiry*.)

Wieand, J. (1983) "Hume's Two Standards of Taste," *Philosophical Quarterly* 34: 129–42. (A discussion of exegetical issues raised by Hume's apparent acknowledgement of two separate standards of taste.)

5

KANT

Donald W. Crawford

Immanuel Kant's seminal work, the *Critique of Judgement (Kritik der Urteilskraft)*, published in 1790 (Kant 1951 [1790]), is generally regarded as the foundational treatise in modern philosophical aesthetics. Plato's *Ion* and *Republic*, along with Aristotle's *Poetics*, were the major writings of the ancients; and there were earlier eighteenth-century writings both on the European continent (Leibnitz, Baumgarten) and in England (such as Shaftesbury, Addison, Burke and Hume). But no integration of aesthetic theory into a complete philosophical system predates Kant's third *Critique*, and its importance and influence is as evident today as in the decades following its publication.

Kant directed his attention to aesthetics relatively late in his philosophical career, having already completed most of his major works, such as the *Critique of Pure Reason* (1781), *Prolegomena to Any Future Metaphysics* (1783), *Foundations of the Metaphysics of Morals* (1785), and the *Critique of Practical Reason* (1788). During his pre-critical period, he had written a minor essay, *Observations on the Feeling of the Beautiful and the Sublime* (1764), which consisted almost entirely of socio-anthropological speculations.

Until the late 1780's, Kant did not consider what we know today as aesthetics to be a legitimate subject for philosophy. He denied the possibility of principles of taste, holding that our judgements about beauty are based simply on pleasure, and being entirely subjective are only a fit topic for empirical studies (anthropology or history). Nor did he regard aesthetic perception as related to the realm of cognitive judgement, understanding and ideas. But Kant's drive for philosophical systemmaticity led him to reconsider whether a critical examination of our faculty of feeling pleasure might discover a third branch of philosophy that would join theoretical philosophy (metaphysics) and practical philosophy (ethics) in being based on a priori principles. The *Critique of Pure Reason* had uncovered a priori conditions for making objective, universally valid empirical judgements, both ordinary and scientific. Space and time are the a priori conditions of our being affected by things (Sensibility) and the categories are the a priori conditions of making judgements (Understanding). The *Critique of Practical Reason* had discovered a priori conditions for making objective, universally valid moral judgements. The question for the *Critique of Judgement*, then, was whether there are a priori conditions for making judgements based on pleasure, with Kant taking as his paradigm the type of judgement everyone believes is based on feeling pleasure, namely the judgement that something is beautiful.

Kant's epistemology and metaphysics are based on a division between Sensibility and Understanding. Sensibility is the passive ability to be affected by things by receiving sensations, but this is not yet at the level of thought or even experience in any meaningful sense. Understanding, on the other hand, is non-sensible; it is discursive and works with general concepts, not individual intuitions; it is the active faculty of producing thoughts. Ordinary experience comes about through the synthesis of these two powers of the mind: the material of sensation coming to be grasped as ordered under a concept, thus resulting in a thought (or judgement), such as 'This [what I am looking at and is giving me visual sensations] is a book.' By 'judgement' Kant simply means experience that results in a claim or assertion about something or, even more generally, an awareness that something is the case. The judgement that something is beautiful he calls a 'judgement of taste.'

The analytic of the beautiful

The beginning section of the *Critique of Judgement* is titled the "Analytic of the Beautiful," which Kant says consists in an analysis of "what is required in order to call an object beautiful" (Kant 1951: §1n). It is divided into four "Moments," corresponding to the headings of the table of judgements in the *Critique of Pure Reason* (A70 = B95): quantity, quality, relation and modality. The fit of the judgement of taste to this table is strained, but the structure serves Kant's purpose of systematic elucidations of the formal properties of judgements of taste, and these elucidations – rather than the architectonic structure – are the heart of his aesthetic theory. They consist in detailed analyses of that to which we are committing ourselves in making a judgement of taste. At the same time, parts of these sections go beyond mere analysis, anticipating and overlapping the content of later sections.

Disinterested pleasure

The judgement of taste is the judgement that something is or is not beautiful. The First Moment (Quality) of the "Analytic of the Beautiful" concludes that in order to call an object beautiful one must judge it to be "the object of an *entirely disinterested* [*ohne alles Interesse*] satisfaction or dissatisfaction" (§1). Thus when beauty is affirmed of the object there is additional content to this affirmation, namely the ability of the object to provide satisfaction to those who judge it disinterestedly.

How does Kant reach this conclusion? He begins with the observation that the judgement of taste is an aesthetic judgement, which he contrasts with a cognitive judgement. In making a cognitive judgement I refer my experiential content to an object by means of a concept: for example, I judge that this (what I am aware of) is print on paper. When I make an aesthetic judgement, on the other hand, I refer the experiential content back to my own subjective state. In judging something to be beautiful, what one is aware of (a painting, a building, a flower) is referred "back to the subject and to its feeling of life, under the name of the feeling of pleasure or displeasure" (Kant 1951: §1). Thus, generically, judgements of taste are a subset of that type of judgement that says that something is pleasing to apprehend; they are therefore subjective rather than objective judgements.

Kant then differentiates the pleasure in the beautiful from other pleasures, by claiming that it is not based on any interest, but is "a disinterested and *free* satisfaction; for no interest, either of sense or of reason, here forces our assent" (Kant 1951: §2). The pleasure we feel in finding something beautiful is not a pleasure based on any interest we have in an object's simply gratifying our senses, such as candy satisfying a craving for sweetness. Nor is it a pleasure based on finding that an object serves a desired practical use (this is the mediately good or the useful). Nor is it a pleasure based on finding that it fulfills moral requirements (this is the morally good). The pleasure in the beautiful, in contrast to the above, is not based on any interest in the *existence* of an object; it is "merely *contemplative*" (ibid.: §5).

Although this explanation of the pleasure in the beautiful as a disinterested pleasure seems merely negative, the notions of *free* contemplation and reflection anticipate Kant's attempt to show the legitimacy of the judgement of taste as a unique type of judgement. For contemplation and reflection are absent in the case of what pleases merely through sensation, and in judging what is useful or moral, the acts of reflection and contemplation are not free but constrained by definite concepts.

Universal pleasure

The Second Moment (Quantity, §§6–9), begins to make this clearer, although the compact text is difficult because Kant goes far beyond merely analyzing the judgement of taste, and anticipates justifying its legitimacy as a class of judgement based on an a priori principle. Its conclusion, that "the *beautiful* is that which pleases universally without [requiring] a concept" (Kant 1951: §9), is badly put, since it is plainly false: a beautiful thing does not please everyone.

The more warranted conclusion is the title given to §6: "the beautiful is that which apart from concepts is represented [*vorgestellt wird*] as the object of a universal satisfaction."

Just as the First Moment encapsulates the common sense notion that one judges something to be beautiful based on the pleasure one feels in apprehending it, so the Second Moment enshrines our belief that the pleasure in the beautiful is not wholly subjective but has some basis that justifies our thinking that others should find the object beautiful as well, while fully recognizing that not everyone will in fact agree with us. Hence Kant says "the judgement of taste itself does not *postulate* the agreement of everyone" (ibid.: §8). Rather, in saying that something is beautiful we think that others should agree with us, which is not the case if we simply say that something is pleasing to us (like the smell of garlic). Kant calls this feature of judgements of taste their "subjective universality" (ibid.: §6).

Kant argues for this universality thesis in two ways, first through the concept of disinterestedness. If one believes the pleasure in finding something beautiful is not owing to any interest, then one naturally concludes that the pleasure does not depend on any private conditions but "must be regarded as grounded on what he can presuppose in every other person . . . Consequently the judgement of taste, accompanied with the consciousness of separation from all interest, must claim validity for everyone" (Kant 1951: §6). Secondly, Kant appeals to semantic considerations:

> to say "This object is beautiful *for me*" is laughable, while it makes perfect sense to say "It is pleasant *to me*" . . . not only as regards the taste of the tongue, the palate, and the throat, but for whatever is pleasant to anyone's eyes and ears.
>
> (Kant 1951: §7)

Thus to say that something is beautiful is (linguistically) to claim universality for one's judgement.

An additional conclusion of the Second Moment is that this implied universality "does not rest on concepts of objects (not even on empirical ones)" (Kant 1951: §8), and hence is not objective but only subjective universality. Kant thinks this follows from that fact that judgements of taste cannot be proved: "there can be no rule according to which anyone is to be forced to recognize anything as beautiful"(ibid.: §8). This theme recurs in Section 34, where Kant emphasizes that no syllogism can force one's assent to a judgement of taste, but that judging something to be beautiful requires that one must *immediately* feel pleasure in experiencing the object. Later this same theme forms the 'thesis' of the "Antinomy of Taste" (ibid.: §56).

At this point Kant's explication of judgements of taste leads to what looks like an insoluble problem. The judgement of taste is based on the feeling of pleasure but also claims universal validity; yet judgements of taste cannot be proved since they do not rest on concepts or rules. Hence it must be the feeling of pleasure itself that one postulates is universally communicable. How can that be? Kant faces this crucial question in §9, which he says "is the key to the critique of taste." The brief answer is that a pleasure can be universally communicable only if it is based not on mere sensation but rather on a state of mind that is universally communicable. And since the only universally communicable states of mind are cognitive states, somehow the pleasure in the beautiful must be based on cognition. Since the judgement of taste is not cognitive in the defining sense of making reference to a concept, though, the pleasure underlying the judgement of taste cannot be based on a particular (or determinate) cognitive state of mind, but only on "*cognition in general*" (Kant 1951: §9). Kant identifies this with the free play of the cognitive faculties – imagination and understanding – in harmony with one another, a harmony we are aware of only through the feeling of pleasure. So the pleasure in the beautiful is dependent on judging (estimating, appraising) the object, which activity is the free play of the cognitive faculties, and the pleasure comes about when the faculties are felt to be in harmony, attaining "that proportionate accord [*Stimmung*] which we require for all cognition" (ibid.: §9). It is as if cognition had successfully occurred, only the result is not the determinate cognition of a conceptual judgement. Nonetheless, the judgement takes the *form* of a conceptual judgement, since we speak of beauty "as if it were a property of things" and say "the *thing* is beautiful" (ibid.: §7).

The form of purposiveness

The Third Moment (Relation) purports to explain what is being related to in the judgement that something is beautiful, the *content* of the judgement of taste. Kant concludes that it is the form of the purposiveness or finality [*Zweckmässigkeit*] of an object, insofar far as this is perceived in it without any representation of a purpose or end [*Zweck*] (Kant 1951: §17). This claim is complex. The straightforward part is that pleasure in the beautiful is owing to the perceived *form* of the object, in contrast to sensations or concepts of it.

Kant argues that a *pure* judgement of taste cannot be based on pleasures of charm or emotion (Kant 1951: §13), nor simply on empirical sensations such as charming colors or pleasing tones (ibid.: §14), nor on a definite concept (ibid.: §16), but only on formal properties. These are essentially spatial and temporal relations, as manifested in the spatial delineation or design (*Zeichnung*) of figures and the temporal composition (*Komposition*) of tones (ibid.: §14). Ornamentation or elements of charm or emotion may attract us to beautiful objects, but judging them purely in terms of beauty requires us to abstract from these elements and reflect only on their form. To this extent Kant advances a formalist aesthetics.

The more difficult part of the Third Moment concerns Kant's concept (or perhaps multiple concepts) of "purposiveness without purpose" (Kant 1951: §10), "the mere form of purposiveness,""subjective purposiveness" (ibid.: §11), "formal purposiveness" (ibid.: §12), "formal subjective purposiveness" (ibid.: §12), and "purposive form" (ibid.: §15). The key here is the concept of purpose, which Kant defines in general as "that whose *concept* can be regarded as the ground of the possibility of the object itself" (ibid.: §15). To say that an object (say a knife) has a purpose is to say that the concept of its being the way it is, having the form it has, came first and is the cause of its existence. It was intended to be the way it is: we "place the cause of this form in a will" (ibid.: §10). The knife's form makes sense because we understand what it is supposed to be; it has a purpose. But experiencing a thing's beauty must be different from apprehending its form as reflecting a *definite* purpose. For this would be to consider it either as something that gratifies us through sensation (thus serving only our individual, subjective purposes), or as serving an objective, useful purpose; and neither of these would satisfy the condition that a judgement of taste not be based on interest or concepts. Kant's fundamental claim is that we can find an object to be *purposive in its form* even though we do not conceptualize a definite purpose; and this harmony in its form belies a harmony in our cognitive powers (imagination and understanding) in our reflection on the object, which harmony is itself the pleasure we experience when we find an object beautiful (ibid.: §12).

Necessary pleasure

The final Moment of the "Analytic of the Beautiful" is that of Modality (§§18–22). Kant concludes that "the *beautiful* is that which without any concept is cognized as the object of a *necessary* satisfaction" (Kant 1951: §22). The beautiful has a necessary reference to satisfaction (ibid.: §18), since when we find something beautiful we think that everyone ought to give their approval and also describe it as beautiful. This cannot be a theoretical, objective necessity, since we cannot prove that everyone will feel the same pleasure; nor can it be a practical necessity, since we cannot prove that everyone ought to act in a specific way. Rather, Kant says, the necessity is "exemplary" (ibid.: §18), "subjective" and "conditioned", based on a "ground that is common to all" (ibid.: §19). He describes this as a "*common sense*" (ibid.: §20) – "a subjective principle which determines [viz. necessitates] what pleases or displeases only by feeling and not by concepts, but yet with universal validity" (ibid.: §20). This common sense is exemplary – an ideal or norm – but is presupposed by us in making judgements of taste.

The deduction of judgements of taste

Strictly speaking, the "Analytic of the Beautiful" was only supposed to "show what is required in order to call an object beautiful" (Kant 1951: §1n): that is, to give an explanation of what a judgement of taste means. In fact in this division Kant also begins to discuss the problem that he later says subsumes the *Critique of Judgement* under transcendental philosophy: whether one can provide a 'deduction' (show the legitimacy) of a class of judgement "which imputes the same satisfaction necessarily to everyone" (ibid.: §36). This is the key question of philosophical aesthetics: is it legitimate to make a judgement based merely on the pleasure experienced in perceptually apprehending something, while implying that everyone ought to agree? By insisting that the implied universality and necessity of judgements of taste require philosophical legitimization (deduction), Kant believes he has established a link to "the general problem of transcendental philosophy: how are synthetical *a priori* judgements possible?"(ibid.: §36).

The path to an answer is initiated in the "Analytic of the Beautiful." In Section 9, Kant claims the pleasure in the beautiful must be based on "*cognition in general,*" which is described as the harmony of the cognitive faculties (imagination and understanding) in free play: that is, not determined by concepts. In §11, this harmony is characterized as the representation of the mere form of purposiveness by which an object is given to us. In §15, the determining ground of the judgement is "the feeling (or internal sense) of that harmony in the play of the mental powers, so far as it can be felt in sensation." And finally in §21 the harmony is described as "a subjective condition of cognition," an "accordance [*Stimmung*] of the cognitive powers" that is "only determined by feeling (not according to concepts)." Thus the judgement of taste presupposes or postulates the universal capacity to experience this feeling, which Kant refers to as a "common sense" (ibid.: §§20–22).

The section of the *Critique of Judgement* actually titled "Deduction of [Pure] Aesthetical Judgements" (Kant 1951: §§30–40) sets up the key issue in the same way posed by the "Analytic of the Beautiful": the need to justify the implied universality and necessity of the judgement of taste, a judgement based on perceptual pleasure and not susceptible of proof through appeal to definite rules or principles. This justification can only succeed by reference to cognition, and specifically to the subjective conditions for making judgements in general. Kant thus claims that "the judgement of taste must rest on a mere sensation of the reciprocal activity of the imagination in its *freedom* and the understanding with its *conformity to law*" (ibid.: §35). The conclusion of the Deduction is clearly stated in §38: it is legitimate to impute to everyone the pleasure we experience in the beautiful because, first, we are claiming that it rests on that subjective element that we rightly can presuppose in everyone as requisite for cognition in general, because otherwise we would not be able to communicate with one another, and second, we are also assuming that our judgement of taste is pure: that is, not affected by charm, emotion, the mere pleasantness of sensation, or even concepts.

Experiencing beauty is thus, for Kant, a doubly reflective process. We reflect on the spatial and temporal form of the object by exercising our powers of judgement (imagination and understanding), and we acknowledge the beauty of an object when we come to be aware through the feeling of pleasure of the harmony of these faculties, which awareness comes by reflecting on our own mental states. In §40 Kant again takes up the idea of a 'common sense,' first introduced in §20, and characterizes it as "an effect of mere reflection upon the mind," which we experience "not as a thought, but as an internal feeling of a purposive state of the mind" (Kant 1951: §40).

The sublime

Kant's examples of the sublime in nature are similar to those used by English theorists and found in the geography and travel books of the time, of which he was an avid reader. He refers to the wide ocean disturbed by a storm, the starry heavens, mountain peaks rising to great heights, and deep chasms with raging torrents. By confining his attention to the sublime in nature, he almost completely ignores the sublime in art. The basic components of Kant's theory of the sublime are not original, but rather are a synthesis of various British and German doctrines. Kant's uniqueness lies in his thoroughly secular treatment and the integrating of the sublime into his philosophical system.

In the "Analytic of the Sublime," Kant develops a twofold division into the mathematically sublime and the dynamically sublime, which relate respectively to nature's vastness and power. Both divisions relate to formlessness, our inability to apprehend nature in definite spatio-temporal measures.

We experience the *mathematically sublime* in encountering and reflecting upon natural objects of great magnitude, such as the sea, huge mountains, vast deserts, the night sky. By selecting some unit of measure (such as a meter) and working logically according to a rule, we can estimate the size of such natural objects. This process of estimating vast magnitudes can continue indefinitely. There is nothing surprising in this, nor anything sublime. The sublime occurs, Kant says, when in this process of logical estimation "the mind listens to the voice of reason" (Kant 1951: §26), which demands a totality and urges us to comprehend the vastness in one intuition, a single presentation for all the members of the progressively increasing series. At some point we realize we cannot do this, that no standard of sense apprehension is adequate to the idea of the infinite. This frustrating realization of the inherent limitations of our powers leads to a feeling of displeasure. And yet our ability *to think* of that which is great beyond all comparison must mean we have a supersensible ability, "a faculty of the mind that surpasses every standard of sense" (ibid.: §26): a faculty which exercises dominion over our own sensible powers (that is, nature in us), always directing us toward a more adequate sensible representation of our ideas, as we strive for a greater and greater totality of systematic knowledge.

The initial displeasure or frustration felt in trying to apprehend that which is too great even for our imagination arises from an apparent conflict between our faculties (sense intuition versus comprehension by reason). But it yields a pleasure if, through this very conflict, we are made aware of the power of our reason to direct sensibility and judgement. Kant says that our feeling of respect for the extensive natural object (such as the vast ocean) in the experience of the sublime is a subreption: a "conversion of respect for the idea of humanity in our own subject into respect for the object" that occasions this idea of our own power of reason over our sensibility (nature in us) (Kant 1951: §27).

We experience the *dynamically sublime* in reflecting upon extremely powerful natural objects and phenomena that are capable of exciting fear:

> bold, overhanging, and as it were threatening rocks; clouds piled up in the sky, moving with lightning flashes and thunder peals; volcanoes in all their violence of destruction; hurricanes with their track of devastation; the boundless ocean in a state of tumult; the lofty waterfall of a mighty river, and such like.
>
> (Kant 1951: §28)

Once again, according to Kant, we experience a displeasure, this time caused by the realization of the inadequacy of our physical powers of resistance to nature's might. Although we are literally helpless in the face of the forces of nature, Kant argues that "we can regard an object as *fearful* without being afraid *of* it" (ibid.: §28), as we notice when we feel secure from actual danger in the presence of such forces. Nature's might makes us recognize our own physical impotence, considered as beings of nature, but at the same time nature discloses to us our unique power of a different kind of resistance. We can come to realize that nature has no dominion over us, even over our physical and sensory responses, since we have the ability, through the use of our reason, to direct our sensible faculties not to feel fear in fearful circumstances. On Kant's view, the awareness of this power of reason over sensibility produces the pleasure marking the feeling of the dynamically sublime.

Kant insists that we speak imprecisely in saying that a natural object is sublime. Sublimity, he maintains, is not really a characteristic of nature; it is a property of the human mind. "Thus the wide ocean, disturbed by the storm, cannot be called sublime. Its aspect is horrible" (Kant 1951: §23). This sublimity in the mind is a form of human self-awareness, *through feeling*, of a transcendental power of the human mind. In Kant's language, it is the consciousness that we are superior to nature within us and therefore also superior to nature without us, insofar as it influences us (ibid.: §28). What is it within us that Kant believes is "superior to nature"? Kant's metaphysics surfaces here, as he refers to his *Critique of Pure Reason* doctrine that behind the empirical, causally-determined self of the empirical world there lies a supersensible, noumenal self possessing free will. The mathematically and dynamically sublime thus are two modes of our supersensible freedom revealing itself and thus providing pleasure in the realization of our nature and destiny.

Judgements on the sublime are aesthetic judgements since they are based on pleasure, although the pleasure arises indirectly. Kant maintains that they exactly parallel judgements of taste in claiming to be universally valid, devoid of interest, subjectively purposive, and necessary (Kant 1951: §24). However he claims that the universality and necessity claimed by judgements on the sublime, unlike judgements of taste, do not require a deduction separate from their analysis, because they make no reference to an object judged in terms of its form (recall reference to nature's formlessness), but only to a state of mind.

Natural beauty

Kant's first characterization of natural beauty in the *Critique of Judgement* begins with the remark: "natural beauty . . . brings with it a purposiveness in its form by which the object seems to be, as it were, preadapted to our judgement, and thus constitutes in itself an object of satisfaction" (Kant 1951: §23). Here Kant seems to think that natural beauty is the exemplar of the 'purposiveness of form' that he earlier (ibid.: §14) claimed was the basis of pleasure underlying the judgement of taste.

The second discussion of natural beauty is reflected in Kant's doctrine of free and dependent beauty (ibid.: §16). Kant says that flowers are "free natural beauties" (§16) in that we do not consider their (reproductive) purpose in viewing them merely as to their form. When they please in themselves, our judgements of their beauty are pure. This contrasts with judgements that attribute beauty based on an object's realization of "a concept of its perfection," how good a thing is of its kind, for example "human beauty . . . the beauty of a horse, or a building (be it church, palace, arsenal, or summer house)" (ibid.: §16). Kant implies that in judging a building to be a beautiful church, we consider its form as dependent on the purpose a church serves, whereas in judging it as free beauty, we either do not know or do not consider its purpose. Nature provides us with the most accessible examples of free beauty.

Kant's third discussion of natural beauty explores whether "the mere universal communicability of feelings must carry in itself an interest for us with it" (Kant 1951: §40). He denies this with respect to art, but concludes that if beautiful forms of nature interest someone immediately, "we have reason for attributing to him at least the basis for a good moral disposition" (ibid.: §42). Kant's reasoning is contorted, but relates to his view that we are intent on finding whether our ideas have objective reality. We have an interest in nature being suitable for our powers of judgement, and experience pleasure when we find it so. Kant says this interest is akin to the moral. For morality is only possible if there is an accord between nature and our exercise of free will, if the ends proposed by reason can be actualized in the natural world. However, this purposiveness of natural beauty for our faculties cannot be shown to be real; it is only ideal (ibid.: §58). When nature appears beautiful, it is *as if* it were designed for our reflective powers of judgement. The beautiful in nature gives us an indication that natural laws and our mental powers are in harmony, a harmony which is necessary if we are to create a moral world: a kingdom of ends.

Fine art and artistic genius

"Nature is beautiful because it looks like art, and art can only be called beautiful if we are conscious of it as art while yet it looks like nature" (Kant 1951: §45). The beautiful in nature appears as if it were designed, made in accordance with rules of art. Fine art [*schöne Kunst*] differs from nature since it is the product of human freedom; it must appear spontaneous although rules may be followed precisely in producing it. Art differs from science in requiring skill in addition to knowledge; it differs from handicraft since its production requires more than following rules (ibid.: §43).

Kant's doctrine of artistic creativity became the cornerstone of Romanticism. Fine art is the art of the artistic genius, who has "a *talent* for producing that for which no definite rule can be given" (ibid.: §46) – something original and exemplary which serves as a model for others. Genius is an innate talent that cannot be taught, and the creative process is ineffable, even to the artist (ibid.:

§§47, 49). Genius requires *creative* imagination, "creating another nature, as it were, out of the material that actual nature gives it," working that material "into something different which surpasses nature" (ibid.: §49). The animating principle of the mind behind such creative activity is spirit [*Geist*], which Kant characterizes as "the faculty of presenting *aesthetical ideas*" (ibid.: §49). Aesthetic ideas are the content of works of art; they are linked to concepts, but not determined by them. In art they are the symbolic presentations of rational ideas (such as love, death, envy) through sensible intuitions (such as images in representational painting or poetry).

Success in presenting aesthetical ideas in works of fine art requires more than creative imagination, however. In particular it requires judgement or taste. "Genius can only furnish rich *material* for the products of fine art; its execution and its *form* require talent cultivated in the schools, in order to make such a use of this material as will stand examination by the judgement" (Kant 1951: §47). Genius must be trained and cultivated, "for all the abundance of the [imagination] produces in lawless freedom nothing but nonsense" (ibid.: §50). In fact, Kant suggests that if imagination and judgement conflict in the creation of art, imagination should be limited by judgement and understanding, otherwise communication in the expression of aesthetic ideas – the ultimate aim of art – will not succeed (ibid.: §50).

Kant's treatment of the fine arts concludes with cursory analyses of the individual arts, an attempt to classify the fine arts in terms of their similarities and differences (ibid.: §51), and a brief comparison of their relative worth in terms of ability to express aesthetic ideas, stimulate mental activity, and promote culture (ibid.: §53).

Aesthetics and morality

Kant discusses the relation between aesthetics and morality in three different places. The first is the "General Remark" following §29, in which he says that both the beautiful and the sublime are purposive in reference to moral feeling: "The beautiful prepares us to love disinterestedly something, even nature itself; the sublime prepares us to esteem something highly even in opposition to our own (sensible) interest."

Then in §42 Kant maintains "that to take an *immediate interest* in the beauty of *nature* (not merely to have taste in judging it) is always the mark of a good soul." It is an interest akin to moral interest, because the latter requires an interest in nature conforming to our faculties. But Kant denies an analogous relationship between an immediate interest in fine art and the moral.

Kant's final discussion of the relationship between beauty and morality occurs in "Of Beauty as the Symbol of Morality" (Kant 1951: §59) and "Of the Method of Taste"(ibid.: §60). The meaning and significance of these sections and their relevance to Kant's 'deduction' of judgements of taste have been variously interpreted, but at a minimum Kant seems to think there is an analogy between the two realms. The pleasure in apprehending and judging beauty (and perhaps the sublime as well) is ultimately based on an awareness of (and pleasure in) our faculty of judgement itself exercising a power over sensibility, which is required if morality is to have a point. Based on this analogy, it is possible for an individual's exercise of taste to transfer to the moral realm, the realm requiring the exercise of our freedom (in judgement, above all) to direct our actions in the empirical world.

Kant's heritage

Kant's aesthetic theory is systematic and comprehensive, relating our experience and judgement of natural beauty and art to basic epistemological, metaphysical and ethical concepts. That heritage is evident in the aesthetic theories after him: by Schiller, Hegel, Schopenhauer, Nietzsche, as well as many twentieth-century writers. Kant's theory encompasses many of the issues in aesthetics still discussed energetically today. His everlasting importance to aesthetics is best revealed through careful reading of the *Critique of Judgement*; however difficult that may seem at first, it repays the effort many times over.

See also Beauty, The aesthetic, Taste, Aesthetic universals, Environmental aesthetics.

References

Addison, J. (1712) "The Pleasures of the Imagination," *The Spectator*, nos. 411-21 (21 June–3 July.

Baumgarten, A. G. (1936 [1750, 1758]) *Aesthetica*, Bari: Jos, Laterza et Filios.

Burke, E. (1958 [1757, 1759]) *A Philosophical Enquiry into the Origin of Our Ideas of the Sublime and the Beautiful*, (ed.), James T. Boulton, London: Routledge and Kegan Paul.

Hume, D. (1963 [1757]) "The Standard of Taste," in *Essays Moral, Political, and Literary*, Oxford: Oxford University Press.

Hutcheson, F. (1974 [1725]) *Inquiry Concerning Beauty, Order, Harmony, Design*, (ed.), Peter Kivy, The Hague: Martinus Nijhoff.

Kant, I. (1951) *Critique of Judgment*, trans. J. H. Bernard, New York: Haffner.

—— (1956) *Critique of Practical Reason*, trans. L. W. Beck, New York: Liberal Arts Press.

—— (1959) *Foundations of the Metaphysics of Morals*, trans. L. W. Beck, Indianapolis: Bobbs-Merrill.

—— (1960) *Observations on the Feeling of the Beautiful and Sublime*, trans. J. T. Goldthwait, Berkeley: University of California Press.

—— (1961) *Critique of Pure Reason*, trans. Norman Kemp Smith, London: Macmillan.

—— (1977) *Prolegomena to Any Future Metaphysics*, trans. P. Carus and J. W. Ellington, Indianapolis: Hackett.

Shaftesbury, Lord (Anthony Ashley Cooper) (1999 [1711]) *Characteristics of Men, Manners, Opinions, Times*, (ed.), Lawrence E. Klein, Cambridge: Cambridge University Press.

Further reading

Budd, M. (1998) "Delight in the Natural World: Kant on the Aesthetic Appreciation of Nature," *British Journal of Aesthetics* 38: 1–18, 117–26, 233–50. (A recent and extended discussion of Kant and environmental aesthetics.)

Cohen, T. and Guyer, P. (eds) (1982) *Essays in Kant's Aesthetics*, Chicago: University of Chicago Press. (A useful collection of articles by leading scholars.)

Crawford, D. W. (1974) *Kant's Aesthetic Theory*, Madison: University of Wisconsin Press. (An introduction to Kant's aesthetics.)

Crowther, P. (1989) *The Kantian Sublime: From Morality to Art*, Oxford: Oxford University Press. (A discussion of the sublime in Kant's aesthetics.)

Guyer, P. (1997) *Kant and the Claims of Taste*, 2nd edn, Cambridge: Cambridge University Press. (A detailed discussion by a leading scholar.)

—— (1993) *Kant and the Experience of Freedom: Essays on Aesthetics and Morality*, Cambridge: Cambridge University Press. (Essays on several elements of Kant's aesthetics.)

Kant, I. (1987) *Critique of Judgement*, trans. W. S. Pluhar, Indianapolis: Hackett. (A recent translation.)

Kemal, S. (1986) *Kant and Fine Art*, Oxford: Oxford University Press. (A discussion of Kant on fine art and culture.)

—— (1992) *Kant's Aesthetic Theory*, New York: St. Martin's Press. (A useful introduction.)

Lyotard, J-F. (1994) *Lessons on the Analytic of the Sublime*, Stanford: Stanford University Press. (A discussion from the perspective of literary theory.)

Makkreel, R. (1990) *Imagination and Interpretation in Kant*, Chicago: University of Chicago Press. (A hermeneutical perspective.)

Saville, A. (1993) *Kantian Aesthetics Pursued*, Edinburgh: Edinburgh University Press. (An elaboration of Kant's aesthetics.)

Zammito, J. H. (1992) *The Genesis of Kant's Critique of Judgement*, Chicago: University of Chicago Press. (An historical perspective.)

6

HEGEL

Michael Inwood

Georg Wilhelm Friedrich Hegel (1770–1831) was, along with Fichte and Schelling, one of the three great 'German idealists' who followed in the wake of Kant. He differed from Kant in several respects. In particular, he believed that human beings acquire their grasp of the world and of themselves not only through prosaic cognition but also through art and religion: they are ways of discovering the world and ourselves, not simply ways of beautifying or sanctifying what we have already discovered. He believed too that our ways of making sense of things – art, religion, even our fundamental categories or thoughts – develop over history. Thus Hegel is concerned not only with the formal features of art, but with its content or meaning. He is also concerned with the history of art and with its changing relationship to its competitors, religion and philosophy (or 'science'). He sometimes presents art, religion and philosophy as progressively satisfactory ways of grasping the 'absolute' or the nature of things: art grasps the absolute in sensory intuition, religion in pictorial imagination (*Vorstellung*), philosophy in conceptual thought (Hegel 1975: 101ff).

Hegel's writings

Hegel's earliest writings, produced soon after his departure from the Tübingen theological seminary, deal with religion and have little to say about art. A fragment in his handwriting now entitled "The Earliest System-Programme of German Idealism" suggests that, like his friends from Tübingen, Hölderlin and Schelling, he hoped for a fusion of beauty, truth and goodness, of poetry, philosophy and morality, in a society that would be, like ancient Athens, a "political work of art" (Hegel 1956: 250). But he soon abandoned this hope, arguing that 'science' or philosophy is quite distinct from poetry, and that modern society is essentially unaesthetic and cannot be remodeled on the Greek city-state.

His first major work, the *Phenomenology of Spirit* (Hegel 1979 [1807]), sets 'science' above both art and religion, but illuminates certain phases of history by art. Greek society, for example, is seen in terms of tragedy, primarily Sophocles's *Antigone*. Art appears again under the title of religion: "Natural Religion" considers the religious artifacts of pre-Greek religions, while "The Religion of Beauty" treats of Greek art and the religion with which, in pre-Hellenistic times, it was closely connected. There follows a section entitled "Revealed Religion," which deals with Christianity and makes no mention of art, implying that art has completed its serious business when Christianity appears on the scene.

Science of Logic (Hegel 1969 [1812–16]), written while Hegel was a headmaster in Nuremberg (1808–16), has little explicit concern with art, but it elaborates a conceptual system which Hegel later uses to comprehend art. In 1817, after gaining a professorship at Heidelberg, Hegel published an *Encyclopaedia of the Philosophical Sciences* to accompany his lectures. In the third part of this, the "Philosophy of Mind" (Hegel 1971 [1871]) art again appears as a prelude to 'revealed religion' and to 'philosophy' (Hegel 1971: 293ff.). However, in the lectures that he was now preparing on aesthetics, he dealt with all the fine arts – architecture, sculpture, painting, music, poetry – and with all periods, from the earliest times known to him – Persia, India, Egypt – down to modern times. He delivered the lectures four times, not at Heidelberg, but at the new university of Berlin where he was a professor from 1818 until his death. The lectures were published posthumously in 1835 and 1842.

The development of the mind

A human being is a mind. A mind essentially knows itself or is, to a degree, self-conscious. What a mind is depends on what it knows itself, or is conscious of itself, as being. For the mind has no static nature or properties, as say a tree does, that would make it a mind independently of what it knows about itself. A mind is, at any given stage, what it knows itself to be. A mind cannot know itself without knowing the external world. For, firstly, a mind stands in contrast to the external world, and in order to know itself it must draw a boundary between itself and what is other than itself. Secondly, a mind is not entirely cut off from what is other than mind. It incorporates parts of the non-mental world as its own, most especially its body, but later its home, its country, and eventually the whole world insofar as it is intellectually and practically involved with it. Thirdly, a mind cannot at first know itself directly. It knows itself by seeing its own reflection in the external world, the deeds it performs, the marks it makes, the words it utters and inscribes.

Self-knowledge is not a matter of all or nothing, but of degree. A mind does not get to know itself all at once. Self-knowledge develops by stages over time. At a given stage a mind is in a state which can be called S1, and is aware that it is S1. Mind's awareness of S1 is however a different state from its simply being S1.

It is a new state, S2. Then mind has to become aware that it is S2, and this in turn propels it into a further state, S3. And so on, until the mind has attained complete self-knowledge, a state such that awareness of that state is not a different, higher, state. A single human being does not acquire self-knowledge on its own. It does so in consort with other minds, together with which it forms a linguistic and cultural network. So intimately associated is one mind with another that Hegel usually speaks of a society as a single 'mind' or 'spirit' (Geist) into which individual minds are integrated. Mind develops both over history and over the life of the individual. An infant's body is initially not in the control of its undeveloped mind and is viewed as strange and alien. As its mind develops it takes over its body and learns to express itself in it. By education – a process which, in Hegel's view, involves alienation such as repressive discipline and the learning of foreign languages at the expense of one's vernacular – the individual is eventually integrated into the culture or 'mind' of the time and made into what is, for the time, a proper human being. Over history human beings gradually expand and deepen their knowledge of themselves and of their world. They do so, in part, by successively reflecting on the stage that they have so far reached. Only after a long journey through the sensory world does the mind purify itself of the sensory and comprehend its intrinsic nature, thought, in the philosophical, conceptual terms appropriate to it.

The role of art

Art serves the development of mind. Thus Hegel is concerned with the beauty of art, not the beauty of nature. ('Beautiful,' schön, does not usually, in Hegel, contrast with 'sublime,' nor is it restricted to surface prettiness; it embraces all artistic value, of both form and content.) Nature is to be mastered and redeemed by mind, not contemplated for its own sake:

> the torch-thistle, which blooms for only one night, withers in the wilds of the southern forests without having been admired, and these forests, jungles themselves of the most beautiful and luxuriant vegetation . . . rot and decay equally unenjoyed. But the work of art is not so naively self-centred; it is essentially a question, an address to the responsive breast, a call to the mind and spirit.
>
> (Hegel 1975: 71)

Art plays a part in the development from infancy to adulthood. The child decorates its body to mark it as its own. It draws pictures of itself, of others and of its environment. It produces effects in the world to contemplate the results of its own activity. Art provides material for contemplation and reflection in a way that purposive activity does not. But Hegel is more interested in art's role in the development of mind over history. Humans have produced art from the earliest times, and art has generally been associated with religion. In the absence of any prosaic theology art was the only medium in which religion could be expressed. Art before the Greeks was 'symbolic' art, expressing its meaning by a sensory entity (such as a vast monument) that supposedly has some feature in common with what it stands for (such as an immeasurable deity), but does not otherwise resemble or adequately portray it. Such art – Indian, Persian, Egyptian – strove to express a message that is too thin and elusive to be expressed adequately in a sensory, or in any other, form. Its forte was architecture, handling the natural forces of matter and weight. The deity towards which such art gestures is too abstract and remote to bring order into the natural world. Nature is left in an unredeemed state, and this is mirrored by the sheer materiality of symbolic art. The human body is not properly portrayed, but often with animal features. Such defects are not to be explained by technical incompetence, but by the deficiency of the world-view that such art expresses. The mind is insufficiently developed and distanced from nature to master its obtrusive disarray. Unsatisfying as it is to us, symbolic art adequately represents the mind of its producers and contemplators.

The Greeks reflected on the art of their predecessors and found it wanting. They expressed in their myths the overcoming of raw natural forces, the Titans, by the Olympian gods. Their forte was sculpture, a genre less dependent on sheer natural forces than architecture, representing the serene human being or the god extricated from the nature it has tamed. Message and medium fit to perfection. The statue does not point towards something unexpressed; no physical detail is superfluous, everything in the statue is needed to express its message. This art is 'classical,' no longer symbolic. The gods, the essence of the world, are conceived in human form. The world thus mirrors the human mind; the Greeks are entirely at home in their world.

The Greeks had other arts too: epics that lay the foundations of their religion and way of life; tragedies that express the insoluble conflicts between different values (such as the family and the state, represented respectively by Antigone and Creon in Sophocles's *Antigone*), conflicts that eventually shattered the world of the Greek city-state; and comedies that show the tendency of things to veer into their opposites. But poetry is, along with painting and music, especially associated not with classicism, but with the third form of art, 'romanticism': a term associated both with medieval Christianity and with the romantics of Hegel's own day. Symbolic art cannot adequately express its message, since it has too little to express; romantic art cannot do so, since it has too much to express. Reflection on art, and in general reflection on the current state of the mind, gave rise to philosophy and to a theology independent of art. Art was now open to philosophical and theological assessment, and no longer the final authority on the absolute. Christianity introduced a novel complexity into our view of the nature of things. Christ can adequately be portrayed in art, and so can the Christian community, which Hegel associates with the third member of the Trinity, the holy spirit that is said, in *Acts* 2, to have inspired the apostles. But the creator god, like the god of Judaism and of Islam, cannot adequately be portrayed in art. Hence although it is not merely symbolic, romantic art loses the harmony of Greek art and points towards hidden, unpicturable depths that can adequately be conveyed only in philosophy and theology.

The human mind too acquires unportrayable depths. The Greeks, before they were contaminated by philosophy, lived close to the sensory surface of things. Their mental life was readily expressed in the demeanor of their bodies and in sculptural representations of them. Under the impact of philosophy and Christianity, the mind developed an inner life of thought and imagination that cannot be so expressed. Medieval Christianity continued to produce great art, albeit art that was not the most adequate expression of the Christian message or of the human mind. Modern art suffers from the generally unaesthetic environment and from the artist's detachment from any particular cause or creed. Hegel attributes such detachment primarily to the 'irony' cultivated by romantics such as Friedrich Schlegel (Hegel 1993: xxviiiff., 69ff., 154ff.). But he also believes that sympathy with art of all periods, genres and creeds is a condition for philosophy of art, and that such catholic sympathy is inimical to the partisan attachment required for great art.

Much post-medieval art is non-religious. But for Hegel the development of the human mind is inconceivable without religion, without the attempt to discern mind at work in the nature of things, even when this takes the form of irreligion. Thus art is never entirely dissociated from religion. He accommodates apparently secular art, such as Shakespeare's, within an overarching Christianity. He conveys this in two images. Architecture provides the temple; sculpture the statue of the god in the temple; painting, music, and poetry treat the worshipers outside the temple. God the Father and God the Son are essentially connected to the Holy Spirit that imbues the community. Human beings are an essential phase of God, who acquires self-consciousness in them. To portray humanity is to portray an essential aspect of divinity.

The romantic arts continue the process of dematerialization that occurred in the move from architecture to sculpture. Painting is one step removed from the full-bodied spatiality of sculpture: it portrays three-dimensional space and objects on a two-dimensional surface. Music abandons space altogether and contents itself with time, which is more 'ideal' than space (Hegel 1975: 88). Moreover, music does not portray events in the external world but the life of the mind itself, though characteristically its emotional rather than its intellectual life. Poetry, finally, reduces the role of the sensory still further. The sound of poetry does not matter in the way that musical sound does. ('Background' music can be enjoyable. Who listens to 'background' poetry?) What matters is the meaning, the conceptions, conveyed: and if these can be transposed into a foreign language without loss, the translation is as good as the original. 'Conception' is *Vorstellung*, which also means 'imagination.' Since imagination is involved in all the arts, poetry exposes the common core of all the arts, removing its sensory garb. Poetry is thus the universal art, not simply the last of the romantic arts. This is why Greece produced poetry that has not been bettered by modernity. Poetry is the most flexible of the arts. It downgrades the sensory in a way that no other art does and thus prepares the mind for an encounter with itself unmediated by the sensory. Hegel thus explains why art has a significant history, and also why there are precisely five fine arts.

The end of art?

Hegel seems to have announced the end of art:

> the form of art has ceased to be the supreme need of the spirit. No matter how excellent we find the statues of the Greek gods, no matter how we see God the Father, Christ and Mary so estimably and perfectly portrayed: it is no help; we bow the knee no longer.
>
> (Hegel 1975: 103)

He does so for several reasons. Art reached its peak in ancient Greece, with a perfect coincidence of message and sensory medium that can never be recovered. Greek art is supremely 'beautiful' in a narrow sense of 'beauty.' In a wider sense of 'beauty,' in which the word covers all artistic value, particularly the truth and profundity of the message expressed, Christian art is more beautiful than Greek. But Christian art is not a full, or the best, expression of the Christian world-view. The art of the eighteenth and nineteenth centuries is inferior to medieval, let alone Greek art. One reason is this. Art does not promote morality (*Moralität*) in the sense of making bad people good. If this were its purpose, art would not be valuable for its own sake, but a means to an end which might be better served by other means. But art expresses and confirms the ongoing social morality or 'ethical life' (*Sittlichkeit*) – the customs, codes, hierarchies, and festivals – of the society it serves. Modern society is, however, irredeemably unaesthetic. The woman taken in adultery provides material for art, even if (as Hegel says) portrayals of her have "seduced many into sin, because art makes repentance look so beautiful, and sinning must come before repentance" (Hegel 1975: 52). The prosaic rules and regulations that govern modern society hinder, rather than help, the artist. What the moderns are good at is reflection on art and philosophy of art. They, and Hegel in particular, have achieved a good understanding of the art of all periods, assigning to each art, and to each art-form, its place in the history of humanity. This too suggests that art has completed its work. Each art has been assigned its place in the 'pantheon' (Hegel 1975: 90) or 'garland' (Hegel 1975: 1236) of beauty (cf. Hegel 1993: 196–7). What more is there for art to do? Art itself cannot reflect on art as a whole and the totality constituted by the arts and artforms. This is a task that can only be performed by philosophy of art, not by art itself.

Occasionally, however, Hegel suggests that the decline of art is a cyclical phenomenon, not its final end: "With the advance of civilization a time generally comes in the case of every people when art points beyond itself" (Hegel 1975: 103). Hegel thus advances at least four theses. First, perfect art of the Greek type will never recur. Second, art will never regain the spiritual importance it had for the Greeks. Third, that modern art is not as good as medieval and renaissance art is perhaps a periodic phenomenon, and art may get better as art. Fourth, however good future art may be, it will make no significant addition to the 'pantheon' of art or to the resources of the human mind.

The suggestion that art had by Hegel's time done everything that art could do is invalidated by the art of the late nineteenth and twentieth centuries, in particular by new arts such as film, but Hegel's thesis of the end of art as a significant vehicle of the human spirit is less easy to refute. He presents us with a dilemma. Either art has a serious message or it is entertainment. In either case art is dispensable. Art may be entertaining; but we have other ways of entertaining ourselves; in any case entertainment is trivial. If art has a message, why can it not be better expressed by philosophy, science, or religion? So far as Hegel's opponent succeeds in explaining the message that art conveys, Hegel's case is confirmed: the message can be put in plain prose and we do not need art to discover it. Plain prose cannot convey the full detail of a work of art; that it cannot do so is part of the point of a statue. But this point too – the incomplete paraphrasability of art – can be expressed in prose. Art is in constant danger of being reduced to second-rate philosophy, necessary only for those too immersed in the sensory to savor the real thing.

Criticizing Hegel

It is not easy to reject Hegel's end of art thesis without further damage to his philosophy. The aim of the mind, he argues, is to know itself as it really is. What the mind really is, is thought. Hence to know itself in a fully appropriate way it must know itself by conceptual thought. The sensory can play only a preparatory part in this. It is true that religion employs pictorial *Vorstellung*, and Hegel does not announce the end of religion. But he should have announced the end of religion, at least as anything more than philosophy for the unreflective masses, and that is a role that he can equally allow to art. The serious business of life is from now on to be conducted in conceptual thought. If art is to be allowed a significant future, Hegel needs to be challenged in one or more of the following ways.

First, we might deny that our rational social order is destined to progress steadily without interruption. Human history may be disrupted by explosions of creative energy that cannot adequately express themselves conceptually, but only by a manipulation of the sensory that qualifies as art. This hypothesis goes beyond Hegel's idea of the cyclical decline and revival of art. It would imply not simply that art may one day become better as art, but that art may once more play a crucial role in the development of mind. It would also imply that the development of mind may not be the relatively steady progress that Hegel envisaged, with a foreseeable terminus in philosophy or science, but a process punctuated by massive upheavals, whose future course and possible terminus we can hardly imagine, let alone foresee.

Second, we might reject Hegel's notion of complete self-consciousness, at least to the extent that it is entirely and unremittingly conceptual and scientific. The sensory, imagination, emotion, even entertainment: all these play a part in human life. Why should self-consciousness require us to downgrade them? They may even have a larger share in our quest for the absolute than Hegel officially allows. The absolute may not be, as he believed, entirely transparent to conceptual thought, so that humanity can ascend by thought to a godlike status. Perhaps art is needed to gesture towards mysteries left by science. Such an admission would grievously impair the symmetry of Hegel's system, which begins with the conceptual thought of the *Science of Logic* and ends with the conceptual thought of philosophy. It would leave no single clear answer to the question what full self-knowledge consists in.

Third, we might resist Hegel's attempt to discern a non-sensory meaning in the sensory and thus to downgrade it. Perhaps painting simply explores shapes and colors, while music creates and explores a world of sound. This too questions Hegel's belief that ultimate meaning always lies in thought, never in sensation or *Vorstellung*. It also raises the question whether art has a single history. One answer to the question may be that, at least since the Greeks, art does not have a history: not, at least, in the way that do science and perhaps philosophy. Modern art does not improve on Greek art in the way that modern physics is an advance on Greek physics. It is just different, with no special claim on our attention apart from its novelty and its appropriateness to our social and cultural circumstances.

Even if we agree that art has a history, it is difficult to accept Hegel's account of it. The fulcrum of that history is for Hegel the perfect harmony of medium and message in Greek art, but the sensory harmony of Greek art is probably deceptive in that respect. Greek myths about the transformation of gods into animal forms suggest an awareness of a residual mystery that is not fully captured by portrayals of gods in human form. Moreover, while the Greeks had no official theology, they had plenty of philosophers, who from the time of Xenophanes (ca. 570–480 BC) criticized the anthropomorphic deities of Greek art. Thus despite the unsurpassed beauty of Greek art and its undoubted importance in Greek life, it is not clear that it was ever the complete and impeccable expression of the Greek world-view that Hegel took it to be.

The end of Hegel?

Hegel's aim was to depict the development of mind in all its rich complexity. He strove to avoid 'one-sidedness,' to encompass with a sovereign objectivity all phases and aspects of the evolution of mind. Despite Hegel's aversion to didactic poetry and to most of the productions of his romantic contemporaries, this objectivity is apparent in his account of art. He has, he believes, devised a system that assigns each art, each artform, every significant work, its appropriate place in the growth of mind. Encompassing objectivity is also apparent in his account of the various aspects of art. The content or meaning of a work is crucial, but this is not to deny the importance of its formal features; certain formal features are required and determined by the content of a work. The centrality of content does not, in Hegel's view, exclude the proposition that a work of art is in some sense an end in itself, valuable for itself, not just as a disposable means to some further end. Again, art may be *both* an end in itself *and* of service to morality, as long as we interpret morality as 'ethical life,' not as the Kantian morality of conscience. In these respects, and many more, Hegel wants to take on board every significant aspect and relationship of art, without excluding any. This has had a twofold implication for his influence.

First, Hegel's systematic enterprise has had few significant devotees or imitators, few, that is, who have had the energy, learning and confidence to discern a coherent logical structure in the ever-expanding world of art. (Spengler's (1926) systematizing and learning are comparable to Hegel's, but he acknowledged no specific Hegelian influence.) Second, however, since Hegel touched on almost every aspect of art, his work has had an enormous piecemeal influence. His end of art thesis, for example, has found support in Danto (1986) and Wind

(1963). Perhaps his most significant impact has been on Heidegger (1971), who, although he suspends judgement on the end of art, is close to Hegel when he argues that a work of art opens up a 'world.'

See also Kant, Art and ethics, Architecture, Sculpture.

References

Danto, A. C. (1986) *The Philosophical Disenfranchisement of Art*, New York: Columbia University Press.

Hegel, G. W. F. (1956) *The Philosophy of History*, trans. J. Sibree, New York: Dover.

—— (1960) *Hegel on Tragedy*, ed. A. Paolucci and H. Paolucci, New York: Doubleday.

—— (1969) *Science of Logic*, trans. A. V. Miller, London: Allen and Unwin.

—— (1971) *Philosophy of Mind: Part Three of the Encyclopaedia of the Philosophical Sciences*, trans. W. Wallace and A. V. Miller, Oxford: Oxford University Press.

—— (1975) *Aesthetics: Lectures on Fine Art*, trans. T. M. Knox, Oxford: Oxford University Press.

—— (1979) *Phenomenology of Spirit*, trans. A. V. Miller, Oxford: Oxford University Press.

—— (1989) "The Earliest System-Programme of German Idealism," in M. Inwood (ed.), *Hegel: Selections*, London: Macmillan.

—— (1993) *Introductory Lectures on Aesthetics*, trans. B. Bosanquet, London: Penguin.

Heidegger, M. (1971) "The Origin of the Work of Art," in A. Hofstadter (ed.), *Poetry, Language, Thought* New York: Harper and Row.

Spengler, O. (1926) *The Decline of the West*, trans. C. F. Atkinson, New York: Knopf.

Wind, E. (1963) *Art and Anarchy*, London: Faber.

Further reading

Bungay, S. (1986) *Beauty and Truth: A Study of Hegel's Aesthetics*, Oxford: Oxford University Press. (An analytical treatment, which relates Hegel's aesthetics to his logic.)

Desmond, W. (1986) *Art and the Absolute: A Study of Hegel's Aesthetics*, Albany: SUNY Press. (Stresses the aesthetic character of Hegel's whole philosophy.)

Harries, K. (1974) "Hegel on the Future of Art," in *Review of Metaphysics* 27: 677–96. (An interesting treatment of the end of art theme.)

Henrich, D. (1964) "Art and Philosophy of Art Today: Reflections with Reference to Hegel," in R. E. Amacher and V. Lange (eds), *New Perspectives in German Literary Criticism*, Princeton: Princeton University Press. (A classic essay by a leading German Hegel scholar.)

—— (1985) "The Contemporary Relevance of Hegel's Aesthetics," in M. Inwood (ed.), *Hegel*, Oxford: Oxford University Press. (An important study of the end of art theme.)

Kaminsky, J. (1962) *Hegel on Art*, Albany: SUNY Press. (A good survey, relating Hegel's aesthetics to his logic and to Kant.)

Steinkraus, W. and Schmitz, K. (eds) (1980) *Art and Logic in Hegel's Philosophy*, Atlantic Highlands: Humanities Press. (Interesting essays, with an extensive bibliography.)

Wicks, R. (1993) "Hegel's Aesthetics: An Overview," in F. C. Beiser (ed.), *The Cambridge Companion to Hegel*, Cambridge: Cambridge University Press. (A masterly survey, with interesting, if controversial, interpretation and criticism.)

7

NIETZSCHE

Ruben Berrios and Aaron Ridley

Friedrich Nietzsche, who was born in 1844, went mad in 1889 and died in 1900, took art more seriously, perhaps, than any other philosopher of comparable stature. All of his published works contain extended discussions of art, and if none of them is quite so explicitly devoted to it as his first book, *The Birth of Tragedy* (Nietzsche 1967a [1872]), this is not, as is commonly held, a sign that art lost its hold on him as his career progressed. Rather, it is a sign of the increasing depth and complexity of his aesthetics. Art became for Nietzsche a principle informing the whole of his philosophy. Relatively inconspicuous because of its very ubiquity, the aesthetic in his later works functions as the site on which Nietzsche's extra-aesthetic concerns are contested: a site that is continually transformed in the process, and so which can be understood only through those apparently extra-aesthetic concerns that animate the surface of his thought. Thus, while the younger Nietzsche effectively rams art down the reader's throat, most unignorably in his claim that "it is only as an *aesthetic phenomenon* that existence and the world are eternally *justified*" (Nietzsche 1967a: 52), the later Nietzsche is more elusive. In what follows, therefore, we will first examine Nietzsche's thoughts about art through his two principal extra-aesthetic concerns – metaphysics and ethics – before attempting to reconstruct the mature aesthetic as it underpins the writings of the late 1880s.

Art and metaphysics

The young Nietzsche was profoundly influenced by the philosophy of Arthur Schopenhauer and, in *The Birth of Tragedy*, he gave full rein to the enthusiasm which Schopenhauer's metaphysics inspired in him. In Schopenhauer's hands, the Kantian distinction between the real world of things as they are in themselves and the apparent world of things as they feature in experience becomes the distinction between the Will and representations of the Will. The world, in its essence, is Will: a blind force which constantly strives for an unattainable resolution, and so serves merely to perpetuate further meaningless striving. The fundamental character of the world is therefore the pain of irreparable lack, and the multiple refractions of this character constitute the world of representation, or experience. Nietzsche found this bleak vision compelling, and constructed his earliest philosophy of art around it.

Two complementary principles, the 'Dionysian' and the 'Apollonian,' dominate *The Birth of Tragedy*. Both of these can be understood under three aspects: the metaphysical, the epistemological and the aesthetic. Under the metaphysical aspect, the Dionysian is Nietzsche's term for the dark "primordial unity" (Nietzsche 1967a: 37) of things: in effect, the Schopenhauerian Will. Under the epistemological aspect, the Dionysian is a state of "intoxication," a state in which the deepest and most "horrible truth" (Nietzsche 1967a: 60) of the world is glimpsed – and can only be glimpsed, since to face it fully would destroy one. Under the aesthetic aspect, the Dionysian is what Kant meant by the 'sublime,' the overwhelming, awe-inspiring and yet elevating experience of things which exceed rational apprehension.

The Apollonian, by contrast, belongs to Schopenhauer's world of representation. Metaphysically, it stands for the false, the illusory, for "*mere appearance*" (Nietzsche 1967a: 34). Epistemologically, the Apollonian indicates a dream-like state in which all knowledge is knowledge of surfaces. Aesthetically, the Apollonian is the beautiful, the world experienced as intelligible, as conforming to the capacities of the representing intellect. Nietzsche's basic claim is that in genuinely tragic works of art the Dionysian and the Apollonian principles cross-fertilize one another, so that the metaphysical horror of existence is simultaneously revealed and made bearable, the ravages of intoxication are transfigured by dreams, and the sublime is beautified by the veil of appearances. It is because tragedy (especially Greek tragedy), and tragedy alone, has the capacity to do this that "it is only as an *aesthetic phenomenon* that existence and the world are eternally *justified*" (Nietzsche 1967a: 52).

Nietzsche did not remain committed to this position for long. By 1878, when the first part of *Human, All Too Human* (Nietzsche 1986) was published, he had repudiated the strong appearance/reality distinction upon which Schopenhauerian metaphysics rests and which lay at the core of *The Birth of Tragedy*. For Schopenhauer, as for Kant, reality and its appearances had logically distinct properties, so that the way that the world was 'in itself' was logically distinct from any of its appearances in experience. Nietzsche's rejection of this position – which is to say, his rejection of traditional metaphysics (Nietzsche 1966: 10) – had a number of consequences which he went on to articulate throughout the 1880s. Two of these are of concern to us here.

The first consequence is that the appearance/reality distinction had to be understood differently. "What is 'appearance' for me now?" Nietzsche asked in *The Gay Science* (Nietzsche 1974 [1882]). "Certainly not the opposite of some essence: what could I say about any essence except to name the attributes of its appearance! Certainly not a dead mask that one could place on an unknown *x* or remove from it!" (Nietzsche 1974: 116). And in the section of *Twilight of the Idols* (Nietzsche 1968a [1888]) called "How the 'Real World' at Last Became a Myth" he is more explicit still: "we have abolished the real world: what world is left? the apparent world perhaps? . . . But no! *with the real world we have also abolished the apparent world!*" (Nietzsche 1968a: 41). On this new conception, the appearance/reality distinction is not a distinction between two logically differentiated 'worlds' – an apparent one and a real one – but a distinction that falls squarely within the ordinary, everyday world of actual experience.

The second consequence is that his aesthetics had to be rethought. Consider the following passage from *The Gay Science*: "as an aesthetic phenomenon existence is still *bearable* for us" (Nietzsche 1974: 163): a claim that echoes the slogan of *The Birth of Tragedy* while also revising its sense in light of Nietzsche's new non-metaphysical realism. "The world" has gone missing from the later passage, because "the world" of the original slogan was the "real" world, now abolished, of things as they are independently of their appearances. What is left is "existence" – not existence as such, but human existence as it is led in the everyday world of experience; and this is no longer to be "eternally justified" but merely made "bearable" – and made bearable, moreover, "for us." The idea of eternal justification has no room for "us" in it: no room, that is, for the points of view of intrinsically embodied, intrinsically temporal creatures such as ourselves. Eternal justification could be offered, if at all, only from a standpoint beyond the world of human experience, from a standpoint logically independent of the way that that world appears (to us) to be. Nietzsche's repudiation of traditional metaphysics insists upon precisely the impossibility of such a standpoint (see Nietzsche 1969b: 119). So the thought that "existence" might be "eternally justified" by the aesthetic gives way to the thought that it might be made 'bearable *for us*' by the aesthetic.

The appearance/reality distinction has thus been transposed back into the real world of human experience. In order to acknowledge the human, all too human dimension of that transposition, moreover, Nietzsche now recasts the original distinction as a distinction between lies and truth (that is, as a distinction falling within the ambit of human discretion, rather than as a distinction marking a metaphysical difference). It is now the lie that performs the task of making life bearable. Art – "in which precisely the *lie* is sanctified and the *will to deception* has a good conscience" (Nietzsche 1969b: 153) – beautifies life by interposing a veil of lies between us and truths about the world that we cannot bear. Nietzsche has abandoned certain details of his earlier terminology, but it is clear that this later conception of art-as-lie is structurally identical to the Apollonian, even if its content has been thoroughly detranscendentalized. It is in this non-meta-physical spirit that he remarks, in a famous unpublished note of 1888, that "we possess *art* lest we *perish of the truth*" (Nietzsche 1968b: 435).

Art and ethics

There is an important sense in which Nietzsche's ethical concerns did not undergo the sort of total transformation that his metaphysics did. Correspondingly, the relation between the ethical and the aesthetic in his thought remains a good deal more stable than does the relation between the metaphysical and the aesthetic. As he notes in one of the more reliable passages from the "Attempt at a Self-Criticism" (Nietzsche 1967a [1886]), *The Birth of Tragedy* already set out to 'tackle' art in the perspective of life; and to the end of his career he remained committed to the thought that art was both a function and the most fundamental symptom of distinctive ways of living. To tackle art in the perspective of life, then, is to seek to understand art as a peculiarly immediate index of the psychological economy, whether cultural or individual, that gave rise to it. The following is a particularly trenchant expression of this methodology: "regarding all aesthetic values I now avail myself of this main distinction: I ask in every instance, 'is it hunger or superabundance that has here become creative?'" (Nietzsche 1974: 329).

In order to understand what is at issue here, and what exactly Nietzsche means, it will be helpful to examine a related passage in some detail:

> what does all art do? does it not praise? does it not glorify? does it not select? does it not highlight? By doing all this it *strengthens* or *weakens* certain valuations . . . Is this no more than an incidental? an accident? Something in which the instinct of the artist has no part whatever? Or is it not rather the prerequisite for the artist's being an artist at all . . . Is his basic instinct directed towards art, or is it not rather directed towards the meaning of art, which is *life*?
>
> (Nietzsche 1968a: 81)

The first thing to notice is the claim that, in selecting and highlighting, certain valuations are strengthened or weakened, not merely incidentally but necessarily. What sorts of valuations are these? Nietzsche's answer is that they are funda-mentally of two sorts: life-affirming valuations and life-denying valuations, a dichotomy which he variously describes in terms of superabundance and hunger, ascending life and declining life, strength and weakness, health and sickness. Thus, in selecting and highlighting certain things rather than others, an artist both reveals his inherent evaluative stance towards life and, in glorifying or celebrating the things selected, strengthens that basic valuation (and so, by contrast, weakens its opposite). Nor does the artist have any choice in this matter. The evaluative stance which he reveals and reinforces in his work is, far from being "something in which the instinct of the artist has no part whatever," instinctive through and through, and it is in this evaluative sense that the artist's "basic instinct" is directed, not towards art, but towards "life." When Nietzsche asks, therefore, whether it is "hunger or superabundance that has here become creative" he is treating art as a symptom of the artist's relation to life, that is, as a symptom of the psychological economy intrinsic to a certain way of living.

The same fundamental evaluative dichotomy also underpins Nietzsche's conception of the various forms of morality, which are themselves treated as symptomatic of life-affirming or life-denying impulses. Thus Nietzsche groups moralities under two heads: "noble morality," he says, "is rooted in a triumphant Yes said to *oneself* – it is self-affirmation, self-glorification of life; it also requires sublime symbols and practices, but only because 'its heart is too full'" (Nietzsche 1967b: 191). "Slave morality," by contrast, "from the outset says No . . . and *this* No is its creative deed" (Nietzsche 1969b: 36). These opposing impulses – the affirmative and the negative – rarely sit on the surface of a morality, however. Rather, they are the deep causes of the surface effects that give moralities their distinctive characters, and they need to be excavated. Which is why Nietzsche claims that "moral judgement is never to be taken literally . . . But as *semiotics* it remains of incalculable value: it reveals . . . the most precious realities of cultures and inner worlds . . . Morality is merely sign-language, merely symptomatology" (Nietzsche 1968a: 55). With a keen enough nose, then, and Nietzsche credited himself with the keenest there has ever been (Nietzsche 1969a: 222), it is possible to detect behind the various systems of moral judgement the seminal Yes or No from which they derive their impetus.

So why is art, and not morality, the most fundamental symptom of a psychological economy? Why is art the "sign language" that reveals most transparently the "precious realities of cultures and inner worlds"? The answer to this is complex, but can be articulated through two overlapping considerations. The first concerns scope. Nietzsche construes the aesthetic very broadly. Art, for him, comprises more than merely "selecting" and "highlighting"; it comprises all "creation and imposition of forms." In the presence of an artist "something new soon arises, a ruling structure that *lives*, in which parts and functions are delimited and coordinated, in which nothing whatever finds a place that has not first been assigned a 'meaning' in relation to the whole" (Nietzsche 1969b: 86–7). Thus art includes any (and every) transformative, interpretative activity; and it is for this reason that Nietzsche insists that the moral domain is "narrower" than the aesthetic (Nietzsche 1967b: 190). Indeed, the moral is simply a special case of the aesthetic. Hence the aesthetic is the more comprehensive index of the "precious realities of cultures and inner worlds."

The second consideration concerns constraint, and comes in two parts. First, morality is practical. Moralities are constrained by the exigencies of the real world in a way that works of art are not. It is always a criticism of a morality, and Nietzsche avails himself of this style of criticism (see Nietzsche 1966: 153–4), to say that it demands the impossible, that it flouts the basic requirement that every moral 'ought' implies a practical 'can.' There is no corresponding style of criticism in the aesthetic domain. Works of art are constrained, if at all, by the imagination alone. Therefore the fundamental affirmation or negation underlying a morality – its seminal instinct – is more likely to be disguised by the demands of practical necessity than the instinct underlying a work of art. Art, as Nietzsche puts it, has "forgotten all sense of shame" (Nietzsche 1967b: 156).

Moreover – and this is the second part – moralities have the form of constraint: every morality involves the regulation of behavior through the repression of (at least some) instincts (to at least some degree). At the lower limit, located by Nietzsche in the noble moralities of human prehistory, that form is minimal: his original nobles are held "sternly in check" only "by custom, respect, usage" (Nietzsche 1969b: 40). There is, in these "man-animals," the smallest degree of repression consistent with self-consciousness: with mutual intelligibility and the collective assignation of meaning. But as human societies become more complex, so too do the patterns of repression characteristic of their moralities, with the result that one needs a very keen nose indeed to detect the seminal instinct underlying their systems of judgement. In art, by contrast, formal minimalism is always possible. It is always possible, in principle, that the largest quantity of unrepressed instinct consistent with intelligibility should find expression. Nietzsche's distinction between "the grand style," indicative of "superabundance," and "miniaturism," indicative of "hunger," is intended to mark the difference between art that realizes this possibility and art that does not (Nietzsche 1968a: 74 and 1967b: 170). In this sense too, then, art is capable of indicating more transparently than any evolved morality the basic evaluative impulse from which it derives. As "semiotics" morality may be of "incalculable value." But art, according to Nietzsche, not only reveals more of the fundamental impulses he is concerned to diagnose (the aesthetic encompasses the moral), it also reveals them more directly.

There is a final reason for privileging art over morality. Nietzsche is convinced that life-denying moralities and interpretations (for instance, Christian ones) have had the upper hand in Western culture for so long that the human soul has been almost irreparably damaged by them. A seminal No (to oneself and the world) has become foundational to the economy of the contemporary psyche. And so he begins to imagine the possibility of an affirmative counter-art of the soul, a counter-art which, while it might, as it were epiphenomenally, entail a morality, is aimed primarily at the restoration to the human soul of a foundational Yes. These attempts to imagine a revolution in the economy of the contemporary psyche constitute one important aspect of Nietzsche's mature aesthetic.

The mature aesthetic

Nietzsche's later philosophy is directed to the possibility of an affirmative evaluative stance toward life as lived in the real, non-metaphysical world of experience, embodiment and temporality. A well known passage from 1882 prepares the ground:

> *One thing is needful.* – To "give style" to one's character – a great and rare art! It is practiced by those who survey all the strengths and weaknesses of their nature and then fit them into an artistic plan . . . Here a large mass of second nature has been added; there a piece of original nature has been removed – both times through long practice and daily work at it. Here the ugly that could not be removed is concealed; there it has been reinterpreted and made sublime . . . For one thing is needful: that a human being should *attain* satisfaction with himself, whether it be by means of this or that poetry and art.
>
> (Nietzsche 1974: 232)

At first sight, it may appear that Nietzsche's idea of giving style to one's character amounts to little more than a recipe for complacent self-deception. But while it is certainly true that self-deception is involved, complacency is not the driving force behind it. Rather, people of stylish character begin with a ruthlessly honest survey of the strengths and weaknesses of their nature: they "open their eyes to themselves" (Nietzsche 1969b: 137) before executing their "artistic plan." The artistry of self-stylization then takes two forms. The first is transformative. Through the addition and removal of "second" and "original" nature, the very materials of the character are forced into an aesthetic unity. The second is interpretative. Those materials which prove resistant to transformation are reinterpreted so that their ugliness is concealed, perhaps by the veil of sublimity.

Despite the fact that these two forms of artistry are directed towards, and indeed expressive of, self-affirmation, the practice of them is grueling. Style, if it is achieved at all, is hard won:

> This secret self-ravishment, this artists' cruelty, this delight in imposing a form upon oneself as a hard, recalcitrant, suffering material and in burning a will . . . into it, this uncanny, dreadfully joyous labor of a soul voluntarily at odds with itself . . . brought to light an abundance of strange new beauty and affirmation, and perhaps beauty itself. – After all, what would be "beautiful" . . . if the ugly had not first said to itself: "I am ugly"?
>
> (Nietzsche 1969b: 87–8)

Self-stylization, then, requires that one be ruthless with oneself both in recognizing one's own ugliness and in transforming or reinterpreting it. "Truth is ugly," says Nietzsche; and so – again – "we possess art lest we *perish of the truth.*"

The first thing to notice about Nietzsche's conception of self-stylization, then, is that it is not a recipe for complacency. In order to understand its full significance, however, it will be helpful to examine the interpretative and the transformative aspects of self-stylization separately. Interpretatively, the notion of giving style to one's character is tied to deception: specifically, to the telling of lies to oneself about oneself and one's relation to the world, so that recalcitrant facts about either are rendered bearable. Take, for example, the large and recalcitrant fact of human suffering. Uninterpreted, Nietzsche thinks, suffering is intolerable. It is the "senselessness of suffering," he claims, rather than "suffering as such" that "really arouses indignation." The challenge, then, is to interpret suffering – to tell lies about suffering – in such a way that it appears, not as "the principal argument *against* existence," but as "a genuine seduction *to* life." Historically, Nietzsche claims, this challenge has been met in two main ways. "The Christian, who has interpreted a whole mysterious machinery of salvation into suffering," makes suffering bearable by positing the existence of a Kingdom of God, of a metaphysically 'real' world in which those who suffer most in this ('apparent') world are duly compensated; and it is in the context of this 'machinery' that the Christian's self-stylization takes place: he construes himself as an immortal soul. The pagan, on the other hand, "understood all suffering in relation to the spectator of it . . . [and] knew of no tastier spice to offer [his] gods to season their happiness than the pleasures of cruelty" – "Every evil the sight of which edifies a god is justified" (Nietzsche 1969b: 68–9). The stylish pagan interprets himself as an actor, as a spectator sport.

Despite the apparent similarity of these two approaches – both, for instance, involve reference to the divine – they are, for Nietzsche, radically distinct. The "seduction to life" offered by the Christian is predicated, paradoxically, upon a seminal No *to* life: the pointfulness of this-worldly suffering is secured only by locating the value of that suffering elsewhere, in a realm that necessarily excludes temporality and embodiment, and so excludes life itself. It is in this sense that "the concept of 'God,'" according to Nietzsche, has been "invented as a counterconcept of life" (Nietzsche 1969a: 334). The life to which the Christian offers a 'seduction' is, to the extent that it is characterized by suffering, worth living only on the presupposition that it is, as such, of no intrinsic value at all. Thus, in Nietzsche's terms, the Christian's version of 'life' is doubly unacceptable: metaphysically, because it presupposes the type of appearance/reality distinction that the late Nietzsche rejects, and ethically, because it is a life-denying symptom of fundamental impoverishment. The pagan, by contrast, has "*nobler* uses for the invention of gods," as is "revealed even by a mere glance at the *Greek gods*, those reflections of noble and autocratic men" (Nietzsche 1969b: 93) who repaid their gods "with interest all the qualities that had become palpable in themselves, the *noble* qualities" (ibid.: 89). A pagan 'god,' then, is, far from being a "counterconcept of life," a "deifi[cation] of life" (ibid.: 1969b: 154), an 'invention' through which the pagan affirms himself and his way of living as uniquely valuable. The pagan's interpretation of suffering, therefore, is a life-affirming – metaphysically harmless – symptom of superabundance. Both Christian and pagan fashion themselves (as immortal soul or actor) in the context of lies (about God or the gods), and both, thereby, turn the fact of suffering to account. But whereas the Christian's lies spring from hunger, and involve the negation of the very conditions of life, the pagan's lies spring from "life and passion through and through" (ibid.: 37).

The transformative aspect of self-stylization, by contrast, involves not invention, but the concrete alteration of the materials of the character. One imposes a new form upon oneself, extracting certain character traits while reshaping and implanting others. As with interpretation, two modes of self-transformation can be distinguished: one life-affirming or 'noble,' the other life-denying. Nietzsche claims that man (noble man) "transforms things until they reflect his power – until they are reflections of his perfection" (Nietzsche 1968a: 72). In the case of self-transformation the noble imposes upon himself a form that is both a symptom and an expression of his native power, his abundance of life. Through his self-transformative activity the "noble human being" honors and affirms "himself as one who is powerful, also as one who has power over himself" (Nietzsche 1966: 205). Since the "*need* to transform into perfection is – art," the noble's need to perfect himself is, for Nietzsche, the fundamental manifestation of the artistic instinct. There is, however, a "contrasting condition, a specific anti-artistry of the instinct," a type of transformation that impoverishes things, and makes them "consumptive" (Nietzsche 1968a: 72). This is the life-denying variety of self-transformation. Like the noble, the life-denier imposes upon himself – with the utmost severity – a new form; but, unlike the noble, he employs his powers of transformation to:

> block up the wells of power. . . . All this is in the highest degree para-doxical: we stand before a discord that wants to be discordant . . . and even grows more self-confident and triumphant the more its own presupposition, its physiological capacity for life, decreases.
>
> (Nietzsche 1969b: 118)

Thus the thought of self-stylization in both its interpretative and transforma-tive aspects constitutes Nietzsche's attempt to imagine how, despite the seminal No which, in his view, underlies so much of contemporary culture, an affirma-tive evaluative stance toward life as lived in the real world of experience might nonetheless be possible. There is no doubt that Nietzsche draws encouragement from history, or from his version of history: his pre-Christian nobles and pagans exhibit very much the styles of character that he is after. Equally, however, he is in no doubt that those styles cannot simply be transposed into contemporary conditions. Modernity, he thinks, is "an age of disintegration" in which "human beings have in their bodies the heritage of multiple origins, that is, opposite . . . drives and value standards that fight each other" (Nietzsche 1966: 111), so that "today there is perhaps no more decisive mark of a '*higher nature,*' a more spiritual nature, than that of being divided in this sense and a genuine battle-ground of these opposed values," that is, of life-affirming and life-denying valuations (Nietzsche 1969b: 52).

> When the opposition and war in such a nature have the effect of one more charm and incentive of life, however and if, moreover, in addition to powerful and irreconcilable drives, a real mastery and subtlety in waging war against oneself, in other words, self-control, self-outwitting, has been inherited or cultivated – then those magical, incomprehensible, and unfathomable ones arise, those enigmatic people predestined for victory and seduction, whose most beautiful expression is found . . . among artists perhaps [in] Leonardo da Vinci.
>
> (Nietzsche 1966: 112)

If history gives Nietzsche encouragement that affirmative self-stylization is possible, and if modernity presents that possibility with its sternest challenge, then the vague and rather hyperbolic quality of his invocation of Leonardo suggests that, for Nietzsche at least, it is uncertain that that challenge either has been, or really can be, met. Perhaps "those enigmatic men," those imagined counter-artists of the soul, are actually only Nietzsche's best hope for the future. Certainly any such counter-artist will need great strength of spirit in order to make good the claim, as Nietzsche requires, that it is only "as an aesthetic phenomenon" that a detranscendentalized existence might yet prove *"bearable."*

Nietzsche is unique among philosophers in the fundamental role he assigns to the aesthetic. For him, indeed, life itself (whether *"bearable"* or not) is an essentially aesthetic phenomenon. The aesthetic, as we have seen, comprises all "creation and imposition of forms," while "the essence of life" consists in those "spontaneous, aggressive, expansive, form-giving forces that give new interpretations and directions" (Nietzsche 1969b: 79). Thus his investigations of metaphysics and ethics (and indeed of science and politics) are, to the extent that those activities involve the creation and imposition of forms, also, and perhaps even primarily, investigations into the underlying aesthetic current of which such activities are strictly the epiphenomena. It is in this sense that, as we said in the introduction, art functions as a principle informing the whole of Nietzsche's later philosophy; and it is in this sense, too, that the mature aesthetic is, because deep, elusive. These characteristics of Nietzsche's investigations ensure that the aesthetic in his hands is not merely not relegated to the periphery of philosophy, but is revealed as inextricably bound up with the nature of philosophy itself.

See also Kant, Value of art, Art and ethics, Style, Tragedy.

References

Nietzsche, F. (1966) *Beyond Good and Evil*, trans. W. Kaufmann, New York: Vintage.
—— (1967a) *The Birth of Tragedy*, trans. W. Kaufmann, New York: Vintage.
—— (1967b) *The Case of Wagner*, trans. W. Kaufmann, New York: Vintage.
—— (1968a) *Twilight of the Idols*, trans. R. J. Hollingdale, London: Penguin.
—— (1968b) *The Will to Power*, trans. W. Kaufmann and R. J. Hollingdale, New York: Vintage.
—— (1969a) *Ecce Homo*, trans. W. Kaufmann, New York: Vintage.
—— (1969b) *On the Genealogy of Morals*, trans. W. Kaufmann and R. J. Hollingdale, New York: Vintage.
—— (1974) *The Gay Science*, trans. W. Kaufmann, New York: Vintage.
—— (1986) *Human, All Too Human*, trans. R. J. Hollingdale, Cambridge: Cambridge University Press.

Further reading

Heller, E. (1988) *The Importance of Nietzsche*, Chicago: University of Chicago Press. (A brilliant series of essays on various aspects of Nietzsche's aesthetic sensibility.)

Kemal, S., Gaskell, I. and Conway, D. (eds), (1998) *Nietzsche, Philosophy and the Arts*, Cambridge: Cambridge University Press. (An uneven affair, but the only collection currently available on the topic.)

Nehamas, A. (1985) *Nietzsche: Life as Literature*, Cambridge, Mass.: Harvard University Press. (An extravagant attempt to neuter Nietzsche by turning him into a text.)

Silk, M. and Stern, J. (1981) *Nietzsche on Tragedy*, Cambridge: Cambridge University Press. (Scholarly and somewhat dull, the only book-length study of *The Birth of Tragedy*.)

Strong, T. (1997) "Introduction" to F. Nietzsche, *Twilight of the Idols*, trans. R. Polt, Indianapolis: Hackett. (A fine exposition of the aesthetic dimension of Nietzsche's later thought.)

Tanner, M. (1993) "Introduction" to F. Nietzsche, *The Birth of Tragedy*, trans. S. Whiteside, London: Penguin. (A deft and suggestive essay, which one could wish had gone on for longer.)

Young, J. (1992) *Nietzsche's Philosophy of Art*, Cambridge: Cambridge University Press. (An accessible, contentious book, describing a Nietzsche who never broke free of Schopenhauer's influence.)

8

FORMALISM

Noël Carroll

The term 'formalism' can refer to many different things. In art criticism, it has been used to refer to the important writings of Clement Greenberg; in literary history, it has been associated with the influential school of Russian Formalism; and in art history it has been used to refer to the writings of Alois Riegl and Heinrich Wolfflin. For the purposes of this essay, however, attention will be paid to its usage in philosophical aesthetics, where 'formalism' denotes a position on the nature of art which has important implications for the limits of artistic appreciation.

Historically, the formalist position finds two of its strongest early polemical statements in Eduard Hanslick's *On the Musically Beautiful* (Hanslick 1986), first published in 1854, and in Clive Bell's *Art* (1914). In both cases, it is possible to see formalism as a historically situated response to significant art world developments: to the triumph of absolute or pure orchestral music, on the one hand, and to the emergence of modern painting, on the other hand. Both books signaled a revolution in taste with regard to their respective artforms. Hanslick questioned whether *all* music trafficked in the arousal of garden-variety or everyday emotions (such as fear, anger and joy) and argued instead that the proper object of musical attention should be musical structure. Bell denied that painting was an affair of representation and of the emotions associated with the representation of events, places and people, and in contrast maintained that the real subject of painting was what he called significant form: the play of striking arrangements of lines, colors, shapes, volumes, vectors and space (two-dimensional space, three-dimensional space and the interaction thereof).

Bell's statement of the formalist position has been particularly important for the development of philosophical aesthetics in the twentieth century. Perhaps the leading reason for Bell's influence has been the fact that he connected his version of formalism with the project of advancing an explicit definition of art. For this reason, Bell can be considered one of the major forerunners of the twentieth century's philosophical obsession with discovering an essential definition of art.

According to Bell, we 'gibber' if we do not base our theories and prognostications about art and its relevant forms of appreciation in an explicit definition of art. Unless we establish what art is, what we say about the value and importance of art, and what we think we should attend to in art works, will be wildly off the mark. We will, from his point of view, go on blathering about the drama and anecdote of something like Poussin's *Achilles among the Daughters of Lycomedes*, rather than attending to its pictorial structures.

As a result, Bell is eminently straightforward about what, in essence, he takes painting-as-an-art-work to be. Essentially, it is significant form. That is, where a painting is a genuine art work, it addresses the imagination like the figures of Gestalt psychology, prompting the viewer to apprehend it as an organized configuration of lines, colors, shapes, spaces, vectors, and the like.

Bell's conception of painting is a rival to other general theories of art. Bell rejects the traditional view that the art of painting is essentially an imitation of nature, a practice defined by a commitment to verisimilitude: to the production of recognizable depictions of persons, places, actions and events. Bell, of course, does not deny that many paintings are representations, but he argues that where paintings qualify as art that is due to their possession of something other than their representational content. It is due to their possession of significant form. Indeed, according to Bell, whether or not an art work possesses representational content is always *strictly* irrelevant to its status as an art work. That is, a painting's being a painting of a horse counts not at all towards its classification as a work of art; only its possession of significant form, if it has any, does.

Similarly, though less explicitly, Bell's theory contrasts with expression theories of art, which maintain that what makes something art is its expression of the emotions of its creator. For Bell believes that a painting, such as a neo-impressionist still life by Cézanne, can be remarkable for its invention of an arresting formal design, while expressing no detectable garden-variety emotions.

With Bell, formalism found its natural home in the realm of painting. Nevertheless, it is easy to extend his view to the other arts. Obviously, most orchestral music is not representational. This was always a vexation for philosophers in the lineage of Plato and Aristotle, who supposed that all art is essentially representational. But it scarcely seems controversial to describe music, especially after the popularization of pure orchestral music, in terms of the temporal play of aural form. In dance in the twentieth century, due to the influential writings of critics like André Levinson, a kind of formalism not unlike Bell's came to be a leading position with regard to ballet, while in modern architecture the idea of form became a shibboleth.

Literature might appear to be a more intractable artform to explicate exclusively in terms of form. However, formalists can point to the centrality of features in poetry like meter, rhyme and generic structures (such as the sonnet *form*); while stories also possess formal features, such as narrative structures and alternating points of view, which theorists can claim lay at the heart of the literary experience. Such formalists, of course, cannot deny that most literature possesses representational content. Instead formalists, notably the Russian Formalists, argue that such content only serves to motivate literary devices, and add that ultimately it is the play of literary devices that accounts for the artistic status of poems, novels, dramas and the like: at least in the cases where the works in question are art works.

Thus the kind of formalism that Bell introduces with reference to fine art (notably painting and sculpture) can be (and has been) turned into a comprehensive theory of art, a competitor to other major philosophies of art, such as the representational theory of art and the expression theory of art. Where those philosophies maintain respectively that art is essentially representation or that it is by its very nature expressive, the formalist says that art is form. Or, to state the matter more precisely, anything x is an art work if and only if x possesses significant form. The possession of significant form is a necessary condition for status as an art work: that is, something is an art work *only if* it possesses significant form. And significant form is a sufficient condition for status as an art work: *if* something possesses significant form, then it is an art work.

To take something of a departure from Bell, it is possible to reconstruct a series of initially compelling arguments in support of formalism. The formalist alleges that a candidate is an art work only if it possesses significant form; this is a necessary condition. But why suppose that this is so? Here the formalist mobilizes what can be called the *common denominator* argument.

The common denominator argument begins with the unobjectionable presupposition that if anything is to count as a necessary condition for art status, then it must be a property possessed by every art work. This is just what it means to be a necessary condition. Next the formalist invites us to consider some of the leading competing proposals for the role of necessary criteria for art status. The two which are most relevant for the formalist debate are that something is art only if it is representational, and that something is art only if it is expressive.

However, not all art works are representational. The bejeweled patterns on Islamic funeral monuments, Bach's fugues, and Ellsworth Kelly's wall sculptures are all pertinent examples here. They are not representational but they are undeniably art. Thus it cannot be the case that representation is a necessary condition for status as an art work.

Similarly, not all art is expressive of the emotions of its creator. Some artists, like John Cage, have adopted aleatoric methods of composition in order to remove any trace of authorial expression from their work. Many of George Balanchine's abstract ballets also attempt to erase expressive qualities for the sake of exploring pure formal qualities. Thus expression is not a necessary condition for status as an art work.

That leaves us with form as the most viable candidate. Moreover, though we have reached this conclusion indirectly by negating the most prominent competing alternatives, the result, it might be said, rings true directly, since all art works do seem at the very least to possess form. It appears obvious that form is the common denominator among all art works the property that they all share whether their medium is painting, sculpture, drama, photography, film, music, dance, literature, architecture or whatever. In searching for a necessary condition for art status, we are looking for a property possessed by every art work. Formalism seems to make the most promising proposal, especially in contrast to rival theories like representationalism and expressionism.

The common denominator argument suggests that form is the most plausible contender we can find for a necessary condition of art status. But this argument does not provide us with a sufficient condition for art status, since many things other than art also possess form. Indeed, some might argue that in some sense everything possesses form. That, of course, is why the formalist speaks of *significant* form. But even with this ostensible refinement, it is still not the case that the formula 'x is art only if it possesses significant form' will differentiate art from many other things. An effective political speech and a theorem in symbolic logic may possess significant form, but they are not art. In order to block such counterexamples, and to establish the sufficiency of the theory, the formalist needs to add something to his or her view. Here the formalist may advert to an hypothesis about the *function* of art works.

Political speeches and theorems in logic may possess significant form, but it is not their primary purpose to display their form. The primary function of a political speech is to convince an audience. The primary function of a logical theorem is to deduce a conclusion. Speech making and logic may result in activities noteworthy for their form, but exhibiting their form is not what they are primarily about. If they lacked significant form, they could still be extremely successful in acquitting their primary functions. Art is different from these and other activities insofar as it is, so the formalist hypothesizes, uniquely concerned with displaying significant form.

No other human activity, the formalist alleges, has the exhibition of form as its special or peculiar province of value. Its primary preoccupation with the exploration of form demarcates the realm of art from other human practices. Whereas representational content is not irrelevant to political speeches or logical deductions, representation is always, the formalist says, strictly irrelevant to art works.

Likewise, though art works may express the emotions, other things, such as battle cries, do so as well. However, art works can be differentiated from battle cries if one supposes that the primary function of art is to exhibit significant form, since battle cries are not uttered in order to foreground their rhythmic structures.

Art works may be concerned with religious or political themes, moral education, philosophical world-views, or martial emotions. But so are many other things. Indeed, many other things, including sermons, pamphlets, newspaper editorials, and philosophical treatises generally do a better job of conveying cognitive and moral information and emotional contagion than does art. What is special about art above all else, according to the formalist, is its concern with discovering formal structures that are designed to encourage our imaginative interplay with art works.

The claim that the primary function of art is the exhibition of significant form can be worked into what we can call the *function* argument. This argument is designed to establish that the exhibition of significant form is a sufficient condition for status as an art work. The argument presupposes that only if x is a primary function that is unique to art can it be a sufficient condition for status as an art work. As in the case of the common denominator argument, the formalist then goes on to canvas the relevant alternatives: representation, expression and the exhibition of significant form. As we have already seen, neither representation nor expression are unique functions of art works. Other activities also share these functions. But the exhibition of significant form is a primary function unique to art. Therefore, it is a sufficient criterion of art status.

Along with the function argument and the common denominator argument, formalism also gains credibility from its apparent capacity to explain certain of our intuitions about art. For example, we often criticize certain films for being too message-oriented, while commending other films for being good of their kind. Why is this? The formalist has a ready answer: a dumb, amoral film may be formally interesting – it may deploy its formal devices (editing, camera movement, color schemes and so on) – in compelling ways. In many such films, the thematic content is negligible, or even silly, but its formal organization is riveting, whereas a film with a big idea, however important and earnestly expressed, may strike us as altogether, as they say, uncinematic. Formalism makes sense of comparative judgements like these.

Likewise, formalism explains why we regard much of the art of the past as worthwhile despite the fact that the sentiments it expresses and the ideas it represents are now known to be obsolete. This contrasts with physics, where discredited theories are long forgotten and rarely consulted. The formalist explains this phenomenon by reminding us that the primary function of physics is to give us knowledge about the universe. The information contained in many past art works is believed to be wrong, but nevertheless we still read Lucretius's *On the Nature of Things*, the formalist hypothesizes, because of its evident formal virtues.

Because of its explanatory power and because of arguments like the common denominator argument and the function argument, formalism is an appealing view. For those who expect an essential definition in response to the question 'What is art?' it provides a tidy response: x is an art work if and only if x is primarily designed in order to possess and to exhibit significant form. (Note: the inclusion of 'designed' in this formula is intended to differentiate art from nature.) Additionally, formalism has important implications about art appreciation, properly so-called.

If the essential, art-making characteristic of a work is its possession and exhibition of significant form, then the pertinent object of our attention to an art work *qua* art is significant form. Art works may contain other features, such as representation and garden-variety emotions, but these are incidental and strictly irrelevant to their status as art works. Thus, when it comes to appreciating art works, attention should be focused exclusively on their formal properties.

Formalism has been an influential doctrine. For decades schoolchildren were taught not to let their attention wander away from the text: not to allow their concentration to become caught up in the story's relation to real life, rather than to savor its formal organization and features (for example, its unity, complexity, and intensity). But formalism does not simply advocate certain protocols for aesthetic experience. It also attempts to ground those protocols in an ambitious philosophical theory.

According to formalism, the intended primary function of exhibiting significant form is a necessary condition for art status. But this cannot be right. Many of our greatest works of art were produced with patently different primary intentions, such as many military monuments whose primary function was to commemorate great victories. In response, the formalist may attempt to modify this condition, arguing that an art work is something that has *among* its primary functions the exhibition of significant form. But this too seems unlikely.

Modern art is full of examples of what are called found objects, or ready-made objects, such as Duchamp's *Why not Sneeze?* These ordinary objects are selected and put forward as art works in order to provoke conceptual insights. Frequently, such objects are chosen expressly because of their palpable lack of what can be called significant form. Inasmuch as these found objects are art, it cannot be the case that the exhibition of significant form is a necessary condition for art status.

Moreover, counter-examples to the formalist thesis can also be located in traditional art. Many cultures produce statues of demon figures whose intended function is to frighten intruders who wander into forbidden precincts. Such figurines are art, coveted by museums and collectors alike. But it is unimaginable that their creators could have in any way intended them as vehicles for the exhibition of significant form. Such an intention would be at odds with their intention to scare off viewers. So, once again we must conclude that the intended function of exhibiting significant form cannot be a necessary condition for art status.

Is it a sufficient condition, however? Here let us return to the case of the theorem from symbolic logic. Such theorems may possess significant form. The formalist, however, maintains that they are not art works because the exhibition of significant form is not among their intended primary functions. However, consider the case of a theorem whose proof has already been established, but by means of a lengthy or cumbersome set of steps. Suppose some logician decides to find a more elegant way of solving the problem, and succeeds in doing so. 'Elegance' is surely a formal property, and in this case the point of the exercise is that the theorem in question possess and exhibit formal beauty. The formalist would appear to be compelled to recognize this as an art work, but this is a fallacious result. Thus, the intended function of exhibiting significant form is not a sufficient condition for art status.

Nor does our argument hinge on this one example. An athlete may have among his or her primary intentions the desire not only to win, but to do it with arresting visual style. And though a baseball catch can be a thing of nearly balletic beauty (and be intended as such), it is not a work of art. (If we refer to it in this way, as we often do, we are, of course, only speaking metaphorically.)

If the intended exhibition of significant form is neither a necessary nor a sufficient condition for art status, what are we to make of the common denominator argument and the function argument? These arguments can be stated in ways that are logically valid, yet logically valid arguments can reach false conclusions when their premises are false. The problem with the common denominator argument and the function argument is that both contain false or misleading premises.

The common denominator argument presupposes that the possession of either representational, expressive or formal properties constitutes a necessary condition for art status. This presupposition can be criticized from two different directions. First, it can be pointed out that this array of alternatives does not spell out all of the relevant options, and that consequently the argument lacks proper logical closure. Unless we know that these are the only candidates available as necessary conditions for art status, we have no reason to accept formalism as the result of an argument by elimination like this one. Furthermore, we have every reason to believe that there are other candidates, such as certain historical properties (Danto 1981) and/or institutional properties (Dickie 1984). These possibilities, especially given the consensus, as already discussed, that 'found objects' can qualify as works of art, may be even more comprehensive than the exhibition of formal properties. Thus, the common denominator argument is false because one of its central premises misleadingly insinuates that it has exhausted all the pertinent alternatives when it has not.

A second frequently-mentioned, though very different, line of objection to the common denominator argument is that it presupposes that there must be a necessary feature shared by all art works. Followers of Ludwig Wittgenstein such as Morris

Weitz (1956) have questioned this. Believing that all art works necessarily possess a common feature seems to be more an article of faith than an established fact. What we call art seems so very diverse. There are so many different artforms and so much variety within artforms. Why suppose that they share a single common property or even a single set of common properties? Is it plausible to suppose that John Cage's *4' 33"* has an essential property that corresponds to an essential feature of the Taj Mahal?

Bell said that we gibber if we cannot adduce a feature common to all art works. But we apply many concepts, like the concept of game, in ordinary language without being able to name an essential property that every object that falls under the concept possesses. Many theories abound about how we are able to do this. Thus, we may not have to worry about gibbering if we deny that the concept of art is governed by necessary conditions. Moreover, if one agrees that one of the alternatives that should be added to the common denominator argument is the possibility that art has no necessary conditions, one may resist the conclusion that formalism is the obvious survivor of the sort of process of elimination the common denominator argument invites.

Similar problems beset the function argument. It too ignores the possibility that there may be no primary function (or set of primary functions) *unique* to art, as well as the possibility that the functions of art may reside somewhere other than in representation, expression or the exhibition of significant form. Thus, the function argument does not compel us to agree that the exhibition of significant form is a sufficient condition for art status.

Moreover, both the common denominator argument and the function argument, along with the general statement of the formalist definition of art, are plagued by a problem that we have so far left unremarked, namely that the concept of significant form that is the central term of the formalist's arguments and definition is regrettably indeterminate. Without some idea of the nature of significant form or some criteria for recognizing it, we must worry (stealing a line from Bell) that when we employ it, we gibber.

What exactly is significant form? The formalist gives us no way to discriminate between significant form and insignificant form. Formalists may give us examples of each, but no principles. What makes one juxtaposition of shapes significant and another not? We have no way to decide. Nor can it be said, as some say of art, that reliable criteria for applying significant form inhere in ordinary language, since 'significant form' is not a term of ordinary usage, but a piece of jargon. Thus, obscurity lies at the heart of formalism; the theory turns out to be useless, because its central term is undefined.

The formalist might say that a work has significant form if it is arresting. But that is not enough, since a work can be arresting for reasons other than formal ones, or even in virtue of formal properties that are not significant in the formalist's sense: such as its unusual, all-over monotone color. How, without a characterization of significant form, will we know whether a work is arresting because it possesses significant form, rather than for some other reason?

Often formalists attempt to repair this shortcoming by saying that significant form is such that it causes a special mental state in the minds of viewers. But this is not a helpful suggestion unless the formalist can define that state of mind. Otherwise we are left with one undefined concept posing as a definition of another, which is effectively equivalent to having no definition at all. Nor can the formalist say that significant form is that which causes the peculiar state of mind in percipients that is the apprehension of significant form, since such a definition is circular. We would already have to possess the concept of significant form in order to tell whether the mental state was indeed an apprehension of significant form.

It is impossible here to review all the different proposals – in terms of notions like aesthetic emotion and aesthetic experience – that formalists have attempted to craft in order to characterize the putative mental state that significant form is alleged to afford. To date, none of these has been anything less than controversial. Thus, at this point in time, the burden of proof falls to the formalist, since on the face of it it appears unlikely that there is a distinctive state of mind elicited by all and only art works. That is, since there are so many different kinds of art work that require all sorts of mental responses, it is doubtful that there is just one mental state which they all induce. Does a feminist novel really engender the same kind of mental state as a Fabergé egg? Is there really some uniform aesthetic experience elicited by all art works? Until that question is answered positively, precisely and persuasively, the idea that significant form can be explicated by reference to aesthetic experience remains moot. But without such an answer, the notion of significant form is too vague to be credible.

Perhaps the most incendiary corollary of formalism is the idea that representational properties in art works, whenever they appear in art works, are strictly irrelevant to their status as art and to our appreciation of them as art works. According to formalists, we must appreciate art works in terms of their purely formal relationships, divorced from the claims and concepts of daily life. But this is a very unlikely doctrine, for the simple reason that what is called significant form frequently supervenes on the representational content of art works.

In order to access the form of a novel – to track its unity and diversity, to appreciate its intensity or its lack thereof – we must attend to its representations of actions, places and characters. We must generally bring to the novel the kinds of schemas, scripts and folk psychology that cognitive scientists tell us we bring to the affairs of ordinary life. But if in order to admire the structure of oppositional relationships among the characters in a novel we must deploy the categories of ordinary life (such as what are called person schemas) to the states of affairs the novelist represents, then the notion that representation and its connection to ordinary experience is strictly irrelevant is grievously mistaken.

Furthermore, it is not difficult to extend observations like this to our apprehension of form in many historical, mythological, religious and otherwise narrative paintings and sculptures, since there too form often comes to light only in the shadows of representational content.

As a heuristic, formalism may be a useful pedagogical standpoint. It reminds us that it is important not to overlook the formal dimension of art works. Artists spend an immense amount of energy designing the structures of art works, and attending to the intelligence disclosed by the form of a work can be a rewarding source of satisfaction for readers, viewers or listeners. However, transforming this near-truism into a philosophy of art, as the formalist does, impoverishes rather than enriches our understanding of art.

See also Definitions of art, The aesthetic, Kant.

References

Bell, C. (1914) *Art*, London: Chatto and Windus.
Danto, A. (1981) *The Transfiguration of the Commonplace*, Cambridge, Mass.: Harvard University Press.
Dickie, G. (1984) *The Art Circle*, New York: Havens.
Fry, R. (1956) *Vision and Design*, New York: Meridian.
Greenberg, C. (1961) *Art and Culture*, Boston: Beacon.
Hanslick, E. (1986) *On the Musically Beautiful*, trans. G. Payzant, Indianapolis: Hackett.
Levinson, A. (1991) "The Spirit of the Classical Dance," in Acocella, J. and Garafola, L. (eds), *André Levinson on Dance*, Middletown: Wesleyan University Press.
Riegl, A. (1992) *Problems of Style*, trans. E. Kain, Princeton: Princeton University Press.
Weitz, M. (1956) "The Role of Theory in Aesthetics," *Journal of Aesthetics and Art Criticism* 15: 27–35.
Wolfflin, H. (1950) *Principles of Art History*, trans. M. D. Hottinger, New York: Dover.

Further reading

Carroll, N. (1985) "Formalism and Critical Evaluation," in P. McCormick (ed.), *The Reasons of Art*, Ottawa: University of Ottawa Press.
—— (1989) "Clive Bell's Aesthetic Hypothesis," in G. Dickie, R. Sclafani and R. Roblin (eds), *Aesthetics: A Critical Anthology*, New York: St. Martin's Press.
—— (1991) "Beauty and the Genealogy of Art Theory," *Philosophical Forum* 22: 307–34.
Lemon, L. T. and Reis, M. J. (eds) (1965) *Russian Formalist Criticism*, Lincoln: University of Nebraska Press.

9

PRAGMATISM

Dewey

Richard Shusterman

There is nothing in Anglo-American aesthetics that can compare with the comprehensive scope, detailed argument, and passionate power of Dewey's *Art as Experience* (1987). Yet though this book initially aroused considerable interest, pragmatist aesthetics was, by the late fifties, totally eclipsed by analytic philosophy of art, which by and large dismissed Dewey's aesthetic theory as "a hodge-podge of conflicting methods and undisciplined specula-tions" (Isenberg 1987: 128; see also Shusterman 1989).

In the last several years, there have been strong signs of a positive revaluation of Dewey's legacy. Many have become tired of the confines of analytic aesthetics, turning to continental aesthetics for deeper discussions of art's sociopolitical dimensions and its practical, ethical, and ideological functions. These topics are very much present in Dewey. In what follows I shall suggest some of the attrac-tions of Dewey's aesthetics by showing how it diverges from the classical analytic aesthetics that dominated Anglo-American philosophy of art since the 1950s, and how it accommodates the most appealing themes of continental theory. I shall then conclude by considering how Dewey's pragmatist tradition in aesthetics has been revived and extended by more recent philosophers who were trained in analytic philosophy and remain appreciative of its resources and style of argument, even in making their more pragmatist points. This should make clear that the series of contrasts I draw between classical analytic aesthetics and Deweyan pragmatist aesthetics does not imply that analysis and pragmatism are essentially incompat-ible orientations which cannot fruitfully be combined by philosophers of art.

The pragmatist alternative

One of the most central features of Dewey's aesthetics is its naturalism. The first chapter of *Art as Experience* is entitled "The Live Creature," and it and all the subsequent chapters are dedicated to grounding aesthetics in the natural

97

needs, constitution, and activities of the embodied human organism. Dewey aims at "recovering the continuity of esthetic experience with normal processes of living" (Dewey 1987: 16). Aesthetic understanding must start with and never forget the roots of art and beauty in the "basic vital functions," "the biological commonplaces" man shares with "bird and beast" (ibid.: 19–20). For Dewey, all art is the product of interaction between the living organism and its environment, an undergoing and a doing which involves a reorganization of energies, actions, and materials. Though human arts have become more spiritualized, "the organic substratum remains as the quickening and deep foundation," the sustaining source of the emotional energies of art which make it so enhansive to life (ibid.: 30–1). This essential physiological stratum is not confined to the artist. The perceiver, too, must engage his or her natural feelings and energies as well as his or her physiological sensory motor responses in order to appreciate art, which for Dewey amounts to reconstituting something as art in aesthetic experience.

The major thrust of classical analytic aesthetics is sharply opposed to naturalizing art and its aesthetic value. G. E. Moore established this attitude with his doctrine of the naturalistic fallacy, a fallacy which "has been quite as commonly committed with regard to beauty as with regard to good" (Moore 1959: 201). Aesthetic qualities must not be identified with natural ones, and are not even reducible or logically entailed by them. This is precisely the point of Sibley's (1959) seminal analysis of aesthetic concepts, and it is why Margaret Macdonald held that "works of art are esoteric objects" (Macdonald 1954: 114).

Art's functionality

Part of Dewey's naturalism is to insist that art's aim "is to serve the whole creature in his unified vitality," a "live creature" demanding natural satisfactions (Dewey 1987: 122). This stands in sharp contrast to the extreme emphasis on disinterestedness which analytic aesthetics inherited from Kant. This emphasis goes beyond the mere Moorean point that beauty, like good, is a purely intrinsic value or end in itself, which can only be misconceived as a means. There is the further characterization of art as something essentially defined by its non-instrumentality and gratuitousness. Strawson explains the impossibility of any general rules for art by defining our interest in art as totally devoid of any "interest in anything it can or should do, or that we can do with it" (Strawson 1974: 178); and Stuart Hampshire likewise tells us that "a work of art is gratuitous, something made or done gratuitously, and not in response to a problem posed" (Hampshire 1954: 161). The underlying motive for such analytic attempts to purify art from any functionality was not to denigrate it as worthlessly useless, but to place its worth apart from and above the realm of instrumental value and natural satisfactions. However noble the intention, this attitude portrayed aesthetic experience as eviscerate and socially irrelevant. No wonder many have turned to the theories of Nietzsche, Bataille, and Foucault for recognition of the bodily factors and desires involved in the aesthetic, just as they turn to continental Marxian theories for greater appreciation of art's historico-political and socioeconomic determinants and instrumental power.

These very themes we can find in Dewey. Though no less devoted than the analysts to defending the aesthetic and to proving its infungible worth, Dewey did so by insisting on art's great but *global* instrumental value. For anything to have human value it must in some way serve the needs, and enhance the life and development, of the human organism in coping with its environing world. The mistake of the Kantian tradition was to assume that since art had no specific, identifiable function which it could perform better than anything else, it could only be defended as being beyond use and function. Dewey's important corrective is to argue that art's special function and value lies not in any specialized, particular end but in satisfying the live creature in a more global way, by serving a variety of ends, and most importantly by enhancing our immediate experience, which invigorates and vitalizes us, thus aiding our achievement of whatever further ends we pursue. The work-song sung in the harvest fields not only provides the harvesters with a satisfying aesthetic experience, but its zest carries over into their work and invigorates and enhances it. The same can be said for works of high art. They are not merely a special function-class of instruments for generating aesthetic experience (as they essentially are for Beardsley (1958), the analyst closest to Dewey's account of aesthetic value and experience); they modify and enhance perception and communication; they energize and inspire because aesthetic experience is always spilling over and getting integrated into our other activities, enhancing and deepening them.

The centrality of the aesthetic

Dewey's recognition of the global functionality of art is related to another view where he seems to differ sharply from analytic philosophers: the philosophical primacy and centrality of art and the aesthetic. For Dewey, the aesthetic experience is the "experience in which the whole creature is alive" and most alive (Dewey 1987: 33). "To esthetic experience, then, the philosopher must go to understand what experience is" (ibid.: 278). While Dewey saw art as the qualitative measure of any society, analytic philosophers saw science as the ideal and paradigm of human achievement. And analytic aesthetics, at least initially, was largely an attempt to apply the logically rigorous and precise methods of scientific philosophy to the wayward and woolly realm of art. Yet Dewey, appreciative as he was of scientific method and progress, could not help but regard scientific experience as thinner than art. For art engages more of the human organism in a more meaningful and immediate way, including the higher complexities of thinking: "the production of a work of genuine art probably demands more intelligence than does most of the so-called thinking that goes on among those who pride themselves on being 'intellectuals'" (ibid.: 52). He therefore held "that art – the mode of activity that is charged with meanings capable of immediately enjoyed possession – is the complete culmination of nature, and that 'science' is properly a handmaiden that conducts natural events to this happy issue" (Dewey 1929: 358).

Continuities versus dualisms

Dewey tries to deconstruct the traditional privileging opposition of science over art not only by reversing the privilege but by denying there is any rigid dichotomy or opposition between the two. He insists that "science is an art," for "esthetic quality . . . may inhere in scientific work" and both enterprises perform the same essential function of helping us order and cope with experience (Dewey 1929: 358). Like Derrida's idea of the general text, Dewey's central continuity thesis was aimed at breaking the stranglehold of entrenched dualisms and rigid disciplinary distinctions which stifle creative thought and fragment both individual experience and social life. He sought to connect aspects of human experience and activity which had been divided by specialized, compartmental-izing thought, then more brutally sundered by specialist, departmentalizing institutions in which such fragmented disciplinary thinking is reinscribed and reinforced. In these ways he also anticipates Adorno and Foucault.

Dewey's aesthetic naturalism, aimed at "recovering the continuity of esthetic experience with normal processes of living," is part of his attempt to break the stifling hold of "the compartmental conception of fine art" (Dewey 1987: 14), that old and institutionally entrenched philosophical ideology of the aesthetic which sharply distinguishes art from real life, and remits it "to a separate realm" – the museum, theater, and concert hall (ibid.: 1987: 9).

Dewey's aesthetics of continuity and holism, however, not only undermines the art/science and art/life dichotomies; it insists on the fundamental continuity of a host of traditional binary notions and genre distinctions whose long-assumed oppositional contrast has structured so much of philosophical aesthetics: form/content, fine/practical art, high/popular culture, spatial/temporal arts, artist/audience, to name but a few. There is no space here to discuss his critique of all such rigid dualisms and distinctions; nor to belabor its affinity to deconstruction and postmodernism, and its radical contrast to analytic aesthetics whose quest for clarity typically advocated "a ruthlessness in making distinctions" (Passmore 1954) combined with a respect for entrenched disciplinary divisions and critical practices (Shusterman 1986, 1992).

The criterion of experience

Analytic aesthetics, pursued under the ideal of science, thus tended to shirk issues of evaluation and reform. The aim was to analyze and clarify the established concepts and practices of art criticism, not to revise them; to give a true account of our concept of art, not to change it. In vivid contrast, Deweyan aesthetics is interested not in truth for truth's sake but in achieving richer and more satisfying experience. For Dewey's pragmatism, *experience* not *truth* is the final standard. The ultimate aim of all enquiry, scientific or aesthetic, is not knowledge itself but better experience or experienced value, and Dewey insists on "the immediacy of aesthetic experience" and its experienced value (Dewey 1987: 294). From this follows his view of the supremacy of the aesthetic: art's "immediately enjoyed," active experience is the "culmination of nature, for which truth or science serves as an auxiliary 'handmaiden'" (ibid.: 33n.). It also follows that aesthetic values cannot be permanently fixed by aesthetic theory or criticism but must be continually tested and may be overturned by the tribunal of changing experience (ibid.: 100–1, 110, 325).

Integrating art and life

A more dramatic and radical consequence of this experiential standard is that our aesthetic concepts, including the concept of art itself, are revealed as mere instruments which need to be challenged and revised when they fail to provide the best experience. This can account for Dewey's obvious attempt to direct his aesthetic theory at radically reforming our concept of art and the aesthetic, an attempt which was alien to the essentially accepting, clarificatory spirit of analytic aesthetics. While analytic aesthetics followed the romantic and modernist tradition of defending art's value and autonomy by identifying the concept of art with the concept (and associated sublimity and genius) of *high art*, Dewey deplores this elitist tradition, which he attacks under the labels of "the museum conception of art"(Dewey 1987: 12) and "the esoteric idea of fine art" (ibid.: 90). The prime motive for his opposition to the spiritualized sequestration of art was not ontological considerations of naturalistic continuity and emergence. It was the instrumental aim of improving our immediate experience through sociocultural transformation where art would be richer and more satisfying to more people, because it would be closer to their most vital interests and better integrated into their lives. The compartmentalization and spiritualization of art as an elevated separate realm set upon a remote pedestal, divorced from the materials and aims of all other human effort, have removed art from the lives of most of us, and thus have impoverished the aesthetic quality of our lives.

More than art suffers from its spiritualized sequestration; nor was this compartmentalization established simply by and for aesthetes to secure and purify their pleasures. The idea of art and the aesthetic as a separate realm distinguished by its freedom, imagination, and pleasure has as its underlying correlative the dismal assumption that ordinary life is necessarily one of joyless, unimaginative coercion. This provides the powers and institutions structuring our everyday life with the best excuse for their increasingly brutal indifference to natural human needs for the pleasures of beauty and imaginative freedom. These are not to be sought in real life, but in fine art, an escape that gives temporary relief. Art becomes, in Dewey's mordant phrase, "the beauty parlor of civilization," covering with an opulent aesthetic surface its ugly horrors and brutalities, which, for Dewey, include class snobbery and capitalism's profit-seeking oppression and alienation of labor (Dewey 1987: 14–16). Here again, we find Dewey anticipating currently influential themes in aesthetic theory which we have imported from the Marxian Frankfurt school.

Social context

Analytic theories of the historicity and institutional nature of art are painfully narrow and rarefied compared to Dewey's, which sees "the compartmentalized conception of fine art" and the austere esotericism of contemporary high art not as an "internal development," but as largely a product of nationalism and imperialism (which fed the museum), and industrialization and world-market capitalism (which deprived art of its "intimate social connection") (Dewey 1987: 14–16). Modern socioeconomic forces have so divided between joyless "externally enforced labor" and free enjoyment, between production and consumption, that the "chasm between ordinary and esthetic experience," art and real life, has become theoretically convincing. Thus, for Dewey, not only art but philosophical theories about art (and everything else) are significantly shaped by "extraneous" socioeconomic conditions; so our concept of art needs to be reformed as part and parcel of the reform of society which has so constituted it.

Art experience versus the art object

I conclude with perhaps Dewey's most central aesthetic theme: the privileging of aesthetic experience over the material object which ordinary, reified thinking identifies (and then commodifies and fetishizes) as the work of art. For Dewey the essence and value of art is not in such artifacts, but in the dynamic and developing experiential activity through which they are created and perceived. He therefore distinguishes between the "art product" and "the actual work of art [which] is what the product does with and in experience" (Dewey 1987: 9). In contrast, analytic aesthetics has been rather suspicious of aesthetic experience (at times even denying its existence), while privileging the art object. It expended enormous efforts in trying to fix the precise criteria for identifying the same art object in its various manifestations (such as copies or performances) and for individuating it from other objects and inauthentic manifestations (such as forgeries). Analytic aesthetics did this because its scientific ideal was objective truth about art rather than the Deweyan goal of enhanced experience. Privileging objective critical truth meant privileging objects. Thus even Beardsley, whose first book followed Dewey in making aesthetic experience the crux of aesthetics, eventually gave uncontested privilege to the object as the guarantor of objective criticism. "The first thing required to make criticism possible is an object to be criticized – something . . . with its own properties against which interpretations and judgements can be checked." He therefore posits the object-centered principles of independence and autonomy: "that literary works exist as individuals" and "are self-sufficient entities" (Beardsley 1970: 16).

Undoubtedly much of poststructuralism's appeal derives from its attack on the static, closed notion of the art work as a fully fixed, self-sufficient and inviolable object, and its ardent insistence on the active role and openness of reading as textual practice which reconstitutes literary meaning. Such themes, central to the fashionable continental theories of Barthes, Derrida, and Foucault, are anticipated in Dewey's move from closed artistic product to open, transformative aesthetic experience. But Dewey's theory seems saner, for while rejecting structural fixity and reification, he clearly preserves the notions of structure, unity, and object by reconstituting them in a functional, contextual form rather than suggesting their total rejection as inescapably rigid, foundational, and retrograde.

Dewey's heritage

The conclusion should be obvious. Since Dewey's aesthetics offers crucial insights usually lacking in the analytic tradition, and obtainable from continental theory but often only at the costly price of conceptual obfuscation and irrelevant theoretical baggage, it represents an excellent point of departure for new aesthetic thinking in Anglo-American philosophy. Though some of Dewey's views are undeniably contestable and dated, pragmatist aesthetics is not simply a curiosity of the past; it points to the most promising future we can envisage for aesthetic inquiry.

Several philosophers, associated also with analytic philosophy, have built on Deweyan insights to enrich the tradition of pragmatist aesthetics and apply it to more contemporary aesthetic issues and artforms: from mass-media arts and multiculturalism to postmodernism and the ethical art of living (Shusterman 1995a, 1995b, 1997, 1992). Nelson Goodman (1976), for example, develops Dewey's theme of the continuity of art and science. Rejecting the idea of autonomous aesthetic objects, valued merely for the pleasure of their form, Goodman urges the fundamental unity of art and science through their common cognitive function. Hence aesthetics should be placed with philosophy of science and "should be conceived as an integral part of meta-physics and epistemology"; and aesthetic value should be subsumed under cognitive excellence (Goodman 1978: 102). Despite Goodman's attempt to supply extremely strict definitions of works of art in terms of authentic objects, he insists with Dewey (and Beardsley) that what matters aesthetically is not what the object is but how it functions in dynamic experience. He therefore advocates that we replace the question "what is art?" with the question "when is art?"

Other philosophers trained in the analytic tradition, such as Joseph Margolis (1989, 1994), Richard Rorty (1989), and Richard Shusterman (1997, 1992), have used pragmatist ideas to show how the interpretation of art works can be meaningful and valid without the need to posit fixed entities as the unchanging objects of valid interpretations. Their arguments show how traditionally entrenched but dialogically open practices can be enough to secure identity of reference for discussion of the work (and thus ensure that we can meaningfully talk about the same work), without positing that there is therefore a fixed, substantive nature of the art work that defines its identity. This basic strategy of distinguishing between substantive and referential identity is formulated in different ways by these contemporary pragmatists. All of them stress the historicity and cultural embeddedness of art works, but only Margolis tries to erect this idea into a ramified metaphysics of cultural objects. In contrast to the idea (shared by Rorty, Margolis, and the literary pragmatist Stanley Fish) that all our aesthetic experience is interpretive, Shusterman argues for some level of experience "beneath interpretation," thus reviving the early pragmatist respect for non-linguistic dimensions of experience shared by James and Dewey.

As Nelson Goodman renews Dewey's continuum of art and science, so Richard Rorty (1989) extends Dewey's pragmatist blending of aesthetics and ethics by advocating 'the aesthetic life' as an ethics of 'self-enrichment,' 'self-enlargement,' and 'self-creation.' If Rorty's vision of the aesthetic life has been criticized for its isolation in the private sphere, its narrowing focus on language and high cultural texts, and its consequent failure to engage with popular artforms and robustly embodied experience, Shusterman's pragmatism argues for the aesthetic experience of the popular arts, of somatic-centered disciplines, and (following Dewey) of democracy itself.

Though Stanley Cavell seems reluctant to bear the label 'pragmatist,' his excellent, detailed work on popular cinema and television certainly helps extend the respect for popular art that Dewey advocated (Cavell 1979, 1981, 1984). Cavell typically takes Emerson rather than Dewey as his mentor, but that is no reason to exclude him from the pragmatist tradition. A good case can be made that Emerson himself anticipated almost all the major themes that we identify as pragmatist in Dewey's aesthetics (Shusterman 1999a). If calling Emerson a pragmatist seems anachronistic because he predates Peirce's coinage of the term, this argument will not hold for another thinker who anticipated many of Dewey's views of art and who studied pragmatism at Harvard. I refer to the African-American philosopher and cultural critic Alain Locke, whose anthology *The New Negro* (1925) served as the guiding light of the Harlem Renaissance (Shusterman 1999b). Here one might even establish a link of influence from Locke to Dewey, since Albert C. Barnes (the art collector and critic) was a contributor to Locke's project on the aesthetics of *The New Negro*; and Dewey claimed that the ideas and discussions of the same Albert C. Barnes were "a chief factor" in shaping Dewey's *Art as Experience*, which was in fact dedicated to Barnes.

References

Adorno, T. (1984) *Aesthetic Theory*, trans. C. Lenhardt, London: Routledge.
Barthes, R. (1977) *Image, Music, Text*, trans. S. Heath, New York: Hill and Wang.
Bataille, G. (1985) *Visions of Excess*, trans. A. Stoekl, Minneapolis: University of Minnesota Press.
Beardsley, M. C. (1958) *Aesthetics*, Indianapolis: Hackett.
—— (1970) *The Possibility of Criticism*, Detroit: Wayne State University.
Cavell, S. (1979) *The World Viewed*, Cambridge, Mass.: Harvard University Press.
—— (1981) *Pursuits of Happiness*, Cambridge, Mass.: Harvard University Press.
—— (1984) "The Fact of Television," *Daedalus* 111: 235–68.
Derrida, J. (1974) *Of Grammatology*, trans. G. Chakravorty Spivak, Baltimore: Johns Hopkins University Press.
Dewey, J. (1929) *Experience and Nature*, Chicago: Open Court.
—— (1987) *Art as Experience*, Carbondale: Southern Illinois University Press.
Emerson, R. W. (1983) *Essays and Lectures*, New York : Literary Classics of the United States.
Fish, S. (1980) *Is There a Text in this Class?* Cambridge: Harvard University Press.
Foucault, M. (1984) *The Foucault Reader*, New York: Pantheon.
Goodman, N. (1976) *Languages of Art*, 2nd edn, Indianapolis: Hackett.
—— (1978) *Ways of Worldmaking*, Indianapolis: Hackett.
Hampshire, S. (1954) "Logic and Appreciation," in W. Elton (ed.), *Aesthetics and Language*, Oxford: Blackwell.
Isenberg, A. (1987) "Analytical Philosophy and the Study of Art," *Journal of Aesthetics and Art Criticism* 46: 125–36.

Locke, A. (1970) *The New Negro*, New York: Atheneum.

Macdonald, M. (1954) "Some Distinctive Features of Arguments used in Criticism of the Arts," in W. Elton (ed.), *Aesthetics and Language*, Oxford: Blackwell.

Margolis, J. (1989) *Texts without Referents*, Oxford: Blackwell.

—— (1994) *Interpretation: Radical but Not Unruly*, Berkeley: University of California Press.

Moore, G. E. (1959) *Principia Ethica*, Cambridge: Cambridge University Press.

Nietzsche, F. (1968) *The Will to Power*, trans. W. Kaufmann and R. J. Hollingdale, New York: Vintage.

Passmore, J. (1954) "The Dreariness of Aesthetics," in W. Elton (ed.) *Aesthetics and Language*, Oxford: Blackwell.

Rorty, R. (1989) *Contingency, Irony and Solidarity, Cambridge*: Cambridge University Press.

Shusterman, R. (1986) "Analytic Aesthetics, Literary Theory, and Deconstruction," *Monist* 69: 22–38.

—— (1989) "Analysing Analytic Aesthetics," in *Analytic Aesthetics,* Oxford: Blackwell.

—— (1992) *Pragmatist Aesthetics: Living Beauty, Rethinking Art*, Oxford: Blackwell.

—— (1995a) "Popular Art and Education," *Studies in Philosophy and Education* 13: 203–12.

—— (1995b) "Rap Remix: Pragmatism, Postmodernism, and Other Issues in the House," *Critical Inquiry* 22: 150–8.

—— (1997) *Practicing Philosophy: Pragmatism and the Philosophical Life*, New York: Routledge.

—— (1999a) "Emerson's Pragmatist Aesthetics," *Revue Internationale de Philosophie* 207: 87–99.

—— (1999b) "Pragmatist Aesthetics: Roots and Radicalism," in L. Harris (ed.) *The Critical Pragmatism of Alain Locke*, New York: Rowman and Littlefield.

Sibley, F. (1959) "Aesthetic Concepts," *Philosophical Review* 68: 421–50.

Strawson, P. (1974) "Aesthetic Appraisal and Works of Art," in *Freedom and Resentment*, London: Methuen.

10
HEIDEGGER

Simon Glendinning

The saving power of art

Martin Heidegger (1889–1976) is best known for his first book, *Being and Time* (Heidegger 1962 [1927]), which propelled him to the centre of the philosophical stage in Europe, radically transforming the 'continental' scene. That book makes only a passing reference to works of art, and that reference is apparently restricted to poetic works (Heidegger 1962: sect. 34). That this is restriction is *only* an appearance will become clearer as we proceed, but on the basis of that book one could be forgiven for thinking that art plays a minor role in Heidegger's thinking. That impression could not arise from a reading of his later essays, and it would be natural to see this as part of a general shift in his philosophy, a shift that might warrant drawing a distinction between an 'early' and 'later' Heidegger, much as we do with Wittgenstein. That may well be misleading even for Wittgenstein, but it is certainly misleading in the case of Heidegger. One of the aims of this chapter is to show that an appreciation of Heidegger's philosophy of art profoundly enriches but never overturns or supplants his early writings.

The abiding and deep significance of art for Heidegger's conception of human existence can perhaps be best introduced by considering its extraordinary appearance at the end of an essay from 1953 entitled "The Question of Technology" (Heidegger 1993). In that essay, Heidegger took up a topic which was widely seen as involving a disturbing new presence in the contemporary world: modern machine technology. In what we will come to see as a 'gear-shifting' gesture utterly characteristic of his thinking, Heidegger regarded contemporary opinion on this matter as completely failing to grasp its essence. Not that Heidegger saw the growing concern as misplaced and modern technology as something to be embraced: if anything, Heidegger thought that the voices of dissent did not go *far enough*.

For Heidegger, what is at stake with the rise of modern technology is not the growing presence in our midst of a distinctive and dangerous new kind of thing, but – and this is the characteristically Heideggerian 'shift of gear' – the holding sway of a distinctive and dangerous new kind of 'midst' within which things show themselves. The idea is that the essence of modern technology, conceived here as what makes it possible for technological instrumentation and equipment to arise in human modes of doing and knowing, is a particular "way of revealing" the actual (Heidegger 1993: 318). This is not just one way of revealing among others, and for Heidegger it certainly is not a neutral way. On the contrary, it is a way of revealing which discloses everything everywhere as measurable, calculable and orderable (under orders or at our command), as what Heidegger comes to call a "standing-reserve" (ibid.: 322).

The dominance of technology obviously connects closely with our own self-understanding too. For Heidegger it is a central characteristic of contemporary modernity that we are more than ever inclined to see ourselves as commanders of nature: we elevate man as the "lord of the earth" (ibid.: 332) who can, through the use of technology, dominate the natural world. Lording it up in this way is not, Heidegger insists, man's true dignity. Moreover, for Heidegger, when the essence of modern technology reigns as the dominant way of revealing, then what is genuinely most distinctive, most human in man threatens to become so deeply eclipsed that "man himself" – the supposed master of the forces and energies of nature – can come to the point where "he himself will have to be taken as standing-reserve," something whose presence is grasped only in terms of something to be measured, controlled and ordered (ibid.: 332). This, in Heidegger's view, is the real threat of modern technology. Nevertheless, as we shall see, for Heidegger there is still hope. A "decisive confrontation" with the essence of modern technology is possible because there is a "saving power" in a realm akin to, yet also fundamentally different from the essence of modern technology. "Such a realm" Heidegger enigmatically asserts "is art" (ibid.: 340).

In this chapter I will explain why Heidegger came to consider art as having such a fundamental role in the destiny of human existence.

Clearing the midst

In order to understand Heidegger's philosophy of art we first need to appreciate that the same kind of 'gear shift' evident in his discussion of modern technology is at the heart of his account of art and works of art. Thus, against the prevailing tendency to conceive art in terms of the object produced by artists (an object of aesthetic appreciation and enjoyment), Heidegger attempts to think the essence of art otherwise than in terms of the presence of a thing.

Yet who would ever think of these things as mere things? Perhaps, Heidegger dryly suggests, the removal men involved in shifting works of art from one gallery to another, "shipped like coal from the Ruhr and logs from the Blackforest," relate to the art-work as a mere thing (Heidegger 1993: 145). Perhaps the cleaners in the museum, who will dust a sculpture and a donation-box alike, do too. But, he acknowledges, those who are supposed to be in the know about the things involved here – and really that is meant to be everyone – know that this is a crude external view of the work. The "actuality" of the work of art cannot be reduced to the presence of a mere thing.

So what is the kind of actuality involved here? Or to put this in other words, what takes place or what occurs when there is a work of art? In its most pervasive dimension this is the question which is in focus in Heidegger's 1936 paper "The Origin of the Work of Art" (1993). The basic proposal of that paper is to fundamentally reject, not only the idea that the actuality of a work of art can be grasped on the basis of its "thingly" character, but quite generally the idea that it might be grasped on the basis of the presence of something in the world at all: even a special kind of thing which is the object of a distinc-tively aesthetic experience. Heidegger 'shifts gear': what is essential to art, what is at work in the work of art, is, like the essence of modern technology for its part, not a (no doubt distinctive) kind of presence in our midst, but the sending our way of a "clearing," the historical coming to pass of a 'midst' or 'world' within which what is actual shows itself or appears. Of course, a work of art, like a piece of technological equipment, also appears in the world. But for Heidegger the "thingly" character of the work must be understood on the basis of what is at work in the work and not the reverse. Heidegger's basic proposal is thus quite astonishing. The work of the work of art, or more precisely what he calls "great art" (ibid.: 166), is nothing short of a "happening of truth" (ibid.: 185), a "happening" which is conceived not in the sense of the taking place of an adequate image or representation of beings or things, but an original opening-up or revealing of beings as such. The essence of art, like the essence of modern technology, is a way of revealing.

From the work of man to the work of art

To understand Heidegger's conception of the essence of art, it will prove helpful to see it against the background of his 'early' work, *Being and Time* (Heidegger 1962) That work remained famously unfinished, an interrupted project. But one of the most striking aspects of his 'later' essays is that they have just the same central target in view as it had: namely, interpretations which conceive man *anthropologically*, that is, as a (no doubt distinctive) presence or entity *within* the world. Heidegger's alternative is one in which the actuality of man (our 'Dasein' to use Heidegger's term) is not conceived in terms of a presence in the world at all. As Heidegger had already insisted in

Being and Time, "Being-present-at-hand [is] a kind of Being which is *essentially inappropriate* to entities of Dasein's character. To avoid getting bewildered . . . the term 'existence,' as a designation of Being, will be allotted solely to Dasein" (Heidegger 1962: 42). 'Existence' is thus sharply distinguished from 'presence,' and the former cannot be understood by starting out from the latter. Thus, Heidegger continues, "Dasein is never to be defined ontologically by regarding it as life plus something else" (ibid.: 50). In "The Origin of the Work of Art" this critique of anthropological tendencies in the interpretation of 'existence' receives its most radical elaboration. Ultimately for Heidegger man is man, that is, man 'exists' in Heidegger's sense, only as (to use Nietzsche's words) an "artistically creative subject". But that conception can be correctly understood only if we can 'shift gear'. As we shall see, for Heidegger, in essence man is not simply 'ontically' but, in a certain way, 'ontologically' creative. That is, man is not just a maker of beings or things, but 'exists' in such a way that, without man, Being "is not" (Heidegger 1993: 211).

I want to begin an explanation of this thought by focusing on a remarkable structural parallel between Heidegger's critique of traditional anthropology and his critique of traditional aesthetics. First, let us look at the question of man. The lowest, most crude interpretation of man is the biologism of what John McDowell has called "bald naturalism" (McDowell 1994: 67). On this interpretation "the essence of man consists in being an animal organism" (Heidegger 1993: 229). Bald naturalism is rife today in philosophy, but it is a position which is rejected not only by Heidegger (massively and comprehensively) but also by traditional philosophical anthropology. For the traditional philosopher, the naturalistic definition is regarded as insufficient and needs to be overcome or offset by attributing man-the-animal with a unique and distinctive trait: man is part of creation but is also unique in that he is created in the image of God; or man is an animal but is an animal which has the power of reason, the character of a person, the possession of language or consciousness or mind or soul or whatever. Man is, in short, "life plus." That is, as Heidegger puts it, "metaphysics thinks of man *on the basis* of animalitas" even if he is then "not equated with beasts" (ibid.: 227).

Heidegger's critique of anthropology involves a certain reversal of this tradition. We are not to understand the humanity of man on the basis of his animality – on the basis, that is, of his presence in the world as a (living) thing – but rather the animality of man on the basis of his humanity. Yes, man is unique, but not because a human being is an entity in the world which has some special property. Indeed, man 'is' not 'there' primarily as a presence in the world at all, but rather has Being-in-the-world as its basic state. Man *qua*

Dasein 'exists' only in virtue of 'being there'. The thought here can be brought out with the question: what occurs when there is a man? According to both naturalism and traditional philosophical anthropology the answer is: a certain kind of entity is present in the world. According to Heidegger, however, Dasein's distinctive openness to entities as entities implies a fundamental contrast with approaches in which man is conceived, in the first instance, as an animal presence in the world. According to Heidegger, animals in general (what he conceives of as, essentially, mere biological organisms) have some access to entities within the world. But such access is, he argues, always circumscribed by the Being of the animal such that it has no access to them *as such*; no access to entities in their Being. The (ontological) difference of man is then expressed with the thought that man 'is' only in an understanding of Being, and hence that "the essence of man consists in his being more than merely human" (Heidegger 1993: 245). On this view, the actuality of man is irreducible to our animal presence in the world. Indeed our presence in the world must be grasped on the basis of our 'existence'; of our standing outside our animal Being and within "the clearing" or the "openness of Being" (ibid.: 252).

Let us now turn from the question of man to the question of art. I shall do so in a way that brings out the structural parallels in Heidegger's accounts, but it should be noted that I am also giving an outline of the first crucial stages in the development of the essay "The Origin of the Work of Art" itself. The lowest, most crude interpretation of art is a kind of brutal physicalism: "works of art are as naturally present as are things. The picture hangs on the wall like a rifle or a hat. . . . Beethoven's quartets lie in the storerooms of the publishing house like potatoes in a cellar" (ibid.: 145). On this interpretation the essence of art consists in being a thing: "all works have this thingly character" (ibid.). As I have already indicated, this conception is rejected not only by Heidegger (massively and comprehensively) but by pretty much everyone, including by traditional philosophical aesthetics. For the traditional philosopher the brutal physicalist definition is regarded as obviously crude and external. It is insufficient and needs to be overcome or offset by attributing the physical work-thing with a unique and distinctive trait: a work of art is a thing but is also unique in that it is "a thing to which something else adheres": namely, "an aesthetic value" (ibid.: 164).

In short, the work is a "thing plus". Thus, "the formulation native to aesthetics" is to think of a work of art on the basis of its thingly character even if it is not then equated with mere things. "The way in which aesthetics views theart work from the outset is dominated by the traditional interpretation of all beings" (Heidegger 1993: 164): namely, in terms of their presence-at-hand. Heidegger's critique of traditional aesthetics, like his critique of traditional philosophical anthropology, involves a certain reversal. We are not to understand what is at work in a work of art, the work's 'workly' character, on the basis of its presence in the world – on the basis, that is, of its 'thingly' character – but rather while "the thingly feature in the work should not be denied . . . it must be conceived by way of the work's workly nature" (ibid.: 165). What then, according to Heidegger, is the kind of actuality that belongs to the work of art if it is not presence-at-hand? Or, to ask our question again: what occurs when there is a work of art if not a new presence in the world?

Heidegger's answer is as clear as it is extraordinary. Yes, the work of art is not a mere thing, but it is not a thing in the world with a special (aesthetic) property either. Rather, according to Heidegger, the work of the work of art is precisely that which makes possible a "world" within which entities with such-and-such properties can be present at all: "the work belongs, as work, uniquely within the realm that is opened up by itself" (ibid.: 167), that is, "the work as work *sets up a world*" (ibid.: 170).

For Heidegger, then, the work of art somehow achieves the disclosure of the "open region" within which beings appear; the disclosure of the "truth of beings". This is not, we should note, because it presents a likeness, an appearance which corresponds to how things or beings appear. Heidegger initially develops his view through a reading of a Van Gogh picture of peasant shoes (see 'Further reading' at the end of the chapter for commentaries on this reading), but his account is perhaps even more clear in connection to non-representational works (Heidegger's principal example here is a Greek temple). In that case too, Heidegger insists, the actuality of the work, what occurs when there is a work of art, is to be conceived as the "happening of truth," and clearly this cannot be thought of as its agreement or correspondence with beings. If art is, as Heidegger suggests, an event of opening up or disclosure, it is never simply the disclosure of the appearance of beings, but rather, the disclosure of their Being, the disclosure of something like a 'world'. Strongly recalling the conception of the world developed in *Being and Time*, Heidegger attributes to the work of the work of art the opening of that "open relational context" (Heidegger 1993: 167) wherein man, uniquely, "dwells" (ibid.: 170).

This is, surely, a profoundly paradoxical position. The work does not appear in a setting of humans, animals, plants and things. Rather, it is the work of art that first gathers these all together, gathers the "earthly" ground so that man can, in Heidegger's sense, 'exist'. Here we have a second, and equally extraordinary, reversal of tradition. It is not that we first have an entity, man, that creates art objects, but rather that we have a happening which lets man be man, that is, lets man 'dwell' such that 'what is' (including man himself) can show itself as it is.

Before developing Heidegger's conception of the work of the work of art further, it is worth remarking that the paradoxical proposal we have just reached *seems* to mark a profound shift from the thinking of *Being and Time*. For the 'early' Heidegger it is man (*qua* Dasein) that is the origin of the disclosed clearing in which he dwells. That is, man "as Being-in-the-world . . . is cleared in itself, not through any other entity, but in such a way that it is itself the clearing" (Heidegger 1962: 171). In "The Origin of the Work of Art" by apparent contrast, the work of "opening the open region," of disclosing a world, is assigned to another entity – the art-work. Is this a shift in Heidegger's view? I do not think so. To see why, however, it will help to look more closely at those aspects of his account of art which suggest that it is.

The autonomous work

Heidegger's account insists that there is a radical autonomy of the work of art *vis-à-vis* the human being whose activity is responsible for the presence of an art-object. The artist, he states, 'remains inconsequential . . . like a passageway that destroys itself in the creative process' (Heidegger 1993: 166). Thus what is at work in the work is made to do without the presence of the artist. That is, the work of the work can 'occur' in the radical absence of the artist as the producer of an object. And as we have seen, what occurs here according to Heidegger is astonishing: "the work opens up a world and keeps it abidingly in force" (ibid.: 169).

This role seems completely mysterious and magical. How could such powers be attributed to a work of art, however its actuality is conceived, and however great it may be? Reiterating the basic dualism of *Being and Time* between entities which do and entities which do not have Dasein's character of Being, Heidegger states at one point that "a stone is worldless. Plant and animal likewise have no world . . . The peasant woman, on the other hand, has a world because she dwells in the overtness of beings" (Heidegger 1993: 170). Yet this 'existence' is possible, it seems, only because of the extraordinary work of the work of art. The artist himself or herself does not escape this. The artist too 'is' only insofar as he or she 'exists' in a world. And that presupposes that there is a world opened up by the work of the work of art, a work of clearing which alone can "establish it in its structure" (ibid.).

Heidegger's paradoxical claim is, in fact, quite general. The work clears the open region in which 'what is' appears as itself. That is, the environment too "comes forth" as itself "for the very first time" by the work of the work: "the rock or stone first becomes rock or stone," and similarly, the work of the work allows "colours to glow, tones to sing, the word to say" (ibid.: 171). Picking up on a word invited by the peasant woman's plodding and weary ways, Heidegger calls what thus appears as itself "the earth" (ibid.): "In setting up a world, the work sets forth the earth. The work lets the earth be an earth" (ibid.: 172). Thus, again, when an art work is actual there is not the presence-at-hand of a new thing. Rather, "an open place occurs," or "there is a clearing" (ibid.: 178). In short, for the Heidegger of "The Origin of the Work of Art" the work of clearing the open region is the work of the work of art, and not the work of man. It is with considerable justice that Heidegger poses the question, two-thirds of the way into his essay "How is it that there is art at all?" (ibid.: 182). How indeed. How on earth could a work of art, even a great work of art, by itself set up a world? Presumably only if it does not happen simply 'on earth.'

The worked work

The 'being there' of the work of art has been interpreted traditionally in terms of presence; the presence of an art-object (the bearer of aesthetic qualities) created by an artist-subject. Heidegger's alternative, by contrast, seems to have bestowed upon the work of art both an impossible role and an impossible autonomy.

Yet even Heidegger's conception of the actuality of the work – the work of the work as the "happening of truth" – has to relate to the work, if not as an object, then at least as a kind of bearer of this happening. As we have seen, however, Heidegger's repeated claim is that the kind of 'thingly' character that we have in view here has to be understood on the basis of the 'workly' character of the work and not the reverse. Thus if there is, as Heidegger puts it, a "bringing forth" involved in the activity of the artist, this cannot be, just like that, the same as the "bringing forth" of a piece of equipment, the making of a thing. Heidegger attempts to bring this into focus with a vivid comparison, a comparison which again suggests a strange parallel between the work of art and Dasein, this time on the topic of death.

In *Being and Time*, Heidegger drew the distinction between Dasein and entities which do not have the character of Dasein in terms of the distinction between 'existence' and 'presence-at-hand.' That contrast gave rise to a profoundly anti-naturalistic, anti-anthropological conception of Dasein in general, including 'Dasein's death.' Heidegger's alternative conception can be brought out by imagining a scene in which an old man is walking with his old dog. Both are alive, and thus both lives can naturally come to an end. Suppose that, on this walk, this happens. Both man and dog, for some reason, cease to live. Now, going by first appearances, the event of ending of a life which here occurs to both would seem to be the same. But for Heidegger, while the end of a dog's life is essentially an event, an alteration or change within the world, what he calls "perishing," the end of the man's life is, in an important sense, something completely different; it is, as it were, the end of a world within which such events take place. As Wittgenstein puts it too, for us human beings "death is not an event in life: we do not live to experience death" (Wittgenstein 1961: 6.4311), and "so too at death the world does not alter, but comes to an end" (ibid.: 6.431). In order to mark this contrast between the coming to the end of life in the case of an animal and man, the distinctive ending of life in man's case is given a different name by Heidegger: man's "demise". But, as an *event*, a demise still contrasts with Dasein's death. Death is not the event of demise but the *possibility* of no-longer-Being-in-the-world that, *as* a possibility, faces every Dasein as long as it is Dasein. And it is only because Dasein can, in this way, be described as 'dwelling mortally' that a man, *qua* Dasein, can meet his demise.

Again we find that Heidegger's analysis of the creation of works of art has an exactly parallel structure. We are trying to grasp the distinction between the "bringing forth" that characterizes the creation of a work of art and the "bringing forth" that characterizes making things like equipment in handicraft. As with the previous case, going by first appearances they are the same: "we find the same procedure in the activity of the potter and sculptor, of joiner and painter" (Heidegger 1993: 184). In Heidegger's view, however, this appearance of sameness masks an ontological difference: a difference, moreover, which maps precisely onto the account of the demise and perishing of man and animals. While the craftsman "brings forth" the presence of something present within the world, makes a change or alteration to the world, "what looks like craft in the creation of a work is of a different sort" (ibid.). Here, according to Heidegger, we do not simply have a new thing 'there' but a coming into presence of a thing whose coming into presence "first clears the openness of the open region into which it comes forth" (ibid.: 187). This is the kind of creation that occurs when there is a work of art, a work which sets free 'what is' to be what it is (ibid.: 189). The working on materials that is involved in its creation "looks like the employment of matter in handicraft." But: "it never is" (ibid.). In both cases, of course, something is produced, but what characterizes the work of the work of art is its enigmatic productivity and autonomy. Seeming to "cut all ties to human beings," the openness of beings in which this being comes forth is "opened by itself" (ibid.: 191). Thus, just as death marks the possibility of an *end* to the world, so the work of art marks the possibility of the *beginning* of a new one. And in neither case is what is at issue the coming in to or out of the world of a human being.

It is sometimes said that while Heidegger's early work gives a place to death, it leaves out birth. But 'Dasein's death' for Heidegger was already something other than a natural event. If there was a missing piece in the analysis of Dasein in *Being and Time*, however, and we can call it 'Dasein's birth' if we like, then it is completed in "The Origin of the Work of Art". Just as we can distinguish between demise and perishing as, respectively, the end of a world and an event in the world, so too we can distinguish creation (of a work of art) and making (of a craftwork) as the beginning of a world and a bringing into the world. And if man can meet his demise only in virtue of 'dwelling mortally,' so too man can create only in virtue of what Heidegger will call 'dwelling poetically'.

Poiesis and techne

In the face of the domination of the essence of modern technology, Heidegger hopes for the possibility of a creative work which can bring about not a new style of art-object but the breaking open of a new open place: a change not in beings but "of Being" (Heidegger 1993: 197). A change that will make possible "a more original revealing" (ibid.: 333)

What is the site for such a possibility? Heidegger has been talking about art, indeed, apparently about great art. But at the end of the essay, drawing on the Greek conception of *poiesis* as a bringing forth out of unconcealment, Heidegger gathers his account together, and reconnects it to the single reference to art in *Being and Time*, with the affirmation that "all art is, in essence, poetry" (ibid.: 197). Poetic composition is thus very broadly conceived, and not confined to linguistic works. Nevertheless, works of art are conceived as essentially discursive in the sense that the "open region" is, as it were, a space of significance or horizon of intelligibility within which truth in the propositional sense is possible. On this conception, even the great works of acknowledged art history pale by comparison to what must stand as the unsurpassably great 'discursive event': the happening of "actual language" (ibid.: 198). Language, actual language, is ultimately "poetry in the essential sense" (ibid.: 199). And with its 'creation' there occurs the irruption or happening into the whole of beings of a being through which beings "break open and show what they are and how they are" (ibid.: 95): Dasein's birth.

With this thought in view we can return to the question of a shift or turn in Heidegger's thought, and in particular the apparent modification to the thought, central to *Being and Time*, that Dasein, as Being-in-the-world, is 'cleared' *in itself*. It had seemed that he later came to suggest that it is really cleared by art, or rather by the work of the work of art. But a closer examination shows no such shift. For what the essay suggests is that man is man (man 'exists') only in virtue of being – in a 'gear shifted' sense – artistically creative. This does not mean that man is that living creature that can make art objects, but that only when man 'exists' is there 'the clearing of Being'. In Heidegger's view, the supreme danger of modern technology is the threat it poses to this extraordinary destiny. It is not that we live in an age without *poiesis*, but that we live in an age in which the mode of *poiesis* which dominates is not art but *techne*. For it should be noted that, for the Greeks, *techne* too names a kind of "bringing forth," and in that sense it too "is something poetic" (ibid.: 318). In Heidegger's view, however, the essence of modern technology is a dangerously exploitative, and in a deep sense an unnatural or perverted mode of such poetic revealing: "the revealing which holds sway throughout modern technology does not unfold into a bringing forth in the sense of *poiesis* [but rather] has the character of a setting upon in the sense of a challenging forth" (ibid.: 320–1). It is, as I noted at the start, a revealing which "orders the actual as standing-reserve" (ibid.: 324). With the dreadful prospect looming that man may come to see himself too only as standing-reserve, Heidegger cleaves to the possible rise of a "saving power" which could start man on a new and more harmonious way of revealing, one which "lets man see and enter into the highest dignity of his essence" (ibid.: 337). For this to occur the "decisive confrontation" with the essence of technology must come from art. However, art here is conceived not in terms of novel art-work things, but as the happening of a new world-disclosing *poiesis*. Ultimately, Heidegger's is an almost Nietzschean hope: a hope for the 'birth' of a new Dasein, one that can let man and earth be what, in essence, they are.

See also Nietzsche, Hegel, Art and ethics.

References

Heidegger, M. (1962) *Being and Time*, trans. J. Macquarrie and E. Robinson, Oxford: Blackwell.
—— (1993) *Basic Writings*, ed. D. Farrell Krell, London: Routledge.
McDowell, J. (1994) *Mind and World*, London: Harvard University Press.
Wittgenstein, L. (1961) *Tractatus Logico-Philosophicus*, trans. D. F. Pears and B. F. McGuinness, London: Routledge.

Further reading

Derrida, J. (1987) "Restitutions of the Truth in Pointing," in *The Truth In Painting*, trans. G. Bennington and I. McLeod, Chicago and London: University of Chicago Press. (A typically thought provoking essay where Derrida questions, among other things, the presupposition held in common by both Heidegger and Shapiro about Van Gogh's picture of old shoes: namely, that it is a *pair* of shoes at all.)
Glendinning, S. (1998) *On Being with Others: Heidegger–Derrida–Wittgenstein*, London: Routledge. (Chapter 4 offers a critical assessment of Heidegger's assumption that we can draw a sharp, ontological, distinction between human beings and other animals.)
Krell, D. F. (1986) *Intimations of Mortality*, University Park, Pennsylvania: Pennsylvania State University Press. (Chapter 6 gives a clear and helpful account of why we should not think

of the early and later writings of Heidegger as involving a break or fundamental shift of position.)

Marx, W. (1971) *Heidegger and the Tradition*, Evanston: Northwestern University Press. (Part VI, Chapter 4 offers helpful observations on the connections between Heidegger and Hölderlin, and the idea of "poetic dwelling.")

Mulhall, S. (1990) *On Being in the World: Wittgenstein and Heidegger on Seeing Aspects*, London: Routledge. (The final chapter includes an interesting reading of Heidegger's response to Van Gogh's painting of peasant shoes.)

—— (1996) *Heidegger and Being and Time*, London: Routledge. (An incredibly useful introduction to Heidegger's *Being and Time* for the uninitiated.)

Sallis, J.(1990) *Echoes: After Heidegger*, Bloomington: Indiana University Press. (Chapter 7 offers a thoughtfully 'Heideggerian' presentation of "The Origin of the Work of Art" and, in particular, its emphasis on poetry.)

Shapiro, M. (1968) "The Still Life as Personal Object," in *The Reach of Mind: Essays in Memory of Kurt Goldstein*, New York: Springer. (A critique of Heidegger's essay "The Origin of the Work of Art" and particularly on what he says there about Van Gogh's painting of peasant shoes.)

Versenyi, L. (1965) *Heidegger, Being and Truth*, New Haven and London: Yale University Press. (Chapter 3 provides a useful presentation of the connections Heidegger draws between art, disclosure and truth.)

11

EXPRESSIVISM

Croce and Collingwood

Gordon Graham

One of the commonest beliefs about art is that it is essentially a form of expression, and what is more, the expression of feeling. This view is so common that it is often simply assumed to be true by students, critics and artists themselves, even very great ones. Thus Tolstoy in *What is Art?* asserts that "art is a human activity consisting in this, that one man consciously by means of certain external signs, hands on to others feelings he has lived through, and that others are infected by these feelings and also experience them" (Tolstoy 1930: 123).

Putting the view even more starkly we may say that artists are people inspired by emotional experiences, who use their skill with words, paint, music, marble, movement and so on to embody their emotions in a work of art, with a view to stimulating the same emotion in an audience. I shall call this view 'expressivism.'

In examining the cogency of expressivism it is worth noting that the temptation to adopt the expressivist point of view arises in part because we live in a post-Romantic world. The modern world is successor to one in which the creation of art works was itself inspired by expressivism: the Expressionist painting of Van Gogh and Manet, the Romantic music of Grieg and Tchaikovsky, the lyric poetry of Byron and Wordsworth. But to take just the case of music: it is only the compositions of the period 1850–1930 (roughly) that are specially suited to expressivist interpretation. A history which takes into account the whole sequence of Baroque to Classical to Romantic will soon detect a movement from music that is marked by largely structural properties (Baroque) to music that is more readily described in terms of feeling and expression (Romantic).

Such a contrast, of course, is precisely between music that is expressive and music that is not, but since it is all equally music, it seems to follow that expressive properties are not properties of music *per se*, but only of a certain style of music. *The Art of Fugue* by J. S. Bach is a work of great genius, but it is far

119

more readily interpreted as a kind of mathematics in sound than as an outpouring or embodiment of feeling. This is not to say that the music of the Baroque cannot be interpreted in accordance with the expressivist theory of art; all it shows is that expressivism is not such an obvious account of art as is often supposed, that it both requires philosophical support and warrants critical examination.

The first section of this chapter will elaborate the philosophical arguments in favor of expressivism as elaborated by one of its most celebrated exponents, the Italian philosopher Bendetto Croce (1866–1952). The second section will then recount some important objections, and the third will turn to expressivism's second best known theorist, R. G. Collingwood (1889–1943), with a view to seeing whether his version succeeds in overcoming them.

Croce: art as 'institution'

The clearest statement of Croce's view is to be found in an essay entitled "What is Art?" (in Croce 1965). This title is undoubtedly a self-conscious reference to Tolstoy's book of the same name, and some commentators have held that by choosing the same title Croce wanted to indicate just how different his view was from that of Tolstoy. But it is not altogether easy to see just where this difference might lie. According to Croce, and in words that have become the defining slogan for his theory of art, art is essentially intuition and

> what lends coherence and unity to intuition is intense feeling. Intuition
> is truly such because it expresses an intense feeling and can arise only
> when the latter is its source and base. Not idea but intense feeling is what
> confers upon art the ethereal lightness of the symbol.
>
> (Croce 1965: 25)

This is expressed in more philosophical language than the passage from Tolstoy quoted earlier, but it says something very similar. The most striking difference is the absence of any reference to art's effect upon the audience, a feature of expressivism to which we will return.

When Croce says "art is intuition" what does he mean and why does he say it? In answering these questions it is best not to start with the first. The term 'intuition' is one which did not catch on widely, and its everyday meaning is unhelpful. But it is sufficient if we take it, for the moment, simply to be a marker for whatever is special and distinctive about art. Croce, along with many other theorists, is primarily interested in pinning down the distinctively aesthetic. Accordingly his method is what theologians in another context call the *via negativa*, the method of determining the nature of something by making clear what it is not.

Croce's first distinction is between art and physical fact. This may seem an odd contrast to draw, but it reflects the inherently plausible claim that art cannot be identified with its physical embodiment; there is more to a painting than pigments on canvas, and it is in this 'more' that the real painting lies. Second, Croce denies that art has anything 'utilitarian' about it. Again this captures a common thought. A painting might prove useful, as an investment perhaps, but this usefulness would be quite tangential to its aesthetic value, and someone who regarded it solely as an investment would have no interest in it 'as art.'

Most people accept this distinction, but Croce adds the further contention that being productive of pleasure is also a utilitarian end, and hence to be discounted. Here, more people would be inclined to disagree, since they see art as intrinsically connected with pleasure. Croce, however, points out that if we also agree, as surely we must, that the fact that a thing gives pleasure is insufficient to make it art, we must invoke a distinguishing and distinctive 'aesthetic pleasure,' and hence still require an explanation of what marks off 'the aesthetic.'

The next thing that art is not is 'a moral act.' "Art," says Croce, "does not originate from an act of will." This is because while it makes sense to say that an artistic image or portrayal can be of something morally praiseworthy or blameworthy, it makes no sense to say that the image is itself either of these things. To try to do so would be "just as valid as to judge a square moral or a triangle immoral" (Croce 1965: 13).

Finally, and most importantly, Croce wishes to deny that art "has the character of conceptual knowledge." It is here that the meaning of the term 'intuition' becomes somewhat clearer. Conceptual knowledge (and under this label we may include philosophy, history and science) is founded upon a distinction between reality and unreality, so that it must compare its hypotheses with 'the world out there.' "In contrast, intuition refers precisely to the lack of distinction between reality and unreality – to the image itself – with its purely ideal status as mere image" (Croce 1965: 14). The idea is (and once again this has a natural plausibility) that a work of art, unlike for example a scientific theory, is sufficient unto itself; to understand its meaning and value we need only look at the work itself and can ignore the world beyond the work. Whether it represents that world in a life-like way (as do Courbet and the Realists) or grossly distorts it (like Dali and the Surrealists) is irrelevant to its aesthetic worth, which is apprehended without mediation: hence the language of 'intuition.' Art is "non-logical."

So much for the *via negativa*. Art is not physical, utilitarian, moral or productive of knowledge. What then does this leave? One approach to this question asks about the value of art. If artistic images are not constrained by external reality, practical value or a moral purpose, what makes them more than idle fancies? Or as Croce puts it, "what function belongs properly to the pure image in the life of the spirit?" (Croce 1965: 21). The answer stated briefly is that properly artistic images are 'symbols.'

> Art is symbol, all symbol, that is all significant. But symbol of what? Signifying what? Intuition is truly artistic, is truly intuition and not a chaotic accumulation of images, only when it has a vital principle which animates it and makes for its complete unit.
>
> (Croce 1965: 23)

So we arrive at the doctrine quoted at the start: "intense feeling is what confers upon art the ethereal lightness of the symbol" (ibid.: 25). In short, the images of art proper are symbolic expressions of feeling.

How good are these arguments of Croce's? In my view they have a plausibility that commands the support of widely-held beliefs about art: its non-physical non-utilitarian character, for instance. If the considerations Croce adduces in favor of 'art as intuition' fall somewhat short of conclusive demonstration, what they suggest is that the burden of proof falls on his critics. Croce has made out a case strong enough for expressivism. The onus is on others to show that he is wrong.

Objections to Croce's expressivism

Upon examination, however, the expressivist picture of the relation between artist, work and audience does generate serious difficulties fairly quickly. Many of these were lucidly cataloged by John Hospers in a famous address he gave to the Aristotelian Society entitled "The Concept of Artistic Expression" (Hospers 1955), and these can be recounted as follows.

First, by defining an art work in terms of its origins, expressivism seems to announce, in advance of considering the historical facts, that it must have been intense feeling which caused Shakespeare, Handel, Michelangelo, Wren and countless others to create in the way that they did. If, on the other hand, in order to avoid this sort of a priorism, expressivism is understood to be offering us an empirical generalization, it seems to be false. Many celebrated artists have expressly denied that emotion lay at the heart of their endeavors.

Second, attributing to each work of art "an intense feeling" which unifies it overlooks the difference between simple and complex works. While it is not implausible to say that a simple love song expresses love, in a complex work with, say, a great array of characters in a variety of relationships, such a wide range of emotions and attitudes is represented that it is impossible to say that any single one is that which the work expresses. What emotion lies at the heart of, unifies, or is expressed by *War and Peace*, for instance? There is much emotion in it certainly, but not, it seems to me, any one emotion which may said to be expressed by it.

Third, a similar doubt arises about the emotional content of certain artforms. Possible examples of emotional expression are easy to find in poetry, opera and the theater. But is it plausible to suggest that modernist works of architecture express emotion? Or abstract paintings? Or musical canons and fugues?

A fourth difficulty is this. The feeling a work expresses must be embodied in that work, because it could be true that the occasion of its creation was an emotional experience, and that its reception was met with emotion on the part of the audience, and yet still be false that emotion was the content of the work. A painter in a spirit of contempt might offer us nothing more that a rehash of a previous work, and we might respond with contempt for his efforts. But this would not make the painting expressive of contempt. So the emotion must be in the work. But how exactly? To say of a song or a painting, not merely that it causes or was caused by sadness, but that it is itself feeling sad, seems quite unintelligible. In reply the philosophers of expressivism usually draw a distinction between 'being an expression of sadness' and 'being expressive of sadness' a distinction explicitly elaborated in defense of an expressivist theory of music by Peter Kivy in *The Corded Shell* (Kivy 1980). This is an important distinction which will have to be looked at further, but for the moment let us record the necessity of its being drawn in the light of this fourth difficulty.

A fifth problem relates to the role expressivism assigns to the audience. Is it true that aesthetic appreciation requires us to feel the emotion that a work of art may be thought to express? It may be true that sad and solemn music tends to induce sadness, and that laughter and gaiety portrayed on stage or in a story engender lightheartedness in the audience. It is certainly often the case that horror and fear are induced in an audience by plays and films. But while some generalizations of this sort may be true, it is plain that this is not a point that extends to all emotions. Jealousy and romantic love are familiar emotions expressed in literature, but I can read a poem expressing all-consuming jealousy in the first person (Browning's "My Last Duchess," for instance) without becoming to the faintest degree jealous myself, just as I can read a love poem without falling in love myself.

It might be claimed, more modestly, that the poem must be counted a failure if it leaves its readers as uncomprehending of jealousy (or love) as before. But this marks a move away from expressivism, towards the idea that a work of art might alter our understanding of emotions, which is different from making us feel them. Since understanding often breeds sympathy, it may be true that those who come to a better understanding of an emotion come to feel differently about it. If so, however, the change is not induced directly but brought about through the intermediary of the understanding.

A sixth objection to expressivism lies in its implausibility as an explanation of the value of art. To regard art in the way that it does seem actually to remove one of its most value aspects: imaginative power. If the emotion expressed in a work should, ideally, be the artist's own, this downgrades just what makes so many works of art remarkable: that they are major feats of imagination. In short, expressivism not only ignores the value of imagination; it actually eliminates it.

A similar question arises about the value of arousing emotion in an audience. Why should greater success in the arousal of emotion count as the mark of higher art? Arguably, the most obvious works which aim to do this, and are often highly successful in this respect, are horror films. The point of these is to induce fear, and that is what they usually do. Moreover, in the main they do it with greater success than more celebrated works of art. But no one could put horror films, as a genre, on a higher level than Shakespearean tragedy.

Given these objections, it seems that as a description of the nature of artistic creation and appreciation, expressivism is seriously flawed, and plainly inadequate as an explanation of art's value. On this second point, one further observation is needed. Expressivism derives a large part of its appeal from the fact that people do indeed find works of art moving, and enjoy being moved by them. What our examination of expressivism has shown, however, is that there is nothing in the nature of art, or in its intrinsic value, that makes this psychological fact significant. We can record that people like being moved, and attach a value to works that move them solely in virtue of this fact. But in so doing we have not arrived at an explanation of the value or the distinctiveness of art.

Collingwood: art as expression

Can these objections be overcome? A sophisticated version of expressivism is to be found in R. G. Collingwood's *Principles of Art* (1938), one of the major works of aesthetics of the twentieth century.

Collingwood's version of expressivism is based on both an admiration for Croce's aesthetics and an awareness of the defects to which everyday expressivism is prone. He thus repudiates several of the features of expressivism on which the objections we have just considered are based. For example, on his view, art is not concerned with the arousal of emotion at all, for the purposes either of amusement (arousing emotion for the sake of enjoyment) or what he calls magic (arousing emotions in order to direct them at concerns in ordinary life). Both of these conception confuse 'art' with 'craft,' a distinction for which Collingwood is famous, but which largely mirrors the category of the 'utilitarian' identified by Croce.

Commonplace versions of expressivism are also mistaken in their supposition that the emotion that is expressed in art pre-exists it. Rather, in the process of creating the work, the artist refines and clarifies an original "psychic disturbance" until it can be recognized as the emotion it is. The activity of feeling and the activity of creating, though "not identical . . . are connected in such a way that . . . each is conditional upon the other" (Collingwood 1938: 304). "Every imaginative experience is a sensuous experience raised to the imaginative level by an act of consciousness" (ibid.: 1938: 306).

As this suggests, in sharp contrast to other versions of expressivism, imagination plays a central role in Collingwood's aesthetic. In fact, art proper as he describes it has two equally crucial elements, expression and imagination. A work of art expresses emotion, certainly, but its creation and appreciation are both acts of imagination, and the work itself can exist only in the imagination. In line with Croce's distinction between art and 'physical fact,' Collingwood holds that works of art must be recreated in the minds of their audience. Just as it is by imaginative construction that the artist transforms inchoate emotion into an articulate expression, so only by imaginative reconstruction can the audience apprehend it. The process of artistic creation is thus not a matter of making external what already exists internally. It is instead a process of imaginative discovery and, since the psychic disturbance is the artist's, a process of self-discovery. Herein, in fact, lies its peculiar value: self-knowledge.

> Art is not a luxury, and bad art is not a thing we can afford to tolerate. To know ourselves is the foundation of all life that develops beyond the mere psychical level of experience. . . . Every utterance and every gesture that each one of us makes is a work of art. It is important to each one of us that in making them, however much he deceives others, he should not deceive himself. If he deceives himself in this matter, he has sown in himself a seed which, unless he roots it up again, may grow into any kind of wickedness, any kind of mental disease, any kind of stupidity and folly and insanity. Bad art, the corrupt consciousness, is the true *radix malorum*.
> (Collingwood 1938: 284–5)

If, as is here alleged, the end of art is self-knowledge, knowledge of our own emotional states, this has the unhappy consequence that artistic creation can only be of real interest to its creator; art becomes a form of introspection. The odd implication of this is that we no longer seem to have any reason to devote special attention to a Leonardo or a Shakespeare.

This is a natural inference to draw, but nonetheless mistaken. Collingwood is aware that his account of art and the artist may easily be construed in this way, and as a result he devotes a whole chapter to the relation between artist and community. In it he argues that it is not 'what I feel' that the artist identifies and articulates, but 'what we feel.'

> The artist's business is to express emotions; and the only emotions he can express are those which he feels, namely his own. . . . If he attaches any importance to the judgement of his audience, it can only be because he thinks that the emotions he has tried to express are . . . shared by his audience. . . . In other words he undertakes his artistic labour not as a personal effort on his own private behalf, but as a public labour on behalf of the community to which he belongs.
>
> (Collingwood 1938: 314–5)

In short, it is not merely artists, but the whole community of which they are a part, that come to self-knowledge in their work. This is why "art is the community's medicine for the worst disease of mind, the corruption of consciousness" (ibid.: 336). Moreover, since it is only in active reconstruction of a work that it can be said to exist for the audience at all, this eliminates the false conception of the passive spectator whose emotions are played upon: "art is not contemplation, it is action" (ibid.: 332), and the function of the audience is "not a merely receptive one, but collaborative" (ibid.: 324).

The *Principles of Art* clearly advances beyond Tolstoy's version of expressivism. Though some of the same difficulties arise, the chief merit of this version is that it centers on the art not the artist. Whereas the Tolstoyan version invites us to scrutinize the artist's history and psychology, Collingwood is scathing about criticism that has been reduced to nothing more than grubbing around for historical titbits about painters and poets.

Still, if there is no way in which the emotion of an artist said to be expressed in his or her work can be specified or even apprehended independently of that work, what reason is there to call the work an expression of emotion? Why infer back from the work to the artist's emotions at all? And if, with Collingwood, we acknowledge that what we find in a work of art is "wholly and entirely imaginative" (Collingwood 1938: 306), why not conclude that the emotion presented to us is presented, so to speak, indifferently as to ownership? It is not anyone's and hence not the artist's.

Moreover, to argue, as Collingwood does, that a specific emotion cannot be attributed to the artist independently of the work, and that imaginative power is an indispensable part of the artist's endeavor, is in effect to agree that the artist's peculiar gift is not a special capacity to feel, but a special capacity to imagine, and this is tantamount to abandoning an important element of expressivism, one to which Collingwood subscribes, namely that "the artist's business is to express emotions; and the only emotions he can express are those which he feels . . . his own."

In a similar fashion the audience's emotional experience also drops out of the picture once we examine Collingwood's expressivism closely. Everyday expressivism holds that emotion is transmitted from artist to audience by being aroused in the audience. Collingwood argues that using art to arouse emotion is a confusion of art proper with craft. Nevertheless, given that the artist's expression of emotion is itself an experience of emotion, and given further that audience participation is a collaborative realization of that experience on the part of both artist and audience, it seems to follow that the artist's emotion is aroused in the audience. In order to avoid this apparently contradictory conclusion, Collingwood must argue that the audience's collaborative activity, like the artist's own, is "wholly and entirely imaginative." This may be true, but if it is, what anyone actually feels on reading a poem or watching a play is as irrelevant as the psychological history of the author. It is as much a mistake to try to determine the merits of a work of art by audience 'reaction' as it is to judge it on the author's 'sincerity.'

Here the distinction between 'being an expression of' and 'being expressive of' is specially important. Some writers sympathetic to expressivism have argued that the errors in the commonplace theory arise from a confusion between the two. 'Being an expression of emotion' implies that there is someone whose expression it is. 'Being expressive of' does not imply any possessor, either artist or audience. To replace the first with the second, therefore, seems a good way to maintain the expressivist's main claim, while avoiding any false psychologism about artists and audiences.

That this distinction is important seems incontestable. Whether it can be used to save expressivism is a different matter. Why is a work's being expressive of emotion something to be valued? To my mind this is a crucial question for expressivism. Collingwood's explanation is that in acting imaginatively upon emotion we bring it to consciousness, discover thereby what our consciousness contains, and come to self-knowledge. Now if what the artist does is not to express emotion, but to formulate expressive utterances or representations of it, then whatever value this has it cannot consist in self-knowledge. If they are not our emotions we come to no further knowledge of ourselves by apprehending them.

To avoid this conclusion we might try to divorce audience apprehension from emotion completely, even where the work in question can indeed be said to be expressive of an emotion. Collingwood himself speaks in this way in places. He sometimes describes the activity of both artist and audience in the language of cognition rather than feeling. So, for instance, he imagines a (right-minded) painter declaring "one paints a thing in order to see it." "Only a person who paints well," he goes on to tell us, "can see well; and conversely . . . only a person who sees well can paint well." Seeing here "refers not to sensation but to awareness. It means noticing what you see. And further: this act of awareness includes the noticing of much that is not visual" (Collingwood 1938: 303–4). On the face of it, this sort of analysis implies that the value of art lies not in its helping us to come to a proper apprehension of personal (or even communal) feeling, but a greater awareness of the world around us. And this remains the obvious interpretation even where, as in expressive representations, 'the world around us' is the world of emotional experience.

The expressivist theory of art, at least in its commonplace version, holds that where a specific emotion can be assigned to a work of art, the work is an expression of that emotion and appreciation of the work consists in feeling that emotion oneself. If now we say that the work is not an expression of, but rather is expressive of, the emotion, appreciating would seem to consist in being brought to a heightened awareness of that emotion. However this does not involve undergoing any element of that emotion. I may, to date, be unaware of the intensity of your jealousy until one day you hit upon an especially expressive word or gesture. My being made aware may indeed give rise to an emotion, but this emotion has only a contingent connection with yours and is neither a necessary nor a sufficient condition of being made aware of it. The expressiveness of your gesture may make me aware of your emotional state without engendering any emotion in me whatever. Conversely, your gesture may arouse an emotion in me (fear, perhaps), though I remain unaware of your true emotional state. What this shows is that the initially innocent substitution of 'being expressive of' for 'being an expression of' signals the abandonment of expressivism. If the function of art is to heighten awareness, the special connection between art and emotion which all forms of expressivism try to articulate and maintain is broken, for art can heighten our awareness of much in human experience besides emotion.

There is reason to think that Collingwood would not deny this. His most extended discussion of a work of art is Eliot's "The Waste Land," and what he says about it is instructive, for he sees Eliot as presenting us with a prophetic vision.

> This poem is not in the least amusing. Nor is it in the least magical. The reader who expects it to be satire, or an entertaining description of vices, is as disappointed with it as the reader who expects it to be propaganda, or an exhortation to get up and do something. To the annoyance of both parties, it contains no indictments and no proposals. To the amateurs of literature, brought up on the idea of poetry as a genteel amusement, the thing is an affront. To the little neo-Kiplings who think

of poetry as an incitement to political virtue, it is even worse; for it describes an evil where no one and nothing is to blame, an evil not curable by shooting capitalists or destroying a social system, a disease which has so eaten into civilization that political remedies are about as useful as poulticing a cancer.

(Collingwood 1938: 335)

In "The Waste Land" Eliot shows "what poetry can be," for "the artist must prophesy not in the sense that he foretells things to come, but in the sense that he tells his audience, at risk of their displeasure, the secrets of their own hearts"(ibid.: 336).

What is important here is not the justice of Collingwood's estimate of Eliot's achievement, but the language he uses to make it. Eliot is said to 'describe,' not feel the present evil, and to 'tell,' not express for, the audience the secrets of their hearts. This is the language of cognition, not emotion. But here Collingwood, following Croce, would warn us against confusing consciousness and intellect. It is the intellect, on Collingwood's view, which orders and organizes the data of consciousness, and establishes relations between them. Art, by contrast, brings those data to consciousness in the first place by realizing the sensuous impact of experience in a form in which consciousness can grasp it. There are thus two kinds of truth, the truth of intellect and the truth of consciousness. Science, broadly understood, is concerned with the former and art with the latter. Thus art may indeed be said to describe, to tell, to prophesy, but since its concern is with the truth of consciousness none of this removes it from the world of emotional experience. Or so at any rate Collingwood contends.

Two observations seem pertinent here. First, if one is to speak of truth in art, some such distinction as Collingwood draws is needed, for whatever we may be said to learn from artists it is not what we learn from the laboratory. At the same time, it is only a lingering loyalty to expressivism that causes Collingwood to go on speaking of emotion in the way he does. For 'emotion' at the end of his analysis means nothing more than sensuous experience brought to consciousness. Even this formulation might be misleading, for the term 'sensuous' is not to be understood as feeling or perceiving in any very restricted sense: it includes feelings of anxiety or loneliness, for instance, and a sense of mystery or foreboding. Moreover, Collingwood allows, insists even, that sensuous experience is not a passive matter of happening to feel; the bringing of an experience to consciousness is essential to having the experience at all.

To say that artists give voice to experience, then, is to say that artists are concerned with the imaginative presentation of immediate experience rather than the construction of abstract reflections upon experience. But this gives no special place to emotional experience and the sensuous. If, with Collingwood, we want to talk about a distinctive truth in art, we need to ask not how art stimulates emotion, but how it directs consciousness. This is to ask about art as a mode of understanding, and it shows that feeling or emotion, ordinarily understood, has been left behind. *Pace* Croce, 'intuition' has no special connection with 'feeling.'

Every theory of art must acknowledge that as a matter of empirical fact and common experience, many works of art do arouse emotion, and that this seems to be one of the ways in which art can give an audience pleasure. Perhaps it is this that sustains the widespread belief in expressivism. But the expressivist holds more than this, namely that the content of art is emotion. A number of familiar problems confront this contention, and Collingwood's interest is that he offers us a more sophisticated version which has the great merit of avoiding what we might call psychologism. On closer investigation, however, its advantages are won through abandoning, in effect, the essentials of expressivism. In the end what emerges is an account of art as a distinctive way of understanding human experience. In short Collingwood's expressivism leads on to a sort of cognitivism in art, a view which, it seems to me, Croce was at pains to deny.

See also Definitions of art, Art and emotion, Value of art.

References

Collingwood, R. G. (1938) *Principles of Art*, Oxford: Clarendon Press.
Croce, B. (1965) *Guide to Aesthetics*, trans. P. Romanell, New York: Bobbs-Merrill.
Hospers, J. (1955) "The Concept of Artistic Expression," *Proceedings of the Aristotelian Society* 55: 313–44.
Kivy, P. (1980) *The Corded Shell*, Princeton: Princeton University Press.
Tolstoy, L. (1930) *What is Art?* trans. A. Maude, Oxford: Oxford University Press.

12
SIBLEY

Colin Lyas

Frank Sibley was born in Lowestoft in England and after war service as a tank commander went to Oxford to read modern languages. There, under the influence of Ryle, Grice, George Paul and Austin, the atmosphere of whose philosophical work was lastingly to imbue his thinking, he became interested in philosophy and in philosophical aesthetics. Already as an undergraduate he was convinced that the clue to understanding problems in aesthetics lay in the careful investigation of what he later called 'praise words,' 'merit and demerit terms' and 'aesthetic terms.' During 1948 and 1949 he collected vast lists of these from various works of criticism found in Oxford libraries. He sorted these into types and began to explore their relationships. This informed his teaching during the 1950s in the USA and equipped him with the extraordinary range of examples and counter-examples for which his interventions in discussions were so notable. It also led to his first and lastingly influential major contribution to aesthetics, "Aesthetic Concepts" (Sibley 1959).

He once observed that he was doing analytical aesthetics before anyone else, aesthetics at that time being still under influence of neo-idealism. Some have claimed that he was influenced by Austin's often quoted remark that in aesthetics it might be profitable to concentrate on modest enquiries into terms like 'dainty' and 'dumpy.' But that remark was made public in 1957, by which time Sibley had been pursuing such enquiries for over ten years. And, another historical note, he could not, as some have claimed, have been influenced by Wittgenstein's remarks on aesthetics. These appeared in 1966, many years after the first of Sibley's major papers. In analytic aesthetics he was an original. His own inaugural lecture put his position succinctly:

> It becomes clear that our common language, flexible, varied and evolved to deal with the complexities of various subject matters, proves, if we explore it with care, to be a repository of conceptual distinctions and discriminations we are able to make and an antidote to false models and simple assimilations.

> (Sibley 1966b)

131

After Oxford Sibley taught at Yale, Iowa State, Michigan and Cornell, where he became chairman of a distinguished department, before returning in to England in 1963 as founding Professor of Philosophy at the new University of Lancaster.

It is convenient to divide Sibley's work in aesthetics, setting aside his striking work on the philosophy of mind and perception, into three groups. The first centers on the paper "Aesthetic Concepts" (Sibley 1959) and the papers radiating from it. The second includes the (soon to be published posthumously) rather different work of his later years. The third group comprises a set of relatively free-standing papers.

"Aesthetic Concepts" and related papers

The essays marking Sibley's best known contributions to philosophical aesthetics, comprise "Aesthetic Concepts" (1959), "Aesthetic and Non-Aesthetic" (1965), "Colours" (1967), "Objectivity and Aesthetics" (1966), "Particularity, Art and Evaluation" (1974) and "General Criteria and Reasons in Aesthetics" (1978). Although the last of these was published much later than the earlier major essays it was in fact written earlier (Lyas 1996). These essays hang together in a developing sequence.

The first, "Aesthetic Concepts," made a lasting impact on philosophical aesthetics. Part of that had to do with the fact that aesthetic philosophy was ready for a change from the somewhat more abstract generalities that had led Passmore, for example, to talk of the "dreariness of aesthetics." In sharp contradistinction, Sibley's paper was embellished with plausible examples of actual critical discourse and was argued with a force, verve and rigor that was then quite startling. Read at a meeting of New York State philosophers it was, at the insistence of George Sabine, then in charge of Sibley's department at Cornell, and against the resistance of Sibley, published, in the *Philosophical Review*. To this day replies and references to it are offered regularly, amounting, so Sibley told me, to some thousands. He publicly replied to only one of these, although an unpublished manuscript contains remarks on rejoinders by Kivy (1973) and Cohen (1973).

"Aesthetic Concepts" asserted rather than argued a relatively simple and apparently straightforward point. Take the remark: 'what makes that picture balanced is the red mass in the lower left hand corner.' Here various things are going on. On the one hand there is reference to the fact that a work possesses a feature, namely, balance. On the other hand, there is a reference to the fact that there is a red mass in the left hand corner of the picture. And there is the assertion that the former in some way depends on the latter. It struck Sibley with some force that anyone in possession of normal powers of vision, could see the red patch. However, it would be possible to see the red patch and not be able to see that the picture was balanced. And it would be possible to see that the picture was balanced without seeing that what gives it balance is a red patch. To see the balance requires taste, and the term 'balance' is, consequently, in Sibley's terminology, an aesthetic, or taste concept.

Such things as balance are also dependent, emergent properties. Change the position of the red mass and the balance might be lost. Fail to see the red mass and one might fail to see what is emergent from it. All this is not so much argued as pointed out using examples.

Now a controversial assertion is made, for although the balance depends on the red patch, there is no logical inference from 'there is a large mass of red in that position' to 'that picture is balanced.' Indeed no knowledge, however comprehensive, of the presence of what are called the 'non-aesthetic' features, color patches, for example, of a work, licences any conclusion as to the presence of such aesthetic properties as grace and balance. Hence follows Sibley's conclusion that aesthetic terms are not positively condition-governed. In this they contrast with terms like 'square,' for here there is a set of conditions which, if fulfilled, entails that something is a square. Similarly, with a term like 'intelligence,' there is an open-ended set of things which might entail that someone is intelligent. But no knowledge of the non-aesthetic properties of a work can entail that a work has this or that aesthetic feature. At most we can argue that some set of non-aesthetic properties may entail that a work will *not* have a certain aesthetic feature. (That it is predominantly in pale pastel colors, for example, will defeat the claim that it is garish.)

All this is dealt with in the first part of "Aesthetic Concepts." Its implications are important. Aesthetic disputes arise not because people cannot see non-aesthetic properties, but they arise because although seeing these properties, they cannot see the aesthetic properties emergent from them. We also have an inclination to believe that disputes are rational if there are decision procedures for their settlement. Those decision procedures are often thought to be reducible to inductive or deductive reasoning. But if Sibley is right, these procedures will not help in cases of aesthetic disputation. This is argued, as a direct consequence of the findings of "Aesthetic Concepts," in the adjunct paper "Aesthetic and Non-Aesthetic" (Sibley 1965). If Sibley is right, from the fact that we have access to a particular piece of non-aesthetic information, for example, that there is a red patch in a certain position, nothing deductively follows about whether or not a work is balanced. There would be no logical contradiction in asserting that although there is red patch in a certain position, the work is not balanced. Induction fares little better. True, we might form the generalization that pictures with color masses in certain positions tend to have certain aesthetic features. But, as every one who has tried to replace taste with inductive rules of thumb will know, not only may the next case let us down, but we still are not led to *see* the quality and so are not led to aesthetic enjoyment.

Sibley draws two conclusions. The first, argued in "Aesthetic and Non-Aesthetic," is about critical explanation. It is often assumed that the task of critics is to prove by arguments that works have this or that property, and the use of the word 'reason' in assertions like 'the reason it is balanced is the presence of this mass' might suggest that a proof is being offered. But 'reason' is ambiguous. What the critic wants is a *reason for inferring* from the fact that work has certain non-aesthetic features that the picture is balanced. If Sibley is right, though, in saying there is no safe inference from statements about non-aesthetic features to statements about aesthetic features, then such reasons are not to be had. The most we can have is explanatory reasons. Thus, having seen that a work is balanced, we can go on to ask on what features of the work that balance depends: for example it might depend on the placing of that mass. But that is a reason for the work being balanced, not a reason for believing it is. Seeing the balance we can, testably, ask on what it depends, testably because if someone says that it depends on that color mass we can, especially with image manipulation, see whether altering the position of the mass spoils the balance. If we cannot see the balance, though, we have nothing to investigate.

If inductive and deductive reasoning are not *a propos*, what is? Here there are two things to be noted. One is that deduction and induction do not exhaust the ways in which we can get someone to see something. Another alternative is perception, and here Sibley's aesthetics becomes a piece with his work on perception. We can get people to see. This is the claim of the second part of "Aesthetic Concepts." There we have a description of the ways in which we might get someone to see something in a picture. We have what Sibley sometimes refers to, always with scare quotes, as 'perceptual proof.' Aesthetics, he repeatedly stresses, is to do with perception. We have to see the qualities for which a work is worth our attention, and argument, though it might get us to believe *that* a work has certain properties, cannot get us to *see* them.

With that claim goes a second area that needs attention. There is a temptation to say that since disputes in aesthetics cannot be settled by deductive or inductive argument, there is something 'subjective' about aesthetics. Here there are two answers. First, the mere fact that aesthetic disputes cannot be settled by ratiocinative proofs does not establish that those disputes are pseudo-disputes about matters of taste. That follows only if it can be shown that these ratiocinative methods are the only ways in which disputes can be settled. But we can also settle disputes by looking and seeing, as we indeed settle disputes as to whether it is raining outside. So to make aesthetics a perceptual matter is not to undermine the possibility that decision procedures exist in aesthetics.

Second, it may be replied that this is not enough. If there is a decision procedure in terms of which disputes can be settled, one might expect those disputes to be settled. But in aesthetics disputes are endemic. There is simply too much disagreement for objectivity to be possible in aesthetics.

It is for this reason that there is a natural connection between the two papers "Aesthetic Concepts" and "Aesthetic and Non-Aesthetic" and the two papers "Colours" (Sibley 1967) and "Objectivity and Aesthetics" (Sibley 1974). Once it is claimed that aesthetics is a perceptual matter, there is room for a proof that its being a perceptual matter is compatible with the possibility of objectivity. Sibley argues thus: first, doubts about the objectivity of our color language are philosophical doubts. In the traffic of life we are happy with the thoughts that the light really was red when the motorist jumped it and that Paul Newman has blue eyes. This being so, we can ask upon what that objectivity is founded. Second, we should ask whether the conditions which make it possible to predicate the truth or falsity of color perceptual judgements might not also be met when we make aesthetic perceptual judgements. If so, then aesthetic judgements can be thought of, for all practical purposes, as being as objective as color judgements in practice are taken to be. So, in "Colours," Sibley asks what it is that underpins our ability to say that grass is green, tomatoes are red and the sky blue. The answer is that this depends upon a certain kind of agreement in judgements among those who use the color language where, when there are disputes, we take the maximum discriminators as the reference group. The next step is obvious. We ask whether that kind of agreement is also possible in the case of aesthetic judgements. Sibley concludes that it is.

In "Colours" Sibley is careful not to tie the reference group of color perceivers to any majority. It is possible that a color language could exist even if a minority of people were fully color sighted, and they only fugitively. Hence it follows that widespread disagreement is not of itself evidence of subjectivity. It also follows that the fact that there are disagreements in aesthetics is not evidence of the subjectivity of that discipline. Indeed we might expect there to be more possibilities of disagreement in aesthetics, for whereas in color perception the sources of disagreement are likely to be physiological in origin (color blindness), in aesthetics there are, as well as physiological factors such as tone-deafness and color blindness, also psychological differences and prejudices to be taken account of (often due to differences in age, temperament and upbringing). (That claim occasions disquiet in a notable reply to Sibley by Michael Tanner (1968).)

Sibley concludes that we have as much reason to say that willow trees are elegant, sunsets sublime, deer graceful as we do to say that tomatoes are red. To that we can add that Sibley believes perception to be educable. This is certainly true of color perception. One can learn to make finer and finer discriminations. So, too, with aesthetic matters. A child who is capable of enjoying simple aesthetic pleasures can, by exposure to objects of greater and greater complexity, come to appreciate more sophisticated things. Aesthetic disagreement might as much be due to the fact that we deprive people of opportunities for aesthetic advancement as to the fact that there is nothing to see. Here a favorite Sibley example was wine tasting which, he believed, shared with aesthetic perception the dependence on a minority reference group of sometimes patchy agreements in judgements honed by experience. It is, however, a skill to which all could aspire through the activity of sampling.

The set of papers which constitutes this first major phase is augmented by the paper "General Criteria and Reasons in Aesthetics" (Sibley 1983). In "Aesthetic Concepts" Sibley had adumbrated a distinction between aesthetic judgements, such as the comment that a line in a picture is graceful, and aesthetic verdicts, or overall judgements, as when we talk about goodness of a whole work. In "Aesthetic Concepts" he asserts that from non-aesthetic judgements, aesthetic judgements do not logically follow. When he comes to the relation between aesthetic judgements and overall verdicts, however, the situation is more complex. On the one hand there are particularists, who argue that no general reasons can be given for aesthetic judgements. The self-same thing that in one work may contribute to excellence can, in another, be the very thing that mars a work. The wit that is admired in a comedy might spoil a tragedy. On the other hand there are generalists, like Beardsley (1958), who argue that there can be general reasons for concluding that a work has merit, although he argues that the relation is probabilistic. Unity, for example, is generally a merit.

Sibley's paper takes issue with both particularists and generalists. Although he agrees that, when the move is from judgements about non-aesthetic features to judgements about aesthetic features, the particularist is right, he thinks the particularists have overlooked the fact that the relation between a non-aesthetic feature and an aesthetic feature (which is not an entailment relation) is quite unlike the relation between an aesthetic feature like wit and an overall feature like goodness. This *is* a logical relation. But on this he takes issue with Beardsley. Beardsley wished to find aesthetic features that would always count positively towards an overall judgement, offering unity and complexity as examples, but he also seemed to think the relation of generality to be an inductive one. Sibley objects to this on two counts. First, there are no features that always count positively for a judgement. Even unity can be the unity of mediocrity. Second, however, the relation between a property like wit, which he calls a 'merit term,' and overall goodness is not simply inductive. For there would be something *logically* odd in saying that the reason why something is bad is that it has the merit of wit. Hence he argues that merit features, such as wit, are *prima facie* merits, a term he borrowed from W. D. Ross. A *prima facie* merit could be defeated as an actual merit by, for example, being out of place in a particular work. But, and this is the important conclusion, there is no algorithm which will tell us for any particular work whether a *prima facie* merit is an actual merit. Nor can we say the more merits the better. The merits have to work and work together, and whether they do so is a matter for judgement.

This phase of Sibley's work is completed by "Particularity, Art and Evaluation" (Sibley 1974). That paper takes up Strawson's (1974) attempt to explain the "putative tautology" that "there are no general criteria of excellence in the aesthetic sphere" as there are in the moral sphere. One striking feature of Sibley's paper is its assertion that the nature of aesthetic appraisal is not clarified simply by clarifying the concept of art. That goes against those, such as Croce (1992), who have argued the exact opposite, and it is related to his later work in which aesthetic judgements of nature take a prominent position. The paper also deals with something implicit in "Aesthetic Concepts," namely a doubt about any easily-made distinction between the evaluative and the descriptive. It also adds to earlier discussions a more careful classification of terms. These now include the solely evaluative ('good,' 'bad,' 'nice' and 'nasty'); the descriptive merit terms ('sharp' used of razors); and evaluation-added property terms like 'elegant,' 'garish,' 'tasty' and 'insipid.' The latter are both descriptive and evaluative. Finally the paper offers a more refined account of the relation between aesthetic qualities and the features on which they depend, in terms of a distinction between determinate properties and determinable properties. Something is valued in terms of some determinate quality (for example, being curved in just that way), rather than by just being curved. This adds strength to his earlier claim that, when the relation between non-aesthetic and aesthetic features is in question, each work must be judged by its own standards. For a determinate property, being a property special to one particular work, will have a unique dependence relation to the aesthetic features emerging from it.

The papers I have grouped together, notably "Aesthetic Concepts," attracted, and continue to attract, substantial attention. Some have attempted to undermine Sibley's distinction between the aesthetic and the non-aesthetic. These include Cohen (1973), who has queried the very possibility of making a distinction between the non-aesthetic and the aesthetic; Kivy (1973), who has argued that there are condition-governed aesthetic features; Scruton (1974) who seems to argue something similar; and Meager (1970) who has objected to any talk of aesthetic properties. Those who are inclined to join the debate ought to be warned of one thing that Sibley continually stressed in private discussions: he was not offering a *definition* of the aesthetic. Indeed not: for non-conditioned governance equally characterizes other emergent properties, such as the expression on a person's face. He was concerned only to remark on what he thought an obvious feature of aesthetic judgements and to explore some of its consequences. He nowhere said that the aesthetic could be defined by reference to this feature. Indeed, as far as I know his only remarks on what makes a feature aesthetic are some fragmentary remarks, to which I shall return, in "Aesthetics and the Looks of Things" (Sibley 1959). However, as well as those who have criticized Sibley's views some more recently have found them a fruitful starting point in discussions of supervenience and realism. Notable here is work by Levinson (1990).

Later publications

After 1965 Sibley's publications became more intermittent. This was owing in part to his devotion to the new University of Lancaster, in the creation of both a major institution and a major department. Those efforts were, at least in part, responsible for a harrowing period of depressive illness followed by a long struggle with the pernicious leukemia from which he was to die. During those years he was immensely influential through his discussions with his colleagues and friends and through the distinctive and sometimes much feared interventions in seminars and conferences. Between 1965 and his death, apart from papers on perception and on thinking, he published in aesthetics his "Inaugural Lecture at Lancaster" (Lancaster 1966b), and a contribution to a symposium with Eva Schaper notable for this rejoinder to those inclined to make aesthetics peripheral in philosophy:

> Indeed far from it being true that aesthetics is peripheral to philosophy, aestheticians encounter ranges of concepts wider than and inevitably inclusive of those studied by most other branches of philosophy. A multitude of terms and concepts – too varied to fit into a few categories of properties and non-properties, but quite as important as the epistemologist's favourites for our characterisation, comprehension and organization of the world and our experience of it – remain to be explored, and it is largely left to aestheticians to explore them.
>
> (Sibley 1966a: 55–69)

During this period of relative silence, it was quite clear to those who knew him, that he was continually working on a wide range of problems. These were given one focus through his meditations on Peter Geach's paper "Good and Evil." That paper essayed a distinction between what Geach called 'predicative' and 'attributive' adjectives. In some cases, we need to know to what class a thing belongs to before being able to ascertain the truth of a statement about it. Thus whether or not a thing is a small something or other depends on the criteria for size in things of that sort. What is small for an elephant would be large for a mouse. That sort of adjective Geach calls attributive. On the other hand there are terms like red. We do not need to know the class to which a thing belongs in order to know that it is red. Sibley was struck by this distinction and worked incessantly on it, for at least the last ten years of his life. This led to a set of papers, to be published posthumously (Sibley forthcoming).

At the basis of this later work there is "Adjectives, Predicative and Attributive" which probes Geach's distinction (Sibley forthcoming). This demonstrates how much more complex was the issue than Geach might have thought. Sibley was in no doubt that there is a distinction between the predicative and attributive uses of adjectives. On the one hand there are cases in which, in order to say that something is beautiful, we need to know what criteria govern beauty for that kind of thing, the criteria for beautiful Tamworth pigs being different from those for beautiful examples of leg ulcers. On the other there are cases, say in talking about a pebble, in which one might make the judgement of beauty *simpliciter*. That there is a difference is suggested by the fact that 'beautiful for a pig' seems all right whereas 'beautiful for a pebble' seems odd.

The area that Sibley explored raises questions about aesthetics, some of which have haunted us at least since Kant. One is about the truth of the claim made, for example, by Savile and Scruton, that 'beauty is always attributive,' so that, Savile claimed, we can only ask whether X is a beautiful A (Savile 1982). That judgement is, given Sibley's later work, in need of careful defense. Second, some, Wollheim (1980), for example, taking issue with Croce (1992), have spoken as if genre judgements are central to aesthetic judgement, so that judgement of a poem might be conditioned by what one knows of the criteria for sonnets. But this implies that aesthetic judgements are attributive, a claim which again requires a clear understanding of the distinction between the predicative and the attributive. Third, Sibley was interested in certain puzzling phenomena in the aesthetics of nature. Why, for example, are toads thought to be ugly? Why, having been moved to delight by a display of daffodils, do we alter that opinion on finding out that they are made of plastic, even though they might still look the same? Here, he thought, matters could be illuminated by the proper understanding of judgements of nature as attributive. This was argued in a paper entitled "Aesthetic Judgements: Pebbles, Faces and Fields of Litter" (Sibley forthcoming). This work has begun to interest those working in the currently topical area of the aesthetics of nature (Foster forthcoming). Time and again Sibley returned to a favorite example: we are shown a framed pink curve and remark with delight on it. The frame is removed and we see that the curve is in fact the curve of a pig's backside. He was much taken with investigating our seeming reluctance to argue as follows: 'this curve is beautiful: this curve is a pig's backside: therefore this pig's backside is beautiful.'

Miscellaneous papers

The third category of papers is somewhat more miscellaneous, though the papers are united by the careful use of examples and close analysis of arguments and distinctions. Some are published. Notable here are a brilliant cameo "Is Art an Open Concept?" Sibley 1960); the inaugural lecture referred to earlier (Sibley 1966b); a paper "Originality and Value" (Sibley 1985), which argues that value is not inherent in the concept of originality; and an early paper "Aesthetics and the Looks of Things" (Sibley 1959). This last paper is notable for two things. First many, following Bullough (1912), have argued that aesthetics is to do with how things look rather than how they are. Against that Sibley, with a characteristic barrage of examples, argues that this account simply will not fit our aesthetic characterizations. A person who says that a line is delicate or graceful is saying that the line *is* these things. Second Sibley, in a startling anticipation of various sociobiological theories of value, of which Dawkins (1999) provides a notable recent example, raises the question why we value the aesthetic properties of things. His answer is that these valuations reflect interests we have as biological beings. His final published paper was "Making Music Our Own" (Sibley 1995), which celebrates, and defends against certain purists, the richness of the figurative language by which we appropriate music.

Other papers will be posthumously published. These are written with a characteristic force but at the same time display the fey, not to say surreal, humor, which his friends cherished and which is not always visible in earlier work. They include the mischievously entitled paper "Why the *Mona Lisa* is not Painting," which attempts to arbitrate between those who wish to identify the *Mona Lisa* with a particular spatio-temporal material instantiation and those wish to treat it as a token of a type. On Sibley's account both are right. Again there is the striking paper in which he takes issue with Scruton's (1974) contention that tastes and smells cannot be objects of aesthetic appreciation. There is also a paper "Art or the Aesthetic. Which Comes First?" which argues, *contra* a line of thinkers from Croce to Savile, that the aesthetic does. For those who wish to hear the master's voice, it is worth remarking that shortly before his death Sibley recorded this paper for the Open University.

See also The aesthetic, Kant.

References

Austin, J. L. (1957) "A Plea for Excuses," *Proceedings of the Aristotelian Society*, 57: 1–30.

Beardsley, M. (1958) *Aesthetics*, Indianapolis: Hackett.

Bullough, E. (1912) "'Psychical Distance' as a Factor in Art and as an Aesthetic Principle," *British Journal of Psychology* 5: 87–98.

Cohen, T. (1973) "Aesthetic/Non-Aesthetic and the Concept of Taste," *Theoria* 39: 113–52.

Croce, B. (1992) *The Aesthetic*, trans. C. Lyas, Cambridge: Cambridge University Press.

Dawkins, R. (1999) *Unweaving the Rainbow*, London: Penguin.

Foster, C. (forthcoming) "I've Looked at Clouds From Both Sides Now," in E. Brady and J. Levinson (eds), *Sibley and After*, Oxford: Oxford University Press, forthcoming.

Geach, P. (1957) "Good and Evil" *Analysis* 17: 103–11.

Kivy, P. (1973) *Speaking About Art*, The Hague: Martinus Nijhoff.

Levinson, J. (1990) "Aesthetic Supervenience," *Music Art and Metaphysics*, Ithaca: Cornell University Press.

Lyas, C. (1996) "Frank Sibley: In Memoriam," *British Journal of Aesthetics* 36: 345–55.

Meager, R. (1970) "Aesthetic Concepts," *British Journal of Aesthetics*, 10: 303–22.

Savile, A. (1982) *The Test of Time*, Oxford: Oxford University Press.

Scruton, R. (1974) *Art and Imagination*, London: Methuen.

Sibley, F. (1959) "Aesthetic Concepts," *Philosophical Review* 68: 421–50.

—— (1959) "Aesthetics and the Looks of Things," *Journal of Philosophy* 56: 905–15.

—— (1960) "Is Art an Open Concept?" *Actes du 4e Congres Internationale d'Aesthetique*: 545–8.

—— (1965) "Aesthetic and Non-Aesthetic," *Philosophical Review* 74: 135–59.

—— (1966a) 'About Taste,' *British Journal of Aesthetics* 6: 55–69.

—— (1966b) *Philosophy and the Arts*, Lancaster: University of Lancaster.

—— (1967) "Colours," *Proceedings of the Aristotelian Society* 68: 145–66.

—— (1968) "Objectivity and Aesthetics," *Aristotelian Society Supplementary Volume* 42: 31–54.

—— (1974) "Particularity, Art and Evaluation," *Aristotelian Society Supplementary Volume* 48: 1–21.

—— (1983) "General Criteria and Reasons in Aesthetics," in J. Fisher (ed.), *Essays on Aesthetics*, Philadelphia: Temple University Press.

—— (1985) "Originality and Value," *British Journal of Aesthetics* 25: 169–84.

—— (1995) "Making Music Our Own," in M. Krausz (ed.), *The Interpretation of Music*, Oxford: Oxford University Press.

—— (forthcoming) *Approach to Aesthetics*, Oxford: Oxford University Press.

Strawson, P. F. (1974) "Aesthetic Appreciation and Works of Art," in *Freedom and Resentment*, London: Methuen.

Tanner, M. (1968) "Objectivity and Aesthetics," *Aristotelian Society Supplementary Volume* 42: 55–62.

Wollheim, R. (1980) *Art and its Objects*, 2nd edn, Cambridge: Cambridge University Press.

13
FOUCAULT

Robert Wicks

Michel Foucault's (1926–84) intellectual brilliance was nobly tempered with a good proportion of modesty. In a 1984 interview, he stated that he was not a great author. In 1982, he mentioned that he was not capable of talking extensively about music, and in 1980 he admitted that he did not know anything about the aesthetics of motion pictures. In 1975, he described his interest in literature as only a matter of passing theoretical interest (Foucault 1988: 53, 307; 1998: 241, 233).

Foucault's widespread academic influence notwithstanding, the above remarks quietly raise the question of whether artistic themes play a significant role in his *oeuvre*. To date, many studies of Foucault have bypassed his reflections on art, and have concentrated upon his discussions of how axiomatic, yet mostly tacit, assumptions about the nature of knowledge – assumptions that appear to vary noticeably over time – can determine effectively a society's modes of inquiry, its institutional structures, and its prevailing conceptions of appropriate behavior. This established understanding of Foucault's intellectual contribution locates his thought at the interface of a variety of realms which include, not particularly aesthetic theory, but sociology, history, politics, linguistics, psychology and philosophy. Foucault's writings, though, are punctuated continually with reflections on art, and these are not merely stylistic embellishments; they can be understood quite directly to inform the trajectory of his philosophical development.

Perhaps one of the most reliable summations of Foucault's general outlook comes from Foucault himself, in a pseudonymously-authored entry for a philosophical dictionary that he wrote under the name of "Maurice Florence" in the early 1980s (Foucault 1998: 459–63). The entry explains how his intellectual project is to reveal the historically-variable social assumptions that mold people into various lifestyles, both as these forces tend to determine the basic attitudes of a social organization, and as they tend to prescribe for people an assortment of general self-conceptions. Foucault regards these historical forces – ones that operate though a diversity of institutional practices and linguistic styles – as so powerful that they can establish what counts as legitimate 'knowledge' for an entire epoch, often to the exclusion and oppression of alternative ways of understanding the world. He notes how his intellectual project resembles that of Immanuel Kant: just as Kant described how human nature, when conceived of as an ingrained mode of rational organization, determines the shape of human experience in general, Foucault describes how, given the probable absence of any universal human nature, historical contexts themselves operate to determine limiting and limited conceptions of knowledge, self and world.

A good portion of Foucault's work reveals how what presents itself frequently in everyday life as being natural, universal and unchangeable is in fact the product of specific social practices relative to a certain place and time. By exposing the mechanisms of these social constructions – ones that typically, and with powerful subtlety, can impose intolerant attitudes which marginalize underprivileged sectors of the population – Foucault's thought embodies liberating values. Contrary to monolithic styles of understanding, he comprehends the world in a more tolerant, multifaceted and perspectival manner, due in a large part to the influence of Friedrich Nietzsche. Foucault's reflections on the importance of art, in light of his concern for open-mindedness and expanded horizons, should not therefore be underestimated: they mesh with his interest in discerning the underlying intellectual shapes of particular historical contexts, his interest in securing liberation from oppressive social fabrications, and his interest in increasing the possibilities for people to exercise a more artistic control over their lives, for the purpose of creating for themselves a more satisfying and healthy personal lifestyle.

The discussions of artistic themes in Foucault's writings cluster around three ideas: first, that works of art can reveal the intellectual temperament particular to a specific historical epoch, either as a whole or in a major part; second, that works of art can bring our existing conceptions of personhood into serious question, and can stimulate radically new modes of awareness; and third, that the concepts of artistic style and creativity can direct how we can positively reinterpret the person, or subject of experience. The third idea aligns with the last phase of Foucault's thought; the first two are more pronounced in his earlier works.

Artistic expressions of the intellectual temperament of an epoch

Velázquez's Las Meninas

The first chapter of one of Foucault's best-known works of the 1960s, *Les Mots et les Choses (The Order of Things)* (Foucault 1973) – a historical-sociological-philosophical study of European modes of knowledge from the sixteenth to the nineteenth centuries – offers a memorable analysis of Diego Velázquez's 1656 masterpiece, *Las Meninas*. Segments from this chapter are perhaps the most often-cited portions of Foucault's writings on visual art, and he makes a daring claim: this painting's compositional structure displays quintessentially the mode of representation that dominated the thought of the seventeenth and eighteenth centuries, or what he describes as the Classical age.

Foucault notes that a relatively detached and abstractive standpoint emerged in Europe during the 1600s, which, in its mappings and orderings of things in a more conventional language, tried to isolate quantifiable and mechanically predictable relationships among objects. An 'objective' apprehension of things was believed to result, if one could detach from consideration all of one's personal expectations, projections and subjective affections within the situation under consideration. In the field of science, this temperament resulted in a quest for, and the major discovery of, natural laws; in the field of aesthetics, it led to theories of aesthetic appreciation that emphasized how a 'disinterested' attitude is necessary for the most unbiased understanding and apprehension of natural and artistic beauty.

According to Foucault, Velázquez's *Las Meninas* displays a subtle and paradox-ical aspect of the neutral Classical outlook: this way of regarding the world does not allow the observer to include itself simultaneously as another object to be observed neutrally. In *The Order of Things*, Foucault elaborately describes Velázquez's painting to explain how its composition illustrates the situation of an observer who, when self-consciously trying to capture his or her own reflection, necessarily fails to represent himself or herself in its capacity as an active center of awareness.

In *Las Meninas*, "representation undertakes to represent itself here in all its elements," but it involves "the necessary disappearance of that which is its foundation – the person it resembles and the person in whose eyes it is only a resem-blance" (Foucault 1973: 16). The painting exemplifies this idea by containing only the twice-removed reflections of the people who are both the implied observers of the painting, and the implied subjects of the painting, namely King Philip IV and Queen Mariana Teresa. The significance of their absence among the actual personages in the painting is conspicuous, since the painting's very subject is Velázquez's act of depicting Philip and Mariana. When these royal personages viewed *Las Meninas* in actual life, the only perceivable representations of themselves which they had before them in the painting were a relatively vague, reflected image of Velázquez's own painted image of them in a distant mirror, and the physical counterpart of themselves in the person of their five-year-old daughter, Margaretha Maria Teresa.

During the twentieth century, and some decades before Foucault wrote *The Order of Things*, Jean-Paul Sartre analyzed this kind of asymmetry between observer and observed, and expanded it into a general account of human consciousness in *Being and Nothingness* (Sartre 1956). As it appears in Western philosophical literature, the core idea extends at least as far back as Immanuel Kant, who stated in his *Critique of Pure Reason* that "I have no knowledge of myself as I am but merely as I appear to myself" (Kant 1965: 169).

Magritte's This is Not a Pipe

Just as Foucault regards Velázquez's *Las Meninas* as illustrative of basic principles that define the intellectual temperament of the Classical period, he discusses the surrealist paintings of René Magritte as indicators of the general mentality typical of Western cultural thinking during the twentieth century. According to Foucault, two principles have ruled Western painting from the fifteenth to the end of the nineteenth century: first, words and images have usually been kept distinct, and when they have been both present in the same painting, one of these has tended to be subordinated to the other in artistic importance, and second, whenever a painted image resembled an object in the world, the image usually served to direct the viewer's attention outside the painting to that object's presence in the world. Words tended to be subordinated to images within paintings, and painted images themselves tended to be subordinated to the actual objects they represented.

Foucault argues that Magritte's *Ceci n'est pas une pipe (This is not a Pipe)* of 1926 is structured in a manner that controverts both these assumptions (Foucault 1983). The painting contains a realistic and straightforwardly-rendered image of a pipe, but it includes the painted sentence, "*Ceci n'est pas une pipe,*" in large letters directly below the pipe's image. In passing, Foucault notes that within this sentence, the word '*Ceci*' ('This') is ambiguous – it could refer to the image of the pipe, or to the sentence "*Ceci n'est pas une pipe,*" or to the entire painting – and he concludes that the painting is intrinsically ambiguous and resists any singular and exclusive interpretation. This capacity for multiple interpretation is also a key feature Foucault assigns to twentieth-century art.

Foucault further asserts that Magritte's painting disrupts the traditional expectation that either the image or the text constitutes the painting's primary message. Rather, he notes that the total composition generates an interpretive oscillation between word and image, much like the experience of perceiving a calligram (an image constructed with the shapes of words whose meanings themselves refer to the kind of object represented by the image). It is also comparable to the experience of perceiving an ambiguous geometrical configuration that stimulates perspective-switches in the viewer, such as the Necker cube. In multiply-interpretable imagery of this kind, none of the projected points of view is given precedence.

Magritte's compositions depart also from the second feature of the fifteenth through nineteenth-century Western attitude towards words and images I have mentioned, namely the assumption that realistically-rendered images refer the viewer naturally to the corresponding objects in the world. In Magritte's own words, his paintings, despite their realistic style, are "farthest from trompe-l'oeil" (Foucault 1983: 43). Magritte intends no deception, and no reinforcement of the relation, or of any assumed priority, between image and object. In this way, his work questions philosophically the traditional conception that words and images refer primarily to actual objects and events. Foucault, in his discussions of Magritte's work, appears to see expressed artistically in the paintings he considers, a general view of meaning which closely approximates that of the linguist, Ferdinand de Saussure: the idea that the meaning of a word is established primarily by the semantic network of associated words within which it operates linguistically, as opposed to an initially clear, unambiguous and independent reference to some specifiable object in the world.

Foucault interprets the imagery in Magritte's paintings as relatively self-enclosed, as essentially self-referent, and as displaying the dissolution of static hierarchies and meanings that are derived from things which straightforwardly present themselves in experience. When, in the perception of a painting such as *Ceci n'est pas une pipe*, a person's interpretive focus shifts from image to word, and from word to image, back and forth continuously, this experience of shifting from one interpretation to another becomes literally the key point to which Foucault aims to draw his readers's attention. Although this point of interpretive transition has no substance of its own – it is a non-entity – the entire dynamism of the ambiguous presentation depends upon this point. He writes, "[Magritte's] incisions that drew figures and those that marked letters communicate only by void, the non-place hidden beneath marble solidity" (Foucault 1983: 41).

Jacques Derrida's notion of *'différence'* bears close affinities to Foucault's analysis of Magritte's surrealist painting insofar as Derrida emphasized the centrality of transitional and differentiating points within the field of linguistic phenomena (Derrida 1978b). Also, Jean Baudrillard's notions of 'simulacra' and 'hyperreality' are foreshadowed by Foucault's analysis of Magritte. The self-contained, and self-referential aspect of the imagery that Foucault emphasizes within his interpretation of Magritte's paintings anticipates Baudrillard's thought that contemporary representations convey the impression that they are "always already reproduced" (Baudrillard 1988: 146).

Foucault's multi-aspected analysis of Magritte's surrealism coincides with the spirit of the 1960s and 1970s post-structuralist intellectual times during which it was written. He reveals, however, that the principles heralded during those decades as distinctly post-structuralist and postmodern were already culturally operative during the 1920s. In this respect, Foucault differs from theorists such as Jean-François Lyotard, who identifies the idea of multi-facetedness as a distinctly postmodern phenomenon (Lyotard 1984).

Borges's Chinese encyclopedia excerpt

Foucault does not limit his examples of historically exemplary works of art to the visual arts. His early reference to José de Goya y Lucientes's well-known etching, *El Sueño de la Razón Produce Monstruos* (*The Sleep of Reason Brings Forth Monsters*) in the conclusion of *Histoire de la Folie* (*Madness and Civilization*, 1965), and his later, more extensive discussion of Velázquez's *Las Meninas*, are complemented by an acknowledgment of Miguel de Cervantes's *Don Quixote* – a literary work which, for Foucault, expresses the transition between the Renaissance and Classical intellectual temperaments (Foucault 1973: 49). Additionally, and with great significance, he regards the work of yet another figure within the Spanish-speaking tradition, Jorge Luis Borges, as embodying the contemporary principles referred to in connection with Magritte. Employing one of Borges's passages as almost a microcosmic description of the contemporary world scene, Foucault prefaces *The Order of Things* with a brief discussion of a passage from Borges's short story, "The Analytic Language of John Wilkins." The story mentions a

> "certain Chinese encyclopedia" in which it is written that "animals are divided into: (a) belonging to the Emperor, (b) embalmed, (c) tame, (d) sucking pigs, (e) sirens, (f) fabulous, (g) stray dogs, (h) included in the present classification, (i) frenzied, (j) innumerable, (k) drawn with a very fine camelhair brush, (l) et cetera, (m) having just broken the water pitcher, (n) that from a long way off look like flies."
>
> (Foucault 1973: xv)

The categories of this encyclopedia, in sharp distinction to the standard practice of formulating clearly partitioned categories of classification (as in biological taxonomy), are sometimes overlapping in scope, sometimes incongruous with each other with respect to their meanings, and sometimes contrary to typical ways of classifying animals. As a whole, they operate without, and defy the postulation of, any underlying conceptual space in relation to which they can be organized into a coherent scheme. The kind of array here is nonetheless not altogether unfamiliar: it expands the more elemental, double-aspected style of incongruity characteristic of Magritte's painting into a multi-sided incongruity, and it displays what Foucault recognizes as a general principle of the twentieth century mentality. It is that the world invites characterization and understanding in a multi-faceted way which can run contrary to logically-grounded and scientifically-interested styles of classification.

There are two important upshots of Foucault's discussion of works of art as exemplars of historical principles. The first is his observation that, as noted, it has been during the entire twentieth century, and not simply during the 1960s and later, that the field of human experience has been perceived as multi-faceted, many-communitied, and filled with incommensurabilities. Many cubist paintings, as well as numerous examples from the Futurist, Surrealist, and Dada movements, display this multidimensional awareness in the history of art; in literary theory, Mikhail Bakhtin's conception of 'heteroglossia' exhibits this tendency as well.

The second upshot of Foucault's discussion concerns his broader interest in drawing our attention to the limits of any given perspective. Those of a traditional mind might find Magritte's paintings to be confusing, and could very likely regard the Chinese encyclopedia as only light-heartedly comical, or, if taken seriously, intellectually indigestible. Yet the very experience of conceptual disorientation that such artistic constructions can generate underscores an important way in which they can reveal the limitations of logically-structured thinking of an Aristotelian sort, and pave the way for a more conceptually prismatic outlook.

Art at the borders of language and self

Ecstatic awareness and the dissolution of the subject

If the underlying principles that govern either a society or a person are dissolved, then the stability and enduring integrity of that society or person will be disrupted. Such upheavals occurred, for Foucault, during the transition from the Renaissance to the Classical period, and from the Classical to the Modern period. With regard to the changes in an individual's perspective, a comparable metamorphosis occurs when a person, upon casting into serious doubt the assumptions which had previously governed his or her life, suffers deep disillusionment, and soon, as a 'new person,' regards her or his previous views as relatively benighted. G. W. F. Hegel's *Phenomenology of Spirit*, for example, extensively describes this phenomenon at a variety of social and individual levels (Hegel 1979).

Foucault believes that language very strongly determines the contours of human consciousness. He is also convinced that a person's sense of 'self' is largely a reformable social construction. So when the assumptions governing a person's life-perspective are cast into radical doubt, the kind of personal 'death' that follows is thought to generate an apprehension of the person's previously-existing linguistic limits and an attempt to express the new experience in a new language. In his discussions of literature, Foucault often refers to authors who apparently succeeded in reaching these borders, and who, by entering new modes of consciousness and attaining a more comprehensive sense of self, developed alternative forms of speaking and writing.

Foucault discerns such linguistic advances in Jean-Jacques Rousseau's *Dialogues*, which issue "from a surge of language that breaks forth from having encountered an obscure barrier" (Foucault 1998: 33), in the writings of the Marquis de Sade, which show "just how far speech may advance upon the sands of silence" (Foucault 1998: 70), and in the work of Raymond Roussel, Antonin Artaud, Georges Bataille, Pierre Klossowski and Maurice Blanchot. He characterizes these writers as having embodied extreme and transgressive forms of language, often in association with a confrontation with death or the experience of intense sexuality.

Such explorers of literary space establish their importance in how they quest, not for a totally comprehensive vision of the world that can be systematically articulated, but for an awareness – as Foucault himself searched for in his own life and work – of the areas where limitations exist, or of those exact points where transgression can take place. This kind of sensitivity leads to writing, and experiencing, at the edge of nothingness, at the edge of death, and at the edge of scandal, the result of which is often literature with a violent erotic content and a disconcerting language of terror. Writing under such conditions can take the entrenched language "as far away from itself as possible" (Foucault 1998: 149). Foucault finds in general that these writers are oriented towards "the void toward which and from which we speak" (ibid.: 89) and he hails them as visionaries and as literary revolutionaries whose words have the power to break through existing patterns of entrenched and habituated modes of world-interpretation.

Foucault believes that at the very limit of this project of trying to take language as far away from itself as possible, the writer must place herself or himself at an extreme personal distance, such as to exclude as much as possible her or his presence in the writing. Language, as it is in itself, will then supposedly appear, untainted by 'subjectivity' – a mode of being present in one's writing that usually carries with it the habitual adherence to ready-made meanings, combined with a drive for systematicity which inevitably results in being too reflective. Once the writer's presence is removed from the writing, then language will present itself in its purity, and its limits will be perceivable. Speaking about the unspeakable will then become possible.

This kind of ecstatic self-removal is apprehended distinctly by Foucault in Maurice Blanchot's writing. He also perceives it in Georges Bataille's imagery of the eye which is upturned and rolled back in either ecstasy or sheer horror, or both. It marks the point where writers ought to aim – the point where one reaches the borders of one's consciousness, faces the void, and is poised for a breakthrough in awareness. In short, Foucault continually celebrates writers who live on the edge, and he considers how their experience-at-the-limit tends to be embodied linguistically. A question which issues from these considerations is whether it is reasonable to require some criteria through which one can distinguish the genuinely illuminating breakthroughs in awareness from the merely offensive, outrageous or fantastic modes. Foucault's overall attitude is to be open-minded and tolerant of transgressive attitudes in general, since he questions seriously whether absolute truth can ever be specified in a once-and-for-all fashion.

The concept of 'authorship' and the dissolution of the subject

In connection with the ideal of eliminating the writer's presence within the meaning of what is written, Foucault reflects upon the nature of art works, upon their interpretation, and upon writing itself. He develops these themes in his essay, "*Qu'est-ce qu'un auteur?*" ("What is an Author?") (Foucault 1998) and observes initially that questions of assigning proper authorship, determining degrees of authenticity, prescribing copyrights, and delineating which items are to be included in the set of an author's 'complete works' are all relatively recent phenomena, and do not determine an exclusive or necessary way to regard literature and art works in general. As is the case for many of Foucault's analyses, he maintains that the concept of an 'author' is largely a historical fabrication and is always subject to further questioning, revision and even dissolution.

In line with his analysis of Magritte's painting, Foucault regards contemporary literature as grounded upon the assumption that it is "an interplay of signs arranged less according to its signified content than according to the very nature of the signifier" – an interplay of signs within "which the writing subject constantly disappears" and that refers "only to itself, but without being restricted to the confines of its interiority" (Foucault 1998: 206). This is to say, as might be expected, that he defines contemporary writing in a manner consistent with Saussure's theory of meaning: written words refer primarily neither to objects in the world nor to the author who wrote them, but to other words. Sometimes, as the words illuminate their linguistic position within the interconnected network of language, they, like a stick of dynamite, can introduce instability and cause a transformation of that existing network.

Foucault's view in "What Is an Author?" has the effect of dissolving the sharp borders and definitive aesthetic functions of concepts such as 'author' and 'work – a point he reiterated in the first chapter of *L'Archéologie du Savoir* (*The Archaeology of Knowledge*, 1972 [1969]), which was published in the same year. He does not regard what has been written as the literal verbal expression of an author's psychological states, and he denies that the assemblages of words which a person of letters composes can be assumed to organize themselves clearly and automatically into that person's 'works.' With regard to the question, for instance, of what counts among Friedrich Nietzsche's works, Foucault notes that it remains perpetually unclear whether a short laundry list should be included. This point was reiterated by Jacques Derrida in *Spurs: Nietzsche's Styles* (Derrida 1978a).

Given the thematic contents of his works in general, Foucault maintains unsurprisingly that the socially constructed idea of 'an author' is an 'ideological product' through which "one limits, excludes, and chooses; in short, by which one impedes the free circulation, the free manipulation, the free composition, decomposition and recomposition of fiction" (Foucault 1998: 221). He also supports the position set forth a year earlier by Roland Barthes in the essay, "The Death of the Author" (Barthes 1977: 142–8), namely that the concept of the author ought to minimized, because it carries with it a fundamentally authoritarian and oppressive conception of literary criticism. Nietzsche's proclamation of the death of God in *Thus Spoke Zarathustra* reverberates here into the realm of contemporary literary criticism, where it transforms itself into a critique of monologue-centered conceptions of literature. Foucault himself anticipates the 'death of the author' simply as a matter of cultural change, and echoing his famous last lines of *The Order of Things* – "one can certainly wager that man would be erased, like a face drawn in sad at the edge of the sea" (Foucault 1973: 387) – he states correspondingly that "at the very moment when [our society] is in the process of changing, the author function will disappear" (Foucault 1998: 222).

Foucault's and Barthes's joint questioning of the author's authority led to significant developments in literary theory in the decades that followed, especially in reference to 'reader-oriented' approaches to criticism advanced by theorists such as Hans Robert Jauss, Wolfgang Iser and Stanley Fish.

Foucault's 'aesthetics of existence'

Foucault's important discussions of 'power' – the very propellers of his many specific sociological analyses – emphasize both the oppressive dimensions of power and its creative ones. In the former instances, power operates as a dominating or repressive force from which liberation would be a reasonable goal; in the latter, power constitutes those productive energies which themselves work to liberate a person from existing social constraints. During his final years, Foucault attended more closely to the positive aspects of power, considering especially how power can be directed towards a kind of 'self-creation' or 'art of life.' In one late interview, he queried, "But couldn't everyone's life become a work of art? Why should the lamp or the house be an art object but not our life?" (Foucault 1997: 261).

Foucault describes his approach to understanding life artistically as an 'aesthetics of existence' – an inquiry which he informs by examining the history of various 'arts of existence' or 'techniques of the self.' These include practices that were cultivated by the members of classical Greek and Roman aristocracy, such as shaping one's body through proper exercise and diet, reflecting upon one's modes of world-interpretation, and adjusting with temperance one's basic rules of social conduct.

Considering Nietzsche's deep influence on Foucault, it is not surprising that the phrase 'aesthetics of existence' can be traced back to Nietzsche's *The Birth of Tragedy* (Nietzsche 1967), which develops an 'aesthetic justification of existence' – a fundamental attitude towards life which issues from the assumption that "life is something amoral" (ibid.: section 5). In the same tradition, a more recent ancestor to Foucault's aesthetics of existence is Albert Camus, who, in his *The Myth of Sisyphus* acknowledged a 'primitive hostility of the world' and maintained that "the present and the succession of presents before a constantly conscious soul is the ideal of the absurd person" (Camus 1955: 47). The noble way to be, for Camus, is to appreciate fully and endlessly the sheer fact of being alive. Foucault transforms these Nietzschean and Camusian aesthetic mentalities into a more practice-centered and body-centered approach, and he considers how to form one's life "into an *oeuvre* that carries certain aesthetic values and meets certain stylistic criteria" (Foucault 1990: 10–11). He emphasizes artistic self-sculpting, in contrast to experiencing simply the intrinsic quality of the existing moment in general, or sensually savoring the constantly-changing display of given aesthetic stimuli, such as the glint of sunlight playing upon the surface of the ocean.

Foucault's 'aesthetics of existence' – an extended meditation which, more accurately, addresses the 'art of living' – is among the most controversial segments of his reflections on artistic themes, and it has been confronted with the same objections that have been leveled against Nietzsche and Camus: giving precedence to aesthetic, artistic or stylistic criteria over moral criteria within the direction of one's life can easily involve the sacrifice of traditional sensibilities regarding what is right and wrong. In Foucault's defense, it should be recognized immediately that artistic criteria and moral criteria are compatible, since it is possible to do the right thing with style. A more crucial problem concerns whether, or when, criteria related to artistic style should override moral criteria in deciding how to behave.

One way to understand this tension is in reference to difficulties that arise for artists in general. This concerns the degree of creative and expressive freedoms that belongs legitimately to an artist, as these freedoms stand in potential conflict with moral responsibilities that can issue from the very fact of any person's active membership in a social community. In general, Foucault's writings call into question the constraints imposed by any given social organization, and his reflections on aesthetics cohere with the revolutionary and adventurous sentiment he displayed throughout his life. Foucault's aesthetics does indeed harbor a sense in which traditional morality is challenged, and in this respect, he remained sympathetic to Nietzsche until the very end.

See also Hegel, Nietzsche, Postmodernism, Interpretation.

References

Barthes, R. (1977) "The Death of an Author" in *Image, Music, Text*, trans. S. Heath, London: Fontana.

Baudrillard, J. (1988) *Jean Baudrillard: Selected Writings*, ed. M. Poster, Stanford: Stanford University Press.

Camus, A. (1955) *The Myth of Sisyphus and Other Essays*, trans. J. O'Brien, New York: Random House.

Derrida, J. (1978a) *Spurs: Nietzsche's Styles*, trans. S. Agosti, Chicago: University of Chicago Press.

—— (1978b) *Writing and Difference*, trans. A. Bass, Chicago: University of Chicago Press.

Fish, S. (1982) *Is There a Text in This Class?*, Boston: Harvard University Press.

Foucault, M. (1965) *Madness and Civilization*, trans. R. Howard, New York: Random House.

—— (1972) *The Archaeology of Knowledge*, trans. A. M. Sheridan Smith, New York: Pantheon.

—— (1973) *The Order of Things*, New York: Vintage.

—— (1983) *This is Not a Pipe*, trans. J. Harkness, Berkeley: University of California Press.

—— (1988) *Politics, Philosophy, Culture: Interviews and Other Writings*, trans. A. Sheridan *et al.*, London: Routledge.

—— (1990) *The Use of Pleasure*, trans. R. Hurley, New York: Vintage.

—— (1997) *Michel Foucault: Ethics, Subjectivity and Truth*, ed. P. Rabinow, trans. R. Hurley *et al.*, London: Penguin.

—— (1998) "What is an Author?" in *Aesthetics, Method and Epistemology*, ed. J. D. Faubion, trans. R. Hurley *et al.*, New York: New Press.

Hegel, G. W. F. (1979) *Phenomenology of Spirit*, trans. A. V. Miller, Oxford: Oxford University Press.

Iser, W. (1980) *Act of Reading – A Theory of Aesthetic Response*, Baltimore: Johns Hopkins Press

Jauss, H. (1985) *Toward an Aesthetic of Reception*, trans. T. Bahti, Minneapolis: University of Minnesota Press.

Kant, I. (1965) *Critique of Pure Reason*, trans. N. Kemp Smith, New York: St. Martin's Press.

Lyotard, J. F. (1984) *The Postmodern Condition*, trans. G. Bennington and B. Massumi, Minneapolis: University of Minnesota Press.

Nietzsche, F. (1966 [1883–5]) *Thus Spoke Zarathustra*, trans. W. Kaufmann, New York: Viking.

—— (1967) *The Birth of Tragedy*, trans. W. Kaufmann, New York: Vintage.

Sartre, J-P. (1956) *Being and Nothingness*, trans. H. E. Barnes, New York: Philosophical Library.

Further reading

Carroll, D. (1987) *Paraesthetics: Foucault, Lyotard, Derrida*. London: Methuen. (Within the general chapters suggested by the book's title, there are some useful observations on Foucault's earlier views on art.)

Nilson, H. (1998) *Michel Foucault and the Games of Truth*, trans. R. Clark, New York: St. Martin's Press. (This book develops an overall interpretation of Foucault's work, grounded on the assumption that his reflections on art are foundational.)

Synder, J. and T. Cohen (1981) "Reflexions on *Las Meninas*: Paradox Lost," *Critical Inquiry* 7: 429–47. (This article provides a brilliant discussion of Foucault's interpretation of Las Meninas and calls into question John Searle's analysis in the same journal.)

Wolin, R. (1986): "Foucault's Aesthetic Decisionism," *Telos* 67: 71–86. (A solid, yet clearly unsympathetic, attack on Foucault's aesthetics of existence.)

14
POSTMODERNISM
Barthes and Derrida
David Novitz

A brief history

What we have come only very recently to think of as philosophical postmodernism is the final, perhaps the most intemperate, stage of a long reaction to the central doctrines of Enlightenment thought. Modern philosophy, and with it the contemporary idea of the natural sciences, hence the idea of modernity itself, stems from the thought of the Enlightenment (Habermas 1987: Lecture I). This is why one cannot properly understand the ideas that constitute *postmodernism* unless one also understands the central tenets of Enlightenment philosophy. And in order to understand this, one has to try and understand how European history and European philosophy come together in the late sixteenth and seventeenth centuries. One has to think of the dreadful power of kings and of the medieval and Renaissance church, and one has to try to remember (and imagine) what life was like in a feudal world where the aristocracy had the power of life and death over most people and where the church could consign the unfaithful not just to persecution and misery on earth, but to eternal damnation. This was a society based on rigid metaphysical and epistemological beliefs: the Earth was the center of the universe, blessed by God, who not only empowered kings, bishops and popes, but who afforded them privileged sources of knowledge not available to ordinary minds, all of which could be challenged only on threat of pains too great to comprehend.

It gradually transpired – first with Copernicus's challenge to Ptolemy and later on with Galileo – that the heavens themselves refused to obey the received version of God's will. The Earth, far from the being the center of the universe, was not even the center of the local planetary system. Astronomy seemed to show that the divine plan, whatever it was, was much bigger, much more diffuse, and much less concerned with 'God's Earth' and 'God's creatures' than the church would ever be willing to concede.

Hence, by the time of the sixteenth-century Renaissance, there was a move away from an uncritical acceptance of the world view that had been dogmatically proclaimed by the church (with alterations and emendations) for nearly fourteen hundred years. There was now a growing emphasis on the importance of the rational capacities of the individual, and on natural ways of coming to know and understand. Mathematics, deductive and inductive reasoning, and empirical observation came gradually and imperceptibly to be held in greater esteem than some of the doctrines of the Christian church. Prayers, it seemed, could not move very much at all, let alone mountains; levers and fulcrums, and a growing under-standing of the laws of dynamics, could and did.

The Enlightenment emphasized the rational powers of the individual: the capacity of all people to reason, in the process to discover the truth, and so to determine autonomously what was or was not morally required of them. In this way, insight, knowledge and understanding were no longer the province of a privileged few; the Enlightenment emphasis on a shared human nature had effec-tively democratized rationality, knowledge, understanding, and moral comprehension. Nor were truths hidden from us: if Hobbes and Locke are to be believed, literal language can convey these to us (Hobbes 1962: 13, 22; Locke 1961: vol. 2, 105–6), so that any ordinary human being can achieve a well-grounded understanding of the world, provided only, that we use those natural ways of coming to know that are part of our shared human nature.

Truth, rationality, the possibility of natural (rather than supernatural) sources of knowledge, the capacity of individuals to understand, to decipher, to invent, discover, discern, and so judge independently of authority, were and remain the perennial themes of modern (Enlightenment) philosophy. What is now called postmodern philosophy begins with the denial of some of these themes in the late nineteenth century. The term itself, we should note, was the invention not of philosophers but of artists. According to Charles Jencks, its earliest appearance "extends to the 1870s when it was used by the British artist, James Watkins Chapman" (cited in Appignanese and Garrett 1998: 3). But it was a term that was used by philosophers only as a result of the growing influence in America of French post-structuralists or deconstructionists like Derrida, Lyotard, and Baudrillard. Even so, there can be no doubt that the tendency in human thought marked by the term 'postmodernism' pre-dates the first appearance of this term among philosophers.

Typically, philosophical postmodernism is critical of the idea that the truth is attainable, if by that is meant that it is possible to determine and so come to know how things really are, in and of themselves, by using our natural faculties. Since one cannot have unmediated access to things themselves, to brute facts, language is not constrained by an extra-linguistic world; rather 'the play of signs' creatively constructs what we mistakenly believe to be a world of brute reality. Thus we find in the work of Jacques Derrida a well-known attack on both the 'metaphysics of presence' and the 'myth of logocentrism': on the ideas, that is, that reality itself, real objects, real meanings can be directly present to us, and on the idea that these presences constrain the way in which people use language (Derrida 1974: 49ff.).

Postmodernism is critical, too, of the idea that there is or could be an unconstructed human nature that is shared by all human beings and that affords them the capacity to be rational. Far from being a natural endowment, rationality is seen as historically and culturally constructed. Indeed, appeals to reason and rationality, far from being an appeal to some neutral, widely-shared arbiter of human practices and judgements, is the product of the common human desire to control others (Nietzsche 1987; Foucault 1989; Rabinow 1984: 3–29), and has nothing at all to do with a naturally ordained and enlightening human capacity.

For the postmodernist, then, there are no foundational truths, no sets of privileged, rationally unassailable propositions, on which our insights and understandings are based. The individual, rather, is historically and socially constituted, and his or her thought processes and understandings are the products of a historical process of which the individual is usually unaware but which is strongly formative and entirely ineliminable (Margolis 1998: 353–5). On this view, then, there can be no neutral, culturally unmediated standpoint from which to view and understand the nature of reality; nor can our natural faculties afford us that unbiased insight into the nature of things that modernism had promised.

The motivation for postmodernism comes from two seemingly different sources. The first is an emphasis on and almost sentimental yearning for community, coupled with a marked hostility to the emphasis placed by Enlightenment philosophy on the natural powers and the autonomy of the individual. This celebration of the individual, coupled with the glorification in liberal thought of the freedom of the individual to satisfy his or her desires, meets with strong initial resistance in the work of G. F. W. Hegel (1956), who mourns the fragmentation of community – especially the loss of what he calls an ethical or an organic community – all brought about, so he thinks, by Enlightenment philosophy. On his view, the individual depends for his well-being and for his particular abilities on a historically shaped community, so that, if one follows an Hegelian line of thought, one would be loath to maintain that the individual has historically and culturally unconstituted faculties or capacities that enable him or her to create or to discern the truth.

A second source of postmodernism is found in an excessive emphasis on the individual rather than on community or history or culture: but in this case on creative powers of the individual. According to Friedrich Nietzsche, who was the first full-blown philosophical postmodernist, there are no known truths. In an early essay, he defends the view that all of what we designate as knowledge is a construct of the fanciful imagination: it is all metaphor, simile and illusion

(Nietzsche 1911). The trouble, though, is that we have an interest in forgetting the origins of our knowledge of the world, and we use words like 'true' and 'rational' to disguise the fact that the various propositions to which we assent and beliefs that we have are no more than a figment of the imagination.

We do so, Nietzsche insists, because we have *an interest* in so doing: it helps cement our values, our security, and our power in the world. "Only by forgetting that primitive world of metaphors," Nietzsche writes, "only by the congelation and coagulation of an original mass of similes and percepts pouring forth as a fiery liquid out of the primal faculty of human fancy . . . does [man] live with some repose, safety and consequence" (Nietzsche 1911: 184).

Although we forget its origins in the imagination, all our knowledge is bred of metaphor (or the imagination), and, in a famous passage, truth is described as nothing more than "a mobile army of metaphors, metonymies, anthropomorphism . . . [which] after long usage seem to a nation fixed, canonic and binding; truths are illusions of which one has forgotten that they are illusions" (Nietzsche 1911: 180).

So, flying in the face of Enlightenment thought, the mature Nietzsche rejected absolute notions of reason, knowledge, and morality. These he saw as the 'idols' of his time: man-made and worshipped by all who wished to be properly a part of society. For him they are idolized because they reflect our deep needs. Talking of works of art, he says "the beautiful and the ugly are recognized as *relative* to our most fundamental values of preservation. It is senseless to want to posit anything as beautiful or ugly apart from this" (Nietzsche 1987: sect. 804). This, it will scarcely surprise you, is how he treats all evaluation, intellectual, religious, and moral. As a result he thinks that there are no absolute facts, no truth, objective values, rationality, and knowledge; what we regard as such is so regarded relative to our own interests, and relative to the perspectives on the world that these interests create.

Postmodernism and philosphy of art

The conflict between the core ideas of modernism and postmodernism underlies many of the more hotly contested issues in contemporary philosophy of art. First, with regard to the theory of interpretation, postmodernists argue that there is and can be no such thing as a true interpretation, while many who are influenced by the central tenets of philosophical modernism argue that any interpretation is either true or false, and that for any work of art there is and must be a single true interpretation. Second, while modernists are of the view that a work of art can be genuinely good, and that it can have intrinsic formal properties that make it so (Bell 1961: 19–46), postmodernists see artistic merit as a function of contingent historical and cultural circumstance, and argue that what makes a work of art 'good' or 'beautiful' is not a set of intrinsic features of the work, but the histori-cally-derived values and conventions that contingently characterize a particular period of a culture. Third, whereas modernists tend to the view that art exists independently of particular cultures and times, and in fact transcends them, so that there are intrinsic art-making features, hence clear boundaries, that distin-guish art from life, postmodernism has inclined some philosophers to be more circumspect about these claims. Such philosophers are of the view that there are no intrinsic features that distinguish art from non-art, or high art from popular art; instead they are inclined to argue that art is a cultural or a social rather than a natural phenomenon, so that the identification of art, high art, or popular art and their properties does not depend on the presence in a particular artifact of some set of stable, publicly available features. It depends rather on an acquain-tance with a certain history and culture, the conventions, traditions and values of that culture, and a grasp of when and how they apply. It is relative to these, the postmodernist argues, that an artifact is identified as art, or as popular rather than high art.

Finally, the dispute between modernism and postmodernism reaches deeply into questions about the proper role or function of art, and the influence that art has over our thinking and understanding. Some modernists have tended to the view that art, as a self-contained, autonomous phenomenon, is not to be appre-ciated in terms of its instructive functions, which, it is argued, are purely incidental to its function as art (Lamarque and Olsen 1994). Others – still modernists – argue that art may properly be considered as instructive; indeed, that its cognitive content is integral to its value as art (Novitz 1992: ch.4; Gaut 1998) but that its powers of instruction are limited by considerations of reason and truth (Novitz 1992: ch.10). As against this, contemporary postmodernists have argued (either directly or by implication) that art in particular, and human cultural products in general, shape human cognition in ways that make it impossible to reach beyond the dominant narratives, texts, discourses, 'vocabu-laries' (Rorty 1989: chs 1 and 2) or paradigms (Kuhn 1970), that mold our thought and our understanding in order to ascertain their truth and so determine their adequacy. On this view, what counts as truth, what counts as 'fitting the facts,' and what counts as 'adequate' is itself culturally determined by the narratives, 'idioms' or 'vocabularies' that, for contingent historical reasons, have come to dominate in our society.

From this it is clear that debates concerning the perennial problems of the philosophy of art – problems to do with the identification of art, its interpreta-tion, evaluation, and cognitive content; problems as well about our perception of art works, and the ways in which works of art exist – all take shape around the divide between philosophical modernism and postmodernism. Even so, it would be wrong to think that all philosophers of art fall neatly into the modernist or postmodernist camp. The two positions represent extremes at either end of a continuum. While it is true, for instance, that analytic aestheticians subscribe to many of the tenets of modernism, it is also the case that many analytic aestheticians are critical of some aspects of modernist thought in its application to art, and deny, for instance, that art is a natural human phenomenon that can be identified independently of cultural practice (Carroll 1993; Novitz 1998), or that there are intrinsic features of art works – formal, affective, or functional properties – that mark the distinction between high and popular art.

The interpretation and evaluation debate

The idea that there are comparatively stable meanings that inhere in a work of art – or at least in some works of art – is the overriding assumption that governs the modernist claim that interpretations can be true and can be known to be true. On this view, there is a single right interpretation for any work of art that has a design or a meaning (Beardsley 1970; Davies 1988, 1995; Novitz 1987: ch. 6; Stecker 1997: ch.7). The postmodernist critique of this idea finds some of its impetus in the deconstructive turn of continental philosophy, exemplified initially in Jacques Derrida's *Of Grammatology* (1974) and anticipated in Roland Barthes's *S/Z* (1974).

Derrida's now famous attack on the 'metaphysics of presence' and 'logocentrism' led to the view that there were no extra-textual or extra-linguistic facts that could be apprehended directly and which could therefore serve to constrain the sense that could properly be derived from any 'system of signs': any utterance, text, or painting. On this view, there is nothing beyond the sign that we can speak of and that can be directly known to us. All we have are systems of signs, where each sign gets its meaning contextually through its relation to other signs. Since there is no extra-textual reality that can tell us how signs are properly to be used and related to one another, and since there is nothing 'out there' to be referred to and consulted in this matter, all that we have is the 'play of signs,' a constant shifting and reconfiguration of the relations of signs and words to one another, with resultant shifts in meaning and understanding. For any seemingly obvious reading that privileges certain construals over others, it is always possible, Derrida contends, to "reverse the hierarchy" (Derrida 1977: 254), to destabilize through argument and so to deconstruct the ways in which signs and concepts are traditionally related to each other. In this way, by adopting an approach that is strongly reminiscent of Nietzsche, he allows that it is always possible to construct and discern other meanings, and in the process offer different but perhaps equally plausible interpretations.

Clearly, on this view the aim of interpretation is not to unlock some or other meaning that "lies hidden in the text" (Beardsley 1970). On the contrary, if the postmodern view is adopted, there is no stable meaning that is there to be discovered; there is, rather, an ongoing 'play' of meaning that can be stabilized only through artifice: by subscribing, that is, to the favored modernist narrative of reason, determinate ascertainable meaning, and literal truth. But this, we are assured, is only one among many discourses or narratives, and to favor it above others is entirely arbitrary, more a function of historical accident than of any way the world is (Rorty 1989).

A similar view is advanced by Roland Barthes. On his view, "the goal of literary work (of literature as work) is to make the reader no longer a consumer, but a producer of the text" (Barthes 1974: 4); it is to make the reader more active, less passive: more, Barthes suggests, like the writer, so that there is a clear sense on Barthes's view in which such a 'writerly' reading or interpretation helps create the meanings that are found in the work. The resultant 'methodological field' of active creation on the part of the reader, Barthes calls the 'Text' (ibid.: 74); and it consists of a ludic or playful response that destabilizes the reader's ordinary beliefs about language. A 'writerly' – as opposed to a 'readerly' – interpretation involves the playful, unconstrained restructuring of our ordinary linguistic beliefs, premised always on the belief that language is itself an infinite network of signi-fications, without a stable foundation on which our understanding of it is to be based. On this view, there is no point in asking whether a given (writerly) inter-pretation is adequate to the text or to the work. Indeed, what Barthes calls the 'Text' (with a capital 'T') is itself "a methodological field" created by such a 'writerly' response.

It plainly is difficult to know how a 'readerly' interpretation, which seeks to be adequate to the text, can be reconciled with a 'writerly' reading, which gives to the reader the freedom to create meanings in ways that we would normally associate with the poet. Writing, for Barthes, is a deeply creative activity; one that is thought of by him as characteristically human since it allows us to rebel against and to change "the intelligible unities" – the categories of thought – that dominate within a speech community at a given time, and to produce alternative ways of thinking and describing. Although Barthes certainly believes that 'readerly' interpretation has a place in literary criticism, this, he seems to think, is so only because of inherited conventional practices and structures that have no more authority than a 'writerly' restructuring of prevailing categories of thought.

The view that readers help complete a work by imputing properties to it has entered deeply into the debate about interpretation in the Anglo-American tradition. Joseph Margolis (1974) insists, for instance, that there is no one true interpretation of a work; that since works of art are 'culturally emergent' entities, and since the cultural myths in terms of which we interpret works of art impart to them the very properties that we 'discover' within them, there is no culturally neutral way of discovering the properties of a work of art in terms of which we adjudge them true. Hence, he contends that the common insistence that there is or must be one true interpretation of a work of art is simply wrongheaded, for this is not an area in which a bivalent logic properly applies. There are many plausible interpretations, Margolis contends, which exclude one another, but there is no neutral way of deciding between them. Hence to subject interpretations of art to the law of the excluded middle does violence to the very notion of art, for works of art, on this view, are always culturally constituted and so inherently unstable, depending on variable cultural practices for the properties that they have (Margolis 1994: chs 1–3; Krausz 1993: ch.1).

The position is problematic. Either it succumbs to a naive cognitive relativism (something that Margolis strives to avoid), or it is guilty of a straightforward non-sequitur, since it does not follow from it that the interpretation of works of art is not subject to a bivalent logic. Let me explain. If it is true, as Margolis and others insist, that works of art are physically embodied and culturally emergent entities, one can straightforwardly come to know that one's interpretation of a particular work of art is true or correct just by acquainting oneself with the cultural background against which the work and its properties emerge. Academic critics regularly do this, and do so with a considerable degree of success. This can be denied only by contending that such cultural knowledge is not really available to them – that they inevitably construe the culture of others in terms of their own location in history, so that they cannot know (and know that they know) the parameters of another culture. But such a claim leads inevitably to a cognitive relativism that is far from robust, since it seems in the end to exclude the possibility of all knowledge, and thus has the embarrassing reflexive consequences that Margolis strives to avoid.

The same sort of considerations apply to the evaluation of art. Even if postmodernists are correct in rejecting the notion of neutral, trans-historical values that attach to particular works of art, all that critics need to do in order to test their evaluation of a particular work is acquaint themselves with aspects of the relevant culture inhabited by the work, against which the properties of the work emerge. In this way, the critic will come to know what values prevailed at a particular time and in a particular culture: what would have horrified and pleased, what would have delighted and disgusted. This will not of course enable the critic to discern universal value in any particular work of art, but it will enable the critic to make true statements of the form: 'This scene would have outraged an Elizabethan audience', or 'This, by Classical lights, is an extremely beautiful building'.

To say that the assessment of artistic value is mediated by an understanding of the culture against which the relevant work emerged is not to relativize value in a vicious way; it is to say no more than that our perception and judgement of value is always made within the bounds of certain genres or categories of art (Walton 1970). Just as a good stroke in tennis will not be a good stroke in golf, so artistic value has to be judged within certain categories, where those categories are discerned and understood only by acquainting oneself with a pertinent culture or period of that culture. To say this is not to deny that one's judgements of value may be more or less reasonable, and may even be shown to be true or correct.

To say all of this is not, of course, to decisively refute philosophical postmodernism. This is a task that I have tried to perform elsewhere (Novitz 1987: ch. 3; 1992: ch. 10). It is only to show that there are reasons for doubting the efficacy of the postmodernist move where interpretation and evaluation are concerned.

Postmodernist art

Thus far I have confined my discussion to postmodern philosophy and its impact on the philosophy of art. It needs to be observed, if only briefly, that in its original application the term 'postmodernism' was used exclusively to describe certain trends in art that marked a break with what we now know as 'modernist art.' Reflecting on this, some commentators contend that there really is no connection between philosophical postmodernism and those trends in art that both artists and critics have described as postmodern. But there is an important connection between the two, and it is worthy of our attention.

As one might expect from its name, the artistic movement known as modernism has its origins in a growing emphasis on the worth, the autonomy, and the achievements of the individual: as both the subject and the creator of art. Influenced by the philosophical doctrines of the Enlightenment, modernism tended to the view that works of art were individual, quite unique, objects of beauty created by the imaginative endeavors of highly talented individuals. The boundedness of art, its separation from life, its intrinsic artistic nature, capable always of a true explanation, and capable of carrying real values that could, and in the best cases would, survive across cultures and times, are all doctrines that are intimately related to the central thought of the Enlightenment, and all help characterize what art critics now refer to as modernism. Coupled with this is the idea of genius: that some people have outstanding natural talents, a natural brilliance, and are capable of designing, more or less from scratch, wholly unique and exceptionally valuable artifacts that are works of art. High modernism, towards the end of the nineteenth century, saw the essence of the visual and musical arts as residing in their formal properties; it was this that distinguished them from life (Bell 1961), as well as from non-artistic artifacts.

Postmodernist art begins with an assault on the modernist boundaries of art; a refusal to see art as purely formal and as distinct from life, hence a willingness to appropriate the ready-made objects of everyday living and to subsume them under the rubric of art. Hence, we can think of Dadaism as the first postmodernist art movement; and there is, of course, a well-documented history of subsequent assaults in contemporary art on the once sacred boundaries between art and life. But it can and has been shown that while the modernist boundaries imposed on art tend to distort and oversimplify the scope and complexity of our artistic endeavors, this fact does not and need not commit us to the philosophical doctrines of postmodernism (Novitz 1992). One can hold the view that modernist ideas about art and the associated practice were needlessly confined, without thereby subscribing to the epistemologies, the anti-metaphysics, the theories of value, interpretation, and meaning advocated by postmodernists like Derrida, Barthes, Margolis, or Rorty.

See also Interpretation, Value of art, Aesthetic universals, Hegel, Nietzsche.

References

Appignanese, R. and Garrett, C. (1998) *Postmodernism for Beginners*, Cambridge: Icon.
Barthes, R. (1974) *S/Z*, trans. R. Miller, New York: Hill and Wang.
—— (1979) "From Work to Text," trans. J. V. Harari, in *Textual Strategies: Perspectives in Post-Structuralist Criticism*, Ithaca: Cornell University Press.
Beardsley, M. C. (1970) *The Possibility of Criticism*, Detroit: Wayne State University Press.
Bell, C. (1961) *Art*, 2nd edn, London: Grey Arrow.
Carroll, N. (1993) "Historical Narratives and the Philosophy of Art," *Journal of Aesthetics and Art Criticism* 51: 313–26.
Davies, S. (1988) "True Interpretations," *Philosophy and Literature*, 12: 290–7.
—— (1995) "Relativism in Interpretation," *Journal of Aesthetics and Art Criticism* 53: 8–13.
Derrida, J. (1974) *Of Grammatology*, trans. G. Chakravorty Spivak, Baltimore: Johns Hopkins University Press.
—— (1977) *Limited Inc*, Supplement to *Glyph* 2: 162–254.
Foucault, M. (1989) *Madness and Civilization: A History of Insanity in the Age of Reason*, trans. R. Howard, London: Routledge.
Gaut, B. (1998) "The Ethical Criticism of Art," in J. Levinson (ed.), *Aesthetics and Ethics*, Cambridge, Cambridge University Press.
Habermas, J. (1987) *The Philosophical Discourse of Modernity*, trans. F. Lawrence, Cambridge, Mass.: MIT Press.
Hegel, G. F. W. (1956) *Lectures on the Philosophy of History*, trans. J. Sibree, New York: Dover.
Hobbes, T. (1962) *Leviathan*, London: Dent.
Krausz, M. (1993) *Rightness and Reasons: Interpretation in Cultural Practices*, Ithaca: Cornell University Press.
Kuhn, T. (1970) *The Structure of Scientific Revolutions*, 2nd ed, Chicago: University of Chicago Press.
Lamarque, P. and Olsen, S. H. (1994) *Truth, Fiction, and Literature*, Oxford: Oxford University Press.
Locke, John (1961) *Essay Concerning Human Understanding*, ed. J. W. Yolton, London: Dent.

Margolis, J. (1974) "Works of Art as Physically Embodied and Culturally Emergent Entities," *British Journal of Aesthetics* 14: 187–96.

—— (1994): *Interpretation Radical but Not Unruly: The New Puzzle of the Arts and History*, Berkeley: University of California Press.

—— (1998) "Farewell to Danto and Goodman," *British Journal of Aesthetics* 38: 353–74.

Nietzsche, F. (1911) "On Truth and Falsity in Their Ultramoral Sense," in *The Complete Works of Friedrich Nietzsche*, trans. O. Levy, London: Allen and Unwin.

—— (1987) *The Will to Power*, trans. W. Kaufmann, New York: Random House.

Novitz, D. (1987) *Knowledge, Fiction and Imagination*, Philadelphia: Temple University Press.

—— (1992) *The Boundaries of Art*, Philadelphia: Temple University Press.

—— (1998) "Art By Another Name," *British Journal of Aesthetics* 38: 19–32.

Rabinow, P. (1984) "Introduction," in P. Rabinow (ed.), *The Foucault Reader*, London: Peregrine.

Rorty, R. (1989) *Contingency, Irony and Solidarity*, Cambridge: Cambridge University Press.

Stecker, R. (1997) *Artworks: Definition, Meaning, Value*, University Park: Pennsylvania State University Press.

Walton, K. (1970) "Categories of Art," *Philosophical Review*, 79: 334–67.

Part 2

AESTHETIC THEORY

15

DEFINITIONS OF ART

Stephen Davies

Definition and its purpose

Defining can take a variety of forms: for instance, pointing to examples, enumerating all the things that fall under the term at issue, or legislating how a term will be used. One particular type of definition, sometimes called 'essential' or 'real' definition, has special power as an analytic tool. A real definition of something, X say, would identify a set of properties such that each and every X has all the properties that make up the set and only Xs have that set of properties. A real definition specifies a group of properties each of which is *necessary* for something's being an X and which, taken as a group, are also *sufficient* for something's being an X. In other words, a definition of X characterizes what all Xs and only Xs have in common. For instance, a widow is a woman who has lost her husband by death and who has not married again. In this case, there are three necessary conditions that together are sufficient for someone's being a widow.

Several points should be noticed immediately. Sometimes a person may be able to identify and refer to Xs without being able to define what makes something an X. For instance, she might acquire a working mastery of the relevant concept as a result of being introduced to a range of typical examples. People could identify water successfully long before science revealed its essential molecular structure. And conversely, someone who knows how Xs are defined might not be able to apply that definition to settle in an uncontroversial way the status of borderline or otherwise 'hard' cases, or even to identify ordinary instances. For example, I can know that a person is bald if his scalp wholly or partly lacks hair, yet not be sure of a particular man whether he is bald; and I might know that the aspidistra are plants of a genus distinguished by shield-shaped leaves and, nevertheless be incapable of identifying an aspidistra as such. Finally, it need not be the case that a thing's defining essence reveals anything about how and why it is important to us. This remains true even in cases in which the definition deals with something created by humans to play an important function in their social lives. For instance, speeding is legally defined as

169

exceeding the maximum rate of progress specified for a given route, but this tells us nothing about why we care to set such limits or to appeal to slogans like 'speed kills.' These observations do not show that definitions always are useless or uninteresting, but they do indicate that it can be a mistake to expect too much from a definition. If the disquotational theory of truth – according to which, for example, 'snow is white' is true if and only if snow is white – is disappointing, this might be because there is more to truth than is captured in its definition.

Early definitions of art

In the past, art has been variously defined as imitation or representation (Plato 1955), as a medium for the transmission of feelings (Tolstoy 1995), as intuitive expression (Croce 1920) and as significant form (Bell 1914). Judged as essential definitions, these are unsatisfactory. There are two ways in which a definition of art could be inadequate: by listing a property that not all art works possess, or by identifying a set of properties that is not exclusive to art works. The theories mentioned seem to fail on both counts. Some musical and painted art works are abstract; they do not imitate or represent any other thing. Some art works deliberately eschew expressiveness, while others lack significant form. Moreover, the features offered as definitional are not, after all, exclusive to art works. Holiday snaps are imitative of the visual arrays they picture, but are not art works. Many of the things that transmit emotion, or give intuitive expression to their creator's feelings, or display significant form, are not art works. For instance, advertisements often succeed in communicating and arousing emotion, keening can be an intuitive expression of grief, and the order in which mileage signs follow each other displays significant form, but none of them counts as art.

Such objections may be surmountable. For instance, if abstract musical works and paintings are expressive, it could be argued that they represent the emotions, or that they are mimetic of patterns and structures underlying the surface of our experiences. It will not be easy, though, to meet all the difficulties that such theories confront. In fact, their protagonists often were not interested in pursuing such issues, which suggests that their views were offered not so much as attempts to characterize an essence that all and only art works display but, instead, either as recommending what art works should be like, or as isolating and drawing attention to distinctive, thematic, prominent, important, and/or valuable features of art works or art forms.

Is the definition of art impossible?

With the failure of these traditional approaches, one might wonder if art is definable. Morris Weitz (1956) argues that art works are united by a web of family resemblances, not by the kind of essence sought by a real definition. The problem with this claim is that everything resembles, or can be made to resemble, every other thing, so the invocation of resemblances cannot explain the unity and integrity of any concept. Weitz also maintains that definitions apply only to closed, unalterable concepts, and that this shows that art, with its changing and unpredictable future, cannot be defined. Again, the claim is unconvincing. The class of meals I have eaten keeps growing and sometimes takes in new and unusual instances, but what alters is the class's membership, not its defining characteristics. It could be part, or a consequence, of the unchanging essence of art that many of its instances are created to be original in some respects. Weitz insists that, when we look and see, we do not find any property common to all art works. He could be right about that, but what might follow is not that art is indefinable but, rather, that the defining properties are non-perceptible, relational ones.

If this last observation is correct, it reveals as misguided the tradition that sought to define art in terms of aesthetic properties, where these were conceived as internal, non-relational features that are perceptible so long as the observer has 'taste' and adopts the appropriate psychological attitude of distanced contemplation.

Definitions since the 1960s

Most definitions proposed in the latter part of the twentieth century identify complex relational properties as essential to art's character. One convenient classification divides recent definitions into functional and procedural ones. Functionalists argue that art is designed to serve a purpose, and something is an art work only if it succeeds in achieving the objective for which we have art. Functionalists can and do differ over art's goal, but a common line suggests that its function is to provide a pleasurable aesthetic experience. By contrast, proceduralists hold that something becomes an art work only if it is made according to the appropriate process or formula, regardless of how well it serves the point of art. Art might have been functional at the outset, but subsequent history shows that the concept operates procedurally. (In the same way, the notion of private property serves important individual and social functions, but it is more or less impersonal procedures and conventions that determine who owns what and when.)

The following, which is defended by Monroe C. Beardsley (1982), is a functionalist definition: an art work is either an arrangement of conditions intended to be capable of affording an aesthetic experience valuable for its marked aesthetic character, or (incidentally) an arrangement belonging to a class or type of arrangement that is typically intended to have this capacity. Whereas functionalism makes the value of art central to its nature, proceduralists' definitions are purely descriptive and non-evaluative. The most famous example of a procedural definition is the 'institutional' account offered by George Dickie. His first definition (Dickie 1974) analyzes 'work of art' as, one, an artifact, two, a set of the aspects of which has had conferred upon it the status of candidate for appreciation by some person or persons acting on behalf of the Artworld. The social character of art is emphasized yet more in the revised definition proposed by Dickie in 1984: first, an artist is a person who participates with understanding in the making of an art work; second, a work of art is an artifact of a kind created to be presented to an Artworld public; third, a public is a set of persons the members of which are prepared in some degree to understand an object which is presented to them; fourth, the Artworld is the totality of all Artworld systems; and finally, an Artworld system is a framework for the presentation of a work of art by an artist to an Artworld public. The "Artworld" is the historical and social setting constituted by the changing practices and conventions of art, the heritage of works, the intentions of artists, the writings of critics, and so forth. Notice that Dickie's later definition is circular, which is thought usually to be a fault in a definition, but which he regards as an accurate reflection of art's inflected nature.

Functional and procedural approaches to art's definition need not be opposed. I have characterized each in terms of a necessary condition that it regards as central, but it could be that something is an art work only if it satisfies *both* the functional and the procedural requirements. Nevertheless, much avant-garde art, which draws on artistic traditions, practices, and conventions but uses these to oppose the generation of pleasing aesthetic effects, forces functionalism and proceduralism apart. One reason why the standing of art works such as Marcel Duchamp's ready-mades is so hotly disputed is because they challenge deeply rooted assumptions about art's nature and purpose. And one reason why they are accepted as art is that they satisfy the 'institutional' requirements. For instance, they are created by an established artist, presented along with other art works, discussed by art historians, and so on.

Functionalism must deal with these objections: it is difficult to find any single or pervasive function that is potentially served by all art works. If all art works are functionally successful to a degree that allows them to qualify as art, the existence of very bad art is not easy to account for. The theory tends to be conservative in dismissing from the realm of art many of the more philosophically stimulating recent works, most of which are widely accepted as art even if they challenge what was thought to be foundational or valuable about their predecessors. Moreover, functionalism does not readily encompass works that are plainly expected to perform social, ritual, or didactic functions, as against aesthetic ones, as is so for much non-Western and popular art.

Proceduralism faces these criticisms: Either the Artworld does not seem to be sufficiently institutionalized to generate a structure of roles and authorities that could explain how the status of art is conferred, or, if the emphasis is placed more on the artist's skill and knowledge than on his or her institutional role and authority, it is not clear that the social practices of art-making are distinctive enough to reveal what distinguishes art works from the products of outwardly similar cultural activities. Moreover, proceduralists have difficulty in acknowledging the art works of isolated artists and of those who operate outside the ambit of the Artworld, such as embroiderers.

Historically reflexive definitions

Arthur C. Danto (1973) has argued that a piece cannot become art unless there is a place prepared for it within the Artworld in consequence of the prior history of art production, both generally and by the given artist. Picasso could make an art work by painting his tie, but Cezanne would not have succeeded in creating an art work had he produced an identical object. Observations like Danto's have made philosophers aware of the dependence of a work's art-status on the art-historical context in which it is created and presented. In turn, this has led to definitions that, unlike those mentioned so far, regard the process by which art's history unfolds as part of art's defining character. I call definitions of this type 'historically reflexive'; they also have been called simply 'historical.'

Historically reflexive definitions have this recursive form: something is an art work only in the event that it stands in the appropriate relation to its artistic forebears. While art works are mentioned on the right-hand side of the equation (the '*definiens*' as it is called), definitions with this form are not viciously circular, because the particular art works being defined always are separable from the different art works with respect to which they are defined. The works being defined are acquiring the status of art in the present, while those to which they are appropriately related already have art-status, having achieved it in the past. That is, art_{now} is defined through its relation to art_{past}.

There are some works that this style of definition cannot accommodate, namely those that came first, and therefore had no predecessors. For completeness, any definition of this form should be supplemented by an account of how the chronologically first art works became such. I have argued (Davies 1997) that it is not convincing to maintain that first art could be stipulated as such (as does Levinson 1979) or that it attains the status of art retroactively (as suggested by Carney 1994). It is more plausible to suppose that it is in terms of their functionality that the first pieces qualify as art, and that the relevant function concerns aesthetic features and the pleasure we take in them, rather than (as maintained in Carroll 1988) in the complex and subtle features of representation, expression, and communication that become prominent in later art works.

My proposal, that something is an art work only in the event that it stands in the appropriate relation to its artistic forebears, is not acceptable as a definition. This is because it is uninformative about the nature of the art-defining relation, except for indicating that it involves a connection between present candidates and established art works. Most theorists agree that the relation can display these various forms: reference, repetition, amplification, or repudiation. They differ over the content of the defining relation, however. Various ways of tying the current piece to its artistic predecessors have been proposed, and each of these results in a different definition.

According to Jerrold Levinson (1979, 1989, 1993), something is art if it is intended for regard in one of the ways in which prior art works have correctly been regarded. He allows that the artist's intention can be referentially opaque; that is, he accepts that something intended for a particular regard would be art in the case where that regard was invited by earlier art works although the intender was not aware of this fact. James D. Carney (1991a, 1991b, 1994) holds that it is in terms of its style that the present candidate is united with prior art works. For Carney, artistic style includes schema for conveying content, as well as characteristic choices of subject matter, materials, and approaches. Noël Carroll (1988) sees the link between the present piece and past art as residing in a narrative that encompasses the two. This narrative must be accurate, must explain later events as generated out of earlier ones, and must track the adoption of a series of actions and alternatives as appropriate means to an end on the part of a person who arrived at an intelligible assessment of the art historical context in such a way that he or she resolved to change it in accordance with recognizable and live purposes of the practice (Carroll 1993a). Though Carroll denies that his proposal is a definition, I treat it as one here because it has the same general structure and function as the definitions offered as such by Levinson and Carney.

Each of these theories has been criticized and defended. (For discussion other than by the protagonists of each, see Davies 1991, Stecker 1997, Dickie 1997.) Rather than debating the detail of individual definitions, I draw attention to a difficulty, which I call 'the Artworld relativity problem,' faced by this general approach. It presupposes the existence of a continuous tradition, of an historically and culturally unified body of work, to which the newly created piece is related in the appropriate fashion. In other words, theories of this kind make art relative to an Artworld. But there is more than one Artworld, more than one tradition of making art works. There may be as many independently generated Artworlds as there are distinct cultures producing their own art works. Most historically reflexive theories are too parochial in that they proceed as if there is only one Artworld, by focusing narrowly on the Western context in which 'high' art is made while ignoring 'low' art and non-Western art.

If, on the other hand, the theory acknowledges that there are several Artworlds, then it is exposed as incomplete. When it is generalized, the theory has this form: what makes something an art work is that the appropriate, historically reflexive, relation holds between it and prior works created within the same Artworld, whether it is the Western 'high' Artworld or the Artworld of some African tribe within which the artist operates, and even if that relation is realized or satisfied differently in distinct Artworlds at a given time. When characterizing the nature of Artworlds, the theories can draw attention to the general pattern of relations they share in common, but not to the detail of the *relata* – the intended regards, styles, or unifying narratives – that generate this pattern, since these details differ from Artworld to Artworld. It is obvious, though, that their historically reflexive character is not distinctive to Artworlds. Many practices that are not art-making ones are historically reflexive in similar ways and thereby exhibit the same abstract form. So, when treated as non-parochial, the theories are incomplete because they do not spell out criteria for distinguishing Artworlds from other social arrangements displaying similar general structures of relations.

Hybrid definitions

I observed earlier that functionalism and proceduralism need not be exclusive. Also, either approach might be combined with historical reflexiveness. For instance, it could be held that art is functional and that the function of art changes through time, depending on how it has been realized in the past. Or it could be claimed that the procedures through which art works gain their standing are themselves subject to historical forces internal to the Artworld. When these various approaches are combined, I call the resulting definitions 'hybrids.' The idea is that hybrid definitions will be superior, because they can combine the advantages of several theoretical perspectives while avoiding the weaknesses that plague each taken in isolation.

Arthur Danto (1997: 195) has suggested that a work of art is to be, one, about something, and two, to embody its meaning. He doubts that these necessary conditions are jointly sufficient. Additional conditions have been intimated in other of Danto's writing (for instance, Danto 1981). Carroll (1993b) sums up Danto's theory as follows: something is a work of art if and only if, one, it has a subject, two, about which it projects some attitude or point of view (has a style), three, by means of rhetorical ellipsis (generally metaphorical), four, which ellipsis, in turn, engages audience participation in filling in what is missing (interpretation), and five, where the work in question and the interpretations thereof require an art-historical context. In Carroll's account, the first condition corresponds to the requirement that the work be about something, and the second, third and fourth explain what is meant by the idea that the work is to embody the meaning of what it is about. Meanwhile, the last condition adds a further constraint that had been stressed by Danto from as early as 1964.

Danto's account (as presented by Carroll) displays elements of functionalism, proceduralism, and historical reflexivity. It suggests that the art work has the purpose of engaging the audience in an interpretation of the subject that the work is about. Moreover, in invoking its art-historical setting as among the determinants of the work's identity, Danto (1986) refers to the structure and roles of the Artworld as well as to art's historical evolution.

The major criticisms of Danto's theory have challenged his claim that art works necessarily are *about* something (see Beardsley 1982) and his methodological assumptions, first, that every art work could be perceptually indistinguishable from "a mere real thing" (which he uses to motivate his rejection of the traditional view, according to which art is marked by perceptible features of a distinctively aesthetic kind), and second, that every art work could perceptually be indistinguishable from a different art work (which he uses to attack the institutional theory according to which otherwise identical items, both of which have achieved art status, have the same aesthetic content). (For clarification and critical discussion of Danto's methodological assumptions, see Fisher 1995.) One might also question whether all art is meant to elicit interpreting and, if so, if such interpretations must be constrained, as Danto maintains, by what was intended by the artist.

Another hybrid definition is defended by Robert Stecker (1997). He maintains that an item is an art work if and only if it is in one of the central art forms at the time of its creation and is intended to fulfil a function art has at that time, *or* it is an artifact that achieves excellence in fulfilling such a function. Though it is primarily functional, this definition agrees with the proceduralist's claim that something can be art without fulfilling one of art's functions; for works produced in central art forms, such as poetry, painting and music, the intention to fulfil is sufficient. The historically reflexive aspect of the theory lies in its treatment of art's functions, which are said to evolve in an open-ended fashion so that there will be resemblance rather than identity between the valuable functions of art in one period and those in another. That is, art of the present relates to art of the past in terms of the historical connectedness of the (changing) functions they serve, or are intended to serve. Meanwhile, Stecker dissociates his own view from some elements that went along with traditional versions of functionalism. The more significant functions of art are experience-causing ones, but the relevant experiences may be cognitive, or emotion-centered, or interpretation-centered, not solely aesthetic. Moreover, he denies both that aesthetic experience must be founded solely on perception and that it must be 'disinterested.' He does not think that only *sensuous* features of art works are relevant to their power to provide aesthetic experience, and he allows that an interest in an item's practical utility could be compatible with a concern with its art-relevant features.

Stecker's brand of functionalism inevitably invites some new questions. Though it surely is an improvement to recognize that the function of art is not singular and unchanging, the more functions one countenances and the more malleable they are, the harder it is to believe that the (intended) purposes of art are distinctive of it.

Artworld relativity again

Whatever their other advantages, the hybrid definitions just mentioned fail to escape the Artworld relativity problem that was described earlier. Any theory that makes arthood depend on historical reflexivity within a given Artworld, while allowing (as it should) that there are different Artworlds each with its own history, fails to complete its analysis satisfactorily if it does not analyze the nature of Artworlds.

The Artworld relativity problem also arises for Dickie's institutional theory, though his definition is not historically reflexive. He defends the ahistoricism of his theory by observing that it can accept and explain the importance of art's history while denying that that historic pattern or process contributes to art's essential nature (Dickie 1997). For him, the crucial relation is between the candidate piece and the Artworld's institutional structure, not between the candidate piece and the Artworld's historical development. Nevertheless, his definition does make art relative to an Artworld, and it leaves him with the problem of distinguishing Artworlds from other social institutions. It is implausible to think that all and only Artworlds exhibit a particular social structure, but, if art is itself Artworld-relative, there must be something common to Artworlds beyond the fact that their products are art works.

Not all definitions are subject to the objection. A theory, such as pure functionalism, that does not make art depend for its nature on its connection to an Artworld can avoid it. On the face of it, though, such views are unattractive for they imply what seems obviously to be false: that any art work would have been such wherever and whenever it was created. And as soon as one allows that a thing's capacity for fulfilling the function or functions of art depends on the social structure of the context in which is made and presented, or on the kinds of pieces that have been accepted as art in the past, the problem returns.

By drawing attention to the ubiquity of the Artworld relativity problem I do not mean to imply that the enterprise of defining art is bound to fail. The point, rather, is that progress in analyzing art's nature is likely to demand of philosophers closer attention to the wider social setting in which art is produced and received, and a greater sensitivity to the variety of such settings, many of which fall outside the ambit of the Artworld of 'high' Western art.

See also Formalism, Expressivism, Aesthetic universals, High versus low art.

References

Beardsley, M. C. (1982) "Redefining Art," in M. J. Wreen and D. M. Callen (eds), *The Aesthetic Point of View*, Ithaca: Cornell University Press.

Bell, C. (1914) *Art*, London: Chatto and Windus.

Carney, J. D. (1991a) "Style Theory of Art," *Pacific Philosophical Quarterly* 72: 272–89.

—— (1991b) "Style and Formal Features," *Southern Journal of Philosophy* 29: 431–44.

—— (1994) "Defining Art Externally," *British Journal of Aesthetics* 34: 114–23.

Carroll, N. (1988) "Art, Practice, and Narrative," *Monist* 71: 140–56.

—— (1993a) "Historical Narratives and the Philosophy of Art," *Journal of Aesthetics and Art Criticism* 51: 313–26.

—— (1993b) "Essence, Expression, and History: Arthur Danto's Philosophy of Art," in M. Rollins (ed.), *Danto and His Critics*, Oxford: Blackwell.

Croce, B. (1920) *Aesthetics*, trans. D. Ainslie, London: Macmillan.

Danto, A. C. (1973) "Artworks and Real Things," *Theoria* 39: 1–17.

—— (1981) *Transfiguration of the Commonplace*, Cambridge, Mass.: Harvard University Press.

—— (1986) *The Philosophical Disenfranchisement of Art*, New York: Columbia University Press.

—— (1997) *After the End of Art*, Princeton: Princeton University Press.

Davies, S. (1991) *Definitions of Art*, Ithaca: Cornell University Press.

—— (1997) "First Art and Art's Definition," *Southern Journal of Philosophy* 35: 19–34.

Dickie, G. (1974) *Art and the Aesthetic*, Ithaca: Cornell University Press.

—— (1984) *The Art Circle*, New York: Haven.

—— (1997) "Art: Function or Procedure – Nature or Culture?" *Journal of Aesthetics and Art Criticism* 55: 19–28.

Fisher, J. A. (1995) "Is There a Problem of Indiscernible Counterparts?" *Journal of Philosophy* 92: 467–84.

Levinson, J. (1979) "Defining Art Historically," *British Journal of Aesthetics* 19: 232–50.

—— (1989) "Refining Art Historically," *Journal of Aesthetics and Art Criticism* 47: 21–33.

—— (1993) "Extending Art Historically," *Journal of Aesthetics and Art Criticism* 51: 411–23.

Plato (1955) *Republic*, trans. H. D. P. Lee, London: Penguin.

Stecker, R. (1997) *Art works: Definition, Meaning, Value*, University Park: Pennsylvania State University Press.

Tolstoy, L. (1995) *What Is Art?* trans A. Maude, Oxford: Oxford University Press.

Weitz, M. (1956) "The Role of Theory in Aesthetics," *Journal of Aesthetics and Art Criticism* 15: 27–35.

Further reading

Beardsley, M. C. (1966) *Aesthetics from Classical Greece to the Present*, London: Macmillan. (A fine survey of the major theories and definitions proposed in the past two millennia.)

—— (1983) "An Aesthetic Definition of Art," in H. Curtler (ed.) *What Is Art?* New York:

Haven. (An elaboration of the theory outlined in Beardsley 1982.)

Carney, J. D. (1994) "Defining Art Externally," *British Journal of Aesthetics* 34: 114–23. (Distinguishes definitions that are 'internal,' in appealing to artist's intentions, from those that are external, in relying solely on what was done or achieved.)

Carroll, N. (1997) "Danto's New Definition of Art and the Problem of Art Theories," *British Journal of Aesthetics*, 37: 386–92. (A critical discussion of Danto 1997.)

—— (ed.) (2000) *Theories of Art Now*, Madison: University of Wisconsin Press. (Contains sophisticated, recent discussions of the topic.)

Danto, A. C. (1964) "The Artworld," *Journal of Philosophy* 61: 571–84. (Introduces and discusses the notion of the Artworld.)

Dickie, G. (1983) "The New Institutional Theory of Art," *Proceedings of the 8th International Wittgenstein Symposium* 10: 57–64. (A concise summary of both versions of the author's institutional theory.)

Diffey, T. J. (1985) *Tolstoy's What Is Art?* London: Croom Helm. (Contains elaboration and criticism of Tolstoy's theory.)

—— (1991) *The Republic of Art and Other Essays*, New York: Peter Lang. (Four papers on art's definition in which an institutional theory is developed; this theory differs from Dickie's not least because of its emphasis on art's historicity.)

Kamber, R. (1998) "Weitz Reconsidered: A Clearer View of Why Theories of Art Fail," *British Journal of Aesthetics* 38: 33–46. (Discussion of Weitz and defense of anti-essentialism.)

Leddy, T. (1993) "The Socratic Quest in Art and Philosophy," *Journal of Aesthetics and Art Criticism* 51: 399–410. (Rejects the historical realism apparent in Levinson's and Carroll's definitions for an anti-essentialism flavored by postmodernist theory.)

16
THE AESTHETIC

Alan Goldman

The term 'aesthetic' was first used in the eighteenth century by the philosopher Alexander Baumgarten to refer to cognition by means of the senses, sensuous knowledge. He later came to use it in reference to the perception of beauty by the senses, especially in art. Kant picked up on this use, applying the term to judgements of beauty in both art and nature. The concept has broadened once again more recently. It now qualifies not only judgements or evaluations, but properties, attitudes, experience, and pleasure or value as well, and its application is no longer restricted to beauty alone. The domain of the aesthetic remains broader than that of aesthetically pleasing art works: we can experience nature aesthetically as well, but understanding the nature of such experience and the properties it encompasses will take us a long way toward understanding how we evaluate and why we value art works. This discussion will focus primarily on aesthetic properties and experience, and on whether a special attitude is involved in the perception of such properties or generation of such experience.

The concepts of aesthetic attitude, aesthetic properties, and aesthetic experience are inter-definable. One can, for example, define the attitude as what is necessary or ordinarily involved in perceiving the properties or generating the experience. Or one can define the experience as what perception of the properties generates or as what the attitude aims to produce. Or the properties can be defined as the contents of the experience or targets of the attitude. Of course, it will be more helpful to avoid this rather small circle. It can be avoided by taking one of these concepts as basic or defining one independently of the others. For the purposes of this discussion, I will avoid as far as possible defining any in terms of the others. Their inter-definability makes the order of presentation a matter of unimportant choice. I shall begin with what is probably the most contested but most widely used of the concepts in contemporary writings, that of aesthetic properties.

Aesthetic properties

The most important early discussion is that in a well known article by Frank Sibley in 1959. While Sibley speaks mainly of the application of aesthetic terms or concepts, he sometimes shifts to more natural talk of properties. For these he initially provides not a definition, but a list that he takes ostensibly to indicate the extension of the concept. His list includes: being balanced, serene, powerful, delicate, sentimental, graceful, and garish. He assumes that, having grasped this list, we could easily extend it, showing a grasp of the general concept of an aesthetic property. And indeed it seems that we can. A formal property (like being balanced) is being loosely woven; an emotion property (like serene) is angry; an evocative property (like powerful) is poignant; a broadly evaluative formal property (like graceful) is elegant; and a second-order perceptual property (like delicate) is vibrant. If we can extend the list in such fashion and exclude other properties of art works like being predominantly red or being rectangular or lasting two hours, then it seems that we can discriminate aesthetic properties from others.

The question for the analytic philosopher then becomes what, if anything, all these properties have in common that leads us to classify them all as aesthetic and to distinguish them from other kinds of properties.

Having offered this list, Sibley's main point in the paper is that no description of works in terms of nonaesthetic properties entails any description in terms of aesthetic properties, although one offers reasons for the latter descriptions by citing nonaesthetic properties in ways that Sibley again indicates ostensibly. That a painting contains pale colors and curved lines does not entail that it is graceful, although one might well point to those features of the painting to support a claim that it is graceful. According to Sibley, the reason for the lack of entailment, as well as an essential feature of aesthetic properties, is that such properties require taste on the part of the subject to pick them out, unlike properties like redness or rectangularity, which require only functioning eyesight. Persons with perfectly good vision can fail to notice that a painting is graceful or delicate, when they cannot fail to notice its predominantly light green color or curved lines. Sibley attributes their shortcoming to lack of taste (but not in the ordinary sense in which people's tastes, their evaluations or aesthetic values, can be said to differ).

His article prompted several skeptical responses, the most thorough from Ted Cohen (1973). Cohen pointed out first that Sibley's definition of aesthetic properties, as requiring taste to be correctly ascribed, already implies that there cannot be sufficient conditions in nonaesthetic properties. Any further argument is superfluous; the position is established by definitional fiat alone. He then argues that we do not in fact require taste in order to apply aesthetic terms correctly. Anyone can distinguish a clear case of a graceful line from its opposite or a somber melody from a cheerful one. Finally, he questions the entire distinction between aesthetic and nonaesthetic properties, mainly by producing a set of terms such as 'daring,' 'powerful,' 'pompous,' 'linear,' 'restful,' which we would hesitate to assign unequivocally to either category.

This point is not decisive, though. It shows only that many terms can pick out either aesthetic or nonaesthetic properties, depending on their context of application and on the objects to which they are applied. This no more calls the category of aesthetic properties into question than the fact that the term 'interest' can refer to a noneconomic object as well as an economic object shows that there are no economic objects, or that economics is not a well demarcated field. 'Powerful,' when applied to a locomotive, generally refers to a nonaesthetic property; when applied to Beethoven's Third or Mahler's Fifth Symphony, it refers to an aesthetic property. 'Pompous,' when applied to an English professor, generally denotes a nonaesthetic property; when applied to a film by Ken Russell, it denotes an aesthetic property. Similarly for 'daring,' when ascribed to a soldier or an avant-garde play; for 'linear,' when applied to an equation or an abstract painting; or 'restful,' when ascribed to a nap or an adagio movement of a chamber piece. That our intuitions are clear in such cases is significant; that the terms can be applied to both sorts of properties is not.

Indeed, Cohen himself accepts that the term 'aesthetic' is meaningful, that it has legitimate uses, and it therefore seems that he must also accept that its use makes some meaningful distinction between what is aesthetic and what is not. If this is not a distinction between types of properties, then one would like to know what sort of distinction it is. How, for example, could we distinguish between objects without distinguishing their properties? Cohen claims that the distinction, even if accepted, is not useful for any theory about art or any description of the ways we appreciate it. But the proper characterization of the nature of aesthetic properties *is* important for a theory of aesthetic evaluation, if, for example, this characterization appeals to an irreducible component of subjective taste in some sense. Cohen can, of course, deny that we value art for aesthetic reasons, but it would take much more argument to erase the implausibility of that claim. The distinction is also useful in a quite mundane way for distinguishing ways of apprehending and appreciating art works. Appreciating the aesthetic qualities of a painting is quite different from noting its intrinsic physical properties (which might be relevant if the painting had to be moved, hung, framed, or restored) or its economic properties (its cost or value on the market, for example).

In regard to Cohen's first point, it does not matter if Sibley's denial of sufficient conditions lacks a supporting argument, if what he is offering is not so much a contested conclusion as a description or clarification of the ways these terms are used or of the nature of these properties. Examples such as the painting with pale colors and curved lines illustrate the absence of entailment without further argument. Cohen is nevertheless perfectly correct to attack Sibley's appeal to taste in his definition of aesthetic properties. It smacks entirely too much of the discredited appeal to a special faculty of moral intuition used to intuit strange, 'unnatural' moral properties. Aesthetic properties would be just as strange if they required some special faculty beyond our ordinary senses to intuit or apprehend them.

Even here, however, there is more than one grain of truth in Sibley's characterization of aesthetic properties. It is true that many of these properties require some training of the subject before they can be apprehended in various art works. We cannot hear the gracefulness in a certain transition passage or modulation in a Haydn quartet without some prior exposure to music in that style. It is also true that taste (in the usual sense in which people have different tastes, that is, they differ in their evaluations of art works) affects which of these properties are perceived and ascribed to various works. What is poignant to one critic is maudlin to another; what is vibrant or powerful to one is raucous, strident, or grating to another. These disagreements can and do occur even among the most knowledgeable critics. They do not imply that ascriptions of aesthetic properties cannot be mistaken, if one is not knowledgeable or is inattentive, for example. The limits of such faultless disagreements, the fact that one critic might find maudlin, but not cheerful, what another finds poignant, indicates that these properties have an objective component. But the disagreements themselves indicate that they also involve a response on the part of the subject, that they are indeed relational properties, and that their ascription must be relativized to competent or ideal critics who share taste in the usual sense. Thus, aesthetic properties are to be analyzed in terms of the shared responses of competent subjects with particular tastes to the intrinsic (usually formal) properties of objects (Goldman 1995).

There are, of course, other relational properties of this sort. We therefore require further distinguishing marks of aesthetic properties. In further characterizing and distinguishing aesthetic properties, Monroe Beardsley (1981) seems to be on the mark when he claims that they are those which directly contribute to the evaluations and values of art works. Since he then characterizes aesthetic value in terms of the production of aesthetic experience, it is clear that, if we follow him here, we have reached the limit in defining aesthetic properties independently of appeal to aesthetic experience. If appeal to value and experience is ineliminable here, that would explain again why aesthetic properties are not only relational, but relative. Since subjects have different experiences of the same works and differ in their evaluations, non-aesthetic base properties must generate different aesthetic properties in relation to these subjects.

Why perception of these properties is of positive or negative value is itself an important question. Some, like gracefulness or gratingness, can produce pleasure or displeasure (involve a positive or negative response) when perceived in themselves. Others generate value only when combined through the interactions and relations among formal base properties in the overall experience of works. Even those that generally involve positive or negative responses on their own do not always do so; all can depend on the broader context. This, together with the fact that the same base properties can produce different aesthetic properties relative to different observers, means that there cannot be principles linking the former properties to the latter; hence there are no principles for constructing successful art works. Not only are there no sufficient conditions for aesthetic properties in nonaesthetic properties, but the former do not even supervene on the latter. The same objective properties produce different responses or experiences, hence different aesthetic properties for different observers. This claim just is the negation of supervenience. To understand further the nature of aesthetic properties and their contribution to aesthetic value we must turn, then, to the nature of aesthetic experience.

Aesthetic experience

Kant focused on aesthetic judgements of beauty and not explicitly on aesthetic experience (Kant 1987). But his account of the grounds of such judgements as lying in the pleasure derived from the free play and felt harmony of the imagination and understanding suggested, first, that experience, the experience of pleasure and subjective harmony in the presence of an object, is central to proper aesthetic judgement. It implied, second, that the key to such experience lies in the mutually compatible functioning of our human faculties. The emphasis on experience is reinforced by Kant's claim that no argument or appeal to principles can convince us that an object is beautiful without our perceiving the object first-hand. Although Kant emphasized the felt harmony of our cognitive powers in perceiving the object, in light of modern art's emphasis on expressiveness, we might want to add to this the exercise of our affective capacities, our emotional faculty. The hallmark of such aesthetic experience then becomes the full exercise of all our sensory, cognitive, and affective capacities in the appreciation of works of art.

The focus on experience becomes natural, even inevitable, once it is recognized that beauty and other aesthetic qualities are not simply intrinsic properties of objects themselves, but essentially involve responses on the part of perceiving, cognizing, and feeling subjects. This becomes the central topic in later aesthetic theories and the exclusive focus of Dewey's aesthetics. Dewey (1958) attributes two main characteristics to aesthetic experience, which according to him occurs not only in appreciating works of art, but also in relation to nature and in daily life. The first is unity and completeness, which together make otherwise amorphous experience into *an* experience: "that which distinguishes an experience as esthetic is conversion of resistance and tensions, of excitations that in themselves are temptations to diversion, into a movement toward an inclusive and fulfilling close" (Dewey 1958: 56). This characterization is reminiscent of Aristotle's account of good form in tragedy as the feeling of necessity (yet surprise) for each element as experienced, with the inability to subtract any without detriment to the whole. Dewey transfers this felt unity or sense of belonging from the object to the experience of it. The second characteristic attributed by Dewey to aesthetic experience harkens more back to Kant's account in terms of the fulfilling engagement of our faculties: "Hand and eye, when the experience is esthetic, are but instruments through which the entire live creature, moved and active throughout, operates" (ibid.: 1958: 50).

As has been noted, the focus of Beardsley's theory too is aesthetic experience, and he adopts with only minor modifications and additions Dewey's characterization (Beardsley 1981). First, he notes that aesthetic experience is controlled by the phenomenal object on which attention is fixed. He emphasizes that the object is phenomenal, that we are focused on the way the object appears to us, that there is an intimate connection here between subject and object. This is close to the point that aesthetic properties are relational, emergent in the experience of observers as they react to the objective formal properties of works. Most important for Beardsley, as for Dewey, is that aesthetic experience is unified or coherent, and complete. He analyzes coherence in terms of continuity of development, and completeness in terms of expectations being resolved or satisfied by later developments. Finally, he describes aesthetic experience as intense or concentrated. What this means is not perfectly clear: in part it consists in the exclusion of extraneous noise or distraction. But it might also suggest a secondary theme that was traced from Kant through Dewey: the full engagement of all our mental capacities, which would generate a felt intensity to experience.

Skeptical attacks against these accounts of aesthetic experience have been launched explicitly by George Dickie and Eddy Zemach. Dickie (1965) questions whether experience can be complete or unified as can a work of art, and whether coherence in experience is any criterion for evaluation at all. Ordinarily we do not speak of experience as unified or complete, and Dickie holds that to do so is simply to confuse perception with its object. Seeing or hearing a unified work does not entail having a unified seeing or hearing. We do sometimes speak of coherent experience, but almost all experience is coherent in this sense except that of an insane person, or perhaps a dreamer, and so coherent experience affords no criterion of value.

Zemach (1997) adds that, even if we can make sense of the notion of a complete experience, we would not describe the experience of good art works in this way, since such experience typically draws on earlier encounters with similar works and reverberates in memory, coloring later encounters with art works and other objects. According to Zemach, the experience of a work is its effects on us, and there is no effect common to even great works: some arouse us and some have a calming effect; some cheer us up and others depress, and so on. Dewey and Beardsley characterize aesthetic experience in only positive terms, but Zemach points out that we experience negative aesthetic properties as well – ugliness, dreariness and so on – so their characterization is both too narrow and has the wrong logical priority between aesthetic experience and aesthetic properties. We must analyze the former in terms of the latter, and not the reverse.

Let us once more mediate this debate over the centrality of aesthetic experience. First, Beardsley appears to make perfectly good sense of the notion of a unified or complete experience. He unpacks the notion in terms of expectations that are raised by works being later fulfilled. The final cadences of most tonal symphonic movements provide clear examples. There is no problem of intelligibility here; nor do Zemach's remarks about prior experience and later effects affect this characterization. But two questions remain. First, if such experience results only from unified works, we might question the point of evaluating according to the property of the experience instead of directly in terms of the property of the work. Second, in contemporary art and music especially, there are many intentionally disunified works that may be better, or at least not worse, on that score. Even in modern tonal music, the sprawling symphonies of Mahler are plausibly judged better, and better for their disunity, than many more tightly classical works.

Regarding the duplication of properties in works and experiences of them, we have seen that there is nevertheless independent reason to focus on the aesthetic experience. Although unity may in some sense exist in a work and the experience of it, the main reason for drawing the distinction lies in the frequent difference between properties of experience caused by objective properties, and objective properties themselves. The movement from the dominant to the tonic chord in tonal music is typically experienced as expectation or tension, and its satisfaction or resolution. Although the tension is not literally in the tones but in our response to them, even a formal description of the work must note the tension. It is precisely our inability completely to distinguish the formal from the expressive in experience that indicates the extent of our engagement by such works. In painting too, objective properties of works may have effects in experience that not only do not duplicate them, but are surprising in relation to them. The rather simple, large, and blurred rectangles in Rothko paintings are experienced as complex, ambiguous spaces that can have a perceptually frustrating yet at the same time calming effect. In light of such relations between objective properties of works and the aesthetic experience they help to cause, there is good reason for emphasizing the distinction and focusing on the latter as the basis for aesthetic evaluation.

Dewey's and Beardsley's characterization of aesthetic experience in only positive terms fits with much common linguistic practice. 'Aesthetic', like 'work of art,' is often used as an honorific or positively evaluative term. Since art works are typically designed to provide rewarding experience, it makes sense at least in some contexts to reserve the term for objects that succeed in fulfilling this intention. And since the term 'aesthetic' is applied primarily (but not exclusively) in the context of appreciating art works, it is natural to apply the term to experience that is rewarding in the way that art works are intended to be rewarding. Zemach is nevertheless also correct in saying that we think of aesthetic properties as those which contribute to the positive *or* negative values of art works.

Some criticism of Dewey's and Beardsley's positive characterization of aesthetic experience was accepted in this argument: not all such experience is aptly described as unified or complete. Dewey and Beardsley would have done better to focus on the other aspect of their description, which derived more directly from Kant's implicit characterization of aesthetic experience: the full engagement of our mental (perceptual, cognitive, affective) capacities and the felt intensity of the experience that results. All great art works, whether they are uplifting or depressing, arousing or calming, engage us in this way, and the value to be derived from such experience is afforded by all the various forms of art, which may nevertheless vary in the degree of their expressiveness, cognitive meaningfulness, perceptual challenge, and so on. Not only does perceptual experience of art works integrate the senses – for example, paintings appear to have tactile qualities, musical tones are described as bright or dark, light or ponderous – but we perceive in them expressive qualities and symbolic meanings as well as ordinary perceptual qualities. The full engagement of our subjective capacities correlates with focus on representational, expressive, symbolic, and higher order formal properties, as these interact and emerge from more basic sensory and formal properties. When we perceive aesthetically objects other than art works (such as the natural environment), we once more use multiple senses and attend completely not only to sensuous and formal properties, but to the natural objects or scenes as expressive, as uplifting or oppressive, majestic or delicate.

While the purpose of art may not be pleasure in the narrow sense, it is the enjoyment, refreshment, and enlightenment that such full experience provides. Great art challenges our intellects as well as our perceptual and emotional capacities. To meet all these challenges simultaneously is to experience aesthetically.

Aesthetic attitude

From the eighteenth century to the present a debate continues over whether a special attitude is involved in perceiving aesthetic objects or aesthetic properties. Originally this attitude was thought to be necessary for proper aesthetic judgement or evaluation, but later the focus shifted to what is necessary for producing aesthetic experience. From the beginning the hallmark of the aesthetic attitude was held to be disinterest. This notion has been defined variously. Its usual meaning outside aesthetics – a lack of bias or an impartiality in judges or mediators of disputes – has little application to aesthetic judgement, and even less to aesthetic experience. The common denotation in aesthetics is a lack of interest in the practical uses of the aesthetic object. We are to attend to the object as an object of contemplation only, to its phenomenal properties simply for the sake of perceiving them. We are to savor the perceptual experience for its own sake, instead of seeking to put it to further use in our practical affairs.

Kant (1987) captured this idea by saying that, for the purpose of aesthetic judgement, we are not interested in the existence of the object (but only in its appearance). We have no interest in the object itself, as opposed to the way it appears, again no interest in its use beyond that of contemplation. Although this would be a misinterpretation of Kant, the notion of contemplation might suggest passivity on the part of the subject, passively taking in the object as it presents itself to our gaze. This would certainly misrepresent the very active perception involved in aesthetic appreciation: anticipation and reconstruction in experience of musical developments, of formal patterns in visual art, or of narrative structure in literature.

In the twentieth century, Jerome Stolnitz (1960) emphasized this active aspect of the aesthetic attitude. According to him, one's attitude always actively guides perception according to one's purposes. In our normal practical attitude we perceive what is relevant to our purposes beyond the perception itself. Aesthetic perception, by contrast, is once more disinterested. It aims at the enjoyment of the experience itself, grasping its object in isolation from other things, instead of classifying or judging it. To the notion of disinterest, Edward Bullough (1912) adds that of emotional detachment. To appreciate a tragic play properly, we must be sufficiently detached not to be tempted to interfere in the action ongoing on stage; to appreciate a storm at sea aesthetically, we must be detached from the fear that prompts precautionary action.

Bullough's characterization of the aesthetic attitude is the easiest to attack. When we cry at a tragedy, jump in fear at a horror movie, or lose ourselves in the plot of a complex novel, we cannot be said to be detached, although we may be appreciating the aesthetic qualities of these works to the fullest. Lack of emotional involvement is not the reason we do not interfere in the action of the tragedy. And we can appreciate the aesthetic qualities of the fog or storm while fearing the dangers they present, although it is also true that the latter can distract us from the former.

Skeptical doubts about the notion of disinterest, as variously interpreted, are once more raised by Dickie and Zemach, among others. Zemach (1997) argues that an aesthetic interest in objects is simply one interest among other possible ones, and a self-centered interest at that, aiming at one's own enjoyment. To call only this interest 'disinterest' is misleading at best. In opposition to Kant's characterization, we *are* interested in the real existence of the objects we perceive aesthetically. We would not enjoy a performance of an opera in the same way if we knew that the singers were only moving their lips to a recording, or if they were only life-sized holograms; similarly if members of a symphony orchestra were only soundlessly moving to computer generated tones. A reproduction of a painting does not affect us in the same way as the original, even if phenomenally indistinguishable from it.

Dickie (1964) claims that the concept of disinterest represents both a confusion of the motivation for perceiving with a way of perceiving, and a trivial demand for paying attention to the aesthetic object itself. What interest motivates one to look at an object can be irrelevant to how one perceives it: a critic may be motivated primarily to write his review and earn his salary, but he may pay close attention to the aesthetic qualities of the orchestral performance because of that motivation. What attitude theorists call disinterested perception is not really a different attitude or way of perceiving or paying attention, but a freedom from distraction by personal associations, fear, economic preoccupations, daydreams, and so on.

In regard to Stolnitz's claim that aesthetic perception aims at the object in isolation from other things, both Kendall Walton (1970) and Arthur Danto (1981) have argued persuasively that how one classifies an art work, where it fits into the art historical narrative, very much affects those aesthetic properties one perceives it to have. What is bold and daring, or graceful, in one style is not in another. Knowledge of the historical context of a work, including its proper classification, is required for proper appreciation of its aesthetic qualities. Even removing certain works from the context of practical affairs prevents proper aesthetic appreciation of them. Much contemporary art reflects the techniques and themes of a technological, mass productive, and materially obsessed age, and the mundane and practical aspects of life in this age. Ignoring the context of practical life loses the point of these works. Older art too may better be appreciated in its narrower practical or concrete context. Taking part in a religious service, using a cathedral for that purpose, can heighten rather than distract from the aesthetic experience of the building (Fenner 1996: 80).

Despite these criticisms, there are once again grains of truth in the traditional account of the aesthetic attitude. It remains the case that ordinary perception is absorbed in and functions in the service of practical action, which normally prompts attention only to aspects of objects insufficient for aesthetic appreciation of them. Nor is it the case that paying close attention to art works or other objects is all that is involved in appreciating them aesthetically. Scientists pay close attention to their experimental data, investors to stock transactions, and baseball batters to pitches coming at them, but none of these contexts ordinarily involve aesthetic appreciation. As noted earlier, the aesthetic properties to which one pays attention are not simply objective properties of works, but relational properties partly constituted by one's responses when fully engaged by the aesthetic object. To be fully engaged is not simply to pay close perceptual attention to formal detail and complex internal relations in the object's structure, but also to bring to bear one's cognitive grasp of those external and historical relations that inform one's aesthetic experience, and to be receptive to the expressive qualities that emerge through this interaction. Knowledge that *can* inform one's experience of a work includes that of the artist's intentions, techniques, attitudes, problems overcome, and so on. Such knowledge is aesthetically relevant only when it *does* inform one's experience of the work.

Such engagement is ordinarily at least partly voluntary, and this is the truth behind the aesthetic attitude theorist's claim that we can adopt or fail to adopt the attitude toward any object, and that whether or not we adopt it affects how we experience the object. Not every object invites or rewards an attempt at aesthetic appreciation, however. Thus the attempt to adopt an aesthetic attitude, or the desire to be fully engaged by an object, is not sufficient to guarantee its own success, to produce aesthetic experience. Nor is it necessary: sometimes we are simply struck by the aesthetic qualities of an art work or natural scene (although engagement is a matter of degree, and full appreciation of an art work usually demands more cognitive preparation than this image of being 'struck' suggests).

When we are so fully engaged in appreciating a work, we often have the illusion of entering another world. We lose ourselves in the aesthetic experience, in the world of the work. This is the truth behind the claim that the aesthetic attitude removes or detaches us from the world of our practical affairs. It is not that we are detached from the aesthetic object in appreciating it: very much the reverse is the case. Nor is it that we are not interested in its existence or relations to other objects, as these relations can affect the object's appearance or our experience of it. But removal from our usual practical affairs is both a typical cause (darkened theaters, quiet museums and concert halls, reading room easy chairs) and a typical effect of aesthetic experience. Escaping such concerns and entering other worlds, even temporarily and metaphorically, is also a major part of its value for us. Whether we call the perceptual and cognitive activity and affective receptivity that generates such experience a special attitude is a purely verbal affair.

See also Kant, Sibley, Aesthetic universals, Taste, Beauty, Fakes and forgeries.

References

Beardsley, M (1981) *Aesthetics*, Indianapolis: Hackett.
Bullough, E. (1912) "'Psychical Distance' as a Factor in Art and as an Aesthetic Principle," *British Journal of Psychology* 5: 87–98.
Cohen, T. (1973) "Aesthetics/Non-Aesthetics and the Concept of Taste," *Theoria* 39: 113–52.
Danto, A. (1981) *The Transfiguration of the Commonplace*, Cambridge, Mass.: Harvard University Press.
Dewey, J. (1958) *Art as Experience*, New York: Capricorn.
Dickie, G. (1965) "Beardsley's Phantom Aesthetic Experience," *Journal of Philosophy* 62: 129–36.
—— (1964) "The Myth of the Aesthetic Attitude," *American Philosophical Quarterly* 1: 56–66.
Fenner, D. (1996) *The Aesthetic Attitude*, Atlantic Highlands, N.J.: Humanities Press.
Goldman, A. (1995) *Aesthetic Value*, Boulder: Westview Press.
Kant, I. (1987) *Critique of Judgment*, trans. W. S. Pluhar, Indianapolis: Hackett.
Sibley, F. (1959) "A Contemporary Theory of Aesthetic Qualities: Aesthetic Concepts," *Philosophical Review* 68: 421–50.
Stolnitz, J. (1960) *Aesthetics and Philosophy of Art Criticism*, New York: Houghton Mifflin.
Walton, K. (1970) "Categories of Art," *Philosophical Review* 79: 334–67.
Zemach, E. (1997) *Real Beauty*, University Park: Pennsylvania State University Press.

17
TASTE

Carolyn Korsmeyer

The idea of taste is embedded in discourse about aesthetic appreciation and art, both in philosophy and in ordinary conversation. People are praised if they display good taste in their choice of art, entertainment, clothes, or behavior to others; they are criticized for dubious preferences and inappropriate demeanor. Popular and public art is sometimes actually suppressed if it appears to violate norms of taste. These activities suggest that 'taste' labels a set of preferences and dispositions that admit shared social standards and public criticism. At the same time, as the saying goes, 'there is no accounting for taste.' Aesthetic responses are also understood as immediate and powerful reactions that are not wholly the result of deliberation or choice. Just as a love of chocolate seems immune to persuasion, taste for decoration, music, movies or other art seems in part to be dependent upon an individual's psychological make-up and personality. How can both these ways of thinking be sound? This question generates what philosophers of earlier times called the 'problem of taste,' for aesthetics has always harbored an uneasy tension between the necessity of critical standards for judging art works and the fact that those standards rely upon the subjective responses of the individuals appreciating art, which are notoriously variable.

A study of taste, therefore, requires consideration of perception and the determinants of appreciation. It raises the difficult question of just what is the *object* of aesthetic appreciation. Are aesthetic qualities so grounded in personal responses that beauty is truly in the eye of the beholder? Or do standards of taste, however indirectly, indicate some degree of realism for the qualities we appreciate in art and other objects? If we maintain that there are standards for the enjoyment entailed by the exercise of taste, how do we distinguish good from bad taste? Moreover, why do we sometimes find ourselves actually preferring things we suspect are in bad taste, changing channels from a concert of classical music by a composer we admire to a cop show, for example? Probably many of us genuinely like certain movies, songs, dances that we acknowledge are not of the highest merit. While aesthetic taste is linked to both quality and pleasure in art, clearly there can be a split between acknowledged high quality and actual appreciative pleasure.

Some of these issues emerge from the very language philosophers have formulated to consider aesthetic response, art, and beauty: the metaphor of taste itself. This term invokes the immediate enjoyment of eating and drinking to elucidate the nature of aesthetic sensibility. Just how apt the metaphor is to account for aesthetic discernment and appreciation has been a matter of philosophical controversy for centuries. To see this, we need to take a look at the genesis of the term in the formative years of aesthetic theory.

The metaphor of taste

Many philosophers have puzzled over the nature of the qualities that make an object or expression beautiful or aesthetically vivid. There is no obvious objective property that can be correlated with all instances of aesthetic appreciation, and though theorists have proposed such qualities as 'harmony' or 'balance' to account for good aesthetic character, these fit only certain works and by no means exhaust the range of artforms that are valued for their beauty, profundity, insight, or accomplishment. Nor do they adequately account for the aesthetic enjoyment of nature or other objects that are not works of art. The language of taste emerges from attempts to account for appreciation of the extreme variety of excellent objects of art and the nearly equally wide range of natural beauties. Use of the term 'taste' and its synonyms in other languages arose in Europe in the sixteenth and seventeenth centuries, and became an established theoretical term in philosophies of beauty in the eighteenth century. The term that gives this field its name, 'aesthetics,' itself came into modern usage at the same time. It was coined to refer to a kind of knowledge gained through immediate sense perception, but it was soon directed to the experience of beauty and the unique experiences of emotive insight that works of art can afford. Speculation about the nature of the aesthetic as well as explorations of taste made for a rich brew of developing philosophical ideas regarding perception, pleasure, art, and beauty in early modern philosophy.

While this essay concerns the concept of taste in western philosophical aesthetics, this is not a culture-bound metaphor limited to philosophy grounded in Europe. Use of taste to refer to aesthetic and artistic appreciation is present in other philosophical cultures as well, most notably in the long tradition that makes use of the concept of *rasa* in India. *Rasa*, which can also mean 'taste' or 'savor,' has been a conceptual foundation for Indian aesthetic theory since ancient times. It forms the metaphoric basis of theories of discernment and appreciation of art and was especially developed to account for the appreciation of emotive expression. Thus these two very different philosophical traditions employ a gustatory foundation to articulate the appreciative and complex apprehension of art.

'Taste' is a term literally employed to refer to one of the five senses, the one that provides gustatory discrimination and enjoyment. As a bodily sense, taste is inevitably linked with *pleasure* or *displeasure*; that is to say, it is a sensory response that tends to carry a positive or negative valance. This affective component is one of the features of gustatory taste that lends itself to employment as a metaphor of aesthetic enjoyment, for the object of taste is not only perceived but also liked or disliked. What is more, the objects of gustatory taste that can be appreciated are enormous, and they vary quite subtly. A person of limited palate may not care whether he or she is eating a well-prepared meal, but one with a finely developed sense of taste is able to discern even small amounts of the seasonings that went into its preparation. The sense of taste, therefore, is the metaphor employed in theories of the appreciation of objects of nature and of art, where one also may be dull or sensitive to subtle perceptual qualities.

One of the most salient features of the use of a sense metaphor for aesthetic appreciation is the requirement of first-hand experience. Discernment of aesthetic properties of art or nature occurs only when one has direct experience of the object, which arouses appreciative pleasure as a signal of the apprehension of aesthetic quality. Just as one cannot decide that soup is well-seasoned without actually sipping it, so one cannot conclude that music is lyrical and moving without hearing it. No second-hand account will suffice to make the aesthetic judgement.

Most early writers on taste agreed that there is a natural disposition to enjoy objects of beauty in most human perceivers, although that disposition requires experience and education to function at its best. As Voltaire put it: taste "is a quick discernment like that of the tongue and palate, and . . . like them, anticipates reflection; like the palate, it voluptuously relishes what is good; and it rejects the bad with loathing; it is also, like the palate, often uncertain and doubtful . . . and sometimes requires habit to help it form." (Voltaire 1971 [1757]: 761) The need to educate taste is important, for the sense metaphor can too easily suggest that taste is just a 'natural' ability. This error is perhaps promoted by the choice of this particular sense as the root metaphor, because the bodily need to eat, which is abetted by the sense of taste, would seem to be built into the human frame for survival purposes. But aesthetic taste, however grounded in natural dispositions, clearly requires cultivation for all but the simplest beauties, and the same can be said for sophisticated gustatory taste, as Voltaire points out. Situations that are likely to promote the cultivation of refined taste, such as leisure, education, and a degree of comfort, tinge the notion of aesthetic discernment with a certain social privilege. (Taste can be a term of manners as well, employed to describe the sensitivity required for polite social interactions and appropriate behavior.) Thinking about taste was incorporated into eighteenth-century debates over mental faculties, specifically whether reason or sense was more central to the perception of beauty. The use of the metaphor of taste weighed in on the side of interpreting aesthetic appreciation as a kind of sensibility, although some theorists such as Edmund Burke insisted on the role of understanding in determining appreciation. In any case, taste soon became the chief term employed to explain the perception of beauty.

As soon as the language of taste entered discourse about art and beauty, certain problems that it raises became the focus of debate. The concept emphasizes the subjectivity of experiences of beauty, understood as a particular type of pleasure, and pleasure is necessarily located in a perceiving subject. But this is not the whole story, for 'judgements of taste' also are about objects: the statement that a work of art is beautiful is not just a report that it pleases the speaker, but a debatable claim that refers to putative qualities of that object (such as harmony, balance, power, profundity) that may be noticed and enjoyed by others. Apt as the sensory metaphor might be to describe varying abilities to perceive and appreciate aesthetic qualities, however, taste is also the sense that by tradition is considered to admit the most variety and idiosyncracy of all the senses. As the ancients put it, *de gustibus, non est disputandum*: there is no disputing about taste. But is there no disputing about art? Hardly. Works of art are among the most scrutinized, assessed, criticized, and lauded of human accomplishments. The metaphor of taste seems right on target to describe the individual attention and response required of aesthetic appreciation; it seems less adequate to accommodate the critical discourse art invites. This realization initiated the central theoretical debate of early modern aesthetics: how and whether *standards* could be developed for taste.

Two influential theorists who contributed to the discussion of standards for taste were the Scottish empiricist David Hume (1711–1776) and the German philosopher Immanuel Kant (1724–1804). Hume makes central use of the idea that taste in art is developed in ways rather similar to taste for food or drink. He regards the recognition of value qualities in objects to be a function of the pleasure and pain responses of perceivers, and the similar constitution of all human beings furnishes the grounds for agreement about matters of value. To function properly, the evaluative sentiments must be in good working order. Just as a person with a bad cold is not in a position to assess the qualities of a meal, so an inexperienced and naive person is not well situated to judge the qualities of art. Hume advances his argument on behalf of standards of taste with an anecdote about two tasters of wine who are ridiculed because they can detect faint traces of metal and leather in a hogshead of wine that no one else can taste. But they are vindicated in the end, because when the cask is drained it is found to contain a key attached to a leather thong, and the discerning tasters are proved to have the most delicate taste, "where the organs are so fine as to allow nothing to escape them, and at the same time so exact as to perceive every ingredient in the composition" (Hume 1898 [1757]: 273).

With practice and education, nearly everyone is capable of developing a degree of delicacy of taste, for Hume is confident that the psychological and dispositional constitutions of all people are as reliably similar as the morphological constancies that govern normally functioning senses. And even those who fail at delicacy can recognize the good taste of critics of finer discernment. Indeed, the ultimate standard of taste in Hume's mind must be the body of sophisticated judges, whose opinions converge over time in agreement about the works of art that most repay attention and deliver the highest degree of appreciation.

Exactly what qualities the delicate taste discerns is a question Hume declined to answer. Unlike many of his contemporaries, who speculated that 'uniformity amidst variety' (Francis Hutcheson) or a 'line of grace' (William Hogarth) might underlie all perceptions of beauty, Hume recognized that the diversity of objects that reward aesthetic attention is too heterogeneous to be reducible to a formula. He never fastens upon any particular objective qualities that correlate with the experience of beauty, preferring to let the verdict of history advance supreme examples of the best art to whet and hone the delicate taste of critics and to perpetuate traditions of good taste. One of the chief means by which one can develop the delicacy of one's own aesthetic taste is to practice enjoying the great works of art that have already achieved recognition and withstood the test of time.

Kant, an appreciative critic of Hume, was wholly unsatisfied with the conclusion that taste emerges as a general agreement among most good critics. He demanded a stronger brand of universality for aesthetic judgements, which requires him to emphasize the distinction between that which is merely pleasant (such as bodily pleasure) and that which is beautiful (Kant 1987 [1790]: 55). Food and drink, for example, afford mere bodily pleasure, which can never achieve the universality and importance of aesthetic judgements. The judgement of beauty indicates a brand of pleasure that is not rooted in individual bodies replete with their idiosyncratic differences. It is grounded in the recognition of a harmony between the form of the aesthetic object and the structures of rationality and understanding, which, being the same in all rational creatures, demand a common recognition and qualify as 'universal' for all perceivers. To account for his analysis of taste, Kant was particular about the type of pleasure that qualifies as aesthetic: it is not sensuous or rooted in the body, it is not a product of satisfied desire, it does not rely even on a preconceived idea of what the object of enjoyment ought to be or what it is for. It is, in short, quite 'disinterested.' In his analysis of taste, Kant advanced the modern distinction between *aesthetic* values and other kinds of values and objects of pleasure or satisfaction: moral, cognitive, instrumental.

Debates over the relativity of taste and the possibility of standards for taste are embedded in consideration of pleasure and of the qualities that trigger that pleasure. The reliance of taste and appreciation on pleasure generates a set of problems for the philosopher of aesthetics. Does the evident subjectivity of pleasure entail a greater degree of relativity for aesthetic judgements than for other value judgements? Do aesthetic qualities have any objective or 'real' standing? In the formative years of early modern aesthetics it was fairly widely granted that 'beauty' properly refers to the pleasure response of perceivers, but the speculation that there are qualities that this pleasure signals never disappeared. Moreover, even if 'beauty' may be analyzed as a way of talking about subjective responses, other aesthetic qualities, such as 'balanced' or 'strident' resist this treatment and seem to demand more particular reference to the properties possessed by the object of appreciation. It is these latter types of aesthetic qualities that Hume's delicate taste seems most appropriate to account for, whereas Kant's pure judgement of taste pertains to beauty. (Kant discussed other judgements of taste as well: notably the dependent beauty of art and the powerful emotion of the sublime. However, it is the pure judgement of taste that, perhaps unfortunately, receives most attention in the overall system of his aesthetic theory.) Questions about the status of aesthetic properties continue to be a subject for contemporary debate.

Contemporary debates about taste

The metaphor of taste entered common parlance and became rather taken for granted in aesthetic theory; but in the mid twentieth century it was injected with new vigor and controversy by the arguments advanced by Frank Sibley in a series of essays that invoke taste in an analysis of aesthetic qualities. Aesthetic objects are not just works of art or objects that we happen to appreciate; they are objects that are assessed and appreciated in virtue of certain qualities. But what kinds of qualities? This question links the standard for taste with the ontological status of aesthetic properties.

Sibley's argument relies on a distinction between aesthetic and non-aesthetic qualities (Sibley 1959). Some qualities of art can be noticed by anyone with normally functioning senses who is paying sufficient attention. For example, the fact that a play contains four characters is a quality readily discernible to anyone who can see or hear and count. This kind of quality is 'non-aesthetic'; other examples of non-aesthetic qualities include square, loud, pale, sonnet, and in a minor key. But these qualities are also value-neutral; they do not label the aesthetic attributes for which one praises or rejects art or any other object. Aesthetic qualities are the properties that distinguish an object as worthy of appreciation or criticism: delicate, elegant, powerful, profound, stiff, awkward, and so on are examples of aesthetic qualities. They are not easily discerned by all perceivers but rather require the exercise of a certain sensitivity that Sibley, following tradition, labels 'taste.' Because there is more variation in taste than there is in sense acuity, aesthetic judgements are more likely to diverge than descriptions about non-aesthetic qualities.

Even assuming that aesthetic qualities ultimately depend upon non-aesthetic qualities, the former cannot be inferred from the presence of the latter. That is, the aesthetic property of being delicate depends upon the presence of non-aesthetic properties such as thin or gently curving. If one praises a vase or bowl as delicate, one might well point to those properties in explanation of the aesthetic predicate. At the same time, the presence of the non-aesthetic properties does not guarantee the aesthetic; they do not constitute sufficient conditions. An object that is thin and curved might be insipid or dull rather than delicate. Therefore one needs taste to discern the aesthetic quality and cannot infer it from the presence of the non-aesthetic qualities. The reason for this relates to the particularity of the aesthetic object; one notes certain unique features in aesthetic evaluation. Sibley's use of taste thus follows closely the reasons invoked in the original coinage of the metaphor, though his analysis of the logic of taste is considerably more exact than one finds in earlier writing.

What is the status of the qualities that taste recognizes? Sibley and others insist that they are not properties that can be picked out by ordinary sense perception the way that color or shape may be. Yet they are also not interpreted as projections on the part of the percipient. There is considerable debate over the ontological status of aesthetic qualities. Some philosophers take a realist stance and argue that aesthetic qualities are actual properties of objects. Perhaps they are 'supervenient' properties dependent upon non-aesthetic properties, such that objects with the very same non-aesthetic properties must have the same aesthetic properties. Or they might be described as 'emergent' properties that result from combinations of more easily discerned qualities. Thus if a piece of music is judged to be strident, this property might emerge from the combination of more readily agreed-upon properties, such as loud, brassy, and discordant. Whether aesthetic properties are interpreted along realist lines, such that they belong to the object, or non-realist lines, such that they are dependent upon the differing responses of perceivers, is another continuing subject of debate.

Good and bad taste

The foregoing issues reveal an ambiguity or duality embedded in the concept of aesthetic discernment that emerges from the taste metaphor. Taste may be considered an ability to discern subtle qualities in objects: in food or drink the person with (fine) taste can notice trace quantities of herbs or other flavors that lie beneath the threshold of detectability for others. Someone with good artistic taste is more able to discern the subtle points of style that distinguish a genuine painting of an old master from a modern forgery; he or she is perhaps able immediately to tell Vivaldi from Bach without looking at the disk label, can order the chronology of Henry James by noticing the ripening style of his writing. Acuity for properties such as these is part of the ability to rank objects of taste in terms of quality as well. The gourmet taster can select the better wine, the more aged cheese, the subtler dish. In art the person of taste is able to discern higher quality artifacts from run-of-the-mill, though to the uninitiated they appear more or less the same. Thus – as the framers of the metaphor would be quick to point out – aesthetic taste no less than gustatory taste can be developed and refined, and when taste refers to an ability to detect fine or subtle qualities it is a term of praise.

A second, related meaning implicit in 'taste' is laden with even heavier normative weight: taste can also indicate a measure of the quality of an object that is gauged by the amount and nature of pleasure that an object affords to a person of *good* taste. For Kant, we recall, the judgement of taste joins an object of perception with disinterested pleasure. And colloquially we speak of having a taste for something, that is, having a preference, which means taking more pleasure or delight in one particular type of object rather than another. Demonstrably, not everyone delights in the same objects, and those who diverge from established norms are apt to be criticized for *bad* taste.

To accuse a person of bad taste is a severe criticism that may invoke failings aesthetic, moral, and social. Especially if one is at the receiving end of such a charge, one may resentfully scoff at the position of the judge and the soundness of the criteria used to distinguish good from bad taste. (The lexicon of this kind of distinction includes terms such as highbrow, lowbrow, and the perhaps much worse middlebrow; high and low art; fine art versus craft and popular art; kitsch, and so forth.) Those who conceive of themselves as having good taste may condescend to those with 'inferior' tastes, while the latter may consider the former mere snobs with no objective standards to support their own preferences. Indeed, the tradition of fine art (as opposed to craft, decoration, or entertainment) is often confounded with the category of 'high' art (as opposed to 'low' or 'merely popular') art.

This blending of concepts suggests that objects of high aesthetic quality must be by their very nature difficult, such that only a few will be able truly to appreciate them. The very popularity of certain types of art (some kinds of movies and music, for example – sometimes called 'mass' art) may seem to be evidence for the absence of aesthetic quality. This ironically splits actual aesthetic pleasure from the idea of the best aesthetic taste. Suspicions leading in this direction have led some theorists to the conclusion that the very idea of taste is more of a social than an aesthetic category, that the elite of any society more or less impose their mandarin tastes on the public, which dutifully acknowledges the superiority of the objects of elite preference while pursuing their own more swinish and amusing tastes. Perhaps the most well-known of such approaches is represented by the French sociologist Pierre Bourdieu (1979), who argues that aesthetic preferences are the product of class distinctions rather than the recognition of standards of quality. While Bourdieu's chief goal is to underscore the class determinants of aesthetic distinctions, his study also revives attention to the sense metaphor. While some seek to include food and drink as legitimate objects of aesthetic appreciation, thereby lifting literal taste to an aesthetic status, Bourdieu argues the converse: different eating habits, which divide people by class and occupation, in fact represent the only manifestation of real taste. The idea of aesthetic taste is social imposition in disguise.

Perhaps the most intriguing split between good and bad, high and low tastes, however, is not exhibited between different social classes, for one and the same individual may harbor tastes for radically different types of art and aesthetic objects. Moreover, one may have an intense liking for art that one considers in highly dubious taste, such as horror movies or sentimental romances or marching bands. Taste describes a disposition to take pleasure in (respond positively to) certain objects and works of art, as well as the ability to discern and assess aesthetic qualities. But there can be considerable disparity between the pleasure that art delivers, especially the immediate pleasure, and art's recognized merit. This observation severs the tight connection between taste and pleasure that forged the first use of the metaphor of taste. Or rather, it leads us to refine the sense of 'pleasure' that is appropriate to describe aesthetic appreciation. There are different kinds of aesthetic pleasure, some of which are so taxing that the use of that particular term seems almost perverse. Bernard Bosanquet (1915) distinguished 'easy' from 'difficult' beauty, and similarly one may consider some pleasures more difficult to achieve than others, albeit more rewarding in the long run. This is only a superficial paradox. Difficult pleasure may include appreciation of art with actually painful subject matter such as tragedy, or of complex works that demand the kind of focus and attention that frequently one is too tired or distracted to undertake. Indeed one way to account for a liking for objects of acknowledged poor taste is that one seeks the immediately pleasant as easier than the truly good but demanding, for complex art can strain both the head and the heart (Levinson 1996). But the easier pleasures of amusement quickly pale and rarely sustain pleasure after repeated exposure. These distinctions help to reconcile any divergence between immediate preferences and the works one recognizes as genuinely worthy objects of taste.

Although the historical framework that lent taste vigor as a philosophical concept crucial to aesthetic theory has receded, there remain a number of points of mystery and argument that keep the concept alive and dense. Some maintain allegiance to the original metaphor, others dispute its suitability to capture aesthetic discernment. Some seek to include literal taste as a sense that affords aesthetic appreciation of food and drink; others continue to insist that only the eyes and ears are inlets for aesthetic perceptual experience. And popular culture and public arts are especially vital grounds for disputes over good and bad taste. Thus centuries after its entry into modern theory, the concept of taste remains alive and controversial.

See also Empiricism, Hume, Kant, Sibley, The aesthetic, Aesthetic universals, Beauty, High versus low art.

References

Bourdieu, P. (1989 [1979]) *Distinction: A Social Critique of the Judgment of Taste*, trans. R. Nice, London: Routledge.
Bosanquet, B. (1963 [1915]) *Three Lectures on Aesthetic*, Indianapolis: Bobbs-Merrill.
Burke, E. (1968 [1757]) *A Philosophical Enquiry into the Origin of our Ideas of the Sublime and Beautiful*, ed. J. T. Boulton, Notre Dame, Ind.: University of Notre Dame Press.
Hogarth, W. (1955 [1753]) *An Analysis of Beauty*, Oxford: Oxford University Press.
Hume, D. (1898 [1757]) "Of the Standard of Taste," in *Essays Moral, Political, and Literary*, ed. T. H. Green and T. H. Grose, 2 vols, London: Longmans, Green.
Hutcheson, F. (1973 [1725]) *An Inquiry Concerning Beauty, Order, Harmony, Design*, ed. P. Kivy, The Hague: Martinus Nijhoff.
Kant, I. (1987 [1790]) *Critique of Judgment*, trans. W. Pluhar, Indianapolis: Hackett.
Levinson, J. (1996) *The Pleasures of Aesthetics*, Ithaca: Cornell University Press.
Sibley, F. (1959) "Aesthetic Concepts," *Philosophical Review* 68: 421–50.
Voltaire (1757) "Taste," in *Encyclopédie*, ed. Diderot and D'Alembert. (In English in A. Gerard (1971 [1759]) *An Essay on Taste*, Menston: Scholar Press.)

Further reading

Bender, J. W. (1996) "Realism, Supervenience, and Irresolvable Aesthetic Disputes," *Journal of Aesthetics and Art Criticism* 54: 371–81. (A contribution to the debate over the status of aesthetic properties.)
Cohen, T. (1973) "Aesthetic/Non-aesthetic and the Concept of Taste," *Theoria* 39: 113–52. (This essay is one of many critical evaluations of Sibley's view.)
—— (1993) "High and Low Thinking about High and Low Art," *Journal of Aesthetics and Art Criticism* 51: 151–6. (Cohen argues for communities of taste that link people together.)
Dickie, G. (1996) *The Century of Taste*, Oxford: Oxford University Press. (A brief history of eighteenth-century aesthetics.)
Eaton, M. (1994) "The Intrinsic, Non-Supervenient Nature of Aesthetic Properties," *Journal of Aesthetics and Art Criticism* 52: 383–97.
Goldman, A. H. (1993) "Realism about Aesthetic Properties," *Journal of Aesthetics and Art Criticism* 51: 31–7. (Both these articles analyze the status of aesthetic properties.)
Goswamy, B. N. (1986) *The Essence of Indian Art*, San Francisco: Asian Art Museum of San Francisco. (The Indian concept of *rasa* is explained in this book.)
Mattick, P. Jr. (1993) *Eighteenth Century Aesthetics and the Reconstruction of Art*, Cambridge: Cambridge University Press. (Essays on eighteenth-century aesthetics that emphasize the social and historical context of the development of taste theories.)
Korsmeyer, C. (1999) *Making Sense of Taste: Food and Philosophy*, Ithaca: Cornell University Press. (A study of the gustatory sense of taste, its history and philosophical fate, and its aesthetic meaning.)
Mothersill, M. (1984) *Beauty Restored*, Oxford: Oxford University Press. (A discussion of beauty that includes a sophisticated analysis of taste in the history of aesthetics.)
Schaper, E. (ed.) (1983) *Pleasure, Preference, and Value*, Cambridge: Cambridge University Press. (Schaper's own essay in this volume is an appraisal and appreciation of Kant's approach to taste.)
Shiner, R. (1996) "The Causal Theory of Taste," *Journal of Aesthetics and Art Criticism* 54: 237–49. (This article is a critique of the taste metaphor for aesthetic appreciation, focusing on Hume's version.)

18
AESTHETIC UNIVERSALS

Denis Dutton

Art itself is a cultural universal; that is, there are no known human cultures in which there cannot be found some form of what we might reasonably term aesthetic or artistic interest, performance, or artifact production: including sculptures and paintings, dancing and music, oral and written fictional narratives, body adornment and decoration. This does not mean that all cultures possess all the various arts. For example, there is no clear analogue in European tradition for the Japanese tea ceremony, which is nevertheless considered by many to be an artform (Okakura 1906). On the other hand there are cases such as the Dinka, a Nilotic herding people who have no developed indigenous visual art or carving. Instead, their aesthetic interests seem to be directed toward poetic expression and, in the visual realm, toward the markings on the cattle that are so important to their lives: they are, so to speak, keen connoisseurs of cattle markings (Coote 1992). Even within the same cultural region there may be sharp contrasts: in the Sepik River region of the northern New Guinea there is an enormous variety of wood carving, while in the Highlands of the same country there is very little carving, with vast effort channeled instead into body adornment and the production of decorated fighting shields.

Universalism in traditional aesthetics

Such diverse genres and cultural variability of ways in which aesthetic and artistic interests are focused and expressed raises the question, might it be possible to identify underlying universal features present in all or nearly all artistic forms? It could be argued that much of the philosophy of art and aesthetics has amounted to an attempt to reveal the most important underlying universal features of art. So, to name three aestheticians, Leo Tolstoy believed the universal essence of art is its communicative capacity to tie people to one another (Tolstoy 1960), Friedrich Schiller argued that art derives from a human impulse to play (Schiller 1967), while Clive Bell found what he considered to be its essential nature in "Significant Form"

(Bell 1914). All such attempts to identify universal features of art share an element in common: they presuppose or posit the existence of a fundamental human nature, a set of characteristics, including interests and desires, uniformly and cross-culturally present in the constitution of human persons. In aesthetics, the emphasis on a stable human nature has been taken to entail two further ideas: first, that artistic activity of some kind will be a predictable component of any society (as predictable as, for instance, the use of language, the making of moral judgements, the existence of family organization and the regulation of sex), and second, that art will itself have predictable content identifiable cross-culturally (just as unrelated languages possess similar syntactic features, kinship systems incorporate some kind of incest avoidance, and moral rules usually forbid in-group homicide).

This universalist conception therefore regards art as a natural category of human activity and experience. This is not in itself a new idea, but goes back to the greatest naturalist of Greek philosophy, Aristotle. He argued that we could expect to find similar arts (by which he also meant technologies) being invented in independent human cultures all over the world. In discussing various ways in which the state has been divided into classes by cultures of the Mediterranean, Aristotle makes his view clear in an aside:

> practically everything has been discovered on many occasions – or rather an infinity of occasions – in the course of ages; for necessity may be supposed to have taught men the inventions which were absolutely required, and when these were provided, it was natural that other things which would adorn and enrich life should grow up by degrees.
>
> (Aristotle, *Politics* 1329b25)

As the existence of these arts and technologies sprang from a shared human nature, Aristotle further believed that their basic forms would also display similarities: so genres of spoken narrative and literary arts would everywhere evolve comedic and serious or tragic forms, there would be carvings, pictures or other representations, and, as with the development of Greek tragedy, these artforms would become more complex over time.

Aristotle regarded the visual and dramatic arts as naturally mimetic, in some manner representing something, whether in words, marble, or paint. He viewed the human interest in representations – pictures, drama, poetry, statues – as an innate tendency, and he was the first philosopher to attempt to argue, rather than simply assert, that this is the case:

> for it is an instinct of human beings from childhood to engage in imitation (indeed, this distinguishes them from other animals: man is the most

imitative of all, and it is through imitation that he develops his earliest understanding); and it is equally natural that everyone enjoys imitative objects. A common occurrence indicates this: we enjoy contemplating the most precise images of things whose actual sight is painful to us, such as forms of the vilest animals and of corpses.

(Aristotle, *Poetics* 1448b)

Aristotle's frame of reference for generalizations was specific to ancient Greek culture, but it is impossible to dispute the claim that children everywhere play in imitation of their elders, each other, even animals and machines, and that such imaginative imitation appears to be a necessary, or at least normal, component in the enculturation of individuals. The other side of Aristotle's mimetic naturalism holds that human beings everywhere enjoy to see and experience imitations, whether pictures, carvings, fictional narrative or play-acting. For Aristotle, the child's fascination with a doll's house with its tiny kitchen and table settings is not to be reduced to a desire for adult power, but in its imitative play is based in the instinctive delight in representation as such. This pleasure, he argues, can be independent of the nature of the subject represented: that is why the sight of a large, black fly walking over ripe fruit might disgust us in the kitchen, but can be a source of delight in a meticulously painted seventeenth-century Dutch still life.

A concept of naturalism akin to Aristotle's, but without its specified content, was advocated in the eighteenth century by Immanuel Kant and David Hume. Kant claimed that judgements about artistic beauty, which he called 'judgements of taste,' are more than expressions of merely personal, subjective liking: they have the necessary property of demanding universal agreement from the rest of mankind (Kant 1987). While Kant's aesthetics treat the demand for universality as a purely logical feature of judgements of taste, he also thought that there was a uniformity of human nature that validated the demand. He called this the *sensus communis*, or shared human sense. The pleasure of beauty for Kant derived from the way in which the experience of a beautiful object engaged the harmonized activity of the imagination and rational understanding in what he called disinterested contemplation, that is, experience of the object cut off from the merely personal and idiosyncratic desires and preferences of the individual. If I receive aesthetic pleasure from a Beethoven sonata, my affirmation of its beauty implies the notion that all other human beings, were they in my position as listener, should agree. Kant's idea of the uniformity of human nature requires this implication, despite the fact that, as Kant also realized, in actual life there is frequent disagreement on questions of beauty: there are too many personal and cultural variables which affect aesthetic judgements to expect agreement in all cases.

David Hume, in his 1757 essay, "Of the Standard of Taste," also acknowledged disagreements in questions of evaluating beauty (Hume 1987). He
nevertheless held, not unlike Kant, that "the general principles of taste are
uniform in human nature." It is such uniformity, in Hume's view, that makes it
possible that the "same Homer who pleased at Athens and Rome two thousand
years ago, is still admired at Paris and London." While we may be temporarily
blinded by fashion or prejudice to the value of classics such as the Homeric
poems, we will sooner or later see their beauties, "which are naturally fitted to
excite agreeable sentiments" in human beings of every epoch. The best works of
art pass Hume's so-called test of time because they appeal to a human nature that
remains constant in different cultures and in different historic periods.

Empirical psychology and universalism

In the twentieth century, research into the existence of universal aesthetic
values came primarily from psychology and anthropology. Although the speculative psychological theories of art in the work of Freud and Jung no longer
excite scientific interest, the same cannot be said for more empirically-based
psychology, especially work centered on perception. D. E. Berlyne's *Aesthetics
and Psychobiology* (1971) summarized the state of psychological aesthetics
and has inspired considerable research since it was published. Following
Berlyne, Colin Martindale has conducted many experiments attempting to
establish universal patterns of stylistic change in art (Martindale 1990). In a
varied series of studies conducted since the late 1960s, Martindale and his
colleagues have shown that artistic change in all cultures rests not on an
instinctive 'will to innovate' but rather on a universal human desire to avoid
repetition and boredom. The craving for novelty is based on well-known
psychological principles of habituation, the principle that predicts the tenth
mouthful of an interesting and delicious food will not be as piquant as the
first, that people will sometimes change perfectly adequate wallpaper, and that
ten Vivaldi concertos in a row may well prove tedious. Martindale calls habituation "the single force that has pushed art always in a consistent direction
ever since the first work of art was made" (ibid.: 11). It is the universal
mainspring of artistic change.

Among many cross-cultural examples adduced by Martindale is the evolution
of similes in French poetry. In the eighteenth century, André Chénier wrote,
"Beneath your fair head, a white delicate neck / Inclines and would outshine the
brightness of snow." The connection between the white neck and snow might
have struck its original audience as fresh; the connection is certainly closer than
one found in Laforgue's later line that the sun "lies on top of the hill . . . like a

gland torn out of a neck." Sun and gland are more remote images, but not as far apart as the relations given in two still later lines from André Breton: "I love you opposite the seas / Red like the egg when it is green." This increase in metaphorical distance – outlandishness – is an example of "a historical movement of similes and metaphors away from consistency toward remoteness and incongruity" (Martindale 1990: 21). This progression can be generalized as follows: in the arts, a form, genre, or style is invented, and once established is gradually elaborated over time by increasing what Martindale calls the general 'primordial content' of the style: its use of emotion, greater complexity and variability, more ornamentation. The 'arousal potential' of the style or genre is gradually increased until some end point is reached where it is fully exploited. Attention then turns to the style itself, which is typically changed or abandoned in favor of a new style. The cycle repeats itself and this new style matures, again through the incremental increase of emotion, complexity and so on. Though Martindale does not refer to Aristotle's evolutionary sketch of the history of Greek tragedy, Aristotle's account – increasing numbers of actors, the introduction of painted sets, complexity of plotting, language and costuming – fits his theory, and so, Martindale is able to demonstrate, do the histories of British, French and American poetry, American fiction and popular music lyrics, European and American painting, Gothic architecture, Greek vases, Egyptian tomb painting, pre-Columbian sculpture, Japanese prints, New England gravestones and various composers and musical traditions. As audiences become satiated, artists increase the psychic impact of artforms by turning up the volume, increasing density of words, vividness of images, making things more emotional, erotic or shocking. The history of movies bears out Martindale's hypothesis well, with general increases in violent and erotic content for the last century. Similar patterns can be seen in the history of music in the progression from baroque to classic to romantic to modern.

The most recent research on universal features in art has come out of evolutionary psychology, which attempts to understand and explain the experience and capacities of the human mind in terms of characteristics it developed in the long evolutionary history of the human species. Evolutionary psychology postulates that human pleasures, such as the pleasures of sex or the enjoyment of sweet or fatty foods, have their genesis in evolutionary history: our ancestors who actively enjoyed sex and consumed fats and carbohydrates survived and left more living offspring than those who did not. The same argument can be applied to countless other aspects of the emotional dispositions of human beings, including, for example, responses to human faces and comportment, or to the threats and opportunities presented by the natural world and its flora and fauna. The argument can also be applied to art and its content.

Studies of human reactions to photographs of landscape habitats show patterns which are stable across cultures (Orians and Heerwagen 1992). Given a series of photographs, older children and adults, familiar with a wide variety of landscape types, showed no pattern of preference for any one type of landscape (scenes included tropical, deciduous, and coniferous forests, desert and East African savannah). Young children, however, demonstrate a preference for open savannahs, even when the children had never seen such landscapes in real life. This predisposition survives from the adaptive history of the early ancestors of contemporary humans, whose emotional responses to the natural world were adaptively formed in the Pleistocene savannahs of East Africa. It is an expression of a general human tendency to prefer landscapes combining open spaces and trees (preferably trees that fork near the ground and so offer escape from predation), water, green flora, flowers, and variegated cloud patterns.

These preferences received unexpected confirmation when two artists, Vitaly Komar and Alexander Melamid, gained financial backing to conduct an extensive, systematic poll of the art preferences of people of ten different countries in Europe, Asia, Africa, and the Americas (Wypijewski 1997). Their poll recorded surprisingly uniform interests in the pictorial content of art worldwide. The most favored color was blue, followed by green. Generally, people expressed a liking for realistic, representative painting, with water, trees and shrubbery, human figures (women and children preferred, or historical figures) and animals, especially large mammals, both wild and domestic. Komar and Melamid used the poll findings as the basis for producing paintings: an *America's Most Wanted* painting and one for each of the nine other countries. The works had obvious tongue-in-cheek elements (the American painting showed children, George Washington and a hippo beside a lake), but they were accurately in line with the poll results, tending to resemble each other, and moreover to resemble much standard calendar art, photographic or painted, of outdoor scenes. In commenting on the poll and their work, Arthur Danto has suggested that the fact the Komar and Melamid paintings looked like realistic European landscape or calendar art, rather than resembling the indigenous art of any of the countries where the poll was conducted, demonstrates the international power of calendars to form and influence conventional artistic taste and content preference. Kenyans, Danto notes, preferred an art that more resembled a realistic Hudson River School landscape than any recognizable African style; they also tended according to the poll to have calendars in their homes (Danto 1997: 134). Danto's explanation, however, begs the wider question: why do calendars worldwide feature landscapes that match the very content evolutionary psychology would predict? The answer to that question may well be the evolutionary psychology hypothesis which posits a Pleistocene genesis for such basic pictorial interests.

Another realm of uniformity of content is in narrative fiction. It has been said that the themes and subjects of literature are limitless. While this may be true in principle, in actual fact most world literatures tend to return a limited list of abiding vital human interests (Carroll 1995). These prominently include questions of life and death, sex and love, conflict in social relations, exploration adventure and struggle and success in overcoming adversity. Aristotle had already noted the tendency for tragic narrative to focus on the disruption of family relations: a mortal dispute between two strangers will be of lesser interest compared to a story of two brothers who fight to the death (*Poetics* 1453). Indeed, conflict within families is one of the most persistent themes in literature, from the Greek tragedies through Shakespeare, the Hindu epics, Chinese and Japanese literature, down to this afternoon's television soap operas.

Joining a long line of philosophic speculation that goes back to Plato, the linguist Steven Pinker has argued that drama and fictional narratives have didactic or instructional value for life. Stories are a way to explore strategies and scenarios for social and family relations and the general challenges of life before they are faced in reality: a kind of practice for living (Pinker 1997). If the basic adaptive value of story-telling for human beings was as practice for survival and reproduction, it should not surprise us that the prevalent, universal themes of the history of literature should also involve questions of survival and reproduction: sex, love, and death, as they would impinge on the life of a protagonist and his or her kin.

The interest in identifying such grand universal themes in literature may be granted, but it is hardly the whole story of art. The content of art which evolutionary psychology both partially predicts and partially explains as universal is not peculiar to high or fine art in any cultural tradition: this content is continuous with the content of the most mundane instances of story-telling, gossip, news gathering (including criteria of what counts as news), household decoration, craft traditions, popular entertainments such as television dramas or sentimental fiction, tourist snapshots and postcards, sporting and patriotic events, landscaping of public parks and private gardens, and on and on, into virtually all areas of life and experience. So what of the so-called high arts? Ellen Dissanayake has theorized that the deepest aesthetic experiences bring together elements that are layered in the aesthetic response to art objects, performances, and occasions. These include the appeal of basic experiential qualities (such as sparkling lights, vivid colors, or arresting rhythms); the incorporation of such experience into rituals and activities which have a power to unite people in a sense of common purpose or shared emotion; the achievement of what she calls 'evocative resonance,' a feeling that there is deep and rich meaning embedded in the experience; and 'satisfying fullness,' the feeling that in the art experience something complete and significant has been accomplished by the percipient (Dissanayake 1997). The sense of intense social involvement in the experience of art is emphasized by Dissanayake, along with the fact that art works of all kinds offer ways in which human beings can enjoy the pleasure putting to work their powers of discrimination and evaluation. The systematic application of these latter capacities, along with extensive knowledge of an artform, becomes connoisseurship.

Universal features of art

Given all that cross-cultural investigation has so far accumulated, it is possible to list the signal characteristics of art considered as a universal, cross-cultural category. The features that follow are not necessarily criteria for the presence of art; on the other hand, it would be difficult to imagine a social practice that was characterized by most of them which was not art in some sense. Every feature on the list is, however, also present in non-art experiences and activities; reminders of these are included in parentheses.

1   Expertise or virtuosity. The manufacture of the art object or execution of the artistic performance usually requires the exercise of a specialized skill. This skill may be learned in an apprentice tradition in some societies, or in others may be picked up by anyone who finds that she or he 'has a knack' for it. Where the skill is acquired by virtually everybody in the culture, such as with communal singing or dancing in some cultures, there still tend to be individuals who stand out by virtue of special talents. Technical artistic skills are noticed in societies worldwide and are generally admired. (The admiration of a recognizable skill extends to all technical areas of human activity where its presence is made apparent, from cooking to public oratory to marksmanship. In modern society, sport is a major area when technical virtuosity is publicly admired and rewarded.)

2   Non-utilitarian pleasure. Whether narrative story, crafted artifact, or visual and aural performance, the art object is viewed as a source of pleasure in itself, rather than as a practical tool or source of knowledge. The embodiment of the art work may be in some respect useful: a tool (a shield, a knife) or a means to information (a sacred poem). Aspects of the embodiment, however, give pleasure in experience aside from these practical or informational/communicative considerations. (This pleasure is called aesthetic pleasure when it is derived from the experience of art, but the pleasure of sport and play, or of watching larks soar or storm-clouds thicken, could equally be 'for its own sake.')

3 Style. Art objects and performances, including fictional or poetic narratives, are made in recognizable styles, according to rules of form and composition. The degree of stylistic determination varies greatly, as much in premodern cultures as in the arts of literate civilizations. Some art objects and performances, typically those involving religious practice, are tightly circumscribed by tradition, while others are open to free, creative, individual variation. A style may derive from a culture, or a family, or be the invention of an individual; styles involve borrowing and sudden alteration, as well as slow changes. (Style is an element in almost all cultural activities beyond art, from language use to table manners; it is crucially but not uniquely important to art.)

4 Criticism. There exists some kind of indigenous critical language of judgement and appreciation, simple or elaborate, that is applied to arts. This may include the shop talk of art producers or evaluative discourse of critics and audiences. Unlike the arts themselves, which can be immensely complicated, it has often been remarked that this critical discourse is in oral cultures sometimes rudimentary compared to the art discourse of literate European history. It can, however, be elaborate even there. (The development of a critical vocabulary and discourse, including criteria for excellence, mediocrity, competence/incompetence and failure, is intrinsic to almost all human activities outside art.)

5 Imitation. In widely varying degrees of naturalism, art objects, including sculptures, paintings, and oral narratives, represent or imitate real and imaginary experience of the world. The differences between naturalistic representation, highly stylized representation and non-imitative symbolism is generally understood by artists and their audiences. (Blueprints, newspaper story pictures, passport photographs, and road maps are equally imitations or representations. While imitation is important to much art – notable exceptions being abstract painting and music – its significance extends into all areas of human intellectual life.)

6 'Special' focus. Works of art and artistic performances are frequently bracketed off from ordinary life and made a special and dramatic focus of experience. While there are plenty of mundane artistic objects and performances (such as decorated parts of Baule looms or communal singing done to pass the time while mending fishing nets), every known culture has special art works or performances which involve what Dissanayake (1997) calls 'making special'. These objects or performance occasions are often imbued with intense emotion and sense of community. They frequently involve the combining of many different artforms, such as chanting, dancing, body decoration and dramatic lighting in the case of New Guinea sing-sings. (Outside

art, or at its fringes, political rallies, sporting events, public ceremonies, such as coronations and weddings, and religious meetings of all sorts also invoke a sense of specialness.)

7   Finally, the experience of art is an imaginative experience for both producers and audiences. The carving may realistically represent an animal, but as a sculpture it becomes an imaginative object. The same can be said of any story well told, whether ancient mythology or personal anecdote. A passionate dance performance has an imaginative element not to be found in the group exercise of factory workers. Art of all kinds happens in the theater of the imagination: it is raised from the mundane practical world to become an imaginative experience. (At the mundane level, imagination in problem-solving, planning, hypothesizing, inferring the mental states of others or merely in day-dreaming is practically co-extensive with normal human conscious life.)

Relativism versus universalism

In the generations that have followed the Second World War, humanistic schol-arship has tended to emphasize the cultural context of all human activities. This has meant that in aesthetics, as much as in popular ethics and social theory, relativism has become a dominant orthodoxy: aesthetic values were understood as having their reality only relative to local cultural and historical conditions. A good work of art was therefore 'good' only in a specific culture; cross-cultural standards were thought impossible to ascertain. A dismissive attitude toward universal values in art has been bolstered by countless anecdotes seeming to illustrate the cross-cultural unintelligibility of the arts. One such oft-repeated story concerns the Indian sitarist who, performing before a naive Western audience, was vigorously applauded when he had finished tuning his instrument.

As mentioned earlier, theories of universal aesthetic value, which are dead set against absolute relativism, go hand-in-hand with hypotheses about the universal nature of human beings; supporters of aesthetic relativism have therefore been generally hostile to such accounts. Scientific theories of human nature have been branded 'essentialist,' and have been portrayed as potentially limiting human creativity and freedom, or as having elements in common with racist varieties of biological determinism used by fascist ideologues in the first half of the last century. The rejection of universalism, and with it the acceptance of culture as the ultimate determinant of aesthetic value, has also been seen by relativists as a way to oppose the notion of a European superiority in cultural value.

Aesthetic relativism, although adopted with the best of intentions, has blinded investigators to the elements arts have in common worldwide. Not every putative cross-cultural misunderstanding can be turned into a general denial of the possibility of universal aesthetic values. It is important to note how remarkably well the arts travel outside their home cultures: Beethoven and Shakespeare are beloved in Japan, Japanese prints are adored by Brazilians, Greek tragedy is performed worldwide, while, much to the regret of many local movie industries, Hollywood films have wide cross-cultural appeal. As for sitar concerts, anyone who has sat through the tedious tuning of a sitar might well want to applaud when the music was finally set to begin. And even Indian music itself, while it sounds initially strange to the Western ear, can be shown to rely on rhythmic pulse and acceleration, repetition, variation and surprise, as well as modulation and divinely sweet melody: in fact, all the same devices found in Western music.

A balanced view of art will take into account the vast and diverse array of cultural elements that make up the life of artistic creation and appreciation. At the same time such a view will acknowledge the universal features the arts everywhere share, and will recognize that the arts travel across cultural boundaries as well as they do because they are rooted in our common humanity.

See also Definitions of art, Taste, Hume, Kant.

References

Aristotle (1920) *Aristotle on the Art of Poetry*, trans. I. Bywater, Oxford: Oxford University Press.

Aristotle (1987) *The Poetics of Aristotle*, trans. S. Halliwell, Chapel Hill: University of North Carolina Press.

Bell, C. (1914) *Art*, London: Chatto and Windus.

Berlyne, D. E. (1971) *Aesthetics and Psychobiology*, New York: Appleton-Century-Crofts.

Carroll, J. (1995) *Evolution and Literary Theory*, Columbia: University of Missouri Press.

Coote, J. (1992) "Marvels of Everyday Vision: the Anthropology of Aesthetics and the Cattle-Keeping Nilotes," in J. Coote and A. Shelton (eds), *Anthropology, Arts and Aesthetics*, Oxford: Oxford University Press.

Danto, A. C. (1997) "Can It Be the 'Most Wanted Painting' Even If Nobody Wants It?" in J. Wypijewski (ed.), *Painting by Numbers: Komar and Melamid's Scientific Guide to Art*, New York: Farrar Straus Giroux.

Dissanayake, E. (1997) *Homo Aestheticus: Where Art Comes From and Why*, Seattle: University of Washington Press.

Hume, D. (1987) "Of the Standard of Taste," in E. F. Miller (ed.), *Essays Moral, Political, Literary*, Indianapolis: Bobbs-Merrill.

Kant, I. (1987) *Critique of Judgment*, trans. W. Pluhar, Indianapolis: Hackett.

Martindale, C. (1990) *The Clockwork Muse: the Predictability of Artistic Change*, New York: Basic Books.

Okakura, K. (1906) *The Book of Tea*, New York: Fox Duffield.

Orians, G. H. and Heerwagen, J. H. (1992) "Evolved Responses to Landscapes," in J. H. Barkow, L. Cosmides and J. Tooby (eds), *The Adapted Mind: Evolutionary Psychology and the Generation of Culture*, New York: Oxford University Press.

Pinker, S. (1997) *How the Mind Works*, New York: Norton.

Schiller, F. (1967) *On the Aesthetic Education of Man in a Series of Letters*, trans. E. M. Wilkinson and L. A. Willoughby, Oxford: Oxford University Press.

Tolstoy, L. (1960) *What Is Art?* trans. A. Maude, Indianapolis: Bobbs-Merrill.

Wypijewski, J. (ed.) (1997) *Painting by Numbers: Komar and Melamid's Scientific Guide to Art*, New York: Farrar Straus Giroux.

Further reading

Aiken, N. E. (1998) *The Biological Origins of Art*, Westport Conn.: Praeger. (A general treatment of emotional cues in art from an evolutionary perspective.)

Brown, D. E. (1991) *Human Universals*, Philadelphia: Temple University Press. (The best account of universals in human life and culture.)

Cooke, B. and Turner, F. (eds) (1999) *Biopoetics: Evolutionary Explorations in the Arts*, Lexington Ky.: ICUS. (Articles examining features as seen in the light of adaptive psychology. Includes writing on art by biologist E. O. Wilson.)

Cooke, B. and Bedaux, J. B. (eds) (1999) *Sociobiology and the Arts*, Atlanta: Rodopi. (Similar to the above anthology, with a wide variety of art themes examined.)

Dissanayake, E. (2000) *Art and Intimacy: How the Arts Began,* Seattle: University of Washington Press. (A discussion of art in terms of the biological propensities of human nature.)

Miller, G. F. (2000) *The Mating Mind: How Sexual Choice Shaped the Evolution of Human Nature*, New York: Doubleday. (An explanation of the development of art and culture in terms of the dynamics of human sexual choice in evolution.)

Turner, M. (1996) *The Literary Mind*, Oxford: Oxford University Press. (A lucid and penetrating examination of how human beings construct narratives in literature and in everyday thinking.)

Van Damme, W. (1996) *Beauty in Context: Toward an Anthropological Approach to Aesthetics*, Leiden: Brill. (An investigation of aesthetic value from a cross-cultural point of view.)

19
VALUE OF ART
Matthew Kieran

What is it for something to be valuable as art? Why, if at all, is good art so important? These are two of the most important questions in philosophical aesthetics. But to see how we may answer them we must first delineate what kind of value we may be seeking to capture. Art works can be valued in all sorts of ways. I may value a work because of its commodity value, sentimental value, historical value or because it tells me certain things I did not know. Yet valuing a work for such reasons is only contingently related to its value as art. I may, after all, learn something from a work which is appalling art.

Instrumental and intrinsic value

One standard approach, as articulated by Malcolm Budd (1995), involves contrasting instrumental and intrinsic value. If we value a work instrumentally, it is merely a contingent means to a particular end. To value Bach's *Cello Suites* just because they cheer me up implies that they are replaceable by anything else that performs the same function as well or better, whether it be a feel-good movie or a night out. However to value a work's intrinsic value is to appreciate the imaginative experience it properly affords, which may be beautiful, moving, uplifting, pleasurable, insightful, profound and so on. But it is the particular nature of the work that prescribes and guides our active mental engagement and responses to it. Hence there is something about the experience of a particular work, if it is artistically valuable, that cannot be replaced by any other.

Consider, in this light, Barber's *Adagio for Strings*. In terms of technical musical complexity the piece is very simple, indeed musical technique in the piece is so backgrounded that the listener is hardly aware of any at all. Yet in terms of its expressivity it is surely a great piece of music. It is a haunting and gravely beautiful piece which develops in a lilting, drawn-out manner one simple, continuous melody. As the melody steadfastly develops there is an emotional arc from the initial melancholic stirrings of the cello through to the increasingly sharp, highly-pitched straining dissonances of the violins which are held for a long period of time. Then we return back down to the lower reaches of the cello, now backed up by violins to give the refrain added substance and depth. It is no coincidence that *Adagio for Strings* has been used for state funerals or the opening and closing music for Oliver Stone's *Platoon*. For though the music may not be *about* anything in the strict representational sense, nonetheless its expressive development affords an analysis of the movement from, and thus interrelations and differences between, melancholy, grief and reconciliation.

Now, another piece of music may well be expressive of the affective attitude of melancholic reconciliation, but not in the very particular way that Barber's *Adagio* is, in terms of the very particular interrelations between the form of the piece and the melancholy expressed. Hence good art works are not dispensable in the way drugs are. How the effect is caused in the case of drugs is beside the point and independent of our will, but in the case of art the experience is a result of our active mental engagement with the work, so quite what and how something is conveyed is not wholly specifiable independently of particular features of the work.

However, despite its initial appeal, such an account is open to challenge. For, like Robert Stecker, one might be skeptical of claims about the intrinsic value of art works (Stecker 1997). Stecker's thought is roughly this. If we value something because of the experience it affords, then we value it because of the end realized. This implies that the value of art is instrumental. We do not value works for their own sake but because they enable us to realize certain ends such as pleasurable experiences. However, a distinction between two different types of instrumental value is required. To value something in purely instrumental terms is to value it solely as a means to the end it realizes. Consider, for example, money. Money as such has no value whatsoever except in terms of those states of affairs it enables us to realize. Moreover its relationship to those ends is an external one. The means of acquisition in the case of money plays no part in shaping or constituting the nature of the ends realized. So too, to take another example, with drugs. Some drugs induce particular pleasurable states by virtue of certain causal powers, but how the state is arrived at is external to why the end state is considered desirable. By contrast, there are many things we value instrumentally, in terms of the ends realized, which are not like this at all. For something to possess inherent value it must not only be the means to a valuable end, but the means must partly constitute and thus be internal to the ends involved. The pleasures afforded by sport, coffee drinking, smoking and good conversation are not wholly specifiable independently of the nature of the objects or activity involved. Just think, for example, how one goes about explaining the interest of sport to the uninitiated. To be sure one might start by claiming that such things give one pleasure, but rapidly one must appeal to how and why pleasure arises in ways intimately bound to the nature of the activity. One cannot specify the kind of pleasures involved in watching football, say, without describing how the game gives rise to the confrontation of combating teams, the kind of individual skills that can be deployed, the tactical guile and nous often required, and how a pass can be elegant and beautiful in its exquisite timing by beating the offside trap. So too with good art generally, and different kinds, forms and genres of art down to the level of the particular work.

Although Budd recognizes that we cannot specify the value of art works without reference to a rich characterization of the ways they afford us valuable experiences, nonetheless, Stecker claims, their value is not intrinsic. For we value such activities, watching sport or engaging with art, by virtue of the general ends they realize. Of course, we do not value them in purely instrumental terms, for the means involved in art partly constitute and shape the nature of the ends. Nonetheless, the value of art must be cashed out in terms of the ends realized. Thus the inherent value of art is a distinct form of instrumental value.

Aestheticism and the distinctive pleasures of art

The dispute over whether art's value is intrinsic or inherent belies a deep dispute in aesthetics over the value of art. The tendency to talk of the intrinsic value of art is the upshot of a tradition stemming from Kant (1928), according to which the pleasures of art should be conceived as being of a very distinct kind: aesthetic ones. Just as we admire the line, colors and complexity of form in nature – its aesthetic qualities – so too in art. Art is thus conceived as the cultural practice geared toward the intentional production of artifacts which by virtue of their grace, elegance and beauty give rise to pleasure in our contemplation and savoring of these qualities. The possible media, shaping and content of art works provide a proliferation of distinct aesthetic pleasures which nature or mere everyday objects cannot afford. True, our appreciation of many of the aesthetic qualities of art depends upon background beliefs about particular artistic categories, genres, forms and artistic intentions. But as long as we have the right kind of understanding of such things, the value of a work as art lies in its rewarding with pleasure the contemplation of its aesthetic virtues, independently of any further end or goal.

It is important not to conflate this general line with the simplistic presumption, famously articulated by Clive Bell, that only the formal qualities of a work count (Bell 1914). Sophisticated aestheticists, such as Beardsley, recognize that form is not necessarily wholly independent of content (Beardsley 1958). In a representational work, the particular way in which colors or imagery have been worked and juxtaposed is significant for what the work is doing, the shaping partly constitutes the content and the content guides the shaping. Consider Picasso's *Weeping Woman*. The paint representing the woman's fingers slashing across her face and the tear drop acidically gouging her face involves complex interrelations between the work's form and the way such form coheres with, and conveys a representation of, a particularly vicious form of grief. Appreciating the work as art does not involve delighting in the represented woman's grief as such. Rather we delight in the way in which the form of the work is an aesthetically artful and apposite means of portraying such grief. Hence the intrinsic aesthetic value of art works, by virtue of the interrelations between a work's formal aspects and its thematic content, inheres in its unity, complexity and intensity. Thus, Peter Lamarque and Stein Olsen (1994) argue, we must keep distinct the cognitive, fictive and aesthetic aspects of a work. We derive pleasure from attending to how artfully the content of a work is conveyed. The content of a work is relevant to a work's value as art, but only as an indirect side-effect. As such, the message of a work or what it represents is irrelevant to the value of a work as art. So sophisticated aestheticism holds that a work's content is relevant to its value as art if and only if the content promotes or hinders the attainment of aesthetic virtues, such as coherence, complexity, intensity or quality of artistic or thematic development, by the work's aesthetic aspect.

The account of art's value afforded by aestheticism has several key virtues. First, it seems to capture why the value of an art work is not reducible to its message. As a schoolboy, a cousin of mine was once awarded a book entitled *Ernie Elton: The Lazy Boy*. Although the ten tales contained therein are undoubtedly worthy, each constituting a moral fable about the dangers of various vices, as literature it is of the most crass kind. Yet a work by Dante may, *ex hypothesi*, have exactly the same message and yet, by virtue of its poetic workings, be of the highest value as art. Hence a good art work is not replaceable by a work merely replicating its content in terms of moralizing, history, sociology or philosophy, because of its aesthetic features, which is what we are concerned with in appreciating something as art.

Second, aestheticism enables us to explain, by emphasizing the need to distinguish a work's fictive, cognitive and aesthetic aspects, why we can appreciate as art, works with whose content we may disagree vehemently. Two art loving friends may disagree fundamentally about the truth or pernicious falsity of Catholicism, and yet both may deeply appreciate as art Evelyn Waugh's *Brideshead Revisited*. Aestheticism gives a neat account of exactly how and why this may be so.

Third, aestheticism marks art appreciation out as a very distinctive kind of activity indeed. For engaging with and appreciating something as art involves attending to the artistic working and maximization of aesthetic features. Thus the nature of art proper is distinguished from mass culture. Mass culture is typically a commercial product which merely aims to please in terms of diverting entertainment, or is didactic in pushing some moral or political message. But merely being absorbing, in the way soap operas are, or didactically striving to communicate a message, as in much propaganda, is insufficient for something to enter the realm of art. Where cognitive concerns predominate, everyday culture cannot hope to rise to the level of art, for the goals and purposes of mass-cultural artifacts are indifferent to the promotion of aesthetic features. Art has as its autonomous goal the promotion of aesthetic values, to which all other considerations are subservient. Hence aestheticism can make sense of a distinction oft drawn between the high or fine arts and mass culture by emphasizing the distinctness of aesthetic pleasures.

Yet as a complete account of artistic value, such a tradition faces severe problems. First, consider conceptual art. Conceptual art often, though admittedly not always, is distinctly lacking in aesthetic qualities. Indeed in much conceptual art, such as Duchamp's, the experience of the work as such often seems to be besides the point, for conceptual art concerns the recognition of a given idea. Hence, it might be objected, not all good art affords the putatively required aesthetic experience.

The aestheticist can just deny that conceptual art is a problem. Jenny Holzer sewing the slogan 'war is bad' on to a camouflage baseball cap creates nothing of aesthetic worth (and one may think even the cognitive content rather adolescent). This explains why many people, rightly on this view, consider conceptual art to be worthless as art. Of course it may turn out that, accidentally, certain pieces of conceptual art do possess aesthetic value, and where they do so, they are to be valued as art for that reason. But where such value is lacking, such art is at best very bad art indeed. Perhaps certain pieces of anti-aesthetic conceptual art may change, alter or sharpen the ways in which people attend to the aesthetic qualities of art works generally. So conceptual art, where it lacks aesthetic value, can at best be something akin to art criticism, but not itself valuable as art.

A more fundamental objection arises when we consider works whose value we take to be diminished due to their content, independently of their aesthetic virtues. Standardly, professional critics and ordinary appreciators alike use critical terms such as sentimental, implausible, profound, insightful, callow, naive, malicious, strident, or simplistic. Such evaluations, as Rowe (1997) has pointed out, often directly concern the content of a work and how we are prescribed to understand it. Renoir's portraits are aesthetically coherent, yet our appreciation of them is somewhat diminished by their cloying sentimentality. So evaluations of a work as art sometimes must make reference to concepts such as truth, an appeal which aestheticism is at pains to rule out.

A sharp division between the purely aesthetic value of a work and the nature of the experience afforded in terms of its emotional depth or cognitive understanding looks difficult to maintain. A work may be aesthetically appealing, artfully contrived and thus absorbing. If a work is exceptionally absorbing and artful in its construction, it may well be great art, for not all great art is serious or profound in terms of its content or emotional resonance. But, importantly, where a work is properly deemed profound we consider it to be a virtue of the work as art. No doubt this pertains more particularly to representational or narrative art. For what matters in such artforms is that the imaginative experience is not merely aesthetically appealing, but enlightens or deepens our understanding of the kinds of characters and states of affairs represented. Thus the artistry and appeal of the narrowly aesthetic features of two works may be the same, and yet where one is merely absorbing and the other cultivates genuine insight, we naturally consider the latter to be better as art.

This leads on to another worry concerning the putatively sharp separation between high art and mass culture, for such a strict divide is out of step with the actual development of art. Far from being independent of non-aesthetic purposes, art has typically been produced to serve a variety of purposes, whether the form of patronage be religious, public, private or commercial. After all, the flattery of patrons, provision of propaganda and focus on material reward which were purposes of the work of Joshua Reynolds, Eisenstein and Hollywood respectively did not preclude them from producing great art. Whether a work of art is produced or not need not depend upon whether the primary purpose of creation is the promotion of artistically worked aesthetic features or the promotion of moral insight, religious worship or provision of housing for Lloyd's insurance underwriters.

Cognitivism and art as craft

A distinct tradition, stemming from Plato (1974), conceives of art as a craft closely tied to much else we value in other activities and human practices. The creation and reception of art is conceived of as a cultural practice which has evolved to realize, albeit peculiarly well, certain cognitive-affective values. Notoriously Plato's estimation of the value of art as such was rather negative, on the grounds that art cultivated the baser affective aspects of our souls so overriding the proper control of reason and thus leading us away from what is true and good. Aristotle (1986) took up Plato's conception of art as a craft but argued that it was to be highly valued. But this is so, contra aestheticism, not because the goals of art are distinct in kind from other activities, but rather because art can realize particularly well certain cognitive-affective ends we properly value in other activities. According to this line of thought, aesthetic virtues, Richard Beardsmore (1971) suggests, only distinguish the means by virtue of which art can realize peculiarly well its cognitive-affective goals. For example, both philosophy and art may seek to deepen our understanding of the human situation, but what is distinctive about art, as opposed to philosophy, is the means by which it seeks to do so.

The presumption is that art is, essentially, a communicative act. Following Walton (1990) we may conceive of representational art works as typically prescribing and promoting, through the use of artistically manipulated conventions, particular imaginings about a given state of affairs. We imagine what the characters, events, states of affairs and worlds, as they are portrayed, would be like. What is distinctive of art is that its physical materials, conventions, genres, artistic styles and forms are developed in order to vivify, guide and prescribe our imaginings and affective responses in ever better and deeper ways. Given that art works prescribe our imaginings about the world of appearances, characters, situations and aspects of the world, then art can inform and enlighten us about different ways we may understand the world. Our cognitively rich, vivid and novel experiences with art works may show us distinct perspectives upon others and the world. So art may expand our cognitive horizons in ways we otherwise would not have realized: art may enable us to see our world in new ways. Travel may well broaden the mind, but it is expensive and dangerous. By contrast, to travel through the imaginative lands evoked by art works is relatively cheap, safe and its pleasures are more easily forthcoming.

This claim is often construed, for example by Adorno (1994), in terms which equate the value of art with confronting or challenging our pre-existent beliefs and understanding. But such cases, as Noël Carroll (1998) has pointed out, are atypical: radical modification is the exception rather than the rule. Standardly, art seeks to deepen our pre-existent understandings by drawing out the implications of certain already-held presumptions. For example, *Brideshead Revisited* may well afford one a deeper understanding of both the attraction and human costs of belief in Roman Catholicism, but this is an enriched understanding of what one had grasped before, not a fundamental alteration in belief. Indeed, art works often do not even so much as deepen our understanding, but serve to revivify impressions or understandings we have already, by foregrounding in peculiarly vivid and striking ways aspects of ourselves, others or the world. This explains why, for example, we value Shakespeare's plays so highly, and moreover why we return to such works again and again. The poetic aspect would be hollow and unaffecting if it were not so tightly intertwined with a deep and profound exploration of the nature of man.

Such an account enables us to underwrite the presumption of art's significance, for good art is not just grounded on a distinctive kind of pleasure. On the aestheticist's account it is difficult to explain just why art is of greater signifi-cance than other kinds of pleasures we may get, whether they be playing pinball or coffee drinking. As Jerrold Levinson (1996) notes, art would seem to rate poorly in terms of hedonistic return. But on this view, good or great art is far from merely decorative or beautiful: it engages with our cognitive-affective attitudes to, and understanding of, the world. It follows from this, on the craft conception of art, that the aestheticists' distinction in kind between high art and mass culture is deeply flawed, for the difference between soap opera and Dickens, say, is one of degree. It is just that Dickens deploys in a more sophisticated and refined manner the means of prescribing our imaginings, attitudes and emotions, in such a way that we are afforded a richer and deeper understanding of what certain situations and characters would or could be like. On this view, the value of art is deeply and intimately tied to our capacity and need to understand ourselves, others and the world. As Matthew Kieran (1996) argues, something is of high value as art to the extent that, through the artistry deployed, it manages to vivify, deepen or, exceptionally, modify our understanding of such things. This explains just why it is that we evaluate art works in terms of their truth to life. If a work is sentimental then it is flawed, for essentially it gives a naive and flawed mischaracterization of that which it is seeking to represent to us.

Nonetheless, worries remain. First, such an account may be viciously reductive in equating the value of a work as art to what it may reveal about the world. *Lord of the Flies* may illustrate the Hobbesian nature of mankind but if this was why we valued such works as art, then surely they would be equally replaceable by works of philosophy or psychology which articulated such views. A different way to make the same point is to claim that two works may afford the same cognitive insight, and yet one may be poorly and clumsily written whilst the other contains poetic imagery which is beautiful, complex and appealing. The difference in the value of two such works as art cannot be a matter of cognitive value. The cogni-tivist is confusing what art may incidentally illustrate with what its distinctive value is, which concerns its aesthetic aspect.

There are two ways a cognitivist may respond. Firstly it may be claimed, as Martha Nussbaum (1990) argues, that there is a distinctive kind of knowledge and understanding that can only be conveyed imaginatively. Propositional knowledge, of the kind involved in philosophy, psychology and history, can tell us things such as that an event happened, how and why human beings have a certain socio-psychological make up, or how practical reason may be linked to moral motivation. But what such abstract principled reason cannot tell us concerns the phenomenology of what it feels like to have certain emotions or attitudes to others and, indeed, to see what is morally required in our relations with others. Such knowledge is a matter of imaginative perception unamenable to principled reason. Hence art can afford us imaginative acquaintance with certain truths that more formalized cognitive activities cannot. However such a strong claim is highly contentious in presuming that certain kinds of knowledge are inherently particularist, a claim many would want to deny.

By contrast, the second response makes no such contentious claims. Rather it claims only that there are different means or avenues to knowledge and understanding. *To Kill A Mockingbird* may afford the same kind of understanding of racism, the need for tolerance and humanity, that principled reason may. But art, as Berys Gaut (1998) suggests, is a particularly valuable way of conveying such an understanding, since it invokes and prescribes a peculiarly cognitive-affective response. In a way philosophy never could, by virtue of engaging our imagination with characters we identify with and affectively respond to in our experience with the work, an art work can get us to care deeply about certain truths or insights, and make us realize their import in a way pure reason either cannot or rarely does. So one need not hold that only art can convey certain truths, but rather that the artistic means employed enable art to do so peculiarly well in a non-abstract, affective fashion. Hence if the artistic means utilized are poor, clumsy or impoverished, then a work has failed to realize the cognitive-affective value of art, for we are then unlikely to care about or take much interest in whatever cognitive insight is implicit in the experience the work affords.

A second objection focuses on whether such an account really could adequately capture the value of art as a whole, for it would seem that the point of many works we value is not to tell us anything significant at all about the world or deepen our understanding of it. Still-life studies, portraits, abstract visual art, certain kinds of sculpture and pure music do not obviously have any significant cognitive content at all, and yet we appreciate many instances of them as great art: something cognitivism is apparently unable to account for.

One move open to the cognitivist is to deny that such works have little or no cognitive content. Superficially one may think Vermeer's realism, as in *Street in Delft*, is just the painterly delineation of bricks, mortar and houses with the odd figure going about ordinary household activity. But once one starts to take in the blank mute facades, closed doors, empty windows, and occasional figures of whom we can only identify their external activities, an impression builds up both that there is interior life and yet that we cannot know the exact nature or content of that interior life in virtue of mere appearances. And this is itself a putative insight into how difficult it may be to fully understand others – what a person is thinking and feeling cannot straightforwardly be read off from observing their behaviour. Similarly, apparently contentless abstract art, pure music or sculpture may be expressive or concern fundamental ways in which we perceive the world. Still, no matter how plausible this may be for many works which belie their cognitive nature, the response cannot be wholly adequate as long as there are at least some works for which such a story cannot be given, and yet which we are inclined to value highly as art.

Lastly, if cognitivism were sound then, the objection goes, it would be deeply puzzling as to why we rate highly works which we take to cultivate a flawed or overly partial understanding of the world. We may admire Francis Bacon's portrayal of humanity as rotten, corrupt and diseased, value his work highly as art, and yet think such a conception of humanity fundamentally mistaken. Yet if cognitivism were sound, surely we would have to consider Bacon's work to be of little value.

A cognitivist may respond, with Bernard Harrison (1991), that truth as such is irrelevant. Rather, what matters is whether the understanding prescribed of the world by the work is interesting, complex, and expands our imaginative horizons. These are the cognitive virtues proper to art, since they pertain to vivifying imaginative possibilities: and whether such possibilities are true or not is neither here nor there, since that is a matter for whichever discourse the envisaged possibilities are properly assessed within. A slightly stronger retort, as articulated by Gordon Graham (1997), involves the claim that truth as such does matter, but truth is only one of many cognitive virtues. After all, something may be true but banal. There are a range of cognitive virtues – profundity, insight, complexity, interest, coherence, consistency, truth to life – and it is in terms of all of these that the value of a work is assessed. Hence, on either the weaker or the stronger retort, a work may have many cognitive virtues and be valued as such even where the possibilities envisaged are ultimately adjudged to be interestingly false. An atheist may still appreciate *Brideshead Revisited* as good art – while, on the stronger claim, possibly judging it to be a lesser work because it commends that which he holds, in the last analysis, should be condemned as false.

One striking explanation as to why these rival traditions have been competing for so long is that both contain important truths about the values of art. Each tradition seems more or less plausible depending on the kind of art one has in mind. Aestheticism speaks particularly to forms such as abstract art or pure music, while cognitivism most obviously applies to representational art. Conversely, one of aestheticism's virtues is its emphasis upon the importance of artistry in representational cases, whereas cognitivism has the virtue of stressing ways in which abstract art or pure music sometimes does have cognitive content. So perhaps the real problem here concerns the ways in which two rival but partial accounts have attempted to generalize indiscriminately over all the arts to give an account of the value of art. Hence it would be more informative to concentrate on such questions in relation to particular artforms and genres. After all, to think one of the two rival traditions could hope to capture everything that is valuable about art, ranging across forms such as pure music, abstract art, sculpture, dance, literature and film and down to genres within a particular form such as light comedy, satire, tragedy and documentary, would appear hopelessly over-ambitious.

See also Formalism, Art and knowledge, Art and ethics, Plato, Aristotle, Kant.

References

Adorno, G. (1994) *Aesthetic Theory*, trans. G. Adorno and R. Tiedemann, New York: Routledge.

Aristotle (1986) *The Poetics of Aristotle*, trans. S. Halliwell, London: Duckworth.

Beardsley, M. (1958) *Aesthetics*, Indianapolis: Hackett.

Beardsmore, R. W. (1971) *Art and Morality*, London: Macmillan.

Bell, C. (1914) *Art*, London: Chatto and Windus.

Budd, M. (1995) *Values of Art*, London: Penguin.

Carroll, N. (1998) "Art, Narrative and Moral Understanding," in J. Levinson (ed.), *Aesthetics and Ethics*, Cambridge: Cambridge University Press.

Gaut, B. (1998) "The Ethical Criticism of Art," in J. Levinson (ed.), *Aesthetics and Ethics*, Cambridge: Cambridge University Press.

Graham, G. (1997) *Philosophy of the Arts: An Introduction to Aesthetics*, London: Routledge.

Harrison, B. (1991) *Inconvenient Fictions: Literature and the Limits of Theory*, New Haven: Yale University Press.

Kant, I. (1928) *The Critique of Judgement*, trans. J. C. Meredith, Oxford: Oxford University Press.

Kieran, M. (1996) "Art, Imagination and the Cultivation of Morals," *Journal of Aesthetics and Art Criticism* 54: 337–51.

Lamarque, P. and Olsen, S. H. (1994) *Truth, Fiction and Literature*, Oxford: Oxford University Press.

Levinson, J. (1996) *The Pleasures of Aesthetics*, Ithaca: Cornell University Press.

Nussbaum, M. (1990) *Love's Knowledge: Essays on Philosophy and Literature*, New York: Oxford University Press.

Plato (1974) *The Republic*, trans. D. Lee, London: Penguin.

Rowe, M. W. (1997) "Lamarque and Olsen on Literature and Truth," *Philosophical Quarterly* 47: 322–41.

Stecker, R. (1997) *Artworks: Definition, Meaning and Value*, University Park: Pennsylvania State University Press.

Walton, K. (1990) *Mimesis as Make-Believe*, Cambridge, Mass.: Harvard University Press.

20
BEAUTY

Jennifer Anne McMahon

What is beauty? What is it about an object which makes it beautiful? What kind of qualities characterize an experience of beauty? In modern philosophy the questions have been: is beauty subjective or objective? Are there properties in the object that count towards beauty in all cases, that are sufficient or necessary for an object to be judged beautiful? What kind of pleasure is the pleasure we experience of beauty? In this chapter, I present an overview of how these questions have been answered by philosophers throughout the ages, and suggest how they might be answered within a physicalist world view.

The history of beauty theory can be divided into two main traditions, according to the kind of pleasurable experience that is recognized as evoked by beauty. Those who recognize the sober, contemplative kind of pleasure evoked by a certain state of formal relations as the only pleasure characteristic of an experience of beauty, can be grouped into the Pythagorean tradition. Alternatively, those who recognize all the pleasures associated with the senses as evoked by beauty can be grouped into the pleasure-principle tradition. One cannot distinguish the two traditions according to the kind of objects experienced as beautiful. Typically however, nature, music and intellectual constructs such as mathematical theories are used to exemplify beauty in the Pythagorean tradition, and those things associated with the pleasures of the senses such as colors, taste and touch are used to exemplify beauty in the pleasure-principle tradition.

A small caveat before commencing: the term 'object' is used here to refer not only to tangible things like paintings and objects of nature, but also to intellectual constructs and temporally extended art works like music and performance.

The Pythagoran tradition

The original Pythagoreans were a school of philosophers in Ancient Greece who believed that the world is beautiful because there is a certain measure, proportion, order and harmony between its elements. They believed that the harmonies of music reveal the same harmonies that underlie nature. These harmonies, according to the Pythagoreans, can be reduced to number. In time, this conception of beauty was modified to accommodate the idea of moral beauty and the beauty of intellectual constructs. Eventually, within this tradition, beauty came to be understood as a relational property. The problems that arise for this conception of beauty are the classic problems of beauty.

Subjectivity and objectivity

To perceive that something is beautiful yet at the same time to claim to be unmoved, untouched by the experience, seems contradictory. Built into the concept of beauty is the notion of a pleasurable response on the part of the perceiver. On the other hand, judgements of beauty can be defended by pointing out the base properties within an object from which the beauty seems to emerge.

Having features pointed out can prompt one to reconfigure the object, and consequently alter one's judgement of beauty. In short, when defending judgements of beauty we behave as though there is a fact of the matter. The modern concept of beauty incorporates both the idea of a pleasurable response and a property of objects.

Traditionally, when we respond to the perception of beauty we are responding to either a reflection or a particular manifestation of the real thing; merely the appearance of beauty rather than beauty proper. When, on the other hand, we conceive of beauty, we are apprehending beauty proper. How we come to conceive of beauty proper varies from theory to theory. Either knowledge of beauty is deeply embedded a priori in our minds (Plato 1997a, 1997b), or beauty is a characteristic of the divine which we come to know through our experience of its manifestations on earth (Aquinas 1964–76). Alternatively, we might have an inner sense or faculty of beauty which is fitted to respond to a certain constitution of parts in an object, and from which we derive our notions of beauty (a common thesis in the eighteenth century). According to the Pythagorean tradition in general, there are two kinds of beauty, one relative and one universal or absolute (with the exception of Hume (1965) whose aesthetic theory only addresses relative beauty). The two kinds of beauty are incorporated into the one theory of beauty either by maintaining that the relative is a manifestation of the absolute (an ancient and medieval thesis), or by postulating that both kinds of beauty are generated from different aspects of the one inner sense/faculty of beauty (again, the eighteenth century idea).

Within this tradition, then, a judgement of beauty does not merely express a personal preference. It has a demand for agreement built into it. Either all rational beings agree, or, depending on what kind of beauty is involved, either all humans agree (absolute beauty) or all members of a culture or shared knowledge group agree (relative beauty).

Principles of beauty

Principles of beauty are usually understood as those qualities of the object which are necessary and/or sufficient for an object to be judged beautiful. Many attempts have been made to identify such principles, but such attempts have failed for a number of reasons. It is generally accepted that for an object to be judged beautiful it must evoke a pleasurable response in the viewer. However, it is always possible to find an object which can be judged to exhibit principles identified as those of beauty but which does not evoke a pleasurable response. Conversely, there may be objects that are experienced as beautiful but which do not exhibit the identified principles. For example, a certain order of the elements in a particular object may be judged as a contributing factor to that object's beauty. However, another object may satisfy these conditions but be experienced as boring and predictable instead of beautiful. When other conditions are added to the notion of order, such as complexity, a similar predicament can obtain. There are no features which can be inducted over a number of cases of beauty to serve as sufficient conditions for beauty, nor can the features of one beautiful object be generalized to account for all cases of beauty.

The problem then arises that if the idea of principles of beauty is given up, it seems a descent is inevitable into the notion of beauty as purely a matter of personal response, which makes a nonsense of the way judgements of beauty are defended in practice. Kant, however, who investigated the nature of beauty through the mental conditions necessary for its experience, concluded that there can be no principles of beauty, yet reasoned that judgements of beauty are universal (Kant 1987).

Kant reasoned that the object of beauty is the imagination's presentation of the form of the object. It might be easier to grasp this in psychological terms. Think of it this way. The perceptual form of an object is provided by the mind during the processing of the incoming perceptual data, which in the case of vision amounts to varying light intensities. Either because the resulting form does not match any of the concepts stored in memory, or because in some cases we can consciously access the perceptual form apart from its concept, we are able to experience the perceptual form provided by the mind. Now, this perceptual form is processed at too shallow a level in the perceptual system to be matched with language schemata. If perceptual form is the object of beauty, then the object of beauty cannot be described simply because we have no language with which to do so. Hence, there can be no principles of beauty, but the basis of judgements of beauty, which is the perceptual form of the object, is universal.

Mary Mothersill (1984) restates the antinomy identified by Kant as a matter of two apparently incompatible theses. The first thesis is that there are no principles of beauty, and the second thesis is that there are genuine judgements of beauty. She argues that the two theses are both true, and that any aesthetic theory must show them to be mutually consistent and to cohere (Mothersill 1984: 169).

As we have seen, a principle of taste is a critical feature or characteristic of an object which counts towards beauty in all cases. Such a feature or set of features could be generalized into defining principles. This would mean that given the presence of these features in any object, one could infer that the object was beautiful. Yet, as Mothersill points out, that is "absolutely impossible" (ibid.: 86). She sets out to answer the question: if there are no such principles, on what basis can genuine judgements of beauty (as opposed to merely an avowal of personal preference) be possible? Mothersill identifies certain mistaken assumptions which she argues are obstacles to solving the antinomy. The mistaken assumptions are that, one, critical reasons can necessarily be generalized to other cases; two, genuine judgements of beauty presuppose aesthetic theory and aesthetic theory presupposes principles of taste; and three, the only alternative to principles of taste is subjectivism (ibid.: 117). Mothersill reconciles the two theses by arguing that critical reasons given in order to support or defend a judgement of the beauty of an individual object do not act as premises from which judgements of beauty can be deduced for unfamiliar objects. There can be critical reasons for a particular judgement of beauty (hence a genuine judgement) which do not translate into principles of beauty. Each beautiful object is beautiful seemingly for unique reasons.

In order to understand how critical reasons which support a judgement of beauty cannot be generalized to other judgements of beauty without undermining the notion of a coherent concept of beauty (hence how judgements of beauty are possible), we need to explain the relation between the constitution of the beautiful object and the mind of the perceiver. This is the task that Kant (1987) set himself. Mothersill does not attempt to translate the transcendental basis of judgements of beauty in Kant's aesthetic theory into a more contemporary metaphysics. Instead, she argues that connecting "a description of what might be called a 'perceived-feature' event with a description of an 'experienced-pleasure' event" will result in a law of taste (Mothersill 1984: 96). As laws are necessarily generalized, she dismisses this possibility on the same grounds that she dismisses principles of taste (ibid.: 100). Mothersill appears to equivocate on this point when she subsequently writes: "in the case of laws, there is at least a surface plausibility to the notion that laws of taste, when finally formulated, will be the consequences of very sophisticated neurophysiological theories which are still in the making" (ibid.: 118). Perhaps she is pointing out that while it might be possible to identify the causal relation between the constitution of the object and the characteristic pleasure evoked by beauty in the subject, the causal relation might be such that it could not be represented as laws of taste. As she herself recognizes, aesthetic theory can enhance understanding without pretending to guide choice (ibid.: 140). The causal relation between the beautiful object and the pleasure it evokes in the subject might be identifiable and illuminating without resulting in laws and hence principles of taste.

Mothersill, however, eschews causal explanation for conceptual analysis. Her definition of beauty rests on the conceptual link between beauty and pleasure. An aesthetic theory's task, she writes, is to explain the difference between the pleasure evoked by beauty and other kinds of pleasure. Her solution is that an object must evoke pleasure in the observer by virtue of its aesthetic properties: this is the basis of a genuine judgement of beauty according to Mothersill. That she recognizes only the sober, contemplative kind of pleasure as evoked by beauty is not explicitly stated but implied in passages such as the following:

> The person who would be disqualified [from making a genuine judgement of beauty] is one who found nothing beautiful, whose pleasure in persons, objects, or events was always explicitly linked to appetite or need . . . all that is required of a subject is that there be something he takes to be beautiful and further that at least one such taking be allowed by him to be an aesthetic conviction. He can then concur in the claim that some judgements of taste are genuine judgements.
>
> (Mothersill 1984: 176)

The identification of beauty in an object pivots on its pleasing us 'in virtue of its aesthetic properties,' which places considerable weight on our ability to distinguish aesthetic properties from other kinds of property. According to Mothersill, aesthetic properties are those qualities of objects that have no simple names and are revealed only by acquaintance, and are grasped only in the apprehension (through considerable attention and contemplation) of the object (ibid.: 342).

Mothersill's aesthetic theory can be understood to represent the extent to which our understanding of beauty has developed under conceptual analysis, within the Pythagorean tradition. She alludes to a possible avenue of further enquiry but does not pursue it herself. This is the causal relation between a beautiful object and the pleasure experienced in its perception/apprehension, which I will take up later.

Disinterested pleasure

Early in the medieval period, writings on beauty refer to a kind of pleasure aroused by the beautiful which is distinct from the pleasures of the sensuous and the good. For example, Erigena (ninth century) wrote that a mind filled with desire for an object cannot perceive its beauty (Tatarkiewicz 1974: 95). For Aquinas (thirteenth century), the pleasure aroused by beauty is distinct from biological pleasures associated with physical desires and satisfactions (Aquinas 1964–76). The mental state required in order to perceive beauty is a state of contemplation which involves both perception and cognition (Tatarkiewicz 1974: 248–50). Shaftesbury (eighteenth century) recognizes in the pleasurable response to beauty an impartiality, a lack of self-interest. He adopts the term 'disinterested' from ethics to describe the pleasure recognized as associated with beauty (Stolnitz 1961: 132–4). Kant (1987) compares the pleasure taken in the agreeable, the good and beauty, and concludes that the pleasure experienced in beauty is disinterested. As such, he reasons that a judgement of beauty must be based on a universal feature of the mind, as no personal concerns are involved.

The pleasure of beauty according to this tradition is a pleasure caused by an object which is not accompanied by desire for the object. It should not be confused with the pleasure taken in the sensuous for its own sake; such as that which sparks that poignant sensation of our physical being in the world. Neither should it be confused with uninterest. Disinterest does not mean disengaged. Disinterested pleasure means that the basis of the pleasure is not egocentric. The pleasure of beauty is like perceiving a solution to a problem, and enjoying it for its own sake, rather than because personal rewards are anticipated. It can feel like a glimpse or intimation through chaos of underlying structures whose relations are harmonious. It feels as if our cognitive apparatus has a connection with some structure beyond itself which underpins what might on the surface appear unfathomable. It makes us feel a part of something larger than ourselves. It is as if we had discovered some profound truth about the world and the nature of being. This is so deeply pleasurable. The pleasure of beauty has been characterized this century (in the tradition of Schopenhauer) as the pleasure of escaping the confines of the ego.

The pleasure-principle tradition

Beauty evokes a pleasurable response. If while perceiving an object you do not experience pleasure, you are not perceiving beauty. While it does not necessarily follow that all pleasure evoked by perceiving an object is a response to an object's beauty, within the pleasure-principle tradition all pleasurable responses to the perception of an object *are* counted as responses to beauty. The aspects of the object relevant to a judgement of beauty can include sensuous properties in isolation such as the pure luscious quality of a certain color or texture, or the smooth rich taste of cheesecake or chocolate. They also include concepts of the object when the object gives pleasure because we anticipate the personal benefits we would enjoy on owning or engaging in some way with the object. In other words, when all pleasures evoked by the perception of the object are counted as pleasurable responses to beauty, beauty is collapsed into the agreeably sensuous and the good.

The pleasure-principle tradition is the tradition of the sophists and Epicureans. To the former, whatever gives pleasure to the eye and/or the ear is beautiful. In similar vein, the Epicureans believe that there is no difference between the good and the beautiful. During the early Christian and Medieval periods, those theologian-philosophers who understand beauty in the sensuous mode (such as Tertullian, third century), denounce beauty as evil; a surreptitious diversion of earthly delights planted by the devil. Within this tradition, conceptions of beauty can waver between the notion that the judgement of beauty expresses merely a personal preference, and the notion that the judgement of beauty does not merely express a personal preference because it has a demand for agreement among cultural or same-experience groups built into it.

In the twentieth century the metaphysics of beauty is conflated with the ontology of art. That is, the answer to the question concerning what and whether beauty is, has mistakenly been understood to depend on whether beauty figures in a definition of art. With the increasing influence of Freud and neo-Darwinism on the conception of art, play and artifice increasingly underpin ontologies of art. According to this conception of art, either art is connected with using up intellectual or physical energies once required for survival, and art in the young is generally a sharpening of the faculties that will in adulthood be used for more serious matters, or art is a legacy of the displays of the mating game. The latter explanations include linking the origin of music to mating calls and explaining the appeal of certain colors as linked to attracting mates. Within such a myopic conception of the arts, any concept linked to art is bound to suffer the same fate. This is one explanation for what has happened to the concept of beauty over the last century. When beauty is conflated with all of the pleasurable aspects of art so conceived, the evolutionary psychologists explain beauty as the kinds of tones and contrasts and shapes which are a sign of fecundity in a person (usually a female). Beauty is conceived as simply a sublimation of desire whose original teleology is procreation (e.g. Sircello 1979).

According to Guy Sircello's pleasure-principle theory of beauty (1975), an 'object' is beautiful when it contains a Property of Qualitative Degree to a very high degree. By 'object' Sircello means both an object (in the broad sense used throughout this chapter) and an aspect of an object. A Property of Qualitative Degree (henceforth a PQD) is a property that cannot be measured in a quantitative sense, such as can temperature or weight. Sircello further delineates a PQD by excluding those qualities that are experienced as deficiencies. He recognizes, however, that whether or not a property is understood as a deficiency is context-dependent. A quality is only a deficiency if it is judged so in relation to the object's nature, function or purpose. Sircello acknowledges that this idea, when left unqual-ified, leaves a certain loophole in his theory. After all, as he points out, the sliminess of a slug and the sourness of a lemon are not deficiencies in the context of a slug's and a lemon's nature. As it stands, this would mean that the slug's sliminess and the lemon's sourness are beautiful. He intends to avoid this conclusion by admitting another condition on the PQD. Those qualities that are not enjoyed are not beautiful. This leads to the question of relativity. For people who enjoy the sourness of a lemon, the sourness of the lemon is beautiful, and for those who don't . . . you get the picture. But Sircello stops short of conceiving of a judgement of beauty as merely a personal response by introducing the connoisseur condition. Sircello says that only those with sufficient experience of the particular quality involved can judge whether it exists in the object to a qualitatively high degree, and hence whether it is beautiful. However, it is not obvious that this condition succeeds in rescuing Sircello's theory from bizarre or trivial consequences. After all, one can easily imagine someone very experienced in tasting lemons, judging the sourness of a particular lemon to be present to a very high degree and enjoying the sourness. This would mean that according to Sircello's theory, the sourness of the lemon is beautiful. Less easy to imagine, but just as theoretically possible within Sircello's theory, is that the sliminess of a slug could qualify as beautiful.

Sircello admits all aspects of objects (from the sensuous to the formal) as possibly counting towards beauty, without accounting for the very different kinds of pleasures evoked between them. While he uses color as his main example of an 'object' which can be beautiful (in a number of possible aspects, such as its vividness), he also discusses a person's morality as a possible 'object' of beauty when it is characterized by properties such as generosity and honesty to a qualitatively high degree. Sircello speculates that the reason the experience of PQDs pleases us is because we only experience PQDs when we are seeing clearly. This in turn pleases us because we feel we are able to be fully aware of our immediate environment and we feel our faculties are in excellent order (Sircello 1975: 138). While Sircello offers this as speculation, it is not an adequate explanation for the pleasure evoked by such beauty as moral beauty. Furthermore, in the case of formal qualities, his claim that formal beauty is the presence of harmony to a very high degree is tautologous. In sum, representing beauty as a matter of the presence of a PQD to a very high degree does not amount to providing a principle of beauty. Instead, given the pleasure-principle idea of beauty, Sircello's theory of beauty is tautologous.

Sircello's theory is more complex and philosophically interesting than the crude Freudian and neo-Darwinian strands of the pleasure-principle tradition, but it does not deliver what we need of a theory of beauty. His theory does not offer logically necessary or sufficient conditions for beauty, and it does not explain how their absence is consistent with genuine judgments of beauty. Sircello's theory broadens out the conception of beauty to include the sensuous, the intellectual and the formal; in fact, every perception that results in pleasure. It does not provide a basis for distinguishing between the agreeable, the good, and beauty, but rather treats them as ascending states on a continuum of approval, with beauty at the summit (Sircello 1975: 78–9). It does, however, elegantly represent a pleasure-principle conception of beauty, and epitomizes the trivializing of beauty which characterizes such conceptions, but as such it does not clarify or advance our understanding of beauty.

A theory of beauty within a physicalist world view

The question we need to answer is what kind of mental processes could simultaneously, one, account for the experience of beauty in such a way that both its subjectivity and objectivity can be understood as complementary, two, provide a rational basis for beauty which does not translate into principles (necessary and/or sufficient conditions), and three, explain the possibility of a disinterested pleasure.

According to what is called a constructivist or structural theory of object recognition by contemporary cognitive scientists, visual processes build visual form in part from visual primitives, during perception. This is necessary because the only information that hits the retina is an array of varying light intensities. Visual form construction is driven by principles of form embedded in the visual system.

Now, imagine that the experience of beauty is a matter of becoming aware of these principles in a limited kind of way (in the sense that we cannot be aware of their source phenomenologically and we cannot accurately match them with language schemata). That is, in the course of perceiving/apprehending what consequently we experience as beautiful objects, we become aware of principles underlying perceptual form construction. This would explain why the exact features of an object which evoke an experience of beauty cannot categorically be defined. These perceptual principles would constitute a part of the architecture of the mind, and as such, could not themselves be represented explicitly and unequivocally in language (could not be matched with language schemata). Further, imagine that other perceptual modules have analogous principles of form construction. The judgement of beauty would be lawful, based on principles of perception. Hence, there would be no principles of beauty as such, but there would be a physical basis (a rational basis) for genuine judgements of beauty. The problem emerges, however, that if we explain beauty according to an awareness of certain perceptual principles, the possibility of mathematical, scientific, moral and intellectual beauty would seem to be precluded. In order to accommodate these kinds of beauty within the explanation provided for perceptual beauty, perceptual principles would need to figure in, either analogously or in some parallel way, higher level judgements of a cognitive kind.

If the conditions listed earlier were satisfied (McMahon 1999, forthcoming), we could further speculate about the way in which the relevant perceptual principles, prompted by certain objective characteristics in the object, need to be employed in order to be brought to our attention. Perhaps certain relations in the object, in the course of being perceived, challenge or stretch the relevant perceptual principles in an unprecedented or non-typical way. On the other hand, the relation of the elements within some objects, such as natural forms (and those art works which mimic these forms) might epitomize these principles. Perhaps when these principles are invoked in any way likely to draw our attention from straightforward object recognition to the process of perception as a solution to a problem, then we are experiencing beauty. That is, when it is as if the very process of perception itself is experienced as a resolution of tensions, or a solution to the problem of constructing a coherent form from the array of perceptual primitives, then we experience beauty.

It might be objected, however, that while various cultures do seem to offer a universal experience of certain aesthetic constants, at the same time, the various cultures can be said to have their own unique aesthetic. For example, we can look at Indian sculptures, Japanese tea ceremonies and Gothic cathedrals, and while we can enjoy their perceptual beauty, we may not be able to experience their intellectual beauty in the way that someone could whose world view was saturated with the outlook exemplified in these works. This objection could be answered if there were a constant perceptual kind of beauty and a dynamic intellectual component to the experience of beauty. The latter would explain the aspects of a culture's aesthetic which are inaccessible to the uninitiated. The apprehension of intellectual beauty, from scientific to moral beauty, would demand a shared background of knowledge or a shared world view. It would be possible for an art work to arouse a response to beauty through its perceptual form without providing the phenomenologically more total beauty experience, which is a combination of relations emerging within and between its perceptual form and conceptual content. It may be that the work simply does not provide the opportunity for the latter, or it may be that the viewer does not share the same world view (metaphysical/religious) as the artist, which makes the intellectual component of the work inaccessible to the viewer. For example, what amounts to a tension between data (facts) for one cultural or shared-experience group, could be apprehended as a balance by another group, depending on how the data is construed. The degree to which a beautiful object prompts an intellectual response, is the degree to which its beauty will be dynamic and relative, rather than constant and universal.

This is not a theory of art. This theory of beauty makes no assumptions about art. Some art is pleasurable on the sensuous level (for example Jackson Pollock's abstract expressionism) without evoking a response to beauty. Furthermore, consider a possible evolutionary justification for our capacity to experience beauty. Perceptual principles have evolved in response to survival pressures exerted by the organism's needs interacting with the environment. Perception has evolved effectively to provide us with information about our environment that assists our survival. Perceptual principles are responsible for converting perceptual input into perceptual output. Hence, we can reasonably speculate that something about the way these principles transform perceptual primitives into a cohesive form, reflects something about principles which underlie what is objectively out there in the world. When we become aware of these principles in themselves, we are experiencing something indirectly about how the world is objectively. When objects (art works and theories) evoke a response to beauty, something about their constitution reflects relational principles out there in the world. Thinking about the relationship between beauty, perceptual principles and principles underlying nature in this way, points to the evolutionary significance of beauty. That is, it explains the connection noted by various mathematicians and scientists between our capacity to experience beauty and our capacity to develop theories that have applications (mathematics and science); and hence between beauty and creativity; and between beauty and truth.

According to such a theory of beauty, a judgement of beauty does not merely express a personal preference because it has a demand for agreement built into it. The agreement may be either that all humans agree (perceptual beauty) or that all members of a shared culture/experience group agree (intellectual beauty). There are no principles of beauty, unless psychological principles of perception could count as such, but there is a rational basis for genuine judgements of beauty. The disinterested nature of the experience of beauty is explained by the fact that the pleasure is based on a solution to the problem of perception; a solution provided by sub-personal levels of perceptual and cognitive processing. In addition, such a theory of beauty provides grounds for distinguishing beauty from the agreeable and the good. It is also able to explain the link intuitively made between beauty and the idea of truth.

See also Plato, Medieval aesthetics, Empiricism, The aesthetic, Taste.

References

Aquinas (1964–76) *Summa Theologiae*, London and New York: Blackfriars.
Hume, D. (1965) "Of the Standard of Taste," *Essays Moral, Political and Literary*, ed. E. Miller, Indianapolis: Liberty Classics.
Kant, I. (1987) *Critique of Judgment*, trans. W. S. Pluhar, Indianapolis: Hackett.
McMahon, J. A. (1999) "Towards a Unified Theory of Beauty," *Literature and Aesthetics* 9: 7–27.
—— (forthcoming) *Aesthetics and Cognition in Visual Beauty*.
Mothersill, M. (1984) *Beauty Restored*, Oxford: Oxford University Press.
Plato (1997a) *Phaedrus*, in *Complete Works*, ed. J. M. Cooper, Indianapolis: Hackett.
—— (1997b) *Symposium*, in *Complete Works*, ed. J. M. Cooper, Indianapolis: Hackett.

Sircello, G. (1975) *A New Theory of Beauty*, Princeton: Princeton University Press.

—— (1979) "Beauty and Sex," in D. F. Gustafson and B. L. Tapscott (eds), *Body, Mind and Method*, Dordrecht: Reidel.

Stolnitz, Jerome (1961). "On the Origins of 'Aesthetic Disinterestedness'" *The Journal of Aesthetics and Art Criticism* 20: 131–43

Tatarkiewicz, W. (1974) *The History of Aesthetics*, The Hague: Mouton.

Further reading

Coleman, E. J. (1991) "The Beautiful, the Ugly, and the Tao," *Journal of Chinese Philosophy* 18: 213–26. (Compares the understanding of beauty in Chinese philosophy with that in the West.)

McAllister, J. (1996) *Beauty and Revolution in Science*, Ithaca: Cornell University Press. (Discusses the role of beauty in science.)

Norton, R. E. (1995) *The Beautiful Soul:. Aesthetic Morality in the Eighteenth Century*, Ithaca: Cornell University Press. (Traces the rise and fall of the idea of moral beauty in eighteenth-century Britain and Germany.)

Sircello, G. (1989) *Love and Beauty*, Princeton: Princeton University Press. (Further discussion of the pleasure-principle theory of beauty).

—— (1990) "Beauty in Shards and Fragments," *Journal of Aesthetics and Art Criticism* 48: 21–35. (Compares his own theory of beauty with Mothersill's.)

Savile, A. (1989) "Beauty and Truth: the Apotheosis of an Idea," in R. Shusterman (ed.), *Analytic Aesthetics*, Oxford: Blackwell. (An account of eighteenth through twentieth-century German philosophers.)

Shaftesbury (1999) "Shaftesbury" in D. Townsend (ed.), *Eighteenth-Century British Aesthetics*, Amityville, N.Y.: Baywood.

Stolnitz, J. (1961) "Beauty: Some Stages in the History of an Idea," *Journal of the History of Ideas*, 22: 185–204. (Concentrates on the eighteenth-century British empiricists.)

Tatarkiewicz, W. (1972) "The Great Theory of Beauty and its Decline," *Journal of Aesthetics and Art Criticism*, 31: 165–80. (Discusses the influence and history of the original Pythagorean notion of beauty).

The following books aim to rekindle an interest in beauty by taking primarily a sociological, non-analytical philosophical, and instrumentalist approach respectively. However, while there is much to recommend these books, they do not address the classic problems of beauty.

Brand, P. Z. (ed.) (2000) *Beauty Matters*, Indiana: Indiana University Press.

Kirwan, J. (1999) *Beauty*, Manchester: Manchester University Press.

Scarry, E. (1999) *On Beauty*, Princeton: Princeton University Press.

21
INTERPRETATION

Robert Stecker

When we interpret works of art and literature we are seeking to understand or to appreciate them, or to improve on our current level of understanding or appreciation. We do this by attempting to discover or, at least, ascribe on *some* basis, a meaning in or to the work in question, or to determine what significance the work has for us.

Around this feat of assigning a meaning or significance to a work of art, many controversies swirl. Some of these controversies will be systematically set out in this chapter. Before doing this, it is worth mentioning why these issues have seemed important enough and uncertain enough to generate so much controversy.

Consider this poem from William Blake's *Songs of Innocence and Experience*:

> *The sick rose*
> O Rose thou art sick.
> The invisible worm,
> That flies in the night
> in the howling storm:
>
> Has found out thy bed
> of crimson joy:
> And his dark secret love
> Does thy life destroy.

First note that there are aspects of the meaning of the poem that it would be natural to say we know prior to interpretation. We know that the poem is ostensibly about a rose that becomes infested with a worm that destroys it. We know the rose is red (crimson), the worm invisible and flies at night in a storm.

We know there is more to the poem than this. We know that we will appreciate the poem only if we can come to some understanding of what this more might be. We also may have some specific puzzles about some lines or phrases in the poem. For example, why is the worm invisible? Is it literally invisible or perhaps barely noticeable? Why does it make its first "appearance" in a howling storm? Why is the vehicle of its destructiveness a "dark secret love"? We need, and for the moment lack, answers to these various questions, general and specific. Clearly these are interpretive issues. Whatever answers we give will result in meanings we find in or assign to the poem in giving an interpretation of it.

There are many views about what we *should* do and what we *may* do in answering these questions. Let us begin to examine these.

Actual intentionalism

One plausible starting point is to focus on the poet, and to see if what we can learn about him helps to answer the interpretive questions raised above about "The sick rose." However, there are different ways of doing this. One can engage in what can be called biographical criticism, in which one tries learn as much as possible about the life of the poet and then tries to, as it were, read off the meaning of the poem from what was going on in the poet's life around the time of writing.

There are several decisive criticisms of this approach. There is no reason to suppose that a poem, or more generally, a work of art, is a direct expression of what is going on in the artist's life. It might be, but then again, the artist may just as likely distance him or herself from his or her life when creating art works. Further, this approach to answering interpretive questions tends to distance the critic from something important: the details of the work. It will be virtually impossible to find non-speculative connections between a poet's biography and his or her writing those precise words. Finally, even if such connections were found between the poet's life and words, these are likely to be private connections and certainly ones that are inaccessible to most readers. This makes them poor candidates for meanings which must be capable of receiving uptake from the poem's audience. Few artists would rely on such connections when creating works to be introduced into the public domain.

A more plausible approach is to ask what a poet (artist) is intending to do or convey with a poem (art work). What was Blake's point in writing about the sick rose, in describing the worm as invisible, in making it first appear in a howling storm, in describing its destructiveness in terms of a secret love?

This approach is plausible because it reflects an important aspect of our explanatory stance when we are trying to understand human behavior and the products of human behavior. We typically explain what people do and make by appealing to their beliefs, and desires and the intentions they form in virtue of these. Why are you writing on that piece of paper? I'm filling out a withdrawal slip and am intending to use it to get money for the weekend. Why are you stirring those ingredients together? I'm making a cake and intending to have it for dessert. Notice it is common to use this explanatory approach when we are concerned with people's semantic doings, that is, when we are trying to understand what they are saying or writing. If we do not understand some part of a conversation, we are apt to say, 'What do you mean?' 'What are you getting at?' Once we are clear on that, our interpretive goals are usually satisfied.

It is plausible to carry over the same strategy to answering the interpretive questions about "The sick rose" and other works of art. On this view, art works are considered expressions of the actual intentions of their creators. Interpretations of art works assert that a work expresses this or that actual intention, and are true only in the event that the intention in question is expressed in the work. In conversation the main source of evidence for inter- pretive claims are the words uttered in context. (So, if your real estate broker says, before the closing on the house that has just sold, "I will meet you at the bank," context tells you that he or she means the financial institution, not the land bordering a river.) Similarly, the main source of evidence for interpretive claims about art works are features of the art work understood in context. However, they are not the only source evidence. Just as we can ask an inter- locutor what he or she means by his or her words, or make inferences about what he or she means from background information we have about the person, we can look for expressions of intention outside the art work or use background information to help generate more plausible hypotheses about the artist's intention.

Actual intentionalism is often misrepresented. It is sometimes confused with the biographical criticism we have already rejected. It is also sometimes identified as the view that the correct interpretation of the work is the artist's interpretation of it. Further, the artist's interpretation is frequently not distin- guished from his or her expressions of intention. This understanding is doubly confused. First, expressions of intention are not, in general, to be identified with interpretations of one's own behavior. "I'm planning on getting to the bank before it closes" is an expression (or at least a report) of intention and not an interpretation. "I think I went to the bank just to get out of the house" is an interpretation of behavior and not an expression (or report) of intention, although there may be certain situations where these two things are hard to distinguish. Second, neither the artist's interpretation of the work, nor his or her expressions or reports of his or her intention that are external to the work, automatically constitute the correct interpretation of the work. The artist's interpretation of the work may be no better, and is often worse, than those of others. Expressions of intention can be inaccurate, insincere, or if issued before the work is completed, discarded rather than realized.

Criticisms of actual intentionalism

We have so far spoken of intentionalism without defining it. To evaluate a view we need a more precise specification of what it says. So, for this purpose, let us define actual intentionalism as the view that the correct interpretation of an art work identifies the intention of the artist expressed in the work.

Despite its plausibility, there are a number of serious criticisms of this view. One frequently expressed worry is whether we can ever know what the artist intends. The thought is that intentions are hidden and inaccessible. However, if they were inaccessible, we would be permanent mysteries to each other. In fact, we can often know another's intentions, semantic and otherwise. The same is true with regard to works of art. As with other cases, some intentions are transparent, some we can figure out even when not obvious, and about some, we can only form hypotheses that will never be confirmed or disconfirmed decisively.

Let us briefly return to "The sick rose" to see how this works in practice. Just as it is obvious that the poem is ostensibly about a rose, it is obvious that Blake intended this, and expressed this intention in the poem. Further, we can be sure that Blake intends the rose, the worm, the storm, to be treated symbolically, to say something about the human condition. (Notice that obvious though this is, we have already broached, if barely, a matter of interpretation.) Finally, the symbolism intentionally concerns, at least in part, human love and sexuality and the destructiveness of certain sorts of relationship or non-relationship having to do with sex and love. We have very good reason to believe this both from the words of the poem (the reference to the rose's "bed of crimson joy" and the worm's "dark secret love") and the surrounding context (the other poems in the *Songs of Experience*, many of which betray similar concerns). What is more a matter of hypothesis is the specific destructive relationship (or non-relationship) that Blake intended to symbolize in the poem – the other poems suggest several possibilities – if he intended something specific at all.

A second criticism is that, even if we can sometimes know what an artist intends, it is a mistake to identify the meaning of a work with the intention of the artist. One of the best arguments for this point begins by noting that we sometimes fail to do what we intend to do. This includes our semantic intentions; we sometimes fail to say what we intend to say. In these cases it is plausible to suppose we have said something, but something other than what we intended to say, and, hence, it is plausible that there is a distinction between what we meant (what we intended to say) and the meaning of our utterance (what we said). Therefore, the two cannot be identified (Levinson 1992, Tolhurst 1979).

A final objection concerns the proper aim of interpretation. Recall that we began by saying that when we interpret, we aim at (better) understanding and appreciating an art work. The present objection claims that we aim at maximizing such appreciation by maximizing enjoyable aesthetic experience (Davies 1991). It is claimed that our interest in promoting enjoyment is best served by permitting a range of interpretations compatible with the art work. The objection to actual intentionalism is that it unduly restricts the range of acceptable interpretations so that the proper aim of interpretation cannot be realized. Notice that this objection does not deny that intentionalism might be the right view in other interpretive contexts, but rather it claims that art and literature create a special context where different rules apply.

These last two objections raise three large issues within the theory of interpretation. One issue concerns whether there is a single proper aim of interpretation in the case of art works, or whether there are many legitimate aims (the proper aim issue). A related issue is whether this aim (or these aims) promote an ideal of a plurality of acceptable interpretations of the same work, or an ideal of a single correct interpretation (the monism/pluralism issue). A final issue concerns whether there is such a thing as the meaning of a work (the work meaning issue). We need to resolve these issues before we can fully evaluate the force of the objections to intentionalism.

The 'proper aim' issue

The last objection claimed that intentionalism is false because it blocks the pursuit of the proper aim of interpretation. How does one decide what we *should* be doing when we interpret a work of art or literature? If there were a set of norms available a priori that we could appeal to, that would settle the matter, but anyone who appealed to such norms would likely be perceived as begging the question. What is available in a non-question-begging way is actual (and possible!) interpretive practice. However, a straightforward appeal to this is not decisive, because what people actually do (much less might do) is not necessarily what they should be doing. Nevertheless, if people engage in certain interpretive practices that make no straightforwardly false assumptions and that aim at valuable goals, then it is not clear how we can object to such practices. The aims of such practices would then at least be among the permissible aims of art interpretation. If there is just one actual or possible aim that passed this test, it would be the one we should be pursuing when we interpret the relevant works, but if not, a number of different aims would be options.

Both common sense and actual practice tell us that there are a number of different interpretive aims that meet the above conditions. There is plenty of critical practice that pursues the goal of identifying the intentions that artists express in works. Furthermore, there is no reason to think that this goal is less valuable here then it is in other interpretive contexts, where it is widely admitted to be the goal of interpretation. Even if the meaning of a work is not invariably identified with the intention expressed in the work, as the second criticism of intentionalism claims, identifying expressed intention may still be a perfectly reasonable aim of interpretation. However, there is plenty of critical practice that doesn't pursue this goal, and aims at other things such as value maximization. It is hard to deny that maximizing value is a valuable goal. These two aims are not the only ones we find when we examine what critics do. Some interpretations aim to find *an* understanding of a difficult work without claiming that it is either the intended way of taking the work or the only way. Some seek out a meaning that the work could have (or have had) for a certain sort of audience. Others attempt to identify how the work would be understood against the backdrop of certain large ideas or theories such as those of Freud, Marx or those of some feminists. There may even be some interpretations that do not literally say anything about a work, but seek to get us to imaginatively contemplate certain actual or possible states of affairs.

We have now suggested a resolution to the 'proper aim' issue: art interpretation does not have a single proper aim. Hence the value maximizers cannot criticize actual intentionalism for blocking the pursuit of this aim. We can, however, level a revised criticism at intentionalism, although it is one that can be raised against value maximization as well. We defined intentionalism as a thesis about *the* correct interpretation of an art work. We now have reason to think that this thesis is false. If art interpretation has a plurality of aims, it is quite possible that there are correct or true interpretations of works arrived in pursuit of some of these other aims that do not make statements about the artist's intention. On the other hand, there can also be perfectly acceptable interpretations that do not aim at, or even contribute to, maximizing our appreciation of the work by maximizing enjoyable aesthetic experience.

The 'monism/pluralism' issue

The second issue was whether the aims of art interpretation promote an ideal of a plurality of acceptable interpretations or of a single correct interpretation.

Those who believe that art interpretation aims at a single correct (true), comprehensive interpretation of a work are critical monists (Beardsley 1970, Hirsch 1967, Nehamas 1981). Those who believe that such interpretation aims at a non-combinable multiplicity of acceptable interpretations are critical pluralists (Barnes 1988, Goldman 1990, Fish 1980). It may seem as if what we have said so far has been in support of the pluralist rather than the monist. After all if there are the wide range of interpretive aims already stated, it will not make sense to combine them all together even if we could do so without outright inconsistency. The result would be a hodgepodge rather than a more comprehensive interpretation.

However, certain aims are properly pursued under the monist ideal while others are not. Actual intentionalist interpretation, for example, aims at finding the uniquely correct account of what the artist intended in the work, even though available evidence may be insufficient for realization of this aim. It would make no difference that the artist's intentions were ambivalent between different conceptions of the work, or if he or she intended the work to be ambiguous in various respects, for a good intentionalist would seek to capture these things in a single interpretation. On the other hand, interpretations that aim at discovering what a work *could* mean, or at finding aesthetically valuable ways of taking a work, are best seen as pursuing the pluralist ideal. This is so regardless of the fact that such interpretations could be combined without inconsistency, since it is not inconsistent to assert that a work could mean that p and that it could mean that *not-p*. Though the interpretations can be consistently bundled together, it typically does not serve the aim of these interpretations to do so.

The 'work meaning' issue

This leaves us with the last of the three issues raised, which we can rephrase as: whether among the numerous aims of interpretation, there is a special one of discovering the meaning of a work? The *meaning* of a work is to be distinguished from the various things that the a work *could mean* or are merely taken to mean in the service of some interpretive aim. It is what the work actually *does* mean either in virtue of the artist's intention or, as the second objection to actual intentionalism suggests, on some other basis. Let us call this 'work meaning,' for short. Is there is such a thing as work meaning?

There is currently no consensus how to answer this question. Some people suppose that, since interpretation is concerned with the ascription of meaning to works, there must be something – the meaning of the work – that is being ascribed. However, we have seen that meanings can be ascribed on many grounds in virtue of the many different aims with which we undertake inter-pretation. So, while we cannot deny that works can bear *meanings*, it does not follow that there is such a thing as *the meaning* of a work. Other people suppose that precisely because there is this multiplicity of aims, and that important among these is the aim of enhancing appreciation of the work, there could not be such a thing as the meaning of work. However, the fact that people interpret with many legitimate aims does not mean either that there is no such thing as work meaning or that one important aim is to discover it.

The challenge that neither of these arguments meet is to show whether we can identify one of the aims of interpretation with the search for work meaning. Utterances provide a good model for seeing how we can make this identifica-tion. An utterance is the use of language on a particular occasion (in speech or writing) to say or do something. 'There are ten sheep in the field' standardly states that there are ten sheep in the field, but on a particular occasion, I may primarily be uttering this sentence to say or do something else. It may be my conventional way of telling you that two sheep, in our twelve sheep herd, have wandered off (in which case I am primarily using these words to say or imply something beyond what the words literally say), or I may even be telling you to go look for the two missing sheep (in which case I am primarily using these words to do something: instruct you to look for the sheep). Notice we can distinguish between what my utterance could mean (what I could say or do in making it) and what it does mean (what I actually say or do). It is the latter that we would identify as *the meaning* of the utterance.

We can extend this model to works of art by thinking of them as utterances of the artists who create them. There are many things one could mean by uttering "O Rose thou art sick." One could be commenting on the state of one's garden. A poet could be commenting on the transitory nature of earthly beauty. Blake was a different sort of poet and was doing neither of these in his poem. By asking what he was doing (intentionally or not) we attempt to find out the (work) meaning of the line on the proposed model. The model applies most straightforwardly to literary works, which are after all, literally complex utterances. However, whatever determines utterance (work) meaning may be applicable to other art works as well.

Meaning and actual intentionalism

It is common ground between actual intentionalists and at least some of their opponents to think of works as utterances. Some of these intentionalists claim that the meaning of an utterance or work is to be identified with the intention expressed in it. (Please notice, however, that this claim is not implied by the definition of intentionalism stated earlier. Intentionalism as it was originally defined made no claim about work meaning, though there are intentionalists, as well as critics of intentionalists, who have uncritically assumed that, if we are engaged in interpreting a work, we must be looking for work meaning.) As we have seen, opponents of intentionalism have shown that we can make utterances (or create works) in which we say or do something other than what we intended, and so the identification between intention and utterance/work meaning does not always hold.

Conventions

If work meaning cannot be *identified* with intended meaning, what might it consist in? There are three main alternatives to consider. The first claims that the work meaning are determined by conventions. For example, the meaning of a literary work is determined by linguistic conventions, literary conventions, and perhaps other cultural conventions (Beardsley 1970, 1982; Davies 1991). In general, artistic, linguistic, and other cultural conventions will be relevant in determining work meaning. (Linguistic conventions are almost always relevant to the meaning of works *not* 'made' out of words – paintings, sculptures, dances, music – for many reasons. For one, most works have titles expressed in language. For another, many of the categories by which we approach these works, such as portrait or sonata, are enshrined in language.) Let us call this view conventionalism. Proponents of this view can, and do, differ about which conventions are operative in fixing work meaning. For example, in the case of literary works, one can disagree about which linguistic conventions are appropriate since such conventions change over time. Are they the conventions in place when the work is written, when the interpretation is offered, or at some other time? Among literary conventions, are conventions of interpretation relevant (if so, again which ones?) or only conventions of writing or genre?

Though a conventionalist would need to answer these questions, they may be moot for us because there seems to be a decisive objection to conventionalism as a stand-alone account of work meaning. The meaning of an utterance is normally not fixed by conventions alone. Context (and, possibly, the utterer's intention) is always relevant. The content as well the truth value of utterances of 'Richard is poor' will vary depending who is being referred to, the relevant sense of 'poor' (which might indicate the wealth, health or another condition of Richard), and what the utterance is being used to do, such as describe Richard's condition or dismiss him as a potential investor. This is equally true of work meaning if it is to be understood on the model of utterance meaning. "The sick rose" cannot be fully understood outside the context of the poems that accompany it in the *Songs of Innocence and Experience*, of its historical period, and so on. An example of this is the choice of the rose as the sick flower. The rose had a conventional significance in Blake's poetic tradition as, for example, a symbol of fragile, transient beauty, but this hardly exhausts its significance in Blake's poetry which can only be determined contextually. (Another poem in the *Songs* tells us, "The modest Rose puts forth a thorn . . . While the Lilly white shall in Love delight.")

Hypothetical intentionalism

The idea of the second account of work meaning is that it is properly identified not as what the actual artist actually intended, but with what an audience should or would understand to be intended, given certain background assumptions. We can call this a *hypothetical* intention, and the view, hypothetical intentionalism. It recognizes that, because art works are the deliberate creations of artists, audiences take the features of works as intended. The innovative aspect of this view is that work meaning is to be identified with the hypothetical intention the audience is most justified in finding in the work. This puts hypothetical intentionalism in a position to take into account the considerations of context with which conventionalism was unable to deal.

The view still needs filling out. It has to tell us more about the audience in question and about the considerations it may use in identifying hypothetical intentions. Is it the audience contemporary with the artist, the audience that the artist intends to address or an ideal audience? Are the considerations that the audience takes into account all items that are *evidence* of the artist's intention, or are other sorts of consideration also to be taken into account, such as whether the postulation of an intention makes the work artistically better? Are there restrictions on the kind of evidence to be brought forward? That all these questions have to be answered is not a criticism of hypothetical intentionalism, but it does indicate a challenge it must meet. There are different versions which answer these questions in different ways, and a hypothetical intentionalist needs to defend the particular version he or she endorses.

The unified view

The last account of work meaning attempts to combine two views we considered earlier and found to be inadequate in their own right as accounts of such meaning. These are actual intentionalism and conventionalism, and the present view, let us call it the unified view, says, roughly, that work meaning is a function of both the actual intentions of artists and the conventions in place when the work is created. When the artist succeeds in expressing his or her intention in the work, that is what we should identify with the meaning of the work, but when actual intentions fail to be expressed, conventions in place when the work is created determine meaning.

Both hypothetical intentionalism and the unified view have problems, though not necessarily insurmountable ones. Perhaps the most serious objections to the former consist in the following purported counter-examples: First, it appears to be quite possible that work W means P, but (perhaps for conventional reasons) P is not intended, and the relevant audience of W has good reason to believe P is not intended. P would then be an example of unintended meaning that hypothetical intentionalism is unable to identify. Second, it may be the case that an artist intends to express P in W, the appropriate audience has good reason to believe this, but P fails to be expressed in W (because we can sometimes see what was intended even while seeing that it is not expressed). Here hypothetical intentionalism would assert that W means P when it does not. The most serious objections to the unified view are that, one, it relies on a notion of successful intention (an intention expressed in a work) which is circular, because there is no way of explaining what success amounts to without an independent notion of work meaning; and two, it lacks a clear account of the way intention and convention jointly determine work meaning. The existence of these objections, and of replies that there is not space here to explore, make the choice between these views not an obvious one.

However, it is also not clear that the choice is an altogether pressing one. This is because the two views have a tendency to reach the same conclusions about the meanings works have, because the intention an audience is most justified in finding in a work will very often be the intention the artist expressed in it. Some hypothetical intentionalists want to restrict the evidence audiences may use to reach conclusions, and to allow them to employ other considerations such as the aesthetic merit an interpretation bestows on a work (Levinson 1992). This seems to imply that the meanings they find in works will differ from those discovered by the unified view. But proponents of the unified view may want to introduce the idea that successful intentions are those that can receive audience uptake which could place similar restrictions on evidence, and they may defend a principle of charity in choosing among rival hypotheses, which could introduce considerations of aesthetic merit. Even if the views do not collapse into each other, they are very close relatives.

Final remarks

We have examined a number of controversies within the theory of interpretation. Does the intention of the artist determine the correct interpretation of a work? What should we aim at when we interpret art works, and is there one dominant aim or a number of legitimate ones? Do we have to choose between critical monism and critical pluralism, or can we actually accept both? Is there such a thing as *the* meaning of an art work, and in what would it consist?

These are not the only controversies that exist in this very complex corner of the philosophy of art. We should at least mention some other important issues that space has not permitted us to discuss. One is the issue raised by relativism. Might the correctness of an interpretation vary according to the different standards of interpretive communities, or, for that matter, of different individual interpreters? Relativists, in essence, say they do, and hence for them there is not one truth about a given work on a given interpretive issue, but many truths relative to these different standards. A second issue concerns the very object of interpretation. We have assumed that this object exists independently of our interpretations, that we have some knowledge of it before we interpret it, and that, while we may assert this or that about the object when we interpret it, we do not thereby add to or alter it. However, not everyone accepts this view. Some claim that interpretation is the process of constructing or altering an object (Krausz 1993, Margolis 1989). Hence, the object of interpretation is in essence made or altered by the interpretation rather than something entirely independent to which it is addressed.

The resolution of these last two issues will not leave unaffected those discussed in more detail earlier in this chapter. A complete theory of interpretation would have to address these matters as well.

See also Criticism, Postmodernism, Fiction, Narrative, Metaphor.

References

Barnes, A. (1988) *On Interpretation*, Oxford: Blackwell.

Beardsley, M. (1970) *The Possibility of Criticism*, Detroit: Wayne State University Press.

—— (1982) "Intention and Interpretation: A Fallacy Revisited," in M. Wreen and D. Callen (eds), *The Aesthetic Point of View*, Ithaca: Cornell University Press.

Davies, S. (1991) *Definitions of Art*, Ithaca: Cornell University Press.

Fish, S. (1980) *Is There a Text in This Class?* Cambridge, Mass.: Harvard University Press.

Goldman, A. (1990) "Interpreting Art and Literature," *Journal of Aesthetics and Art Criticism* 48: 205–14.

Hirsch, E. D. (1967) *Validity in Interpretation*, New Haven: Yale University Press.

Krausz, M. (1993) *Rightness and Reasons*, Ithaca: Cornell University Press.

Levinson, J. (1992) "Intention and Interpretation: A Last Look," in G. Iseminger (ed.), *Intention and Interpretation*, Philadelphia: Temple University Press.

Margolis, J. (1989) "Reinterpreting Interpretation," *Journal of Aesthetics and Art Criticism* 47: 237–51.

Nehamas, A. (1981) "The Postulated Author: Critical Monism as a Regulative Ideal," *Critical Inquiry* 8: 133–49.

Tolhurst, W. (1979) "On What a Text is and How it Means," *British Journal of Aesthetics* 19: 3–14.

Further reading

Carroll, N. (1992) "Art, Intention, Conversation," in G. Iseminger (ed.), *Intention and Interpretation*, Philadelphia: Temple University Press. (A recent defense of intentionalism.)

Currie, G. (1993) "Interpretation and Objectivity," *Mind* 102: 413–28. (A defense of hypothetical intentionalism.)

Davies, S. (1982) "The Relevance of Painters' and Writers' Intentions," *Journal of Aesthetics and Art Criticism* 41: 65–76. (A criticism of intentionalism.)

Iseminger, G. (ed.) (1992) *Intention and Interpretation*, Philadelphia: Temple University Press. (An excellent collection of essays arguing every side of the issue.)

—— (1996) "Actual Intentionalism vs. Hypothetical Intentionalism," *Journal of Aesthetics and Art Criticism* 54: 319–26. (A defense of intentionalism.)

Juhl, P. D. (1980) *Interpretation: An Essay in the Philosophy of Criticism*, Princeton: Princeton University Press. (A defense of intentionalism.)

Nathan, D. (1992) "Irony, Metaphor and the Problem of Intention," in G. Iseminger (ed.), *Intention and Interpretation, Philadelphia: Temple University Press*. (A criticism of intentionalism.)

Stecker, R. (1994) "Art Interpretation," *Journal of Aesthetics and Art Criticism* 52: 192–206. (A discussion of the aims of interpretation, monism and pluralism.)

—— (1997) *Artworks: Definition, Meaning, Value*, University Park: Pennsylvania State University Press. (A defense of the unified view and a critique of alternatives.)

Wimsatt, W. K. and Beardsley, M. (1976) "The Intentional Fallacy," in D. Newton-de Molina (ed.), *On Literary Intention*, Edinburgh: Edinburgh University Press. (Though the *locus classicus* of anti-intentionalism, many of the arguments are at least as much directed against biographical criticism.)

22
IMAGINATION AND MAKE-BELIEVE

Gregory Currie

Art and imagination are universally acknowledged to be connected, but the precise nature of the connection, like the nature of imagination itself, remains unclear. This may be because there are a variety of relations between the different arts and different kinds of imagination. In order to reduce the problem to manageable proportions, this essay will focus on one kind of imagination and one kind of art: the fictional. Under this heading something will be said about depictive as well as about literary arts, but the role of imagination in artistic creation will largely be ignored. Instead, this essay focuses on our engagement with works already created.

Two kinds of imagination

We can make a distinction between two kinds of imagining. For imaginings of the first kind, there is an important relation between the imagining and something of which the imagining is what might imperfectly be called a copy, or a counterpart, and in terms of which it seems we have to describe the imagining. But we must not suppose that the imagining need be anything like a replica of this other thing; we should think of it as a copy in the same way that a toy car is a copy of a real car, without it resembling a real car in all or even many respects. A better way to describe the relation would be to say that imagination simulates this other thing, borrowing a term that has recently acquired a special sense in the philosophy of mind (Davies and Stone 1995a; 1995b). One advantage of this term is that it suggests that the similarities between imagining and what it simulates are similarities of function; we shall see that this is exactly where some of the relevant similarities lie. Imaginings of the second kind are not like this; they are not to be described in terms of something else, which they simulate.

What cases genuinely fall into the first, simulative category is a matter of debate, but obvious candidates would be the modes of mental imagery. Visual imagery is a copy, in our special sense, of visual experience, and it is in terms of visual experience that we must describe that imagery. Imaginings of this simulative kind raise a problem. As Malcolm Budd puts it, "the root of the problem raised by these concepts of the imagination is the nature of their relationship with their apparent counterparts" (Budd 1989: 100). Understanding this kind of imagination is very largely a matter of understanding this relationship.

We might call this kind of imagination the 'recreative imagination,' not because the imaginative event is always or even usually the literal recreation of some specific actual event, but because it cannot fully be described without reference to the kind of event of which is a copy. I can see in imagination something no one has ever seen or will see, but my act needs to be described in terms of seeing that thing.

The second, nonsimulative, kind of imagining is exemplified when someone puts together ideas in a way which defies expectation or convention: the kind of imaginative 'leap' that leads to the creation of something valuable in art, science or practical life. We may call this the 'creative imagination.' An instance of imagining can belong to both kinds, as when I imagine saying something witty and brilliant. But the recreative imagination need not be creative. People have said that strong mental imagery is no proof that the subject is imaginative, a point that we can now put by saying that such a person possesses at least one element of the recreative imagination, but lacks creative imagination.

Both kinds of imagination play an important role in the arts. While the creative imagination is of obvious importance for the production of art works, it can be important for the successful interpretation of complex works as well; symbol and metaphor invite us to create meaning, and to see connections that are far from obvious. The recreative imagination is fundamental to a proper engagement with many art works, particularly where the work has a strong representational content. It is likely also that the recreative imagination subserves the creative imagination of many artists and interpreters, though the exact relations here must be complex, with wide variation between cases. But neither kind of imagining is proprietary to the arts. The recreative imagination has been important for devising thought experiments in science, and hence for creative breakthroughs in scientific theorizing.

The recreative imagination is more amenable to description and analysis than the creative, which Hume understandably called "magical" and "inexplicable" (Hume 1902: 24). The recreative imagination is also the kind most closely connected with make-believe. So we can afford to devote our attention here to recreative imagination. Unless there is indication to the contrary, that is what I shall mean by 'imagination' hereafter.

Imagination, representation and fiction

That there is an important connection between imagination and representational art has been powerfully argued by Kendall Walton (1990, esp. ch. 1). Walton claims that paintings, plays, films and novels are representational works of art because they are props in games of make-believe; they prompt us to imagine various things. Indeed they are normative with respect to imagining: they authorize certain imaginings and proscribe others, as *The Old Curiosity Shop* authorizes us to imagine that Nell dies, and proscribes our imagining that she lives on into a happy old age. That which a work authorizes us to imagine is what the work makes fictional. Where the work asks us not to imagine something, it makes fictional the negation of that thing, as *The Old Curiosity Shop* makes it fictional that Nell does not live to old age. Where the work does not pronounce one way or the other we are in the realm of the indeterminate, as it is neither fictional that Holmes was born on an even-numbered day of the month, nor fictional that he was not. But indeterminacies need not be trivial; they can be crucial to the work's effect, as it is with Hamlet's motives which, at least in detail, are indeterminate. So now we have explained being fictional (what is sometimes called 'truth in fiction') in terms of imagining.

There are two things worth saying about this proposal. The first is that someone might complain that it is wrong to say that we imagine that Nell dies, when the text plainly says that she does, there is no indication of narrative unreliability in this instance, and the assumption of her death coheres well with the rest of the story. 'Imagining' sounds better in contexts which involve a hermeneutic effort, as when we are struggling to make sense of a story and hit on the idea that the character's motive was so-and-so: now we can make sense of it, and we do so by imagining something about the character's motive. But this objection confuses the creative and the recreative imagination. Imagining that little Nell dies takes only the latter; imagining that, say, the governess in *The Turn of the Screw* is deluded, would, at least at one time, have required imagination of both kinds. Works of fiction prescribe acts of recreative, and not of creative, imagination.

The second point concerns the claim that we can explain being fictional in terms of imagining. Take the idea that the work makes it fictional that Nell does not live to a ripe old age because it asks us not to imagine that. Arguably, an appropriate (or at least intended) engagement with the work requires one to greet her death with a sense of sorrow and loss; imagining her living to a ripe old age might be a good way of making that loss vivid. It remains true that the work does not prescribe that one imagine her living to old age; no doubt there are appropriate responses to the work that would not involve this. But saying that it is merely optional whether we imagine her living to old age fails to distinguish this case from cases where imagining is optional because it is indeterminate whether the thing to be imagined is part of the story, and Nell's living to a ripe old age is not merely indeterminate so far as the story goes: it is ruled out. It seems that we need to distinguish imagining things as part of the project of imagining what is fictional, and imagining things which are not fictional but the possibility of which informs our response to what is fictional. It is not immediately clear how this can be done in a way that would save the proposed analysis of being fictional in terms of rules of imagining. Perhaps we need to distinguish different 'levels' at which imagining takes place.

We apply the concept fiction to characters as well as to works (to Hamlet as well as to *Hamlet*), and it is not immediately clear how we could account for fictional characters in terms of imagining; to say that fictional characters are imaginary does not explain anything. One response would be to say that the problem is not really a problem about fictional characters. Fictional characters are those that occur in fictions, and they can be real, as Napoleon is a character in *War and Peace*. The problematic cases are where there really is no such person or object as the character in the fiction, as with Pierre Bolkonski. But this problem is not especially a problem about fiction, since we often use terms which appear to be proper names, only to discover that they do not refer to anything, as with 'Vulcan.' So what we need is a semantics for empty names in general, which can then be applied to the case of nonexistent characters in fiction. We should not expect imagination to be useful in solving that problem (see Currie 1990).

Insofar as imagination is explanatory of the literary arts, it is explanatory only of those works which are fictional. Darwin's *Origin of Species* might be regarded as a work of art but it does not authorize imaginings, though imagining may be involved in our encounters with it in various other ways. Since there is a distinction to be drawn between fictional and non-fictional literature, it would be natural to expect a similar distinction within the pictorial realm. Some pictures – formal portraits of real people, for example – do not seem to be fictions. Documentary films are not usually wholly pictorial works since they involve commentary as well as speech and sound internal to the action, but it would be odd to claim that they are partly fictional just because they are partly pictorial. Similarly with 'still' photography. Karsh's photograph of Churchill presents him as defiant; apparently, his appearance at that moment was expressive of petulant anger. There is a tension here that treating this picture as fictional does not illuminate. The photograph asks us to believe, falsely as it turns out, that Churchill's look expresses defiance. It does not merely mandate us to imagine that his look expresses defiance. My own view is that many 'hand-made' portraits similarly serve primarily to induce belief rather than to authorize imagining, though such cases are less clear than those concerning photographs.

In Kendall Walton's treatment, however, pictures always count as fictions. He claims, quite generally, that the depictive content of a picture is what it authorizes us to imagine. Why treat literature and pictures so differently, with a fiction/non-fiction category that cuts right across the one, and no corresponding dissection of the other? One argument would be that linguistic representations do not require imagination in order merely to be understood; we have instead a faculty of language comprehension that is by and large isolated from other cognitive systems, and which is certainly not dependent on imagination. If you pick up a book unsure whether it is fiction, and hence unsure whether to take the attitude of imagining to its contents, this does not prevent you from understanding the meanings of the words and sentences in it. It is then a further question as to what attitude you ought to take, or consider taking, towards its contents: belief if it is non-fiction, imagining if it is fiction. It is at that point that we need the distinction between fiction and non-fiction for literary works. But with pictures it is different because understanding even the depictive contents of pictures does require imagination. So imagination is an 'entry-level' requirement for depictions, and they all therefore count as fictional.

It can be argued, however, that picture recognition depends on perceptual and not on imaginative capacities, where these perceptual capacities are at least as automatic and isolated from the rest of cognition as language processing seems to be. One argument for this appeals to the idea that the essential 'trick' of picture recognition is that a picture of an X has the capacity to trigger one's visual X-recognition capacity; it has been argued that only on this assumption can we explain how it is that we are capable of recognizing pictures we have never seen before (Schier 1986). As it stands, this argument is no more than suggestive, since picture recognition might be argued to involve imaginative as well as perceptual capacities. We might then look for evidence from so-called cognitive deficits: cases where someone is impaired on one kind of cognitive task and intact on others. So if there turn out to be people who are impaired on what would generally be acknowledged to be tasks involving imagination but not on picture-recognition tasks, that would be evidence for Schier's proposal. There is some evidence that people with autism fall into this category.

If we enforce a distinction between fictional and non-fictional pictures, we concede that picturing itself cannot be explained in terms of imagining, while holding to the view that pictures are fictional when they do mandate imaginings. But it needs to be emphasized that understanding and appreciating pictures of all kinds (just as with literary works of all kinds) may be enhanced by and even require imagining, both creative and recreative. Much contemporary scepticism about the fiction/non-fiction divide, based on the claim that works of all kinds engage the imagination, collapses when we enforce the distinctions between the recreative and the creative imaginations, and between works that authorize specific imaginings and works which involve imagination in other ways.

Recreative imagination and belief

I have said that the recreative imagination is marked by its instances being copies, or counterparts, or simulations of other things. I began by saying that we would focus here on the recreative imagination. But in what sense is imagining the events of a fictional story recreative? What do these imaginings copy or simulate? One answer is that these imaginings are copies of the events which are being imagined and which the story describes. But it is a mistake to think that when I imagine a battle, there is something going on which is a copy of a battle. That mistake leads to the view that mental imagery involves mental pictures of the things imaged, whereas in fact the counterpart of my having a mental image of something is my seeing it, not the thing itself. It also leads to the confused opinion one hears to the effect that while Hamlet does not exist in the real world, he exists 'in the mind.'

In the case of imagery, we said that what is simulated is perceptual experience. But what of the nonimagistic imagining that is going on when I read a novel? The answer is that in such cases our imagining simulates the having of a propositional attitude, and for the time being we can take the attitude of believing to be the case to focus on. So the view being proposed is that there is a kind of imagining which stands to belief as imagery stands to perceptual experience. Indeed, this kind of imagining is often called 'make-believe.' When we 'make as if to believe' something, we do something that is rather like believing it.

That this is so is suggested by the fact that imagining behaves inferentially like belief. If, as part of your engagement with a piece of contemporary fiction, you imagine that a character was in London one day and in Chicago the next, you will also imagine that he flew there, unless there is some strong indication in the work itself that he got there by another means. It will be much more difficult to know what to imagine if this occurs in a Conan Doyle story about Sherlock Holmes; you will probably conclude that there is some mistake of chronology and give up the attempt to match your imagining to this bit of text. In general, we let our imaginings mingle with our beliefs, and further imaginings emerge which, so far as their contents go, are identical with what would emerge from the operation of inference on belief alone. There are occasions where imagination seems to licence inferences that belief would not; one can be much more willing to infer a magical cause within the scope of a fiction than outside it. But when as readers we imagine P, and infer a magical cause for P, this is best explained by supposing that we are operating on the basis of the, perhaps tacit, acceptance of a further, general bit of imagining to the effect that magical causes operate in cases like P. And if we believed that P-events had magical causes, we would make precisely that inference in belief.

There is more to be said about the ways in which imagining copies believing; one further way that will be of significance later is that imagining someone in danger can have some of the affective and emotional consequences that believing they are in danger does. But it is time to consider a contrary proposal: that imagining is really just a species of believing. That would undermine entirely the claim that this kind of imagining is recreative, because it would show that imagining is believing, rather than being a counterpart of believing.

People often say that an engrossing fiction is one we come to believe, and that it is this believing on our part which explains our often intense concern for the story, its character and their fates: a problem to which we shall return. While not many people would argue that imagination is just the same as belief in the strongest or most complete sense, there seems to be support for the idea that imagination is an attenuated kind of belief, a kind of state that occupies one end of a spectrum of belief states. To the objection that few people would go to, or stay in, the theater if they believed that real murders were going to take place there, an attenuated-belief-theorist will respond that arguments like this simply show that imagining is not believing in any of the very demanding senses that philosophers have proposed. For instance, philosophers sometimes say that whether or not one believes that P is a matter of whether one is disposed to act in a way that is appropriate, given that P is true. It is not plausible that we believe fictions in this sense of 'believe.' One the other hand, we might want an account of belief which makes it possible to believe P without being disposed so to act; it might be enough to give sincere verbal assent to P, for example. And then we might be tempted to say that imagining, with its inferential and affective similarity to belief, really is believing in this broader sense. Would it be more than a terminological stipulation to reject this idea?

The similarities between imagining and believing are important, and a significant clue to the nature of imagining, but they are not grounds for classing imagining as a kind of belief, for the following reason. We may well want to take a liberal view of what counts as a belief, but belief, however weakly conceptualized, is normative in the following sense: an agent who has contradictory beliefs (in any sense of belief) is in a less than ideal epistemic situation. Suppose for example that someone has the belief that P, but also has, in some sense or other, the belief that not-P. This latter might be a very marginal case of a belief. Nevertheless, there is something wrong with this agent's epistemic condition; his or her condition would be improved by finding a way to give up either P or not-P, provided that doing so could be motivated by respectable reasons. The agent's situation need not be a desperate one, it is simply not epistemically *ideal*. Also, from other points of view, there might be benefits in being in this state; perhaps people are more interesting when there is some tension in their views. Again this is not the issue; the question is whether the agent's condition is *epistemically* ideal.

This principle does not govern the relations between beliefs, however weak, and imaginings. It is simply no defect in a person's epistemic condition that he or she imagines things contrary to what he or she believes, in any sense of 'believes'; an otherwise consistent and coherent believer who imagines that Desdemona is murdered is not in any way failing to meet constraints of epistemic virtue. In that case we ought to say that, while imagining is like belief in various ways, it is not to be classed with beliefs, even in a weak sense of 'belief.' And given that this is so, we may continue to explore the imagination-as-simulated-belief proposal.

Imagination and emotion

The strength of that theory can really be seen only through its capacity to solve problems. Here is one: the supposed paradox of fiction, that we often care, and care deeply, about the fates of fictional characters when we know that they do not exist and so do not act and suffer. Let us see briefly how this paradox can be resolved.

The problem is that there is an inconsistency in the conjunction of the following three rather plausible propositions:

1 We fear for characters in fictions who are in danger.
2 To fear for someone we must believe they are in danger.
3 We do not believe in the dangers described in fictions.

(I have stated the paradox in terms of fearing for; it will be see that the paradox arises for a number of other attitudes.) The conjunction of any two of these entails the negation of the remaining one; no one of them alone entails the negation of any other.

Philosophers have taken a variety of positions on this problem. In an influential piece which launched the contemporary debate about fiction and the emotions Colin Radford seems to be taking the view that there are cases where all of (1) to (3) are true, and that this reveals a contradiction or incoherence in our approach to fiction (Radford 1975: 78). A number of philosophers have denied (1), some arguing that the real objects of our emotions are not the fictional characters but other things: real people and events (McCormick) or real thoughts (Carroll, Lamarque). These writers seem to accept that we experience fear, but claim that fictional characters are not the objects of our fear. But one might read Carroll and Lamarque instead as saying that unasserted thoughts, rather than beliefs, are required for fear, and hence as denying (2). Others who deny (1) deny that what we experience is genuine fear. Kendall Walton, for example, says that the film viewer does not really fear the slime in the horror movie, though it is fictional that he does (Walton 1990, sect. 5.2 and 7.1). Some philosophers have denied (2), arguing that we can have emotions concerning things we do not believe in (Yanal).

Someone who adopts the approach to fiction and the imagination outlined here will say that while (3) is true, we can do something like believing in the dangers described in the fiction; we imagine them, and our imaginings are like believings in their internal functional roles. One of the internal function connections of belief is to affect; we are fearful because we know that we are in danger. And imagining, conceived of as simulation of belief, can be expected to have the same effect. It would then be a matter of further decision whether we say that there is a kind of fear which depends not on belief but on imagining (in which case we deny (2)) or whether we say that while we do not fear for characters in fiction we do something very like fearing for them (in which case we deny (1)). The latter option will be favored by the many philosophers and psychologists who hold that emotions are best understood as states which motivate, guide and monitor our actions, since these connections to action are exactly what is lacking in the fictional case. We need not resolve that issue here.

What about those responses to creatures of fiction which do not involve affect, as when I judge, in a remote sort of way, that Othello is naive? The same problem arises for these cases: surely I cannot believe that someone is naive if I do not believe that person did anything which indicates naivete, and indeed believe that person does not exist? When I evaluate someone as naive I typically believe that he or she is, wish that he or she were not, and register my sense that naivete (at least in this sort of situation) is disvaluable. What is happening in the Othello case is like that, except that the first two components – a belief and a desire – are replaced by counterparts from imagination. Again, it will then be a further question whether we choose to say that this really is making an evaluation of naivete, or merely doing something which, from the inside, seems very like it.

Imagination and desire

I spoke just now about belief and desire having counterparts in the imagination, whereas I have so far officially acknowledged only imaginative counterparts of belief. But if we acknowledge that there are states of imagining which are functionally like belief, it is hard to see why we should resist saying the same for desire. And certainly, if our responses to fiction require us to postulate imagination-based counterparts for beliefs, they require us to postulate imagination-based counterparts for desire, and for the same reason. Just as we react to fictions in ways that seem to depend on beliefs that we do not really have – as we do not believe in Othello – so we react to fictions in ways that seem to depend on desires we do not have. This can manifest itself in interesting ways: peaceful folk can seem, even to themselves, to desire violent revenge to be visited on a fictional character, and lovers of justice can desire (so it seems) likeable rogues to escape the punishment they deserve. It is plausible that these are people who simulate, for the duration, desires they do not really possess.

By treating imagination as a family of states parasitic on other kinds of mental states, we have been able to make some progress in understanding the role of imagination in our responses to some works of art. We have concentrated here on the kind of imagining which is parasitic on attitudinal states like beliefs and desires, ignoring the role of imaginings which have as their counterparts states with a distinctive 'feel' such as states of seeing, hearing, and action that involves movement of the body. Imaginings of these kinds doubtless play an important if less easily regimented role in responding to works that may or may not be representational. It is a familiar suggestion that imagined dispositions or movements of the body are called forth by pictorial, sculptural and even by musical works. Science has made some advances in locating and monitoring the mechanisms in the brain that underlie these capacities, and we can look forward to some fruitful empirical study of these responses.

See also Fiction, Interpretation, Literature, Pictorial representation, Art, expression and emotion.

References

Budd, M. (1989) *Wittgenstein's Philosophical Psychology*, London: Routledge.
Carroll, N. (1990) *The Philosophy of Horror*, New York: Routledge.
Currie, G. (1990) *The Nature of Fiction*, New York: Cambridge University Press.
Davies, M. and Stone, T. (eds) (1995a) *Mental Simulation*, Oxford: Blackwell.
—— (eds) (1995b) *Folk Psychology*, Oxford: Blackwell.
Hume, D. (1902) *A Treatise of Human Nature*, Oxford: Oxford University Press.
Lamarque, P. (1981) "How Can We Fear and Pity Fictions?" *British Journal of Aesthetics* 21: 291–305.
McCormick, P. (1985) "Real Fictions," *Journal of Aesthetics and Art Criticism* 43: 375–83.
Radford, C. (1975) "How Can We Be Moved by the Fate of Anna Karenina?" *Aristotelian Society Supplementary Volume* 49: 67–80.
Schier, F. (1986) *Deeper into Pictures*, Cambridge: Cambridge University Press.
Walton, K. (1990) *Mimesis as Make-Believe*, Cambridge, Mass.: Harvard University Press.
Yanal, R. (1994) "The Paradox of Emotion and Fiction," *Pacific Philosophical Quarterly* 75: 54–75.

Further reading

Currie, G. (1995) *Image and Mind: Film, Philosophy and Cognitive Science*, Cambridge: Cambridge University Press. (Extends this author's earlier account of the psychology of fiction by appealing to simulation theory.)
Feagin, S. (1996) *Reading with Feeling*, Ithaca: Cornell University Press. (An account of empathy with fictional characters based on the idea of mental simulation.)
Hjort, M. and S. Lavers (eds) (1997) *Emotion and the Arts*, New York: Oxford University Press. (An important collection of essays, many concerned with the paradox of emotional responses in fictional contexts.)
Oatley, K. (1992) *Best Laid Schemes*, Cambridge: Cambridge University Press. (A leading psychologist advocates the view that fictions present us with opportunities for simulation.)

23
FICTION

David Davies

Few concepts in the arts are as central to our ordinary commerce with art works yet as philosophically problematic as that of fiction. While we seem to have little difficulty employing the concept in everyday life, a number of very thorny problems continue to preoccupy philosophers. Most obviously, the very nature of fiction calls for clarification: what distinguishes those verbally or visually presented representations which are fictions from those which are not? Second, there are questions about the notion of 'fictional truth,' or, less paradoxically, 'truth in a fiction.' Third, there are possibly deeper questions about what may be termed 'truth *through* fiction,' the capacity of fictions to furnish us with knowledge of the actual world. Fourth there are questions about the mode of existence enjoyed by those characters and events, described in fictional narratives, upon which the truth or falsity of claims made about those narratives seems to depend. Finally, there are apparent paradoxes arising out of our emotional responses to representations acknowledged to be fictional. I shall examine in some detail how the first three questions might be answered, and briefly locate the remaining questions in the broader philosophical terrain.

What is a fiction?

However unified or patchwork a 'theory of fiction' may turn out to be, its core must be an account of what it *is* for something to be a fiction. While some (e.g. Walton 1990) have taken a broader view, we may focus upon fictionality as a property of certain *narratives*. This allows for a derivative sense in which there are 'fictions' that are not themselves narratives, but that have subjects drawn from fictional narratives: the 'fictionality' of a painting of Mr Pickwick might be so understood. Fictional narratives need not be works of literature, in the evaluative sense. Further, a fictional narrative may be presented in a non-literary medium: cinema, theater, painting, or dance, for example.

Paradigm fictional narratives (*Treasure Island*, 2001) differ from paradigm non-fictional narratives (*The Voyage of the Beagle*, a cinematic history of space exploration) in both the manner in which the narrated events are presented, and the extent to which the narrative portrays actual happenings and actual agents. But such differences cannot be constitutive of the fictionality of fictions. As to the manner of narration, there are uncontroversially fictional works that utilize narrative structures characteristic of non-fiction (the diary, for example, or the 'academic' style adopted by Borges in many of his short stories), and non-fictional works that utilize narrative structures characteristic of fiction (some historical narratives, and works of 'literary journalism' such as Mailer's *The Executioner's Song*, for example).

As for the portrayal of actual happenings and actual agents, most fictional works contain at least some narrative elements that, taken as assertions, make true claims about real existents. For example, true claims about Victorian London can be found in *Bleak House*. On the other hand, some non-fictional works – such as discredited histories and early scientific texts – fail to represent actual events and contain expressions that do not refer to any real person, place, or entity. Nor can we take the proportion of true to false claims to be the distinguishing feature of fiction, for this will account neither for massively false works of non-fiction (texts on alchemy or witchcraft, for example), nor for the possibility of largely or wholly true (but *accidentally* true) works of fiction.

This suggests that the fictionality of a narrative may be a matter of *how it functions*, or *how it was designed to function*. In the former case, what matters is the function conferred upon a narrative by its users. For example, it has been suggested that a narrative is fictional when its socially recognized function is to serve as a certain kind of resource in games of make-believe (Walton 1990). Just as children employ 'props' in their imaginative play, so readers may use a text as the basis for an exercise of the imagination. Where this use is socially sanctioned for texts of a given kind, those texts are fictions. Fictionality so conceived is independent of the intentions of a narrator. It is a matter of the accepted ways of using a thing, rather than the uses for which it was designed.

One problem with any such account of fiction is that it has difficulty preserving the intuitive distinction between a narrative's *being* fictional, and its being *treated as* or *believed to be* fictional – the distinction we need to make sense of the idea that a text we have been treating as non-fiction may really be a work of fiction, or vice versa. This distinction is preserved if we take fictionality to be a matter of the function the maker of a narrative *intends* it to perform. According to some philosophers, language (verbal and non-verbal) is typically used in the performance of actions, called 'speech acts.' The paradigm speech act is that of asserting that something is the case. On one account of fictionality

(Searle 1975), fiction is the product of an agent's *pretending* to perform the speech act of asserting the sentences that make up a narrative. A problem for this view is that there seem to be pretended assertions that do not result in fictions: for example, acts of mimicry. On an alternative account (Wolterstorff 1980: 219–34; Currie 1990: ch. 2; Lamarque 1996: ch. 2), fiction arises when an agent performs a genuine speech act, but one distinct from that of assertion in one significant respect. Whereas it is a condition for assertion that the speaker intends her audience to *believe* what she states, in fictive utterance the author intends that her audience *make-believe* what is narrated. This requires what Lamarque terms a 'practice of fiction making': there must be publicly recognized conventions that allow for the suspension of certain standard commitments involved in assertion, so that an author can invoke these conventions, and an audience, recognizing this, can respond appropriately by making believe, rather than believing, the narrated propositions.

'Speech act' theorists hold that the fictional status of a text stems from its originating in an act of pretended assertion or fictive utterance. However, they usually insist that this is not sufficient for the fictionality of a text: it is also thought necessary that, if the narrated events correspond in every detail to actual events, this is purely accidental, the utterer's belief being that, in a substantial part of the narrative, he or she is presenting and describing imaginary people and/or events (Currie 1990: 42ff.; Lamarque 1996: 25). This is meant to exclude from the realm of fiction any text whose author truly believes that the narrated events fully correspond to an actual sequence of events. However, we might ask why no such text can be fictional, if, as 'intended function' theorists maintain, fictionality derives from an author's intention that her audience make-believe the narrated events. First novels frequently draw heavily upon an author's own experience, although it is clearly intended that the audience make-believe, rather than believe, what is narrated. For example, in Joyce's *Portrait of the Artist as a Young Man* the narrated events closely parallel happenings in Joyce's own life, but we rightly read the work as fiction. Suppose we were to discover that *all* of the events narrated by Joyce actually occurred in the order narrated. Since the truth of the narrated events does not, by itself, prevent the narrative from being fictional, why should the author's knowledge of their truth make a difference as long as the appropriate fictional intention is present? The answer, perhaps, is that it *does not* matter, unless this knowledge plays a particular kind of role in the construction of the narrative.

This point can be clarified if we look more closely at the constraints under which narrative construction takes place in acts of fiction-making (Davies 1996). We can shed light on the nature of these constraints by asking how *reading* a text as fiction differs from reading it as non-fiction. Suppose a text, T, narrates a particular sequence of events. As a reader I may ask, 'why *those* events in *that* order?' In asking that question, I posit a generative process that has produced the narrative. To read the text as non-fiction is to assume that the selection and temporal ordering of *all* the events making up the narrative was constrained by a desire, on the narrator's part, to be faithful to the manner in which actual events transpired. We take non-fictional narratives to be governed by what we may term the 'fidelity constraint': the author is presumed to have included only events he or she believes to have occurred, narrated as occurring in the order in which he or she believes them to have occurred. To read the text as fiction, on the other hand, is to assume that the choices made in generating the text were not governed by this constraint, but by some more general purpose in story-telling. This is not, of course, to deny that *some* beliefs about the actual world constrain the construction of fictional narratives: Dicken's beliefs about Victorian London constrained his construction of *Bleak House* because he wished to compose a fictional story *set in that location*.

Suppose we conjoin this idea – that fiction-making involves narrative choices governed by certain kinds of constraints – with the idea that something is a work of fiction insofar as it is the product of an act of fiction-making, as the latter notion is understood by 'speech act' theorists. On the resulting view, the fiction-ality of a text generated with the intention that receivers make-believe the narrated events depends neither on whether the narrated events correspond to some actual sequence of events, nor on whether the author of the text knows of, or is unconsciously guided by, the actual sequence of events in question. It depends, rather, on whether the fidelity constraint was taken, by the author, as the constraint that the ordering of events in T must satisfy. This allows an author to select, as the narrative content of a fiction, a sequence of events he or she knows or believes to have actually occurred, as long as it is the satisfaction of some other constraint by this sequence of events that governs the choice. For example, aiming to tell a story with certain kinds of thematic or structural properties, the author selects these actual events because they exemplify the properties in question. A narrative can fail to be fictional either because its construction *was* governed by the fidelity constraint, or because the narrator lacked the necessary intention that readers make-believe what is narrated.

Truth in a fiction

Fictional narratives, we have seen, may contain statements that are true of the actual world. But to say that a fictional narrative 'contains' such statements is to say that such statements are themselves part of the story narrated, and are thus not only true *simpliciter* but also true in the story. We need to ask, then, as to the conditions under which something is true in a story or fiction.

The simplest account of truth in a fiction would be as follows: it is fictionally true in a story N that p if and only if it is explicitly stated in the text T, in which N is narrated, that p: where it is 'explicitly stated' in a text that p if and only if the text contains, as a proper part, an expression of p. (The rider 'as a proper part' is necessary if the content of expressions occurring in direct or indirect quotation in a text is to be excluded from what is 'explicitly stated.') Being explicitly stated in the text of N is neither necessary nor sufficient for being true in N, however. It is not necessary because we must allow at least some things to be true in the story though they are neither explicitly stated nor immediately derivable from what is explicitly stated – for example, characters in adventure stories presumably eat and sleep in between their explicitly described exploits. It is not sufficient, on the other hand, because we must allow for the 'internal narrators' of stories to be deceivers or deceived (as in Nabokov's *Pale Fire*), or disposed to understate, exaggerate, or employ irony.

The second of these problems is easier to resolve, for we encounter, and generally surmount, analogous difficulties in understanding non-fictional narratives. If we believe the author of such a narrative to be informed about the subject, truthful, reliable, and speaking literally in a language we understand, then we generally infer the truth of whatever is explicitly stated by the speaker. When we distrust the speaker, or believe him or her to be ignorant of the subject, or think that he or she is not speaking literally, we make appropriate adjustments in the inferences we draw from what is explicitly stated. In our attempts to determine what is true in a fictional story, we can employ much the same strategies, as long we are able to gauge, from the fictional text, when the narrator is trustworthy, or deceived, or speaking non-literally. Similarly, we can bring to our reading of fictions the same interpretive skills that enable us to determine when a speaker, in saying one thing, intends to communicate something else. For example, if I respond to your inquiry as to how I did in an exam by remarking on the weather, you may infer that I did not do well. Philosophers talk here of our capacity to grasp 'conversational implicatures' (Grice 1975).

No such easy solution presents itself when we consider those fictional truths that are neither explicitly stated in, nor conversationally implicated by, a text. We infer such truths on the basis of what we take to be 'given,' in the understanding of a story, as unstated background. For example, unless informed to the contrary, we assume that characters in novels are individuals possessed of those features and capacities characteristic of human agents, and we infer certain non-explicit fictional truths on the basis of such assumptions. However, in reading fictions we cannot utilize the same strategy that furnishes us with a background for our understanding of non-fictional narratives. In interpreting the latter, we take as unstated background whatever is independently known to be true of the actual world. In the case of standard fictional narratives, however, many if not most things that are explicitly true in the story are not true in the actual world. If we were to take everything independently known to be true of the actual world as unspoken background in our reading of a fictional story, we would usually render the narrative inconsistent, and even incoherent. Indeed, whole genres of fiction ('superhero' comics, fantasy, fairy stories, 'magic realist' fiction) are predicated on the assumption – known to the competent reader – that the world of the story differs fundamentally from the actual world.

Thus a theory of fictional truth faces a distinctive problem in specifying how we determine, for a given fiction, the unspoken background that is non-explicitly true in the story, and that governs legitimate inferences from what is explicitly true or conversationally implicated. One approach here utilizes what philosophers term 'possible worlds': roughly speaking, alternative ways that the actual world might have been. The suggestion is that what is true in a story N can be captured by appeal to possible worlds in which those things that are explicitly true or implicated in the text of N are *actually true*. We may term these the S-worlds for that story (Lewis 1983). By definition, the S-worlds for N agree concerning everything that is explicitly true or implicated in the text of N. However, they differ dramatically from one another in other respects. In the different S-worlds for *Bleak House*, for example, every feature of the actual world not explicitly mentioned or implicated in the text of the novel can vary in countless ways.

The strategy is to identify the 'unspoken background' for N with what is common, over and above those truths that all S-worlds share, to some sub-set of the total set of S-worlds for N. This requires some principle that will pick out the relevant sub-set. For example, we might select those S-worlds that most closely resemble the actual world, or perhaps those S-worlds that most closely resemble the way we believe the actual world to be. The proposal, in each case, would be that what is true in N is what is true in every S-world of the specified type. But these proposals lead to counter-intuitive results when we consider fictions generated in cultures whose beliefs about the world differ sharply from our own, or from the truth. Additionally, to tie what is true in a story to *our* beliefs about the world entails that what is true in that story changes over time as our beliefs change.

An alternative proposal would select those S-worlds that most closely resemble the way the author of the narrative believes the actual world to be. Being true in each such S-world for N, however, is neither necessary nor sufficient for being true in N. It is not sufficient because an author may have strange and idiosyncratic beliefs that are completely orthogonal to what is explicitly true in the story. And it is not necessary because we want to allow for non-explicit truths in a story that contradict the author's actual beliefs: for example, non-explicit truths about the fire-breathing capacities of dragons in a fairy story.

Lewis himself proposes that what is true in N is what is true in those S-worlds for N that most closely resemble the way members of the intended audience for N believe the actual world to be. However, this faces a more general problem that confronts any account of fictional truth based on the notion of truth in a set of possible worlds. It seems that no such account can deal with stories in which *inconsistent* truths obtain, for example, certain sorts of time-travel stories. The problem is that possible worlds must themselves be *consistent* in order to be possible. To resolve this problem, Currie (1990) proposes an analysis of truth in a story not in terms of possible worlds in which a given set of beliefs is true, but rather in terms of belief-sets themselves. He maintains that, in reading fictional narratives, readers imagine, as part of their make-believe, that they are being informed about the events in the story by a reliable source, the so-called 'fictional author' of the story. The fictional author is *not* to be identified with the actual author, nor, crucially, with the narrator internal to the story: the latter, as we have already noted, may be deceived or deceiving, whereas the fictional author is assumed to be both completely trustworthy and completely knowledgeable about the narrated events. The reader forms an impression of the character and beliefs of the fictional author based on the text of the narrative and assumptions about its provenance. It is by reference to the beliefs attributable to such a fictional author that the reader determines what is true in the story, since the fictional author, as noted, is taken to be a completely reliable source of information about the narrated events.

A ruling assumption in the literature just surveyed is that a philosophical analysis of truth in a story, of 'story meaning,' is *basic* to an account of fiction, both in the sense that it is presupposed by any attempt to understand the 'meaning' of a fictional work in any deeper sense, and in the sense that the problem of story meaning is independently tractable. It may be argued, however, that our engagement with story meaning must often proceed in tandem with our attempt to grasp more thematic meanings intended by the *real* author (Lamarque 1996: ch. 4; Davies 1996). For example, the reader's decision that the Currian 'fictional author' of Marquez' *100 Years of Solitude* believes that the magical events narrated in the story really occurred (rather than believing them to be the imaginings of a deceived narrator) rests upon an assessment of what Marquez himself was attempting to do in telling the story. Indeed, it may be a feature distinguishing those narratives we treat as 'serious fiction' – as works of literature in the evaluative sense – that a reader who has not inquired as to the point of this story being told in this way can be held to have failed to exercise a properly responsible attitude towards the work.

These observations can be connected with the earlier suggestion that fiction-making involves narrative construction guided by certain kinds of constraints.

The inferences of the reader engaged in a game of make-believe with a particular text address what are taken to be the fruits of an intentional act of fiction-making on the part of the person who authored the text. The reader posits certain constraints guiding the narrative choices made by the (real) author, and, to the extent that he or she treats the text as serious fiction, posits these constraints by reference to a purpose ascribed to the author in telling *this* story in *this* way. As a result, determining what the fictional author believes, or what the real author invites us to make-believe, may require determining what the real author wants us to *believe*. If this is the case for much serious fiction, then issues of 'truth *in* fiction' and 'truth *through* fiction' – the subject of the next section – are not as distinct as some would have us think.

Truth through fiction

How is 'truth through fiction' possible? In what ways can we learn about the real world by reading narratives whose construction is not guided by the fidelity constraint? Two kinds of cognitive value have been ascribed to fiction. First, it is claimed that fictional narratives furnish us with knowledge of the real world, distinct from our learning what is true in the story. Second, it is claimed that reading fictional works effects cognitively valuable changes in the reader's emotional and perceptual dispositions. I defer consideration of the second kind of cognitive value to the following section.

There are at least four ways in which fiction might be represented as a source of knowledge or understanding of the real world (for a related and more detailed analysis, see Novitz 1987: ch. 6). First, it may serve as a source of factual information about the world. If, as has been shown, authors incorporate true statements about the real world into their narratives, then readers may come to believe those statements as a result of reading a work. That truth-in-the-story can overlap with truth in this way is built into the manner in which readers characteristically apprehend fictional narratives. Such apprehension is not, usually, in terms of qualitative features of the characters or situations, but in terms of their being fictional characters or events placed in an x-world, where 'x' picks out some real-world events or circumstances. For example, Holmes is a fictional detective in Victorian London. One advantage for the author in setting a fiction in an x-world is that he or she can rely upon readers' prior knowledge of what an x-world is like. Second, fiction may serve as a source of propositional understanding. The narrated events may explicitly or implicitly exemplify and make salient general principles – moral, metaphysical, or psychological – which might be taken to govern the unfolding of events in the real world. This is one way of understanding Aristotle's claim that poetry is more philosophical than history. Third, fiction can serve as a source of categorial understanding. In presenting the fictional world, the narrative may employ novel categories or kinds, natural or psychological, whose application to the real world illuminates certain matters of fact (Goodman 1976: 258ff.). Finally, fiction can be a source of affective knowledge, knowledge as to what it would be like to be in a particular circumstance. Some writers have argued that this plays a valuable part in the development of our moral sensibility (Putnam 1978, Nussbaum 1990).

The claim that fiction furnishes us with knowledge of the real world is, however, open to the following objection. Granted that we form beliefs of the sorts described, and granted that some of these beliefs may be true, to what extent can the acquisition of beliefs in this way satisfy our requirements for genuine learning? Knowledge, after all, has traditionally been taken to require beliefs that are not only true but also justified. Perhaps the most we can get from reading fiction is *hypotheses* about the general ordering of things in the world, or *beliefs* about specific aspects of the world, or *potentially insightful* ways of categorizing things in our experience. Talk of 'learning' from fiction is justified only to the extent that the fruits of our reading are subject to further verification. Only if those hypotheses or beliefs pass further tests can they acquire the status of knowledge, it might be claimed.

Whether this presents a serious obstacle to the cognitive claims of fiction depends, in part, upon more general issues in epistemology. There are, however, interesting but little-studied questions that present themselves in this context. For example, it is undeniable that some fictions leave us with the feeling that our understanding of the world has been deepened. Is this because we somehow *test* the thematic or affective hypotheses in the fiction in the very process of reading? Are there features of a fiction that lead us to trust an author to have got it right? Can we explain why, as Geertz (1988) puts it, we listen to some narrative voices but not to others?

Fiction and the emotions

Some have ascribed cognitive value to fiction on the grounds that reading fictional works effects cognitively desirable changes in the emotional or perceptual dispositions of the reader. For example, Iris Murdoch (1967) claims that reading fiction helps us to develop a clearer 'vision' that sees the real world objectively, rather than in terms of our own self-interest. Again, on one plausible reading of Aristotle's *Poetics*, the 'catharsis' produced by the experience of tragic drama shapes our emotional dispositions so that we pity and fear those things that rationally merit such emotional responses, thereby harmonizing emotion and reason.

The latter claim raises much-discussed issues concerning our affective responses to fictions, however. Catharsis – the 'tragic effect' – seems to presuppose that we can be moved to emotions such as pity and fear in watching what we take to be a tragic fiction. But if we take a narrative to be fictional, we generally do not believe that what we are viewing or reading is a representation of actual events that have occurred to actual people. In that case, it is unclear how we can be moved by the narrated events to feel pity, fear, or other emotions for the protagonists. For it is widely assumed that there is an essential cognitive component to emotions, so that one can respond emotionally to the death of Cordelia, for example, only if one believes that she is an actual person who is undergoing or has undergone the trials described in the story. It seems, therefore, that we must either, implausibly, maintain that we are not actually moved in reading or watching known fictions, or, again implausibly, reject the idea that emotional states have an essential cognitive component.

Two strategies are open to us here if we wish to preserve a cognitivist conception of the emotions. First, we may preserve the idea that we feel genuine emotions in our encounters with fiction by proposing, for these emotions, objects with respect to which we do have the appropriate sorts of beliefs. One possible object for our emotional responses to fictions would be *fictional characters* recognized as such. On such a view, the object of my pity is indeed Cordelia, whom I believe to exist as a fictional character who suffers a particular fate. This option is not promising, however, for at least two reasons. First, the sense to be given to our talk about fictional characters is itself a matter of considerable debate. If we say that a reader who asserts that Cordelia is cruelly rewarded for her honesty and is therefore to be pitied is using the expression 'Cordelia' knowingly to refer to a fictional character, we must explain what sort of thing a fictional character is, and how such an entity can ground our talk about fictions. Philosophers responding to this challenge have drawn on recent technically sophisticated work in metaphysics and the philosophy of language (for a detailed treatment of these issues, see Currie 1990: ch. 4). But, second, even if the mode of existence of fictional characters is clarified, this is unlikely to illuminate our affective responses to presumed fictions. For we must also explain how we can be moved emotionally by the fate of what we take to be a fictional character.

Other proposed objects for genuine emotional responses to fictions seem more promising. Some have suggested that we feel genuine emotion for real people in analogous circumstances to fictional characters, or that it is the idea of such things happening that moves us (Carroll 1990). Alternatively, if we maintain that the objects of our affective states are situations which, as presumed fictions, we do not believe really to obtain, we can preserve the cognitivist conception of the emotions by denying that what we feel in respect of fictions are genuine emotions. Either we merely make-believe that we are feeling real emotions (Walton 1990), or our genuine affective responses are not real emotions but something phenomenologically similar accompanied by make-belief rather than belief (Currie 1990). Proposed solutions to the 'paradoxes' of fiction along all of the preceding lines continue to be debated in the literature.

See also Literature, Narrative, Imagination and make-believe, Interpretation, Art and Knowledge, Art, expression and emotion, Tragedy, Aristotle

References

Carroll, N. (1990) *The Philosophy of Horror*, New York: Routledge.

Currie, G. (1990) *The Nature of Fiction*, Cambridge: Cambridge University Press.

Davies, D. (1996) "Fictional Truth and Fictional Authors," *British Journal of Aesthetics* 36: 43–55.

Geertz, C. (1988) *Works and Lives*, Stanford: Stanford University Press.

Goodman, N. (1976) *Languages of Art*, 2nd edn, Indianapolis: Hackett.

Grice, P. (1975) "Language and Conversation," in P. Cole and J. L. Morgan (eds), *Syntax and Semantics*, New York: Academic Press.

Lamarque, P. (1996) *Fictional Points of View*, Ithaca: Cornell University Press.

Lewis, D. (1983) "Truth in Fiction," *Philosophical Papers*, New York: Oxford University Press.

Murdoch, I. (1967) *The Sovereignty of Good*, London: Cambridge University Press.

Novitz, D. (1987) *Knowledge, Fiction, and Imagination*, Philadelphia: Temple University Press.

Nussbaum, M. (1990) *Love's Knowledge*, Oxford: Oxford University Press.

Putnam, H. (1978) "Literature, Science, and Reflection," in *Meaning and the Moral Sciences*, Boston: Routledge.

Searle, J. (1975) "The Logical Status of Fictional Discourse," *New Literary History* 6: 319–32.

Walton, K. (1990) *Mimesis as Make-Believe*, Cambridge, Mass.: Harvard University Press.

Wolterstorff, N. (1980) *Works and Worlds of Art*, Oxford: Oxford University Press.

24
NARRATIVE

Paisley Livingston

'Narrative' and related terms (such as 'narration,' 'story,' and the many cognates in other languages) have been put to a variety of uses in many scholarly fields, including aesthetics, history, psychology, linguistics, and anthropology. Historians debate the role of narration in historical knowledge, psychologists speak with increasing frequency of 'the narrative of the self' (and even of 'the self as narrative'), anthropologists describe storytellers and their cultural contexts, and literary theorists, aestheticians, and film scholars seek to describe the artistic and rhetorical features of narrative works. Philosophers reflect on these and other sorts of claims about narrative, and sometimes discuss the narrative dimensions of philosophical writings.

The burgeoning theoretical literature on narrative has engendered some rather striking claims concerning both the nature and importance of narrative. Narrative has been blamed as a deceptive ideology (for example, by self-proclaimed postmodernists who say they reject the Enlightenment's 'Grand Narrative' of progress). And narrative has been praised as an especially valuable mode of knowing, sometimes because it is perceived as an alternative to the 'natural-scientific model,' and sometimes because it is held to be a constituent of successful scientific research. Similar polemical stances with regard to the place of narrative within the arts have also emerged. Sometimes decried as the very essence of bourgeois ideology's influence on the arts, narrative is also presented as a unique and invaluable source of moral insights, the very condition of possibility of literature's contribution to worthwhile knowledge.

That such strong and contrasting claims are prominent in the literature motivates a careful look into the basic conceptions of narrative at stake. What sort of thing is a narrative? What does and does not fall within the term's extension? If actual usage of the term is multifarious and contradictory, how can we construct some alternative, reasonably restricted notion of narrative, capable of better serving our descriptive and explanatory needs?

A first question concerns the genus or overarching category to which narratives belong. In one tradition of research on narrative (beginning with French 'narratology'), it is uncontroversial to use the term 'discourse' (or 'text') to mark this first definitional condition. All narratives are discourses, though there may be some discourses that are not narratives. 'Discourse,' however, is rarely given an explicit definition, nor does a cogent conception implicitly orient such theories. In the theoretical excesses of semiology and poststructuralism, every artifact, gesture, and world-historical epoch is a discourse, and one wonders what is not. An alternative approach is to replace 'discourse' with a Grice-inspired usage of 'utterance,' construed broadly to designate any act or performance (or product thereof) expressive of thought or belief, where expression requires that the action be performed in order to indicate some attitude (Davis 1992). A motorist's intentional flashing of the turn signal is, then, an utterance, but sunsets, driftwood and entire civilizations are not.

Another clarificatory issue concerns the relation between narrative utterances and fictional ones. On an account of fiction favored by poststructuralists, all narratives are thought to be fictions because it is assumed that all narratives, *qua* discourses, involve a selective, conventional, arbitrary, and ultimately misleading manner of organizing and presenting experience. Yet on a more plausible, pragmatic account of the distinction between fictional and non-fictional utterances, narratives fall on both sides of the distinction, and can involve sincere or deceptive assertions as well as invitations to engage in imaginative thoughts and feelings. I return later to the issue of narrative's epistemic value.

What is a narrative?

How do narrative utterances differ from non-narrative ones? A common response, which is that 'narratives tell or convey a story,' only shifts the burden onto the story/non-story distinction. Under what conditions does someone's utterance express or convey a story? Usually the way this question is approached is to try to say what must figure within an utterance's contents if it is to be a story. It should be noted that this relatively uncontroversial move has the consequence of making the concept of narrative depend on assumptions about how an utterance's content is determined, a difficult issue that cannot be surveyed here.

We can, however, list some of the more prominent proposals concerning the requisite ingredients of the contents of any storytelling utterance. It has been proposed, then, that to be a story, an utterance's contents must include the following:

1   At least one event, or a change of state from one situation or state of affairs

to another, for example, some object instantiates at least one new property (Prince 1973). It follows that 'The leaf fell from the tree' is a story.

2   At least two events standing in the right kind of relation to each other. Proposals for the relation in question include:

   (i)   a temporal ordering: a story is "*at least two* real or fictive events or situations in a time sequence, neither of which presupposes or entails the other" (Prince 1982: 4).

   (ii) a causal sequence, such as "The wind blew the leaf off the tree" (Prince 1973; Danto 1985: 251–2).

   (iii) a more general 'x occasions y' relation, such as "Autumn came, and the leaf fell" (Hobbs 1990).

   (iv) at least one event manifesting some agent's problem-solving activity, that is, some (intentional) action or goal-directed activity, such as "The leaf decided to leave the tree.'"

   (v)   two or more actions involving purposeful activity, with the additional requirement of a form of 'closure,' meaning that there must be events that function as a coherent sequence of purposeful activity, with a beginning and resolution (provided, for example, when some agent realizes or abandons some overarching goal), such as "John was hungry, so he put on his coat, went to the restaurant, ordered a meal, and ate it" (Wilensky 1983).

3   The same as in 2(iv) or 2(v), with an additional, pragmatic requirement to the effect that the actual storyteller or author of the narrative effectively design the pattern of story events so as to convey some 'point' or to achieve some other expressive or communicative goal. An example is Brewer and Lichtenstein's (1982) proposal that an intended function of all stories is to 'entertain' an audience. Another idea in this vein is that relative to some set of expectations, the agent's goal-oriented actions must involve either unusual or interesting goals, conflicts, or efforts to solve these problems.

4   The same as one of the above proposals, plus the additional requirement that the events include either an implicit or explicit telling of these events: in every narrative there must be at least one narrator who narrates what happens in the story. This figure's manner of conveying the events could be what satisfies the requirement evoked in (3).

Are there good grounds for accepting any one of these proposals? Theorists arguing for a favored usage of 'narrative' typically appeal to our 'intuitions' concerning which examples should and should not count as a story. It is far from clear, however, that any detailed and coherent bed of intuitions awaits any of the theories. Intuitions clash and blur. Attempts to conduct empirical surveys on children's and adults' 'story intuitions' reveal that it is hard to disentangle opinions about what counts as a story and intuitions about what is a 'good story,' or at least one deemed worth telling in some context (Stein 1982, Stein and Policastro 1984). Yet to opt for a strongly normative stipulation seems a mistake, since we sometimes want to say that an utterance conveys an incoherent, imperfect, or boring story, but is still a narrative.

Humanists are ill-served by broad construals of narrative that embrace most of the utterances made by chemists, astrophysicists, and geologists. Cannot the events in a chemical reaction manifest a beginning, middle, and end, if not the 'three unities' required by the classical poeticians? The latter consideration gives us a reason to prefer some conception of story based on agency, as in (2) (iv), yet even this modest first step remains controversial, for reasons that are not always pellucid. Sometimes opposition to an agential understanding of narrative seems to be motivated by broadly 'anti-humanist' worries that liberal individualism or a 'great man theory of history' is being smuggled in. Yet to say that events involving agency must figure in every narrative utterance need not be taken as an especially severe restriction, particularly if one recalls that in the context of a narrative's content, the most diverse array of items can appear as agents. In Stanislaw Lem's story, "The Washing Machine Tragedy," the central character is a planet-sized agglomeration of sentient self-organizing computers that evolve when overly sophisticated home appliances rebel. In other tales, the ultimate agent is God, Spirit, Language, Textuality, or the history of Being. The requirement, then, is not that narrative utterances represent agency truthfully, but that their contents truly include some representation of agents and their purposive strivings.

Another objection to proposal (2)(iv) is that it is too liberal because it allows that trivial and incoherent recountings of various agents' doings count as narratives. Taking this objection seriously motivates the shift to (2)(v). Yet some complain that this is insufficient because a description of banal, successful problem-solving is not a narrative. The latter contention plainly clashes with ordinary usage (for example, 'Sigmund bored me to tears with his tedious narrative'). It would seem that moves to a stiffer, pragmatic restriction in the spirit of (3) have the problem of being either too vague, or of yielding contradictory judgements (because what counts as an unusual or entertaining chain of events in one context may not be deemed so in another). In sum, even with regard to the basic elucidation or construction of a reasonably well delimited concept of narrative, controversy reigns supreme.

Narrators and narration

Must the cast of characters include a narrator? Many theorists have said so (e.g. Chatman 1990: 115; Levinson 1996: 250–1). Central to such claims is the assumption that the narrator, speaker, or presenter deemed necessary to every narration is a *fictional* entity distinct from the work's actual or implied authors, just as this fictional narrator's imagined performance, such as the telling of the story from one or several perspectives or 'points of view,' must not be confused with the actual author's expressive or communicative acts.

Yet this sort of strong thesis about a link between narrations and fictional narrators has not gone unchallenged (Wolterstorff 1980: 163–79; Pettersson 1990: 104–13). A first qualification specifies that the putative necessity of fictional narrators to narration can pertain only to works of fiction, for in non-fiction narratives, an author can speak in his or her own voice, and no separate, narrating agent should be imagined. Arguably, then, the narrator of John Stuart Mill's autobiography is Mill himself, and not some fictional figure. It can still be recognized that within a work of non-fiction, the author may chose to employ one or several fictional narrators. Perhaps Descartes was fictionalizing when he began his second mediation by referring back to his meditations of 'the day before.'

A second, more controversial objection is that within the category of fictional narration, we may distinguish between works in regard to which it is and is not fictionally true that the story is told or presented by a narrator. Although disagreement on this topic can be found already in discussions of verbal story-telling, controversy is greatest with regard to visual and audio-visual fictions.

Advocates of the view that narrative entails a narrator are typically moved by what could be called the epistemic constraints on story knowledge: if story events are to be known at all, there must be some way in which information about them is conveyed or made manifest, and this within the reader's or spectator's make-believe. It is, then, correct for interpreters to ask themselves questions about what is either explicitly or implicitly indicated concerning the provenance of such information, and such questions pertaining to the imaginative content of our experience of the fictional events cannot be answered in terms of the activities of the author, real or implied.

Opponents of this sort of thesis can point to the many visual fictions where there is at least apparently no textual or other evidence warranting us to imagine a presentational activity 'at work' alongside the occurrence of the story events. Mime performances and narrative paintings – cyclical, continuous, or static – are sometimes thought to be examples. Given the controversy that surrounds the definition of narrative, as well as entrenched practices among art historians, there is no obvious basis for holding that paintings cannot narrate a story. A painting can depict one or several events, and these can satisfy most if not all of the constraints sketched in the proposals evoked earlier. The attentive and imaginative observer discovers a story element implicit even in pictures belonging to such seemingly non-narrative genres as still-life and landscape. Thus if it is allowed that John Everett Millais' painting *Ophelia* narrates at least part of a fictional story, one may add that the discerning observer still need not imagine the presence or activity of a fictional presenter.

The conflict over the putative necessity of narrators to narrative is sharpest with regard to what Gregory Currie (1995: 265–6) calls a 'controlling narrator,' that is, a narrator whose mode of presenting the story is imagined to coincide with the work's text or structure as a whole. The first-person narrator of Kazuo Ishiguro's *The Remains of the Day* is a controlling narrator because it is true in the fiction – and it is appropriate to imagine – that the words in the text are his words, and not those of some other authorial or narrating figure. Esther is not the controlling narrator of Charles Dickens's *Bleak House* because the chapters that we are to imagine as having been written or spoken by her are accompanied by chapters narrated by someone else, and she explicitly refers to her own account as her 'portion of these pages.'

With regard to the distinction between controlling and non-controlling narrators, there would seem to be a basic difference between the possibilities available within visual and verbal fictions, since in some verbal works of fiction, the title and ensuing text can coherently be imagined as the very means a fictional narrator has used to tell the story; yet it is hard to see why we should imagine that the entire audio-visual display presented to us at a film screening is the product of a narrator who somehow exists within the world of the fiction. Where, one wonders, was this narrating figure standing as he or she recorded these startling close-ups of the lovers' private conversations? This and many other questions one may raise about the presence and activities of internal storytellers or narrators seem totally irrelevant to the works, which may warrant the conclusion that the fiction should be recognized as perfectly indeterminate with regard to them. Thus, we need not bother to think about how a manuscript could have been written by an illiterate storyteller, just as we need not wonder how cinematic or some other sort of representations or images of the protagonist's private doings have been obtained and made available to an audience (Wilson 1997). This insight concerning story indeterminacy can be extended even further, so as to cover a wide range of cases where engaging in determinate make-believe about narrators and their activities is at the very least highly controversial, and perhaps quite pointless. If we can imagine a fictional showing without thinking how this showing could be possible within the terms of the story, can we not also imagine perceiving something without also imagining how this can occur? The burden of proof is placed on the shoulders of those who claim that we ought to engage in such imaginings.

Resistance to such a minimalist proposal may be motivated by the idea that it runs contrary to standard desiderata concerning the appreciation of the arts of fiction, beginning, for example, with a necessary attunement to differences between reliable and unreliable fictional rhetorics. In response one may contend, along with Currie (1995: 265–80), that unreliability is best viewed as a strategy employed by a fiction's author. Thus, if the first-person voice of Edgar Allan Poe's "The Tell-Tale Heart" is clearly that of the work's fictional narrator, attunement to unreliability requires us to attend to the stylistic devices the author has used to highlight the irrationality of the character's account. In cases of cinematic and other narrations without narrators, unreliability is discerned within the author's rhetorical design.

It should be clear from this brief survey that controversy surrounds some of the most basic conceptual steps involved in our uses of 'narrative.' Such a lesson may fruitfully be brought to bear on the numerous eager theorizings in which some stipulative take on narrative is applied to one or more major topics in some discipline or collection of fields. Perhaps the single most influential trend in this vein has been reflection over the nature and status of historical knowledge, for here we have a rather large and influential literature in which contesting accounts of narrative, knowledge, and their relations abound (see Carroll 1990 for a thorough presentation and insightful criticisms of relevant publications).

Within theoretical writing on the arts, similar trends have arisen with regard to at least two key topics: one, the role of narrative in our descriptions and evaluations of the history of the arts, and two, the relation between narrative and the values of some work, style, movement, or artform. With regard to the first of these, it is safe to say that the debates recapitulate many of the moves and positions characteristic of the previously-mentioned controversies within philosophy of history. If 'narrative' is equated with speculative eschatological machines (as in Hegel's manner of narrating the world-historical development of the arts), then one wants to agree that historical studies of the arts should be freed from this baleful influence. Yet we should not let a stipulative decision convince us that narratives as such are the problem. What is more, if the proposal is that research in art history should be conducted without reference to artists and their efforts to identify and solve creative problems, the critique of 'narrative' has been carried rather too far. Once one works with a thin or minimalist construal of narrative, it becomes difficult to distinguish between historical knowledge claims and the descriptive efforts of scientists in other fields, and consequently more difficult to make narrative *per se* the object of any warranted praising and blaming.

Narration, history, and value

Much of the critical discussion of narrative's putative vitiation of historiographic knowledge hinges on a conception of narrative involving some more or less strict idea of closure and emplotment, as in (2)(v) above. The immense array of events that may be associated, say, with the history of literature contains neither a (knowable) beginning nor an end, and hence no middle, and thus any narrative of it satisfying the norms of closure can only be misleading, or at best reveal a metaphoric sort of insight. Such an argument is trenchant with regard to some imaginary Procrustean effort to compass the whole of literary history within a single narrative, yet is hardly telling with regard to modest, piecemeal stories focusing on smaller sequences of literary activity. For example, Virginia Woolf's completion of *The Years* in 1937 was the end of a long and complex sequence of events in which she struggled to write a work involving certain historical themes; the closure brought by this event was not the product of some commentator's discourse or utterance, and a biographer's narrative can either convey or fail to convey the pattern of events, or story, immanent in this aspect of the writer's activity.

Closure may not, in fact, be the most plausible candidate for the epistemic vice that supposedly lurks within the very form of narrative. Narrative utterances are products of human action, and we have good reason to suspect that their makers sometimes select and arrange story events in ways foreign to actual sequences of events. One such mode is proleptic anticipation or prefiguration. Knowing the story's outcome, the storyteller imbues earlier events with the property of being a prefiguration of subsequent events, just as John the Baptist is made to foreshadow Jesus in the Christian understanding of 'figura' (or 'allegoria' and 'typus', Auerbach 1959). For the non-prophetic historian, no such proleptic property or significance is properly applicable to the prior event at the time of its occurrence, nor can an event, once past, acquire new properties. Thus, when Woolf had completed *The Waves*, she began working on what she imagined as a 'novel-essay' to be entitled *The Pargiters*, and only years later did she abandon this scheme and settle on the design of *The Years*. *The Pargiters* neither anticipates nor prefigures *The Years*, yet at the time of its writing, *The Years* was the successor to, and culmination of, the writer's work on the earlier project. That a work can become influential, or acquire the status as a break-through only years after its completion, means not that the bygone event has taken on new properties, but that in its continued existence, the work itself has done so in a process which involves no anachronistic influences. Yet even if this criticism of proleptic presentations of events is warranted, it hardly seems plausible to say that the error is somehow endemic to all narratives.

A valid argument to the effect that narrative entails a fundamental epistemic error is to contend first of all that 'narrative' designates utterances, the contents of which include agents and their intentional doings as a central constituent. One then contends, along hard determinist or eliminativist materialist lines, that agency is an illusion. It follows that narratives, or at least the non-fictional variety, are inimical to knowledge. The argument's assumptions and conclusion, however, are hard to live with, and probably unsound. And if agency figures among the 'necessary illusions,' there would at least be a place for narrative fiction in this scheme.

With regard to the second issue, or the general issue of narrative's relation to artistic and other forms of value, it seems safe to say that the interesting generalizations have yet to be discovered. Who can tell us under what conditions conveying a story, or a story having a certain form or content, does or does not contribute to the value of a work of art? The search for norms or principles is problematic, even with regard to some reasonably well-defined generic category. In such a context, one of the aesthetician's tasks is to critique the reductive proposals that critics and philosophers have set forth. An example is Gilles Deleuze's (1983) manner of praising certain films by means of wild claims about how they 'free themselves' from some horrific constraints of narrative. A closer look shows that 'narrative' is undefined, and that on any of the broader construals surveyed earlier, the films in question would have to be acknowledged as telling stories. Another source of examples is current debate over literary narrative's contributions to moral insight and education. Only on some rather stringent restriction of the extension of 'narrative' is it plausible to extol the unbroken stream of morally rewarding experiences and insights flowing to us from the 'genre.' The mainstream movie industry finds its mainstay in fictional stories that are hardly morally insightful, a central pattern of which is the 'resolution' of crises by means of the heroic, violent extermination of some 'evil' party who functions as a ritual scapegoat. Thus it is not narrative *per se* that is a source of moral value, but some sub-set thereof, and those who extol the essential virtue of narrative are in fact working with some stipulative definition. Given that these stipulations would most likely appear highly counterintuitive and be open to many counterexamples, it is unsurprising that they are rarely m ade explicit.

The moral of *this* story, finally, is that in theory, what we get from our concept of narrative is often just what we put into it.

See also Fiction, Interpretation, Imagination and make-believe, Literature, Art and knowledge.

References

Auerbach, E. (1959) "Figura," in *Scenes from the Drama of European Literature*, New York: Meridian.

Brewer, W. F. and Lichtenstein, E. H. (1982) "Stories are to Entertain: A Structural-Affect Theory of Stories," *Journal of Pragmatics* 6: 473–86.

Carroll, N. (1990) "Interpretation, History, and Narrative," *Monist* 73: 134–66.

Chatman, S. (1990) *Coming to Terms: The Rhetoric of Narrative in Fiction and Film*, Ithaca: Cornell University Press.

Currie, G. (1995) *Image and Mind: Film, Philosophy, and Cognitive Science*, Cambridge: Cambridge University Press.

Danto, A. C. (1985) *Narration and Knowledge*, New York: Columbia University Press.

Davis, W. (1992) "Speaker Meaning," *Linguistics and Philosophy* 15: 223–53.

Deleuze, G. (1983) *Cinéma 1: L'image-mouvement*, Paris: Minuit.

Hobbs, J. (1990) *Literature and Cognition*, Stanford: Stanford University Press.

Levinson, J. (1996) "Film Music and Narrative Agency," in D. Bordwell and N. Carroll (eds), *Post-Theory: Reconstructing Film Studies*, Madison: University of Wisconsin Press.

Pettersson, A. (1990) *A Theory of Literary Discourse*, Lund: Lund University Press.

Prince, G. (1973) *A Grammar of Stories*, The Hague: Mouton.

—— (1982) *Narratology: The Form and Function of Narrative*, Morton.

Stein, N. L. (1982) "The Definition of a Story," *Journal of Pragmatics* 6: 487–507.

—— and M. Policastro (1984) "The Concept of a Story: A Comparison Between Children's and Teachers' Viewpoints," in H. Mandl, N. L. Stein and T. Trabasso (eds), *Learning and Comprehension of Text*, Hillsdale, N.J.: Lawrence Erlbaum.

Wilensky, R. (1983) *Planning and Understanding: A Computational Approach to Human Reasoning*, Reading, Mass.: Addison-Wesley.

Wilson, G. (1997) "*Le Grand Imagier* Steps Out: The Primitive Basis of Film Narration," *Philosophical Topics* 25: 295–318.

Wolterstorff, N. (1980) *Works and Worlds of Art*, Oxford: Oxford University Press.

Further reading

Carr, D. (1991) *Time, Narrative and History*, Bloomington: Indiana University Press. (Promotes narrative as adequate to our experience of temporality.)

Carroll, N. (1998) "Art, Narrative, and Moral Understanding," in J. Levinson (ed.), *Aesthetics and Ethics*, Cambridge: Cambridge University Press. (Excellent survey of question of narrative's contributions to moral knowledge.)

Colby, B. N. and Colby, L. M. (1981) *The Daykeeper*, Cambridge, Mass.: Harvard University Press. (Insightful anthropological study of a storyteller's craft and cultural context in a Guatemalan village. Presents and employs functionalist 'story grammar' models.)

Lamarque, P. (1990) "Narrative and Invention: The Limits of Fictionality," in C. Nash (ed.), *Narrative in Culture: The Uses of Storytelling in the Sciences, Philosophy, and Literature*, London: Routledge. (Comprehensive discussion of relations between narrative and fiction.)

Mitchell, W. J. T. (ed.) (1980) *On Narrative*, Chicago: University of Chicago Press. (Influential collection containing significant essays by Hayden White, Paul Ricoeur, Louis O. Mink, Nelson Goodman, Frank Kermode, Victor Turner, and others. A diverse array of contrasting claims about narrative.)

Prince, G. (1987) *A Dictionary of Narratology*, Lincoln: University of Nebraska Press. (A very reliable and time-saving digest of the results and claims of narratology.)

Wilson, G. (1986) *Narration in Light: Studies in Cinematic Point of View*, Baltimore: Johns Hopkins University Press. (A rich and original investigation of a range of issues related to narration in cinema.)

25
METAPHOR

Garry L. Hagberg

It is evident that metaphors are common in the arts and in art criticism as well as in our talk about the arts more generally. Thus an account of metaphor will form part of a complete understanding of the arts. But some have argued that metaphor is not just something of which the arts avail themselves; it is at the root of the arts (or shares a common root with them). Why this is so will be clear once we better understand the nature of metaphor. We will thus consider, first, a number of prominent philosophical accounts both ancient and modern (including reductivist accounts, conceptual-comparison accounts, accounts emphasizing the creative nature of metaphor, and some recent alternative accounts) and, second, conceptions of the relation between metaphor and the arts and the role metaphor plays within them.

Accounts of metaphor

Reductivist accounts

It is Aristotle who gives the – to put it one way – foundational account of the subject. He writes, "metaphor consists in giving the thing a name that belongs to something else; the transference being either from genus to species, or from species to genus, or from species to species, or on grounds of analogy" (*Poetics*: 1778457b). It was in the *Poetics* that Aristotle laid down the influential structural analysis of metaphor in which A is to B as X is to Y. This form, when filled with content such as 'life is to old age as day is to evening,' yields metaphors such as 'the evening of life' and 'the old age of the day.'

Quintilian, in the first century AD, introduced metaphor through simile, suggesting that 'Achilles is like a lion' (in battle) is more readily comprehensible than the metaphorical 'Achilles is a lion' (Quintilian 1996). The simile is immediately accessible because it does not generate problems of the truth-conditions for the assertion. Whether Achilles is like a lion in battle is straightforwardly determinable as true or false, but the metaphorical assertion

'Achilles is a lion' is of course *literally* false, and yet – and here the complexities begin – in a different sense, true. Thus some have preferred theories of metaphorical meaning suggesting that the meaning of the metaphorical assertion is different from the literal (and false) assertion identical in words but not in meaning to the metaphorical assertion. The simple thesis here is the theory of the elliptical simile: a metaphor condenses the content of the simile by removing, but still implying, the explicit comparison (the 'like' or 'as' phrase), thus making the same assertion as the simile, via elliptical implication. The metaphorical assertion 'Achilles is a lion' only appears to put forth a claim that is both false and different in meaning-content from the parallel simile, and the distinct problem of metaphorical meaning on this account evaporates. It will be evident that that conception of metaphor greatly emphasizes the central place occupied by literal assertion (and by extension, literal description) in our larger account of meaning and communication; the metaphorical assertions are made descriptively palatable by transforming them back into their 'parent' similes, which again have far more readily available truth-conditions.

Similarly, metaphor has often been construed as a conceptual comparison in which the primary subject, Juliet for example, is compared to a secondary subject, in this case, the sun. More precisely, the reader is invited to imaginatively compare various similarities as they are suggested, not by the *writer* in terms of a pre-cognized and closed set of specific qualities or attributes, but by the conjoined *words* themselves. And as every schoolchild knows, the context will determine which qualities or attributes are consistent with the intention (but again where this intention of metaphorical meaning is not fully pre-specified); thus 'Juliet is a fiery ball of burning gas exerting enormous gravitational influence' is fairly wide of the mark. 'Juliet is the very source of light and warmth, necessary for life itself, and indeed the center of Romeo's universe' is considerably more on target.

It is conceptually far less complex to ascertain the coherence or compatibility of any two literal utterances than any two metaphorical ones. The assertions 'life is easy' and 'life is difficult' are, in the absence of further specifics, each more readily verifiable or falsifiable, and taken together more obviously incompatible than the related pair of assertions 'life is a bowl of cherries' and 'life is no bed of roses.' And claims such as 'all the world's a stage' can seem to move us rapidly toward epistemic disorientation: one is not at all sure how to begin to determine the truth-conditions for such an utterance. Indeed, the search for truth-conditions seems strangely irrelevant to the meaning, or to the understanding, of that Shakespearian observation; it seems to propose a way of seeing the world, a distinct perspective upon it, rather than making a true-or-false assertion.

Here, however, we move outside the general reductive consensus that the apparent simile is the true (or false) content of the metaphor. In sum, the reductive impulse in dealing with metaphor is fueled by fundamental concern for descriptive truth. This concern motivates Hobbes's surely too extreme remark that reasoning with metaphors is nothing more than "wandering amongst innumerable absurdities" (Hobbes 1968: 117) and that, in the "rigorous search of Truth," all metaphors are "in this case utterly excluded. For seeing they openly professe deceit; to admit them into Councell, or Reasoning, were manifest follies." Similarly, Locke remarked that metaphors are "for nothing else but to insinuate wrong ideas, move the passions, and thereby mislead the judgement" (Locke 1975: 508). For such extreme reductionists, metaphors are best avoided, and, if unavoidable, then reduced to epistemologically manageable similes.

Metaphor and creation

The revolution in the recent discussion of metaphor dates to Max Black's 1955 essay, which builds on the foundations laid down by I. A. Richards (1991). Black developed the claims that metaphors possess a cognitive value internally of a kind that cannot be reduced to literal paraphrase. Thus he rejected substitutive conceptions (A is to B as X is to Y), comparison conceptions (Juliet is comparable to the source of warmth, light, and so on) and elliptical-simile reductionism. Black articulated a decidedly *creative* conception of metaphor, arguing that the similarities into which a metaphor offers insight are created through the novel conjunction of terms, and *they* do not merely describe a set of similarities already resident in the perceptual world. The distinctive interactions of the sets of ideas associated with each of the two terms of a metaphor – or at least a good one – offer a unique insight that is neither possible in strictly literal terms nor 'sayable' within those terms.

Black's position constitutes the emancipation of metaphor from the domination of the literal assertion and has opened the way to detailed studies of the relations between artistic and metaphorical-linguistic practices. Although this revolution is still under way, it was Nietzsche (1979) who anticipated it in characteristically extreme form, asserting the primacy of the metaphorical over the literal. Metaphor, for Nietzsche anything but a rhetorical device for the generation of writerly color, is the essential foundation not only of linguistic meaning but of all cognition. In places he argued that perception itself is a metaphoric process, setting the stage for more recent discussions of the metaphoric structure of the arts. He argued that drawing the line demarcating the literal and the metaphorical is not itself a simple task, because common parlance is very heavily populated (so to speak) with dead metaphors, that is, metaphors that are no longer recognized for their novel insight-generating admixtures of terms. Non-philosophical instances are plentiful and unproblematic: we quite naturally now speak of a clock's face and hands.

Philosophical instances are also plentiful but considerably more problematic in determining the precise extent to which a phrase is in fact metaphorical. Given

Nietzsche's position we naturally must face the question whether the phrase 'the foundations of knowledge' is an architectural metaphor. If so, is it epistemologically misleading? And do spatial metaphors, once adopted, subsequently determine our thinking about philosophical psychology? Examples (not Nietzsche's, but illustrative of his view) are readily found in phrases such as thoughts 'in the head,' 'the back of the mind,' 'the inner recesses of the mind,' 'the motivations behind the utterance,' and 'the privacy of the mind.'

It is thus not a simple matter even to say that we would do well to consider the arts *in the light of* the linguistic practices to which they stand parallel (and that motivate the use of the commonly-employed phrase 'visual language,' for the very phrase 'in the light of' is metaphorical, although certainly moribund if not deceased). Speakers of language, it is thought by the proponents of this Nietzschean view, naturally forget, or cover over, the metaphoric nature of all utterance. Truth is "a mobile army of metaphors" which "after long usage seem to a nation fixed, canonic, and binding" (Nietzsche 1979: 180). It is art that reawakens the slumbering sense of novel, insightful, perceptual-perspectival conjunctions of terms, of images, and of their creatively converging sets of associated ideas. On this radical view, the very idea of a fixed literal truth is only a dead metaphor disguised as literal fact.

Recent views

Before proceeding to an examination of the artistic side of the comparison of metaphorical and artistic practice, however, it is necessary to glance at a few more chapters in this still-unfolding history of the theory of metaphor. Donald Davidson, in a widely influential paper, put forth a powerful argument concluding that there is no such thing as metaphorical meaning apart from the literal meaning of the words contained in the metaphorical expression: "metaphors mean what the words, in their most literal interpretation, mean and nothing more" (Davidson 1979: 30). Davidson identifies the view that "a metaphor, has in addition to its literal sense or meaning, another sense or meaning" (ibid.) as the central mistake of the field to date. He agrees, with many others, that a metaphor cannot successfully be paraphrased, but for the very different reason that, rather than there being a form or variety of meaning not amenable to literal propositional encapsulation, there is no special metaphorical meaning to be paraphrased in the first place.

Davidson builds his argument on the distinction between what words mean on the one hand, and what they are used to accomplish on the other. This broad distinction is not difficult to illustrate. An ironic 'nice work' or a sarcastic 'oh sure' suggests the splitting-off of use from meaning (where meaning is, if controversially, thought to be identifiable in isolation from usage). Thus 'all the world's a stage,' while it means just what it says, is used to make an observation on the theatrical, role-playing aspect of life. With metaphor thus located wholly in "the domain of use," Davidson (like a number of earlier writers on metaphor) regards it as "something brought off by the imaginative employment of words and sentences," but then adds (very much unlike those earlier writers) "and depends entirely on the ordinary meanings of those words and hence on the ordinary meanings of the sentences they comprise" (Davidson 1979).

Although Davidson's analysis is far too detailed to recount here, he argues against comparison, novelty, ambiguity-analogies (that a metaphor, like an ambiguous phrase, has two separate meanings), elliptical similes, extended-meaning theories (that the use of 'face' in the phrase 'upon the face of the water' extends the settled or familiar use of 'face'), the analogy between using a metaphor and telling a lie (that in both cases we assert something we know to be literally false) and others, indeed, against most of the history of the subject. And with metaphor having no special or distinct meaning, there is, for Davidson, no distinct metaphorical truth – that is, in the *sentences* – for "this is not to deny that there is such a thing as metaphorical truth, only to deny it of sentences" (Davidson 1979: 39).

It is important to see that his position is not by any means an eliminative one (although he is denying the very motivation for other theories of metaphor, the problem of metaphorical truth of sentences): he allows that there is such a thing as metaphorical truth, for "metaphor does lead us to notice what might not otherwise be noticed, and there is no reason, I suppose, not to say these thoughts, and feelings inspired by the metaphor, are true or false"(Davidson 1979: 39). Poetic metaphor can "intimate much that goes beyond the literal meaning of the words." But if "intimation is not meaning," one may wonder why intimation cannot constitute an aspect of meaning when we naturally call it that in certain contexts. Apart from such detailed concerns, however, the openness of metaphorical interpretation or paraphrase is given a secure place: Davidson holds that "the endless character of what we call the paraphrase of a metaphor springs from the fact that it attempts to spell out what the metaphor makes us notice, and to this there is no clear end" (ibid.: 45). And this claim is clearly linked to our frequently finding the interpretation of a work of art inexhaustible.

Another view of metaphor is that of Lakoff and Johnson (1980), who argue for the pervasiveness of metaphor throughout our language and thought, emphasizing the undetected influence of unconscious central metaphorical concepts that we pre-reflectively take as literal. Unlike Davidson, they believe that metaphorical content holds truth value: the cognitive content of the metaphor, distinct from literal meaning, can be true or false. This cognitive content of the metaphor is constituted by the transference of a mapping (itself a cartographical metaphor) of one distinct domain of experience onto another. Lakoff and Johnson investigate a broad range of cases, integrating material from cognate fields such as anthropology, psychology and linguistics, and find that bodily experience is a powerful influence on – indeed they say the source of – our thought, demarcating the range of possible metaphor.

The description of mental phenomena in the terminology of visual experience provides an example of experience-domain transference: 'casting light' on a subject, 'illuminating' it, 'seeing' the point, 'clouding' the issue, and so forth, are usages drawn from bodily experience and projected onto the realm of pure cognitive experience. Indeed, Lakoff and Johnson argue that one layer of metaphorical description often stands, not on literal fact, but on another hardened layer of metaphorical description. For example, in alluding in conversation to the 'foundational issues' or the 'fundamental point,' one is not thus alluding to a basis of fact upon which the conversation is constructed, but in turn just to other architectural metaphors. That position has been extended by Lakoff and Turner (1989) into an analysis of poetic metaphor, showing not only the power of fundamental metaphors on our thought and speech but also on our conceptions of, and practices of, emotional expressivity.

A fairly extreme view relates metaphor to metaphysics. Paul Ricoeur (1977) has argued that the employment of metaphor can liberate us from the referentially-static or fixed conception of the world that literal language is thought to enforce, allowing not only a changed metaphor-induced perception of the world, but more extensively, a changed ontology, indeed a changed world. Metaphor is construed by Ricoeur as a re-organizational force in metaphysics, and many (such as Hesse and Arbib 1986) who do not endorse that extreme ontological thesis have still investigated with great profit the role – some would say a leading role – that metaphorical speech (and thus thought) has played throughout the history of scientific thought.

Another rather extreme view has been advanced by Richard Rorty (1989), who has argued that linguistic change – roughly the move from one Wittgensteinian language-game to a subsequent, different game – is the result not of rational progress along a developmental continuum, nor of the improved matching of corre-spondences between our language and the way the objective external world really is, but rather the result of strong new vocabularies that are often fundamentally metaphorical in nature, and that simply take root in our culture's ongoing conversation and thus shape subsequent thought and talk. Freud, for example, developed what became a culture-wide hybrid or metaphoric language of psychodynamics from the pre-existent language of hydrodynamics, so that we speak of mental pressure, force, flow, blockage, outlets, and so on. Rorty's view is profoundly relativistic: it is not the aptness, or the accuracy, or again the correspondence to reality that makes truth, it is the conventions that happen to be in play at a given time and place. A metaphoric assertion, if true, is true by acceptance, by practice, and not by virtue of a matching of the metaphorical description to the objective features of the object or person described. Metaphoric language is thus cut loose from its moorings to any extra-linguistic or ontologically objective world of stable referents. The very idea of such moorings is exposed as another contingent and practice-entrenched metaphorical image that is, in truth (if a difficult – indeed it may be argued self-contradictory – concept to wield within this theory) no more epistemologically privileged than any other. Like some of the other views we have considered, metaphors are here believed to shape the contingent conceptual and perceptual world in which we live.

Metaphor and the arts

It will be clear that the foregoing issues and views are immediately relevant to the verbal arts. One need not even speak of an *application* of those issues and theories to verbal arts, precisely because they are already resident within them. The obvious fact is that metaphors are richly woven throughout fiction, poetry and the other verbal arts, and the full explication of the meaning of those works – whether we speak of a distinct metaphoric meaning or only of distinct metaphoric usages of literal meanings – will inevitably entail a consideration of those issues and views. But what of the non-verbal arts? How does the concept of metaphor, however articulated in detail, cast light on the visual and musical arts? A number of writers have extended the concept of metaphor into non-verbal or extra-literary domains, and a number of ways of proceeding present themselves.

The first, building on the broad conception of the non-verbal arts adumbrated by Susanne Langer (1953), is to construe the work of art most fundamentally as a symbol. However this is achieved in detail, the symbolic content of art can then enter into metaphoric relations with other terms or symbols, allowing for the transference of meaning or of associated ideas from one symbolized content to the other. Among countless examples one might choose Goya's court portraits, infamous for having depicted the members of the royal court with horse-like faces. The picture of the king is thus a symbol, the hint of equine physiognomy another, and their merger within the visual content of the painting, each with its own set of associations, produces an image that functions metaphorically. Interestingly, parallel problems of paraphrase emerge here: the metaphorical sentence 'the king is a horse' fails to capture the particular gesture made in the painting, and although one could go on in attempting to capture that visual meaning verbally, it is – as Davidson suggested in the verbal case – unclear just where to stop or just where one has finished the visual-to-verbal interpretative-paraphrastic task.

A second way of understanding non-verbal metaphor is as the result of an interaction between two visual forms, each of which is familiar and again brings its complement of connotations, but which, when the two are united, creates a 'way of seeing' not previously contained within either visual form and not previously resident in the perceptual world. The main exponents of this view have been Virgil Aldrich (1968) and Carl Hausman (1989). The parallel to the verbal version is clear. One example is Cézanne's landscape painting, in which houses are depicted as volumetric masses contained organically within the landscape, and conversely masses comprising geological or topological features of the landscape assume a 'constructed' aspect or identity. In direct analogy to one conception of verbal metaphor, an unperceived or insufficiently-perceived similarity is brought to the fore by the metaphoric function of the picture. The conceptual result is a way of seeing, or an insight into, an ontological continuity between the natural and the constructed environment that one can only verbally characterize as a

'Cézanne-landscape-way' of seeing, but that is strong enough to change perception. Indeed, this kind of conceptual-visual change is one way to give content to the commonly-heard phrase 'learning the visual language' of one artist or another.

A third way of developing the concept of metaphor in visual form is found in inter-art-work relations: just as two terms interpenetrate, so may visual forms. Turner, in making clear that he wanted certain of his sunset-seascapes hung next to Claude Lorrain's influential paintings in the same genre, stipulated – to put the matter one way – that the two 'terms' of the metaphoric structure be within visual 'reach,' thereby displaying complex interactions of form, light, design, palette, representational content, technique, and related matters. And they are metaphorically structured; they do *interact*. We see the Claude differently after having seen the Turner. One might express this by identifying Turner as a 'strong' painter who, in changing the 'vocabulary' of our visual culture, changed, if not, like Freud, the way we speak, then certainly the way we see, including paintings that preceded his own. This leads to the perception of relational properties that link the two works, even though the first painter may not have known of the latter (just as any pre-Turner painting of a vortex now visually resonates with Turner's work). In this respect particularly, the metaphoric structure of the inter-art relations is, as it was said to be on one model of the linguistic case, creative.

A fourth way (or perhaps an amalgamation of the earlier ways), now applied to music, is found in the case of a composer, freed of all referential or representational moorings, writing a first theme, a transition, a second theme, and then a full treatment through the interaction of the two themes in a development section of a work in the sonata-allegro form. That is followed by a recapitulation, in which what one heard in the preliminary exposition is now heard differently, owing to the interaction of the two themes, and the final coda reflects back in a way that could reasonably be characterized as an end-of-work insight gained through the full articulation, development and interaction of those themes. Here, a historically contingent 'language-game' is developed within compositional practice, and is 'right' only internally, and not in reference to any outward or extrinsic standard against which the musical work is compared in the interest of verifying a true correspondence. (Many musical forms would fit as well; I choose sonata-allegro because of its particularly good fit to one of the conceptions of verbal metaphor.) In another way, this musical case does invite questions of matched and justified correspondence, but between the metaphorical language we use in critical descriptions of musical work, and the works that are thus metaphorically described; of course similarly structured questions arise in all the arts.

A fifth way, put forward by David Summers (1991, 1998), has been to develop the concept of what he calls *real* metaphor. Building on the foundational etymological point that the word 'metaphor' comes from the Greek '*metapherein*,' meaning 'to transfer, to bear' or 'to carry over or across,' Summers argues that we should reawaken our sense, from our knowledge of and participation in cultural rites and customs, that the absent entities, persons, or power can be made 'present' through substitution. Stones in place of gods, subsequent anthropomorphized images, and still subsequent ritualistic painting, and paradigmatically, sculptural objects have functioned, and indeed still function, in this way. The objects function not so much by referring to or representing the absent entities but rather by standing in for them, rendering their associations present. One may question the use of the word 'real' here, since the associated ideas are (really) present while the real entity is not, but for Summers, the transference of meaning, or of idea-association sets, is the vital issue. The creative physical objects – with which we engage in ritualized contexts or in a culturally customary way (such as in museums) – thus carry the transferred meaning of the depicted images, just as a stone may take the place in a given culture of a deceased chieftain, "in order for his power to continue to be addressed" (Summers 1998: 219–21).

As Summers tellingly observes, the words 'statue' and 'monument' preserve this fundamental metaphoric power in sculpture into the present day. Like Lakoff and Johnson, he emphasizes the embodied experience of spatiality and the physical presence of the art object. Parallel to their claim that we derive from metaphor a good deal more of our thinking about the mind and bodily experience than we may initially realize (and that our mental talk is thus metaphorical to its core), Summers proposes that the development of Western optical naturalism and vanishing-point perspective is a "construction of virtual space," a conventional depiction of the receding third dimension that derives from our embodied, single-viewer conception of the experience of real space. He adds, also parallel to views of verbal metaphor, that artistically-created virtual space as structured in our or in any of a number of alternative ways, is not "reducible . . . to the structures of language." Artistic space, as it functions metaphorically, is not 'sayable,' and thus not paraphrasable.

It will be obvious that there are many further contributions to the understanding of metaphor since Aristotle, and countless examples of both metaphorical usage in the verbal arts and metaphorical structures (or, variously, analogies to the verbal structure of metaphor) throughout the non-verbal arts, the examination of which space does not allow. But this glance at the issues suggests that a distinctive kind of light can indeed be shed on the arts by investigating metaphor. This is so precisely because in those cases – very many cases – where a metaphor or metaphoric structure is housed within a work of art, a fuller understanding of the power, scope, and significance of that work is invariably afforded by a fuller understanding of the nature and function of the metaphor contained within it.

See also Interpretation, Literature.

References

Aldrich, V. (1968) "Visual Metaphor," *Journal of Aesthetic Education* 2: 73–8.

Aristotle (1984) *Poetics*, in J. Barnes (ed.), *Complete Works of Aristotle*, Princeton: Princeton University Press.

Black, M. (1955) "Metaphor," *Proceedings of the Aristotelian Society* 55: 273–94.

Davidson, D. (1979) "What Metaphors Mean," in S. Sacks (ed.), *On Metaphor*, Chicago: University of Chicago Press.

Hausman, C. R. (1989) *Metaphor and Art: Interactionism and Reference in the Verbal and Nonverbal Arts*, Cambridge: Cambridge University Press.

Hesse, M. and Arbib, M. A. (1986) *The Construction of Reality*, Cambridge: Cambridge University Press.

Hobbes, T. (1968) *Leviathan*, ed. C. B. Macpherson, Harmondsworth: Penguin.

Lakoff, G. and Johnson, M. (1980) *Metaphors We Live By*, Chicago: University of Chicago Press.

Lakoff, G. and Turner, M. (1989) *More than Cool Reason: A Field Guide to Poetic Metaphor*, Chicago: University of Chicago Press.

Langer, S. K. (1953) *Feeling and Form: A Theory of Art Developed from Philosophy in A New Key*, New York: Scribner.

Locke, J. (1975) *An Essay Concerning Human Understanding*, ed. P. H. Nidditch, Oxford: Oxford University Press.

Nietzsche, F. W. (1979) "On Truth and Lie in an Extra-moral Sense," *Philosophy and Truth: Selections from Nietzsche's Notebooks from the Early 1870s*, trans. D. Breazeale, Brighton: Harvester.

Quintilian (1996) *Institutio Oratoria*, Books I–III, trans. H. E. Butler, Cambridge, Mass.: Harvard University Press.

Richards, I. A. (1991) *Richards on Rhetoric*, ed. A. E. Berthoff, New York: Oxford University Press.

Ricoeur, P. (1977) *The Rule of Metaphor: Multi-Disciplinary Studies of the Creation of Meaning in Language*, trans. R. Czerny, K. McLaughlin and J. Costello, Toronto: University of Toronto Press.

Rorty, R. (1989) "The Contingency of Language," in *Contingency, Irony, and Solidarity*, Cambridge: Cambridge University Press.

Summers, D. (1991) "Real Metaphor: Toward a Redefinition of the Conceptual Image," in N. Bryson, M. A. Holly and K. Moxey (eds), *Visual Theory: Painting and Interpretation*, New York: Harper Collins.

—— (1998) "Metaphor and Art History," in M. Kelly (ed.), *Encyclopedia of Aesthetics*, New York: Oxford University Press.

Further reading

Beardsley, M. (1962) "The Metaphorical Twist," *Philosophy and Phenomenological Research* 22: 293–307.

—— (1978) "Metaphorical Senses," *Noûs* 12: 3–16. (Two lucid papers investigating the effect and the meaning of metaphors.)

Black, M. (1977) "More about Metaphor," *Dialectica* 31:3–4: 431–57. (Further refinement of the view examined here.)

Cicero (1948) *De Oratore*, trans. H. Wrexham, Cambridge, Mass.: Harvard University Press. (Classical examination of metaphor in the context of rhetoric and persuasion.)

Cohen, T. (1975) "Figurative Speech and Figurative Acts," *Journal of Philosophy* 72: 669–84. (Finely analytical study of the performative dimension of metaphorical speech.)

—— (1976) "Notes on Metaphor," *Journal of Aesthetics and Art Criticism* 34: 249–59.

Fogelin, R. J. (1988) *Figuratively Speaking*, New Haven: Yale University Press. (Astute and concise study, building on Wittgenstein and Grice, emphasizing the participatory role of the interpreter of a metaphorical text, giving an account of metaphorical inexhaustibility.)

Hausman, C. R. (1998) "Metaphor and Nonverbal Arts," in M. Kelly (ed.) *Encyclopedia of Aesthetics*, New York: Oxford University Press. (Compact statement of the position articulated at length in Hausman (1989), with emphasis on the metaphorical structure of non-linguistic art.)

Johnson, M. (ed.) (1981) *Philosophical Perspectives on Metaphor*, Minneapolis: University of Minnesota Press. (Useful collection of influential papers in the field.)

—— (1998) "Metaphor: An Overview," in M. Kelly (ed.), *Encyclopedia of Aesthetics*, New York: Oxford University Press. (Helpful introduction.)

Kittay, E. F. (1986) *Metaphor: Its Cognitive Force and Linguistic Structure*, Oxford: Oxford University Press. (Analyzes the cognitive power of metaphor in representing the world.)

Moran, R. (1989) "Seeing and Believing: Metaphor, Image and Force," *Critical Inquiry* 16: 87–112. (Develops an account of the significance metaphor holds for perception.)

Ortony, A. (ed.) (1993) *Metaphor and Thought*, 2nd edn, Cambridge: Cambridge University Press. (Useful collection of writings from throughout the field of metaphor studies.)

Sacks, S. (ed.) (1979) *On Metaphor*, Chicago: University of Chicago Press. (Rich collection of papers investigating the roles of metaphor in ethics, epistemology, philosophy of language, religion, art, education and literary criticism.)

Searle, J. (1979) "Metaphor," in *Expression and Meaning: Studies in the Theory of Speech Acts*, Cambridge: Cambridge University Press. (Sturdy analysis of metaphor in the theory of speech as action.)

Stern, J. (1998) "Metaphor and Philosophy of Language," in M. Kelly (ed.), *Encyclopedia of Aesthetics*, New York: Oxford University Press. (Concise review of the fundamental questions to which metaphor gives rise in the philosophy of language, with a review of major positions as responses to these questions.)

26
PICTORIAL REPRESENTATION

Mark Rollins

Pictures are everywhere, and we can usually recognize what they represent with ease. It might be thought, therefore, that we can also *explain* with ease how pictures represent. Unfortunately, we cannot. For one thing, there are five standard theories of pictorial representation, each of which seems to give obvious and common sense answers to two basic questions: What is a picture? And how do pictures have content? Pictures are representations of some sort; the first question is about how to distinguish them from other forms of representation. Individual pictures are identified by the contents they have; the second question asks how to distinguish one picture from another. These standard theories explain depiction in terms of convention, resemblance, causal relations, mental constructions, and information, respectively. Although each has some intuitive appeal, they cannot all be right. Moreover, there is a tendency to treat them as types in a taxonomy. They may be taken to define the range of categories into which theories of pictorial representation fall. But this standard list is not the best way to divide up the turf. Not only do the categories overlap to some extent, describing them in the traditional way ignores or obscures some important dimensions of theories of depiction. Specifically, it cuts across a basic contrast between *perceptual* and *non-perceptual* accounts (Lopes 1996).

This division is basic for two reasons. First, it opens the door to certain further subdivisions (primarily among perceptual theories) that are essential for a clear understanding of notions like resemblance or mental construction. Second, the subdivisions come from recent work in cognitive science, which the standard taxonomy antedates. If human psychology is at all relevant to understanding pictures (as it surely is), this work must be reckoned with. In particular, current perceptual theories are divided up along two dimensions. On the most general dimension, there are *indirect* and *direct* models of perception. The former make perception depend on complex internal representations, whereas the latter do not. Then, within the indirect camp, there are *modular* and *non-modular* accounts: those that sharply distinguish perception from cognition versus those that do not.

These distinctions define a fuller, more revealing taxonomy within which the five standard theories can be located as follows. Under the heading of non-perceptual accounts fall convention and resemblance. In the latter case, what are said to be similar are the picture and the object it represents. But resemblance can also be reconstrued in terms of similarities between the *visual experiences* of the picture and the object; in which case, the theory is perceptual. Thus under the banner of perceptual accounts fall four types of theory: resemblance (recon-strued), causal, mental construction, and information-based accounts. The first three of these accounts of depiction presuppose an indirect theory of perception. On the last one, perception is direct. Among the indirect accounts, the first two accept a modularity thesis, while the third rejects it. I shall discuss these theories in the order just laid out and identify different versions of some of them, where the variations have been the focus of debate.

Non-perceptual theories

Convention

Conventionalism in its strongest and most fully developed form is due to the work of Nelson Goodman (1976). On his account, pictures are language-like artificial symbol systems. Both their status as pictures and their contents are determined by the syntactical and semantic properties they are deemed by common agreement to have. Because these properties are assigned by convention, their assignment is said to be *arbitrary*. On this view, pictures are distinguished from words by the fact that they represent the properties of objects in a continuous, analogue form; that is, between any two marks repre-senting features there will be a third mark representing another feature, and there are no distinct grammatical roles among features that allow for the expression of discrete propositions. However, there is no natural connection between a representation having that form and what it represents. Of course, depicted objects will look more realistic if the properties attributed to them are familiar ones, but any object–property association can become familiar or (in Goodman's term) 'entrenched.' More importantly, the means by which such associations become entrenched does not constrain them in any way that contributes to the specification of pictorial content. Thus, the role of perception in becoming familiar with the 'language' of paintings or photographs (or 'reading' representations in it) is only of tangential interest.

This theory is appealing on several counts. First, pictures clearly do have language-like semantic properties: they can denote objects and are typically meaningful compositions. Second, it would be gratifying to have a unified approach to verbal language and visual art, both of which are forms of communication. And third, there is, in fact, much diversity across cultures in systems of pictorial representation, which could be explained if such systems were wholly conventional. Nonetheless, there are several reasons to reject this account.

One problem is that the evidence is not all on the conventionalist's side. Pictorial systems are simply not as varied as the theory would lead us to believe. While it may be true that anything can denote anything, it does not seem to be true that anything can depict anything, just as a matter of fact.

The second problem is related: picture-object relations are not arbitrary. It is important to recognize how radical Goodman's conventionalism is in this regard. It is sometimes said, rightly, that an interest in the psychology of learning is consistent with conventionalism, and that the latter is compatible with a perceptual theory that explains visual experience in terms of acquired knowledge. But if an account of depiction is actually grounded on such a perceptual theory, then picture–object relations will not be arbitrary; rather, they will depend on the laws of psychology. And while a conventionalist of Goodman's type may agree that we learn to recognize picture–object relations in accordance with some psychological laws, it does not follow that the relations are determined by those laws for him. To the contrary, the facts of human psychology do not matter for such a conventionalist, because those facts could be something quite different than they happen to be, and his formal, logical analysis of symbol systems would remain unaffected. But this is precisely where Goodman's conventionalism goes astray.

Resemblance

According to this second theory, what a picture represents depends on what it looks like. More precisely, pictures are said to represent *in virtue* of similarity, and representing in that way is distinctive of the class of representations to which they belong. Thus a portrait is said to be a picture of Rembrandt because it resembles him. The name 'Rembrandt,' on the other hand, does not represent the man in that way.

This theory, too, has intuitive appeal. Pictures often do resemble their objects. And the experience of picture recognition does seem, on the face of it, to be one of seeing similarities between the picture and what it represents. But resemblance theory faces some notorious problems. First, as Plato pointed out, everything resembles everything in some respect or other. Thus, the appeal to resemblance is empty, unless one can answer the question, 'resemblance with respect to what?' Pinning down the relevant similarity would seem to require something other than resemblance; an interpretation, a description, or a title, perhaps. Second, it is a well-known point of Goodman's (1976) that resemblance does not distinguish the representation from what it represents. Resemblance is both symmetrical and reflexive: a picture and its object each resemble the other; a picture resembles itself more than anything else. But objects do not represent pictures, nor do pictures represent themselves. Therefore, resemblance is not a sufficient condition for pictorial representation. It is not a necessary condition, either, if any of the other four accounts are correct. For they show how something might count as a picture, despite the absence of any significant similarity to its object.

Perceptual theories

Resemblance reconstrued

One way of pinning down the respect in which a picture resembles its object is to invoke a perceptual theory; a theory of how viewers *see* picture–object similarities. Such a theory has been defended recently in terms of David Marr's theory of vision (Marr 1982, Gilman 1992; see also Peacocke 1987 for a related account). According to that theory, vision depends on certain basic operations shared by all perceivers, operations that are not affected by differences in background knowledge. Early vision is thus *modularized*, that is, segregated from other sense modalities and higher cognitive processes. Vision is informationally encapsulated (any knowledge on which it depends is restricted to basic visual knowledge), and the processes that define it are activated only by a limited type of (visual) stimuli. On this view, not only is vision unchanged by differences in the beliefs, values, or theories held by the viewer, it is also isolated from other senses. Marr's argument, then, is that when the task is object recognition, the same modularized operations that are used in ordinary perception are also used in picture perception. It is in that sense that pictures 'look like' their objects: information is extracted from them in order to identify their objects by the very same mechanisms that would be brought into play by the objects themselves. This is supposed to translate into similarities in perceptual experience (Gilman 1992: 186). Thus a human figure is recognized both in the flesh and in Picasso's *Rite of Spring* because its contours and basic components are registered through processes that are in both cases, and for every viewer, the same.

However, there are important reasons to believe that, at least in a strong form,

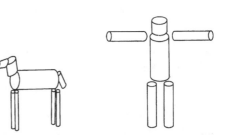

Figure 26.1 Picasso's *Rite of Spring* shows how shape information is contained in silhouettes

Figure 26.2 The organization of stored shape descriptions for bipeds and quadrupeds

Source for both figures: David Marr, *Vision*, San Francisco: W. H. Freeman, 1982. Used with permission.

the modularity thesis is probably false. First, psychological evidence shows that even basic visual functions can be affected by background knowledge, and studies of the primate visual system, along with human brain imaging research, indicate that there are reciprocal, top-down pathways that reach areas of visual cortex devoted to early visual processes. It is reasonable to assume that these pathways link psychological functions, and thus that they are possible avenues by which early vision is affected by higher order cognition. In addition, there appears to be communication across different sense modalities. Finally, it is clear that the brain is highly plastic: damage to an area of the brain normally responsible for a particular perceptual task need not result in a loss of function, because other areas can take over that function and compensate for the loss. That implies that structures in the normal brain are not simply and permanently dedicated to a single function.

In any case, even if early vision were strongly modular, that would not be enough to motivate a resemblance theory of pictorial representation in any interesting sense. The reason is that early visual modules impose only limited constraints on higher-order conscious processes, constraints that can effectively be superseded (Wollheim 1993, Churchland 1988). That is, they provide certain kinds of input to subsequent processes, such as elementary shapes, on the basis of which objects are recognized. But the more complex representations, concepts, and beliefs on which perceptual experience presumably depends can vary widely nonetheless. In light of that, any assurance of a perceived resemblance between a picture and its object largely disappears. Because higher-order processes do have access, in principle, to all sorts of background knowledge, objects in pictures may not look similar to the same objects in the world. Knowledge may simply be brought into play in different ways when the picture and its object are perceived. Thus, even if there were modularized early visual processes, they could not sustain the weight that a resemblance theory requires them to have.

Causal relations

Traditional accounts

The next approach to pictorial representation explains depiction in terms of a causal chain. The chain begins with the object or scene toward which a camera is pointed or an artist directs his attention during picture production. It ends with the picture perceiver's response. It seems almost obvious that the content of a picture should be identified with the object or scene that stands at the beginning of this chain (Walton 1984, Thomas 1997). For example, the surface of a prize-winning pumpkin reflects the light that enters the camera lens and results in a certain pattern on the film. The salient cause in this chain of events is the pumpkin (or its surface); therefore, that is what the photograph is supposed to depict.

However, the account is so far incomplete. The reason is that, in speaking simply of 'what a picture represents,' we have glossed over a distinction between two components of representation: pictorial *reference* and pictorial *meaning*. The former involves the picture standing for a particular object or individual of a certain type; the latter concerns the attribution of properties to the individual in question. For example, a picture of a cat may refer to a real individual named Morris. And it may represent him as being orange, having a striped tail, or wearing a sailor's hat. That these are distinct (yet possibly related) components is seen in the fact that two pictures can refer to the same individual, but show different aspects or features of him. Thus, establishing the referent of a picture by tracing its casual history to an individual is not enough to specify the picture's content. Indeed, in some cases, the actual referent even seems irrelevant. Does it really matter who the anonymous model posing as Jesus was, for a description of the picture's content? Probably not always. In other cases, there will be no referent at all; for example, in paintings of imaginary objects.

One solution to these shortcomings might be to say that pictures refer to instances of *properties*, as well as to individuals. In that case, the content of a picture could in principle be specified in traditional causal terms, by describing the causal history of the properties as they are depicted. This also opens the door to an account of imaginary objects. Mental representations in the artist or perceiver are, in that case, composites – they are composed of more basic representations of previously perceived features, which are attributed to the depicted object. Those features are individuated by causal histories of their own.

However, even if we overcome the problems of incompleteness and imaginary objects in this way, an important objection still remains. It is not obvious how the 'actual cause' of a picture can be described in any case. Any effect will be the result of a chain of causes, and items in the chain can be described in many ways. Which item, then, under what description, should be said to stand at the beginning of the chain and provide the content of the picture? It is true that some of the causal indeterminacy can be overcome by knowing the nature of the visual system (Dretske 1986). The causal relation involves a law-like covariation: one sort of change (the presence or absence of the depicted object) corresponds regularly with another (the presence or absence of an image on film, and then of a certain kind of neural, psychological, or behavioral response in the perceiver). But each of these changes occurs in a medium, so to speak, the properties of which impose limitations on it (such as the structure of the camera or the perceiver's brain). This establishes a range, at least, of possible causes. However, establishing points in the causal chain to which the visual system is responsive does not tell us how best to describe the items found at those points. This is as true for properties as it is for objects.

We might try to avoid this problem by shifting the emphasis from the cause of a picture to its effects on perceivers. However, the idea that a significant part of a picture's content depends on the perceiver's response leads to a causal theory of a rather different sort from the traditional account we have so far considered.

Recognition theories

According to Flint Schier (1986), what a picture represents is determined by a perceiver's ability to recognize objects in it: pictorial content derives from the use of ordinary perceptual abilities. A picture, P, represents an object, O, if a perceiver interprets P rightly, based just on his ordinary perceptual ability to recognize O. Although some learning and conventions are involved in interpreting pictures, they are limited. In contrast to language learning, picture perception is distinguished by the fact that, once an initial successful interpretation has been made, the perceiver who made it can then interpret novel pictures without further training. This is a distinctive feature of pictures called *natural generativity*. Given this fact, Schier says, "if you can see it the chances are you can see it in pictures" (Schier 1986: 43).

This is a causal theory in two respects. First, it presupposes a causal theory of reference. What makes the perceiver's response a correct or veridical one is the fact that P refers to O, which is determined by the fact that O stands in the proper causal relation to P (Schier 1986: 91–3; cf. Lopes 1996). Second, although it is not required by their basic construal of pictures, recognition theories of depiction have been grounded on a causal theory of perception (Schier 1986: 49; Lopes 1996). In both philosophy and cognitive science, object recognition is usually explained in terms of percepts or other mental representations. According to the most influential account, the content of those representations is determined by the items with which they causally covary. The recognitional abilities involved in picture perception can be described in similar terms.

For example, on this account, a picture of Mont Saint Victoire refers to that mountain if it stands in the appropriate causal relation to it. That a mountain is what is depicted depends on the fact that the picture activates the same mental representations that mountains ordinarily activate; for instance, a certain perceptual prototype. It is because mountains ordinarily activate this type of mental representation that it has the identity that it has. Thus, in general terms, we might say: if the perceiver were to see a certain object, O, a certain mental representation – the O-representation – would ordinarily be activated. A picture represents an O if it activates the O-representation too.

It is here, however, that recognition theories – as much as the more traditional causal accounts – begin to founder, for causal indeterminacy now simply reappears to plague the individuation of mental states. It is just as hard to single out the relevant cause of a mental representation as it is of a picture.

Mental constructions

As an alternative to causal accounts, we might consider explaining pictures in terms of relations among mental states. There are three major theories of this type. They emphasize make-believe, illusion, and 'seeing-in,' respectively, as the modes of mental activity that play the central roles in picture perception.

MAKE-BELIEVE

According to Kendall Walton (1990), pictures come in two basic types. On the one hand, there are photographs, which refer to their objects in virtue of a causal connection. On the other hand, there are hand-made pictures, which do not refer at all. Whether they depict existing entities or not, all of the latter are non-literal representations that are defined by their roles in a game of make-believe. On this view, a picture represents a certain object, O, if it enjoins its perceivers to pretend or imagine that they are seeing O. In so far as it severs the causal links that would establish reference to objects in the world, and because it makes depiction depend on propositional attitudes and higher-order cognitive abilities, Walton's theory of make-believe is constructivist in spirit.

However, one problem with this theory is the lack of psychological evidence that picture perception involves mental pretending in a game-like, rule-governed way. In fact, it is not clear even from ordinary experience that picture perception depends on imagination in any elaborate sense. Further, pictures often provide us with information. It seems unlikely that, in order to extract that information, we have to engage in a game of mental pretend. In light of these concerns, it is appropriate to consider constructivist theories of depiction that are more explicitly based on constructivist perceptual psychology.

ILLUSION

Perceptual constructivism is usually identified with the New Look psychological movement (Bruner 1957). On that approach, perception depends on inference, which in turn depends on knowledge possessed by the perceiver. This implies that all perceptual processes are, in effect, *theory-laden*. The knowledge on which perception depends consists, not of isolated bits of information, but of an interrelated set of ideas drawn from an integrated conceptual framework or scheme. E. H. Gombrich (1960) draws heavily on the New Look school. The assumption that perception is *theory-laden* (or at least highly knowledge-dependent) can be seen in the famous declaration that "there is no innocent eye." Three ideas are central to Gombrich's account of art: schema-and-correction, seeing-as, and illusion. According to the first idea, perceptual recognition depends on matching the visual stimulus to familiar forms, which are modified over time if the fit is repeatedly too inexact. Although Gombrich views schemas as invented pictorial techniques, these clearly rest on psychological mechanisms. The matching-and-correction process reflects a 'principle of the adapted stereotype,' which suggests that schemas are like perceptual prototypes; not strict rules or definitions for classifying objects, but overlapping sets of features that provide criteria for judging degrees of similarity among members of a class.

The idea of schema-and-correction is used by Gombrich to explain the history of art. That, he claims is driven by a process of hypothesis-and-testing. Gombrich follows Popper in grounding the selection of visual hypotheses on a principle of falsifiability. This fits well with his use of the concepts of information and illusion, which at first may seem inconsistent. His view is that, insofar as pictures represent correctly, a perceiver will derive no false information from them. Thus, one may properly apply certain concepts to the picture and see it as the sort of

Figure 26.3 Birds and Schema by Van de Passe

Source: E. H. Gombrich, *Art and Illusion*, Princeton: Princeton University Press, 1961. Reprinted by permission of Princeton University Press.

object it represents. In that sense, art is illusion. But the illusion is only 'of the eye' and not of the mind. The perceiver ordinarily does not believe that the picture is the object he sees it as. This does not mean, of course, that the perceiver makes-believe that the picture is its object. If I pretend that one thing is another, then I harbor no illusions about them. Seeing P as O is quite different from pretending or imagining that P is O.

But do we always see P as O? One obvious objection to the illusion theory is that it over-generalizes from a small sub-set of pictures, in applying the claim about illusion to the entire range. In the case of many paintings, there are reasons to think that, even if we apply the concept of a certain O to them, their surface properties so compel our attention that illusion is really out of the question. In more general terms, even if picture perception is as dependent on concepts, theories, or schemas as Gombrich suggests, that by itself does not warrant the view that art is illusion. While pictorial content may derive from what perceivers know, a better understanding of perceptual dynamics may show that, for most pictures, there is never a moment in which the eye is simply tricked.

At any rate, it is not clear that picture perception is actually theory-laden or fully concept-dependent. If it is not, then a major premise in the argument for illusion is undercut. There are two lines of argument against this view, one theoretical and the other empirical.

The theoretical objection concerns the way in which mental content is most plausibly identified on this account. Pictorial representation on Gombrich's theory is a function of mental representations formed by picture perceivers; the contents of the latter are a function of their relations to other mental states. Although his eclectic use of psychological theories and philosophical ideas makes it hard to identify a single theory of mental representation, this suggests a conceptual role semantics for mental states and, by extension, for pictures.

To be specific, the hallmark of conceptual role semantics is its *holism*. Mental contents can never be identified in isolation, but only as part of an interrelated network of mental states. This interdependence of schemas, concepts, and beliefs is apparent in Gombrich's account when he speaks of the "tendency of our minds to classify and register our experience in terms of the known," on the one hand, and "the influence which acquired patterns or schemata have on the organization of our perception," on the other (Gombrich 1960: 168).

Such a view stands in contrast to the resemblance and causal theories we have considered. Like constructivist accounts, they treat pictorial content in terms of complex mental representations. But they also impose important constraints on perception that are missing from constructivism. Specifically, certain 'assumptions' are said to be built into perceptual processes by natural selection; for example (in Marr's theory), an assumption is that objects are more-or-less rigid. These are necessary for perceptual systems to get a unique, correct identification of an object. Building them in is nature's way of tuning our sensory receptors to the kind of world in which we live. Such assumptions are, in a sense, the axioms from which we derive more elaborate models, theories, and beliefs about the visual world. They must, therefore, be construed as elements that are unaffected by their use in further information processing. To that extent, the views we have considered are atomistic rather than holistic, at least in regard to early stages of perception.

The motivation for this sort of atomism comes from the need to provide some grounding for higher-order mental contents. If all knowledge and memory is fully embedded in a holistic conceptual framework, then the analysis of mental content will be regressive or circular, and it will be impossible to find a fixed point of reference from which to attribute mental content to a perceiver. The first objection to treating picture perception as thoroughly knowledge dependent, then, is that it lacks a grounding in just this sense. The result is that pictorial content will be as unstable as mental content is, if we accept Gombrich's more holistic account. What a picture represents will depend on an elaborate network of schemas, concepts, knowledge, and beliefs. This network is ever changing, both within the individual perceiver and across viewers in different places and times.

The empirical problems with the theory can be brought out by considering two related objections that have been raised against constructivism, one in cognitive science, the other in aesthetics. First, the perceptual plasticity that is supposed to show that perception is theory-laden has not always been due to the effects of theory or concepts (Fodor 1984). For instance, a perceiver's ability to switch between different ways of seeing an ambiguous figure (such as a Necker cube or duck-rabbit) often depends more on a redirection of attention than on background knowledge. Second, Wollheim (1974) has criticized Gombrich for ignoring our ability to detect visually (and not just understand conceptually) differences between surface properties of paintings and their objects, while simultaneously seeing objects 'in' them. This ability requires dividing attention, rather than just switching it back-and-forth between surface properties and representational content. Both objections suggest that, in order to understand how pictures represent, we must know more about the constraints that are imposed on perception by attentional mechanisms. These constraints are at odds with the idea that art is illusion, which makes picture perception depend primarily on inferential and conceptual relations among mental states.

SEEING-IN

According to Wollheim's (1988) model of picture perception, it is necessary to conceptualize pictorial content; but conceptualizing does not require that the perceiver believe (or make-believe) that the picture is its object; nor must he or she see the one as the other. Instead, one can *see in* the picture whatever object it represents, which is to say that one applies the concept of the object to the picture, while at the same time attending to, and being aware of, for example, the color and shading, or the layers of paint or lines of ink, as design features of the painting or drawing. Seeing-in is not limited to picture perception; we can also see the shapes of objects in water stains and clouds. But pictures are distinguished by the fact that, in order to see something correctly in them, we must see what the picture producer intended. Still, the question remains: in what does seeing-in consist?

Wollheim does not himself offer a full account of seeing-in. This is an obvious weakness in the argument for the theory. However, some recent models in psychology allow for the simultaneous division of attention, in which information about meaning or content can be processed along with information about shapes, sounds, or locations (e.g. Treisman and Gelade 1980). These open the door to an empirically grounded analysis of seeing-in.

However, integrating theories of attention with a mental construction account also points to a hybrid model in which elements of both indirect and direct theories of perception are combined. Before discussing this model, we must consider Gibson's account of depiction, which is born of a view of perception as entirely direct, unmediated by mental representations.

Information

According to James Gibson (1978), pictures contain the same information as the scenes they depict. In particular, both pictures and the light surrounding the objects they represent embody gradients of texture density. These gradients are said to 'specify' properties of the objects. For instance, size is a function of the number of textural units displaced by the object, which is constant over different locations in space. This is because texture compression varies regularly with distance. On Gibson's direct realist account, such information can be 'picked up' by the perceiver without any intervening mental processes.

This information theory initially faces the same kind of symmetry problem that resemblance theory confronts: if the same information can be picked up from a picture and the object it represents, and pictorial representation is explained as being owing to that fact, then the object would seem to count as a representation of the picture. However, the problem is avoided by an appeal to attention: a perceiver can notice aspects of a painting not found in the scene

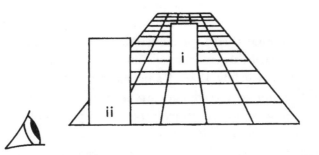

Figure 26.4 Size constancy as a function of the number of textural elements covered by an object where it touches the ground

Source: Julian Hochberg, *Perception*, 2nd edn, Upper Saddle River, N. J.: Prentice Hall. Reprinted by permission of Prentice-Hall Inc., Upper Saddle River, N. J.

or object it depicts. While Gibson cannot invoke theoretical knowledge in the mind of the perceiver to distinguish picture from object, he can cite practical know-how, especially skills or abilities like attention.

Moreover, Gibson's ecological approach allows him to argue that pictures have higher-order relational properties not found in other artifacts, and vice versa. These properties fall under the heading of *affordances*. Gibson was liberal in describing properties that could be directly perceived: a cake, for instance, might be seen as edible, whereas a picture of a cake would not. Thus the real cake affords its perceiver opportunities not available with the picture. The picture, in turn, presents possibilities for perceptual training which the ordinary object does not present.

Information theory is appealing, because it seems to correspond well to our sense that picture perception is a natural, unlearned ability that we all use without thinking. And it emphasizes the fact that both the world of objects and pictures of them are rich in prestructured information that does not depend on mental constructive activity in its perceivers. Nonetheless, Gibson's theory is unable to explain how pictures have a particular content. As Gibson himself notes, two surfaces at different distances, but slanted at appropriate angles, could have textural features that are represented in pictures in the same way. Pictures can thus be ambiguous. Concerns of this sort led Gibson to emphasize the importance of perceiver's movements through his environment to help pick up disambiguating information. But that is a source of information that is unavailable in pictures, where the point of view and spatial perspective are fixed by the artist. Shifting attention over the surface of the picture, through movements of the eyes and head, can lead us to discover new details; but it cannot change that perspective.

A new hybrid: strategic design theories

In recent years, several theories of perception have emerged that combine elements of indirect and direct accounts. This suggests a new avenue for developing a perceptual theory of depiction. The combination takes several forms, referred to variously as 'active,' 'directed,' or 'utilitarian' theories of vision (Ballard 1991, Cutting 1986, Ramachandran 1990). Generally the idea is that vision does not require the construction of detailed, complete mental representations of a scene or object; partial representations will suffice, because the visual system can use attentional and other strategies to facilitate the performance of perceptual tasks. These strategies allow the visual system to take representational shortcuts, so to speak. Perceivers make do with incomplete information by attending to diagnostic features, by using psycho-logical resources not specifically designed for the task, by moving through the environment or using the motor system in other ways, and by exploiting assumptions about the correlation of one type of information with another. For example, the shape of an object can be recognized without a full delineation of its contours, because the shading of its surface will take distinctive forms, regardless of the location of the light (Lehky and Sejnowski 1988). A theory of depiction in these terms has not yet been fully developed, although a discussions of work in this direction can be found in Cutting and Massironi (1998) and Rollins (1999).

Pictures are perceptual objects. The challenge for a theory of pictorial representation is to find the right theory of perception. This is true for sculpture, film, theater, and even literature as well, to the extent that these are representational arts that depend on visual and auditory perception. Although much is known, in particular, about the visual system, there is currently no clear consensus regarding the nature and extent of mental representation in perception. However, recent research points in the direction of compromise. Some of the work discussed here suggests that perception depends on both internal representations and attentional or other strategies. This opens the door to a better understanding of picture perception and thus of pictorial representation.

See also Interpretation, Imagination and make-believe, Painting, Photography, Sculpture.

References

Ballard, D. (1991) "Animate Vision," *Artificial Intelligence* 48: 57–86.

Bruner, J. (1957) "On Perceptual Readiness," *Psychological Review* 64: 123–52.

Churchland, P. (1988) "Perceptual Plasticity and Theoretical Neutrality," *Philosophy of Science* 55: 167–87.

Cutting, J. (1986) *Perception with an Eye for Motion*, Cambridge, Mass.: MIT Press.

Cutting, J. E. and Massironi, M. (1998) "Pictures and Their Special Status in Perceptual and Cognitive Theory," in J. Hochberg (ed.), *Perception and Cognition at Century's End*, San Diego: Academic Press.

Dretske, F. (1986) "Misrepresentation," in R. Bogdan (ed.), *Belief: Form, Content, and Function*, Oxford: Oxford University Press.

Fodor, J. (1984) "Observation Reconsidered," *Philosophy of Science* 51: 23–43.

Gibson, J. J. (1978) "The Ecological Approach to the Perception of Pictures," *Leonardo* 11: 227–35.

Gilman, D. (1992) "A New Perspective on Pictorial Representation." *Australian Journal of Philosophy* 70: 174–86.

Gombrich, E. H. (1960) *Art and Illusion*, Princeton: Princeton University Press.

Goodman, N. (1976) *Languages of Art*. 2nd edn, Indianapolis: Hackett.

Lehky, S. R. and Sejnowski, T. J. (1988) "Network Model of Shape from Shading," *Nature* 333: 452–4.

Lopes, D. (1996) *Understanding Pictures*, Oxford: Oxford University Press.

Marr, D. (1982) *Vision,* San Francisco: Freeman.

Peacocke, C. (1987) "Depiction," *Philosophical Review* 96: 383–410.

Ramachandran, V. S. (1990) "Interaction Between Motion, Depth, Color and Form: The Utilitarian Theory of Perception," in C. Blakemore (ed.), *Vision: Coding and Efficiency,* Cambridge: Cambridge University Press.

Rollins, M. (1999) "Pictorial Representation: When Cognitive Science Meets Aesthetics," *Philosophical Psychology.*

Schier, F. (1986) *Deeper Into Pictures,* Cambridge: Cambridge University Press.

Thomas, L. (1997) "Junk Representations." *British Journal for the Philosophy of Science,* 48: 345–61.

Treisman, A. M. and Gelade, G. (1980) "A Feature Integration Theory of Attention," *Cognitive Psychology* 12: 97–136.

Walton, K. (1984) "Transparent Pictures," *Critical Inquiry* 11: 246–77.

—— (1990) *Mimesis as Make-Believe,* Cambridge, Mass.: Harvard University Press.

Wollheim, R. (1974) "Reflections on Art and Illusion," in *On Art and the Mind,* Cambridge, Mass.: Harvard University Press.

—— (1988) *Painting as an Art,* London: Thames and Hudson.

—— (1993) "Danto's Gallery of Indiscernibles," in M. Rollins (ed.), *Danto and His Critics,* Oxford: Blackwell.

Further reading

Arnheim, R. (1966) *Art and Visual Perception,* Berkeley: University of California Press. (A classic discussion of pictures from the point of view of Gestalt psychology.)

Danto, A. (forthcoming) "Seeing and Showing," *Journal of Aesthetics and Art Criticism.* (A non-resemblance account of pictorial representation committed to the modularity of vision.)

Turvey, M. T. *et al.* (1981) "Ecological Laws of Perceiving and Acting," *Cognition* 9: 237–304. (Helpful discussion of Gibson and the intentionality of perception.)

Part 3

ISSUES AND CHALLENGES

27

CRITICISM

Roger Seamon

Criticism in the broadest sense is a ubiquitous human activity. It is addressed to whatever people do or make, and it is an inherent part of human cultures. Some major objects of criticism are tools (artifacts with a distinctive purpose), deeds (actions judged from a moral perspective), theorems (claims about what is true), and performances such as we find in sport and art, where common abilities like balancing, running, singing, and telling stories are more highly developed than utility demands. Any act or artifact may appropriately be judged on different grounds. My wearing an amber necklace to class may be assessed as a tool ('He'll never attract women that way'), a theorem ('He wants to show that the correlation of jewelry with gender can be deconstructed, but that is hardly original'), a deed ('It is immoral for a professor to use his position of authority to undermine conventional ways of distinguishing men from women'), and a performance ('That necklace, though handsome and well-made, is much too heavy for his delicate features'). Although Plato clearly recognizes the value of the Homeric epics and tragic drama as performances, he, like many contemporary critics, also treats poems as both bad theory and bad deeds. While the determination of how to take something is, finally, up to the person criticizing, people do and make things within a context of expectation, and the person criticizing normally takes that into consideration.

Criticism in the narrower and usual sense – which is how I shall henceforth use the term – is addressed primarily to artistic performances. While there are restaurant and wine critics, a critic is commonly understood to be someone who comments formally on the arts as performances. To take something as a performance means taking it as something that someone did or made, and

> The notion of getting something done includes that of succeeding where one might have failed, the idea of an achievement, so that, to that extent, the concept of a performance is inescapably evaluative. So if criticism is

to be all and only that discourse that is peculiarly appropriate to performances as such . . . everything said implies that the performer was doing
something in which he might succeed or fail, the point of that activity
being to succeed.

(Sparshott 1983: 237)

Criticism is discourse that takes performances as its object: "to regard something made or done as a performance is, precisely, to regard it as a potential
object of criticism. What is criticized is always a performance, and criticism and
performance become correlative terms" (Sparshott 1967: 42). Aesthetic sports
such as figure skating and gymnastics are also performances, as are the culinary
arts, but the fine arts, probably because they primarily employ cognitive, rather
physical or gustatory, capacities (dance is the obvious exception to the former),
tend to be more highly valued, and so the criticism of them is much more developed. Criticism has been a highly refined and complex activity for over two millennia, and it encompasses a variety of practices, often within a single discourse.

Legislative criticism

The description of the scenes on Achilles's shield in the *Iliad* captures the nature
and qualities of the object, and, by implication, Homer's sense of what is
valuable in it, and that is still the central aim of much art criticism today.
However, from antiquity to the eighteenth century criticism did not consist
primarily of such appreciative descriptions (though there was a formal practice
– *ekphrasis* – of describing visual art), but of learned discourses on the principles
governing artistic practices. Aristotle's *Poetics* is the most famous and influential example of such *legislative criticism* (Watson 1986: 13–14), and some of the
best known critical documents in the literary critical tradition, such as Horace's
Art of Poetry, Longinus's *On the Sublime*, Wordsworth's "Preface" to the
second edition of *Lyrical Ballads*, and Ezra Pound's "Imagist Manifesto" are of
this kind. There are also many such guides to the making of music and visual
art. Legislative criticism treats artistic performances as arts in the classical
sense, that is, what we might call crafts. Today it is a part of commercial culture
(one can buy guides to writing screenplays), and it is also found in studio and
creative writing courses. It is, however, no longer taken seriously as a form of
intellectual inquiry.

The decline of legislative criticism began toward the end of the seventeenth
century, when the function of the critic changed from legislating artistic practices
to filtering increasing artistic production and educating a public in the appreciation of art. This dramatic change was brought about mainly by the wide

dissemination of more and more works of art to a new and larger public, who needed – and still need – guides to contemporary artistic production, something that had been unnecessary in court and popular culture, where intimacy with a limited number of works was taken for granted. The change was especially dramatic in literature, as printed books became cheap and numerous. Secondly, the advent of "the modern system of the arts" (Kristeller 1985) transformed technē, or crafts, into fine arts that called for refined discrimination and a self-conscious education in taste. A bit later, the romantic shift of power from critic or theorist to the artist elicited the need for the interpretation of works of genius, and so the critic now was not so much a judge of quality as a guide to the significance of works of art. These changes meant that critics became reviewers, re-appraisers, and interpreters rather than legislative theorists, although the earlier role lingered on in the imperiously judgemental tone that much early reviewing took. This had to be overcome for criticism to perform its new function of respectful mediation between work and audience rather than artist and work, although the critic could, of course, be severe on artists who betrayed their now-exalted calling. The academic version of the change meant, speaking emblematically, that Brooks' and Warren's *Understanding Poetry*, a handbook on how to describe, evaluate, and interpret poems, supplanted Aristotle's *Poetics*, a handbook on how to make them.

Appreciative description

Appreciative description, which of course includes its depreciative sibling, was the central form of criticism from the late eighteenth to well into the twentieth century, when it came to be rivaled by interpretation. In appreciative description the critic functions as an intermediary between the work and the audience. The critic is presumed to have better taste, greater sensitivity to meaning, and more extensive relevant knowledge than the audience. While any given piece of criticism may be a complex mixture of purposes, there are logical stages in the process of appreciation, and these are reflected in what appreciative critics do.

Recognizing something *as* a performance is the first step in appreciation. Walking through a park I see a crowd standing around a man stretched out motionless on the ground. For a moment I am unsure about what is happening, but from various clues I infer that this not a medical emergency but a performer about to begin a performance. Doubt about whether something is or is not an artistic performance is especially important in modern art in which recognition is made problematic. When Marcel Duchamp placed a shovel in an art exhibition, the object itself did not, as was customary, constitute the performance. The performance consisted of the conceptual implications of Duchamp's exhibiting the shovel, and it took considerable critical effort to make this clear.

Having established that something is a performance, one must then determine what sort of performance it is. Performances are of a certain kind, even if original, and in order properly to appreciate a work we must correctly identify the medium, genre, and so on. That is often overlooked since we take so much of this for granted (Walton 1970). To illustrate this point, let us return to the prone man in the park. Having determined that the man is a mime, the audience's next task is to identify what is being imitated; we have to make sense of those slowly accelerating twitches and the change from flat out to bent at the joints. It suddenly dawns on some that he is imitating a piece of bacon being fried, and when they pass on this complex inference, they engage in the basic critical task of bringing others to see what is being performed. The critic who tells us that a ballet portrays first love, or that tragedy consists of the fall of a good person because of a weakness, is carrying out this basic critical function, whose aim is to put detailed appreciation – which is the major aim of attending to artistic performances – on a solid foundation.

Usually critics readily identify performances, but uncertainty can force the issue into the open. Thus P. N. Furbank has no problem recognizing that a book he is to review is a satiric novel, and not reportage of contemporary life, but he is not sure just what sort of novel it is:

> How shall one classify this novel? One is tempted at first to suppose its genre is philistinism: the vindictive philistinism of the campus novel (a tiresome genre) or of 'Tom-Stoppardism' – a matter of getting your own back on culture 'knowingly.' . . . But actually, I think what may be involved is something else altogether. . . . He is making a genial unspoken joke to the effect that these [Heidegger, Lacan, and the deconstructionists], their theories and the tags from them, now constitute a social orthodoxy as Horace and Virgil did for the Augustans.
>
> (Furbank 1994: 35)

It will require considerable labor sometime in the future for a critic to acquire the knowledge necessary to make – or perhaps even revise – Furbank's judgement, and considerable imagination to recapture the significance of what the novelist has done.

As the last sentence implies, we are not equally intimate with all performances, and that means that for some works we must inquire in order to identify the performance. Relative difficulty in identifying the specific character of performances defines their remoteness. We are, of course, never absolutely sure we have correctly identified a performance, and, therefore, the rock critic reviewing his favorite band is, in principle, in the same position as the art historian commenting on Greek vases: they must both identify the perform-ance, which gives them the relevant criteria for description and appraisal. In practice, however, the difference between intimacy and remoteness is crucial. If the rock critic had to explain his view to someone unfamiliar with the tradition and current bands, he would be giving a course not writing a review. It is the aim of such historical criticism

> to equip the reader or viewer with the information needed to respond to the work's power which, after all, can be lost as concepts change or be inaccessible because of the outward difficulties of the work, which the received cultural equipment is insufficient to accommodate.
>
> (Danto 1981: 174)

Thus, when E. H. Gombrich tells us, after carefully taking us through the steps that led him to his conclusion, that for Raphael "to combine the intimacy of a *genre* group [in the *Madonna della Sedia*] with the hieratic tradition of a direct contact with the beholder was indeed a daring stroke" (Gombrich 1966: 69), he has made it possible for us to grasp a value in the painting that would not be available to those who lacked the relevant contextual knowledge.

Such criticism can, however, have the paradoxical effect of making the work more distant experientially, even though it may be better understood. In an essay on "A Modest Proposal," Claude Rawson claims that Swift's satire is not the right-minded attack on the dehumanizing nature of social engineering it is commonly taken to be:

> the complicated interplay of compassion and contempt [for the poor] is not to be taken as a finely textured, sensitively judicial blend, a mellowly pondered product of the liberal imagination. It is an explosive mixture, and Swift's feelings oscillate starkly among extreme positions.
>
> (Rawson 1985: 128)

It is doubtful that well-off people in our culture can unselfconsciously feel con-tempt for the poor, so we cannot experience the work as originally meant. At the same time, Rawson's essay makes it harder, if not impossible, to continue to read "A Modest Proposal" in the conventional way. We may know more about Swift's satire, but that does not translate into the immediacy of a full literary experience. That dilemma is intrinsic to the recovery of earlier meanings whose force depends on the attitudes the author assumed in his audience. The history paintings that evoked such powerful responses in earlier audiences now languish in museums because the Biblical and classical foundation on which they were built has crumbled. The degree to which we can recover and internalize the "relevant tacit knowledge" (Hirsch 1967: 165), which may range from the contemporary significance of an historical event to attitudes to women, varies considerably.

The next and most important stage in the critical journey is reached when critics are on intimate terms with performances and can presume that audiences share the relevant contexts. The most familiar *locus* of this stage in criticism is the review. George Bernard Shaw's account of a performance of Bach's *St Matthew Passion* is typical:

> No doubt it was something to have brought the chorus to the point of singing such difficult music accurately and steadily. But a note-perfect performance is only the raw material of an artistic performance; and what the Birmingham Festival achieved was very little more than such raw material. In the opening chorus, the plaintive, poignant melody in triple time got trampled to pieces by the stolid trudging of the choir from beat to beat. The violins in the orchestra shewed the singers how it ought to be done; but the lesson was thrown away; the trudging continued.
>
> (Shaw 1978: 89)

Such criticism does not consist of arguments in support of verdicts, but of efforts of the critic to express through appreciative description the basis upon which a work is judged. "Trudging" is an attempt to say just how something was bad. Appreciative description is "discourse grounding evaluation" (Sparshott 1967: 61), and evaluation is implicit in the description itself. One cannot properly describe a performance without implicit evaluation, since the very point of the performance is to do something well that is worth doing.

The difficulty for appreciative critics is not understanding, but expression. An extreme view of the problem was taken by the great Austrian critic, Edward Hanslick: "The language of prose is not only poorer than that of music; as far as music is concerned, it is no language at all, since music cannot be translated into it" (Hanslick 1950: 241). The difficulty, however, did not stop Hanslick, nor has it stopped countless others, from trying, and for good reason, for such 'translation' shares with the artistic performances themselves the possibility of being done better or worse: criticism is itself a performance, not a science or academic discipline. Along with sensitivity to artistic meaning, the ability to find words for what one has read, seen, or heard is at the heart of the critic's art:

> In his Symphony in C Minor, Brahms plunged with desperate passion into a dark Faustian struggle in the very first dissonant measures. . . .

The symphony No. 2 is a peaceful, often pastoral counterpart. While the thunder of the old Beethoven is still heard receding in the distance, we hear the voices of Mozart and Haydn as if from celestial sanctuary. The Symphony No. 3 is really something new. It repeats neither the unhappy fatalism of the first, nor the cheerful idyl of the second; its foundation is self-confident, rough and ready strength.

(Hanslick 1950: 243)

Appreciative description is often carried on through images and other figures, which can best convey the subtle qualities that characterize even commonplace works of art. We can see this in the passage from Hanslick and in this comment by Nicolas Penny:

In the center of the most beautiful painting by Correggio in the Louvre there is a knot of flesh as intricate and lively as a swimming octopus. It consists of the left hand of the Virgin Mary delicately supporting the slightly smaller right hand of Saint Catherine, while the much smaller hand of the infant Christ tenderly picks out the Saint's ring finger. This is a miniature example of an effect at which Correggio excelled: actions inspired by a sentiment of breathless intensity are somehow endowed with angelic grace and with a formal complexity which is delightfully difficult to disentangle.

(Penny 1998: 18)

Or this, by Randall Jarrell on Robert Frost's "Design," a poem that portrays a plump white spider on a white flower holding a white moth it has captured, killed, and will devour:

This is the Argument from Design with a vengeance; is the terrible negative from which the eighteenth century's Kodak picture (with its *Having wonderful time. Wish you were here* on the margin) had to be printed. . . . And this little albino catastrophe is too whitely catastrophic to be accidental, too unlikely to be a coincidence.

(Jarrell 1959: 42)

It is hard to imagine a better phrase than "little albino catastrophe" to capture at once the eeriness of the poem and Frost's semi-ironic elevation of an insignificant event to cosmic horror. The usefulness, or perhaps even the necessity, of images to convey the critic's impressions is one of the main things that makes criticism itself an art.

Descriptions of performances can be excellent even when the appraisals they are meant to support seem quite wrong and the principles upon which they are based are misguided: "The best art critics are indeed less notable for the inerrancy of their taste than for the vividness, aptness, and tellingness of their descriptions" (Sparshott 1967: 104). A passage from Henry James's review of "The Impressionists" illustrates the point:

> The young contributors to the exhibition of which I speak are partisans of unadorned reality and absolute foes to arrangement, embellishment, selection, to the artist's allowing himself, as he has hitherto, since art began, found his best account in doing, to be preoccupied with the beautiful. The beautiful, to them, is only a metaphysical notion, is what the supernatural is to the Positivists – a Metaphysical notion, which can only get one into a muddle and is to be severely let alone.
>
> (James 1956: 114)

James's appraisal and the principles upon which it is based have proved inadequate as a basis for appreciating impressionist painting, but his description is good, for he sees what the painters are up to and even makes a shrewd connection between a contemporary philosophical position and the implicit attitude of the artists. James' taste means that he cannot deal adequately with impressionist painting, yet his criticism is illuminating, because the paintings were meant to be unsettling against the background of traditional art. We cannot recapture the shock of what was then new, and James could not see that impressionism was, after all, another instance of beautiful art.

What we want from a critic is description that permits us to understand how it could be seen that way, even if we disagree with the appraisal:

> The point [of the movie *Germinal*] is plain, and inarguable: that in nineteenth century France, as anywhere else, miners toiled under infernal conditions for woeful wages, and deserved better. . . . As social history, all this looks impeccable; as a campaign for justice, it is flushed with fine feelings; as drama, however, it's got problems. Call me a thrill junkie, but I find there's only so much excitement to be had from watching angry debates about the redistribution of timbering costs.
>
> (Lane 1994: 90)

Germinal may be a great didactic movie, as it is a great didactic novel, and so Lane may be wrong, but he makes it quite clear how he can describe and evaluate it as he does. Had he asserted that *Germinal* – movie or book – was a splendid miniature that portrays the finest nuances of thought and emotion in the manner of Henry James, we would wonder what he was talking about. That we agree with Lane's verdict does not make him a good critic; what matters is that he has made it possible for us to see the movie from his perspective (and of course the perspective must be plausible for us to imagine seeing it that way) and thus to understand the basis for his judgement. That, in turn, might lead us to alter our own view. This is the form that argument usually takes in criticism. Appreciative description is a branch of rhetoric not logic, and, as in art itself, anything goes that 'works.'

Analytical criticism

The vagaries of taste and the rhetorical art of the appreciative critic presented a problem when the fine arts, most notably literature, became university subjects in the late nineteenth century. This led to efforts to make criticism systematic in order to put the study of the arts on the same footing as philology, sociology, or psychology, and to distinguish it from the 'impressionistic' discourse of appreciative critics. Thus, R. S. Crane wrote that

> Criticism, as distinct from mere aesthetic perception or appreciation, is reasoned discourse, that is to say, an organization of terms, propositions, and arguments the peculiar character of which, in any instance, depends as much upon factors operative in the construction of the discourse itself as upon the nature of the objects it envisages or the mind and circumstances of its author.
>
> (Crane 1967: 6–7)

The word 'mere,' the complex syntax, the latinate diction, and the budding obscurity are signs of the academic effort to make criticism a discipline with a distinctive vocabulary that reflects its discovery of meanings and structures (the key term for modern academic commentary on the arts) that are not made evident in appreciative criticism. Such criticism is often called 'analysis' in order to suggest its systematic and rigorous character, in contrast to the subjectivism of appreciative descriptions. Analytic criticism is closely tied to a formalist theory of the arts that takes the underlying organization of works of art as their distinctive value, thus subordinating the mimetic and expressive appearances that are dominant in descriptive criticism. Formal analysis, of which New Criticism is perhaps the best-known school, claims "that it can analyze out and reveal the very structure or principle of formal organization to which the work owes its being" (Gombrich 1966: 73) and, by implication, its value.

The commonest method of analysis, which we might call 'thematizing,' is most often applied to literary works, but its application is general:

> The process of academic criticism begins, then, with reading a poem through to the end, suspending value-judgments while doing so. Once the end is reached, we can see the whole design of the work as a unity. It is now a simultaneous pattern radiating out from a center, not a narrative moving in time. The structure is what we call the theme, and the identifying of the theme is the next step. By 'identifying' a theme I do not mean spotting it: the theme is not something in the poem, much less a moral precept suggested by it, but the structural principle in the poem.
>
> (Frye 1963: 65)

The New Criticism, analyses of paintings that speak of space, mass, diagonals, and verticals, the Schenkerian method in music, and the once-ubiquitous structuralist schemas are varieties of analytic criticism. Here is an example, an extreme version of New Criticism:

> In summary, the following seventeen relationships between rhyme and meaning (R–M's) are found in "Sailing to Byzantium":

SEMANTIC CONGRUITY		SEMANTIC DISPARITY	
Symbol	3	Antithesis	7
Synonym	1	Irony	4
Metonymy	2		—
	6		11

> **Grand Total: 17**
>
> (Perloff 1970: 131)

When formal analysis remains closely tied to artistic practice, as it does, for example, in the teaching of musical composition, it can be successful. However, the claim that the formal structure of artistic performances is what *really* determines their value and 'real' meaning and that the relationship between form and value can be demonstrated has not been realized.

Interpretative criticism

Criticism does not stop when the critic has offered a descriptive appraisal of new works or a re-appraisal of earlier ones. Having appreciated a performance, we want to connect it to the world, and thereby say what its significance might be (Hirsch 1967). The *interpretive criticism* that produces significance is usually directed to canonical works, and it serves a function similar to that of the re-staging of dramatic works. Both provide continuity not by historical reconstruction, which takes us backward in time, but through the making of meanings that bring them forward to us. One of the most powerful such interpretations in this century is Simone Weil's essay, "The *Iliad* or The Poem of Force," in which the modern belief in the dehumanizing effect of war is given expression through commentary on an ancient text:

> The true hero, the true subject, the center of the *Iliad* is force. Force employed by man, force that enslaves man, force before which man shrinks away. . . . The cold brutality of the deeds of war is left undisguised; neither victors nor vanquished are admired, scorned, or hated. . . . As for the warriors, victors or vanquished, those comparisons which liken them to beasts or things can inspire neither admiration nor contempt, but only regret that men are capable of being so transformed.
>
> (Weil 1941: 163, 190)

It does not matter if Homer meant this or not. It is a meaning that makes the poem significant for us, and it is through such interpretive criticism that the canonical works are adapted to the concerns of contemporary readers.

Interpretive criticism is commonly carried out by means of the allegorization of non-allegorical works: it is *force*, not Achilles, that is now the hero of the poem, just as in Marxist readings it is social classes that are the 'real' agents. Interpretation was once directed almost exclusively to sacred texts, which have been replaced in western secular societies by works of art as the major objects of hermeneutic attention. Greek commentators allegorized Homer, and Christian writers did the same for classical literary works. Psychoanalytic interpretation is a well-known instance of this process, which is endlessly flexible, and in which selected elements of the performance are abstracted and related to ideas that are significant to the interpreter and his audience. The most common form of allegorization is through thematic oppositions such as appearance and reality, chaos and order, good and evil. Thus Alvin Kernan writes: "In some ways I have schematized *Othello* as just such a morality play, offering an allegorical journey between heaven and hell on a stage filled with purely symbolic figures" (Kernan 1963: xxxiv). In "Against Interpretation," Susan Sontag's well-known essay attacking such allegorization, Sontag herself cannot resist allegorizing even as she claims to be offering a different, more 'sensual,' kind of reading:

> Taken as a brute object, as *an immediate sensory equivalent fo*r [i.e. an allegorical parallel to] the mysterious abrupt armored happenings going

inside the hotel, that sequence with the tank is the most striking moment in the film. Those who reach for a Freudian interpretation of the tank are only expressing their lack of response to what is there on the screen.

(Sontag 1967: 9–10; my emphasis)

Allegorical interpretation, which had long been in intellectual disrepute, first gained acceptance in literary studies, then spread to film (Bordwell 1989), and has now reached the visual arts:

A shift from history [in the study of visual art] to discourse theory, as Craig Owens once remarked, is the hallmark of the new 'allegorical' approach, which he distinguishes from traditional hermeneutics. The conviction is not that later commentators, after much hard research, will be able to restore an original meaning that may have been obscured or lost, but that critics in the present, schooled in congeries of poststructuralist ideas of subjectivity and ideology, will be able to add to the image new meanings never seen before .

(Holly 1996: 174)

Interpretive criticism was a staple of academic commentary long before the advent of poststructuralism. Such criticism should, but often does not, acknowledge its creative nature. The pervasiveness of interpretive criticism as an academic practice has the unintended effect of making meaning rather than aesthetic qualities the central concern of criticism. This may also entail making meaning the criterion of value, rather than, for example, grace, vividness, inventiveness: in short, the qualitative aspects of works of art. *The Waste Land* is good because it requires so much effort to get at such deep meaning. Interpretive criticism is often an over-elaborate extension of the routine ways that we connect performances back to the world and our immediate concerns. Of course some performances – allegories themselves – do the connecting for us, which is why, Northrop Frye shrewdly remarks, "The commenting critic is often prejudiced against allegory without knowing the real reason, which is that continuous allegory prescribes the direction of his commentary, and so restricts its freedom" (Frye 1957: 90). The extravagances of interpreters are an expression of that freedom.

Cultural criticism

There is another form of critical discourse, which is common today and which is usually called *cultural criticism*. It takes us another – and final – step away from works of art as performances. This notion of criticism as social critique began in the nineteenth century – one thinks of Marx's 'critical criticism' – and it was advanced by Matthew Arnold in "The Study of Criticism at the Present Time," where he contrasts it to "polemical practical criticism" (Arnold 1962: 271), that is, reviewing. Criticism has here almost wholly lost its meaning as discourse grounding the evaluation of performances, and instead uses commentary on art and culture as a basis for social criticism. Such criticism "serves the cause of perfection" and not artistic performance (ibid.: 274). For the cultural critic the words of Samuel Johnson still ring true: "criticism [of performances]. . . is only to be ranked among the subordinate and instrumental arts," and, he adds, "there are laws of higher authority than those of criticism," by which he means moral judgement, and from which performances are not immune (Johnson 1968: 208). That takes us back to Plato and Aristotle and the perennial uncertainty about the status of performances in the range of human activity. For Plato, Johnson, and contemporary cultural critics there are, indeed, "laws of higher authority" before which performances must appear, whereas for Aristotle performances also had an authority of their own, and his task was to ensure that they were done well. Criticism in the narrow and usual sense is, ideally, the servant of artistic performance. It is an effort to foster appreciation of particular works and maintain standards of artistic performance. Cultural criticism returns us to criticism in the broadest sense, where works of art are not judged primarily as performances but as theorems and deeds.

See also Interpretation, Metaphor, Value of art.

References

Aristotle (1987) *The Poetics of Aristotle*, trans. S. Halliwell, Chapel Hill: University of North Carolina Press.

Arnold, M. (1962) *Lectures and Essays in Criticism*, ed. R. H. Super, Ann Arbor: University of Michigan Press.

Bordwell, D. (1989) *Making Meaning: Inference and Rhetoric in the Interpretation of Cinema*, Cambridge, Mass.: Harvard University Press.

Brooks, C. and Warren, R. P. (1976) *Understanding Poetry*, 4th edn, New York: Holt, Rinehart and Winston.

Crane, R. S. (1967) "History vs. Criticism," in *The Idea of the Humanities and Other Essays Critical and Historical*, vol. 2, Chicago and London: University of Chicago Press.

Danto, A. (1981) *The Transfiguration of the Commonplace: A Philosophy of Art*, Cambridge, Mass.: Harvard University Press.

Frye, N. (1957) *Anatomy of Criticism: Four Essays*, Princeton: Princeton University Press.

—— (1963) "Literary Criticism," in J. Thorpe (ed.), *The Aims and Methods of Scholarship in Modern Languages and Literatures*, New York: Modern Language Association of America.

Furbank, P. N. (1994) "Marshmallowing," *New York Review of Books* (January 13): 35.

Gombrich, E. H. (1966) *Norm and Form: Studies in the Art of the Renaissance*, London: Phaidon.

Hanslick, E. (1950) *Vienna's Golden Years of Music: 1850–1900*, trans. H. Pleasants III, Freeport, N.Y.: Books for Libraries Press.

Hirsch, E. D. Jr. (1967) *Validity in Interpretation*, New Haven: Yale University Press.

Holly, M. A. (1996) *Past Looking: Historical Imagination and the Rhetoric of the Image*, Ithaca: Cornell University Press.

James, H. (1956) *The Painter's Eye: Notes and Essays on the Pictorial Arts*, ed. J. L. Sweeney, London: Hart-Davis.

Jarrell, R. (1959) *Poetry and the Age*, New York: Vintage.

Johnson, S. (1968) *Essays from the Rambler, Adventurer and Idler*, ed. W. J. Bate, New Haven: Yale University Press.

Kernan, A. (ed.) (1963) "Introduction," *The Tragedy of Othello, The Moor of Venice*, New York: New American Library.

Kristeller, P. O. (1985) "The Modern System of the Arts," in *Renaissance Thought II: Papers on Humanism and the Arts*, New York: Harper and Row.

Lane, A. (1994) "The Shaft," *New Yorker* (14 March): 90–1.

Penny, N. (1998) "Why is Christ playing with the Magdalene's Hair?" *London Review of Books* (2 July): 18–19.

Perloff, M. (1970) *Rhyme and Meaning in the Poetry of Yeats*, The Hague: Mouton.

Rawson, C. (1985) *Order from Confusion Sprung: Studies in Eighteenth Century Literature from Swift to Cowper*, London: Allen and Unwin.

Shaw, G. B. (1978) *The Great Composers: Reviews and Bombardments*, ed. L. Crompton, Berkeley: University of California Press.

Sontag, S. (1967) *Against Interpretation and Other Essays*, New York: Farrar, Straus and Giroux.

Sparshott, F. (1967) *The Concept of Criticism*, Oxford: Oxford University Press.

—— (1983) *The Theory of the Arts*, Princeton: Princeton University Press.

Walton, K. (1970) "Categories of Art." *Philosophical Review* 79: 334–67.

Watson, G. (1986) *The Literary Critics: A Study of English Descriptive Criticism*, London: Hogarth Press.

Weil, S. (1941) "The *Iliad* or the Poem of Force," in S. Miles (ed.), *Simone Weil: An Anthology*, New York: Weidenfeld and Nicolson.

Further reading

Rugh, T. F. and Silva, E. R. (eds) (1978) *History as a Tool in Critical Interpretation*, Provo, Utah: Brigham Young University Press. (Essays on the relationship between historical inquiry and appreciative criticism.)

Williams, R. (1977) *Marxism and Literature*, Oxford: Oxford University Press. (One of Williams's many, excellent, and influential works of cultural criticism.)

28
ART AND KNOWLEDGE

Eileen John

The central debates about art and knowledge concern art's potential as a *source* of knowledge. Do we learn things from art? If so, what kinds of things do we learn and how does the learning occur? I believe we indeed learn things from art, and I take that to be a relatively uncontroversial claim among non-philosophers. But it is a controversial claim within philosophy, and the reason for that lies in the difficulty of answering the 'what' and 'how' questions satisfactorily. I will survey some of the most promising answers to those questions here.

Two extremes

In thinking about art as a source of knowledge, two extreme approaches are tempting. On the first, art is embraced enthusiastically but rather loosely as a source of insight and fresh awareness. Sometimes this approach includes the view that the special insight cannot be put into words, but perhaps allows us to perceive the world in a new way. On the second, opposed approach, art or experience with art is rejected as not meeting requirements for the production of knowledge, knowledge being defined along traditional lines as true, justified belief. Art may be critiqued for not asserting or conveying true beliefs, or for not providing justification for any beliefs it may convey. Sometimes this approach includes the charge that even if true knowledge claims are occasionally presented in a work of art, those claims are uninteresting in content.

These approaches generally share the assumption that, if art is a source of knowledge, its way of fulfilling that function must reflect something essential to its nature and value as art. The 'insight' enthusiast may interpret this quite strongly, taking a particular insight to be provided uniquely by the experience of a particular work of art. The knowledge cannot be reached by any other route and cannot be detached from awareness of that work of art. While such a uniqueness claim makes it clear that the knowledge reflects what is essential to a given *work*, it leaves it less clear how the knowledge reflects the general nature of art, since each work is taken to provide insight in its own way.

Meanwhile, when this assumption is made by the advocate of traditional requirements for knowledge, it works to place a seemingly impossible demand on art. Art is supposed to engage us in an epistemically respectable, yet characteristically artistic, practice of knowledge-gathering; however, if this practice is genuinely artistic, then it is apt not to look epistemically respectable (Stolnitz 1992). As with the work-specific uniqueness claim, this demand may further include the idea that art should provide knowledge in a *uniquely* artistic way.

While these extremes each receive support from our experiences with art, each is unsatisfying. We do not want the knowledge gained from art to seem so nebulous in content and so inscrutably produced that it can be dismissed as either uninteresting or illusory. Worthwhile knowledge must have some recognizable and usable substance to it, and it must be able to 'travel' at least a bit beyond the site of its acquisition: you should be able to rely and build upon it in other contexts. However, we should not set up at the outset too many demands based on traditional models of knowledge-gathering, often derived from theories of science, as if we already understand everything about knowledge, and thus what learning from art would have to be like. Given that many people say they learn things from art, we should explore that as a live option, recognizing that our understanding of knowledge may change as a result.

In exploring the middle ground, I will work with three fairly loose constraints. First, learning from art requires some degree of awareness of what the new knowledge is. Second, the engagement with art should provide some form of justification or confirmation, some reason to accept and trust the change in one's thinking, feeling, perception, or behavior. These two constraints reflect in a very general way the concerns of the advocate of traditional epistemological standards. Knowledge is supposed to have withstood some kind of scrutiny: it is supposed to be tested, well-considered, based on relevant evidence. The awareness constraint is intended to demand more specification of what has been learned than is required for affirming, say, that 'I see things differently now.' These constraints go some way toward maintaining a distinction between learning from art and the more inclusive category of being influenced or changed by art. Not every way in which art influences us is a matter of learning from art, and my provisional way of isolating the narrower category is by requiring that the results of learning be recognized and supported in some way.

The third constraint endorses the assumption mentioned above: accounts of learning from art should make it clear how the learning depends on and reflects the nature and value of art. Cynthia Freeland articulates this position succinctly, in stating the central theses of 'cognitivist' views of art:

(1) Artworks stimulate cognitive activity that may teach us about the world. . . . (2) The cognitive activity they stimulate is part and parcel of their functioning as artworks. (3) As a result of this stimulation, we learn from artworks: we acquire fresh knowledge, our beliefs are refined, and our understanding is deepened. (4) What we learn in this manner constitutes one of the main reasons we enjoy and value artworks in the first place.

(Freeland 1997: 19)

The underlying support for cognitivism lies in fleshing out how cognitive stimulation and learning are 'part and parcel' of the artistic functioning of art works. A satisfying cognitivism should require, again, first, that the content of the learning be specifiable (*what* is it we learn); second, that demands for justification be respected (*how* does the knowledge emerge?); and third, that these accounts of learning appeal to characteristic features of artistic experience. With regard to whether these accounts should show unique, distinctively artistic means of knowing, I do not find it plausible that art provides knowledge in unique, *sui generis* ways. I assume that learning from art engages us with knowledge-gathering practices we use in many contexts; I would rather argue for differences of degree. Learning from art is often marked by the degree of intensity, focus, surprise, and richness of the learning experience.

Cognitive stimulation

Even those who doubt that art is a source of knowledge generally grant that it is a source of cognitive stimulation. To be cognitively stimulating means at the very least to prompt activities in conscious life: thoughts, feelings, perceptions, and desires. Usually it carries a more positive evaluative meaning: art is cognitively stimulating because it has a *stimulating* effect, prompting conscious activity which is interesting, new, provocative, intense, suggestive. Such activity may or may not lead to knowledge, but clearly the fact that art has this capacity is relevant to its potential as a source of knowledge. Studying art's powers of cognitive stimulation is an important step in understanding *how* art provides knowledge.

Many works of art, in order to be appreciated and enjoyed as art, call out for understanding, as opposed to sheer awe or delight. This understanding often requires cognitively lively or demanding activity, as we try out ideas, feelings, and attitudes important to understanding the work. For example, Alice Walker's *The Color Purple* begins with a number of letters addressed to God, and that striking feature of the novel needs to be mulled over and understood in order to reach a satisfying reading of the novel. We need to consider what writing to God means to the girl writing the letters, and we may feel some of the desolation that leads her to write to God. So, even if we just set out to enjoy a work, we often pursue cognitive stimulation en route to that goal.

Art's particular ways of stimulating us are frequently highlighted as distinguishing art from other cognitive influences. In discussions of literature and moral knowledge, for instance, emotional and imaginative responses to literature are used to contrast learning from literature with learning from traditional works of moral philosophy. Traditional moral philosophy is presented as stimulating thought and argument primarily about general moral principles and metaethical theories. Literature, on the other hand, is presented as prompting a richer, more complex kind of engagement. Of Henry James's novel *The Golden Bowl*, Martha Nussbaum says, "To work through these sentences and these chapters is to become involved in an activity of exploration and unraveling that uses abilities, especially abilities of emotion and imagination, rarely tapped by philosophical texts" (Nussbaum 1990: 143). Such works call upon us to take fictional characters seriously as moral agents, to enter imaginatively into the concrete circumstances of their lives, and to have the kind of complicated evaluative and felt responses to them that we can have to real people. We often also imagine things about ourselves in response to art. Traditional philosophical works ask for active reasoning and critical participation, but they generally do not ask for the imaginatively constructive, perceptual, morally evaluating, and emotionally sophisticated participation appropriate to many works of art.

One overarching important feature of engagement with art is that it integrates pleasure-seeking into cognitive activity. With art, it is appropriate to make associations which are interesting or funny or somehow satisfying. We are supposed to be teased and tempted into inferring something from the subtle elements of a work; and we are often encouraged to develop conceptions holding complexity, ambiguity, and irony, as much by relying on a feeling for what details and ideas it is intriguing to bring together, as on a sense of their logical relations. In general, we often develop ideas in response to art, moving cognitively from point A to point B, because of the fun or interest or satisfying quality of making that move. David Novitz, for instance, argues for the cognitive role of fiction by emphasizing that it triggers the 'fanciful imagination,' by which he means "the ability which people have to fabricate or invent by combining ideas, images, beliefs, words, or physical objects howsoever they choose" (Novitz 1987: 27). The fanciful imagination enables us to guess and speculate when faced with gaps in knowledge. David Hills suggests, with respect to metaphors, that "we try to enjoy them in order to understand them," so that we are guided in interpretation partly by "various kinds of prospective pleasure" (Hills 1997: 145–6). If we are guided in responding to art by factors such as which ideas hint of pleasure and which fabrications and guesses we choose to make, it seems reasonable that this activity would generate cognitive results which would be hard to arrive at otherwise.

Content and justification of knowledge

That art has a wide-ranging cognitive impact on us is accepted; the real controversy concerns whether art affords us knowledge, where knowledge, again, requires some form of justification. Why should we accept ideas we acquire from art? Does experience with art provide evidence or carry some kind of authority? The questions of justification are linked closely to questions of content, since what is being learned affects what kind of justification is needed.

Perhaps we learn from art because the artist has knowledge which is transmitted through the work: the work of art has authority because its maker is an authority. One problem with this is that, while artists may have relevant knowledge, they need not use their art to offer sincere expressions of what they know (Jacobson 1996: 331). That is, our experience of the work would have to be accompanied by external evidence either supporting what the artist knows or showing the relevant authority of the artist, and in that case it does not seem we are learning from *art* (Stolnitz 1992: 198). In general, the connection between what an artist knows and how we experience the artist's work is too indirect and unreliable to give the work epistemic value.

In seeking alternatives, however, we should resist assuming that the confirming force must lie solely in the intrinsic features of the work itself. This is not even a reasonable model of how we learn from such things as philosophical essays, since in that context we must either assess the truth of the premises and the strength of the reasoning ourselves, or trust what the essay says on the basis of independent support for the writer's authority. Similarly, features of our interaction with works of art should be considered in establishing whether we can learn from art.

Experiential knowledge

Perhaps the most straightforward argument defends art's role in providing experiential knowledge, especially knowledge of emotion. Experiential knowledge is knowledge of what it is like to experience something. How would it feel to undergo something, to observe a certain kind of event, to experience things from a certain perspective, or to feel a certain emotion? The assumption is that this kind of knowledge in part requires experiential justification. It is a necessary condition of confirming an experiential belief – a belief about what a certain experience is like – that one's experiential evidence be reasonably taken to give access to the qualities of such an experience.

The fact that works of art can inspire imaginative participation and emotional response is used to argue that art can be a source of this kind of knowledge. Novitz explains,

> our imaginative involvement in fiction allows us to respond emotionally or feelingly to the tribulations and triumphs of creatures of fiction. It is as a result of these experiences . . . that we often come to hold certain beliefs about what it must feel like to occupy situations akin to those of our favorite heroes and heroines.
>
> (Novitz 1987: 120)

For example, I read Virginia Woolf's novel *To the Lighthouse* as capable of putting me experientially 'inside' a particular set of social and psychological relations, in which men and women with various forms of power ask for, give, and resist giving sympathy. Clearly works of art can lead us at least to acquire experiential beliefs. But those beliefs can be mistaken. We can be experientially misled by art, as one might, for instance, get a quite unhelpful sense of "what it is like to be in love" from many works of fiction (Jacobson 1996: 327). What makes it reasonable to take experience with such works to have justificatory force?

Novitz addresses the justification of experiential beliefs, which he calls 'empathic beliefs,' by requiring support from our broader experience: "if [empathic beliefs gained from fiction] turn out to have some basis in, or to cohere with, our future or past experiences, they will pass as empathic knowledge" (Novitz 1987: 120). On the one hand, this is obviously right. As with any kind of contingent knowledge of human life, we need to confirm putative experiential knowledge in the long term, on the basis of coherence with other related experiences. But it is not entirely clear, on Novitz's view, whether there can also be reason for trusting our experience with a work of art, for treating it as knowledge – granting that it is revisable and defeasible in light of further experience – based on the relatively short-term encounter with the work. Should we use these experiential beliefs only as provisional suggestions for what to expect in future experiences, or can we have grounds for accepting them with some conviction? Does experience with the work itself have confirming power or must we turn to external sources?

I think we can have good reason for taking these experiences to have justificatory force, in part because our encounter with the work already incorporates some of the confirming evidence to which Novitz refers. We draw on the emotional, experiential knowledge we have acquired to that point, both in the sense that we respond according to dispositions we already have, and in the sense that we interpret our experiences with art, and fiction in particular, using rich knowledge of the generating circumstances, causes, effects, and 'feels' of various emotions and experiences. Past experience allows us to assess whether or not a position taken up in imagination is furnished adequately with the components of a particular kind of experience. We are capable, for instance, of having an emotional response to a story, perhaps weeping, while rejecting it as an untrust-worthy response, because we can sense that the story does not genuinely support the emotional experience. It seems, then, that we sometimes have the resources to tell that our responses are being manipulated, and similarly it seems we may sometimes have the resources to tell that an experience has arisen out of a reasonably complex and relevant set of factors.

Furthermore, in the phenomena of *recognizing* one's past experience in an experience evoked by art, or of *being* in circumstances relevant to the work, it seems that one's circumstances and recognitional experience can allow one to serve as an authority of sorts, such that one's trust in the awareness provided by the work is reasonable. When someone sent me a few lines from a Sylvia Plath poem about her infant son, shortly after I had had a baby, I found the lines were powerfully evocative of how it felt to look at my son. In this case, I think my circumstances and recognitional experience made it reasonable for me to trust my sense that the poem was experientially revelatory.

Moral knowledge

There are a number of arguments for the view that we learn morally from art. Typically they depend on art's ability to provide experiential and emotional stim-ulation. This stimulation is taken to be important to moral agents' need to perceive morally relevant elements of experience, to have morally sensitive and apt emotional responses, and to take up morally challenging perspectives in imagination.

The first type of argument stresses art's capacity to give us exemplars of, and exercise in, these morally pertinent activities. In experiences with art, and especially with literary fiction, we learn in the sense of getting training or practice in *doing* things which are central to responsible moral life (Murdoch 1971: 86–91; Nussbaum 1990, Diamond 1991, Jacobson 1996, Kieran 1996). Furthermore, the substance and style of a work can demonstrate the relevant virtues of perception, feeling, and imagination, so we can also learn from a work by taking it as an exemplar or model of morally excellent sensibilities. So Nussbaum says of James's *The Golden Bowl* that "The text itself displays, and is, a high kind of moral activity" (Nussbaum 1990: 161). Learning from doing and from encountering an exemplar provides moral knowledge in the sense of developing skills required for responsible moral agency; thinking in these terms means taking knowledge to include learned abilities or 'know-how,' as well as propositional knowledge.

With respect to justification of such knowledge, it seems that we need reason to believe that the exercise is good exercise and that the exemplar is a good exemplar. Is my imaginative perception morally deep or shallow? Are Henry James novels really discerning or artificially complex? I doubt there is any neat justificatory story to tell here. It seems that we indeed scrutinize works such as novels in this regard, and that we can be aware of whether a work presses us to notice and feel in a more acute way. Perhaps we also get confirming evidence in our futures as moral agents, if we find ourselves perceiving and feeling with greater sensitivity. But in general there are hard, unresolved questions concerning how to assess the worth of the exercise and models provided by art. Do we learn from any stretch of the moral imagination, or just from exercise that gets us to perceive *correctly*, according to substantive moral standards?

Second, it is argued that we can acquire specific substantive moral knowledge from art (Murdoch 1971, Nussbaum 1990, Kieran 1996, Brudney 1998, Freeland 1997). A very general pattern of argument appeals, again, to art's power to give us imaginative access to experiences which are relevant to moral judgement and knowledge. The fact that we feel certain emotions in certain imagined circumstances helps us to know the moral import of those circumstances (for example when Jane Austen's Emma makes a cruel remark, we know it is cruel largely because of how it makes us feel and how fervently we wish she had not said it). Hence our experience with a work of art can show us, it seems, about the moral import of pertinently similar events, real or imagined.

One justificatory idea is that the quality of the imaginative and emotional activity involved in generating putative moral knowledge can be an indicator of trustworthiness (Brudney 1998). The idea is that if we have a vivid, rich, gripping imaginative response, that is evidence of genuine, scrupulous engagement with the imagined circumstances, and evidence that the imagined circumstances are relevant to real human concerns. We cannot end up working imaginatively in such a sustained, compelling way unless there is coherence and substance to our activity. This is a relative of the Cartesian view that the clarity and distinctness of an idea carry epistemic weight. It is also a nice way of linking the artistic and the cognitive value of art, since it makes the artistic goal of providing rich experiences directly relevant to how we learn from art. I think this is the justificatory idea implicit in many of Nussbaum's accounts of literature and moral knowledge, since she emphasizes so heavily the complex particularity, subtlety, and affective richness of a reader's activity. This idea may also be implicit in Rosalind

Hursthouse's discussion of getting a "dominatingly vivid" image of the terrible-ness of war, from Picasso's *Guernica* and Goya's war paintings (Hursthouse 1992: 278–9). Perhaps a dominatingly vivid experience can have justificatory force, if the fact that some experiences *cannot* be ignored serves as provisional evidence that they *should* not be ignored.

On this view, not just any kind of aesthetic virtue or beauty is claimed to carry justificatory force. Rather, a very specific kind of great aesthetic experience, in which we think and feel acutely and, as best we can tell, conceive of and understand the context of our experience clearly, is taken to count as evidentially relevant. Certainly it may turn out in any given case that we have not imagined scrupulously or critically enough: we are capable of having stimulating encounters with morally distorted works without realizing it. Suppose, for example, that one is powerfully stirred by songs which celebrate white racist identity, perhaps even feeling that the lyrics give one new insight into race relations. It would be nice if we could say that the qualities of such an experience, powerful though it may be, could nonetheless be exposed as aesthetically lacking in some way (too crude, shallow, or confused, perhaps), allowing us to discount the apparent justificatory force of the experience. Perhaps aesthetic qualities can sometimes be questioned and used to discount an experience in this way, but it seems implausible that we can do this systematically and reliably when undergoing a striking aesthetic experience.

One last suggestion relevant to justification concerns the role of commentaries on works of art. Citing controversies over recent cases of morally challenging art, Cynthia Freeland argues that,

> often the confusion and lack of dialogue . . . show that to understand an art work's moral content requires fairly complex acts of artistic interpre-tation. Islamic fundamentalists don't *understand* the vocabulary of magical realism; Mapplethorpe's critics don't *understand* his gay urban S&M aesthetic; and Serrano's critics don't *understand* that *Piss Christ* could mean something other than 'Piss on Christ'.
>
> (Freeland 1997: 31)

Our experience of such works may be quite inadequate and morally off-target, unless we allow our experience to be informed by commentaries which discuss the techniques, intentions, and moral import of a work. Taking experience with art to be part of a public conversation about works of art means that we can rely on some of the virtues of public discourse in claiming to have learned from a work. We can appeal to the benefits of other people's perspectives and to the authority of people with wider artistic and cultural experience, as well as to the generally good epistemic effects of comparing one's experience to another's: we tend to scrutinize, question, and go further in our thinking with an external 'provocateur.' This idea of course opens the door to the objection that learning in this way is not a matter of learning from *the work of art*. I think the force of Freeland's examples shows this objection to be not so compelling. To give accompanying commentaries a central role in learning from art still leaves the work of art as the originating stimulus for learning, and it is still the work of art and how it can be experienced which sets the terms for how we assess the commentaries. But to embrace commentary in this way does shake up our sense of what we ought to be doing with art, by suggesting that public discourse, along with individual response, should be part and parcel of the cognitive functioning of art.

Art and categories of knowledge

Finally, one other important way in which art is portrayed as a source of knowledge involves the role of art in creating or shaping the categories of knowledge. Sometimes the claim is that art has a role in giving us conceptual knowledge (Hagberg 1994, John 1998, Wilson 1983). In the Woolf example mentioned earlier, for instance, I would argue that the experiential knowledge of sympathy I gain from *To the Lighthouse* contributes to my learning something general about the concept of sympathy.

A more radical claim is that art in various ways helps shape what can be known. So Nelson Goodman says that if an artist's picture

> is recognized as almost but not quite referring to the commonplace furniture of the world, or if it calls for and yet resists assignment to a usual kind of picture, it may bring out neglected likenesses and differences, force unaccustomed associations, and in some measure remake our world. And if the point of the picture is not only successfully made but is also well-taken, if the realignments it directly and indirectly effects are interesting and important, the picture – like a crucial experiment – makes a genuine contribution to knowledge.
>
> (Goodman 1976: 33)

If the innovative constructions provided by a work of art suit our needs and turn out to be projectable in future thought and practice, they will prove themselves to belong in our understanding of the world.

How might art works have such powerful effects? The following claims made by an art historian and a literary theorist are suggestive. Anne Hollander thinks that movies "have taught us to recognize the presence of meaning in uneventful scenes full of vivid objects," and in movies, furthermore, "the world is presented in a fluid medium that depends on incompleteness, quick change, and often on ambiguity" (Hollander 1989: 17, 7). Dorrit Cohn, on the portrayal of the psychological domain in realist fiction, says that

> the most real, the "roundest" characters of fiction are those we know most intimately, precisely in ways we could never know people in real life . . . the special lifelikeness of narrative fiction . . . depends on what writers and readers know least in life: how another mind thinks, another body feels.
>
> (Cohn 1978: 5–6)

Perhaps these artforms gave us new ideas about what knowledge of the world can be like, whether by giving ordinary aspects of life potential for meaning, by making fluid vision seem possible and desirable, or by giving a new sense of how people could be known. If these ideas about how to know the world have been 'well-taken,' they seem like plausible illustrations of Goodman's view.

It is controversial whether art, in having such an impact, would provide *knowledge*. Would it be better construed as an example of art influencing rather than educating us? Perhaps the idea that novels of a certain genre could give us new and appropriate standards for knowledge of the human mind is just not plausible; maybe this case must be rejected as an example of art imposing on us an unworkable fantasy of knowledge. But it seems that the fact of being adopted, of acquiring a stable role in our repertoire of categories, distinctions, and ways of knowing, could amount to a 'vindication' of such artistic influences (Elgin 1991: 206–7).

The issues raised by considering art as a source of knowledge are important to our understanding of art, but they are also of general epistemological interest. This is in part because, in its content, what we learn from art is apt to lie in epistemologically challenging domains. It is difficult to give accounts of perceptual, experiential, psychological, and moral knowledge in general, so any insights we get about those domains of knowledge, based on learning experiences with art, will be valuable. Thinking about art and knowledge also presses important issues about the range of types of knowledge. Art is one of the phenomena which show traditional models of propositional knowledge to be inadequate. We need a theory of knowledge which embraces such things as knowing how to perceive, imagine, and feel aptly, and knowing what a certain experience is like. Finally, the cognitively stimulating powers of art are a good resource for studying the role of such factors as creativity, surprise, interest, and choice in the emergence of new ideas.

See also Plato, Aristotle, Hegel, Imagination and make-believe, Fiction, Value of art, Art and ethics, Art, expression and emotion, Literature.

References

Brudney, D. (1998) "*Lord Jim* and Moral Judgment: Literature and Moral Philosophy," *Journal of Aesthetics and Art Criticism* 56: 265–81.

Cohn, D. (1978) *Transparent Minds*, Princeton: Princeton University Press.

Diamond, C. (1991) "Having a Rough Story about What Moral Philosophy Is," in *The Realistic Spirit*, Cambridge, Mass.: MIT Press.

Elgin, C. (1991) "Understanding: Art and Science," *Midwest Studies in Philosophy* 16: 196–208.

Freeland, C. (1997) "Art and Moral Knowledge," *Philosophical Topics* 25: 11–36.

Goodman, N. (1976) *Languages of Art*, 2nd edn, Indianapolis: Hackett.

Hagberg, G. (1994) *Meaning and Interpretation: Wittgenstein, Henry James, and Literary Knowledge*, Ithaca: Cornell University Press.

Hills, D. (1997) "Aptness and Truth in Verbal Metaphor," *Philosophical Topics* 25: 117–53.

Hollander, A. (1989) *Moving Pictures*, New York: Knopf.

Hursthouse, R. (1992) "Truth and Representation," in O. Hanfling (ed.), *Philosophical Aesthetics*, Milton Keynes: Open University Press.

Jacobson, D. (1996) "Sir Philip Sidney's Dilemma: On the Ethical Function of Narrative Art," *Journal of Aesthetics and Art Criticism* 54: 327–36.

John, E. (1998) "Reading Fiction and Conceptual Knowledge: Philosophical Thought in Literary Context," *Journal of Aesthetics and Art Criticism* 56: 331–48.

Kieran, M. (1996) "Art, Imagination, and the Cultivation of Morals," *Journal of Aesthetics and Art Criticism* 54: 337–51.

Murdoch, I. (1971) *The Sovereignty of Good*, New York: Schocken.

Novitz, D. (1987) *Knowledge, Fiction and Imagination*, Philadelphia: Temple University Press.

Nussbaum, M. (1990) *Love's Knowledge*, Oxford: Oxford University Press.

Stolnitz, J. (1992) "On the Cognitive Triviality of Art," *British Journal of Aesthetics* 32: 191–200.

Wilson, C. (1983) "Literature and Knowledge," *Philosophy* 58: 489–96.

Further reading

Lamarque, P. and Olsen, S. (1994) *Truth, Fiction, and Literature*, Oxford: Oxford University Press. (A comprehensive critique of literature as a source of knowledge.)

Robinson, J. (1995) "L'Éducation Sentimentale," *Australasian Journal of Philosophy* 73: 212–26. (An account of literature as a source of complex knowledge of emotion.)

Young, J. (1999) "The Cognitive Value of Music," *Journal of Aesthetics and Art Criticism* 57: 41–54. (A defense of music as a source of knowledge.)

29
ART AND ETHICS

Berys Gaut

The issues

The relation of art to ethics has been at the forefront of several recent controversies about art: the dispute over Robert Mapplethorpe's homoerotic
photographs; the protests over the sexism and violence seemingly advocated in
the music of 'gangsta' rappers such as Ice-T; the controversy over the violence of
many Hollywood movies, such as *Natural Born Killers*; and the fatwah declared
against Salman Rushdie for publishing *The Satanic Verses*. Those who think of
art as a kind of pleasant and harmless pastime might do well to reflect on these
disputes: popular passions have raged, law suits have been threatened, criminal
proceedings have been enacted, and a death-sentence has been promulgated. Art
has real power: power to disturb, power to pummel against the bulwarks of our
ethical convictions.

Such controversies are not merely the ephemeral froth of contemporary media
hype. Worries about the relation of art to ethics run deep in the mainstream of
the Western intellectual tradition. Plato in *The Republic* famously attacked
almost all kinds of mimetic art for undermining reason at the expense of the
unseemly stimulation of emotion and the advancement of a mere simulacrum of
knowledge. A great deal of the subsequent debate about the value of art has been
shaped by this seminal attack, so that the issue of the relation of art to ethics has
been of recurrent and central interest both to philosophical aesthetics and to
literary theory.

The general issue of the relation of art to ethics admits of several distinct
questions which need to be disentangled. One, most overtly posed in the
contemporary popular debate, is this: does exposure to works of art which are
ethically suspect (because of their advocacy of violence, sexism, and so on) tend
morally to corrupt their audiences? This is essentially a causal, empirical
question: we need to find the answer from psychological and sociological
experiments. A second question concerns censorship: does the ethical badness

of certain works of art justify their suppression? Some of the points made in the present chapter will be relevant to answering that question, but we will not address it directly: it is chiefly a question in political philosophy, and a full answer would have to develop a general theory about freedom of expression. A third question concerns what are sometimes called the 'moral rights' of art works: do we have moral obligations towards art works to preserve them in certain ways: for instance, do we have obligations not to colorize movies? Again, we will not address that question here. A fourth question, of great interest to eighteenth-century philosophers, including Hume and Kant, is whether there are structural parallels between aesthetic and moral judgements: are both kinds of judgements, for instance, objective or relative, are they governed by principles, are they about response-dependent properties, and so on? This question will also not be addressed here, since it would lead us away from the core issues which have animated the debate about art and ethics.

What interests us is a question distinct from all of the above. Put most simply, it is this: are the ethical flaws (or merits) of works of art also aesthetic flaws (or merits) in them? Consider Leni Riefenstahl's famous film, *Triumph of the Will*, which is a glowingly enthusiastic account of the 1934 Nuremberg Nazi Party rally. Is the film aesthetically flawed because of its advocacy of Hitler's cause? It has frequently been denounced as bad art because of its message. Or is its immoral stance simply an irrelevance to its merit as a work of art? Many regard it as a good, even a great, work of art. Or is it in contrast a great work of art partly because of its immorality? If great art disturbs and challenges our convictions, then this film could surely qualify as great art.

As the example illustrates, there are three plausible contending answers to our question. They will need refining later, but we can initially roughly characterize them as follows. Autonomism (or aestheticism) holds that ethical flaws or merits of works of art are never aesthetic flaws or merits in them: ethical assessment is irrelevant to aesthetic assessment. The other two views deny this claim of irrelevance, but differ as to how the ethical and aesthetic relate. Immoralism holds that works of art are sometimes aesthetically good because of their ethical flaws. Moralism (or ethicism) in contrast holds that works of art are aesthetically bad because of their ethical flaws. The goal of this chapter is to establish which of these three views is correct. And in answering this question, we will have discovered the answer to one of the core questions which has animated the long debate about art and ethics.

Before proceeding, we need to clarify what counts as an ethical flaw in a work of art. Ethical flaws should not be understood in terms of the causal powers of works to affect audiences, since assessing this would be relevant chiefly to the causal question. Rather, we should understand flaws in terms of the intrinsic properties of works. We will characterize these flaws thus: a work is ethically flawed just in case it manifests ethically reprehensible attitudes. For instance, *Triumph of the Will* is ethically flawed because of the attitudes it displays of worshipful adoration and wholehearted approval of Hitler and Nazism. Its causal power to convert some audiences to Nazism is conceptually distinct from this (though of course this power partly rests on its intrinsic ethical flaws).

Autonomism

An extreme version of autonomism would hold that it makes no sense morally to evaluate works of art, in the same way that it makes no sense for instance morally to evaluate numbers. Now perhaps some kinds of art works cannot be morally evaluated (this may be true of some music without a text), but as a general claim, there is little to recommend this view, for it is clear that works of art, such as *Triumph of the Will*, can express views which it is proper to evaluate morally, and indeed many, especially narrative, works are constructed so as deliberately to engage their audiences' moral responses (see Carroll 1996).

A more moderate and plausible autonomist view is that works of art can be morally evaluated, but that their ethical flaws or merits are never aesthetic flaws or merits in them. The ethical has nothing to do with the aesthetic. When it seems that ethical flaws in works are aesthetically relevant, it is in fact not their ethical badness, but some other features of the expression of these flaws which is relevant. The autonomist Monroe Beardsley discusses Ezra Pound's *Cantos*, some passages of which are anti-Semitic, others of which denounce usury. Both views are false and ethically flawed, but Beardsley holds that only the anti-Semitic passages are aesthetically flawed, because they express anti-Semitism in a cheap and vulgar, insensitive and imperceptive way, whereas the anti-usury views are expressed in a serious tone with rough and strong images and are related to the complexities of things (Beardsley 1981: 427–8). It is the aesthetic manner of expression, in short, that matters aesthetically, not the morality or truth of the attitudes expressed.

Why might one be an autonomist? First, some works of art are ethically deeply flawed, for instance *Triumph of the Will*, yet they are good, or even great, works of art. That being so, it might be argued that the ethical cannot be aesthetically relevant. Now the example certainly proves something: if one held that moral merits are the *only* kind of aesthetic merits which there are, then one must aesthetically condemn the film. And some writers have held a version of extreme moralism, which would fall to this kind of objection. Tolstoy in *What is Art?* for instance maintains that the value of art lies in its evocation of a feeling "of joy and of spiritual union with another" (Tolstoy 1930: 227). But this extreme moralism is highly implausible: we praise works for a wide variety of features, such as their beauty, unity, complexity or profundity, features which have no necessary relation to morality (see also Beardsmore 1971: ch. 2). The moralist should, in short, be a pluralist about aesthetic values; and then he or she can hold that the film is aesthetically flawed insofar as it is immoral, but that it has many aesthetic merits, such as its unity and complexity, which overall make it a good work of art.

A second reason for being an autonomist derives from an appeal to the aesthetic attitude. The main support for autonomism has come from formalists such as Beardsley and Clive Bell; and formalists generally have held there to be an aesthetic attitude, an attitude we adopt when we assess art works aesthetically. If this attitude were insensitive to moral considerations, autonomism would be established. Many aestheticians have been skeptical about the existence of an aesthetic attitude; but let us suppose that it exists. Is it insensitive to moral considerations?

The aesthetic attitude is sometimes defined in terms of detachment or disengagement from practical concerns, being an attitude of pure contemplation towards the aesthetic object (the idea derives from the Kantian notion of disinterest). However, even if one accepted this disputable characterization, it would not follow that moral considerations played no role in aesthetic assessment. I am forced to take a merely contemplative attitude towards historical figures such as Napoleon, since I can do nothing to alter the past; but it does not follow that I cannot make moral assessments of their conduct.

Alternatively, the aesthetic attitude might be defined by reference to those features of works of art at which it is directed. Bell, for instance, holds that aesthetic emotions are directed at the significant form of an art work, and that significant form in the case of the visual arts is merely "a combination of lines and colours" (Bell 1987: 12). Certainly, this would exclude moral considerations from bearing on aesthetic emotions. But even for the visual arts it is an untenable view of what is aesthetically relevant. Our aesthetic interest is directed not just at lines and colors, but also at how the art work presents a certain subject-matter: the ideas and attitudes it manifests towards its subject. Consider Picasso's great anti-war painting *Guernica*. Someone who reacted to it merely as a set of lines and colors in Cubist style would be missing out on a central item of aesthetic interest: namely, how Picasso *uses* Cubist fragmentation to convey something of the horror of war and Fascism. Our aesthetic interest is directed, in part, at the mode of presentation of subject matter; and the way it is presented can and often does manifest ethical attitudes.

Beardsley broadens out aesthetically relevant features to encompass unity, complexity and the intensity of what he terms "regional properties" (which mainly includes expressive properties) (Beardsley 1981: 456–70). But it is hard to see how ethical properties could legitimately be excluded from this list: they certainly can exhibit intensity, and ethical terms are commonly applied to art works when assessing them aesthetically. Indeed, Beardsley himself appears to succumb to this temptation. In condemning an anti-Semitic passage in Pound's *Cantos* he says that "its tone is insensitive and imperceptive" (ibid.: 428). Beardsley's aesthetic evaluation of the passage is purportedly non-ethical. But can one really understand his words in a non-ethical sense? What would be a *sensitive* presentation of an anti-Semitic view? Even formalists find it hard to embrace autonomism when it comes down to detailed criticism.

There is a general reason for this: our aesthetic practices are laden with ethical evaluations. We often aesthetically praise works for their ethical characteristics, for their compassion, moral insight, maturity, sensitivity, and so on; and think them less good works for their gross insensitivity, sadism and cruelty. Indeed, as the literary critic Wayne Booth has noted, up to the end of the nineteenth century the legitimacy of ethical criticism of art was mainly taken as a given (Booth 1988). Though the formalist high-point of the mid twentieth century saw ethical criticism go into relative decline, the recent burgeoning of feminist and radical literary criticism represents a strong renewal of the ethical tradition. Further, many authors exhibit ethical intentions in their writings; and it would be heroically implausible to hold that this had nothing to do with the aesthetic value of their works. Imagine trying to ignore the ethical evaluations in George Eliot's *Middlemarch* while aesthetically evaluating only its other features: to do this is simply impossible, since her ethical stance pervades the work's narrative structure, its descriptions of characters and situations, its style, its authorial tone and persona. One cannot set aside Eliot's ethical stance while keeping anything remotely resembling her novel before one's view.

Immoralism

Autonomism should be rejected: but that does not yet show that moralism is correct, for one might be an immoralist. Immoralism is a little discussed position; yet it is, in my view, a more interesting and powerful rival to moralism than is autonomism. Extreme immoralism would hold that the only aesthetic merits of a work of art are its ethical flaws. However, a view which made the Marquis de Sade one of the greatest writers of all time, and George Eliot one of the worst, has little to recommend it. In contrast, moderate immoralism would hold that the ethical flaws of a work can *sometimes* be aesthetic merits in it. This is compatible with holding that sometimes ethical flaws are aesthetic flaws, and also with holding that there is a plurality of aesthetic values. This (moderate) immoralism looks attractive.

Why might one be an immoralist? First, art is sometimes praised for its transgressive or subversive qualities; so if art sometimes subverts our moral values, couldn't it be *ipso facto* good? Something like this view is defended by Lawrence Hyman. Hyman claims that there is often a tension or conflict between our aesthetic and ethical responses to works: a work's aesthetic power can act to undermine our moral values, and the moral resistance we feel can enhance the work's aesthetic worth. Discussing passages in *King Lear* where Lear condones adultery by equating human and animal sexuality, and cruelly jokes at the expense of blind Gloucester, Hyman remarks that "the dramatic effect requires our moral disapproval" (Hyman 1984: 154).

However, though the immorality of Lear's attitudes are *represented* in the play, it does not follow that these attitudes are *shared* by the play itself (in fact, given the play's account of Lear's gradual achievement of moral wisdom, clearly they are not). Ethically sound works can represent immoral characters and their attitudes without the works sharing those attitudes. But it is the attitudes manifested in a work that are relevant to the dispute between moralists and immoralists. Secondly, we need to distinguish two senses in which a work can be transgressive. It might ask us to *question* some of our moral attitudes; but that hardly makes the work ethically flawed: moral attitudes can be questioned without immoral attitudes being endorsed (moral philosophers frequently do this, after all). If on the other hand immoral attitudes are actually *embraced* by a work, then we can plausibly deny that this is an aesthetic merit: de Sade's enthusiastic endorsement of sexual torture and enslavement gives one reason to be revolted, not aesthetically enraptured.

A second argument for immoralism appeals not to transgression but to inseparability. The moralist holds, roughly, that a moral flaw in a work is an aesthetic flaw: so it seems he or she should claim that were the moral flaw removed, this would aesthetically improve the work. But, the objection goes, this is clearly false. Some aesthetically good features of a work may depend on its moral flaws: for instance, Riefenstahl's film is great not just because of the formal beauty of its images, but because of the continuity of its political and aesthetic ideas, the unity of its form and content. "The moral defects of the film are not aesthetic blemishes, because they are inseparable from the work's aesthetic value" (Jacobson 1997: 192–3).

One can raise doubts about the treatment of this particular example (for a moralist appraisal of the film, see Devereaux 1997). But let us consider the more general point made. Moralists may sometimes seem to suppose that removing a moral flaw in a work would invariably lead to a better work, but there is no need for them to make so strong a claim. Consider the notion of a *pro tanto* principle: this holds that something is good *insofar as* it possesses a certain property. Morality is often thought to involve such principles: an act is morally good insofar as it is an act of kindness, an act is morally bad insofar as it is a lie. Whether it is *all things considered* morally good can be determined only by looking at details of the context. Suppose my aged aunt proudly shows me her new hat, a monstrous confection of lace and silk which sits on her head like a sagging blancmange. 'Do you like it?' she wants to know. I cannot choose silence: it would be all too clear what I thought; so I decide to lie: 'It's great.' My action is good insofar as it is kind, bad insofar as it is a lie. Let us suppose that in this particular case lying is less bad than being unkind, so all things considered, it is good to say that I like her hat.

Now if I decided instead not to lie to my aunt, my action would be improved in respect of its truthfulness: but it would *ex hypothesi* be, all things considered, a worse action. *Pro tanto* principles are indeed general: it is always the case that an act is bad insofar as it is a lie. But it does not follow that improving an act *in a particular respect* (by telling the truth) would *all things considered* improve it. For by improving it in this respect, I might remove some other good-making feature it possesses (such as its being kind). So there may be general *pro tanto* principles, but there need be no all-things-considered principles. And this is because certain properties of actions are interactive. I cannot in this instance be kind, except at the expense of lying; the presence of truthfulness here undermines the presence of kindness. But note that my action of telling my aunt that I like her hat is still morally flawed.

The moralist about aesthetics can appeal to *pro tanto* aesthetic principles: notably, that a work is aesthetically bad *insofar as* it is ethically flawed. But he or she need not hold that removing that ethical flaw must *all things considered* aesthetically improve the work. For removing the ethical flaw might remove some other good aesthetic qualities which depend on that flaw (for instance the work may be very original and this may be reduced if its morality is improved), just as in the case of my aunt, removing the flaw in respect of truthfulness would all things considered make it a worse action. Again one must look at details of the particular context to determine what will result all things considered. For aesthetic properties are interactive (sometimes put by saying that art works possess organic unity), in the same way that moral properties are.

So the moralist can insist on a *pro tanto* principle that the work is aesthetically bad insofar as it is ethically flawed, but should not embrace the all things considered principle that a work is always aesthetically improved when its morality is improved: that is too strong. The moralist can consistently agree with the immoralist that removing a moral flaw might not make a work all things considered aesthetically better; but she will maintain, nevertheless, that insofar as a work is immoral, it is aesthetically flawed.

A third argument for immoralism appeals to offensive jokes: are not certain jokes funny precisely *because* they are cruel and wounding, and is that not enough to show that moralism is false (Jacobson 1997: 171–2)? As thus stated, the objection fails: jokes as a genre are at best analogous to works of art, and moralism is a thesis about works of art, not jokes. But the objection might be pressed by noting that humor is an aesthetically relevant feature of many works of art, and humor can be effective because it is offensive.

Suppose the immoralist were right about humor, and a comic play were made less funny by having its immorality sanitized. Drawing on the strategy just noted, we could agree that the revised play would be less good insofar as its humor was lessened, and might also agree that the play would be, all things considered, aesthetically worse. But we could still consistently hold that the revised play would be aesthetically improved insofar as it was no longer vicious. That said, however, the moralist can make a stronger claim; for the immoralist is wrong about humor. He or she ignores the complexity of our reactions to vicious jokes. Sometimes we are indeed amused by them, but we may judge on reflection that they were not really funny: for the notion of the funny is not a merely causal one (what causes amusement) but a normative one (what merits amusement). Also the immoralist has a hard time explaining our reactions to racist and sexist jokes (he or she ought to hold that they are simply hilarious). Moreover, contrary to what the immoralist alleges, the moralist about humor need not hold that immoral jokes are not funny at all: rather, if he or she is a pluralist about value, he or she can hold that they are flawed in their humor (because of their viciousness), but may nevertheless hold that they have other features which strengthen their humor (they may be very clever, for instance). The moralist who is a pluralist can in fact give a much better account of the complexity of humor than can the immoralist (see Gaut 1998; note that 'moralism' there refers to what I am here calling 'extreme moralism').

Moralism (ethicism)

Since we have rejected autonomism and immoralism, we should be moralists. Contemporary defenders of moralism have also rejected Tolstoy's extreme moralism; and to make this clear, they have sometimes termed their positions moderate moralism (Carroll 1996, 1997), or ethicism (Gaut 1997, Kieran 1996).

We have seen that this kind of modest moralism, or ethicism, should be formulated using a *pro tanto* principle. However, ethicism as roughly characterized up to now needs refining; for the ethicist should not allow any ethical flaw at all to count as an aesthetic flaw. Consider a novel which simply added a list of morally dubious claims to its final chapter ('kindness is a sign of weakness,' 'lying is a good thing'): the novel would be ethically flawed, but we might well think that it was not aesthetically flawed (or if it were, it would be because of the irrelevance of this list to what went on in the novel). So the ethicist should hold that ethical flaws are only sometimes aesthetically relevant. Ethicism then would hold that a work of art is always aesthetically flawed insofar as it possesses an ethical flaw which is aesthetically relevant. One might hope to discover a general condition for aesthetic relevance, but it is not essential to do so to argue successfully for ethicism.

Three main arguments can be advanced for ethicism. (For a further argument based on befriending an author, see Booth 1988.) The first is a *best-fit* argument: when we consider our evaluative practices and judgements, the best fit to them is ethicism, not autonomism, immoralism or extreme moralism. The ethicist can appeal to the dominance of ethical criticism in the Western tradition, and its widespread influence today. As we have noted, appeal to such practices and judgements undermines extreme moralism; indeed, Tolstoy was lead to condemn all of his own works with the exception of two short stories because of his espousal of that view (Tolstoy 1930: 246). Any theory which denounces *War and Peace* and *Anna Karenina* as bad art should be rejected. The immoralist also claims that his or her theory better fits our evaluative practices than does ethicism; we have argued against that claim in the previous section. The case of autonomism is more complex, since formalists actually implemented their autonomist convictions in their critical practice. The replies are to note how autonomists have fallen foul of their own ethical ban (recall Beardsley's problems with anti-Semitism), to demonstrate the poverty of autonomist criticism (recall the inadequacy of Bell's notion of significant form), and to engage in a general critique of the theoretical assumptions of autonomism (recall our discussion of the aesthetic attitude). The best-fit argument, then, draws on philosophical critique and close attention to critical practices to give support to ethicism.

A second, *cognitivist*, argument for ethicism is probably the most popular (Beardsmore 1971, 1973; Carroll 1997; Kieran 1996; Nussbaum 1990). The basic argument appeals to the fact that works of art can teach us, and what they can teach us includes moral truths and how we ought morally to feel. Strong versions of the view even hold that *only* certain great works of literature, such as the novels of Henry James, can teach us very fine-grained moral truths (Nussbaum 1990). That claim looks highly implausible: the world is full of morally sensitive people who are happily innocent of the works of Henry James and his ilk. But a more modest view holds that art is one of the sources of moral knowledge. Many literary works, including those of James, Dostoevsky and Shakespeare, convey important moral insights.

To make this cognitivist argument work it is not enough to show that art can educate us morally. One also has to show that its capacity to teach us is an aesthetic merit in it. An art work can teach us a great deal about the world without this having anything to do with its artistic merit: photographs of Victorian Britain are an important source of information about that society, but that does not make them better as art works. Historical value is not the same as artistic value. So the cognitivist must show that when art teaches us morally, this is at least sometimes an aesthetic merit in it. (One can allow that it need not always be an aesthetic merit: for, as we noted, not all ethical flaws and merits should be held to be aesthetically relevant.) Few cognitivists have seen this point: one who has is R. W. Beardsmore, whose important work on art, cognition and morality has been sadly neglected in the recent debate. Beardsmore argues that *what* art teaches us is essentially connected with *how* it teaches us. So for instance in Donne's beautiful comparison of parted lovers to a pair of compasses, what is conveyed about love is essentially connected with the particular metaphor and words by which it is conveyed (Beardsmore 1971: 59). If this is correct, then at least in some cases cognitive content (including moral content) is essentially connected with the aesthetic features of the vehicle which carries that content. So the aesthetic relevance of cognition in those cases is established. And in general, it is plausible that when cognitive insights are conveyed in rich and detailed descriptions of characters and situations, they achieve aesthetic relevance.

The third argument for ethicism, the *merited response argument*, goes back in one version to Hume. Hume is an ethicist about art, but not it seems a cognitivist. He writes that

> where vicious manners are described, without being marked with the proper characters of blame and disapprobation; this must be allowed to disfigure the poem, and to be a real deformity. I cannot, nor is it proper I should, enter into such sentiments
>
> (Hume 1907: 282)

The core of this argument rests on an appeal to affective responses ('sentiments'), and Hume claims that we cannot enter into the immoral sentiments which the work asks us to feel. This seems (unhappily) false, for an evil person might be able to enter into such sentiments with enthusiasm, and applied to his case, the argument might conclude in establishing immoralism. However, Hume also adds, "nor is it proper that I should," and that ought to be the core claim: the responses must be *merited*, not simply the ones we actually have.

A contemporary version of the argument, which highlights the role of merited responses, proceeds as follows. As noted in the first section, a work is intrinsically ethically flawed just in case it manifests ethically reprehensible attitudes. When works manifest attitudes, they do so by prescribing or inviting their audiences to have certain responses: de Sade's *Juliette* manifests its sadistic attitudes by inviting readers to have erotic responses towards the scenes of sexual torture it depicts. Responses which works prescribe are not always merited: for instance, a horror film invites us to be horrified by the events it recounts, but if those events are ineptly presented, they may merit amusement, not horror. Now one ground for holding a response to be unmerited is that it is unethical: for instance, it is wrong to find torture erotically attractive. If an art work prescribes responses which it does not merit, then that is a failure in the work. And it is an *aesthetic* failure in the work, given the aesthetic importance of these prescribed responses: for instance, tragedies which do not merit fear and pity, horror films which do not merit horror, comedies which do not merit amusement, and so on, all fail aesthetically. So putting together these points, we can conclude that ethical flaws manifested in prescribed responses are in such circumstances aesthetic flaws in a work (Gaut 1997: 192–7; a related though less general argument is in Carroll 1996; Jacobson 1997 criticizes both arguments).

These three arguments for ethicism need, of course, further development and defense against objections, but each argument has a good deal of plausibility. Since, as we have seen, there are reasons to reject autonomism, immoralism and extreme moralism, and there are plausible arguments for ethicism, we should conclude that in the long debate over art and ethics, ethicism wins.

See also Plato, Aristotle, Empiricism: Hutcheson and Hume, Kant, Nietzsche, Formalism, The aesthetic, Value of art, Art and knowledge, Humor.

References

Beardsley, M. (1981) *Aesthetics: Problems in the Philosophy of Criticism*, 2nd edn, Indianapolis: Hackett.
Beardsmore, R. W. (1971) *Art and Morality*, London: Macmillan.
—— (1973) "Learning from a Novel," *Royal Institute of Philosophy Lectures* 6: 23–46.
Bell, C. (1987) *Art*, ed. J. B. Bullen, Oxford: Oxford University Press.
Booth, W. (1988) *The Company We Keep: An Ethics of Fiction*, Berkeley: University of California Press.
Carroll, N. (1996) "Moderate Moralism," *British Journal of Aesthetics* 36: 223–38.
—— (1997) "Art, Narrative, and Moral Understanding," in J. Levinson (ed.), *Aesthetics and Ethics*, Cambridge: Cambridge University Press.
Devereaux, M. (1997) "Beauty and Evil: The Case of Leni Riefenstahl's *Triumph of the Will*," in J. Levinson (ed.), *Aesthetics and Ethics*, Cambridge: Cambridge University Press.

Gaut, B. (1997) "The Ethical Criticism of Art," in J. Levinson (ed.), *Aesthetics and Ethics*, Cambridge: Cambridge University Press.

—— (1998) "Just Joking: The Ethics and Aesthetics of Humor," *Philosophy and Literature* 22: 51–68.

Hume, D. (1907) "Of the Standard of Taste," in *Essays Moral, Political, and Literary*, ed. T. H. Green and T. H. Grose, London: Longmans.

Hyman, L. (1984) "Morality and Literature: The Necessary Conflict," *British Journal of Aesthetics* 24: 149–55.

Jacobson, D. (1997) "In Praise of Immoral Art," *Philosophical Topics* 25: 155–99.

Kieran, M. (1996) "Art, Imagination, and the Cultivation of Morals," *Journal of Aesthetics and Art Criticism* 54: 337–51.

Nussbaum, M. (1990) *Love's Knowledge: Essays on Philosophy and Literature*, Oxford: Oxford University Press.

Plato (1997) *Complete Works*, ed. J. M. Cooper, Indianapolis: Hackett.

Tolstoy, L. (1930) *What is Art?* trans. A. Maude, Oxford: Oxford University Press.

30
ART, EXPRESSION
AND EMOTION

Derek Matravers

The primary use of such terms as 'sadness' and 'joy' is to refer to the mental states of people. In such cases, the claim that someone is sad is equivalent to the claim that they feel sad. However, our use of emotion terms is broader than this; a funeral is a sad occasion, a wedding is a happy event. In such cases, a justification can be given for the use of the word. For example, it is part of what is meant by 'sadness' that it is an appropriate reaction to occasions such as funerals. Sometimes in criticism (I shall follow practice and use this term broadly) a similar justification can be given; it explains, for example, why the death of Little Nell is sad. On other occasions, such a justification is not available. A poem can express sadness without representing a sad state of affairs. More obviously, to take a medium that is not representational, a piece of music can be sad. What we need is some way of making sense of these uses of the emotion terms.

Expression theories

An obvious and appealing solution is to take the words to be referring to the mental state of the artist. The artist feels an emotion that he or she transmits to the audience by way of the work. This position, generally known as 'the expression theory' found a vigorous exponent in Tolstoy:

> Art is a human activity consisting in this, that one man consciously, by means of certain external signs, hands on to others feelings he has lived through, and that other people are infected by these feelings and also experience them.
>
> (Tolstoy 1930: 123)

There are two separate claims that are part of this position:

1   At the time of creation, the artist was in mental state F.
2   In virtue of possessing the property P, the work expresses F.

The classic expression theory claims that the two are linked in virtue of the fact that the artist expresses F by causing the work to possess P. Opposition to the expression theory stems from the claim that for this to be true, P must be the vehicle for the artist's expression. How is this to be explained? It cannot be simply that the artist caused P when he was feeling F; not everything we do when we are sad expresses sadness. It must be some fact about P. However, the account of how P itself can express the artist's emotion seems to be the account of the nature of expression; the causal account of how P came into existence is no longer relevant. It follows from the logical independence of cause and effect that it would be fallacious to infer the nature of P from the nature of its causes (the so-called 'genetic fallacy').

In reply, expression theorists have attempted to claim that (1) and (2) stand not only in causal, but also in a logical relation. One way in which this is attempted is to point out that the relevant descriptions of a work of art also refer to the intentional actions that bought them into existence. Works *present* ideas, *view* scenes, *observe* events, for example. Guy Sircello has dubbed these 'artistic acts' (Sircello 1972: 406). He argues that

> Precisely in virtue of their artistic acts and of the similarity they bear to common kinds of expressions, works of art may serve as expressions of those feelings, emotions, attitudes, moods and/or personal characteristics of their creators which are designated by the anthropomorphic predicates applicable to the art works themselves.
>
> (Sircello 1972: 412)

Sircello's view is that the manifestations of emotion are logically connected to the inner state that caused it. To see a smile is not to see an appearance and infer a happy state of mind, but to see the happy state of mind in the face itself. The 'act' and the 'thing' are inseparable (ibid.: 409).

It is plausible that there are logical connections between the nature of mental states and their outward manifestations. Is this enough to establish that, on any particular occasion in which there is an outward manifestation, there is a mental state being expressed? No, because expressive appearances do not necessarily have mental states for their causes. A sad face might be caused by slicing onions, in which case there is no relevant mental state to which the appearance is connected. Just as we can discuss what makes a face sad without being committed to the existence of a prior mental state, the appearance in art of emotion can be discussed and analyzed as an appearance, independently of the state (if any) which caused it. As Alan Tormey put it, "the particular mistake . . . arises from assuming that the existence of expressive qualities in a work of art implies a prior act of expression" (Tormey 1971: 425).

Can the actual artist be removed from the story without any loss to criticism, as Tormey's view implies? In particular, are the intentions of the artist necessary to establish a standard of correctness? That they are is part of the account of expression put forward by Richard Wollheim. The account, devoid of some of its complexity, is as follows. Human beings have the capacity to 'project' their internal states on to natural objects, a capacity that is rooted deep in our psychology. The objects on to which we project state F (for example) are those which 'correspond' to F. A rocky landscape with a solitary tree, for instance, might correspond to melancholy. This projection results in the person viewing the object as being 'of a piece' with their state; the projected properties are genuinely seen in the object. At a later stage of development, human beings are able to see objects as those on which "we might have or could have" projected the state (Wollheim 1993: 154).

Expression in art is an extension of this. Here we see a marked surface as being 'of a piece' with our mental state. The property of the work that enables us to do this is one that has been put there intentionally by the artist. Hence, in the case of art, "there is now imposed upon expressive perception a standard of correctness and incorrectness" (Wollheim 1987: 85). The actual intentions of the artist are not, however, the only way to provide such a criterion (we shall consider another in a moment), so Wollheim needs a further argument. He attempts to provide one by appealing to how we come to recognize that a work is expressive: "when we assign expressive value to a work of art, we invariably draw upon our knowledge of, or our beliefs about, the artistic processes involved" (Wollheim 1993: 155). For example, we discern the significance of a style of brush stroke for the artist through our awareness of the artist's technique discerned from his wider *oeuvre*.

Wollheim's argument is not conclusive. Even if we grant that assigning expressive value involves drawing on beliefs about the artistic processes, one could still maintain that the standard of correctness is given by the intentions not of the actual author, but of some hypothetical author. That is, interpreting a work could be a matter of asking not what the actual painter meant by making the surface as he did, but what an artist could have meant by making the surface as he did (Levinson 1996: 100). In other words, the aesthetic qualities are those plausibly attributed to the artist rather than those actually intended by the artist. Establishing the ground rules for such plausible attribution is a question that would take us too far from our topic here.

The semantic theory

Nelson Goodman's *Languages of Art* (1976) is an attempt to explain the central features of art within a theory of symbols. A expresses E, according to Goodman, if one, A possesses E metaphorically, and two, A exemplifies E (Goodman 1976: 95). Goodman is a nominalist; he does not believe in explanations in terms of properties, but rather in terms of the extension of terms (although he does use the term 'property' as shorthand; something I will also do here). Hence, for A to possess E metaphorically, is for A to fall within the extension of E used as a metaphor. For example, a picture may possess 'square' literally, and 'sad' metaphorically. An object exemplifies a predicate or property if it refers to it. For example, a tailor's swatch possesses many properties; it has a color, size, and absolute value. However, it only refers to the first of these; exemplification is possession plus reference (ibid.: 53). Hence, our picture not only is sad, it exemplifies sadness.

Both parts of Goodman's definition have been criticized (Davies 1994: 137–50; Matravers 1998: 104–8). What is it for A to fall within the extension of E used as a metaphor? Goodman says that "in metaphor . . . a term with an extension established by habit is applied elsewhere under the influence of that habit; there is both a departure from and deference to precedent" (Goodman 1976: 71). It is an open question whether metaphor can be defined in terms of the nature of the use of a term in a way that distinguishes a metaphorical use from other possibilities, such as a novel use or a slip of the tongue. What seems to be needed is an account in terms of the nature of the picture: what is it about the picture that justifies the application of 'sad' to it, albeit metaphorically? Goodman shifts between two replies. The first is to reject resolutely the need for justification: "the predicate must apply to all the things it must apply to" (ibid.: 78). This will be unsatisfactory to anyone but a convinced nominalist. The other is to take metaphorical possession of a property not as a linguistic fact, but as a *way* an object might possess a property. However, this is not only apparently incompatible with nominalism, but, without further explication, is wholly mysterious.

An air of mystery also surrounds the claim that A exemplifies E. The problem is to distinguish between those properties an object exemplifies, as opposed to those it merely possesses. Recalling the tailor's swatch, one might think it is best done by reference to those properties for which the object is a sample. However, this has no obvious place in an account of expression. This was not a problem to which Goodman had any satisfactory solution.

The local quality theory

I referred above to Alan Tormey's claim that expressive qualities are logically independent of acts of expression. This suggests the 'local quality' theory, probably the most widely accepted in the recent literature (for classic texts, see Beardsley 1981: 325–32; Bouwsma 1954). It maintains that expression is to be analyzed in terms of expressive qualities which are recognized in works of art. Such qualities can be analyzed independently of the state of mind of their creator. They are not logically distinct from other qualities, such as grace, unity or balance, and, like those other qualities, are perceived as part of the form of works of art.

The medium in which such an account works best is music. Hence, I shall consider the account as it applies there, assuming that if it fails where it is most likely to succeed, such a failure can be generalized.

Given that we do not obviously experience the natural expression of sadness in an expressive work, it is tempting to think that the predicate 'is sad,' when used aesthetically, picks out a *sui generis* aesthetic property. To claim that the music is sad is to claim that it possesses some particular musical property. This, however, would not work. For if 'is sad' picks out a musical property when used aesthetically, and a mental state when used centrally, this would make the term systematically ambiguous. Furthermore, given that almost any term that has an aesthetic use has a non-aesthetic use, such ambiguity would be widespread. If this were so, it would be possible in principle to disambiguate the language by replacing all the aesthetic uses of terms with new words, without loss of meaning. Such a conclusion is absurd; the same concept is being appealed to in both aesthetic and non-aesthetic uses (Scruton 1974: 38).

The predicate needs to pick out a property of the work of art that is sufficiently akin to the natural expression of emotion to avoid the ambiguity. A popular candidate in the literature is resemblance between the purely musical properties (in particular, movement) and the natural expression of emotion (Bouwsma 1954; Kivy 1989; Davies 1994; Ridley 1995). This appears to fulfil both desideratae. First, the appearance of expression is logically independent of a prior mental state. A person or object can present the appearance of sadness without actually being sad. Second, resemblance is a property of the music and presumably can be experienced as such.

Despite its obvious merits, the theory faces several difficulties. First, there are, without doubt, some pieces of music that resemble a cry, or a falling away of the voice, but in general the resemblance between music and the natural appearance and behavior associated with an emotion is slight. Music no more resembles the expression of emotion than it does many other things: the waves of the ocean, the rise and fall of the stock market (Kivy 1989: 61–2). Secondly, how is the theory to characterize the experience of expressive art? Hearing music as sad is not hearing it as the natural expression of emotion, nor is the listener conscious of resemblances between the music and the natural expression of emotion. However, if resemblance plays no part in the experience of expression, in what sense is an appeal to resemblance the account of expression?

Both these problems can be overcome with a single change to the theory: to put resemblance forward not as an analysis of expression, but as the property of the music that *causes* us to experience it as expressive. That is, the resemblance between a piece of music and the natural expression of emotion causes the listener to experience the music as expressive. That the resemblance is only slight does not matter; it is an empirical claim that such slight resemblances have this effect. Second, there is no longer any claim that the resemblances feature in the experience itself; they merely cause the experience.

This change, however, only introduces additional problems. First, we are left with no account of the nature of expression (as opposed to its causes). Local quality theorists have endeavored to provide such an account in terms independent of resemblance, which I will consider later. Second, once it is conceded that resemblance is merely a cause, it becomes a pressing question why anyone should think it is the only cause. The major chord and the minor chord resemble expressive behavior as much (or as little) as each other. However, their expressive quality is discernibly different. Peter Kivy has introduced an additional cause here, in terms of convention (Kivy 1989: 77). Why stop there? Might it not be that, for hidden evolutionary or cultural reasons, people simply find some combination of sounds expressive? Once it is conceded that resemblance is merely one of a number of possible causes of expression, the philosophical significance of resemblance diminishes.

What account of the local aesthetic qualities can be given independently of resemblance? The question of what provides the link with the emotions could be separated from the question of the nature of the experience, given the link. Building on the work of earlier local quality theorists, in particular, Peter Kivy, Jerrold Levinson has argued that the link with the emotions is *sui generis*, before going on to put forward a particular account of the nature of the link (Levinson 1996: 107). The introduction of *sui generis* elements into the account is some kind of a defeat although, given the apparently intractable nature of the traditional formulation of the problem, this at least provides a way forward.

Arousal theories

What further options are there for those who reject the local property approach? There is one obvious solution we have not yet considered: namely, that expressive properties are 'response-dependent': that is, that they depend for their nature and existence on the response of the audience. This too has obvious advantages. If my claim that a work is sad is justified by the fact that it makes me sad, this provides little scope for ambiguity. It also, as we shall see, has some apparent drawbacks.

The so-called 'arousal theory' can be stated in plausible and implausible versions. The claim that a work expresses an emotion if it arouses the full-blooded emotion in every member of the audience has little to recommend it. It is, however, plausible to claim that amongst the mental states caused by a work, is some non-cognitive state that has a role to play in our experience of the work as expressive. Roger Scruton made this claim as part of a general aesthetic theory in his *Art and Imagination*: "the experience of hearing the sadness in the music is in some irre-ducible way analogous to hearing the expression of sadness – say, in another's voice" (Scruton 1974: 127). Scruton's postulation of an irreducible analogy rested on the claim that the thought content of an experience cannot be specified independently of the experience. Hence only the total experiences can be compared. The claim is not plausible, the content of an experience can be stated in propositional form, and Scruton has since revised his account (Budd 1985: 147; Scruton 1997: 140–70).

Further attempts to elucidate Scruton's analogy leave us with something like this: A expresses E if, among the mental states caused by A, is some non-cognitive state which stands in the right kind of relation to the appropriate reaction to the expression of emotion in the central case (Matravers 1998: 146). However, this account still faces a number of problems of which I will mention only three. First, 'dry-eyed critics' (to use Bouwsma's phrase) claim both to experience a piece of music as expressive and not to be in any feeling or emotional state. Second, the expressive quality seems located in the wrong place; to hear music as sad is not to hear music and feel sad, it is to hear the sadness in the music. Finally, the capacity to cause feelings or emotions is not distinctive to expression. Many things sadden me which are not thereby expressive of sadness.

The arousal theory needs to be supplemented with an account of what is happening in the mind of the listener. The non-cognitive mental state aroused by the music is present in the listener's consciousness along with the music. The existence and nature of the former is immediately causally dependent on the latter; as the music changes, so does the nature of the non-cognitive state. Furthermore, there is no immediate link between the number and nature of mental states attributed by a theory, and the subject's experience of those states. Put simply, the arousal theory is not committed to the claim that the listener experiences the states as separate.

If this is accepted, an attempt can be made to solve the three problems described. First, the claim not to be experiencing a feeling does not entail that no non-cognitive state can be attributed to the listener, provided one has other reasons for doing so. Second, as I said earlier, the non-cognitive state and the music are not necessarily experienced as separate. Having said this, it is not clear that nature of the experience implied by the criticism is correct. Arguably, expressive qualities are not perceived as simply another audible property of the music (Elliott 1967: 146). Finally, the arousal theory uses only those feelings that play the distinctive psychological role specified. Any other aroused feelings will not be relevant to expression (Matravers 1998).

Feelings in appreciation and evaluation

The role of feelings and emotions in the arts is broader than that of expression. Can anything be said about the kinds of emotions involved in the appreciation of art? Are such emotions simply things we might happen to feel, or are they the kind of things we ought to feel? In other words, is feeling these emotions something the work justifies?

The role of emotion in appreciation can only be a proper part of criticism if it is intimately tied to the work. A work of art may well trigger some idiosyncratic association. In such a case, exposure to the work may well provoke an emotional reaction, but it would be bizarre to consider this was relevant to the appreciation of the work considered as a work of art. Hence, in subsequent discussion such cases will be ignored.

Works of art can be divided into two sorts: representational works (those with propositional content) and non-representational works (those without propositional content). (The situation is complicated with respect to pictures. 'Representational' denotes works that have pictorial space, which includes most abstract works. 'Figurative' denotes works that depict some state of affairs. Hence, with respect to pictures, I mean non-figurative). I shall consider each in turn. The former divides further into two cases: those in which the emotions felt in appreciation are justified by the propositional content, and those that involve a feeling which is justified, but not justified by the propositional content. An example of the first would be feeling sadness on reading of some misfortune that has befallen our hero. Imagining the misfortune not only causes this sadness, but it justifies our sadness as well. There are various philosophical problems in justifying an emotion by reference to the sufferings of a character we do not believe exists, which I will say no more about here.

Before moving on to the second case, it is worth being more precise about terminology. It is generally agreed that emotions are some combination of a cognitive state (usually a belief) and some phenomenological and physiological states. For example, fear involves some manner of assent to the proposition that one is threatened, combined with feelings of anxiety, discomfort and such things as increased heart rate and adrenaline flow. The propositional element usually is the cause of, and also provides the object of, the emotion. My belief that there is a burglar in the kitchen causes the other elements, and then, in combination with the other elements, constitutes the emotion. My emotion takes the burglar as its object; that is, I am afraid *of* the burglar in the kitchen. Such states can be contrasted with similar states that lack the propositional element: free-floating anxiety is an example. Such states obviously have their causes, although unlike the former case, such causes do not justify the feelings nor do they provide their object.

What of our second case: emotions (or feelings) felt in response to representational works that are not justified by its propositional content? Cases such as these provide a plausible answer to a puzzle as to the value of poetry. It is clear that what we find valuable in poem goes beyond its propositional content (a paraphrase will not do as a substitute). There are various candidates for the bearer of this extra value, the most obvious being the pragmatic charge of the language used. The nature of criticism of poetry would suggest that at least part of this pragmatic charge lies in the feelings the poem evokes. Noël Carroll has suggested a further role for such feelings, by including a capacity to evoke revulsion and disgust in his definition of horror (Carroll 1990: 28). Works that evoke feelings such as fear and suspense are not properly horror; to be properly horror, the work needs to evoke revulsion or disgust.

Unlike the first case, in which the emotion can be justified by appeal to the content of the work, the feeling in the second case is, as yet, without justification. Some justification will be needed to build an element of normativity into our response to art. There are three possible sources of the normativity. The first is to specify some property of the work that makes the response reasonable. There are two problems with this approach. First, it will always be possible to find plausible candidates for such properties. For example, certain metrical arrangements in poems are plausible candidates for causes of feelings that figure in the experience of reading the poems, yet metrical arrangements are not easily seen as providing a reason for having a certain feeling. Second, it is difficult to identify such properties independently of their capacity to provoke a response. There is little point in justifying a response by appeal to a property A, if A is identified only as 'that property which causes the response.' The second possible source of normativity is to identify the appropriate response with an ideal appreciator. For example, the ideal appreciator might be someone with knowledge of the background out of which the work emerged, and someone who can make fine discriminations. The problem with this approach is that it is unclear why the response of an appreciator so defined should be identified as the correct one. The third possible source of normativity is to defend the feeling as having a role within a larger appreciation of the work. The supposition is that the author deliberately set out to provoke certain effects (Feagin 1996; Carroll 1997). Hence, such effects can be justified as being something the author could reasonably have expected, given his or her overall intentions regarding the piece.

Although our second case concerns figurative works, the fact that such a work is figurative plays no essential role in the explanation and justification of the feeling. The feeling is not necessarily caused by some proposition, and is not directed towards the content of some proposition. This makes it easy to apply the same account to feelings aroused by non-figurative works. If the meter of the poem can provoke certain effects that are part of the experience of the poem, then the rhythm, harmony and melody of a piece of music might similarly provoke certain effects that are part of the experience of the music. This is akin to the view of the arousal theories described earlier, although here the feeling is only part of the appreciation of the work, and does not necessarily play a role in expression. Some philosophers, opposed to the arousal theory, have allowed for the existence of feelings in appreciation but denied that they have any connection to feelings felt in the ordinary commerce of life. Peter Kivy has claimed that, in responding to music, we feel a *sui generis* musical emotion: "music moves us by its (perceived) beauty" (Kivy 1989: 231; cf. Kivy 1990: VIII). Feelings, whether expressed by a work of art or merely felt as part of the experience of a work of art, are clearly an important element in our appreciation of art.

See also Expressivism, Imagination and make-believe, Fiction, Interpretation, Metaphor, Value of art, Tragedy, Music.

References

Beardsley, M. C. (1981) *Aesthetics*, 2nd edn, Indianapolis: Hackett.
Bouwsma, O. K. (1954) "The Expression Theory of Art," in W. Elton (ed.), *Aesthetics and Language*, Oxford: Blackwell.
Budd, M. (1985) *Music and the Emotions*, London: Routledge.
Carroll, N. (1990) *The Philosophy of Horror*, London: Routledge.
—— (1997) "Art, Narrative and Emotion," in M. Hjort and S. Laver (eds), *Emotion and the Arts*, Oxford: Oxford University Press.
Davies, S. (1994) *Musical Meaning and Expression*, Ithaca: Cornell University Press.
Elliott, R. (1967) "Aesthetic Theory and the Experience of Art," in H. Osborne (ed.), *Aesthetics*, Oxford: Oxford University Press.
Feagin, S. (1996) *Reading with Feeling*, Ithaca: Cornell University Press.
Goodman, N. (1976) *Languages of Art*, 2nd edn, Indianapolis: Hackett.
Kivy, P. (1989) *Sound Sentiment*, Philadelphia: Temple University Press.
—— (1990) *Music Alone*, Ithaca: Cornell University Press.
Levinson, J. (1997) "Musical Expressiveness," in *The Pleasures of Aesthetics*, Ithaca: Cornell University Press.
Matravers, D. (1998) *Art and Emotion*, Oxford: Oxford University Press.
Ridley, A. (1995) *Music, Value and the Passions*, Ithaca: Cornell University Press.
Scruton, R. (1974) *Art and Imagination*, London: Methuen.
—— (1997) *The Aesthetics of Music*, Oxford: Oxford University Press.
Sircello, G. (1972) "Expressive Properties of Art," in J. Margolis (ed.), *Philosophy Looks at the Arts*, 3rd edn, Philadelphia: Temple University Press.
Tolstoy, L. (1930) *What is Art?* trans. A. Maude, Oxford: Oxford University Press.
Tormey, A. (1971) "Art and Expression," in J. Margolis (ed.), *Philosophy Looks at the Arts*, 3rd edn, Philadelphia: Temple University Press.
Wollheim, R. (1987) *Painting as an Art*, London and New York: Thames and Hudson.
—— (1993) "Correspondence, Projective Properties and Expression in the Arts," in *The Mind and its Depths*, Cambridge, Mass.: Harvard University Press.

31
TRAGEDY

Alex Neill

Philosophical interest in the art of tragedy, an interest which is as ancient as tragedy itself, has tended to centre around two thoughts, both of which were presaged in the first sustained philosophical discussion of tragic drama, Aristotle's *Poetics* (1987). One is the thought that tragedy is in one way or another an especially philosophical genre of art; a thought for which many have found encouragement in Aristotle's claim, in *Poetics* 9, "that poetry is more philosophical and more serious than history." The other is the thought that there is something deeply puzzling about the nature of the response that tragedy appears to demand from its audience; a thought inspired by Aristotle's description, in *Poetics* 14, of the tragic poet's task as being "to provide the pleasure which derives from pity and fear by means of *mimesis*." Given that the experience of tragedy is one which involves fundamentally passions that are by nature 'negative,' how can that experience be one of pleasure? The focus of this essay will be on reflection on these thoughts in the western philosophical tradition. (On the history of critical theories of tragedy, see Wellek 1955. On psychoanalytic theory and tragedy, see Kuhns 1991.)

The experience of tragedy

Works of tragedy, whatever else they may be, are narratives of human suffering, and at its simplest, the question posed by Aristotle's characterisation of our experience of tragic art in terms of pleasure is that of how we can take pleasure in representations of human beings in pain. This has been taken by some (e.g. Burke 1990: 41–4) to be a question about human psychology: why is it that our responses to suffering as it is depicted in tragedy differ from our responses to suffering in everyday life, in which context it rarely elicits pleasure? By others (e.g. Nietzsche 1993), it has been seen as a question of morals: there would be something repugnant about a person or culture who or which commonly took pleasure in watching others suffer; yet isn't this precisely what we are doing when we enjoy tragic works of art? And it is also a question of aesthetics: tragedies are among our most highly valued works of art, and the value that we attach to them lies in the nature of the experiences which they offer us. But if those experiences involve our taking pleasure in the portrayal of suffering, then the value that we attach to tragedy itself starts to look problematic.

One of the oldest answers to these questions, and one which echoes Aristotle's suggestion that the pleasure that we take in tragedy is in one way or another dependent on the fact that its object, the tragic work of art, is a *mimesis* (to put it crudely, a creative imitation), suggests that the key to understanding the pleasure that we take in tragedy lies in recognising that what tragedy presents us with is *fictional*. We can unproblematically take pleasure in tragedy's portrayal of suffering, it is maintained, precisely because we know that no one is really suffering up there on the stage; what we are responding to is, after all, only a story. By itself, however, this suggestion does not get us very far. For one thing, pointing to the fact that the suffering depicted in a tragedy is fictional hardly explains why we might take pleasure in its depiction. For another, it is far from clear that we *do* regard the content of tragedy as merely fictional; to the contrary, over the centuries it has been maintained in a variety of ways that part of the value of tragedy lies in its capacity to show us something of profound truth and importance about ourselves. Finally, the appeal to the fictional status of tragedy to explain the pleasure that we take in it fails to address the real difficulty implied by Aristotle's characterization of tragic pleasure. For given Aristotle's account of the matter, what looks problematic about our experience of tragedy is not simply that it involves pleasure in the portrayal of suffering, but rather that it is an experience which involves both pleasure *and* the arousal of emotions such as pity and fear, emotions which Aristotle himself, in the *Rhetoric*, defined partly as feelings of *pain*. Appeal to our awareness of the fictional status of tragedy renders the latter aspect of our experience of tragic art all the more mysterious, for the awareness of fictionality that is supposed to allow us to take pleasure in what is depicted would, if it were effective in this respect, seem likely to be an effective prophylactic against our being distressed by tragedy at all.

A different account of our experience of tragedy that does try to acknowledge both delight and distress as elements of that experience holds that these elements are distinct, and aroused by different aspects of the work: distress by what the work depicts (roughly, its content), and delight by the manner in which it depicts it (roughly, the formal aspects of the work). (A recent version of this suggestion is defended in Eaton 1982, for example.) However, this suggestion again fails to address the real difficulty implied by Aristotle's characterisation of tragic pleasure. For Aristotle's suggestion is precisely that the pleasure experienced by the audience of tragedy is *not* something distinct from the 'negative' emotions of pity and fear that the audience experiences; it is, rather, the pleasure "*of*," or "*derived from*," those emotions. As Hume puts it, "it seems an unaccountable pleasure which the spectators of a well-written tragedy *receive from* sorrow, terror, anxiety, and other passions that are in themselves disagreeable and uneasy" (Hume 1987: 216.) What looks puzzling about our experience of tragedy, that is, is not simply the fact that one and the same work can be a source of both distress and delight, but rather the fact that in the experience of tragedy, distress and delight appear to be somehow bound up together, so that the audience, as Hume puts it, "are pleased in proportion as they are afflicted" (ibid.: 217).

Just what Aristotle himself had in mind when he wrote that the pleasure 'appropriately' provided by tragedy is "the pleasure which derives from pity and fear by means of *mimesis*" is far from clear. He says in *Poetics* 6 that the aim of tragic *mimesis* with respect to pity and fear is to effect the *katharsis* of these emotions, which suggests that tragic pleasure is somehow a function of *katharsis*. Unfortunately, however, Aristotle never says explicitly in the *Poetics* just what he takes *katharsis* to involve. The term has been interpreted as referring to processes of emotional purgation or release, of moral and spiritual purification, of emotional education and of intellectual clarification, among other things, and these different interpretations of *katharsis* imply differing conceptions of the pleasure that tragedy provides its audience. It is unlikely that we shall ever be able to be certain which of these, if any, was Aristotle's own conception, though debate about the nature of *katharsis* continues to be one of the staples of philosophical aesthetics.

Philosophical interest in the nature of our experience of tragedy reached its highest point in the eighteenth century, during which it was discussed by most of the distinguished philosophers of the time, as well as by host of others. Two accounts of the matter put forward during this period were particularly influential. The first, advocated by Adam Smith among others, attempted to relate the distress and the delight involved in our experience of tragedy by identifying the psychological mechanism underlying the distressing emotions experienced as sympathy, and arguing that the operation of sympathy, because of its social utility, is naturally pleasurable to human beings even when the emotions communicated sympathetically are painful. (A contemporary version of this sort of account can be found in Feagin 1983.) The second, advanced by Hume, held that while the audience's delight and distress are responses to different aspects of a work of tragedy – the distress to what the work depicts, the delight to the 'eloquence' and 'genius' with which it depicts it – these responses merge as the delight, which is dominant, overpowers and somehow 'converts' the distress in such as way as to reinforce the former: "the impulse or vehemence, arising from sorrow, compassion, indignation, receives a new direction from the sentiments of beauty. The latter, being the predominant emotion, seize the whole mind, and convert the former into themselves" (Hume 1987: 220).

Both of these accounts of our experience of tragedy are open to criticism. Hume himself objected to the former on the grounds that the operation of sympathy is not always pleasurable; and the claim that sympathy underlies all of the audience's distress in response to what is depicted in tragedy might also be questioned. Hume's own account, on the other hand, suffers from the obscurity of the notion of 'conversion' to which he appeals. A more general criticism, however, is that both accounts – and in this they are typical of accounts of our experience of tragedy advanced in the eighteenth century – take the question posed by that experience to be essentially one of psychology, to be answered primarily if not entirely in psychological terms, with very little thought about the workings of tragedy as a form of art. Their question, in effect, is 'what sort of creatures must we be for the peculiar combination of delight and distress characteristic of our experience of tragedy to be possible?' And this represents a radical departure from Aristotle's approach, which is guided rather by the question 'what sort of a thing must tragedy be to provide us with the distinctive sort of experience that it does?' Or, to put the point slightly differently, while Aristotle saw tragedy primarily as raising interesting philosophical questions about art and the making of it, the eighteenth-century theorists typically saw it primarily as raising questions about human psychology. In the move from the former emphasis to the latter, tragedy itself, as a distinctive form of human expression, largely dropped out of the picture. In the nineteenth century, it began to come back into focus. Although the nature of our experience of tragedy was never far from the minds of the great nineteenth-century philosophical theorists of tragedy, their primary concern was more Aristotelian, at least in the sense that their focus was more on the form and content of tragic art than on the psychology of its consumers. And this brings us to the other thought identified at the beginning of this essay: the thought that there is something distinctively philosophical about the art of tragedy.

Tragedy and philosophy

Although Aristotle is often thought of as the source of the idea that tragedy is in some more or less unique way a philosophical genre of art, in fact the statement from *Poetics* 9 quoted at the beginning of this essay, when it is understood in its context, provides no direct endorsement of that idea. The temptation to see Aristotle as defending tragedy's philosophical credentials stems largely from the widely-shared recognition that one of his concerns in the *Poetics* is to respond to the criticisms of tragic poetry and other forms of mimetic art made by Plato, most notably in the *Republic* and the *Ion*. Plato, in turn, was concerned to respond to the traditional Greek conception of their poets as teachers and philosophers in the literal sense of 'lovers of wisdom.' In short, Plato saw poetry, and in particular tragic poetry, as a rival to philosophy, whose claims to purvey wisdom were potentially damaging both to individuals and to the state, and hence needed to be quashed; thus one of his main charges against poetry was that it is not grounded in and expressive of genuinely philosophical understanding. In seeing Aristotle as accepting Plato's challenge, in *Republic* 10, to "champions who love poetry" to come forward to defend her, then, it is not surprising, particularly given the claim that he makes in *Poetics* 9, that many have also seen Aristotle as attempting to defend tragedy's philosophical respectability.

In a sense, indeed, he was. However, it is no part of Aristotle's defence of poetry to show that the tragic poet is doing the work of the philosopher, far less that tragedy is itself a species of philosophy. His response to Plato's charge that poetry is not grounded in reason consists rather in an extended and subtle attempt to show that the writing of tragedy is a *technê*, a productive activity which employs rational means in the pursuit of a predetermined practical end. His statement in *Poetics* 9 that the tragic poet deals in universals rather than particulars is subordinate to this project: the end aimed at by tragedy, Aristotle holds, is the *katharsis* of pity and fear through *mimesis*, and 'speaking' in terms of universals rather than particulars – and in that sense being 'more philosophical' than the historian – is one of the means by which the tragic poet is best able to achieve this end. Aristotle's response to Plato, to put it very briefly, is that tragedy is an art informed by reason and knowledge, and one that has cognitive value, but it is not itself a species of – and hence it is no rival to – philosophy.

The relationship between art and philosophy, and between tragedy and philosophy in particular, is much closer in Hegel's thought than it is in Aristotle's. For in Hegel's view, art and philosophy have the same aim: that of grasping and expressing the nature of reality, or what Hegel calls 'the Absolute.' The difference between the two lies in the kind of form which each gives this expression: while philosophy expresses the Absolute in conceptual thought, art does so in sensory forms. The history of art, according to Hegel, is part of the history of the development of our grasp of the Absolute and of our attempts to express it in sensory forms. The significance of tragedy in this history is that in its most developed form, tragedy lies on the boundary between art and philosophy, marking the end – the highest and final point – of art's development. In tragedy of the Romantic stage (which in Hegelian terms stretches from the medieval to the modern periods), art comes as close as it can to fulfilling its "supreme task" of "bringing to our minds and expressing the Divine, the deepest interests of mankind, and the most comprehensive truths of spirit" (Hegel 1975: I, 7). Beyond Romantic tragedy, Hegel believes, art cannot fruitfully go: once the sense of the Absolute which is the content of art progresses beyond that which is given expression in Romantic tragedy, it has progressed to a point where it cannot be expressed in sensory forms, and art gives way to philosophy and to religion.

But if tragedy came closest to philosophical thought in the Romantic stage of its development, it was at its most beautiful during the Classical period. For beauty, in Hegel's view, is a function of the harmony of artistic form and content, and this, he argued, reached perfection in Classical art, in which the artistic forms employed by the Greeks were perfectly adequate to the sense of the Absolute which they were used to express. He argues that the purpose of Classical tragedy is to demonstrate "the validity of the substance and necessity of ethical life" (Hegel 1975: II, 1222). It achieves this first by showing the 'collision' between different aspects of the ethical that occurs when the latter is fragmented and particularised in human social life: thus, in his favourite example, Sophocles' *Antigone* dramatises the collision between the authority of the state (symbolized by Creon) and family love (symbolized by Antigone). These aspects of ethical life collide because "each of the opposed sides... can establish the true and positive content of its own aim and character only by denying and infringing the equally justified power of the other" (ibid.: II, 1196). The business of tragedy is then to show the 'resolution' of conflict of this sort, which it can do in a variety of ways. From the aesthetic point of view, Hegel holds, the most satisfying form of resolution involves the destruction of the characters who embody 'false one-sidedness,' as happens in the *Antigone*, for these characters, just in virtue of their one-sidedness, are in conflict not only with others but with themselves: since the power that they oppose is as justified as the power that they one-sidedly represent, "they violate what, if they were true to their own nature, they should be honouring" (ibid.: II, 1217), and hence in effect self-destruct. Even when a tragedy is resolved in this fashion, however, its message is positive; it affirms the fundamental unity of the ethical – "the eternal substance of things emerges victorious" – "because it strips away from the conflicting individuals only their false one-sidedness, while the positive elements in what they willed it displays as what is to be retained, without discord but affirmatively harmonized" (ibid.: II, 1199).

Although Hegel has been criticised on the grounds that some of his interpretations of the Greek tragedies (and in particular of the *Antigone* (see e.g. Bungay 1984: 165 ff.)) are less than fully supported by the works themselves, it is a significant aspect of his discussion that it is based on thought about particular works of tragic art, and is sensitive to the differences between those works. Thus, for example, he recognizes that forms of tragic resolution which do not involve the annihilation of the protagonists are also possible. The most significant of these is that represented in what Hegel describes as "the eternally marvellous" *Oedipus at Colonus*, where "the unity and harmony of the entire ethical order" is affirmed in "an inner reconciliation" in the character of Oedipus who, before he dies, "expunges all his own inner discord and is purified within" (Hegel 1975: II, 1219). The significance of this form of resolution, in Hegelian terms, lies not least in the fact that it shows how Classical tragedy, while expressive of the sense of the Absolute that is the content of art at this stage of its history, is also a force in the development of that sense into something more adequate. For in the move from the type of resolution that we see in *Antigone* to that which we see in *Oedipus at Colonus* there is a move away from the emphasis on objectivity which is the hallmark of the classical stage of art, during which "the spiritual was completely drawn through its external appearance" (ibid.: I, 517), towards the occupation with subjectivity that is the hallmark of the Romantic stage, during which the content of art is man's sense of the 'inner world' of spirit. (Thus, as Hegel might, if tendentiously, have put it, Antigone and Creon are essentially symbols, while Oedipus is the beginnings of a person.) And it is in Romantic tragedy, Hegel believes, that art comes closest to an adequate representation of spirit. The subject matter of tragedy by this stage of its development is "the subjective inner life of the character," and at its best, in Shakespeare's hands, these characters are "concretely human individuals," "complete men," and, crucially, "free artists of their own selves" (ibid.: II, 1227–8).

Hegel's claim that the importance of tragedy lies in what it reveals about the nature of reality is echoed by Schopenhauer. Like Hegel, Schopenhauer saw the arts in general as engaged fundamentally in the same task as philosophy; both "work at bottom towards the solution of the problem of existence" (Schopenhauer 1966: II, 406). However, since Schopenhauer's metaphysics are very different from Hegel's, he develops a very different picture of tragedy and the precise nature of its philosophical significance.

Schopenhauer argues that the nature of reality is quite different from that which is presented to us in sense experience. Reality, he argues, is Will, a single arational and impersonal force that is constantly in flux. This Will manifests or 'objectifies' itself in Platonic Ideas, which differ with respect to the clarity with which it does so in them. With the important exception of music, Schopenhauer holds, the function of the arts is the 'expression and presentation' of these Ideas. The greater the clarity with which Will is manifest or 'objectified' in an Idea, the more valuable, because the more revelatory of the nature of reality, is the artform which presents and expresses that Idea.

The Idea which is the subject of poetry, that of "man in the connected series of his efforts and actions" (Schopenhauer 1966: I, 244), is the Idea in which Will manifests itself most clearly; hence of all the representational arts, poetry is the most valuable. And tragedy, Schopenhauer holds, is "the summit of poetic art." For in representing "the unspeakable pain, the wretchedness and misery of mankind," tragedy reveals to us more clearly than anything else the most important feature of reality: "the antagonism of the will with itself" and the fact that "chance and error" are "the rulers of the world" (ibid.: I, 252–3).

However, in Schopenhauer's view tragedy is significant not merely because of the importance of what it reveals to us concerning the nature of reality, but also because in the experience of tragedy we come to recognize the only appropriate response to the terrible truth it presents. This is to adopt an attitude of 'resignation:' the spectator "becomes aware . . . that it is better to tear his heart away from life, to turn his willing away from it, not to love the world and life" (Schopenhauer 1966: II, 435). The greatest tragedies, Schopenhauer holds, are those in which this attitude of resignation is not only suggested by a work but also represented in its characters.

At this point, an important difference between the approaches to tragedy taken by Aristotle, Hegel and Schopenhauer begins to emerge. Like Schopenhauer, Aristotle has a view about what makes a work of tragedy good, a view based on an account of the purpose or function of tragic art. But in Aristotle's case, this account is grounded in his extended consideration of the art of tragedy itself: Aristotle's account of tragedy is, so to speak, empirically based. Something like this is also true of Hegel's account of tragedy: given that his business is to provide an historical account of the development of art, it is essential for Hegel that his discussion of tragedy is grounded in and true to what tragedy, as a form of art, has in fact been like. Whether Aristotle and Hegel get things right in this respect is another matter, of course; but it is a matter which, as both philosophers would have accepted, is central to the assessment of the theories of tragedy which they offer.

Schopenhauer, however, is very different. He cheerfully concedes that "rarely in the tragedy of the ancients is this spirit of resignation [which in the best tragedies is 'exhibited' in the characters] seen and directly expressed." But then so much the worse, he says, for Classical tragedy: "the tragedy of the moderns is at a higher level than that of the ancients." However, even "many of the moderns are also content to put the spectator into the mood" of resignation, without representing it the characters of the drama themselves (Schopenhauer 1966: II, 434–5); again, he implies, so much the worse for these 'moderns.' What this indicates is that Schopenhauer's theory of tragedy is grounded not so much in consideration of what tragic art has been and is, as in his own metaphysics. 'Given what I have said about the nature of reality and about the general purpose of art,' he is in effect saying, 'this is what *must* be true concerning the purpose and value of tragedy.' In short, Schopenhauer's theory of tragedy is unfalsifiable by any considerations about what might be called the practice of tragedy; even if there were *no* actual works of tragedy which matched the theory, all that that would show would be that no work has yet reached "the summit and goal of tragedy" (ibid.: II, 435).

In the end, then, Schopenhauer is not so much doing philosophy of art as he is doing something else – broadly speaking, metaphysics – into the service of which art, or some more or less abstracted idea of it, is being pressed. And something similar might be said of Nietzsche in *The Birth of Tragedy* (1993), although in this case it is harder to characterize what it is that is being done: 'philosophy of culture' is perhaps as good a description as any. For Nietzsche is less interested in *tragedy* – in the sense of a literary genre instantiated in a body of actual works of art – than he is in *the tragic,* in the sense of something like a condition of human sensibility. In *The Birth of Tragedy*, Nietzsche's infrequent references to particular works of Greek tragedy betray very little of the knowledge of this part of literary history that he surely had; and the Aeschylus, Sophocles and Euripides whom he discusses in that work are little more than caricatures of these authors and their achievements. Now a charge of this sort against Aristotle's *Poetics* or Hegel's *Aesthetics* would, were it accurate, be devastating; laid against *The Birth of Tragedy*, however, it is simply indicative of point-missing. For the Classical tragedians and their works, as they appear in Nietzsche's essay, figure not as artists in a history of a genre of art, but rather as symbols of different cultural points or tendencies in Nietzsche's working out of a genealogy of the tragic spirit.

The main symbols in this genealogy are those of Dionysus and Apollo, Greek deities whom Nietzsche uses (again in creative rather than scholarly fashion) to stand for both metaphysical and artistic categories. The Apollonian spirit is that which is concerned with appearances; what it offers us is "beautiful illusion" (Nietzsche 1993: 16). The Dionysian spirit is that through which this illusion is shattered, and what is revealed to us is reality as it truly is: the Schopenhauerian Will, in which there is merely endless and pointless struggle of things in flux. As its objects are illusory, the Apollonian vision is too fragile to sustain human beings indefinitely. But with its object of what Nietzsche describes as a "witch's brew" of lust and cruelty (ibid.: 19), the Dionysian vision is too terrible for human beings to survive. The 'supreme goal' of art, Nietzsche thinks, is to allow us to escape this dichotomy. Art, at its highest, does not attempt to evade the Dionysian truth but rather, by somehow (and in a way that Nietzsche is never very clear about) mediating it through the Apollonian, renders it bearable and even something to be exulted in.

The capacity to bear and indeed rejoice in the "witch's sabbath of existence," which is the achievement of the tragic spirit, is made possible by art, but not only and not always by tragedy, if the latter is understood, as it is by Aristotle and by Hegel, in literary-historical terms. For in Nietzsche's view, after Aeschylus and Sophocles the tragic spirit was extinguished in tragedy (in the literary-historical sense), snuffed out by Euripides' rejection of Dionysiac wisdom in favour of Socratic rationality. Nor is the tragic spirit to be found in post-Renaissance tragedy, in which music, through which the Dionysian wisdom is expressed, plays no substantial role. In fact, Nietzsche believed, at least at the time when he wrote *The Birth of Tragedy*, the only art capable of rediscovering the spirit of tragedy was the music-drama of Richard Wagner.

Philosophy and tragedy in the twentieth century

Philosophical thinking about tragedy was at its most alive in the eighteenth and nineteenth centuries, and has been much less fashionable in the twentieth. But this is not to say that recent philosophy has had nothing to say about tragedy. In contemporary aesthetics, widespread interest in the role of emotional response in our understanding and appreciation of art works, together with work by historians of the philosophy of art, particularly on Aristotle and Hume, has fuelled a minor resurgence of the eighteenth-century interest in the nature of our experience of tragedy. Much of the recent writing on this topic persists in the eighteenth-century tendency to see the issues involved as primarily psychological (e.g. Morreall 1985), but the most valuable contributions to the contemporary debate, of which Schier's (1983 and 1989) are outstanding examples, are those which have resisted this tendency and attempted to illuminate the nature of our experience of tragedy by reference to the nature of tragic art itself.

The nineteenth-century thought that tragedy is in one way or another an artform of special philosophical significance has done less well in recent years. The rise of 'analytic' philosophy in the early years of the twentieth century was built largely on disdain of the sort of large-scale theorizing about metaphysics, history and culture out of which the nineteenth-century philosophical concern with the nature of art in general and of tragedy in particular grew; and while the 'continental' tradition in philosophy has been far more receptive to reflection on culture and history, it has too often been underwritten by relativism to have been able to take seriously the idea that tragedy has a special significance by virtue of its capacity to reveal reality and convey truth. This notwithstanding, the idea that tragedy is a particularly valuable source of insight for philosophy is far from extinct, and contemporary efforts to engage philosophically with tragedy while taking it seriously as a form of art, though still rare, are showing signs of becoming more philosophically respectable. Particularly influential have been Nussbaum (1986) and Williams (1993), both of which focus on Classical tragedy as a source of ideas about morality and ethics: the former to illuminate Greek ideas about human vulnerability to 'moral luck,' the latter to investigate the evolution of contemporary ideas of human agency, responsibility and necessity. Cavell (1987) reads Shakespearean tragedy as studies of epistemological skepticism, arguing that "the study of tragedy can and should entail reconceptions of what drives skepticism," and that Shakespearean tragedy, in particular, indicates "a path of recovery" from skepticism that philosophy itself has been unable to find. Work of this sort and calibre promises that philosophy's interest in the art of tragedy will be as abiding as it is ancient.

See also Plato, Aristotle, Hegel, Nietzsche, Art and emotion, Art and knowledge, Art and ethics.

References

Aristotle (1987) *Poetics*, trans. S. Halliwell, London: Duckworth.

Aristotle (1984) *Rhetoric*, in J. Barnes (ed.), *Complete Works of Aristotle*, Princeton: Princeton University Press.

Bungay, S. (1984) *Beauty and Truth: A Study of Hegel's Aesthetics*, Oxford: Oxford University Press.

Burke, E. (1990) *A Philosophical Enquiry*, ed. A. Phillips, Oxford: Oxford University Press.

Cavell, S. (1987) *Disowning Knowledge in Six Plays of Shakespeare*, Cambridge: Cambridge University Press.

Eaton, M. (1982) "A Strange Kind of Sadness," *Journal of Aesthetics and Art Criticism* 41: 51–63.

Feagin, S. (1983) "The Pleasures of Tragedy," *American Philosophical Quarterly* 20: 95–104.

Hegel, G. W. F. (1975) *Aesthetics: Lectures on Fine Art*, 2 vols, trans. T. M. Knox, Oxford: Oxford University Press.

Hume, D. (1987) "Of Tragedy," in *Essays Moral, Literary and Political*, ed. E. F. Miller, Indianapolis: Liberty Classics.

Kuhns, R. (1991) *Tragedy: Contradiction and Repression*, Chicago: University of Chicago Press.

Morreall, J. (1985) "Enjoying Negative Emotions in Fiction," *Philosophy and Literature* 9: 95–102.

Nietzsche, F. (1993) *The Birth of Tragedy*, trans. S. Whiteside, ed. M. Tanner, London: Penguin.

Nussbaum, M. (1986) *The Fragility of Goodness*, Cambridge: Cambridge University Press.

Schier, F. (1983) "Tragedy and the Community of Sentiment," in P. Lamarque (ed.), *Philosophy and Fiction: Essays in Literary Aesthetics*, Aberdeen: Aberdeen University Press.

—— (1989) "The Claims of Tragedy: An Essay in Moral Psychology and Aesthetic Theory," *Philosophical Papers* 18: 7–26.

Schopenhauer, A. (1966) *The World as Will and Representation*, 2 vols, trans. E. F. Payne, New York: Dover.

Wellek, R. (1955) *A History of Modern Criticism*, 2 vols, New Haven: Yale University Press.

Williams, B. (1993) *Shame and Necessity*, Berkeley: University of California Press.

32
HUMOR

Ted Cohen

Humor is a marvelous subject for philosophers of art. The breadth of the subject is enormous. Humor is to be found in canonical works of art: plays, movies, stories, novels, paintings, operas and so forth. And it is found in contexts not typically associated with art: jokes, wit in ordinary conversation and even in events to be witnessed in the world, like umbrellas blowing inside-out, dogs chasing their tails or a baby grabbing the nose of an intrusive adult.

Thus humor is found both in and outside art, in both fictional and real contexts. This suggests, what is almost certainly true, that there can be no general, overarching 'theory' of humor, unless the theory is so general and probably vague as to be utterly uninformative. There have been such theories, and they can be found described in the excellent encyclopedia entries listed in this essay's bibliography, but they will be discussed only briefly in this essay. Instead, this essay will suggest a more general theory, but also say why neither this theory nor any other is likely to be definitive.

Eighteenth-century philosophers were accustomed to thinking of some human capacity as a 'sense of beauty,' by which they meant a capacity to be affected by beauty. Although that way of thinking has lapsed, along with thoughts of a 'sense of morality' or 'sense of virtue,' it is still common to speak of a 'sense of humor,' presumably meaning by that a capacity to be affected by humorous things; and this is not a bad way to begin thinking about humor. For instance, one might start with an innocuous formulation like this:

H is humorous if and only if *P* finds it funny.

This formulation is reminiscent of eighteenth-century ethics and aesthetics, where we find propositions like these:

B is beautiful if and only if *P* is pleased by it.
V is virtuous if and only if *P* is pleased by (or approves of) it.

The immediate problem with these formulations, all of which say that something is beautiful or virtuous or whatever if and only if the thing is reacted to in some way by people, is that not all such things have the relevant effect upon all people. Thus the formulation must be refined. Unrefined, it will not do. For instance, one might establish that something is beautiful by showing that it gratifies people of taste; and one might establish that someone has taste by showing that he is gratified by things of beauty. But one cannot do both, because one could not get started. There will have to be an independent specification, either of beauty or of taste. No one understood this more clearly than Hume, who undertook first to say what makes one a competent judge, and then to identify beauty in terms of its effect upon such judges.

This problem is present acutely when we try to understand humor. It may well be true – how could it not? – that something is humorous if and only if it is found funny by someone with a sense of humor; but it seems plain that there is no chance of saying either what humorous things are, or what a sense of humor is, independently. The reason why is twofold. First, the range of humorous things is enormous, encompassing things both inside and outside art, including plays by Aristophanes and Shakespeare, Marx Brothers movies, pratfalls, cartoons, riddles and drawings, to name only a few. This bewildering array is made even more diverse and intractable when we recall an observation of Aristotle's, namely that some things which give no pleasure have 'imitations' that do give pleasure. This distinction, if anything, is even more conspicuous in the case of humor. In movies, literature, and elsewhere we find depictions of objects and events, which depictions are humorous, while the objects and events would not be humorous if encountered in real life.

The second reason why such formulations are unlikely to succeed is that virtually no one's sense of humor reaches to every humorous thing. Someone with a richly humorous sense of wordplay and wit, likely a fan of Oscar Wilde, may well abhor the movies of the Three Stooges.

If the formula were to be acceptable, it would have to be in some refined version, on the order of something like this:

> H is humorous if and only if P finds it funny under certain appropriate conditions and P is the right kind of person.

Such a proposition may be true once the relevant conditions and kind of person are specified, but only if the most important questions are begged. But however the proposition fares, it leads to the question of what, as a matter of fact, it is about H on account of which P finds H funny. That is, what are the properties of H that make H funny? It is in answer to this question that theories of humor are offered.

It is generally agreed that there have been three major general 'theories of humor,' and it should be agreed that none of them can succeed as a theory of all humor. The three theories might be called the incongruity theory, the superiority theory, and the relief-from-tension theory.

The idea that humorous things are *incongruous* is present in the works of Schopenhauer, Kierkegaard, Hazlitt and Kant, among others. Kant puts this by saying that "laughter is an affection arising from a strained expectation being suddenly reduced to nothing" (Kant 1928: 199). In order for this theory to have even an initial plausibility, the idea of 'incongruity' must be understood broadly, so that things count as incongruous if they are logically impossible (or paradoxical), merely odd or somehow out of place or simply very unusual. And, of course, it may be the thing itself that is incongruous, or it may be that the incongruity is due to the thing in its context. Thus a bear riding a bicycle, a poor, badly-dressed man at a fancy ball and a popcorn salesman at an opera all count as incongruous, and their humor is written off to their incongruity.

Even if some version of the incongruity theory is right about these things, right to find them humorous, and right to locate their humor in their incongruous display, the feebleness of the theory is readily apparent as soon as we notice that many, many incongruities are not found humorous, and many humorous items display no evident incongruity, however broadly the idea of incongruity is construed.

The idea that humor appears when one finds oneself feeling *superior* to someone is present in at least some works of Plato, Aristotle and Bergson (1956), but it is probably best known in the works of Hobbes, who declared that "laughter is nothing else but sudden glory arising from some sudden conception of some eminency in ourselves, by comparison with the infirmity of others, or with our own formerly" (Hobbes 1928: 9.13).

Surely this is an apt description of the humor arising when fun is *made of* someone, when someone is presented as clumsy, inept, incompetent or unfortunate. And it is worth noting that this felt superiority can arise on either side, either on the side of those who truly are in superior positions, or on the side of those whose positions are inferior. In either case, the other side – the oppressors or the oppressed – are represented as inferior to the one who laughs. It makes considerable difference whether the one who laughs in expression of his own superiority is in fact truly in a superior position, as, for instance, when the members of one race make fun of the race they have enslaved or dominate; or whether it is the downtrodden who find humor in *pretending* that their superiors are actually inferior, as, for instance, in jokes made about Nazis and Soviet Communists by those being brutalized by those people, exactly because the Nazis and Communists were in superior positions. It is a typical lack in superiority theories that they do not attend to the fact that the jokes, cartoons or skits in question are, after all, *fictions*, but fictions that are sometimes taken to represent genuine truths and sometimes not. What, after all, is the difference between chancing upon a stupid person doing something that strikes one as humorous, and encountering a joke or cartoon in which a stupid person is portrayed as doing something that strikes one as humorous? Our engagement with fictions is not at all well understood, not how we engage fictional characters, how we feel for them or about them, and to the extent that this is not understood, it is difficult to see just how to make sense of the superiority theory as a general theory.

Even if the superiority theory could make good on its need to deal with fictional elements, the theory would still founder on the simple facts that not all cases of felt superiority are humorous, and that not all examples of humor have anything remotely to do with superiority. Consider a nature documentary film showing the behavior of orang-utans in Indonesia. Whenever I have seen this film, I and everyone else in the audience have been amused by one particular episode in which an extended family of orang-utans is shown making its way through the jungle. All but one of the family are young and relatively small, and they make their way by swinging from vine to vine. The oldest male, however, has grown too heavy to swing from vines, and although he tries from time to time, he always comes crashing down as his weight pulls the vine loose. He is reduced to running as fast as he can along the jungle floor trying to keep up with his airborne relatives. Why is this funny? Do I feel superior to the overweight beast? I don't think so. I just find it funny. Is it somehow incongruous that he should be running and puffing while others are swinging and gliding? I don't think so.

The best known exponent of the idea that humor comes with *relief* or the *release of tension* surely is Freud (1976), although Spencer (1911) had such a theory at about the same time. The idea, roughly, is that social and psychological constraints make it impossible for us to express certain thoughts and feelings, and so those mental phenomena, as it were, build up in us and finally are given expression in the laughter promoted by jokes about the very things we have been forbidden to express ourselves about ingenuously: for instance, our sexual impulses, and our instincts for aggression. This is an extremely useful idea, probably with even wider application than Freud gives it. There are any number of things we find ourselves constrained not to speak of, or give active voice to, because of political, social, moral or other strictures that seemingly declare these things out of bounds. And yet we think about them, wish to declare our interest in them, and have a need to express ourselves about them. So we do this with jokes, perhaps partly for the reason Freud suggests, that these things are just bursting out of us anyway, but also because we take advantage of a presumption to the effect that humor is light, good-natured, benign and therefore virtually universally acceptable.

Again, however, it is undeniable that there are myriad examples of humor that have nothing to do with this kind of release of tension.

Each theory has indeed identified a feature characteristic of some examples of humor. But it is almost immediately apparent that none of these characteristics is either necessary or sufficient for humor. That is, not every incongruity is funny, nor is everything funny incongruous, and so on for the other two theories. Indeed there are no necessary or sufficient conditions for humor, at least as far as this essay's author can see.

An oddity of theories in aesthetics – and for that matter elsewhere in philosophy – is that it is not always clear in what sense they are *theories*. What do they explain? What do they predict? How are they to be tested? This seems especially problematic in aesthetics, perhaps most acutely when one is considering humor. It is a commonplace that the effects of works of art cannot, in general, be realized by substitutes for the works. That is, no description of a musical work, or a novel, or a painting can do what the music, writing, and painting do. With regard to humor, the point virtually is enshrined in the saying 'you had to be there.'

Consider: in music, a movement from the leading tone to the tonic will sound satisfying. Is that true? The answer, surely, is: sometimes, but not always. And similarly with humor. Is incongruity or absurdity funny? The answer is: sometimes; it depends. How about a dog wearing sunglasses? A painting of some dogs playing poker? A small child firing a shotgun? A man giving birth? Anyone faced with these questions, if prudent, will say that it is necessary to experience the thing oneself. The descriptions alone are insufficient.

The theories are still worth considering, however, if only as partial descriptions of some humor, especially if it is possible to regard them as three parts of a single theme. It may be possible to do this if we fudge a little and take them to be relatively narrow descriptions of what, in general, are kinds of *anomaly*.

Now just as none of the three theories is comprehensive, neither is the idea of anomaly wide enough to capture the three. But it may be an interesting idea to the extent that it captures something yet more general that is suggested by each of the three common theories. Still, just as with the three theories, neither is anomalousness either a necessary or a sufficient condition for humor. Yet it may be worth looking into the fact of anomalousness to ask just why, when it is, it is humorous.

An anomalous thing is irregular, unusual, unexpected and often unsettling. We may ask, when an anomaly is funny, why is it funny? What is the humor in anomaly?

A provisional answer to this question discovers a striking oddity, namely that there seem to be two reasons why anomaly is (sometimes) funny, and these reasons are virtually opposites of one another. The first is that anomalies can suggest that we have power over the structures that usually restrain us, while the second is that an anomaly can exhibit our powerlessness to comprehend and subdue the world in which those structures exist.

It has been noted that humor often arises when one feels superior. Hobbes seems to have thought laughter is almost always associated with something like the conquest of one's enemy. But the idea of *power*, power over something or someone, extends into more subtle areas. The humor of wordplay and related forms of wit, for instance, may fairly be thought of as incorporating a sense of power, the power to free oneself from the normal strictures of language. More generally, the humor of anomaly regularly involves the placement and action of things – including people – in circumstances not regularly permitted by society or by nature. This is, perhaps, the humor of *freedom*. It is our freedom, at least in imagination, from the linguistic, social, cultural and natural constraints that are the inhibitions of our normal lives.

Although it has been less commonly noted, the humor of anomaly sometimes bespeaks not power but powerlessness. When an anomaly has the form of extreme incongruity, so exaggerated that the situation is truly absurd, then the joke (or cartoon or other form) presents something genuinely incomprehensible. In such a case one does not imagine oneself with power over anything, and yet one may find humor. One is not in a mood of exultation or triumph, but of something quite different. It is not the opposite mood. It is not merely a mood of resignation, as if one were submitting to a greater power. It is a mood of acceptance, of willing acknowledgment of those aspects of life that can be neither subdued nor fully comprehended.

It is a wonderful thing about humor that it is the province of the powerful and of the powerless, that it is a response to weakness and to strength. Small wonder that no theory is able to say just what makes a humorous thing humorous. It would be a shame if it could, because then the pervasive possibility that we humans cannot tell when and where we might laugh would disappear, and human life would be so different as not to be recognizably human.

See also Taste, Fiction.

References

Bergson, H. L. (1956) "Laughter," trans. C. Brereton and F. Rothwell, in W. Sypher (ed.), *Comedy*, Baltimore: Johns Hopkins University Press.

Freud, S. (1976) *Jokes and their Relation to the Unconscious*, trans. J. Strachey, Harmondsworth: Penguin.

Hobbes, T. (1928) *The Elements of Law, Natural and Politic*, ed. F. Tonnies, Cambridge: Cambridge University Press.

Hume, D. (1985) "Of the Standard of Taste," in *Essays Moral, Political and Literary*, ed. E. Miller, Indianapolis: Liberty Classics.

Kant, I. (1928) *The Critique of Judgement*, trans. J. C. Meredith, Oxford: Oxford University Press.

Spencer, H. (1911) "The Physiology of Laughter," in *Essays on Education*, London: Dent.

Further reading

Carroll, N. (1991) "On Jokes," *Midwest Studies in Philosophy* 16: 280–91. (A useful discussion of jokes.)

Cohen, T. (1999) *Jokes*, Chicago: University of Chicago Press. (Jokes, the conditions for understanding them and their importance in human life.)

Dauer, F. W. (1988) "The Picture as the Medium of Humorous Incongruity," *American Philosophical Quarterly* 25. (A rare discussion of visual humor.)

Levinson, J. (1998) "Humour," *Routledge Encyclopedia of Philosophy*, London: Routledge.

Lippitt, J. (1992) "Humour," in D. Cooper (ed.), *Companion to Aesthetics*, Oxford: Blackwell. (With Levinson, a helpful overview of theories of humor.)

Morreall, J. (1983) *Taking Laughter Seriously*, Albany: State University of New York Press. (An extended account of humor.)

33
AUTHENTICITY IN PERFORMANCE

James O. Young

In recent years, authenticity has become an end valued by many performing artists and audiences. Authentic performance could be a goal in any performing art: drama, dance, or music. The authentic performance of music has, however, generated the most attention. The so-called early music movement is responsible for a phenomenal growth of interest in the authentic performance of music. This movement is one of the most striking developments in the history of music performance, and amounts to little less than a revolution in musical taste. In view of this development, the concept of authentic performance, particularly as it applies to music, has received philosophical analysis.

Authenticity in performance became an issue because modern performances of old works can differ dramatically from the original performances of the same works. Consider, for example, an eighteenth-century performance of a composition by Bach and some modern performances of the same work. The musical instruments of the eighteenth century differ dramatically from the instruments of our time. For example, baroque violins were strung in gut, were played with short, convex bows and had finger boards shorter than those on modern instruments. Performance practices have also changed. While players of modern violins use almost continuous vibrato, most eighteenth-century violinists used it only sparingly, as a special effect. As a result a modern performance of a work by Bach can sound quite unlike an eighteenth-century performance. Significant changes have also taken place in dramatic performance. In Shakespeare's day, for example, all dramatic roles were taken by males. Boys acted the parts of women.

Several philosophical issues arise from reflection on authenticity in performance. The first issue is conceptual. We need to analyze the concept of authentic performance and decide what counts as an authentic performance. Once authentic performance is defined, questions emerge about the value of such performances. We need to ask whether reasons can be given for thinking authentic performances are aesthetically superior to non-authentic ones. Moral issues also arise. Perhaps moral reasons can be given for or against the authentic performance of some works. These normative and definitional issues are intertwined, and cannot completely be separated.

We should begin an analysis of the concept of authentic performance by identifying the desiderata a good definition of the concept will satisfy. For a start, we do not want a stipulative definition of authentic performance. Rather, a good definition will capture and refine what performers of early music and informed audience members mean when they talk about authenticity. A good definition of authentic performance will also represent it as a goal that performing artists can attain, at least some of the time. Finally, authentic performance should be characterized in such a way that it represents an attractive aesthetic goal. That is, authenticity is supposed to be an aesthetic good and, if possible, it should be defined in such a way that it is represented as such. We cannot rule out the possibility that no definition can satisfy all of these desiderata.

Before we can proceed with the examination of these proposals, a couple of preliminary points should be made. For a start, we need to consider the requirement that authentic performance be defined in such a way that authentic performances are attainable. This requirement should not be applied too strictly. Each definition of authenticity establishes a goal for performers. No matter which definition is adopted, our ignorance of parts of music history may make these goals unattainable in some cases. This is most obviously true in the cases of works which are partially lost. Modern performers cannot give a completely authentic performance of an incomplete work. (Musicians could, fortuitously, play all the notes in an incomplete work, but this would not be an authentic performance of the work. As we will see, authenticity involves fidelity to something in the past, and accidental reproduction of a work is not fidelity to something historical.) Even when complete scores survive, authentic performances may not be possible. We may be too ignorant of the performance practices of certain periods (the early Middle Ages, for example) for the authentic performance of some works to be attainable. The fact that authenticity is not always achievable should not be taken to establish that the concept of authentic performance has no application. Authenticity should, however, be defined in such a way that it is a goal performers can reasonably hope to achieve on a regular basis. Fortunately, our musicological knowledge is quite good, and such a definition should be available.

The second preliminary point identifies the sort of authenticity we are trying to define. The authenticity of concern to the early music movement is historical authenticity. This sort of authenticity is to be contrasted with personal authenticity. A personally authentic performance is faithful to a performer's individual genius. That is, a performance characterized by personal authenticity is not a slavish recapitulation of another performance. Rather, it is the product of a performer's individual interpretation. Historical authenticity involves fidelity to something historical. As we will see, different accounts are given of the item to which historically authentic performances are faithful.

It has been claimed that performances cannot be both personally and historically authentic, but there is no necessary incompatibility. For a start, every performance of an existing work, even the most personally authentic, is historically authentic to some degree. (Without some degree of fidelity to the past, a performance could not be a performance of an existing work.) Even a high degree of historical authenticity is, however, compatible with personal authenticity. The two sorts of authenticity are only incompatible if historical authenticity demands complete fidelity to the past. Historical authenticity can, however, be defined in such a way that performers have scope for individual creativity. Given such a definition, a work can be completely historically authentic and personally authentic. To the extent that creativity in performance is an aesthetic good, a satisfactory definition of historical authenticity will not demand complete fidelity to past performances. (For the rest of this article, talk of authenticity is talk of historical authenticity, unless otherwise specified.)

The key to defining authenticity is specifying the sort of thing to which an historically authentic performance is faithful. Three main proposals have been presented. According to the first proposal, an authentic performance is one faithful to the sound of performances at the time of composition. (This version of the proposal applies only to the performance of music. If it were extended to cover opera and drama, it would also have to mention fidelity to how performances looked.) Alternatively, an authentic performance of a work is one faithful to the intentions of the work's composer (or author). The third proposal suggests that the authentic performance of a work involves fidelity to a score and the performance practices employed at the time of the work's composition.

Let us begin by considering authenticity as fidelity to the sounds of past performances. I will call this the acoustic definition of authenticity. Fidelity to past sounds can be understood in two senses. In the first sense, an authentic performance reproduces audible phenomena of the past. That is, an authentic performance reproduces vibrations of the air of the type which occurred in the past (by the means originally employed). Peter Kivy calls this sonic authenticity (Kivy 1995). Alternatively, performers could aim at the reproduction of the sort of experience possessed by past audiences. Authenticity would then be defined in terms of the faithful reproduction of past experience (by the means employed in the past). Again following Kivy, we can call this sensible authenticity. A definition of authenticity in terms of fidelity to past sounds, however this is understood, faces problems. Perhaps, however, the severity of some of these problems has been overestimated.

An immediate problem faces the acoustic definition, however fidelity to past sounds is understood. Some compositions were never performed. As a result, there are no past sounds to which present performances of these works can be faithful. Consequently, the acoustic definition leads to the conclusion that authentic performances of works not performed in the past are impossible. This seems to be an unacceptable consequence, but the acoustic definition can be modified to avoid it. The definition's advocates could hold that when a composition was not performed in the past, authenticity is to be defined counterfactually. That is, an authentic performance of a previously unperformed work would be a performance which sounds as the work would have sounded, had it been performed at the time of composition.

The acoustic definition faces other, more serious problems. In particular, questions arise about whether sonic and sensible authenticity represent attractive and attainable aesthetic goals.

Consider first sonic authenticity. Sonic authenticity will often be attainable. Whether it represents an attractive goal is, however, open to question. Performance standards have varied over time, and performers sometimes did not do justice to works at the time of their composition. If modern performers can produce better performances, sonic authenticity is not always an attractive aesthetic goal. (The reproduction of past vibrations of the air might have historical value, but authenticity is an aesthetic end.) Sometimes, of course, sonic authenticity is desirable. For example, Bach was the supreme interpreter of his own keyboard works, and the reproduction of the sound of his performances (were it possible) would be of enormous aesthetic value. Authenticity should, however, be defined in such a way that it is a valuable goal in performances of all valuable works.

Notice that this version of the acoustic approach results in a definition of historical authenticity which is incompatible with personal authenticity. This is the case since performers aim to replicate a past performance, rather than to develop an original interpretation.

Questions arise about both the attainability and attractiveness of sensible authenticity. For a start, sharing the experience of past audiences is not always an attractive aesthetic goal. Any time sonic authenticity is aesthetically undesirable, sensible authenticity would also be undesirable. After all, sharing the experience of someone who heard a bad performance is not appealing. Even when past performances were good, sensible authenticity is not always desirable. Audiences in the past did not always experience works as aesthetically valuable. For example, many of Beethoven's first audiences found his works uncouth and bombastic. The second version of the acoustic definition could be revised in an effort to deal with this difficulty. The definition could incorporate a reference to selected audience members. For example, some members of Beethoven's audience (including, presumably, Beethoven himself) had an aesthetically valuable experience of original performances of his works. Sharing the experience of such listeners would be attractive. Still, it is doubtful whether sensible authenticity is a universally attractive aesthetic goal.

Doubts have also been raised about whether sensible authenticity is attainable. Members of modern audiences have had very different sorts of experience than, say, eighteenth-century audiences. Our experience and, in particular, our experience of music (and other arts), is bound to influence how things sound to us. For example, modern listeners are raised on Beethoven's music and the works of later composers. As a result, it has been argued, we cannot hear his works as shocking, even bizarre, as contemporaries did. It would follow that sensible authenticity is not an attainable goal. This objection can be challenged on a number of grounds. One could question whether musical experience has changed so very much, or suggest that our imaginations make it possible to recapture past experience. Still, enough doubts have been raised about the various versions of acoustic authenticity to motivate the search for an alternative definition.

Stephen Davies has advocated an idealized version of acoustic authenticity (Davies 1987). On his view, an authentic performance of a work is one which sounds as it would have sounded at the time of composition, had conditions been optimal for the time. When Mozart's musicians performed the overture to *Don Giovanni* at first sight, the conditions were not anything like optimal. According to Davies, an authentic performance of this work should not be understood in terms of fidelity to this performance. Rather, he holds, an authentic performance of the overture is one which sounds as it would have sounded in 1787, had Mozart had at his disposal good, well-rehearsed musicians, playing good instruments. (Here, 'good' is understood as 'good by the standards of 1787.') Davies' definition of acoustic authenticity is much preferable to versions which do not idealize the sound to which authentic performances are faithful. So long as it is understood that an ideal performance is a personally authentic one, it seems to meet all of the desiderata listed above.

Consider next the definition of an authentic performance of a work as a performance that sounds (and, in the case of opera, drama and dance, looks) as its composer intended. I will refer to this as the intentional definition. This definition faces some troublesome questions. The definition appears to capture what many performers of early music mean when they talk about authenticity. Whether it actually does, however, depends on what a composer's intentions for his or her work are taken to be. A question also arises about whether fidelity to composers' intentions is always aesthetically desirable.

Consider the intentions a composer may have had. At first, determining a composer's intentions for the performance of his works seems easy enough. The score will reveal a good deal about a composer's intentions. For example, Bach's score explicitly states that the *Goldberg Variations* are to be performed on a harpsichord with two keyboards. Information about the performance practices of the composer's time will also reveal a great deal. A composer probably intended that his works be performed on the instruments of the time and in the contemporary style. A composer may, however, have had other intentions. He or she may have intended that the works be performed on the most modern instruments available. A composer may have considered that future performers would develop interpretations of the works which had not occurred to him or her. He or she may have intended that, if such interpretations were aesthetically successful, they should be employed.

Suppose that a composer intended that the latest musical style be employed in the performance of his or her works. Or suppose he or she intended that the works be performed on the most modern (or the loudest) instruments available. (Beethoven may have had such an intention for some of his piano works.) If a composer had such intentions, fidelity to these intentions will not result in what many people regard as historically authentic performances of the works. Certainly fidelity to such intentions will not result in performances such as those sought by members of the early music movement. Consequently, a definition of authenticity in terms of composers' intentions fails to meet the first desideratum.

There are other reasons to reject the intentional definition. Suppose that we could be certain that a composer only intended a work to be performed with a certain interpretation and on the instruments of the day. The question of whether fidelity to these intentions is aesthetically desirable still arises. Sometimes fidelity is aesthetically desirable. A composer will often be the best interpreter of his or her own works. Composers who were great virtuosi, such as Bach and Handel, probably were. These performers also chose the instruments best suited to their compositions. In such cases, fidelity to a composer's intentions is probably the best aesthetic policy. (We should not be surprised if Bach's keyboard works sound better on harpsichord than on modern piano.) Modern performers may, however, have developed interpretations of some works which are superior to the interpretations intended by the composer. Here, fidelity to a composer's intentions is not desirable. That is, authenticity, construed as fidelity to a composer's intentions, is not a characteristic of the best performances of some works.

There may be reasons, besides aesthetic reasons, for respecting composers' intentions. Kivy once believed that performers are under a moral obligation to respect composers' intentions (Kivy 1993). Performers could be under such an obligation, even when fidelity a composer's intentions results in performances less aesthetically good than ones that result from infidelity. When composers are dead, the existence of such an obligation depends on the claim that the dead can be harmed by performers who disregard their intentions. The claim that the dead can be harmed is controversial, but not indefensible. The fact that testamentary wishes are generally respected can be taken as evidence that the dead can be harmed.

Even if it is accepted that the dead can be harmed, and that performers have a moral obligation to respect composers' intentions, respect for composers' intentions may not be morally obligatory. Other moral considerations may override an obligation to respect these intentions. Sometimes respecting a composer's intentions will obviously be immoral. This will be the case when the composer intended that an aria be sung by castrati. (If a boy is accidentally castrated, he should be given hormone therapy, not singing lessons.) One could also argue that performers have right to interpret works freely. The interests of audiences also enter into moral questions about performance. Consequentialists could argue that an audience's interest in hearing the best possible performances could override a composer's interest in having his or her intentions respected. They might reason that any harm to a composer is more than outweighed by harm to audiences denied access to the best possible performances.

One definition of authenticity remains to be considered. According to this definition, an authentic performance of a work is faithful to the work's score and to the performance practices employed at the time of the work's composition. More precisely, on this definition, an authentic performance is faithful to the performance practices which affect the sound of performances. This qualification must be added, since some performance practices (for example, the use of walking sticks as batons) have no impact on sound, so there is no aesthetic reason to observe them. This definition may be referred to as the technique definition, since an authentic performance is the product of a certain sort of practice or technique.

On this definition, an authentic performance is faithful to a score when all of the directives contained in a score are followed. A performance of some work is also faithful to the performance practices of a period when it employs the instruments, performing forces, and style of a period. So, for example, an authentic performance of one of Handel's trio sonatas will employ baroque violins, accompanied by a continuo group of cello and harpsichord. The tempi will be rather quicker than is common in non-authentic performances, sparing use will be made of vibrato, but other ornaments will be added, and so on.

The technique definition incorporates some of the best features of the other two. On this view, an authentic performance is not the reproduction of the sound of a past performance. When fidelity to scores and performance practices is the touchstone of authenticity, however, a good authentic performance will sound something like an ideal performance would have sounded at the time of composition. Something of the intentional definition is also preserved, since fidelity to a score involves fidelity to a composer's intentions. Fidelity to performance practices also involves respect for composers' intentions, since composers often intend their works to be performed in accordance with the practices of their period. As well, composers' intentions, in part, determine the performance practices of a period. Consequently, fidelity to past performance practices involves fidelity to composers' intentions.

For practical purposes, the differences between the technique definition and Davies' idealized acoustic definition are not great. The two definitions are extensionally equivalent. That is, they classify as authentic the same class of performances. The technique definition is, perhaps, preferable because it makes clear that a performance can be both historically and personally authentic. Since statements about counterfactual states of affairs (for example, about how music would have sounded, had conditions been ideal) are the source of considerable philosophical confusion, the technique definition also has the advantage of avoiding reference to such states of affairs.

If the technique definition is accepted, an authentic performance leaves scope for performers' creativity. Two performances can be equally faithful to some score (particularly scores of the eighteenth century and earlier) but quite different from each other. Fidelity to the performance practices of a period also leaves performers the freedom to cultivate individual interpretations of compositions. Consequently, on the technique definition, a performance can be both historically and personally authentic. Indeed, historical authenticity will sometimes require personal authenticity. This will be the case, for example, when a composer directs on the score that performances of a work include an improvised cadenza.

The technique definition easily meets two of the three desiderata identified above. Performers of early music often carefully study scores and aim to revive the performance practices of the past. So the technique definition captures a good deal of what performers mean when they speak of authenticity. The second desideratum is also met, since the goal established by the technique definition can often be attained. Many scores survive together with instructions for their performance. Our knowledge of the instruments of many periods is quite good, and instruments are often the best guides to past performance practices. Surviving performance manuals provide valuable insight into the performance practices of the past, and musicologists have discovered a great deal of additional evidence. We still need to ask, however, whether the technique definition establishes authenticity as a desirable aesthetic goal.

Before we can answer this question, we need to ask how we can tell whether authenticity (as defined by the technique definition) is an aesthetic good. One way to decide the question would be empirical. Imagine the following experiment. Authentic and inauthentic performances of works are recorded. The authentic and inauthentic performances are by equally good musicians. Qualified audiences are then presented with two recordings works, one authentic and one inauthentic. (There will, of course, be some question about what counts as a qualified audience member.) If these audiences prefer authentic performances to the inauthentic ones, then authenticity is an aesthetic good.

The experiment just described has, in effect, been carried out on massive scale over the past few decades. (Many recent recordings of early music are properly classified as authentic.) The results of this experiment are inconclusive. Various qualified listeners given different verdicts on authentic performances. (Some dogmatic observers on both sides of the question hold that the truly qualified listeners are unanimous. I will disregard this possibility.) Some qualified audience members report that they prefer authentic performances. They often note that authentic performances are characterized by a greater clarity than inauthentic ones. For example, Bach's counterpoint emerges more clearly on a harpsichord than on a modern piano. Other listeners admire the wider range of tone colors offered by baroque instruments. Still others prefer authentic performances since the style of performance matches the style of composition. For example, performances of baroque compositions in a baroque style may be unified in a way that a performance of the same work in a romantic style is not. Some qualified audience members, however, do not like fidelity to period performance practices. They prefer the lush, full sound of modern instruments. The tone of a fortepiano might seem feeble when compared to that of a concert grand. Some listeners also prefer the big sound of modern orchestras to the more intimate sound of small baroque ensembles. A third segment of the qualified audience is happy to listen to good authentic and good inauthentic performances. These listeners are indifferent about historical authenticity and simply seek out personally authentic performances.

Even given this lack of unanimity among qualified audiences, one conclusion can be drawn. Authenticity, as defined by the technique definition, is an aesthetic good. At any rate, it is an aesthetic good on the assumption that if listeners seek something out, then it is (for them) good. On this account, however, the aesthetic goodness of authenticity is relative to some listeners. Some people are dissatisfied with this relativism, and inclined to search for a way to establish that either authentic or inauthentic performances are preferable. Such people claim that listeners who prefer inauthentic (or authentic) performances are guilty of bad taste. A satisfactory case for such a claim would depend on the resolution of long-standing debates about what makes one performance or interpretation of a work better than another. Still, it is possible to sketch a line of argument for the conclusion that, all other factors being equal, an authentic performance is superior to an inauthentic one.

Whether relativism can be avoided depends on the nature of music. If musical performances are valuable simply as sources of pleasure, it is hard to see how relativism about their value can be avoided. Relative to listeners who receive more pleasure from authentic performances, authenticity is an aesthetic good. Relative to audiences who receive more pleasure from inauthentic performances, authenticity is bad. If, however, performances are a source of more than pleasure, perhaps thoroughgoing relativism can be avoided. Suppose that music can have content. That is, suppose that it can express or represent non-musical phenomena such as emotions. If music has such content, it is (potentially) the source of insight as well as pleasure. If so, there is a basis for saying that authentic performances are better than inauthentic ones.

What a work expresses depends in large measure on how it is performed. Consider, for example sonatas of the seventeenth century. In the seventeenth-century standard, pitches were up to a full tone or more below modern concert pitch. When a work of the period is performed at the lower pitch, it often displays a character it lacks in an inauthentic performance. It becomes expressive of emotions which it does not express at modern pitch. When the composer wrote the piece he or she (presumably) took into account the pitch of the period. If audiences are interested in experiencing what a work expresses, they will prefer authentic performances of seventeenth-century sonatas. Many similar examples could be provided in support of the claim that performances best reveal the content of compositions.

It is important to note that many musicians in the early music movement no longer take authentic performance as their goal. The reluctance to take authenticity as the goal of performances is the product of two considerations. Musicians are concerned (perhaps unduly so) about whether authenticity is attainable. Performers of early music are also aware that their practices sometimes deliberately depart from historical ones. Consequently, performers of early music often take historically-informed performance as their goal. People have different conceptions of historically-informed performance, but the general idea is clear enough. Historically-informed performance has much in common with authentic performance, as defined by the technique definition.

Historically-informed performance involves fidelity to original scores, but does not demand complete fidelity. Similarly, a historically-informed performance involves a measure of fidelity to the performance practice of a period, not complete fidelity. Rather than being completely faithful to something in the past, a historically-informed performance is faithful to a tradition of performance practice. A historically-authentic performance is faithful to something in the past, such as the performance practices of a period. A tradition of performance practice, however, does not exist completely in the past. It continues to exist and evolve in the present. The difference between authentic and historically-informed performance is, then, that one is faithful to something in the past, and one is faithful to something continuing in the present.

A couple of examples will illustrate how a performance could be historically informed, but inauthentic. The liturgical music of the renaissance was sung entirely by males. The treble parts were taken by boys or castrati. Today, women often sing the upper parts, even in ensembles within the early music movement. Performances by these ensembles are inauthentic, since they depart in an essential way from past performance practices. At the same time, the performances are historically informed since they are faithful to an evolving tradition of performance practice. The performance practices of the renaissance still inform the performances of these ensembles. They employ the tempi, ensemble sizes, interpretive practices (for example, there is little use of vibrato) of the period. The tradition has evolved in such a way, however, that women's voices may be employed. The evolution of instrument building has also affected whether performances are authentic. In the renaissance, people were smaller than they are today. Lutes that were comfortable for the players of the period can be awkwardly small for modern players. Some luthiers compensate by building slightly larger lutes. A performance on such a lute is inauthentic, since the practice of the period was to perform on small instruments. It can still be historically informed in the sense of being faithful to an evolving tradition of performance practice. A performance on a large lute can be faithful to the evolved tradition of performance practice.

A performance can also fail to be faithful to a score, but count as historically informed. Members of the early music movement frequently arrange baroque compositions for instruments other than those the composer specified. Performances of these arrangements are not faithful to an existing score. Arrangement was, however, an accepted practice in the baroque period. So long as the arrangements are faithful to a tradition of arrangement, performances of the arrangement can count as historically-informed performances.

See also Music.

References

Davies, S. (1987) "Authenticity in Musical Performance," *British Journal of Aesthetics* 27: 39–50.

Kivy, P. (1993) "Live Performances and Dead Composers: On the Ethics of Musical Interpretation," in *The Fine Art of Repetition*, Cambridge: Cambridge University Press.

—— (1995) *Authenticities*, Ithaca: Cornell University Press.

Further reading

Godlovich, S. (1988) "Authentic Performance," *Monist* 71: 258–77. (A general discussion by a lutenist and luthier.)

Haskell, H. (1989) *The Early Music Revival*, London: Thames and Hudson. (A history of the early music movement.)

Thom, P. (1983) *For an Audience: A Philosophy of the Performing Arts*, Philadelphia: Temple University Press. (A version of the technique definition.)

Young, J. (1988) "The Concept of Authentic Performance." *British Journal of Aesthetics* 28: 228–38. (Expresses skepticism about whether authentic performance is a useful concept.)

34
FAKES AND FORGERIES

Nan Stalnaker

Underlying much philosophical discussion of forgery is this question: Why do people prefer a genuine work of art to a copy of it when they cannot tell the difference between the two? One common assumption is that, whatever the reason is, it is not aesthetic. It is plausible to think that when the indiscernible copy is a forgery, we object to it for moral reasons, just as we would object to any deception, but not on aesthetic grounds: that is, grounds relevant to its appearance or other sensory qualities. But the moral explanation cannot account for why we prefer to see the original rather than the copy even when there is no deception involved; when, for example, the copy is clearly identified as a copy. If, to accommodate the crowds, the *Mona Lisa* and a well-labeled, exact copy were hanging in different parts of the Louvre, most of us would still choose to line up in front of the real thing, even though we would not be able to tell if the works were accidentally switched. What is controversial is why this is so.

One possible explanation is that we associate copies with forgeries, since close copies can easily be used to deceive. But this attitude seems hardly justified since copies are not typically forgeries: there is a long tradition of benign copying, either to train art students or, before photography, to provide access to widely admired art. Rubens, for example, copied many of Titian's works, copies that have long been prized and collected.

The formalist view

Against this backdrop, some theorists have argued that, judged on purely aesthetic grounds, exact copies ought to be as highly valued as originals, given that they must be just as beautiful. Underlying the claim that original works and their exact copies are aesthetically equivalent is the Appearance Theory, the view that only the appearance of an art work should affect its aesthetic value (Meiland 1983: 116). The Appearance Theory is implicit in the formalist views of early twentieth century art critics Clive Bell and Roger Fry, who defined visual aesthetic value in terms of response to purely formal, sensory qualities, such as a painting's line, color and spatial organization (Bell 1914). For such formalists, the intentions of the artist, the deceit of the forger, and the historical context of a work are irrelevant to its appreciation. So, any physical array of marks or sounds that produces the exact same perceptual experience in the viewer or listener as the original is its aesthetic equivalent.

The original fake

In response to the formalists, others argue that although the copy and the original are identical in appearance, the two are not identical in aesthetic value, since the genuine art work is original, while the copy is not. In this view, even though originality is not a feature of a work's appearance – it concerns a work's historical relationships to the works that came before it – it is an aesthetic value, one that the copy lacks.

Perhaps, then, we prefer genuine works of art because they are more original than copies. Yet even forgeries that are in one sense original are thought to lack aesthetic interest. Up until now, we have taken a forgery to be an exact copy of an existing art work, where the copy purports to be the original work. But another kind of forgery, sometimes called a fake, is not copied from an existing work, but has a composition invented by the forger, who emulates merely the style of a well-regarded artist. For example, in one of the most celebrated cases of painting forgery, Hans van Meegeren painted a work called *The Supper at Emmaus*, which purported to be an early Vermeer, but was not a copy of an existing work. Partly because there were few early Vermeer works for comparison, van Meegeren's forgery deceived some well-known critics at that time. But although van Meegeren's fake Vermeer was more original than a copy, it is doubtful that it has any higher value than one. Even the inventive fake is not valued as art.

Van Meegeren's fake Vermeer was, however, original in only one sense of the term: in this sense an original work is one conceived by the artist who painted it or caused it to be painted by others under his or her direction. In a second sense, an original work is one that is groundbreaking, unconventional, or innovative. To call a work original in the first sense is not to make a claim about its quality: the original work of a pedestrian painter will probably be uninteresting. On the other hand, a copy may have considerable aesthetic value. Rubens's *Rape of Europa*, for example, is a beautiful painting, even though it is not Rubens's own, original work, but a copy of Titian's *Rape of Europa*.

The contextualist view

Opponents of the formalist view emphasize the importance of context in under-standing an art work; they argue that originality is only one aspect of aesthetic value that the Appearance Theory cannot explain. To the contextualist, everything we know about an art work's history, cultural role and moral qualities enters into our idea of its aesthetic value. It may seem irrational that Etruscan statues long enjoyed for their beauty were removed from view at the Metropolitan Museum when they were discovered to be forgeries (Meyer 1983: 78). But the contextualist insists that a work of art is valued not just for its appearance but also for its connection to a culture. Thus, the forged Etruscan objects, because they are not genuine, may subtly reflect the culture and time in which they were copied in ways that misrepresent Etruscan culture.

As described so far, the contextualist emphasizes the cultural milieu as one source of the meaning and value of art. But another kind of contextualist emphasizes the conceptual context, by locating an art work's value in the individual artist's intentions or ideas. For such intentionalists, lack of conceptual interest or individuality is what makes a copy lower in value than the original work it so closely resembles. In support of this, copies that exhibit the distinctive qualities of their maker, like Rubens's version of Titian's *Rape of Europa*, are often considered more aesthetically valuable than slavishly accurate copies.

From the formalist point of view, the contextualist (and intentionalist) mistake lies in suggesting that the value of an art work is determined partly by what we know about it rather than simply by the beauty we discover with our eyes. From the contextualist point of view, the Appearance Theorist's (and formalist's) mistake lies in suggesting that the appearance of an art work can be insulated from what the viewer knows, unaffected by whether one is an art expert or a casual museum-goer, a pre-Renaissance monk or a modern teenager. Both objections have merit: neither the formalist or the contextualist seems able to account fully for our most basic intuitions about art.

Goodman's hybrid view

In *Languages of Art* (1976) Nelson Goodman argues for a position that combines elements of both views. Goodman sounds like a contextualist when he argues that our knowledge of a work's authenticity affects our aesthetic encounter with it, but he shows a formalist sensibility in linking knowledge of an art work's authen-ticity to its appearance: not its current appearance but the way it may possibly be seen in the future. He asks us to imagine we have in front of us two paintings, one we know to be Rembrandt's *Lucretia* and the other, an indiscernible copy of it. Goodman argues that even though we cannot see any difference between the two, the copy still differs aesthetically from the original. The aesthetic difference comes from our knowledge that one was produced by Rembrandt and that the other was not: knowing this, he claims, we cannot rule out the possibility of learning in the future to see a subtle difference between the two that we cannot see currently.

Goodman can be seen to be making a plausible empirical point. We may, for instance, be unable initially to distinguish two wines by their taste. But if we are told of a difference – for example, that one is produced in oak barrels – we can eventually learn from repeated comparisons, tasting for oakiness, to distinguish them easily. We apparently have at our disposal sensory information – the oak taste – that we cannot make use of without the concept for doing so. Similarly, Goodman suggests that knowing a work to be a Rembrandt prepares us to see what visually distinguishes Rembrandt's work from works that, to the untrained eye, look identical.

The empirical interpretation of Goodman's claim suggests a bolder contextualism than the one described earlier: while the cautious contextualist claims that the aesthetic value of an art work is affected by the work's cultural and moral value, the bold contextualist claims that what we know about an art work's history changes its aesthetic qualities by changing the very way it looks to us, altering even its formal qualities. If Goodman is seen as making an empirical claim, then he appears to belong in the camp of the bold. But as we shall see in connection with Arthur Danto's contribution to the discussion, Goodman's claim that knowledge enters into aesthetic experience can be interpreted in several different ways, some more boldly contextualist than others.

To bolster his claim, Goodman points to the van Meegeren forgery, which passed for a fine Vermeer in its own time, but today is easily seen to be a clumsy work, distinguishable even by non-experts from a genuine Vermeer (Goodman 1976: 110). Although, in this case, an exact copy is not being compared with an original, the van Meegeren story does suggest that differences not discernible to one generation of viewers are obvious to another, and that this increased visual discernment is caused by our knowledge of possible differences. In further support of Goodman's empirical point, copies and original paintings are said to differ in characteristic ways that allow experts to distinguish them: copies often look labored, lacking the fluid integration of overall conception and detail that is seen in originals (Friedlander 1941a: 147).

The capacity of experts to see such differences, though relevant to an empirical version of Goodman's claim, does not speak to another more theoretical issue raised by his argument: if there were a perfect, molecule for molecule copy of *Lucretia*, perhaps made by a computer, would it differ in aesthetic value from the Rembrandt original? It seems plausible that, knowing how the two were produced, we would look at and describe the two identical-looking works differently in ways that bear on aesthetic value: the genuine Rembrandt might be described as weathered by age, or lovingly crafted, while the copy might be said to be convincingly old-looking, or a remarkable feat of engineering. If this is right, then objects can have different aesthetic properties even though no one will ever be able to distinguish them from each other visually. So despite its empirical plausibility, Goodman's argument does not succeed in explaining all aspects of aesthetic value in terms of possible visual differences.

Forgery across the arts

Central to Goodman's aesthetic theory is his claim that there are two different kinds of symbol systems within the arts, and that this distinction is related to whether a particular kind of art can be forged. By his definition, a forgery is "an object falsely purporting to have the history of production requisite for the (or an) original of the work" (Goodman 1976: 122); by 'object' Goodman appears to mean physical objects and also concrete, token-events such as performances, both of which he considers forgeable (ibid.: 118). Forgeable arts, like painting, and sculpture, Goodman calls 'autographic'; in these arts, the identity of a work depends on the history of the production of a unique object, which can be falsified. Speaking of the etcher's original plate, Goodman explains its autographic character this way: "even the most exact copy produced otherwise than by printing from that plate counts not as an original but as an imitation or forgery" (ibid.: 114).

Music and literature, on the other hand, Goodman terms 'allographic': in allographic arts, the identity of an art work is determined by a particular sequence of symbols, such as musical notes or words. Goodman claims that in music, mere conformation to a score is sufficient to make a musical composition an instance of that work. This claim has been often disputed: Jerrold Levinson persuasively argues that the history of production of a musical composition – that it was produced by a certain composer at a certain time – is essential to that work's identity (Levinson 1990: 95–7). In Levinson's view, the application of the allographic/autographic distinction to music is more complex than Goodman suggests.

Goodman's claim that only autographic arts are forgeable can also be questioned. His definition of forgery – an object that falsely purports to have a certain history of production – is nonetheless a useful starting point. It neatly explains the fact that a forgery need not copy an existing work. Thus, by Goodman's definition, van Meegeren's *Supper at Emmaus* counts as a forgery, since it falsely represents itself as painted by Vermeer, even though what was forged was not a particular work, but early Vermeer style. But if you can forge a painting by copying a painter's style, then it would seem that you can forge a musical or literary work as well, by copying its musical or literary style; for an allographic art the forger would copy certain characteristic relationships among symbol sequences, in order falsely to identify the work as the product of a certain maker or period. Musical compositions that falsely purport to be produced by Mozart, sonnets that falsely purport to be Elizabethan, twentieth-century violin works composed by Fritz Kreisler and attributed to eighteenth-century composers: all these are musical or literary fakes closely related to forgery as Goodman defines it. Forgery of autographic art works can thus be seen as a special case of a more general concept of forgery that applies equally to allographic artforms: a forgery would be an object, either abstract/symbolic or physical, with intentionally falsified origins. Given this definition, then the distinction between autographic and allographic symbol systems – assuming there is one – cannot be drawn by forgeability (Beardsley 1983: 225; Levinson 1990: 102).

If we accept Levinson's critique of Goodman's idea of musical identity, and if we accept the argument advanced earlier that all forms of art can be forged, then should we conclude that, despite the intuitive plausibility of the autographic/allographic difference, it has no significance? The distinction can perhaps be salvaged if it is recast as a difference in the way intentions are formulated and expressed in creating art. In some arts – performance arts, painting, sculpture, photography – the artist's intentions are expressed in the production of a unique physical or token event: a performance, a finished painting, an etched plate or an exposed negative. In other arts – musical composition, poetry, and conceptual art – the artist's intentions are expressed by creating a kind, or type, of object or event – a type of performance, reading, or situation – by means of a score, sequence of words or other notation.

Of course, as Goodman recognized (Goodman 1986: 291), artists can, and frequently do, work against the grain of standard practice, and blur the lines between these two ways of creating art (Ralls 1972: 6–8). Though painting is considered the most thoroughly autographic artform, the painter Sol Le Witt reportedly described his murals as musical scores that anyone could perform (Radnóti 1999: 148). Though music is usually considered allographic, jazz in its purest form is autographic, created as a unique token event.

For Goodman, forgeability determines an artform's allographic/autographic status, but the following relationship seems more plausible: how an art work is created, whether in allographic (notational) or autographic (physical) terms, determines how (not whether) it can be forged. If, for example, we take Le Witt at his word, then he has created allographic works, so that anyone could produce genuine 'Le Witts' by following his score. In this case, Le Witt's work could not be forged by copying: following his score would count as a performance. One could, however, forge Le Witt's work by inventing new painting scores in the Le Witt style and attributing them to him.

Similarly, Rubens's way of producing art works, by using studio assistants to execute works he composed and sketched, suggests he thought of 'a Rubens' as a type of picture rather than a unique physical product of his hand. A work from Rubens's studio might contain relatively little work by his own hand, though he often added finishing touches and final corrections. Rubens's assistants, some of whom were artists of great talent, can be seen as analogous to musical performers, in that their artistry consists in interpreting the composing artist's ideas. As a result, any work painted by an assistant that was based on the master's sketches and painted under his direction would count as genuine. But if Rubens had represented such paintings as 'autograph' work, or work from his own hand, then they would count as forgeries perpetrated by Rubens himself. It is also possible to imagine a disgruntled assistant setting up a personal shop and producing paintings based on discarded Rubens sketches. These would be forgeries insofar as they were falsely represented as exemplifying 'the Rubens type' as judged by Rubens's eyes.

Such cases reveal that Goodman's formulation – that a forgery is an object that falsely purports to have the history of production requisite for the (or an) original of the work – refers only obliquely, if at all, to the role of the artist's activities. Yet these intentional activities are central to what Goodman calls the 'production requisite' for the art work. Exactly how Rubens was engaged in making a particular work determines whether it is appropriately represented as a genuine Rubens, a genuine work from his workshop, or a forgery.

Similarly, with the phrase "object that falsely purports," Goodman glosses over the intentional activities of the forger. Though his phrase suggests it is the character of an object that determines a forgery, rather, whether something is a forgery or not is determined by the character of the copier's or forger's intentions. A clearly labeled copy is not a forgery, even though, if it were labeled falsely (and not falsely by accident), it could be one. Forgery thus requires deliberate deception (Beardsley 1983: 226). It is true that in the most familiar examples of forgery an object is crafted to suggest a false history of its origins. But Goodman's formula does not recognize a widespread form of forgery, in which an innocently crafted object is misrepresented; this occurs when a genuinely old workshop copy is sold as an original, or the work of a less well-known artist is attributed to more famous one (Friedlander 1941b: 195).

Some years after *Languages of Art*, in response to a criticism, Goodman acknowledges that the distinction between copies and forgeries depends on the intention to deceive (Goodman 1986: 291; Kennick 1985: 3–12). But because

Goodman's earlier definition of forgery does not mention deceptive intentions, it does not succeed in distinguishing innocent copies from forgeries. In a sense, even an innocent copy can be seen as falsely purporting to be old when it is painted in a currently archaic style. Even a restoration, however well-intentioned, suppresses an object's history when it hides all signs of its own painstaking role in creating the work's current appearance. By eliminating tears, cracks, and yellowing varnish, it falsely suggests that the history of the object stopped after its original production. Neither copies nor restorations, though they suggest false histories, are forgeries, however, because neither intends to deceive. In the case of restoration, erasing some of the object's more recent history is intended to allow us to appreciate its aesthetic character in close to its original form. Whether this is justified or not is a hotly debated issue, but the aim of restoration, which is not in question, is to allow the object to be seen and appreciated for what it is. Art forgery, on the other hand, requires that someone intentionally misrepresent an object's history, usually in order to inflate its aesthetic interest or value.

Danto and the appearance theory

While Goodman attempted to reconcile conflicting intuitions about the Appearance Theory, Arthur Danto more recently delivered it a direct blow. Danto argues that not only can identical-appearing objects differ in aesthetic value, but some of them may not be art works at all. He imagines a series of identical plain canvas squares painted in red; among them, one is a work by a minimalist artist, another is a "clever bit of Moscow landscape called 'Red Square,'" (Danto 1981: 2), and another happens to be painted the same color and shape for reasons that have nothing to do with art; perhaps it is a paint sample. Some of these rectangles, he claims, are works of art that vary in aesthetic significance and one is not art at all, even though there is nothing visual that distinguishes between any of them.

Despite the interest of Danto's intriguing series, its lesson should not be overdrawn. Though we can imagine a series of identical minimal art works, of the kind Danto describes, generated by independent ideas or even by chance, this scenario is not credible for traditional paintings. One cannot conceive of a series of painted canvases looking exactly like *Lucretia* each made independently with a different intention, including one that had no connection with art at all. Certainly few of us would believe that a present day painting indistinguishable from Rembrandt's *Lucretia* was not derived from it. In focusing exclusively on minimalist works (works in which appearance plays a minimal role) Danto's argument may make us forget that the most important knowledge we have of the intentions of painters or sculptors we derive from the precise appearance of their art works, not from the sort of verbal account of intentions that Danto uses to set up his example.

In the context Danto provides, however, we can see that Goodman's empirical claim – that what we know may change the way an art work looks to us – can be interpreted in at least three ways. First, in the spirit of Danto's red canvases, what we know may impose an external framework on a work of art, and thus change how we look at the work without changing anything we could visually identify within the work. Second, what we know may change how we identify and describe internal features of the work. This applies to the molecule-for-molecule replica of *Lucretia*, discussed earlier, which because it is machine-made rather than man-made, prompts our attention to features relevant to its machine-made origins. Here we might also think of Wittgenstein's much cited duck/rabbit picture, a simple line drawing that may look like either a duck or a rabbit, but not both at once. Knowing that it was intended by the artist as a duck might focus our attention on its duck features, and thus act on our visual experience of the drawing without changing its molecular structure. Third, what we know may give us access to data that is present in the work that we previously were unable to access. This is what happens when we begin to identify Rembrandt's special qualities of style from comparisons of his works with very similar non-Rembrandts. Concerning these three ways in which knowledge can affect a work's appearance, only the third way supports actual discrimination of an art work from its copy. In the first two ways, knowledge affects aesthetic experience even in the absence of any possible future discrimination. In the end, it is difficult to say which of these three interpretations best represents Goodman's position.

Originals and historical authenticity

Finally, however, our original question remains unanswered, either by Goodman's claim that a copy may someday be distinguishable from the original, or by Danto's radical, appearance-independent intentionalism. Why do we prefer an original art work over a copy when we cannot tell the difference? Recalling Danto's red canvases, it is hard to see why one would care if the particular canvas the minimal artist painted were switched with the paint sample, since either one would serve equally well to convey the artist's idea. As for Goodman, he tells us that an original Rembrandt may be some day distinguishable from a copy, but he gives us no justification for preferring to see originals rather than copies. After all, examining copies, just as much as examining originals, is part of learning to distinguish originals from copies. To make the case for preferring a Rembrandt, what is required is not just any visible distinguishing difference but a difference that provides grounds for such a preference.

One tempting answer to our original question invokes historical authenticity: people want to see a real Rembrandt or a real work of the minimalist painter for the same reason they want to see Martin Luther King's toothbrush. Though it is without aesthetic merit, the toothbrush is a causal connection between King and the visitors to his home who see it. No doubt this kind of physical link to a past life figures in our desire to see a genuine Rembrandt. Yet the desire to see a Rembrandt painting is different in some respects from our desire to see King's actual toothbrush. If we were promised we would see a molecule-for-molecule replica of the toothbrush, it would not satisfy our desire for actual contact with King and his life, even though the exact replica would give us the same visual information as the original toothbrush. When our attachment to an object is based on sentiment, as it is with a favorite teddy bear, a family heirloom, or an historical icon, an exact replica will not do. In the case of seeing the Rembrandt painting, however, the desire to have certain exact visual information is at least as important as the desire for authenticity: if there were an actual Rembrandt work that was too dirty or damaged to see very well, we might well prefer to see an exact copy of the painting as it originally was, if one were available. It is true that some degree of dirt and damage is tolerated in originals, perhaps on the grounds that if the object is not new it should not mislead us by looking new; the objections to the brand-new look of the restored Sistine Chapel ceiling may have such a basis. Nonetheless, when an art work is lost to sight completely by the ravages of time, we feel a great loss, even when the physical object remains as a relic of the artist's life. Our desire is not primarily for contact with Rembrandt – though we may desire that also – but for contact with the precise visual experience that Rembrandt envisioned that viewers would have. With the copy, we are uncertain whether the copyist inadvertently introduced alterations that the artist would have rejected. But if we are looking at the actual work from Rembrandt's hand, the causal connection tells us we are certainly seeing something of what he actually saw.

It is precisely because we ourselves cannot see much difference between original and copy, that we must trust to what we know: we want to know that what we see traces back to the original artist's acts of seeing. It has been pointed out that in the cases in which the original work is missing, as is the case with Greek sculptures we know only by way of Roman copies, we value the copies more highly than we would if the originals were available. This is taken to mean that we are not consistent in our preference for originals, or are unduly prejudiced against copies when originals do exist. But we may be expressing a perfectly consistent and sound policy: we wish to get information that is as close as possible to the originating source of a valued visual work. We in general prefer works that do not interpose another act of seeing, such as the copyist's, between our eyes and the artist's. But since our aim is to trace our own experience back to the originating visual experience, this aim can be, if need be, fulfilled in alternative ways.

In the original question, much is made of the fact that, in preferring the artist's own work, we are relying on what we know about the art, and not on what we can see. It has even been suggested that this is sheer snobbery, a result of what has been dubbed 'the Sotheby effect,' meaning that when we are told the work is great we read greatness into it to seem sophisticated (Harrison 1967–8: 121). But Goodman's intriguing argument suggests there is something legitimate in our preference for original art: we appear to recognize, even if not explicitly, that we are not always immediately conscious of how what we see (or taste or hear) is affecting us. It is because we know that art can affect us slowly, with repeated exposure, that we go to see Rembrandt whether or not in the short term we can see for ourselves anything special in his work.

The preference for quality

Our trust that an original Rembrandt will affect us over the long run is tied to assumptions about the quality of Rembrandt's work. If it were the practice to copy mediocre paintings line for line, it is not at all clear that people would prefer originals to copies. Certainly seeing a great Rubens copy is preferable to seeing a mediocre original. The widespread silence on the issue of quality in discussions of forgery and copies is understandable, given the difficulty of defining quality in art. But since it is too important to ignore, one can say at least this: one striking characteristic of a high-quality painting is the seamless integration of the ideas it expresses and the way it looks, which gives conceptual significance to even the smallest sensory detail. In Bellini's *The Madonna of the Meadow*, for example, because of the resonance between the deep, pure blue of the Virgin's robe and the transparent blue of the distant sky, we must attend to the exact hue of the robe to appreciate Bellini's idea of the Virgin's moral simplicity and heavenly nature. If concept and sensation are so closely linked, then we need a reasonably accurate idea of the work's conceptual content to grasp the salience of particular visual details.

Can it possibly be justifiable, on aesthetic grounds, to prefer to look at something because of what we know about it rather than what we can see in it? Yes, if what we know about a work of art and what we are able to see in it are so closely integrated that the smallest change in one can affect the other. There is a famous passage from Kant that bears on this point. In it, he speaks of the beauty of the sound of a nightingale on a summer evening, and comments that if we were to discover the sound is actually produced by a mischievous boy, "who knew how to produce this sound exactly like nature," the song would lose its charm (quoted in Sagoff 1983: 141). This phenomenon can be described somewhat differently: when we hear the sound of the boy while believing it to be a nightingale, we are deaf to all the sensory details that reveal that it is a boy. Our access to the concrete details that indicate human whistling depends on our having accurate beliefs about the cause of the sound.

For Kant the change experienced in identifying the boy as the sound's cause is a loss of charm; another listener, however, might discover added charm in a boy's skillful whistling, when the song is heard as such. An analogous added charm is felt when we learn that an ordinary-looking painting is, for example, an early Matisse. This added charm may come from the Sotheby effect. But knowing the work to be a Matisse may also give us access to subtle sensory information that was present to us but not put to conscious use before. We will be blind to these features, as we are deaf to the human sounds in the counterfeit nightingale song, if our ideas of a painting are too misinformed or too conventional (compared with the artist's) to attend to the subtleties that were the artist's concern. It may be, that is to say, a prerequisite for aesthetic response that we be fitted with concepts close enough to the artist's to provide access to the sensory discriminations that were built into the work. At the very least, this means seeing copies as copies and originals as products of the artist's mind, eyes and hand, synchronized to give conceptual weight to the subtlest sensory detail.

See also Art and knowledge, Painting, Music, Formalism.

References

Beardsley, M. (1983) "Notes on Forgery," in D. Dutton (ed.), *The Forger's Art*, Berkeley: University of California Press.

Bell, C. (1914) *Art*, London: Chatto and Windus.

Danto, A. (1981) *The Transfiguration of the Commonplace*, Cambridge, Mass.: Harvard University Press.

Friedlander, M. (1941a) "Artistic Quality: Original and Copy," *Burlington Magazine* 78: 143–51.

—— (1941b) "On Forgeries," *Burlington Magazine* 78: 192–6.

Goodman, N. (1976) *Languages of Art*, 2nd edn, Indianapolis: Hackett.

—— (1986) "A Note on Copies," *Journal of Aesthetics and Art Criticism* 44: 291–2.

Harrison, A. (1968) "Works of Art and Other Cultural Objects," *Proceedings of the Aristotelian Society* 68: 105–28.

Kennick, W. E. (1985) "Art and Inauthenticity," *Journal of Aesthetics and Art Criticism* 44: 3–12.

Levinson, J. (1990) "Autographic and Allographic Art Revisited," in *Music, Art, and Metaphysics*, Ithaca: Cornell University Press.

Meiland, J. (1983) "Originals, Copies, and Aesthetic Value," in D. Dutton (ed.), *The Forger's Art*, Berkeley: University of California Press.

Meyer L. (1983) "Forgery and the Anthropology of Art," in D. Dutton (ed.), *The Forger's Art*, Berkeley: University of California Press.

Radnóti, S. (1999) *The Fake: Forgery and its Place in Art*, Lanham: Rowman and Littlefield.

Ralls, A. (1972) "The Reproducibility of a Work of Art," *Philosophical Quarterly* 22: 1–18.

Sagoff, M. (1983) "The Aesthetic Status of Forgeries," in D. Dutton (ed.), *The Forger's Art*, Berkeley: University of California Press.

Further reading

Bowden, R. (1999) "What is Wrong with an Art Forgery?: An Anthropological Perspective," *Journal of Aesthetics and Art Criticism* 57: 333–43. (Discusses the differences between modern Western and nonliterate cultures with respect to art forgery, art copies and creativity.)

Dutton, D. (ed.) (1983) *The Forger's Art*, Berkeley: University of California Press. (Includes essays representing a range of views by important contributors.)

Janaway, C. (1997) "Two Kinds of Artistic Duplication," *British Journal of Aesthetics* 37: 1–14. (Argues against the possibility of autographic forgery in music and literature.)

—— (1999) "What a Musical Forgery Isn't," *British Journal of Aesthetics* 39: 62–71. (Takes issue with Levinson's account of music forgery.)

Margolis, J. (1998) "Farewell to Danto and Goodman," *British Journal of Aesthetics* 38: 353–74. (Compares and rejects the views of Danto and Goodman on art works, forgery, and perceivable differences.)

35

HIGH ART VERSUS LOW ART

John A. Fisher

Hamlet versus Bugs Bunny; string quartets versus rap music; Joseph K versus Sam Spade. Such contrasts instantly evoke a familiar cultural divide, typically expressed as the distinction between 'high' and 'low' art. In spite of its familiarity, however, there are different intuitions about the general contrast. Is it, for example, a contrast between *artforms* (for example poetry versus video games) or between genres *within* artforms (such as avant-garde versus romance novels), or is it a distinction between *individual works* in the same artform or genre (*Moses and Aaron* versus *Turandot*, *Lawrence of Arabia* versus *Plan 9 From Outer Space*, *I'm Looking Through You* versus *Louie, Louie*)?

The fuzziness of the distinction raises a number of basic questions. Do the terms express one fundamental distinction? Is that distinction theoretically coherent? Does it mark significant aesthetic differences? Finally, what is the relation of this distinction to the concept of art?

A paradoxical distinction

'High art' is the clearer half of the contrast. In typical use it certainly refers to paradigms of art: *Hamlet*, Eliot's *The Waste Land*, Beethoven's *Eroica*, *Swan Lake*, the paintings of Cézanne: indeed, museum paintings generally, classical music generally, poetry generally, and so forth. Now, if 'high art' denominates the central cases of art, and if by being central they delineate what it is to be art, it is natural to think of the term that contrasts with high art as denoting objects that are not really art, that are labeled 'art' only at best in a non-literal sense: art by courtesy only. In short, there is natural line of thought that suggests that the distinction between high and low art approximates the art/non-art distinction.

But then is low art *non*-art? As Ted Cohen wonders:

> If the distinction between high art and low art is like the distinction between art and non-art, then why do we need *both* distinctions? Suppose

409

I am already lumbered with an art/non-art device, shouldering it because I cannot seem to get along without it. Why do I also drag along a wedge for separating high art from low art? What extra work does it do?

(Cohen 1993: 152)

In spite of what he clearly sees as a puzzling relation between the two distinctions, Cohen contends that each distinction seems logically distinct and indeed indispensable.

One point seems clear: even though 'high' and 'low' read as adjectives of contrasting quality, we should not equate the high/low distinction with a third distinction, that between good and bad art. Although 'high art' certainly brings to mind canonical works in various artforms, there is much high art – paintings, poems, chamber music – that is uninspired, mediocre, minor, derivative, and so forth. Conversely, it does not seem plausible that *all* 'low art' could turn out to merit the status of art but be all bad. *If* rock music is art, then *some* recordings or performances – for example, by the Beatles, Bob Dylan, and Jimi Hendrix – are surely successful and important examples of art. Thus we cannot equate high art with good art and low art with bad art.

The distinction between high and low art is narrower than a distinction between high and low *culture*. The relation between the two distinctions is brought out by the sociologist Herbert Gans, who embeds the artifacts of high and low art in what he calls 'taste cultures.' These "consist of values, the cultural forms which express these values . . . and the media in which these are expressed . . . and insofar as ordinary consumer goods also express aesthetic values or functions, furnishings, clothes, appliances, and automobiles" (Gans 1974: 10). He then defines a taste public: "users who make similar choices of values and taste culture content will be described as publics of an individual taste culture, or *taste publics*" (ibid.: 11). Gans claims that there are *five* taste publics, defined by a combination of aesthetic values and socio-economic position: high culture, upper-middle culture, lower-middle culture, low culture and quasi-folk low culture. He thinks of each public as preferring and consuming different artforms. For example, "although it shares [television] with lower-middle culture publics, initially network programming catered extensively to low culture, for example, by providing Westerns, the comic action of Lucille Ball and Red Skelton, and situation comedies like 'Beverly Hillbillies'" (ibid.: 92).

Gans's analysis suggests that the high/low art distinction is based on distinctions of taste. Cohen (1999) supports the idea that there are high and low audiences. However, he does not accept the common assumption that high art is more important than low art, nor that works cannot appeal to both high and low audiences. He suggests, for example, that many of Hitchcock's movies have a 'bilateral' capacity to appeal to both audiences.

Contra Gans (1974, see also Bourdieu 1984), it may not be useful to think of the notion of taste as explained by social class. Noël Carroll (1998) rejects the idea that high art is art that appeals to "the dominant social classes" and in general that we can understand the distinction along class lines. As he notes, "a taste for popular art and an aversion to high art seems to cut across class lines, at least in contemporary American society" (Carroll 1998: 180). It seems safe to assume moreover that the main 'consumers' of high culture are people from the educated middle class.

It is plausible to think that, in fact, there are several overlapping but different distinctions that can underlie ordinary uses of 'high art' and 'low art.' Two are most significant from the perspective of aesthetics. The first is a distinction between two classes, either of media or of artforms/genres; for instance, between oil painting and television (media) or abstract paintings and television situation comedies (forms). This makes the distinction an offspring of the modern system of the arts. According to Kristeller (1992), eighteenth-century thinkers for the first time grouped the arts together into a separate and coherent group of activities and artifacts with a distinctive character. This group comprised: painting, sculpture, architecture, music, and poetry. Obviously, such a grouping was the foundation of the notion of art with a capital 'A,' which developed at the same time.

Since the eighteenth century new media have developed for a mass society: mass-produced books and visual prints, photography, motion pictures, radio, television, sound recordings, computers, the Internet, and so on. The technological and social changes during the last two hundred years have also led to a proliferation of artforms and genres, from Ukiyo-e prints to radio soap operas to horror movies and rock recordings. High/low construed as a distinction between groups of forms or genres, comes to this: certain traditional forms, those growing out of the modern system, are thought of as 'high art,' whereas the new forms tend to be thought of as 'low.' For example, at first movies were regarded as a 'low' artform compared to theater. Under this reading, it becomes clear why the high/low art distinction seems so closely related to the art/non-art distinction.

The second way of framing the distinction is more fine-grained; it is a distinction that classifies works *within* a pre-existing medium or artform. Starting with the contrast between folk or popular culture and aristocratic culture before the eighteenth century, consider that with the wide distribution and accessibility of cultural artifacts the taste and values of popular audiences came to play a significant role in the various artforms already in place. This led to the development of new sub-forms (penny novels, romance novels) as well as genres of standing artforms that appealed to popular taste (naive/folk painting of the nineteenth century, motel painting of the twentieth). In the twentieth century this has fueled a tendency for the most sophisticated instances of an artform, such as the novel, to become much more difficult (as in the work of Joyce and Pynchon) while simultaneously there has been a parallel development of works within the same artform appealing to a very broad audience (such as mass-market romance and gothic horror novels).

Some theorists (Novitz 1992, Levine 1988) write as if the high/low distinction is a twentieth-century bias. However, there has always been a tendency to rank and to divide artforms into higher and lower. Ranking the arts was a common activity of thinkers from the renaissance through the eighteenth century. Leonardo, for instance, argued that painting was the supreme art, superior to poetry, music and sculpture (Kemp 1989). Equally important was the influential distinction in the classical rhetorical tradition between high, middle and low styles. Dionysius of Helicarnassus, for instance, divided styles into the elegant, the middle and the severely plain (Wimsatt and Brooks 1957).

The history of rock and roll music illustrates the continuing tendency to subdivide and rank genres. Young consumers of rock music today distinguish many genres just within electronic pop music: jungle, rave, house, deep house, tech house, drum and bass, ambient, trip hop, big beat, bhangra, acid, and they do so to embrace some and reject others. They regard some forms of pop music as superior and ultra-sophisticated and other forms as beneath contempt (consider the common view of disco). Such hierarchies may function to create a distinctive identity and to provide a means for fans to distinguish themselves (Bourdieu 1984) from others who prefer a different type of music. So, relative to classical music and its audience, all pop genres may seem 'low' art, whereas to fans of electronica, main-stream rock may seem hopelessly naive and common compared to their music. The same story can be told for comics. While comic strips are a low or mass artform relative to other artforms, the artform subdivides into low or mass strips (Dagwood) and sophisticated, high strips (*Zippy, The Pinhead*).

No doubt the value difference between high and low disturbs modern egalitarian thinkers. Where does this hierarchy come from? It could lie in the different audiences meant to receive the different styles or forms and the differential status of these targeted audiences. In the tradition, there is also a suggestion, contained in the notion of elevated versus common taste, that the high/low distinction lies within ourselves, that it refers to those aspects of spectators (knowledge, opinions, mental functions, behavior and values) which are presupposed by a given text or art work. Consider that comedy, for example, as a stimulus to laugh has always been cast into the realm of lower art. One familiar thought is that comedy, as Plato suggests in Book X of *The Republic*, appeals to certain human weaknesses. Yet comedy is arguably as important, valuable and necessary as other more 'elevated' forms of performance or writing. Rock music has also been attacked because of the perception that it appeals to inferior aspects of the listener. As Shusterman notes, for cultural critic Alan Bloom, "the problem with rock is its deep appeal to 'sensuality' and 'sexual desire'... It is not only not reasonable, it is hostile to reason" (Shusterman 1991: 206).

It is plausible to conclude that the value difference implied by the high/ low art distinction has been influenced in part by our tendency to grade the types of cognition and character involved in appreciating various genres of artifacts. As such, it appears to presuppose unexamined, traditional ideas about the value of various mental states and attitudes.

Is the high/low distinction real?

In spite of the fact that the high/low distinction in various guises runs deeply through our cultural life, some thinkers have questioned whether it is philosophically legitimate. Two questions can be raised. Are there two distinct classes of cultural artifact? And if there are, is there in fact a distinct difference in aesthetic value between the two classes?

Before formulating different positions on the distinction, we should note that because it sounds less pejorative, theorists usually speak of 'popular' art rather than low art, and they accordingly examine the contrast between high art and popular art. Another common contrast is between high art and mass art. (Whether the concepts of popular art and mass art are identical will be posed later.)

Kaplan (1972) finds many characteristic differences between popular art and high art. Popular art is dominated by a need for familiar forms, an intolerance of ambiguity, a tendency toward easiness and indulgence in stimulated emotion. In spite of all this he thinks there "is a time and place even for popular art. Champagne and Napoleon brandy are admittedly the best of beverages; but on a Sunday afternoon in the ballpark we want a coke or maybe a glass of beer" (ibid.: 62). We might call this the 'tolerant hierarchical' view: there are two characteristically different classes of works: art and popular 'art'; the former is superior to the latter, but the latter has its place. By contrast, critics of popular art (discussed later) accept that there are two groups of artforms with significant characteristic differences, but they find popular art to be essentially flawed. We can call their position 'intolerant hierarchicalism.'

Cohen (1999) argues that there are two classes of works, but he is more than simply tolerant of them. He finds each group significantly valuable. Suppose then, one thinks there is a sort of hierarchy, yet each group meets important but different aesthetic needs (recall comedy and tragedy). We might call such a position 'pluralistic hierarchicalism.' Such a position should be distinguished from a *relativistic* position, which holds that there are two or more taste cultures, to use Gans's term, but that there are no grounds for grading any one or its set of artifacts as higher than another: "all taste cultures are of equal worth" (Gans 1974: x–xi).

Novitz (1992) rejects all these positions, even relativism, because they all suppose that there are two or more classes of art works that have significant aesthetic differences. (Relativism supposes that there are characteristically different artforms for different social groups.) The relativist merely denies that any one class is superior to any other. Novitz denies in particular that there any substantive aesthetic differences between popular art works and high art. It is merely a matter of social convention to differentiate them. Call this the 'conventionalist' position. Novitz notes that the customary way of ascribing a higher status to high art and a lower status to popular art (as by hierarchical-ists) is to ascribe systematic differences to works in the respective categories. Yet, there are no essential differences of the kind claimed: "there are neither formal nor affective properties which distinguish the high from the popular in art" (Novitz 1992: 24), nor is there a difference in the way works are produced, such as the difference between the individual genius and a production team.

Since there is no substantive aesthetic difference between low and high art, Novitz suggests that the distinction is artificial and socially constructed to serve a political function, namely to make that art that avoids political, moral and economic issues, in short, *high art*, the only acceptable art. High art is art that does not threaten the interests of the dominant classes. Levine too suggests that the distinction is of recent origin and has a social function. He points out that Shakespeare and opera were enjoyed by all classes in the nineteenth century. Not quite as conventionalist as Novitz, Levine notes that "like Shakespearean drama. . . opera was an artform that was *simultaneously* popular and elite" (Levine 1988: 88). As against this free exchange of cultural products between all classes, cultural products came to be removed from the marketplace, rescued and "placed, significantly, in concert halls, opera houses, and museums that often resembled temples, to be perused, enjoyed and protected by the initiated – those who had the inclination, the leisure, and the knowledge to appreciate them" (ibid.: 230). Levine's account suggests another way to put conventionalism: works in themselves are neither high nor low, instead high or low depends on how art works are regarded and treated. Indeed, it is clear that works migrate between the categories. Not only have plays and operas migrated from popular to high, but works by Mozart, Beethoven, Leonardo and Monet have moved out of concert halls and museums to movie soundtracks and T-shirts. In Levine's view, high art's lack of 'accessibility' is a matter not so much of its intrinsic features but of the patterns of behavior that have become gatekeepers for entrée into the temples of culture.

Mass art

Noël Carroll (1998) argues that the key theoretical concept is not that of popular art but of *mass art*. He thinks of mass art (art that is mass-produced and distributed in multiple quantities) as a *species* of popular art, which he defines as either the art of the 'common people' or "art that is liked by lots of people" (Carroll 1998: 185). He notes that societies throughout history have had popular art. In contrast to traditional popular art, he proposes that something quite distinctive has occurred in industrial societies over the last two centuries, amounting to the creation of a new sort of art characteristic of mass, industrial society.

The most prominent forerunner of Carroll's idea is Walter Benjamin's account of the effects of mass reproduction on art. Benjamin (1969) argued that the capacity to reproduce art works photographically had altered the nature of art, erasing its 'aura' by removing its uniqueness and inaccessibility. Benjamin thought that the new forms of mass art, for example, movies and photography, were appropriate to a new historical era. He proposed that they were able to foster new and potentially progressive forms of consciousness. For example, movies, he thought, function very differently from stage performances. The camera's independence from the actor both removes the actor's aura and gives the audience a critical distance that it previously lacked. Movies, then, not only express the next epoch in consciousness but are potentially liberating.

Carroll's theorizing begins with the many criticisms of popular and mass art that have been offered by prominent twentieth-century thinkers, such as Dwight MacDonald (1957), Clement Greenberg (1986), R. G. Collingwood (1958) and Theodore Adorno. He points out that the arguments of these thinkers – whether advanced against "amusement art" (Collingwood) or the "culture industry" (Adorno) – apply principally to mass art not to popular art in general.

What sort of worries have theorists expressed concerning mass art? Carroll identifies several (see also Shusterman 1992):

1 *Massification.* In order to appeal to a mass audience, the mass work must gravitate "toward the lowest level of taste, sensitivity, and intelligence" (Carroll 1998: 23). This is not compatible with distinctive expression (unique expression flowing from a personal vision), yet distinctive expression is what art should aim at.
2 *Passivity.* Genuine art should require active spectatorship. But mass or popular art, in order to generate broad appeal and accessibility, abets passive reception. It is easy and safe.
3 *The formulaic.* A common complaint is that popular or mass art is formulaic, whereas real art is original in its conception and in its goals.
4 *Autonomy.* Many theorists view the arts from the perspective of political

theory. Adorno, for example, held that a central function of art is to provide a critical perspective on society; its goal should be liberation from the social, economic and political realities. To that end, it needs to be free from commercial pressures (Carroll 1998; Gracyk 1996). But to be popular, arts such as pop music and jazz have to sacrifice their autonomy. They must mix structural predictability with a dash of what Adorno called 'pseudo-individualization,' in the form of passages of improvisation. The end result is merely to reinforce the economic system and social reality rather than to encourage a more radical and liberated consciousness.

These objections tend to criticize mass or popular art relative to 'genuine' art. They urge either that mass art works are not genuine art or that they do not perform the same functions as genuine art (and these functions are either aesthetically valuable or good for society). One prominent tendency of the critics is to deny the status of art to all popular art. But is this going too far? As Shusterman notes, "what philosophers need to consider . . . is the validity of arguments claiming to show that popular art is *necessarily* an aesthetic failure" (Shusterman 1992: 337, emphasis added). Against such a strong claim, Shusterman and Carroll show that there are counter-examples, that is, examples of popular or mass art that are not, for instance, any more formulaic than examples of high art.

What is Carroll's account of 'mass art'? He proposes three conditions that are individually necessary and jointly sufficient for something to be mass art. It must be:

1 a multiple instance or type art work
2 produced and distributed by a mass technology
3 "intentionally designed to gravitate in its structural choices (for example, its narrative forms, symbolism, intended affect, and even its content) toward those choices that promise accessibility with minimum effort . . . for the largest number of untutored (or relatively untutored) audiences" (Carroll 1998: 196).

The first condition contains two claims about mass art works. First, by using the term 'art works,' Carroll literally means to define mass works as art in the same way that string quartets and sculptures are art. The artifacts in question also have to be capable of having multiple tokens, such as copies of a novel or screenings of a movie. Since string quartets and cast sculpture are capable of multiple instances, it is the second and third conditions that distinguish *mass* art.

The second condition requires that the work be mass-produced and mass-distributed. This eliminates multiple-instance traditional art. It also rules out traditional popular art: "mass art is popular art, but a noteworthy subspecies, distinguished by its reliance upon mass delivery systems capable of reaching non-overlapping receptions sites simultaneously" (Carroll 1998: 199). Thus pop recordings qualify as mass art, whereas live performances of a computer-composed string quartet would not. Radio broadcasts can count – for example, Goon shows – but they must meet the other conditions. A broadcast of a live musical performance, *qua* broadcast, would not meet the first condition of being an art work.

The second condition has the odd consequence that a rock concert, although a paradigm of low or popular art to many thinkers, is not mass art. Even though a rock concert is produced by electronic technology, it is not delivered to multiple sites simultaneously. So neither a rock concert nor a broadcast of a rock concert is mass art, for Carroll, although if the broadcast contributes a layer of additional manipulation (as in Scorsese's movie of The Band's last concert, *The Last Waltz*), it could itself be a mass art work.

The third condition reflects the influence of popular taste on mass art. Carroll allows that some avant-garde art works could meet the first two conditions: avant-garde films or novels. What rules them out as mass art is the third condition, which turns a common complaint about mass art – its easy accessibility – into one of its defining characteristics. Carroll notes that to make a work broadly accessible, it must be constructed to avoid the difficulties and challenges of avant-garde art as well as the need to have extensive background knowledge. It must incorporate content that has broad appeal.

Many questions could be raised about Carroll's theory. The first condition will be troubling to those who doubt that works of mass art are genuine art. This condition says that it follows as an analysis of the concept of mass art that *all* mass art works are art. Carroll is not saying that we ought to *extend* the notion of art to include mass art works, but rather that we already *do* count them as art. However, it is unclear that we possess a concept of mass art for which this strong claim is true.

What are we to include in the class of mass arts? Carroll suggests that "roughly stated, the extension of the items that I intend my theory to capture includes: popular commercial films, TV, commercial photography, pop music, broadcast radio, computer video games, comic strips, world wide web sites, and pulp literature" (Carroll 1998: 173). But the first condition of the analysis gives us no guidance on what to include and what to exclude. There are many artifacts that appear to meet conditions (2) and (3) but are not obvious examples of art: talk radio shows, Levi blue jeans, ads on TV, designer table-settings, board games, and automobiles.

We thus require a further restriction on which mass-produced types of artifact count as mass art. Carroll proposes that "inasmuch as mass art-forms are descended from traditional art-forms, they have a prima-facie claim to art status"

(Carroll 1998: 197). This suggests that mass art works are those types of mass-produced multiple-instance artifacts meeting conditions (2) and (3) *and* which are descended from traditional artforms. This fits some artforms well, especially movies, which could be regarded as descended from stage plays. Perhaps also photography can be regarded as in a way descended from more traditional visual arts, such as painting and lithography. But then any use of photography would still count as art, including any commercial photography (since it would be descended from earlier artforms). Although Carroll says that he wants to include 'commercial photography,' one would think that not *all* commercial photographs – such as those in newspaper advertising supplements – ought to be regarded as art works (even bad ones). It appears then that the suggested principle rules out very little. The counter-examples suggested above might all be left in. For instance, nationally syndicated talk radio programs bear similarities to paradigm artforms: they are entertainments involving story-telling, role playing, and collaborative improvization that might be regarded as descended from earlier radio and folk genres.

We should note that these counter-examples to Carroll's first condition do not invalidate his whole analysis. Subtracting the claim that all instances are art, the rest of the analysis might still stand as an adequate account of mass art.

Carroll's third condition claims, as a defining feature, that mass arts are easy and undemanding. Carroll theorizes that this is a necessary design characteristic required to achieve mass popularity. But even if we think in terms of statistical tendencies, rather than in terms of essential conditions, it is not as obvious as many assume. Undoubtedly, each genre makes *different* demands, but it can be questioned whether serious artforms on average make more demands on their audiences than popular artforms (Gould 1999). There are of course, obvious differences that do not necessarily imply aesthetic value, such as the difference in length between the average rock song and the average classical piece of music. But length is not everything anyway: both techno pop music and minimalist art music pieces tend to be long with slowly evolving repetitive structures, and neither would be regarded as difficult. Similarly, popular novels are frequently as long as so-called 'literature.' Moreover, while being formally simple, rock songs may make greater demands on listeners in terms of the raw emotions expressed and the sheer power and discordance of the sounds than the average piece of chamber music. Are the demands, intellectual and emotional, of a Hitchcock or Kubrick movie, an episode of the TV program *Homicide* or a Hannibal Lecter novel easy? Are the lyrics of pre-1968 Bob Dylan or the Brazilian Caetano Veloso any less demanding than the average poem? Is Auden any wittier than Lorenz Hart or Cole Porter? Is a typical avant-garde narrative any harder than the backwards episode of *Seinfeld* which starts with the last event in a time sequence and works sequentially backward?

Two points might be made against such counter-examples. First, works of popular art may have several levels. Although there is always more to analyze in any Hollywood movie or pop song, the average viewer does not have to think about those issues to enjoy it. Still, possessing an accessible surface does not appear to separate mass art from high art. With the exception of some avant-garde art, does not most high art include an accessible level? A second point is that highlighting the very best examples of mass art does not refute the notion that *on average* mass art must be easier and more predictable than high art. Yet, it is suggestive that *Seinfeld* was for a time one of the most popular shows on television even though it was based on imaginative, even absurdist premises that were arguably as original as the average new play or literary novel.

Attending to low/mass art

Whether fully justified or not, it is clear that popular and mass artforms are being taken more and more seriously by a wide range of thinkers. This should have far-reaching effects on aesthetics. It is no exaggeration to say that crafting a theory to fit avant-garde art works, such as Duchamp's urinal, *Fountain*, has been the major preoccupation of art theorists in the twentieth century. The original institutional definition of art (Dickie 1969) with its appeal to an art world able to confer the status of art onto anything, was one such attempt. Attempting to accommodate popular artforms may be the next major preoccupation of theories of art.

There may also be ontological consequences. Carroll (1998) holds that mass art works merit their own general account of what sorts of things they are. Mass art works are neither unique physical objects (like paintings) nor performed and inter-preted objects (like plays and musical works). He suggests that an account of the ontology of movies can be extended to other mass-artforms, such as photography, broadcast radio and television, and sound recordings. His idea is that all such art works are types that have tokens mechanically generated from a template (film print, CD, and so on). In a similar vein, others have argued that in rock music the recording and not the 'song' in the traditional sense is the primary art work (Gracyk 1996, Fisher 1998) and that tokens of the rock musical work are produced by playback of the original authentic recording. This contradicts the usual view that musical works may be identified with an abstracted sound structure that musicians can instantiate any time they play a work's score. Accounts that emphasize the importance of the recording in rock music imply that the ontology of rock musical works is more like that of lithographs than it is like classical musical works.

To take popular and mass arts as seriously as high art is finally to question some of the central ideas of aesthetic theory. Because such artforms are commercial and often functional (as is a Donald Duck mouse pad), they lack the autonomy traditionally expected of art; they are not instances of art for art's sake in any sense. Not only are they controlled by commercial and functional goals, but the type of response expected from a normal audience member scarcely conforms to traditional notions of aesthetic judgement. At one extreme, some mass artforms may not be consciously attended to, as is the case, for example, in movie sound-tracks and Muzak. Moreover, when popular or mass art works are attended to, they may not be approached with psychological distance (consider a rock concert) or disinterest (consider the commitment of fans). As opposed to the free play of the cognitive faculties of imagination and understanding that is the sole mechanism of aesthetic response in Kant's aesthetic theory, the appreciation of popular music, for example, involves non-intellectual bodily responses: dancing, singing (Shusterman 1991). Lastly, the very notion of an independent art object may be undermined by the interactive musical, textual and visual works now being developed for computers and the internet. It seems likely that many of the favored concepts and attitudes of traditional aesthetics will at the very least have to be revised as the attention of aestheticians shifts to mass and popular art works.

See also Taste, Definitions of art, The aesthetic, Aesthetic universals, Humor, Photography, Film, Criticism.

References

Adorno, T. (1997) *Aesthetic Theory*, trans. R. Hullot-Kentor, Minneapolis: University of Minnesota Press

Benjamin, W. (1969) "The Work of Art in the Age of Mechanical Reproduction," *Illuminations*, trans. H. Zohn, New York: Shocken.

Bourdieu, P. (1984) *Distinction: A Social Critique of the Judgement of Taste*, Cambridge, Mass.: Harvard University Press.

Carroll, N. (1998) *A Philosophy of Mass Art*, Oxford: Oxford University Press.

Cohen, T. (1993) "High and Low Thinking About High and Low Art," *Journal of Aesthetics and Art Criticism* 51: 151–6.

—— (1999) "High and Low Art, and High and Low Audiences," *Journal of Aesthetics and Art Criticism* 57: 137–43.

Collingwood, R. G. (1958) *The Principles of Art*, Oxford: Oxford University Press.

Dickie, G. (1969) "Defining Art," *American Philosophical Quarterly* 6: 253–6.

Fisher, J. (1998) "Rock 'n' Recording: The Ontological Complexity of Rock Music," in P. Alperson (ed.), *Musical Worlds: New Directions in the Philosophy of Music*, University Park: Pennsylvania State University Press.

Gans, H. (1974) *Popular Culture and High Culture*, New York: Basic Books.

Gould, T. (1999) "Pursuing the Popular," *Journal of Aesthetics and Art Criticism* 57: 119–35.

Gracyk, T. (1996) *Rhythm and Noise: An Aesthetics of Rock*, Durham: Duke University Press.

Greenberg, C. (1986) "Avant-Garde and Kitsch," in *Collected Essays and Criticism*, vol. 1, Chicago: University of Chicago Press.

Kaplan, A. (1972) "The Aesthetics of the Popular Arts," in J. B. Hall and B. Ulanov (eds), *Modern Culture and the Arts*, 2nd edn, New York: McGraw-Hill.

Kemp, M. (ed.) (1989) *Leonardo on Painting*, New Haven: Yale University Press.

Kristeller, P. O. (1992) "The Modern System of the Arts," in P. Kivy (ed.), *Essays on the History of Aesthetics*, Rochester: University of Rochester Press.

Levine, L. (1988) *Highbrow/Lowbrow: The Emergence of Cultural Hierarchy in America*, Cambridge, Mass.: Harvard University Press.

MacDonald, D. (1957) "A Theory of Mass Culture," in B. Rosenberg and D. M. White (eds), *Mass Culture: The Popular Arts in America*, New York: Free Press.

Novitz, D. (1992) *The Boundaries of Art*, Philadelphia: Temple University Press.

Plato (1997) *Complete Works*, ed. J. M. Cooper, Indianapolis: Hackett.

Shusterman, R. (1991) "Form and Funk: The Aesthetic Challenge of Popular Art," *British Journal of Aesthetics*, 31: 203–13.

—— (1992) "Popular Art," in D. Cooper (ed.), *A Companion to Aesthetics*, Oxford: Blackwell.

Wimsatt, W. and Brooks, C. (1957) *Literary Criticism: A Short History*, New York: Knopf.

Further reading

Adorno, T. (1995) "On the Fetish Character in Music and the Regression of Listening," in A. Neill and A. Ridley (eds), *The Philosophy of Art: Readings Ancient and Modern*, New York: McGraw-Hill. (A good introduction to Adorno's critique of the culture industry.)

Brantlinger, P. (1983) *Bread and Circuses: Theories of Mass Culture as Social Decay*, Ithaca: Cornell University Press. (An extended treatment of critiques of mass culture that interpret it as a symptom of social decay.)

Shusterman, R. (1992) *Pragmatist Aesthetics: Living Beauty, Rethinking Art*, Oxford: Blackwell. (Chapters 7 and 8 offer a treatment of the high/low distinction from the point of view of pragmatism.)

36
ENVIRONMENTAL AESTHETICS

Allen Carlson

Environmental aesthetics is one of the two or three major new fields of aesthetics to emerge in the second half of the twentieth century. It focuses on philosophical issues concerning aesthetic appreciation of the world at large and, moreover, the world as it is constituted not simply by objects but also by larger environmental units. Thus, environmental aesthetics extends beyond the narrow confines of the art world and our appreciation of works of art to the aesthetic appreciation of environments, not only natural ones, but also our various human-influenced and human-constructed environments. However, although the field has come into its own only recently and treats human as well as natural environments, it has historical roots in earlier work on the aesthetics of nature. To understand the current state of the field, it is useful to briefly examine this historical background and the developments that followed from it.

Historical roots

The historical roots of environmental aesthetics lie in the ideas about aesthetic appreciation developed in the eighteenth century and given classic expression by Kant. Central to this approach was the concept of disinterestedness, in virtue of which aesthetic experience was construed as distanced from everyday interests, such as the practical and the personal. The coupling of the concept of disinterestedness with the eighteenth-century fascination with the natural world resulted in a rich tradition of landscape appreciation. With the aid of disinterestedness not only could domesticated, rural countrysides be seen as beautiful, but even the wildest of natural environments could be appreciated as sublime. Moreover, between the beautiful and the sublime, disinterestedness made space for the emergence of a even more powerful mode of landscape appreciation, the picturesque. Initially the idea of the picturesque was tied to a particular sort of landscape having those features common in the landscape paintings of the day. However, it ultimately developed as a more general mode of appreciation that could facilitate the aesthetic experience of any kind of environment simply by focusing attention on picture-like qualities involving sensory surface and formal composition. The upshot was an eighteenth-century aesthetic synthesis having disinterestedness as the central theoretical concept, landscapes as the paradigm objects of aesthetic appreciation, and formalistic, picturesque appreciation as the favored mode for such objects.

The eighteenth-century aesthetic synthesis, however, did not come down to the present completely intact, and the current state of environmental aesthetics is as much a function of the changes it underwent as of the synthesis itself. Chief among these changes were the ascendence of works of art and the decline of landscapes as paradigm objects of aesthetic appreciation. This shift in emphasis may be traced to a number of sources, such as the solidification of the so-called modern system of the arts, the prominence given to art as opposed to nature in Hegel's philosophical system, and the expanded importance of the artifactual as opposed to the natural in western civilization as a whole. Whatever the causes, however, and in spite of the Romantic period's seeming infatuation with nature, the overall result was that within philosophical aesthetics the aesthetic appreciation of the natural world was increasingly marginalized. Under the lingering spell of the picturesque, it ultimately came to be equated with little more than the appreciation of those landscapes especially suited for disinterested, formalistic appreciation: grand scenes that could be easily composed to enhance picture-like sensory and formal qualities.

Although lacking the nature world as their main focus, the other key elements of the eighteenth-century synthesis, disinterestedness and the formalistic mode of appreciation, nonetheless survived into the twentieth century. Indeed, at the beginning of the century each was given renewed life, as exemplified by the classic reinterpretation of disinterestedness in Edward Bullough's psychical distance theory and by the uncompromising formalism of Clive Bell's theory of art. Moreover, with Bullough and Bell the theoretical marginalization of the aesthetic appreciation of anything other than art was strongly reaffirmed. Although Bullough mentioned the appreciation of fog at sea, his main example was *Othello,* and psychical distance was designed to function primarily in the appreciation of art. Bell was even more extreme in the exclusiveness of his focus on art, suggesting that the paradigmatic aesthetic response, a special aesthetic emotion, was typically evoked only by art.

Background

The relevance of the early twentieth-century retrenchment of disinterestedness and formalism to the development of environmental aesthetics is to be found in the fact that a major theme of mid-twentieth century analytic aesthetics involved the rejection of both disinterestedness and formalism. The rejection began with the development of the expressionist theory of art and reached its climax in the institutional theory of art. The result was a change in the concept of aesthetic appreciation significant enough to be thought of as a paradigm shift: a change from the old idea of disinterested contemplation of the sensory and formal qualities of an isolated and solitary object of art to a new paradigm of emotionally and cognitively rich engagement with a cultural artifact, intentionally created by a designing intellect, informed by both art-historical traditions and art-critical practices, and deeply embedded in a complex, many-faceted art world. Somewhat ironically, the relevance of this paradigm shift to the development of environmental aesthetics lies in the fact that the new paradigm was tailored almost exclusively to suit art appreciation. The resources introduced to replace the doctrines of disinterestedness and formalism – the designing intellect, the art-historical traditions, the art-critical practices, and the art world itself – have little if any application to the appreciation of anything other than art. Thus, the aesthetic appreciation of the world beyond the art world was left behind, seemingly involving at best only distanced contemplation of sensory and formal qualities.

In the second half of the twentieth century, this state of affairs expressed itself in two developments, which constitute the immediate background to the rise of environmental aesthetics. The first was that in developing and defending the new paradigm of aesthetic appreciation, analytic aesthetics completely abandoned any remaining interest in the aesthetics of anything other than art. The abandonment was institutionalized by virtually equating philosophical aesthetics with philosophy of art. The key textbook in the field was subtitled *Problems in the Philosophy of Criticism* and the two major anthologies bore the titles *Philosophy Looks at the Arts* and *Art and Philosophy*. With a total of 1,527 pages among them, none of these three volumes, each a classic of its kind, even mentioned the aesthetics of nature. Moreover, when nature was alluded to by analytic aestheticians, its appreciation was typically treated as basically subjective and, in comparison with that of art, of less aesthetic interest. This was in part just because nature lacks key features of the new paradigm, such as the designing intellect, the art-historical traditions, and the art-critical practices, that were taken to give art appreciation both objectivity and interest. This development reached its extreme in the idea that not only is philosophical aesthetics equivalent to philosophy of art, but, moreover, aesthetic appreciation itself is limited to art. In line with the new paradigm and its apparently exclusive tie to art, some philosophers contended that the appreciation of the natural world is simply not aesthetic appreciation. (Mannison 1980, Elliot 1982).

The second development constituting the immediate background to the rise of environmental aesthetics involved the real world beyond both philosophical aesthetics and the art world. It related to the new public awareness of the aesthetic quality of the environment that began to evolve early in the second half of the twentieth century (Blake 1964, Lewis *et al.* 1973). The awareness caused a difficulty, since, given the developments in philosophical aesthetics, individuals concerned about the aesthetics of the world at large were left with few theoretical resources other than the old paradigm of distanced contemplation of sensory and formal qualities. This had two ramifications. On the one hand, those charged with addressing the concerns about the aesthetic state of the environment, such as landscape architects, environmental planners, and landscape assessors, embraced assessment, planning, and design approaches that focused primarily on sensory, formal qualities of scenic views (Litton 1968, USDA 1972). On the other hand, many individuals, whose concerns can be characterized as environmentalist, reacted negatively both to the old paradigm itself and to its utilization in landscape management. Some saw the old paradigm as improperly accenting the scenic to the exclusion of the rest of the environment (Leopold 1966). Others, suspecting that aesthetic appreciation of the natural world is inherently subjective and trivial, flirted with the idea that it has little positive or perhaps even negative influence on environmental issues (Shepard 1967).

The rise of environmental aesthetics

The rise of environmental aesthetics was initially in direct response to the two developments just mentioned. It originated in the renewed theoretical interest in the aesthetics of nature that surfaced shortly after mid-twentieth century. This is evident in the title of the article that almost single-handedly launched the renewal: Hepburn's "Contemporary Aesthetics and the Neglect of Natural Beauty" (Hepburn 1966). Reacting to the treatment of the appreciation of nature within analytic aesthetics, Hepburn argued that those features that other philosophers viewed as aesthetic deficiencies in the natural world, and thus as reasons for deeming its appreciation trivial, subjective, and/or even non-aesthetic, are actually sources for a different kind of and potentially very rich aesthetic experience. He emphasized the fact that since the natural world is not constrained by things such as designing intellects, art-historical traditions, and art-critical practices, it facilitates an open, engaging, and creative mode of appreciation. However, Hepburn also demonstrated that there is in the appreciation of nature, as in the appreciation of art, a movement from trivial to serious aesthetic experience. He argued that if we are to realize this serious kind of aesthetic experience of nature, then the open, engaging, creative appreciation must be guided by an understanding of the real nature of the natural world.

In this way, Hepburn addressed both the problem of the differences between art and nature concerning the resources available for constituting aesthetic appreciation, and the problem of the appreciation of the natural environment being limited to the old paradigm of distanced contemplation of sensory and formal qualities. His work laid the foundation for a new paradigm for environmental aesthetic appreciation: a paradigm that, in stressing both the openness of the natural environment and the significance of our understanding of it, facilitated an aesthetic experience of the natural world that is as emotionally and cognitively rich as that which we can have with art. This new paradigm stands at the center of environmental aesthetics. Its reflection may be seen in many of the developments in the field that occurred in the last part of the twentieth century, as well as in the general shape that the field has come to have. To appreciate the current state of environmental aesthetics, it is useful to examine each of these developments.

Some of the relatively early developments in environmental aesthetics focused on the applied side of the field. They involved the critique of empirical work that was being done in response to the growing public concern about the aesthetic state of the environment. The critique paralleled Hepburn's rejection of the assumptions implicit in the old paradigm of distanced contemplation of sensory and formal qualities. For example, Carlson argued that the landscape assessment, planning, and design techniques being used in the practical management of landscapes were inadequate in being fixated on picturesque scenery and committed to formalism, and that in general the public debate over the aesthetic state of the environment presupposed an overly narrow, formalistic idea of what constituted aesthetic quality (Carlson 1976, 1977). Appleton identified similar problems and attributed them to a lack of adequate theoretical work, charging that empirical research was being carried on in what he termed a "theoretical vacuum" (Appleton 1975b). The call to fill this vacuum resulted in various responses: there were attempts to provide sociobiological underpinnings for the aesthetic appreciation of nature, such as Appleton's prospect-refuge theory (Appleton 1975a), as well as a wide range of theoretical models of aesthetic response grounded in, for example, developmental and environmental psychology (Kaplan and Kaplan 1989, Bourassa 1991). There are a number of overviews of this kind of work (Zube 1984, Cats-Baril and Gibson 1986, Carlson 1998) as well as some useful collections (Saarinen et al. 1984, Nasar 1988). In addition, there were periodic attempts to link empirical and applied research with theoretical work originating in the more philosophical side of environmental aesthetics (Sadler and Carlson 1982, Eaton 1989, Carlson 1990).

The developments on the philosophical side of environmental aesthetics can be grouped around two focal points. Each involves a reaction to one aspect of the old paradigm of aesthetic appreciation as distanced contemplation of sensory and formal qualities, and each was foreshadowed by a central theme in Hepburn's seminal article. One of the two is a direct response to the traditional idea of aesthetic appreciation as distanced contemplation, and is related to Hepburn's suggestion that the natural environment facilitates an open, engaging, and creative mode of appreciation. The other is a reaction to the old paradigm's nearly exclusive focus on sensory and formal qualities, and pursues Hepburn's insight that aesthetic appreciation of the natural world, although open, engaging, and creative, must yet be guided by an understanding of its real nature.

The aesthetics of engagement and related views

The former of the two philosophical developments mirrors the rejection of disinterestedness as central to the aesthetic appreciation of art. Analytic aesthetics' attack on disinterestedness helped to clear the ground for the new paradigm of art appreciation. However, since the resources replacing disinterestedness seem appropriate only for art, the rejection of the distanced contemplation paradigm for appreciation of the natural world requires further argument. Berleant addresses this issue by stressing the similarities between the appreciation of art and nature. He rejects not only disinterestedness but also various art world-related dogmas that place art on a pedestal separating it from the world at large (Berleant 1990). Thus, Berleant puts the issue on its head, modeling the appreciation of art on the open, engaging, creative appreciation that the natural environment facilitates. He proposes what he terms an 'aesthetics of engagement' as a paradigm for the appreciation of both nature and art. The aesthetics of engagement advocates transcending traditional dichotomies, such as subject/object, and diminishing the distance between the appreciator and the appreciated, aiming at a total, multi-sensory immersion of the former within the latter, be it nature or art (Berleant 1992). Moreover, the aesthetics of engagement is not limited to nature and art, but constitutes a model for the appreciation of any environment (Berleant 1997). Thus, it is a major factor in shaping environmental aesthetics as a field not simply focusing on natural environments, but encompassing our aesthetic appreciation of the world at large. In this way, it well illustrates how environmental aesthetics has important implication for aesthetics generally.

The aesthetics of engagement stresses our immediate sensuous involvement with any object of appreciation. Other positions in environmental aesthetics also emphasize this and closely related dimensions of our appreciation of natural and other environments, arguing that these dimensions, although not exhaustive of such appreciation, are nonetheless essential to it. For example, Carroll argues that the emotional arousal that nature often immediately and directly elicits from us is an important and legitimate aspect of its aesthetic appreciation (Carroll 1993).

Along somewhat similar lines, Foster promotes the significance of the almost ineffable, "feeling of being surrounded by or infused with an enveloping, engaging tactility," which she terms the 'ambient' dimension of aesthetic experience (Foster 1998). The multi-sensory and encompassing nature of our appreciation of environments is also emphasized by Fisher, who defends the importance of the 'sounds of nature' (Fisher 1998). And the ineffable quality of our experience of nature is stressed by Godlovitch, who argues that nature is aloof and distant, suggesting that appropriate appreciation involves a sense of mystery, of appreciative incomprehension (Godlovitch 1994). Such views frequently note the role of feelings of awe and wonder in our appreciation of the natural world, and thus recall the historical roots of environment aesthetics and the notion of the sublime.

In granting a central position to our immediate sensuous and emotional responses, the aesthetics of engagement and positions such as the arousal and the ambient views draw attention to what is an important component of aesthetic experience. However in doing so, they emphasize the trivial end of the movement from trivial to serious aesthetic appreciation elaborated by Hepburn (1966, 1993). Thus, they face a number of problems (Carlson 1995). First, these views allow appreciation, although no longer distanced, to remain focused primarily on sensory and formal qualities. Second, they thereby do not fully address the worries of environmentalists and others that aesthetic appreciation is basically a trivial and subjective approach to nature; and, third, they leave open the possibility of reinstating the barrier between the aesthetics of art and that of the rest of the world, for the former, in light of the new paradigm of art appreciation, clearly involves more than simply sensuous and emotional engagement with sensory and formal qualities. Addressing such problems requires one to pursue Hepburn's suggestions that although open, engaging, and creative, the aesthetic appreciation of the natural world, if it is to be serious rather than trivial, must yet be guided by knowledge and understanding. This insight is at the heart of the other major philosophical development in environmental aesthetics, which focuses on the cognitive dimensions of our appreciation of the world at large.

The cognitive approach

The cognitive line in environmental aesthetics was initially a response to the old appreciative paradigm's obsession with sensory and formal qualities. The line of thought is developed by Carlson who maintains that aesthetic appreciation of nature must be conceptualized in other than purely formal terms, in part by taking into consideration the expressive qualities of natural environments (Carlson 1976). Similarly, Sagoff stresses the significance of nature's expressive as well as symbolic qualities (Sagoff 1974). Consequently, Carlson contends that appreciation of nature must be freed from old approaches modeled on formalistic appreciation of isolated objects or picturesque appreciation of scenic beauty (Carlson 1979). However, he argues that this necessitates neither reducing aesthetic appreciation of nature simply to sensory and emotional responses nor abandoning it to trivial subjectivism (Carlson 1981). Rather, analogous to the way in which, under the new paradigm of art appreciation, serious, appropriate aesthetic appreciation of art is cognitively informed by reference to both art-historical traditions and art-critical practices, the aesthetic appreciation of nature, in order to be equally serious and appropriate, must be cognitively informed by reference to natural-historical and scientific information. Thus, Carlson finds a central place in the aesthetic appreciation of the natural world for the knowledge provided by sciences such as geology, biology, and ecology (Carlson 1981, 1984).

The basic idea of grounding the appropriate aesthetic appreciation of nature in scientific knowledge has proved fruitful in a number of ways. It is interpreted as an "ecological aesthetic" in the tradition of Aldo Leopold, who linked the beauty of nature to its ecological integrity and stability (Leopold 1966, Callicott 1987), and it is embraced by philosophers concerned to bring our aesthetic appreciation of nature in line with our ethical duties to maintain nature's ecological well-being (Rolston 1995, Eaton 1997a, Saito 1998). It also yields applied results in suggesting a cognitive framework for landscape assessors, planners, and designers who are attempting to address public concerns about the aesthetic quality of environments, and thus it assists in filling the so-called theoretical vacuum (Carlson 1993b, Eaton 1997b). Moreover, given its emphasis on scientific knowledge and objectivity, the cognitive approach helps to counter the worries of environmentalists and others that the aesthetic appreciation of nature must be trivial and subjective. The approach also has theoretical ramifications in offering an explanation for the development of the somewhat counter-intuitive view known as 'positive aesthetics,' which holds that untouched, pristine nature has only or primarily positive aesthetic qualities. In linking aesthetic appreciation of nature to science, the cognitive approach suggests that positive appreciation of nature is nurtured by the scientific world view that increasing interprets the natural world as having positive aesthetic qualities such as order, balance, unity, and harmony (Carlson 1984, 1993a). The positive aesthetics view, along with the link between science and nature appreciation, is pursued in various directions (Thompson 1995, Godlovitch 1998, Saito 1998).

Elaborations of the cognitive approach

The general cognitive approach connecting the appreciation of natural environments to scientific knowledge occupies a central position in environmental aesthetics. Moreover, it is elaborated in two related ways that fill out and give shape to the field: first, in its application beyond nature to the world at large, and, second, in its expansion to consider information other than that provided by science. These elaborations are suggested by the explanation for the relevance of scientific knowledge to the appreciation of nature: the fact that, concerning nature, it is primarily science that gives knowledge about why it is, what it is, and what it is like (Carlson 1993a). Considering nature *as nature*, as Budd puts it, is at the heart of its appropriate aesthetic appreciation (Budd 1996). Likewise, in appreciation of the world beyond the natural world, what is aesthetically relevant is knowledge of why it is, what it is, and what it is like, whether or not that knowledge is, strictly speaking, scientific. Thus, for environments such as, for example, the landscapes of agriculture, what is relevant to appropriate appreciation is a rich mix of information about what they are like and why they are as they are, information about their histories, their functions, and their roles in our lives (Carlson 1985). The same is true of other human environments, whether rural countrysides, urban cityscapes, or simply our private living spaces (Melchionne 1998). At this point, environmental aesthetics makes contact with the aesthetics of borderline artforms, such as gardens (Miller 1993, Ross 1998) and architecture (Carlson 1994), as well as with related fields, such as landscape ecology (Nassauer 1997), cultural geography (Conzen 1990, Groth and Bressi 1997), and the tradition of what may be called, for lack of a better phrase, landscape criticism (Watts 1957, Jackson 1980).

The application of the cognitive approach to the aesthetic appreciation of the world beyond nature demonstrates the aesthetic relevance of information other than that provided by natural science. However, in light of this, the question of the relevance of such information to the appreciation of more purely natural environments arises. The idea that scientific knowledge is the primary, or perhaps even the only information relevant to the appreciation of nature is challenged from various perspectives (Saito 1984, Carroll 1993, Godlovitch 1994, Stecker 1997, Brady 1998, Foster 1998). Some of these discussions, in noting the role of what may be called cultural knowledge in our appreciation of landscapes, stand in a venerable tradition. The aesthetic relevance of such information seems especially evident for environments that constitute important places in the histories and cultures of particular peoples. This sense of place is investigated by Tuan who elaborates it in terms of cultural and artistic heritages (Tuan 1974). Similarly, Sepanmaa, in his extensive study of environmental aesthetics, notes the influence of Finnish nature poetry on the aesthetic appreciation of Finnish landscapes (Sepanmaa 1993). Landscape descriptions contained in literature also seem to be aesthetically relevant to appreciating various landscapes, such as, for example, the novels of Hardy and Hillerman to, respectively, the rural countrysides of southwest England and the desert landscapes of southwest America (Carlson 2000). In addition to poetry and literature, other artforms, such as film (Sitney 1993), environmental art (Crawford 1983), and painting (Ross 1998), are explored and/or re-explored regarding their roles in shaping aesthetic appreciation of environments. Such investigations avoid the old pitfall of imposing restrictive artistic models on the natural world.

In spite of their obvious impact, however, the ideas, images, and associations contained in art and literature may not be the most significant cultural forces in shaping aesthetic appreciation of environments, natural or otherwise. Perhaps more important are the ideas embodied in mythology, religion, and metaphysics. Sepanmaa and others find an important place for folklore and mythology in particular peoples' aesthetic appreciation of particular landscapes (Sepanmaa 1993, Saito 1998, Carlson 2000). Similarly the aesthetic significance of religion, for example Christianity in the West and Buddhism in the East, has not been overlooked (Saito 1985). The aesthetic relevance of such information, like that provided by art and literature, may point toward a rather pluralistic or even relativistic account of environmental appreciation. However, the hope of a more objective account may lie in another aspect of our culture heritage, which, like scientific knowledge, is seemingly more universal. This possibility is suggested by Hepburn in arguing for the aesthetic relevance of what he calls the metaphysical imagination (Hepburn 1996). According to this view, our imagination interprets the world as revealing universal metaphysical truths: insights about the meaning of life, the human condition, humankind's place in the cosmos. Given the central place that this view grants to the human imagination in the appreciation of nature, it, as others mentioned earlier, harks back to some of the historical roots of environmental aesthetics (Brady 1998).

Current environmental aesthetics

What then is the shape of the emerging field of environmental aesthetics? In conclusion, three points should be emphasized. The first is that the field has forged, by way of the convergence of the engagement and the cognitive lines of thought, a viable alternative to the old paradigm of appreciation as distanced contemplation of sensory and formal qualities. Moreover, the new paradigm for aesthetic appreciation of environments is comparable to the new paradigm for appreciation of art. The latter, as noted, is that of emotionally and cognitively rich engagement with a cultural artifact, intentionally created by a designing intellect, informed by both art-historical traditions and art-critical practices, and deeply embedded in a complex, many-faceted art world. The former may be characterized as emotionally and cognitively rich engagement with an environment, created by natural and cultural forces, informed by both scientific knowledge and cultural traditions, and deeply embedded in a complex, many-faceted world. The parallelism between the two paradigms reinstates the traditional symmetry between appreciation of art and appreciation of the world at large, which was gradually diminished between the eighteenth century when the roots of environmental aesthetics were put in place and the mid-twentieth century when that symmetry was almost lost.

The second point concerns the scope of environmental aesthetics. Given the richness of the new paradigm for the aesthetic appreciation of environments, the scope of the field is essentially limitless concerning factors such as variety, size, and quality. First, variety extends from pristine nature to the borders of traditional art, and may even be construed as including the latter. The field ranges from wilderness, through rural landscapes and countrysides, to cityscapes, neighborhoods, amusement parks, shopping centers, and beyond, reaching into the art world itself. Second, concerning size, environmental aesthetics stretches from large environments that fully surround us – dense forests, endless fields of grain, the downtowns of our cities – to smaller and more intimate ones: our backyards, our offices, our living spaces. Third, the scope of the field ranges over quality, from the extraordinary to the ordinary, from the exotic to the mundane. Just as environmental aesthetics is not limited to the large, it is not limited to the spectacular. Ordinary scenery, commonplace sights, and our day-to-day experiences are proper objects of aesthetic appreciation. Environmental aesthetics is the aesthetics of everyday life.

The last point is that, in light of the new paradigm of aesthetic appreciation and in line with the limitless scope of the field, environmental aesthetics embodies the view that every environment, natural, rural, or urban, large or small, ordinary or extraordinary, offers much to see, to hear, to feel, much to appreciate aesthetically. The different environments of the world at large can be as aesthetically rich and rewarding as are the very best of our works of art.

See also Kant, Formalism, The aesthetic, Beauty, Architecture.

References

Appleton, J. (1975a) *The Experience of Landscape*, London: Wiley.
—— (1975b) "Landscape Evaluation: The Theoretical Vacuum," *Transactions of the Institute of British Geographers* 66: 120–3.
Beardsley, M. (1958) *Aesthetics: Problems in the Philosophy of Criticism*, New York: Harcourt, Brace.
Berleant, A. (1990) *Art and Engagement*, Philadelphia: Temple University Press.
—— (1992) *The Aesthetics of Environment*, Philadelphia: Temple University Press.
—— (1997) *Living in the Landscape: Toward an Aesthetics of Environment*, Lawrence: University Press of Kansas.

Blake. P. (1964) *God's Own Junkyard: The Planned Deterioration of America's Landscape*, New York: Holt, Rinehart and Winston.

Bourassa, S. C. (1991) *The Aesthetics of Landscape*, London: Belhaven.

Brady, E. (1998) "Imagination and the Aesthetic Appreciation of Nature," in A. Berleant and A. Carlson (eds), *Special Issue: Environmental Aesthetics, Journal of Aesthetics and Art Criticism* 56: 139–47.

Budd, M. (1996) "The Aesthetic Appreciation of Nature," *British Journal of Aesthetics* 36: 207–22.

Bullough, E. (1912) "'Psychical Distance' as a Factor in Art and as an Aesthetic Principle," *British Journal of Psychology* 5: 87–98.

Callicott, J. B. (1987) "The Land Aesthetic," in J. B. Callicott (ed.), *Companion to a Sand County Almanac: Interpretive and Critical Essays*, Madison: University of Wisconsin Press.

Carlson, A. (1976) "Environmental Aesthetics and the Dilemma of Aesthetic Education," *Journal of Aesthetic Education* 10: 69–82.

—— (1977) "On the Possibility of Quantifying Scenic Beauty," *Landscape Planning* 4: 131–72.

—— (1979) "Appreciation and the Natural Environment," *Journal of Aesthetics and Art Criticism* 37: 267–76.

—— (1981) "Nature, Aesthetic Judgement, and Objectivity," *Journal of Aesthetics and Art Criticism* 40: 15–27.

—— (1984) "Nature and Positive Aesthetics," *Environmental Ethics* 6: 5–34.

—— (1985) "On Appreciating Agricultural Landscapes," *Journal of Aesthetics and Art Criticism* 43: 301–12.

—— (1990) "Whose Vision? Whose Meanings? Whose Values? Pluralism and Objectivity in Landscape Analysis," in P. Groth (ed.), *Vision, Culture, and Landscape: The Berkeley Symposium on Cultural Landscape Interpretation*, Berkeley: Department of Landscape Architecture, University of California.

—— (1993a) "Appreciating Art and Appreciating Nature," in S. Kemal and I. Gaskell (eds), *Landscape, Natural Beauty and the Arts*, Cambridge: Cambridge University Press.

—— (1993b) "On the Theoretical Vacuum in Landscape Assessment," *Landscape Journal* 12: 51–6.

—— (1994) "Existence, Location, and Function: The Appreciation of Architecture," in M. Mitias (ed.), *Philosophy and Architecture*, Amsterdam: Rodopi.

—— (1995) "Nature, Aesthetic Appreciation, and Knowledge," *Journal of Aesthetics and Art Criticism* 53: 393–400.

—— (1998) "Landscape Assessment," in M. Kelly (ed.), *Encyclopedia of Aesthetics*, vol. 3, New York: Oxford University Press.

—— (2000) "Landscape and Literature," in *Aesthetics and the Environment: The Appreciation of Nature, Art and Architecture*, London: Routledge.

Carroll, N. (1993) "On Being Moved By Nature: Between Religion and Natural History," in S. Kemal and I. Gaskel (eds), *Landscape, Natural Beauty and the Arts*, Cambridge: Cambridge University Press.

Cats-Baril, W. L. and Gibson, L. (1986) "Evaluating Aesthetics: The Major Issues and a Bibliography," *Landscape Journal* 5: 93–102.

Conzen, M. P. (1990) *The Making of the American Landscape*, London: Harper Collins.

Crawford, D. (1983) "Nature and Art: Some Dialectical Relationships," *Journal of Aesthetics and Art Criticism* 62: 49–58.

Eaton, M. (1989) *Aesthetics and the Good Life*, Cranbury, N.J.: Associated University Presses.

—— (1997a) "The Beauty that Requires Health," in J. I. Nassauer (ed.), *Placing Nature: Culture and Landscape Ecology*, Washington: Island Press.

—— (1997b) "The Role of Aesthetics in Designing Sustainable Landscapes," in Y. Sepanmaa (ed.), *Real World Design: The Foundations and Practice of Environmental Aesthetics*, Helsinki: University of Helsinki.

Elliot, R. (1982) "Faking Nature," *Inquiry* 25: 81–93.

Fisher, J. A. (1998) "What the Hills Are Alive With: In Defense of the Sounds of Nature," *Journal of Aesthetics and Art Criticism* 56: 167–79.

Foster, C. (1998) "The Narrative and the Ambient in Environmental Aesthetics," *Journal of Aesthetics and Art Criticism* 56: 127–37.

Godlovitch, S. (1994) "Icebreakers: Environmentalism and Natural Aesthetics," *Journal of Applied Philosophy* 11: 15–30.

—— (1998) "Valuing Nature and the Autonomy of Natural Aesthetics," *British Journal of Aesthetics* 38: 180–97.

Groth, P. and Bressi, T. W. (eds) (1997) *Understanding Ordinary Landscapes*, New Haven: Yale University Press.

Hepburn, R. W. (1966) "Contemporary Aesthetics and the Neglect of Natural Beauty," in B. Williams and A. Montefiore (eds), *British Analytical Philosophy*, London: Routledge and Kegan Paul.

—— (1993) "Trivial and Serious in Aesthetic Appreciation of Nature," in S. Kemal and I. Gaskell (eds), *Landscape, Natural Beauty and the Arts*, Cambridge: Cambridge University Press.

—— (1996) "Landscape and the Metaphysical Imagination," *Environmental Values* 5: 191–204.

Hook, S. (ed.) (1966) *Art and Philosophy*, New York: NYU Press.

Jackson, J. B. (1980) *The Necessity for Ruins and Other Topics*, Amherst: University of Massachusetts Press.

Kant, I. (1987 [1790]) *Critique of Judgement*, trans. W. S. Pluhar, Indianapolis: Hackett.

Kaplan, R. and Kaplan, S. (1989) *The Experience of Nature: A Psychological Perspective*, Cambridge: Cambridge University Press.

Leopold, A. (1966) "Conservation Esthetic," in *A Sand County Almanac with Essays on Conservation from Round River*, New York: Oxford University Press.

Lewis, P. F., Lowenthal, D. and Tuan, Y. (1973) *Visual Blight in America*, Washington: Association of American Geographers.

Litton, B. R. (1968) *Forest Landscape Description and Inventories – A Basis for Land Planning and Design*, Berkeley: USDA Pacific Southwest Forest and Range Experimental Station.

Mannison, D. (1980) "A Prolegomenon to a Human Chauvinistic Aesthetic," in D. Mannison, M. McRobbie, and R. Routley (eds), *Environmental Philosophy*, Canberra: Australian National University.

Margolis, J. (ed.) (1962) *Philosophy Looks at the Arts*, New York: Scribner.

Melchionne, K. (1998) "Living in Glass Houses: Domesticity, Interior Decoration, and Environmental Aesthetics," *Journal of Aesthetics and Art Criticism* 56: 191–200.

Miller, M. (1993) *The Garden As Art*, Albany: SUNY Press.

Nasar, J. L. (ed.) (1988) *Environmental Aesthetics: Theory, Research, and Applications*, Cambridge: Cambridge University Press.

Nassauer, J. I. (1997) "Culture and Landscape Ecology: Insights for Action," in J. I. Nassauer (ed.), *Placing Nature: Culture and Landscape Ecology*, Washington: Island Press.

Rolston, H. (1995) "Does Aesthetic Appreciation of Nature Need to be Science Based?" *British Journal of Aesthetics* 35: 374–86.

Ross, S. (1998) *What Gardens Mean*, Chicago: University of Chicago Press.

Saarinen, T. F., Seamon, D. and Sell, J. L. (eds) (1984) *Environmental Perception and Behavior: An Inventory and Prospect*, Chicago: Department of Geography, University of Chicago.

Sadler, B. and Carlson, A. (eds) (1982) *Environmental Aesthetics: Essays in Interpretation*, Victoria, B.C.: Department of Geography, University of Victoria.

Sagoff, M. (1974) "On Preserving the Natural Environment," *Yale Law Journal* 84: 205–67.

Saito, Y. (1984) "Is There a Correct Aesthetic Appreciation of Nature?," *Journal of Aesthetic Education* 18: 35–46.

—— (1985) "The Japanese Appreciation of Nature," *British Journal of Aesthetics* 25: 239–51.

—— (1998) "Appreciating Nature on its Own Terms," *Environmental Ethics* 20: 135–49.

Sepanmaa, Y. (1993) *The Beauty of Environment: A General Model for Environmental Aesthetics*, 2nd edn, Denton: Environmental Ethics Books.

Shepard, P. (1967) *Man in the Landscape: A Historic View of the Esthetics of Nature*, New York: Knopf.

Sitney, A. P. (1993) "Landscape in the Cinema: The Rhythms of the World and the Camera," in S. Kemal and I. Gaskel (eds), *Landscape, Natural Beauty and the Arts*, Cambridge: Cambridge University Press.

Stecker, R. (1997) "The Correct and the Appropriate in the Appreciation of Nature," *British Journal of Aesthetics* 37: 393–402.

Thompson, J. (1995) "Aesthetics and the Value of Nature," *Environmental Ethics* 17: 291–305.

Tuan, Y. (1974) *Topophilia: A Study of Environmental Perception, Attitudes, and Values*, Englewood Cliffs: Prentice Hall.

USDA (1972) *National Forest Landscape Management*, vol. I, Washington, D.C.: Government Printing Office for United States Department of Agriculture Forest Service.

Watts, M. T. (1957) *Reading the Landscape*, New York: Macmillan.

Zube, E. H. (1984) "Themes in Landscape Assessment Theory," *Landscape Journal* 3: 104–10.

Further reading

Berleant, A. and Carlson, A. (eds) (1998) Special Issue on Environmental Aesthetics, *Journal of Aesthetics and Art Criticism* 56. (Ten original articles by some of the main philosophical researchers in the field.)

Bourassa, S. C. (1991) *The Aesthetics of Landscape*, London: Belhaven. (An overview of and contribution to the empirical and applied research in aesthetic appreciation of environments, with a very good general bibliography.)

Carlson, A. (1999) *Aesthetics and the Environment: The Appreciation of Nature, Art and Architecture*, London: Routledge. (A set of studies in the cognitive approach to environmental appreciation.)

Kemal, S. and Gaskell, I. (eds) (1993) *Landscape, Natural Beauty and the Arts*, Cambridge: Cambridge University Press. (A collection of twelve original articles on environmental aesthetics by individuals from a number of different, but primarily humanities-centered disciplines.)

Nasar, J. L. (ed.) (1988) *Environmental Aesthetics: Theory, Research, and Applications*, Cambridge: Cambridge University Press. (A collection of thirty-two articles of differing lengths and technical detail, mainly by individuals representing various empirical and applied approaches to environmental aesthetics, with an excellent bibliography of empirical work.)

Nassauer, J. I. (ed.) (1997) *Placing Nature: Culture and Landscape Ecology*, Washington: Island Press. (A collection of ten original articles by individuals representing a very wide range of different disciplines, but generally focusing on landscape ecology; many articles have suggestions for further reading.)

Sepanmaa, Y. (ed.) (1997) *Real World Design: The Foundations and Practice of Environmental Aesthetics*, Helsinki: University of Helsinki Press. (Twenty-two short pieces on environmental aesthetics by individuals representing a number of different countries, approaches, and philosophical traditions.)

37
FEMINIST AESTHETICS

Sarah Worth

The making and experience of art are gendered in a significant way, and this must be taken into account if we are to understand art fully. However, the influence of gender has not been sufficiently accounted for within aesthetics. Feminist aesthetics is not a way of evaluating art or our experience of it, but rather examines and questions aesthetic theory and its attitude toward gender. In what follows I spell out some of the main goals and tenets of feminist aesthetics and also show how it can serve as a useful critique of two historically dominant aesthetic theories.

Background and goals

Although feminist work in literary criticism, film theory and art history is well established, feminist aesthetics is a relatively young discipline, dating from the early 1990s. The earliest work in feminist aesthetics was published as a special issue of *Hypatia* in 1990. Since then, there have been a handful of special issues of journals and anthologies on the topic: notably, Hein and Korsmeyer's *Aesthetics in Feminist Perspective* (1993), which was developed from the *Hypatia* issue, and Brand and Korsmeyer's *Feminism and Tradition in Aesthetics* (1995), which was an outgrowth of a special issue of the *Journal of Aesthetics and Art Criticism* (1990). Because of its relatively recent beginnings, feminist aesthetics is still a discipline without a canon. In fact, several writers resist the idea that feminist aesthetics should have a canon at all, since they believe that work in this field needs to develop as women artists and theorists do themselves. Moreover, since it draws upon several brands of feminism and feminist work in other disciplines, feminist aesthetics is rarely concerned to respect disciplinary boundaries. Finally, one of its primary tasks is to broaden our concept of what counts as art, and enable the discipline to include more varied perspectives on artists, art appreciators, and the wider contexts in which art develops.

Gender and art

Men and women in our society have access to different kinds of opportunities to education and the institutions of the art world. These differences produce a varied outcome in product, but more importantly, in kinds of experiences. Although women often perform similar tasks to men, their work is rarely accorded the same status because of the different sphere in which it is performed. For example, women's art is often seen as tied to the spheres of nature, the private and the domestic, rather than to the realms of culture and public life.

One of the distinctions the art world has given us is that between art and craft. A feminist examination of this suggests that there exists not only a division between the two, but also a hierarchy that regards art as higher or more inherently valuable than craft. The lower arts, or crafts – or the decorative arts – are assigned a lesser degree of intellectual effort or appeal and a greater concern with manual skill and function. Very often, these are women's arts, such as the traditional domestic arts: quilting, embroidery and needle-point, for example. The association of women with feminine and domestic arts takes their work out of the realm of fine or high art.

The social definition of femininity affects not only the evaluation of what women do, but also how much value can be assigned to what they do. Often, women were identified with the kind of subjects they worked with in their art. For example, women artists were compared to the dainty flowers they would paint. Until this century it was not considered appropriate for women to paint nudes, and they were not taught this skill in art schools. It would clearly be absurd to compare Michelangelo's *David* and its masculine physique with the artist himself, but this sort of comparison was commonplace with women artists and their subjects in the past.

Art itself is also gendered because of the way women appear as subjects in works of art. Women, often nude, are intended to be the subjects of "disinterested contemplation" and are held up as representative of idealized beauty, according to a standard set by men. This puts all women in the place of being the objects of male contemplation, in and out of the art world. If we acknowledge that this is the case before we attempt to define a unified feminist aesthetic theory, the result will probably be more all-encompassing and accurately representative of our experience.

Assumptions of feminist aesthetics

It is important to keep in mind, however, that feminist aesthetics does not claim that women necessarily produce different kinds of art from men, nor that women necessarily have different experiences of art from men. Not only is there no clear distinction between women's art and men's art, there is also no clear similarity among all women's art. The different kind of art men and women produce is less significant than the recognition that they have different kinds of experiences in response to art, because of the social definition of gender. By starting with the assumption that art and the way we experience it are gendered, feminist aesthetics acknowledges the different kinds of experiences art can produce, and hence can take more varied kinds of experiences into account. There is no assumption that the differences are essential; the assumption is that prevailing notions of gender inform the experiences of art enjoyed by men and women.

Almost all feminist scholarship challenges the view that there is a generic perceiver of, or participant in, art. Awareness of gender informs the content of perception itself, so that what is perceived and how it is perceived depends on whether the perceiver occupies a more or less privileged social and political position. This overturns the traditional use in philosophical aesthetics of the ideal of the generic perceiver to produce theoretical analyses that apply uniformly in all kinds of contexts to all kinds of people. It is much easier to understand the relationship between a work of art and its perceiver if we have some static notion of what kind of person the perceiver might be. This relationship is complicated enough to account for (is the 'art' in the object? in the perceiver? in the interplay between the two?) without having to consider the possibility that men and women, black and white, educated and less educated, will all encounter art differently. But this is exactly what feminist aesthetics wants to point out. There is not one, standard experience of art.

Feminist aesthetics maintains that aesthetics is not and should not be gender neutral, and it begins by recognizing how art and artists are privileged and affected by gender. Standard aesthetic theory oppresses women by assuming a gender-neutral, disinterested ideal spectator who in fact embodies a privileged, white male perspective. Moreover, understanding that gender influences the viewer, and accounting for the varied spectators that we do have, are not the same. Feminist aesthetics goes beyond the acknowledgment that gender matters to consider *how* it matters and how different women create and experience art.

Critiques of traditional aesthetics

Although rejected by most contemporary philosophers, the doctrines of formalism and disinterestedness have dominated traditional aesthetics. By examining feminist aesthetics' critique of these doctrines, we can illuminate its contextual approach to art and consider our more varied experiences.

Formalism

Formalist or autonomist aesthetics includes three main elements. First, formalism attempts to define art and explain it as a distinct activity which stands apart from other cultural practices, separated from craft and any other functional or practical activity. Second, formalism isolates particular *objects* of art; that is, art works are taken out of context, away from their original settings and symbolic meanings in human experience. For example, museums often isolate paintings or artifacts from their cultural surroundings so that the work can be contemplated separately or disinterestedly and without interruption from extraneous influences. Third, formalist aesthetics uses structurally-oriented concepts for judging and evaluating art works. It claims that formal elements such as line, shape and color are the primary generators of aesthetic value. Formal value is also understood to be independent of other characteristics of an art work such as meaning, reference or utility.

In response to these formalist paradigms, feminist aesthetics calls for us to replace our concept of the art work as object (only) with a more all-encompassing description (but not a categorizing definition) of art, moving from the autonomous realm of value to the everyday realm of the social, political and even functional. Denying an art work its context can deprive it of important cultural, personal or political significance that need not be lost. The fact that the work of art is made by a particular (gendered) person at a particular place and time can further a more developed appreciation and understanding of the art object. Thus, by recognizing the context of a work of art, one can reach beyond art history proper to define, describe, and understand the art work as part of the everyday world.

Second, feminist aesthetics wants to allow art works to remain in their context, rather than isolating them and putting them on display separately in a museum. This might mean displaying a traditional African mask in a museum not alone, but with accouterments used along with the mask, and a video of the ceremony in which the mask was worn. Feminist aesthetics might also encourage performance art or interactive dance concerts, or interactive plays rather than traditional ways of performing which do not include audience inter-action or response. In essence, a feminist approach will allow for the meaning of the creation to reveal itself in more diverse ways because of the contexts that are included in its presentation.

The third way feminist aesthetics works against traditional formalism is by reconsidering the relationship between art and the established artistic traditions. Whereas formalism assumes a standard, ideal spectator or appreci-ator, feminist aesthetics believes that art can speak for and to all of us, across genders in considerably more varied ways.

Disinterestedness

Feminist aesthetics also challenges the notion that a pure, disinterested state of contemplative attention characterizes ideal aesthetic appreciation and the appropriate apprehension of art. According to the doctrine of disinterestedness, the perceiver of an aesthetic object must adopt a special kind of attitude or way of attending to the art object. Edward Bullough (1912), one of the more influential attitude theorists, characterizes this attitude in terms of 'psychical distance.' This is understood to be the mental distance one places between oneself and an object. Bullough draws an analogy with the distance that enables a passenger on a boat to see a dense fog and sense the danger, and yet also know that it is far enough away not to cause harm. If the passenger feels it too intensely, he or she will be too frightened to function, and if he or she feels it not intensely enough, he or she will not take the proper precautions. In the case of the aesthetic, Bullough explains that the practical side of appreciation should be inhibited so that one can focus on the aesthetic qualities of the object. Although the attitude of distance for Bullough is temporary (whereas for Jerome Stolnitz (1960) the aesthetic attitude is something one can adopt in viewing the world long term), the distance is said to be crucial to the appreciation of many works of art. For Bullough, distance comes in degrees. Too much distance would mean the loss of connection with the work of art. Not enough distance would not allow the appreciator to set aside his or her immediate, personal responses.

In general, disinterestedness is the distance felt between the viewer and the object perceived. It is not that the viewer should be *un*interested in the work of art, but that he or she should not feel any personal connection to it which might influence the pure understanding of the work. For example, the viewer should not value a painting because it is of her childhood home, or a male spectator should not be drawn to a painting of a woman who he might want to possess, if he is truly disinterested. The focus should be on line, form and color, rather than aspects of the work of art that are personally significant in one way or another. Only with such a disinterested attitude was it believed that one could properly appreciate a work of art.

Although disinterestedness has had a great impact on aesthetics, it has an odd consequence for appreciating art. It means that in order for something to be appreciated as art, it must be perceived and understood as cut off from its present surroundings, its history or its practical use. This fuels the notion that the value of an object *qua* art object is unrelated to whatever other value it might possess. It is not that art must be impractical, but rather that its perceived practical value, if any, is irrelevant to its value as art or our experience of it as art. This view of art eliminates much of the work traditionally made by women – such as quilts, needlepoint, and even still-life paintings of flowers – because these are not the kinds of objects we tend to view with disinterest.

Not all feminist aestheticians reject the concept of disinterestedness altogether. Peggy Zeglin Brand (1998) suggests that spectators fluctuate between interested and disinterested attention. Since we cannot fully train ourselves to see only one way or the other, with interest or without, Brand suggests that what we do is switch between them (much like the duck–rabbit picture: we cannot see them both at the same time, but we can train ourselves to switch back and forth once we have seen it both ways). Disinterested attention has an important place, according to Brand, but there is no reason, especially with feminist or political art, not to examine the work with interested attention as well. Brand claims that these two ways of seeing complement each other, since being able to appreciate something with interest and without allows an appreciator a more comprehensive experience. She suggests we actually use both in order to understand the art works we encounter more fully.

To admit that gender, among other contextual factors, does matter in art is to admit that we need a new approach to aesthetic theory, and that the negative aspects of disinterested and formalist theory need to be disengaged. We can begin to understand this new approach, first, by seeing that art is not produced in an atmosphere which is in any way transcendent of gender identification. One of the primary functions of feminist aesthetics is to promote a new way of looking at the context in which art is produced. It identifies art not by proscriptive definition, but by attempting to understand the complex relation of circumstances which produces art objects and experiences in the first place.

Feminist alternatives

Feminist aesthetics offers not merely a critique of traditional aesthetics but alternatives as well. First, traditional formalist theory defines art exclusively in terms of formal characteristics and principles. But this leaves aesthetics always striving toward a definition that will ultimately, always, come up short. Feminist theory, on the other hand, seeks to describe, rather than define, art, and thus is able to take account of its changing nature.

Second, formalism gives priority to products of artistic endeavors that are viewed disinterestedly, and gives priority to the view that art objects should be viewed disinterestedly. Conversely, feminist aesthetics emphasizes the connection between art and life. Feminist aesthetics takes art works not only to be objects but also performances, environments (gardens perhaps), and other interactive programs viewed within their contexts.

According to formalist theory, what is considered to be good art or high art transcends nature and culture. Art is often said to be dependent upon artistic genius and disinterested contemplation by trained critics. Feminist aesthetics, on the other hand, claims that good art is challenging but makes life sensible to its audience. Good art often transcends its particular culture and suggests alternative ways of being and understanding the world. Whereas formalist theories make hard and fast distinctions between aesthetic versus moral versus epistemological ways of looking and assessing, feminist theory suggests that aesthetic value arises in *conjunction* with the moral and epistemological and not in opposition to them. By combining the significance of these things, one can form a more comprehensive understanding of art works, their contexts and our experiences of them.

Within formalist theories, there is a clear separation between art and artist which allows for claims of universality. That is, there is a clear separation between artist as maker and art work as object. Feminist aesthetics recognizes this distinction, but also allows for an understanding of how the artist influences and is influenced by his or her art work. Taking this into consideration, universal claims of disinterestedness or pure formal value are more difficult to accept. With feminist aesthetics there is an appreciation of the interaction between the experience of the artist and his or her environment. Claims of universality yield to situated contexts. The focus is not on understanding or expressing the universal, but understanding and presenting what can only be found in a particular context: understanding how the nexus of relationships works.

According to a formalist theory, a perceiver should appreciate a work of art as a thing in itself, on its own, for its own sake. He or she should evaluate the work of art in terms of success or failure as it measures up against significant form. According to feminist aesthetics, on the other hand, the perceiver focuses on the relationship of art to artist, culture, nature, and ultimately to its context. Adopting this approach allows one to take into consideration religious, political, social, and economic considerations that are important to the context, in addition to other formal characteristics. This allows one to evaluate the work of art in terms of its effect on cultural understanding.

By taking a feminist approach to aesthetics, we allow art to return to its social context. Estella Lauter explains that

> feminist theory enhances our experience of art by accounting for it more accurately. It expands the range of what we consider to be art and prepares the way to legitimate new art forms; opens the community of artists; revalues subjectivity in art and augments it to include women's experiences; allows us to reconnect aesthetic values with political activity; stimulates criticism of obsolete aesthetic standards and validates new ones; valorizes new modes of production; and supports more active responses.
>
> (Lauter 1993: 33)

Feminist aesthetics has not provided us with a new set of standards by which to judge art or aesthetic theory, but offers a new way of approaching and appreciating what has come before.

The male gaze

Although feminist aesthetics begins with the recognition that gender matters in art, it should not be confused with feminist art history or feminist art criticism, which also begin with the same assumption. The fact that women are oppressed as subjects of art does play a part in the acknowledgment that gender is influential, but it is not necessarily all that matters. There is a bias in painting (and print media) toward female subjects (often nude women perceived as passive and wanting to be looked at) and male artists (always in control, always doing the looking). What this feminist view of art history produces is our recognition of the "male gaze," which is a significant part of feminist aesthetics. In this case, feminist aesthetics has contributed something that traditional aesthetics has not so much gotten wrong as overlooked entirely.

The discussion of the way women are viewed by men in different kinds of contexts is influenced by John Berger's characterization of it in his book *Ways of Seeing* (Berger 1972). Clearly here – even in the early 1970s – the view was being developed that perspective and context mattered. Undoubtedly, as Berger has shown, many of the paradigms for putting women as seen objects by men developed from the tradition of Western easel painting. Elaborate ways of presenting the female body (and especially the female nude) as representative of beauty were devised, presenting the female body frozen in time. She is the ultimate in passive contemplation, existing merely for admiration and disinterested contemplation. Currently, the more accessible print media fulfills the same purpose: everything from *Good Housekeeping* to *Playboy* shows how women are not the thinkers in this culture, but rather the ones who can keep a house, cook dinner, maybe even hold a job, and still look good doing it. Women function not only as the historical objects of attention throughout the history of painting and sculpture, but even now, as objects of pornography, commercial advertising, film and general media, and even still in the art world (see Duncan 1989). Feminist aesthetics takes on the task of making us aware of the gaze which we use to look at, interpret, and judge our world. This is part of the context in which art works are made, and it is part of the context in which we need to understand them.

Although the notion of the male gaze was originally introduced by Laura Mulvey (1989) in reference to film theory, it has worked its way into aesthetic theory to characterize *a way of looking* or a *way of seeing*. It is one way in which we (men and women both) are *trained* to perceive women, inside and outside of the art world. Mulvey's study of framing techniques and camera angles revealed that the vantage points of spectator, film maker, and actor virtually always reinforce a masculine position in relation to the action of a film and toward the bodies of the female characters. Even when women are not specifically referred to or acknowledged as objects of aesthetic experience, there are clearly parallels between the characteristics that make something an appropriate aesthetic object (something worthy of male contemplation) and those characteristics that exemplify traditional femininity. Both aesthetic objects and the feminine characteristics are necessarily passive, available for admiration and exist primarily for validation from a more active (male) spectator. Thus, with the male gaze as well, women are to be seen and characterized by this passive, wanting-to-be-looked-at susceptibility.

To say that the gaze is male is to say that there is a way of seeing which takes women to be its object. In this broad description of a way of seeing the world, the gaze is male whenever it directs itself at women, or takes pleasure in viewing women as erotic objects. Feminists claim that most art, most of the time, places women in this position: in the position of being seen. The man is the bearer of the gaze and woman is his object.

An interesting feature of the gaze so characterized is that women are just as susceptible to adopting it as are men. Neither men nor women simply watch, view or look. The way both sexes look – where they look, when they look and what they look at – imitates a particular way of thinking about the world and acting in that world. It represents particular ways of judging what is seen and the responsibilities one has toward what one sees. Women judge women in the same way men do because this is the standard way of seeing and apprehending the world. It is in this way that *seeing* never escapes a *way of seeing*. We can never be divorced from our own ingrained, culturally induced perspective. Whether we take this to be an asset or a detriment to relations between the sexes, it is a much more culturally accurate starting point for aesthetic theory.

A related element of film viewing (and art viewing) is scopophilia. This is the pleasure one takes in looking and also from being in the position of being able to do the looking. The notion stems originally from Freud, who associated scopophilia with taking other people as objects, subjecting them to a controlling and curious gaze. Mulvey notes of scopophilia that "the position of the spectators in the cinema is blatantly one of repression of their exhibitionism and projection of the repressed desire onto the performer" (Mulvey 1989: 17). Thus it is not only the male looking at the female which becomes incorporated into our understanding of the interplay between subject and object, but also the pleasure that the spectator derives from being in the privileged position of being the one who gets to look. The fact that these gender inequities can clearly be identified gives feminist aesthetics a good starting point for developing either an aesthetic theory that either takes this inequity into account, or one which attempts to diffuse it from the outset.

Both feminist aesthetics and feminist art criticism have focused on the imbalance between the subject and object of aesthetic contemplation, and both want to initiate an important blurring of clear distinctions between them. Further, there is an emphasis on the aesthetic dimensions of everyday life and the importance of seeing art as an activity rather than a product. Feminist analyses attempt to link aesthetic judgement and the resultant implied meaning and value of works of art to beliefs and desires in everyday life. It is only here, in the complicated nexus of social circumstances surrounding the creation of art, that we can fully understand its significance.

See also The aesthetic, Formalism, Kant, Value of art.

References

Berger, J. (1972) *Ways of Seeing*, London: Penguin.

Brand, P. (1998) "Disinterestedness and Political Art," in C. Korsmeyer (ed.), *Aesthetics: The Big Questions*, Oxford: Blackwell.

Bullough, E. (1912) "'Psychical Distance' as a Factor in Art and as an Aesthetic Principle," *British Journal of Psychology* 5: 87–98.

Duncan, C. (1989) "The MoMAs Hot Mamas," *Art Journal* 48 (Summer).

Lauter, E. (1993) "Re-Enfranchising Art," in H. Hein and C. Korsmeyer (eds), *Aesthetics in Feminist Perspective*, Bloomington: Indiana University Press.

Mulvey, L. (1989) *Visual and Other Pleasures*, Bloomington: Indiana University Press.

Stolnitz, J. (1960) "The Aesthetic Attitude," in *Aesthetics and Philosophy of Art Criticism*, New York: Houghton Mifflin.

Further reading

Battersby, C. (1989) *Gender and Genius: Towards a Feminist Aesthetics*, Bloomington: Indiana University Press. (A discussion of women and their perceived inability to achieve genius.)

Brand, P. and Korsmeyer, C. (eds) (1995) *Feminism and Tradition in Aesthetics*, University Park: Pennsylvania State University Press. (An anthology focusing on gender within historical and current debates in aesthetics.)

Devereaux, M. (1995) "Oppressive Texts, Resisting Readers and the Gendered Spectator," in P. Brand and C. Korsmeyer (eds), *Feminism and Tradition in Aesthetics*, University Park: Pennsylvania State University Press. (A discussion of women as gendered readers.)

Felski, R. (1989) *Beyond Feminist Aesthetics: Feminist Literature and Social Change*, Cambridge, Mass.: Harvard University Press. (A feminist approach to literary theory.)

Hein, H. and Korsmeyer, C. (eds) (1993) *Aesthetics in Feminist Perspective*, Bloomington: Indiana University Press. (An anthology unified by a focus on the nature of 'feminist,' 'feminine,' or 'female' art, creativity and interpretation.)

Korsmeyer, C. (1998) "Perceptions, Pleasures, Arts: Considering Aesthetics," in J. Kourany (ed), *Philosophy in a Feminist Voice: Critiques and Reconstructions*, Princeton: Princeton University Press. (A summary of the feminist position in analytic aesthetics.)

Nochlin, L. (1998) "Why Are There No Great Women Artists?" in V. Gornick and B. K. Moran (eds), *Woman in Sexist Society*, New York: Basic Books.

Part 4

THE INDIVIDUAL ARTS

38

LITERATURE

Peter Lamarque

The term 'literature' is used with different senses, not necessarily related to art. In the most general sense it encompasses virtually all printed matter, as when we speak of the literature on urban planning or the Ford Sierra. In a second, more restricted, sense – literature as 'belles-lettres' – the term applies only to 'fine writing,' writing that has 'literary merit.' This would include the King James Bible, Hume's *History of England*, the Gettysburg Address, as well as certain philosophical or theological treatises, biographies, memoirs, letters, even some journalism. The occasional essay was considered an important literary form in the nineteenth century. When Bertrand Russell and Winston Churchill received the Nobel Prize for Literature this second connotation was assumed.

A third sense narrows the meaning further and is largely a modern (post-eighteenth century) innovation, under which literature denotes 'works of the imagination.' Thus some, but not all, poems, novels, dramas, short stories, sagas, legends, satires, would be included, while more fact-oriented writing of the kind listed would be excluded. This third sense is strictly a subclass of the second, for the evaluative component of 'literary merit' still applies. Not all works of the imagination are deemed to be 'literature,' in this sense, and much popular fiction or drama or light verse would not be so classified. Publishers have even come to recognize a particular genre of fiction as 'literary fiction,' in contrast to other genres, crime, fantasy, horror, war, science fiction, which are rarely classed as 'literature.' What these other genres are thought to lack, as well as 'fine writing,' is a kind of moral seriousness which is taken as a further essential mark of 'imaginative literature.'

Literature as an art

This third sense of 'literature' – fine writing of an imaginative/creative kind imbued with moral seriousness – engages with aesthetics, for in this sense literature has come to be classified as one of the high arts.

A number of questions arise. Can this conception be sharpened up sufficiently to provide a useful and substantial demarcation of discourses? What modes of interpretation and evaluation are appropriate for literature as art? How does imaginative literature relate to fictionality, truth, ethics, ideology? One charge sometimes made against 'literature' so conceived is that it is already deeply tainted with historically situated political and ideological presuppositions (Eagleton 1983). This, so the charge goes, belies its aspirations to embody timeless and universal values. The very idea of a 'canon' of great literary works, especially associated with a 'national literature,' has been thought to be motivated by considerations far removed from the purely aesthetic (Bourdieu 1993).

Although the notion of 'imaginative literature' as described is relatively modern, the idea that writing can be a form of art is one of immense antiquity. Of course 'art' itself has evolved in meaning, with the distinction between 'fine art' and 'craft' also stemming from the modern age. The craft of writing (and speaking) was prominent in education from ancient Greece to eighteenth-century Europe, and literary skills were imparted through the teaching of rhetoric (one of the subjects, along with grammar and logic, in the Trivium, the lower division of the Seven Liberal Arts). But poetry has long been thought an 'art,' both in the sense of something crafted and as writing that is highly valued. Horace's notion of an '*ars poetica*' would have been familiar to pre-Socratic thinkers. Indeed poetry, which includes not just the lyric and the epic (such as the *Iliad*) but also the great tragedies of Sophocles and Shakespeare, epitomized what we now call the literary arts right up to the late seventeenth century. Until the advent of the novel (and prose drama) in the early eighteenth century there was no call for a new category of 'imaginative literature' because 'poetry' captured all that was needed for a distinct artform. To lump the emerging novel, and other forms of imaginative prose-writing, together with poetry under the broad heading of 'literature' was in many ways a surprising move, and doubts are still raised whether there really is a viable category of this kind.

Literary language

Whatever else it is, literature is essentially linguistic, and the attempt to define a distinctive literary language has been at the heart of modern poetics or the theory of literature. Formalistic accounts of literary language focus on stylistic, syntactic and rhetorical features, from poetic 'devices' like meter, rhythm, euphony, imagery and metaphor, to more general rhetorical figures like repetition, accumulation, hyperbole, and climax as associated with the 'sublime' style described in the *Peri Hypsous* of Longinus (Wellek and Warren 1973, chs 13–14). In the popular mind, 'literary' language is contrasted with the 'everyday' in being more ornate, structured or self-conscious. It seems unlikely, though, that any purely formal linguistic properties could provide either necessary or sufficient conditions for literature, in our third sense (Lamarque 1996). All 'fine writing' exhibits rhetorical features, but some modern novelistic writing, for example, is quite devoid of poetic ornateness.

Other features, of a more or less formalistic kind, have been proposed as definitive of literary language. I. A. Richards, in the 1920s, suggested that literature highlighted the 'emotive' function of language, in contrast to the 'referential' function exhibited by the sciences. His student William Empson identified 'ambiguity' as the key to poetry, to which the American critic Cleanth Brooks, in the 1940s, added 'paradox,' 'tension,' and 'irony.' Such attempts sought to find distinctive semantic properties associated with literary language, this being thought an advance on earlier emphases on stylistics. This direction of thought was epitomized in what came to be known as the 'semantic definition of literature' offered by Monroe C. Beardsley, according to which literature could be defined as a type of discourse with 'semantic density,' that is, exhibiting a high level of 'implicit meaning' (Beardsley 1958).

Parallel developments arose out of the Russian and Czech formalist schools, again from the 1920s onwards, where the essence of 'literariness' was sought in such notions as 'defamiliarization' (Shklovsky), 'foregrounding' (Mukařovský) or 'the palpability of signs' (Jakobson). One central idea, which became a prominent feature of the later structuralist movement, was that literary language draws attention to itself, even to the point of becoming self-referential, rather than being a vehicle for describing an outside world. (For a useful anthology of these, and other theories, see Selden 1988.)

However, in spite of capturing recognizable aspects of the literary, these semantic or formalist accounts face fundamental difficulties. The first is that they fail to isolate the literary: they do not apply to all literary works ('paradox' and 'tension,' for example, might characterize metaphysical poetry but not the nineteenth-century realist novel), and they apply to writing that is not literary (puns and obscenities draw attention to themselves without being literary). The second problem is that the presence of formally-defined linguistic properties cannot explain the value ascribed to literature (Lyas 1969). There is nothing inherently valuable in any of the properties mentioned. Ambiguity or semantic density or foregrounding can only be attributed literary value as a means to some further (valued) end. Now we see the difficulty in finding a formal definition of 'literariness' adequate to capture even the 'fine writing' aspect of literature. The linguistic qualities admired in poetry are not necessarily those admired in the novel, so we have not yet established what makes literature itself admirable.

The institution of literature

If linguistic properties cannot capture the essence of literature as an art, where can we turn next? A promising move is to look at literature not atomistically – one work at a time – but institutionally. On this view literary works are defined not by their intrinsic properties but by the role they play in a human practice (Olsen 1987). An analogy is sometimes drawn with units of currency. What gives a five-pound note its monetary value is not its value as a piece of printed paper (or its color, weight, size) but the function it performs within a social institution (the nation's banking system). Users of the currency recognize its range of uses and the conventional value vested in its material form. Without the institution there would be no units of currency (just bits of metal and paper, at best). Similarly, so this argument goes, there would be no literary works without the 'institution' of literature, that is, without established conventions for creating, appreciating, and evaluating literary discourse. The mere existence of ornate or finely-structured language does not constitute literature. Literary works are not 'natural kinds' but institutional entities determined by social interactions. If this is right then the role of the aesthetician is to identify the defining characteristics of the institution. This is a subtly different task from seeking common features intrinsic to all literary works.

The theorist must focus on 'relational' properties, notably between texts, authors and readers, with prominence given to the attitudes, expectations and responses conventionally attached to texts by participants in a 'literary practice.' It might be thought that nothing sufficiently determinate could be said about the conventions of reading and appreciating literature, given the heterogeneity of responses to literary works. Yet if we direct attention to literature as art, with the focus on the broad constraints already mentioned – including the 'imaginative/creative' aspect and 'moral seriousness' – we soon find that substantive indicators are identifiable.

The best place to start is to ask what it means to adopt a 'literary point of view' towards narrative, drama or poetry, and what distinctive expectations that raises. Clearly, not every approach to a text could be classed as a 'literary approach', so there should be general characteristics recognizable (Lamarque 1996). First, as with all art, a fundamental expectation regarding a literary work (treated as such) is that the parts cohere, more or less, into a unifying whole, that there is a design or purposiveness in the elements. Note that this does not rule out the avant-garde or 'nouveau roman,' which rejects 'closure', and plays with disjointedness, for design can reside in apparent randomness. Second, it is expected, in line with the 'moral seriousness' requirement, that whatever the surface subject matter (narrative event or poetic metaphor) there will be underlying themes of a broadly human interest, indeed that reflection on the subject matter will elicit reflection, of an imaginative kind, on these broader themes. Third, there is an expectation that the work will reward a process of interpretation which reveals the literary interest in the work, notably by showing in detail how the themes are sustained or developed by the work's elements and design. Finally, the value of the work, as a literary work, will emerge as a function of the three other features, that is, in relation to the rewards delivered by the work in these respects.

We can consider such a template as specifying at least some of the conventional attitudes and expectations which constitute the 'literary point of view' and thus the institution of literature. This approach has several advantages. By applying equally to the short lyric and the triple-decker novel, it accommodates the seemingly incommensurable variety of literary works. It abandons the search for a linguistic definition of literature, but without sidelining the obvious centrality of language to literature. Literary works are linguistic artifacts, and the aim of literary reading is to appreciate how linguistic properties – from poetic devices to narrative structure – are utilized to the end of producing a coherent form capable of sustaining imaginative (thematic) interest. Just as there is no prescription in the template about what literary forms are available, neither are restrictions placed on subject or thematic content.

Nevertheless, this broad sketch of the 'literary institution' raises a number of further issues: about content, about interpretation, about value.

Literature and fiction

The first problem is that the account offered is not, on the face of it, able to distinguish our second and third senses of 'literature.' For do not the King James Bible, Hume's *Treatise*, and the Gettysburg Address also conform to the definition? They are 'fine writing,' imaginative, and morally serious; they have a purposive design, they develop themes of human interest, they are subject to interpretation, they are regarded as of high literary value. There are many who would welcome this inclusiveness (Williams 1983: 152–5). Others, though, insist that the imaginative component of literature, in the third sense, implies fictionality (Wellek and Warren 1973: 25), which would exclude non-fictional works like the *Treatise*; speech act accounts of literature often have this consequence (see Ohmann 1971, Beardsley 1970).

Are literary works essentially fictional? No satisfactory answer can be given without an adequate conception of fiction, yet that concept has proved remarkably elusive to definition. It can mean 'false,' or 'unreal,' or 'invented,' or 'product of the imagination.' It can have both positive and negative connotations. Objects can be fictional (characters or events in novels) as also can descriptions (stories, statements). Being false is not sufficient for fiction, or else Aristotle's *Physics* and Bede's *History of the English People* would, counterintuitively, be classed as fictional. Arguably fictions can be compatible with a high degree of literal truth, as with many historical novels. Nor does fiction, as normally understood, imply the presence of fictional (that is made up) characters; again, historical fiction can be exclusively about real people.

Perhaps the best way of accounting for fictionality is not by appeal to falsehood or unreality or failure of reference but – as with literature – by reference to the intentions and attitudes of those who engage with fictions. Works of fiction encourage a certain kind of 'cognitive detachment,' in the sense that readers are invited not to believe in the literal truth of what they read but only to 'make-believe' (Currie 1990). Fictional works are imaginative not just in the sense that they emanate from the imagination, but because they invite an imaginative response in those who read them.

What makes Hume's *Treatise* non-fictional, according to this account, is not its truth-value but its primary purpose (Lamarque and Olsen, 1994). Hume is making assertions, inviting our rational assent, hoping to affect our beliefs. So it is with histories, scientific tracts, essays, and biographies. Fictional works might also seek to change our beliefs but the focus of their effort is make-believe, they aim to stir our imagination, to transport us into their own worlds.

The concepts of literature and fiction are not identical: the terms have different meanings. 'Literature,' for example, possesses an evaluative component not present in 'fiction.' Nor are they extensionally equivalent: not all works of fiction are deemed to be literature. Nevertheless, there are connections, most evident when we recall what it is to attend to a work 'from a literary point of view.' To read Hume or Bede or the Bible as literary works is different from reading them primarily from a philosophical, historical or religious standpoint. The literary reading attends to such matters as: the congruence of structure and content, the aptness of the linguistic qualities as a vehicle for a thematic vision, the way the parts cohere into an aesthetically satisfying whole. This is not the same as attention to rational persuasion, factual accuracy, or theological doctrine. In fact it fits more naturally with the response invited by fictions: imaginative involvement, immersion in fictional worlds, an emphasis on make-believe over belief.

What this suggests is that it is at least characteristic of literature (if not definitive, on our third sense) that such works be read as if they were fiction (Culler 1975: 128; Lodge 1977: 6–8). Some paradigmatic literary works – Shakespearean drama, the novels of Austen, Dickens, and Trollope – display their fictionality overtly. Other paradigmatic literature (usually poetry) – Shakespeare's sonnets, Wordsworth's *Prelude*, Robert Lowell's Notebooks – is much less obviously fictional, though can (perhaps should) be read, from the literary point of view, as the projection of fictional personae rather than as unequivocally autobiographical. That leaves the wider class of works belonging to our second category – the histories, treatises, speeches – which on this view can be appropriated into the narrower third category, but only by setting aside their principal function (as philosophy, history, and so on) and reading them as if they were works of the paradigmatic kind. They become 'honorary' literary works, under a certain reading. This move might not afford the sharp division of discourses that some theorists seek, but it seems to accord best with ordinary usage, and it affirms the intuition expressed earlier that being a literary work is not an intrinsic quality of a text, but a role in a social practice that some texts perform better or worse than others.

Literature and truth

The question of whether literary works can convey special kinds of knowledge, wisdom or truth applies exclusively to the paradigmatic works, treated as fictions. There is no controversy over whether Hume's *Treatise* is a legitimate vehicle for truth. Historically the truth debate about literature concerned poetry, the nature and claims of 'poetic truth.' Again the debate is ancient. The issue exercised Plato because he confronted a standing assumption that the great tragedians (notably Sophocles) were moral teachers, somehow in competition with philosophers. Plato's worry was that the poets' methods of teaching – through mimesis or imitation – were less than fully rational and could beguile the unwary into beliefs that lacked rational (philosophical) foundation. The Platonic thought that poetry (including drama) can be deceptive, dangerous, and immoral has surfaced continuously through European history, promulgated by both Church and State, prompting repeated 'defenses of poetry' of which Sir Philip Sidney's and Shelley's are simply the most well known.

The standard defense against these charges was first aired by Plato's pupil Aristotle, who argued that poetic drama, of a suitably structured kind, could both educate the emotions and transmit truths of a universal nature. In fact the truths that Aristotle associated with poetry – "what such-and-such a kind of man will probably or necessarily say or do" (*Poetics* 1451 b, 4) – seem curiously downbeat. It was left to the Romantic Shelley to express the highest aspirations for poetry which "makes immortal all that is best and most beautiful in the world" and "awakens and enlarges the mind itself by rendering it the receptacle of a thousand unapprehended combinations of thought" (Shelley 1965).

One difficulty with the truth debate concerns just how narrowly (or broadly) truth is conceived in connection with poetry. It is generally agreed that poetic truth is not reducible to a species of scientific or empirical truth. But what then is it? Shelley revered the imagination as "the great instrument of moral good" and saw the cognitive worth of poetry in terms of "enlarg[ing] the circumference of the imagination." That notion fits well with the accounts given earlier of both literature and fiction. However, it does not force an interpretation in terms of 'truth.' The imagination could be enlarged without truths as such being imparted. Those modern aestheticians who have sought to redefine poetic truth have invariably relied on qualified conceptions of truth: 'truth to reality' (John Hospers), a kind of verisimilitude, or 'authenticity' (Dorothy Walsh) or 'ontological truth' (Colin Falck) or a kind of empathetic truth, 'knowing what it is like' (David

Novitz). Iris Murdoch has explained artistic truth in terms of an artist's way of 'looking at the world.'

Behind these theories is the strong, and plausible, intuition that literary works have cognitive benefits, that we can learn as well as derive pleasure from them, that we can be improved by them. This is the intuition behind Horace's dictum *utile et dolce*. It is debatable, though, whether the intuition is best captured by appeal to 'truth' or even 'knowledge.' In Western culture these terms are so closely integrated into the scientific enterprise that to suppose there is a kind of 'imaginative truth' not accessible to science but revealed by art is only to court mystification. It seems wiser to focus on distinctively literary qualities. We have spoken of the presumption of 'moral seriousness' in literature. Works can be judged morally serious, in terms of the themes they develop, the complexity of characterization, the psychological subtlety of motive and action, the coherence of any vision expressed, without being judged as literally true or false (Lamarque and Olsen 1994). Readers can learn and feel morally uplifted by having their imaginations stretched, without thereby acquiring new knowledge. There is a danger that by trying to assimilate literature into philosophy the features which make literature distinctive will become diluted.

Criticism and interpretation

If the reading process integral to literature is not a search for truth, it is often thought to be a search for meaning. The idea of looking beyond the surface of a text to hidden meanings beneath came into prominence in Biblical hermeneutics in the early Middle Ages when different levels – the literal, allegorical, tropological, and analogical – were ascribed to scriptural meaning. The development of allegorical poetry – the *Faerie Queen*, the *Divine Comedy*, *Pilgrim's Progress* – continued this scriptural tradition, with the works themselves inviting 'levels of interpretation.' However, the idea that all literature, or literature *per se*, demands complex styles of interpretation is again relatively modern, accompanying the rise of hermeneutical methods in the human sciences (Wilhelm Dilthey) and also the intellectual currents of psychoanalysis and Marxism.

By the 1920s many factors – the establishment of 'English' on university syllabuses, the proliferation of popular culture, the eroding of a consensus on artistic value, the influence of positivism in the social sciences – created the felt need for a 'new criticism' which could inject discipline, scientific method, and objective judgement into critical practice. In Britain, I. A. Richards, T. S. Eliot, and F. R. Leavis, in the United States John Crowe Ransom, Allen Tate, R. P. Blackmur, Cleanth Brooks and W. K. Wimsatt (among others) brought to bear on the essentially humanist tradition of nineteenth-century critical methods a new rigor, attention to detail and fine-grained linguistic analysis. A far-reaching revolution in critical practice was born; it took poetry as paradigmatic (metaphysical, not romantic, epitomized by Donne, Eliot and Pound), it treated individual works atomistically and ahistorically (as 'verbal icons'), it was anti-psychologistic, and promoted the virtues of multiple meaning, complexity and 'organic unity.'

A key tenet of the New Criticism was the exposure of an 'Intentional Fallacy' in criticism (coined by M. C. Beardsley and W. K. Wimsatt, although anticipated by C. S. Lewis and T. S. Eliot) and the insistence that an author's actual intentions have no final authority in either interpreting or evaluating a literary work. Although the doctrine of 'autonomy' came to permeate the practice of critics, it has always remained controversial at a theoretical level. The critic E. D. Hirsch championed the opposite position, that authorial meaning must predominate in interpretation (Hirsch 1967), and subtle variants of these views have been developed (Stecker 1997), notably a compromise 'hypothetical intentionalism' which gives priority to the 'best hypothetical attribution of [an author's intention], formed from the position of the intended audience' (Levinson 1992: 224). The reason the debate drags on unresolved is that it occurs at a fault line between irreconcilable conceptions of literature: as vehicle of personal expression (Romanticism), as impersonal 'imitation' of timeless truths (Classicism), as pure linguistic artifact (Modernism).

A more radical anti-intentionalism appears in the doctrine of the 'death of the author' (Barthes 1977), which underpins poststructuralism. Literary works, on this view, are merely instances of *écriture* (writing), the author is an abstraction of the text, and meaning is determined by the reader. Related to this doctrine is the distinction between 'text' and 'work,' the former a mere concatenation of signs subject to multiple interpretations, the latter constrained by purpose, context, and genre. By assigning priority to texts over works, poststructuralists in effect sideline altogether the category of literature; mere *écriture* is undifferentiated.

However, the importance of retaining a conception of 'work' has been emphasized by humanistic critics (Lamarque 1996). Interpretation of texts *per se*, independently of any conception of what works the texts are of, is futile if not impossible. Poems, political speeches, legal statutes, hieroglyphics, or cryptic remarks might need interpreting, but the methods used and ends sought will be different. Literary interpretation must be consonant with the aims determined for literature as art. On the account sketched earlier this will mean that the focus of interpretation will lie in seeking to elicit themes from the work's subject, showing how parts cohere with the whole, and how linguistic means further aesthetic ends. Theorists who import extraliterary paradigms, even linguistic ones, as models of literary interpretation – semiotics (Barthes 1977), metaphor (Beardsley 1958), conversation (Carroll 1992), utterance meaning (Stecker 1997) – are in danger of losing sight of the specificity of these literary functions (the point is made forcefully in Olsen 1987).

A greater danger, though, to the humanistic conception of literature and criticism arises from the attempted assimilation of literature into wider theoretical frameworks, such as Marxism, Freudianism, structuralism, postmodernism, and feminism. These movements are all in varying degrees reductive, challenging the autonomy of literary qualities and seeking to explain (or explain away) literary production and reception through political, psychological or social parameters.

Literary value

There is no more controversial topic in literary studies than that of literary value, either the value assigned to particular works or that of literature itself. Criticism, as its name implies, has always involved value-judgements, yet modern critics have been loath to make these explicit.

We need to distinguish different levels of evaluation. At the base level there are judgements about specific details in a work: the aptness of phrase or image, the coherence of a scene, the predictability of plot development, the psychological insight of character interaction, the obtrusiveness of narrative voice. To judge such an element a success or failure presupposes that significance has been assigned it in the work, under an interpretation. A segment that fulfills its assigned function poorly is weak, although there might be room for debate over what that function correctly is (hence even at this level there is a connection between evaluation and interpretation).

At the next level, value judgements can be made about whole works. These judgements are more likely to be considered controversial. For one thing, they are associated with the formation of 'canons' or 'great traditions' in literature; also they are more likely to be dismissed as 'matters of taste' or at any rate culturally conditioned. The question of the objectivity of aesthetic value judgements has been much debated, especially in the eighteenth century when the sources of 'taste' became the key issue in aesthetics. We will come to canon formation in a moment, but first we should note that it is not obvious that the evaluations of whole works are of a different order from those of a work's components. Indeed the former judgements seem to presuppose the latter. A work with flaws at a structural or content-based level will not be the highest artistic achievement. Nor is it obvious that we lack objective criteria for judging literary works. Once a conception of literature is determined, then evaluations will be based on the extent to which the defining conditions are satisfied. Our account of literature as art already has evaluative criteria built into it: fine writing of an imaginative/creative nature with moral seriousness. A good literary work is one that rewards attention from the literary point of view, with these aims in mind. The criteria are different from those governing a philosophical, historical, or sociological perspective.

It is one thing to state the criteria in general terms, another to make specific judgements. As Hume insisted, making aesthetic value judgements calls for skill and discernment, experience and sensibility. It is important to emphasize that judging a work for its literary value is not purely formalistic, not simply based on 'poetic diction.' We have seen that the 'fine writing' aspect concerns not intrinsic qualities of 'literariness' but the consonance of linguistic means to literary ends. The literary ends can be determined only through an interpretation which assigns symbolic, figurative, or thematic significance to a work's elements. Aesthetic appreciation of literature can recognize no deep division of 'form' and 'content.' The 'seriousness' of the moral 'content' must always be a function of the imaginative exploitation of linguistic means.

The question of 'content' still haunts discussions of literary value. How can works like the *Iliad*, the *Divine Comedy*, the *Faerie Queen* and *Paradise Lost* continue to command our attention when the intellectual presuppositions on which they rest are so remote from, even at odds with, those of our own time? And could a work that we find morally reprehensible nevertheless be valued aesthetically (Levinson 1997)? We do not need, though, to force a dichotomy between aesthetic value and moral (or intellectual) content. A work fails aesthetically if it elicits and cannot resolve a dissonance between its (informed) readers' beliefs and its own literary aims. Literary appreciation is sufficiently flexible to allow imaginative engagement with a work's themes under most underlying presuppositions (as in the works mentioned). But it cannot always do so – for example, confronting extreme moral dissonance – and then there is literary failure.

The account given presupposes a more or less stable conception of literature and broad agreement on the highly valued (canonical) works. For some literary theorists this stability and agreement are largely illusory and products of ideological conditioning. Their reasoning is partly that the aesthetic itself is not a universal category but deeply embedded in historical circumstance, and partly that aesthetic criteria by no means exclusively determine canon formation. What counts as a canonical work, on this view, is determined not by inherently literary values but by political interests. So, for example, Shakespeare's canonical status has as much to do with the ideological construction of an English national identity as with the quality of his plays.

Perhaps the best response to these sociological attacks on literary value is just to look at individual cases and argue again for the values they exhibit (Bloom 1994). This takes us to the third and final level of literary evaluation, that of the 'institution' of literature itself. On the institutionalist account, literary works owe their very existence to a social practice, so *ipso facto* the values of literature are also defined by, and internal to, the practice. The works have no value outside the institution, yet within it their values are universal and recognized by all participants.

But is the institution itself of value? Do we need the discriminations and modes of appreciation that it defines? Those who see literature merely as part of (an undesirable) bourgeois ideology would reply negatively. By emphasizing rhetoric over literary criticism, texts over works, instrumental over intrinsic values, ideology over aesthetics, they reject not just the canon but the very concept of literature. Yet it is hard to imagine a culture without literary art, without a tradition of revered writings, without literary education.

It seems unlikely that recognition of an art of literature will cease altogether, that cultural studies will supplant literary criticism. A practice ends only when there are no more practitioners. But defenders of the humanistic values on which a literary education is based should not be complacent about its continued survival.

See also Fiction, Imagination and make-believe, Interpretation, Art and ethics, Art and knowledge, Criticism, Narrative.

References

Aristotle (1987) *The Poetics of Aristotle*, trans. S. Halliwell, Chapel Hill: University of North Carolina Press

Barthes, R. (1977) *Image–Music–Text*, trans. S. Heath, New York: Hill and Wang.

Beardsley, M. C. (1958) *Aesthetics*, Indianapolis: Hackett.

—— (1970) *The Possibility of Criticism*, Detroit: Wayne State University Press.

Bloom, H. (1994) *The Western Canon*, New York: Harcourt Brace.

Bourdieu, P. (1993) *The Field of Cultural Production*, trans. R. Johnson, New York: Columbia University Press.

Brooks, C. (1947) *The Well-Wrought Urn: Studies in the Structure of Poetry*, London: Methuen

Carroll, N. (1992) "Art, Intention and Conversation," in G. Iseminger (ed.), *Intention and Interpretation*, Philadelphia: Temple University Press.

Culler, J. (1977) *Structuralist Poetics*, London: Routledge and Kegan Paul.

Currie, G. (1990) *The Nature of Fiction*, Cambridge: Cambridge University Press.

Dilthey, W. (1910) "Der Aufbau der geschichtlichen Welt in den Geisteswissenschaften" (The Formation of the Historical World in the Human Sciences), trans. R. A. Makkreel and F. Rodi, in R. A. Makkreel anF. Rodi (eds), *Dilthey: Selected Works*, Princeton, N. J.: Princeton University Press (forthcoming).

Eagleton, T. (1983) *Literary Theory*, Oxford: Blackwell.

Empson, W. (1930) *Seven Types of Ambiguity*, London: Chatto and Windus.

Falck, C. (1989) *Myth, Truth and Literature*, Cambridge: Cambridge University Press.

Hirsch E. D. Jr. (1967) *Validity in Interpretation*, New Haven: Yale University Press.

Hospers, J. (1946) *Meaning and Truth in the Arts*, Chapel Hill: University of North Carolina Press.

Jakobson, R. (1960) "Closing Statement: Linguistics and Poetics" in T. A. Sebeok (ed.), *Style in Language*, Cambridge Mass.: MIT Press

Lamarque, P. V. (1996) *Fictional Points of View*, Ithaca, N.Y.: Cornell University Press.

Lamarque, P. V. and S. H. Olsen (1994) *Truth, Fiction, and Literature*, Oxford: Oxford University Press.

Levinson, J. (1992) "Intention and Interpretation: A Last Look," in G. Iseminger (ed.), *Intention and Interpretation*, Philadelphia: Temple University Press.

—— (ed.) (1997) *Aesthetics and Ethics*, Cambridge: Cambridge University Press.

Lodge, D. (1977) *The Modes of Modern Writing: Metaphor, Metonymy and the Typology of Modern Literature*, Ithaca, N.Y.: Cornell University Press.

Lyas, C. (1969) "The Semantic Definition of Literature," *Journal of Philosophy* 66: 81–95.

Mukařovský, J. (1964) 'Standard Language and Poetic Language' in P. L. Garvin (ed.), *A Prague School Reader on Aesthetics, Literary Structure and Style*, Washington, D.C.: Georgetown University Press.

Murdoch, I. (1970) *The Sovereignty of Good*, London: Routledge and Kegan Paul.

Novitz, D. (1987) *Knowledge, Fiction and Imagination*, Philadelphia: Temple University Press.

Ohmann, R. (1971) "Speech Acts and the Definition of Literature," *Philosophy and Rhetoric* 4: 1–19.

Olsen, S. H. (1987) *The End of Literary Theory*, Cambridge: Cambridge University Press.

Richards, I. A. (1924) *Principles of Literary Criticism*, London: Routledge and Kegan Paul.

Selden, R. (ed.) (1988) *The Theory of Criticism: From Plato To the Present*, London: Longman.

Shelley, P. B. (1965) *A Defense of Poetry*, Indianapolis: Bobbs-Merrill.

Shklovsky, V. (1965) "Art as Technique", in L. T. Lemon and M. J. Reis (eds), *Russian Formalist Criticism: Four Essays*, Lincoln: University of Nebraska Press.

Stecker, R. (1997) *Artworks: Definition, Meaning, Value*, University Park: Pennsylvania State University Press.

Walsh, D. (1969) *Literature and Knowledge*, Middletown, Conn.: University of Connecticut Press.

Wellek, R. and Warren, A. (1973) *The Theory of Literature*, 3rd edn, London: Penguin.

Williams, R. (1983) *Keywords*, rev. edn, Oxford: Oxford University Press.

39
FILM
Murray Smith

Film and the established arts

Arguments against film as an art

I will take as my focus in this essay the relationship between film and art (and assume, following most theorists of film, that the notions of film aesthetics and film art can be treated as synonymous, thus bracketing the largely unexamined issue of the relationship between art and the aesthetic in the context of film). Where the relations among film and art have been discussed, the outcome has often been a disdain for the artistic dimensions, achievements or potential of film. A usefully extreme version of such disdain can be found in the work of the conservative philosopher Roger Scruton who, in his discussions of photography and film, excludes the mass of popular fiction film making from the possibility of aesthetic achievement or distinction, dismissing it as the "mass marketing of sentimentality under the guise of imaginative drama" (Scruton 1981: 86).

Scruton writes of the "fictional incompetence" of cinema (Scruton 1983: 112), suggessting that the fictional dimension of a film is held in check by the fact that the fiction depends on the recording, visually and aurally, of an actual space and time. The fiction of Rhett Butler and Scarlett O'Hara embracing in an antebellum mansion in Georgia depends on a depiction of Clark Gable and Vivien Leigh embracing under arc lights in a studio in California. Now, the importance of this is that it reveals a particular type of aesthetic criterion: a fiction, as a type of aesthetic object, must not be bound to a mere *recording* of (some part of) reality. "It is only because of their absolute *lifelikeness* – their absolute truth to the ways things appear – that these [cinematic] images exert their fascination . . . Before the imagination can arrive at its truth, it must pass through the world of fiction" (Scruton 1981: 86). The aesthetic object is such by virtue of a creative or imaginative transformation of what it represents, and film, due to its character as a recording device (a 'phonograph for the eyes,' as

463

Thomas Edison conceived of it), is 'incompetent' in performing this function: films can perform an aesthetic function, but only so far and never very well.

Scruton is not a major theorist or critic of film, and his arguments are not extensively developed, but they serve to introduce two traditions of thought about the aesthetic potential of film which are of greater significance. First, Scruton's attitudes to film, and popular film in particular, were in many ways prefigured by the Marxist philosopher and aesthetician Theodor Adorno. For Adorno, the aesthetic potential of film was corrupted by the mechanical and commercial nature of film making, this commercial function conflicting with the 'autonomous' development necessary for art, debasing the Kantian 'purpose-lessness' of art into the barren 'purpose' of commerce (Adorno and Horkheimer 1979: 158). Adorno's hostility to film and its aesthetic potential was, however, far from the dominant attitude among early and classical film theorists (those writing up to roughly 1925, and those writing from around 1925 through the 1950s, respectively). It is among such figures that we find the second overlap with Scruton, though their arguments move in the opposite direction to those of Scruton. Theorists such as Rudolf Arnheim, Béla Balázs and Sergei Eisenstein also examined film in the light of traditional aesthetic criteria, in order to demonstrate that film *was* capable of aesthetic achievement, rather than to expose its (supposed) failings in this regard. The major project of early and classical film theory was to demonstrate that film was truly the 'seventh' art (or the sixth or the eighth, depending on how you count). Writing in 1922, Eisenstein and fellow Soviet film maker Sergei Yutkevich proclaimed that "the genius of Charlie Chaplin" had taken "the eighth seat in the Council of Muses" (Eisenstein 1988: 29).

Arguments for film as an art

Along with those of Lev Kuleshov, V. I. Pudovkin and Dziga Vertov, Eisenstein's theoretical writings grew out of, and developed in relation to, film making practice, both his own and the practice of other directors and other traditions of film making. Writing and filming from the early 1920s onwards, the revolu-tionary social and political context of Eisenstein's work inflected his use of, and perspective on, the concept of art, drawing it away from considerations of 'beauty' or 'disinterest,' and towards its role in galvanizing an audience in relation to the practical matters of revolution and social change: Eisenstein wrote of "an ever deeper immersion in the dialectical principles of militant mate-rialism in the field of art" rather than a concern with "aesthetics" (Eisenstein 1988: 244; see also 161–2). Abstract as this declaration sounds, his theoretical work is in fact littered with concrete examples, focusing on the construction of films at every level: the composition of the shot, the editing of the sequence, the overall force of a film. This is a vestige, perhaps, of his early training as an engineer, and very much part of a general (anti-Kantian) emphasis on the utility of art, on didacticism and tendentiousness, and the prioritizing in the early Soviet Union of the arts of design, architecture, documentary ('factography') and propaganda. The central organizing concept for Eisenstein was, of course, the notion of *montage*. Although conceived initially in terms of the editing of shots, the concept came to refer more broadly to the creation of new, higher levels of meaning and experience through the juxtaposition of any more basic elements. Eisenstein discriminated different types of montage and elaborated the notion in numerous directions (see, for example, Eisenstein 1988: 161–94).

Eisenstein's theoretical work represented the reflections of a film maker on his own and others' film making, and neither aspired to nor achieved a completeness or systematicity. A very different and more academic approach was undertaken by Arnheim, who produced the most systematic pre-war treatise on film-as-a-traditional art, *Film als Kunst* (1932) (translated into English in 1933 as *Film*; shortened and revised in 1957 as *Film as Art*). Arnheim's education was in Gestalt psychology, philosophy and art history, and his work is infused with Kantian assumptions and precepts (though he seldom makes explicit reference to philosophical aesthetics). The key assumption derived from this tradition was the definition of art as embodying 'purposiveness without purpose': the notion that aesthetic objects (whether natural or man-made) are distinctive because of the manner in which they are cut loose from practical ends. (The color red in a stop sign is telling you to do something in the world; red as it is used in a Rothko painting, or a film by Hitchcock, is simply inviting your attention.) This disengagement from practical purposes enables aesthetic objects to be used for purely *perceptual* or *contemplative* purposes: roughly speaking, the aesthetic object becomes an occasion for reflection rather than action. In order to fulfill this aesthetic role, however, an art work must exhibit certain properties: it must possess qualities of 'form' which distinguish it from that which it represents, its 'mere subject matter' (Arnheim 1983: 55). In other words, to be worthy of this disengaged, aesthetic attention, a work of art has to be more than a mere imitation of the world, or some part of it: it must also be a trans*form*ation of the world. Arnheim's Kantianism is tempered, however, by a suspicion of pure formalism as an artistic practice, and a recognition that 'informative' modes of film making – like the documentary – are as legitimate an arena of artistic expression as the fiction film. Arnheim cites Goethe's dictum "art is instructive long before it is beautiful" in order to stress the potential significance of propositional content, and as a corrective to pure formalism as a critical practice (Arnheim 1997: 76; see also Arnheim 1983: 114–29).

The idea that films might creatively shape that which they represent could hardly be taken for granted during the first decades of cinema's existence; indeed, as we have seen, arguments are still occasionally put forward denying film's status as an art in this sense. Photography and film were regarded by many as nothing more than advanced technologies of recording, and thus unable to effect that transformation of 'material' vital to art. As such, Arnheim's principal goal was to demonstrate the manifold ways in which film in fact *did* transform what it represented – in spite of its apparent ability to attain 'absolute truth to the way things appear' – and the ways in which this fact of transformation could be enhanced and accentuated by creative control of the medium. Film – silent, black-and-white film of the type that formed Arnheim's corpus – reduces a three-dimensional world to two dimensions, so a film maker has the creative choice either of fostering the appearance of three dimensions, or of stressing abstract, two-dimensional forms. Similarly, film takes a world of color and renders it in shades of grey; it takes an unlimited and continuous visual field and frames it; it takes a world of sound and renders it, if at all, by visual means. Thus Arnheim praises Josef von Sternberg's *The Docks of New York* (1928) for the way in which it evokes the sound and impact of a gunshot through a shot of a flock of birds suddenly taking flight, expressively shaping – and not merely recording – the event depicted. (Of course, this skirts the difficulty of any claim that it is possible to *record* a *fictional* event, but this was not a problem debated by Arnheim and his peers.) Encapsulating his overall argument, Arnheim writes: "Art begins where mechanical reproduction leaves off, where the conditions of representation serve in some way to mould the object" (Arnheim 1983: 55). Obvious as this view might seem to those trained in aesthetics, it conflicts with an assumption in popular film history which was particularly active in the late 1920s when Arnheim wrote: the idea that *technological* advances in the 'mechanical repro-duction' of reality correlate with *artistic* advances. Arnheim vigorously protested against the synchronized sound film, and did so, it is worth noting, by modeling his argument on a classic text of philosophical aesthetics, Gotthold Ephraim Lessing's *Laocoön* (1962).

The specificity of film

As Arnheim's appeal to Lessing's *Laocoön* suggests, the search for the 'specificity' of film was an abiding concern of classical film theory. As another important theorist of the period, Lev Kuleshov, wrote: "a film ought to be filmic, or it is not worth making" (quoted in Bordwell 1997: 27). This concern arose as a corollary of the concern to establish that film was an art, insofar as film might be seen to be merely parasitic upon existing artforms, such as painting and theater; to establish that photography and film should not be "regarded as the dull under-workers of true art" (Carroll 1988b: 24). Arnheim and other classical theorists effectively asked the questions: what are the specific or essential capabilities and features of film that allow it to function as a medium of art? For the Hungarian theorist (and occasional film maker) Béla Balázs, an important part of the answer lay with the close-up as a technique, and the 'microphysiognomy' that it brought to light, especially in terms of the human face. He argued that close-ups functioned both texturally, by revealing a microscopic landscape beneath the threshold of ordinary vision, and dramatically, in depicting dramas as they are revealed through tiny gestures and intimate details which, again, escape ordinary perception (Balázs 1970: 65–6, 75).

For Arnheim, the specificity of film lay in its being a visual, black and white, moving photographic medium. As such, dialogue was anathema to film as an art, threatening its degeneration from a creative art into mere 'canned theater.' The arrival of synchronous sound was thus problematic for Arnheim in two ways. In closing the gap between our perception of reality and our perception of film, the expressive possibilities open to the artist narrowed. And this depletion of the specific artistic resources of film was compounded by a corrupting contamination by, and dependence on, dialogue, the specific resource of theater. As with many – though not all – theorists of the silent era, Eisenstein shared this suspicion of synchronous sound, though he combined it with practical proposals for an alter-native conception of 'contrapuntal' or 'asynchronous' sound cinema based on the application of montage principles to sound (Eisenstein 1988: 113–14). More generally, although Eisenstein treated montage as the *sine qua non* or 'nerve' of film (ibid.: 163; see also 77–81), he was far less concerned with questions of specificity, often conducting his enquiries into montage and other aspects of film *via* the consideration of other artforms, including the theater (the field in which his own first artistic forays were ventured), the novel, poetry, painting, and music.

Film and the transformation of traditional artistic criteria

All classical theorists reveal an interest in defining the specificity of film, but where those discussed so far attempted to demonstrate how such medium-specific features enabled film to function aesthetically according to traditional criteria, other theorists argued that its value lay in its transformation of these very criteria. Two of the most notable figures in this regard are the German cultural theorist Walter Benjamin, and the French film critic André Bazin. Both recognize, as Scruton does, that film does not operate like any traditional art, indeed that its specificity might be said to lie in this fact; but unlike Scruton, both Benjamin and

Bazin, each in their own way, celebrates the transformation of familiar aesthetic experience effected by film.

According to Benjamin (1973), the traditional artistic object possesses an 'aura' which arises from the fact that the object is unique. Benjamin sees art as a descendant of religion; the aura of an artistic object is the secularized equivalent of the mystical or divine qualities thought to inhere in religious icons and artifacts, like the wine and wafer of Catholic communion. The advent of techniques of mechanical reproduction – initially in such techniques as lithography, and then more fully with the arrival of photography and the cinema – sweeps away any such aura, by undermining the uniqueness of the artistic object. One can go and see *the Mona Lisa* in the Louvre, but one cannot in an equivalent sense see *the* film of *Citizen Kane*. One can of course see reproductions of the *Mona Lisa* almost anywhere, but these are, as it were, degraded 'tokens' of the original painting. In the case of film, however, what we see in particular cinemas or videotapes are all *equally* valid tokens of the type *Citizen Kane* (assuming that all of these prints are complete and legible). For Benjamin – like Eisenstein, a Marxist – this releases the viewer of the artistic object from awed contemplation, which for Benjamin amounts to a kind of authoritarian trance imposed on the viewer. Released from this transfixed state, the viewer can then see the world in a new way, as it is revealed to him or her by the modern (and modernist) techniques of cinematography: the revelation of normally imperceptible or 'optically unconscious' sights through the close-up, and the dynamic rush and interplay of objects and events embodied by montage (Benjamin 1973: 237–40). Although opposing himself to traditional conceptions of aesthetic experience, then, Benjamin's ideas nevertheless overlap with those of his contemporaries working to a greater extent within those traditional frameworks, such as Balázs and Eisenstein.

Bazin's (1967) thinking about film represented a more significant departure from that of the silent 'creationists' (Carroll 1988b: 90) – those theorists who formulated their theories in relation to 'silent' cinema and who stressed the importance of creative transformation – and insofar as synchronous sound enhanced the recording capacity of film, Bazin is philosophically as well as historically the first great theorist of the sound era. For Bazin's account of film begins with the intuition that we have already noted in relation to other theorists: that photography and film are uniquely powerful mechanisms in the recording of reality, and the manner in which they represent the real world is qualitatively different from all traditional media. Bazin stressed the ability of film to represent the continuity of the world, temporally and spatially: the cinematic frame implying a continuous field of space merely 'masked' by the frame, a continuous shot capturing a slice of reality in real time (an example of what Greg Currie has termed *automorphic* representation, in which the time of representation and represented are identical (Currie 1995: 97)). Briefly sketched, Bazin's theory might sound rather like a version of the resemblance theory of depiction, where film occupies the role of the most compelling and pure case: films possess a special realism because of their 'absolute *lifelikeness*', that is, their utmost resemblance 'to the way things appear' (see Carroll 1988b: 122–5).

There is more to Bazin's theory than a notion of extreme resemblance, however. Bazin conceived of photographic representation as a kind of 'imprint' or 'trace' left by the world on the film, comparable to the way in which a shroud takes on the imprint of the body within it (Bazin 1967: 9–16). The key feature of filmic representation is the direct causal link between representation and reality, not the high degree to which representation is said to resemble reality; in the terminology of Charles Peirce, Bazin focuses upon the *indexical* rather than *iconic* dimension of photographic representation. Indeed, writing of the idea of the replication of phenomenal reality by film through resemblance, Bazin scorned the 'myth of total cinema,' arguing that no matter how sensuously refined the filmic image became, it would never be indistinguishable from reality. And more starkly, Bazin also celebrated a moment in Marcel Ichac's documentary *Annapurna*, when an avalanche sweeps away the camera and denies us footage of the climactic ascent of the mountain, a moment which captures a real event not through any kind of 'positive' resemblance, but rather through its obverse, the loss of any representation at all (ibid.: 161–2; see also 14).

How, then, does this feed into an evaluation of the aesthetic capacity of film outside of traditional conceptions of the aesthetic? Where Arnheim and Eisenstein stress the need for film to *transcend* its status as a mechanical recording device in order to underline its 'formative' aesthetic qualities, Bazin celebrates precisely its uniquely direct relationship with that which it represents. Thus, Bazin values the continuous long take and mobile camera work over the principle and the techniques of montage, so central for Eisenstein. And if, for Scruton, 'fictional truth' is corrupted by what he sees as the literal realism of film, for Bazin the unique 'ontology' of cinema rather enriches filmic fiction (Bazin 1967: 15; Smith 1995b: 116).

Contemporary developments

Contemporary film theory

The rise of semiotics – the study of signs, usually modeled on and assuming natural language as the pre-eminent sign system – in the 1950s and 1960s led to the temporary eclipse of the study of film *as an art*, as a focal topic in film theory. Questions concerning art and the aesthetic were dissolved into the broader notions of symbolism, language, representation, mind, and culture; in some quarters, the aesthetic is not merely ignored or marginalized, but explicitly attacked as an outmoded and bankrupt notion (Bennett 1987, Taylor 1998). It is in this context that we see the emergence of debates around issues like the status of film as a language, or the nature of film spectatorship, which first began to be addressed systematically during this period. The major figure in these developments was Christian Metz – the first professional film theorist of all those discussed here – who wrote the defining works of both the 'first semiotics' (which analyzed film in relation to the theory of language expounded by one of the founders of semiotics, Ferdinand de Saussure) and the 'second semiotics' (in which the principal point of comparison became a synthesis of the Saussurean-influenced psychoanalysis of Jacques Lacan, and the Lacanian-influenced Marxism of Louis Althusser) (Metz 1974, 1982). While often having relevance for aesthetic questions, these debates do not themselves directly focus on such questions. The one partial exception to this trend was the debate around the idea that there might be a specific 'feminine aesthetic,' that is, a form of aesthetic expression whose characteristics were deemed peculiarly or especially 'feminine' (whether conceived as a biological or cultural category) (de Laurentis 2000).

Historical poetics and the philosophy of film

Since the 1980s, however, debates centered on film art and aesthetics have reignited. The sources of this rebirth are twofold. First, there are those film critics and theorists who focus on the aesthetic dimensions of film, and do so in part by drawing on pre-semiotic traditions. Two such traditions have been particularly influential: that of Bazin and that of the Russian Formalists, a circle of literary theorists who also contributed to the creationist strand of film theory in the 1920s and 1930s (Eagle 1981). The influence of Bazin is evident in the work by and inspired by Stanley Cavell (1979), V. F. Perkins (1972) and Dudley Andrew (1984), all of whom stress the importance of critical attention to particular films in the formulation of broader theories of film. The Russian Formalists are a principal source for the 'historical poetics' – so called because of its focus on artistic norms and practices in historical contexts – of David Bordwell (1985, 1989, 1997, 1998), Kristin Thompson (1988) and those they in turn have influenced, such as Edward Branigan (1992), Carl Plantinga (1997) and Murray Smith (1995a).

The second source of the rebirth of debate on film art arises from philosophy. Film has become an object of debate among contemporary analytic philosophers to the extent that the philosophy of film has now been recognized as a distinct domain of philosophical inquiry, which approaches the questions of film theory with the 'methods' of analytic philosophy (Allen and Smith 1997; cf. Carroll 1988a: 263). Key figures here include Gregory Currie, who has analyzed some of the theses of classical film theory, especially those associated with Bazin, in the context of the philosophy of mind (Currie 1995). George Wilson (1986) has more explicitly pursued the Bazinian legacy, as well as offering arguments on the nature of film narration which overlap with those Bordwell, Branigan and Smith. The crucial linking figure here is Noël Carroll, who has written on a wide array of topics, and occupies an important role in debates in both philosophical aesthetics and film theory. Moreover, two anthologies have appeared in which representatives of both the philosophy of film and film theory are gathered together (Bordwell and Carroll 1996, Allen and Smith 1997). Both anthologies, and the work of all the figures mentioned here, testify to the way in which the philosophy of film maintains the broad focus, indeed the grand ambition, of semiotic film theory, while nevertheless arguing for the need to specify particular subdomains of inquiry – like those of art and the aesthetic – with their own particular problems and questions (see Bordwell on 'middle-level research' (Bordwell and Carroll 1996: 26–30) and Carroll on 'piecemeal' theorizing (Carroll 1988, 1996)).

Bordwell's entire oeuvre has stressed what would traditionally be thought of as an aesthetic perspective on film; indeed, his collaborator Kristin Thompson has overtly contrasted their work with that of contemporary semiotic film theorists in terms of its "assumption of an aesthetic realm distinct from (though dependent upon) a nonaesthetic realm" (Thompson 1988: 9). More specifically, Bordwell's keen attention to style and technique mark his commitment to the analysis of film as an art. This concentration on style echoes the work of classical theorists like Eisenstein (on whom Bordwell has written) and Arnheim, as does his use of scientific psychology (cognitive psychology taking the place of Gestalt psychology in Arnheim, and Soviet biomechanics and reflexology in Eisenstein). Moreover, Bordwell has argued for the existence of 'style-centered' films, which appeal to us more through their abstract dimensions, of rhythm and graphic play, than through their depiction of particular subject matter; and he has stressed that these formal dimensions play a significant role even in our appreciation of the most 'content-laden' of films (Bordwell 1985: 274–310). This idea receives its most forthright expression in his arguments against critical approaches favoring inter-pretation, or hermeneutics: approaches – overwhelmingly dominant in semiotic theory – which deem the sole or main role of criticism to be the revelation of the meaning or 'thesis' of a film (Bordwell 1989: 249–74). Bordwell insists on the distinctness (and even primacy) of the perceptual and cognitive *experience* of art works, as opposed to any meaning or moral we may take from them.

All of this is supported by one of the cornerstones of Bordwell's approach: the notion of *defamiliarization*. Derived from the Russian Formalist Viktor Shklovsky, defamiliarization refers to the perceptual and cognitive 'making strange' of our everyday perceptions and conceptions (Shklovsky 1990). This experience of 'estrangement' or 'seeing anew' is regarded as more significant than any thesis or 'message' about the subject matter which might be implied. Such a position can be regarded as a contemporary version of one of the founding statements of modern aesthetics, Alexander Baumgarten's *Aesthetica* (1961), in which Baumgarten argued for the integrity of perception as an end in itself, and not merely as a mere means to (conceptual, cognitive) knowledge.

In this regard, Bordwell's position can be likened to that of such figures as Adorno and Susan Sontag (1964), who have (in different ways) argued against the adequacy of interpretation as a mode of critical inquiry into and appreciation of the power of art; and contrasted strongly with that of Arthur Danto, who sees artistic expression – and thus art criticism – as inescapably and centrally concerned with questions of meaning and interpretation (Andrew (1984: 11) argues for a similar position within film theory). Indeed for Danto, whose premises are traceable to Hegel rather than Kant, art and the aesthetic are to be contrasted, rather than treated as largely overlapping, as they are for most of the figures discussed in this essay (Danto 1996).

Bordwell's work has developed in tandem with that of Noël Carroll, though the latter's work has always had a more overtly philosophical character (indeed, while Carroll began his career in film studies he has become a professional philosopher). Carroll's interest in aesthetic questions is evident throughout his work, but particularly in his earliest essays and first book, which discussed classical theorists like Arnheim and Bazin, and later writers like V. F. Perkins whose work has been defined in part by an engagement with classical film theory and the issues it focused upon (Carroll 1988b). Carroll's view of classical theory is divided. On the one hand, Carroll has contested the viability and value of essentialist, medium-specificity arguments. On the other hand, he has noted the great value of the "close examination of characteristic cinematic structures" (Carroll 1988a: 91) – that is, practices which have in fact been widely or successfully used by film makers, regardless of whether they are in any sense 'specific' to the medium – which arises in the course of the medium-specific arguments of classical film theory (such as Arnheim's on camera positioning or Bazin's on the exploitation of depth of field and deep staging) .

Moreover, Carroll has conducted an investigation into, and defense of, the artistic potential of popular art in general, with commercial film – 'the movies' – as a major example. Carroll accounts for 'the power of movies' by analyzing the way in which standard filmic conventions (concerning framing, point-of-view and so forth) are designed to exploit our perceptual and cognitive endowments in a direct, untutored and thus cross-cultural fashion (like Bordwell, Carroll draws extensively on contemporary cognitive and evolutionary theory in mounting this argument). *A Philosophy of Mass Art* (Carroll 1998) tackles the many arguments and prejudices to be found within traditions of aesthetic theory against the very idea of popular *art*, while Carroll's *The Philosophy of Horror* (1990) makes the case for a particular genre of popular art through the patient examination – conceptual and empirical – of a vast array of problems and examples (including the definition of horror, the notion of character identification, and various paradoxes of fiction and of horror).

In line with his arguments questioning the value of medium specificity, Carroll's corpus of horror encompasses literary and painterly as well as filmic examples. Thus, while Carroll refuses to separate film from the other popular arts on the grounds of medium specificity, he takes up in this broader context the defense of the idea of popular art which was always an implicit, and sometimes explicit, concern of many of the classical film theorists (insofar as most traditions of film making have been popular, rather than elite or esoteric, traditions). The remarkable interweaving of themes taken from the philosophy of art with those derived from film studies can be discerned in the various ways in which Kant crops up in *A Philosophy of Mass Art*. On the one hand, Carroll notes that the wide accessibility of mass art enables "what Kant called the sociability of art" (Carroll 1998: 13); on the other hand, he argues that a major source for 'philosophical resistance' to mass art is the illegitimate transfer, by later philosophers and art historians, of Kant's arguments concerning the aesthetic (the beautiful and the sublime) to the field of art (ibid.: 89–109). So Kant still has a role to play in our discussions of the movies and mass art more generally, but not the role that most theorists and philosophers have assigned to him.

In all but a few benighted corners, film has been accepted as an art. But the way in which it fulfils artistic criteria, given its distinctive technological character – a character which has evolved and continues to evolve – is a fascinating and far from settled matter. The continuing value and interest of the early and classical theorists derives from the novelty of the problem they faced, and the severity of the prejudices they opposed. Extravagant as some of the claims of such figures as Arnheim, Bazin and Eisenstein may seem today, their insights continue to inspire – as theses to defend, to modify, and to critique – the efforts of contemporary theorists and philosophers of film to analyze the distinctive nature of film art.

See also High versus low art, Photography, Pictorial representation, Kant, The aesthetic, Formalism, Interpretation, Imagination and make-believe, Fiction.

References

Adorno, T. and Horkheimer, M. (1979 [1947]) *The Dialectic of Enlightenment*, trans. J. Cummings, London: Verso.

Allen, R. and Smith, M. (1997) *Film Theory and Philosophy*, Oxford: Oxford University Press.

Andrew, D. (1984) *Film in the Aura of Art*, Princeton: Princeton University Press.

Arnheim, R. (1983 [1957]) *Film as Art*, London: Faber.

—— (1997) *Film Essays and Criticism*, trans. B. Benthien, Madison: University of Wisconsin Press.

Balázs, B. (1970) *Theory of the Film: Character and Growth of a New Art*, New York: Dover.

Baumgarten, A. (1961 [1750]) *Aesthetica*, Olms, Okla.: Hildesheim.

Bazin, A. (1967) *What is Cinema?* trans. H. Gray, Berkeley: University of California Press.

Benjamin, W. (1973) "The Work of Art in the Age of Mechanical Reproduction," in *Illuminations*, trans. H. Zohn, London: Fontana.

Bennett, T. (1987) "Really Useless 'Knowledge:' A Political Critique of Aesthetics," *Literature and History* 13: 38–57.

Bordwell, D. (1985) *Narration in the Fiction Film*, Madison: University of Wisconsin Press.

—— (1988) *Ozu and the Poetics of Cinema*, London: British Film Institute.

—— (1989) *Making Meaning: Inference and Rhetoric in the Interpretation of Cinema*, Cambridge, Mass.: Harvard University Press.

—— (1997) *On the History of Film Style*, Cambridge, Mass.: Harvard University Press.

Bordwell, D. and Carroll, N. (1996) *Post-Theory: Reconstructing Film Studies*, Madison: University of Wisconsin Press.

Branigan, E. (1992) *Narrative Comprehension and Film*, London: Routledge.

Carroll, N. (1988a) *Mystifying Movies: Fads and Fallacies in Contemporary Film Theory*, New York: Columbia University Press.

—— (1988b) *Philosophical Problems of Classical Film Theory*, Princeton: Princeton University Press.

—— (1990) *The Philosophy of Horror; or, Paradoxes of the Heart*, New York: Routledge.

—— (1996) *Theorizing the Moving Image*, Cambridge: Cambridge University Press.

—— (1998) *A Philosophy of Mass Art*, Oxford: Oxford University Press.

Cavell, S. (1979) *The World Viewed*, 2nd edn, Cambridge, Mass.: Harvard University Press.

Currie, G. (1995) *Image and Mind: Film, Philosophy, and Cognitive Science*, Cambridge: Cambridge University Press.

Danto, A. (1996) "From Aesthetics to Art Criticism and Back," *Journal of Aesthetics and Art Criticism* 54: 105–15.

de Laurentis, T. (2000) "Rethinking Women's Cinema: Aesthetics and Feminist Theory," in R. Stam and T. Miller (eds), *Film and Theory: An Anthology*, New York: Blackwell.

Eagle, H. (1981) *Russian Formalist Film Theory*, trans. H. Eagle, Z. Breschinsky, A. Lawton and E. Sokol, Ann Arbor: Michigan Slavic Publications.

Eisenstein, S. (1988) *Eisenstein: Writings 1922–1934*, trans. R. Taylor, London: British Film Institute.

Lessing, G. (1962) *Laocoön*, trans. E. A. McCormick, Indianapolis: Bobbs Merrill.

Metz, C. (1974) *Film Language: A Semiotics of the Cinema*, trans. M. Taylor, Chicago: University of Chicago Press.

—— (1982) *Psychoanalysis and Cinema: The Imaginary Signifier*, trans. C. Britton, A. Williams, B. Brewster, and A. Guzzetti, London: Macmillan.

Perkins, V. F. (1972) *Film as Film*, Harmondsworth: Penguin.

Plantinga, C. (1997) *Rhetoric and Representation in Nonfiction Film*, Cambridge: Cambridge University Press.

Scruton, R. (1981) "Philosophy and Literature," in *The Politics of Culture and Other Essays*, Manchester: Carcanet.

—— (1983) "Photography and Representation," in *The Aesthetic Understanding*, London: Routledge.

Shklovsky, V. (1990) *Theory of Prose*, trans. B. Sher, Elmwood Park: Dalkey Archive.

Smith, M. (1995a) *Engaging Characters: Fiction, Emotion, and the Cinema*, Oxford: Oxford University Press.

—— (1995b) "Film Spectatorship and the Institution of Fiction," *Journal of Aesthetics and Art Criticism* 53: 113–27.

Sontag, S. (1964) *Against Interpretation*, New York: Dell.

Taylor, C. (1998) *The Mask of Art: Breaking the Aesthetic Contract – Film and Literature*, Bloomington: Indiana University Press.

Thompson, K. (1988) *Breaking the Glass Armor*, Princeton: Princeton University Press.

Wilson, G. (1986) *Narration in Light: Studies in Cinematic Point of View*, Baltimore: Johns Hopkins University Press.

40

PHOTOGRAPHY

Patrick Maynard

Despite the great importance of photography to many aspects of life, philosophy, including aesthetics, has paid this strikingly modern kind of image-making scant attention, neglecting philosophy's traditional roles of asking meaningful questions, inventing basic conceptions, drawing important distinctions, and in general critically searching into the meaning of a topic in relation to other things that matter to us. A bibliography of philosophical writing on photography could be printed on a single page, with little of that about *art* photography. Not only in philosophy, but in aesthetics generally, cinema is a far more developed topic: indeed, some of the better known 'aesthetic' essays on photography are prefaces to film theories (Bazin 1979, Cavell 1971, Kracauer 1979, Scruton 1990). 'Essay' is the word for most of the best selling, impressionistic, occasional pieces on photography by the *philosophes* of time, who not only display but declare light acquaintance with their subject (Barthes 1981, Berger 1980, Sontag 1977). Fortunately, over the last decades serious, well-researched, attractively presented photographic histories have been written, and, with the stronger presence of photography in art exhibitions, fresh lines of photo interpretation, criticism and critical history have sprung up, filling a gap between the steady tradition of technical writing and spikes of journalistic interest signaling the arrivals of new processes such as digitalization. All this provides rich conceptual material for philosophy, but it is not philosophy.

Therefore our treatment will be of a 'protreptic' kind: not a survey of an autonomous philosophical tradition, but an identification and shaping, for philosophical investigation, of photo-aesthetic topics as they arise in practice. First, basic, nontechnical, distinctions are called for in an area of perennial perplexity, arguments at cross-purposes and equivocation. Following the analyses, we will consider the interrelations of what we have distinguished, in order to clarify issues of meaning for photographic art.

Photography, art and aesthetics

It might be said that photography no more came into existence to serve art than the printing press arrived to produce poetry. In less than two hundred years of existence, photography's rapidly evolving uses have become integral to so many aspects of modern people's lives (Goldberg 1993), with so many different and important meanings, that the issue of photography's place among the pictorial fine arts can never claim central interest, practically or theoretically. Thus some of the most important philosophical issues about photography lie outside art, aesthetics, and the scope of this article. Yet, while useful in some ways, analogies to print technologies have limits. Artistic uses were, after all, among the aims of the first inventors of photography and its many subsequent re-inventors. One simple reason for this is the close association between fine art and making pictures and representations generally. There is still much truth to the old idea of art as representation, as the extremely high proportion of real or putative works of visual art that are straightforwardly representational could hardly be an accident. Conversely, there is a strong, if careless, tendency to use the word 'art' for any process of making meaningful visual images, particularly representational ones. Thus the many successful general histories of photography (Gernsheim 1986, Newhall 1982, Rosenblum 1997) include much photo *art* history, depend on recognized works of photographic art, identify photo artists, and deal with kinds of photo aesthetics.

If practitioners, theorists, and historians of photography cannot avoid matters of aesthetics, philosophers of art, in turn, have much to learn from photography. Conceptual debates about the status, or the very possibility, of photographic art have arisen recurrently since the introduction of the medium, in different guises, with changes of photo-technologies, activities and uses, as well as with changes in modern conceptions of visual art itself. This very ambivalence should be of particular interest to philosophers, as whenever we encounter both attraction and resistance to including one important conception within another, we are challenged critically to examine both.

Three issues immediately arising from the above seem to call for philosophical treatment. First, if we are to consider the relationship of photography to the visual arts, both provide moving targets, as rapid changes in the technology and use of photography must be correlated with the notoriously shifting modern conceptions of visual art itself. We must also consider their interactions: changes in photography will be affected by changed attitudes and practices in the arts, and – as is often pointed out – the modern arts themselves have been affected, possibly transformed, by the evolving phenomenon of photography (Benjamin 1981). Second, encouraged by the demonstrated force of photographic images, some have denied the relevance of artistic and aesthetic categories to the medium; some have even held that photography, together with other modern media, has helped to make art and aesthetics outdated institutions ('art is superfluous'). Besides questions of ratification, we have declarations of independence and attempted revolutions.

Third, as we look into the sources of ambivalence concerning photo art, distinctions are called for, as some sources have to do with the aesthetic *appearance* of photographs, others with the *processes* of producing them, still others with their *uses*. This is a seemingly simple set of distinctions but, as we shall be emphasizing, distinct factors may be highly interactive: we might call this conceptual 'photo chemistry.' Thus the mix of uses of photography for illustration, commerce, propaganda and science has long raised issues regarding photography as art. For example, many photo artists have supported themselves with commercial work, sometimes (as with Steichen) attempting to integrate the two, sometimes (for example Adams, Michals, Weston) insisting on their separation. Furthermore, most written histories and large private or museum collections of photo art include commercial work, notably portrait and fashion photography (by, for example, Avedon, Beaton, and Karsh). They also include press and documentary photography, where some of the best-known works of artistic photography occur, including images by photographers like Capa who do not call themselves artists. A complex situation is made more interesting by later shifts in conceptions of visual art. In the radically heterogeneous climate of artistic practice of the 1970s and 1980s, a number of visual artists took up photography while refusing to call themselves photographers, often disdaining photo history and existing photo aesthetics. Still later photographers, sometimes called 'postmodern' (such as Levine, Prince and Sherman), often did the same (Davis 1999).

To suggest what philosophers of art might learn from such issues about photography, and to encourage philosophical attention to photo aesthetics itself, I will consider photography in terms of some familiar ideas about art: ideas about the aesthetic, representation, self-expression, and art considered culturally.

The aesthetic

The term 'aesthetic' is generally understood, like the older term 'beauty,' to concern delight (or the reverse) in the activities of *perceiving* things. While this idea of 'perceiving' is strongly rooted in sensual activity, it gets extended to activities of imaginative apprehension in order to include such fine arts as literature. 'Aesthetic' then has a qualifying, adjectival and adverbial, use, usually as a term of contrast, as in 'aesthetically interesting' (or, as one philosopher wrote, "aesthetic this and aesthetic that"). The term 'aestheticism' denotes a high placing of such experiences among all values, practical, ethical and social. (For example, within photography, the art and writings of Stieglitz (1980) and Weston are noted – often criticized – for their aestheticism.) By derivation, 'aesthetic' also has an important *noun* use: we speak in plural of different 'aesthetics' of societies, epochs, styles, media.

One important line of photographic aesthetics has the aim of identifying a generic photographic aesthetic, notably one based on its material and sensual characteristics, which – along with the mobility of the small camera and nearly instantaneous image production – have combined to provide a variety of new image forms (Adams 1980, 1983, Borcoman 1993, Edwards 1980, Evans 1980, Kracauer 1979, Moholy-Nagy 1980, Strand 1980, 1981, Szarkowski 1966, Weston 1980a, 1980b). On this modernist understanding, photographers explore the nature of their medium, thereby revealing aspects of the world. Such medium features usually include extreme sensitivity to gradations of light, the perspectival features of camera images, a tendency to record incidental detail, and the trace nature of the image. Some of the most influential modern writing on photography exists in those histories (Eder 1978, Galassi 1981, Gernsheim 1986, Newhall 1982), which – given the clearly technologically driven history of its media – find a strong narrative line in materials and processes. Recent advances in research and the development of large public photo collections (such as the Société Française de Photographie, the National Museum of Photography, Film and Television, the George Eastman House, the Getty Foundation, the Metropolitan Museum, and MoMA) are producing increased appreciation of the distinct aesthetics of different kinds of photography (Adams 1983, Frank 1958). Publications on specific historical processes such as daguerreotype and early paper methods are notable (Jammes and Janis 1983, Trachtenberg 1998), and benefit from great improvements in book plate-reproduction.

An opposed stream of anti-modernist practice and theory denies the importance – or even existence of – unique physical media bases for photography (Coleman 1981, Marien 1986, Snyder 1989, Solomon-Godeau 1991, Uelsmann 1981). These writers call for histories of photography alternative to the mainstream, with not only different categories but different data, for a different conception of photographic art (though it proves one thing to criticize the successful modernist histories, another to write the alternatives). Radical attempts at basic reconsiderations clearly open up philosophical territory, as does another anti-modernist trend, which favors critical studies of the historical and cultural contexts of art works and their presentations (Bolton 1989, Taft 1938, Trachtenberg 1989).

Do such critical positions represent *anti*-aesthetic approaches to photo art? In a narrow sense some do, by rejecting a visual 'poetics' (Phillips 1989) of photography based on material-perceptual characteristics of the medium. But in a wider sense they do not: after all, Aristotle denied material causality as the essence of poetry, yet we attribute an aesthetic – indeed a poetics – to him. We need to consider the aesthetic by way of perception. Although certain habits of speech about art may suggest viewer passivity (with terms such as 'impact,' 'effect,' 'exposed to'), modern studies of visual perception insist that seeing is an activity, a thing we do. Furthermore, art works and aesthetic objects tend to be not only completely absorbing ones, but also ones that implicate us and encourage our participation. Whenever a certain aspect or look of a kind of photograph is recommended, a visual activity on our part is recommended. This is seen clearly in appreciations of different kinds of photography: in what is said about the aesthetics of daguerreotypes, machined photographs, small snapshot or large view, soft or hard focus, monochrome or color, family albums, magazine advertising, street and social documentary, previsualized or postvisualized, single or serial, 'straight' or combined, minimalist, postmodern, mass or high art. Each of these may develop and reward, or discourage, frustrate or affront perceptual activities. Thus, even anti-sensual approaches to photography still express aesthetics that favor perceptual activities. Even the most 'conceptual' work, by taking on the *look* of being conceptual, becomes itself sensually perceptual. Given the speed at which perceptual adaptation usually occurs, truly anti-aesthetic movements will be difficult to sustain.

Depiction

Since, as has been remarked, photography is most strongly associated with a diverse class of visual figurative images, thought about the perception of photo images leads directly to questions of depiction. First, we must note that access to images of all kinds is one of photography's greatest contributions to the arts: photographic *reproduction*, together with photographs of sculpture and architecture, has made the enjoyment and study of the arts accessible to billions, changing our relationships to works of art in various ways. Nor should we disregard the aesthetic judgement necessary in making and using reproductions. We might also be skeptical of the common idea that photographs themselves are indefinitely reproducible. Besides the material limits, particularly of chemical negatives, anyone of aesthetic perception can easily notice the wide range of differences among reproductions made from a given negative: features that made a picture worth taking are often lost in technically acceptable prints and reprints. Finally, with modern artistic self-criticism, photo reproduction has been itself a frequent subject of art and theory (Benjamin 1981, Savedoff 1997).

In any discussion of photo depiction, especially in relation to art, it is essential to avoid obscurities around the everyday notion of a 'photograph of' something.

It is necessary to distinguish what a photographically-made picture *represents* from what it is a *photograph of*; next it is necessary to distinguish what such a picture, artistically, may be *about*. It is routine practice to photograph one thing in order to depict another: in cinema and in advertising, for example, photos are taken of actors and props in order to depict different things: sometimes non-existent entities or events, so that there can be no question of these causally producing the image. Furthermore, some have argued that an extremely valuable feature of photography is owing to the following: that what is depicted may also be one of the factors that causally affects the film via a mechanical linkage, although of course many of the other causal factors involved are not depicted (Arnheim 1979, Kracauer 1979, Maynard 1997, Walton 1984). We look at photos to detect any of a host of causal features that have produced the image: exposure length, aperture, lens type and condition, camera action, film speed and condition, characteristics of the light, the development process, as well as physical characteristics of the thing photographed. It is likely that none of the former is shown or depicted by the resulting picture, though they may *show up* and may be detected from it: after all, this is how we diagnose difficulties with film, camera settings or actions, development and other causal factors that afflict our attempted photo-depictions. Normally only the physical characteristics of what is photographed, perhaps with characteristics of the light, can be candidates for what a photograph depicts, or 'is a picture of.'

Still, in photo art, any of the other undepicted causal factors – such as the position or motion of the camera – can be important parts of the content or meaning of the picture. The position of the photographer and the very act of taking the exposure (such as in a photo that has the appearance of being a hand-held snapshot), while not represented, are often significant aspects of the meanings of pictures. So is the time (not always a 'moment') of exposure, although – contrary to cliché – photos are no more necessarily limited either to depicting or to registering their periods of exposure than are any other kinds of pictures or trace-recordings.

Our double use of photographs in a variety of contexts, both to show or depict, and to detect causal factors, sets the use of photos markedly apart from the use of other pictures. A source of confusion concerning whether photos can 'lie' is a simple failure to consider this overlapping double function. By a simple analogy, two characteristics of knife blades – being wide in one dimension and narrow in another – allow them to perform the distinct functions of dividing and spreading, which we combine in different ways, as we sometimes divide in order to spread and spread in order to divide evenly; sometimes in continuous motions, as with a palette knife, which is used to lift and spread or apply again. This analogy of blended color also reminds us of the variety that can come from combining a few clearly distinguishable elements.

Since photo depiction so often works as a 'user friendly' mode of access to detection, we can be careless or misled about what we can detect thereby. A benign example is the posed photo, in which, for example, a photo of someone saying 'cheese' is used to depict someone smiling. Much commercial use of photography is simply an economical form of depiction, reinforced by a vague impression that one is detecting some traits or other of the main subject. By contrast, technical uses of photography for detection take place against controlled background conditions and with specially trained personnel. Most digitalization of photographs does not disturb this information channel, but rather makes the information more easily accessible. Wider use of digitized images from the 1980s is thought to have widened the old gap between what a picture represents and what we can detect from it, although it might rather be said to have raised problems about technologies that make non-photographic images (sometimes made out of photographs) that are indiscernible from photographs of things.

Two extreme responses to these multiple functions should be noted. One extreme is so to emphasize the causal linkage and detective value of photography as to deny that photographs are depictions at all. Thus an early commentator termed photography "a new form of communication . . . neither letter, message, nor picture" (Eastlake 1980), and a recent philosopher has held that photographs are not even depictions (Scruton 1990). The opposite extreme is to deny the singularity of any photo-detective function (Snyder and Allen 1975). One philosopher even asserts that, regarding photo images, "the causes cannot be read in the effects – the former are limited to only causing them," a statement whose truth would be a blow to medical diagnostic imaging, historical archives, aerospace programs and the like (Michaud 1998: 736).

Photography's double functions have implications for the specifically aesthetic matters discussed earlier. As the aesthetic is a matter of the perceptual activities of viewers, the photo double function makes possible striking new perceptual activities and blends, and thereby new aesthetic possibilities. Also, as already noted, the perceptual content of a photo can go far beyond what it pictures or depicts. Here it should be observed how, on a very narrow construal of the aesthetic, which once gripped aesthetic thought, the detective function of photo images could not be aesthetic, as that would constitute an instrumental use of the image, allegedly incompatible with treating it as aesthetic: that is, as an 'end in itself.' This is a view whose presupposition is still popularized through metaphors of 'reference' such as an arrow pointing away or 'transparency' as a window. When we think in such crude cartoons our complacency courts confusion. Among several failures of these views are their sharp separation of means and ends: itself, ironically, a most unaesthetic approach to experience, and to life.

Much appreciative writing on photographs, from its earliest days to the present, reflects fascination with the many ways in which depiction and visual detection combine – not always amicably – while drawing in other mental and psychological processes. A striking case is the art of documentary – including war and catastrophe – photography, where the devices of the pictorial arts must be brought into play unobtrusively against the situation we detect as recorded and revealed: there are often moral reasons for this. Here, as with the variety of other cases and contexts, it is important that philosophers draw significant distinctions and think things through, not in an a priori manner but with informed sensitivity about the diversity of actual photographic practice, working from particular cases, which suggest new, interesting general conceptions. Typically, photo *artists* make play with the associated functions we have considered. A close matching of what is depicted by a photo and what can easily be detected by it is one feature of documentary photography. However volumes could be written on the great variety of meanings and effects that artists continue to explore in the tensions, balances and many other relations between under-standing the depiction and detecting a situation. Finally, we must bear in mind that in some cases this double function of photos may not count for very much, or not at all, to aesthetic or artistic meaning: above all, the image itself may be what interests us.

These considerations help us see another essential distinction: that it is as true of photography as of other 'representational arts' that what a photo is *of* – even what it represents – need not be what it is *about* (Snyder 1989). While many photographers will agree (in different ways) with Callahan's "it's the subject matter that counts" (1981) some photos are more about the light which produced them than they are about the illuminated objects, situations and events involved or depicted. Some influential photo aesthetics give more emphasis to photo-graphic tonal gradations and contrasts than to any objects; most stress all-over composition; some stress 'space-filling' and the negative spaces between depicted objects (Davis 1999). As was mentioned earlier, others strongly 'thematize' the action of taking the picture, including spontaneity or careful control, camera action, photographer's position or action, complicity in or reaction of the subject to the picture-taking act, and so on. Finally, with a general artistic turn to social criticism – notably acute self-criticism – in the decades following the 1960s, photographic depiction and detection became themselves much-worked subjects, not only of art writing but of the photographic works of that very era in which photo art came strongly into the art world, in exhibition, criticism and collecting. Although the point holds for all epochs of photo art, anyone approaching the minimalist, postmodern or deconstructive photographic works of those decades will have especially great difficulty identifying photographic art works as 'photo-graphs of,' or even as depictions of things, situations and events.

Agency and expression

From its earliest times and processes, a strikingly peculiar feature of photos has been the way in which, as is often said, they are not made 'by hand' (Arnheim 1979, Barthes 1981, Bazin 1979, Holmes 1980, Talbot 1980). This 'automatic' or 'mechanical' aspect of photography has several implications regarding art and the aesthetic; three in particular need distinguishing and closer study. First, a feature much remarked since the earliest days of photography is that its images, whether chemical or electronic, are not usually experienced as put together by sequential processes of working physical surfaces with tools ('by hand'), applying materials to build up an image, or – as with much drawing and painting – depositing materials with significant tactile and optical properties. This sometimes makes our aesthetic or perceptual activities with photos significantly different from those with other pictures. A second and more commonly noticed issue concerns whether photographs, understood as stages in engineered, filtered and maintained information channels for detection, can have artistic status.

Closely linked to these is a third issue, concerning human agency and self-expression. Human agency is, after all, a component of the general idea of art. Even at the eighteenth-century origin of the modern idea of 'fine arts,' when many arts were considered aesthetically – that is, as means of craft production of 'fine' objects for luxury markets – craft was valued in terms of intentional human activity. Yet that was never taken as sufficient. Room was always made for 'genius,' as what goes beyond craft rules, even beyond the aesthetically-valued feature of admired formative skills. 'Genius' being a term for spirit, the individual spirit of the maker was thereby given value, as was, increasingly, the wider spirit of a people. Succeeding centuries greatly developed these ideas along broader political lines of individual and cultural freedom. Thereby, creativity and self-expression, with strong implications of freedom, became bywords of art, and the idea of fine art came increasingly to represent these wider motives. Indeed, photography is often recommended in this manner, as a medium whose technological advantages lie not simply in saving labor, but in opening wider fields of self-expression for artists and amateurs.

Paradoxically, these very advantages have also been a source of misgiving about photo art. Since it is clear from everyday actions that people express themselves by the way they do things, it would be foolhardy to suppose that the procedures bypassed by photography were merely technical ones. Indeed, the very labor-saving advantages of photo-technologies have seemed to some (Emerson 1981, Kracauer 1979, Scruton 1990) so to weaken the scope of mind – the degree of conceptualized content – in photography, as to compromise or even defeat its status as fine art. Accepting these considerations, some photographers have actually been sanguine about photography's being something other than art (such as Brassaï), whereas others have either defended the degree of photographers' control (Weston 1980b, 1981), or redefined it as a perceptual, not a physical, action. Yet one can hardly consider such matters without first identifying the *entity* or *aspect* that is or is not controlled or conceptualized. When we say that an artist made a sculpture, we do not mean the piece of marble, the calcium carbonate (synthesized by prehistoric marine creatures), the calcium (product of an ancient star). For example, as already pointed out, in pictures, and certainly in works of art generally, the representation is only *one* of the relevant candidates for identity.

Such are points that philosophers need to clarify, especially as it is by now amply evident that different photo-artists have achieved distinctive, recognizable self-expressive styles characterized by all the normal terms of psychological attitude. But in addition to such analysis, philosophy is also called on to follow the more philosophical intentions of the artists themselves. As noted, some photo traditions deny the importance of the physical processes of production; by contrast, another broad tradition is happy to accept the photographer's actions as an integral part of a wider system of contributing physical causes, among which the situation photographed, the light, and other causes also feature. This latter view not only fits the experience of many photographers (Lange 1980, White 1980, Weston 1981, Adams 1983); it fits the experience of artists in other media, times, and cultures, who are less interested in self-expression than in self-realization, understood as taking part in what their work manifests.

Art

Although the aesthetic, like representation, has strong associations with art, we also apply 'aesthetic' to nature. Besides not all the aesthetic being art, some argue the converse as well, that not all art is aesthetic or, more strongly, that there is no essential connection between the two. Denials of essential connections between art and the aesthetic may express either a rejection of a sensual conception of art (as described earlier) or a rejection of a spectator or 'consumer' conception of art. For photography, a separation of art and the aesthetic helps explain why many who are unconcerned with whether there is photographic art or what it is – or even deny that there is (Emerson 1981) – nonetheless have distinctive views on, or pronounced practices of, photo-aesthetics. It also explains how some who make a case for photo-art can reject aesthetics (Levine 1979).

Our third component, self-expression, can now be more closely compared with the aesthetic. If self-expression approaches to art can be found sometimes to conflict with aesthetic construals of art, once again the matter is not simple. An 'aesthetic' – a sensibility – is self-expressive of individuals as well as of groups. It is a way in which they make their social, religious, ethical and other values perceptible; indeed, it typically becomes *part* of those values. As applied to photography, those who favor particular kinds of photo-aesthetics usually make broad claims for photo 'vision,' notably as expressive of modern times (De Zayas 1980, Léger 1980, Levine 1979, Moholy-Nagy 1980), sometimes even hoping to usurp the role of other figurative arts or to reshape everyday visual experience. In any case, each succeeding movement in photo art is usually taken as expressing its era (Davis 1999).

This helps to explain why there should be a general issue about photo art, and why recently there has been sharp criticism of the very effort to bring photography into the class of fine arts (Coleman 1981, Crimp 1989, Keller 1984, Phillips 1989, Sekula 1981, Solomon-Godeau 1991, Sontag 1977). Although the idea of fine or high art in Western societies is often criticized as marginalizing other arts, it is normal for cultures (and sub-cultures) to designate certain of what we would call their arts – even certain artists or art works – as canonical, as particularly expressive and close to their own sense of values, identity, meaning and importance (rather as they regard their languages, customs and histories). Thus as photo-imaging technologies continue their powerful course through modern societies, vying for this position with the visual arts, questions about photo art recur. Ironically, the merging of electronic and computer forms of imaging further complicates the situation, with some even heralding a post-photographic imaging age (Mitchell 1992). However, just as the announcement in 1839, when photography was introduced, that 'painting is dead' soon rang hollow, history seems to show that, rather than new forms and conceptions in art and aesthetics simply supplanting older ones, we find layerings of new forms over preceding ones, which persist, and indeed work interactively with the newer ones to produce other aesthetic and artistic possibilities. Amid this changing, interesting, perplexing and culturally important complexity, philosophers have their work to do.

See also Expressivism, Definitions of art, The aesthetic, Formalism, Art, Expression and emotion, Value of Art, Pictorial representation, High versus low art, Film, Painting.

References

Adams, A. (1980) "A Personal Credo," in B. Newhall (ed.), *Photography: Essays and Images*, New York: Museum of Modern Art.
—— (1983) *Examples: The Making of 40 Photographs*, New York: Little Brown.
Arnheim, R. (1979) "On the Nature of Photography," in P. Petruck (ed.), *The Camera Viewed: Writings on Twentieth-Century Photography*, New York: Dutton.
Barthes, R. (1981) *Camera Lucida*, New York: Farrar, Straus and Giroux.

Bazin, A. (1979) "The Ontology of the Photographic Image," in P. Petruck (ed.), *The Camera Viewed: Writings on Twentieth-Century Photography*, New York: Dutton.

Benjamin, W. (1981) "The Work of Art in the Age of Mechanical Reproduction," in V. Goldberg (ed.), *Photography in Print: Writings from 1816 to the Present*, Albuquerque: University of New Mexico Press.

Berger, J. (1980) "Understanding a Photograph," in A. Trachtenberg (ed.), *Classic Essays on Photography*, New Haven: Leete's Island Books.

Bolton, R. (1989) "The Contest of Meaning: Critical Histories of Photography," in R. Bolton (ed.), *The Contest of Meaning: Critical Histories of Photography*, Cambridge, Mass.: MIT Press.

Borcoman, J. (1993) *Magicians of Light: Photographs from the Collection of the National Gallery of Canada*, Ottawa: National Gallery of Canada.

Callahan, H. (1981) "Statement," in V. Goldberg (ed.), *Photography in Print: Writings from 1816 to the Present*, Albuquerque: University of New Mexico Press.

Cavell, S. (1971) *The World Viewed*, New York: Viking.

Coleman, A. D. (1981) "The Directorial Mode," in V. Goldberg (ed.), *Photography in Print: Writings from 1816 to the Present*, Albuquerque: University of New Mexico Press.

Crimp, D. (1989) "The Museum's Old/ The Library's New Subject," in R. Bolton (ed.), *The Contest of Meaning: Critical Histories of Photography*, Cambridge, Mass.: MIT Press.

Davis, K. (1999) *An American Century of Photography*, 2nd edn., New York: Abrams.

De Zayas, M. (1980) "Photography and Artistic-Photography," in A. Trachtenberg (ed.), *Classic Essays on Photography*, New Haven: Leete's Island Books.

Eastlake, E. (1980) "Photography," in B. Newhall (ed.), *Photography: Essays and Images,* New York: Museum of Modern Art.

Eder, J. M. (1978) *The History of Photography*, 4th edn, trans. E. Epstean, New York: Dover.

Edwards, J. P. (1980) "Group f.64," in B. Newhall (ed.), *Photography: Essays and Images,* New York: Museum of Modern Art.

Emerson, W. H. (1981) "The Death of Naturalistic Photography," in V. Goldberg (ed.), *Photography in Print: Writings from 1816 to the Present*, Albuquerque: University of New Mexico Press.

Evans, F. (1980) "Frederick H. Evans on Pure Photography', in B. Newhall (ed.), *Photography: Essays and Images,* New York: Museum of Modern Art.

Frank, P. (1958) *The Americans*, Zurich: SCALO.

Galassi, P. (1981) B*efore Photography: Painting and the Invention of Photography*, New York: Museum of Modern Art.

Gernsheim, H. (1986) *A Concise History of Photography*, 3rd edn, New York: Dover.

Goldberg, V. (1993) *The Power of Photography: How Photographs Changed Our Lives*, 2nd edn, New York: Abbeville.

Holmes, O. W. (1980) "The Stereoscope and the Stereograph," in B. Newhall (ed.), *Photography: Essays and Images*, New York: Museum of Modern Art.

Jammes, A. and Janis, E. P. (1983) *The Art of the French Calotype*, Princeton: Princeton University Press.

Keller, U. (1984) "The Myth of Art Photography," *History of Photography* 8: 249–75.

Kracauer, S. (1979) "Photography," in P. Petruck (ed.) *The Camera Viewed: Writings on Twentieth-Century Photography*, New York: Dutton.

Lange, D. (1980) "The Assignment I'll Never Forget," in B. Newhall (ed.), *Photography: Essays and Images,* New York: Museum of Modern Art.

Léger, F. (1980) "The New Realism – The Object: Its Plastic and Cinematic Value," in B. Newhall (ed.), *Photography: Essays and Images*, New York: Museum of Modern Art.

Levine, L. (1979) "Camera Art," in P. Petruck (ed.), *The Camera Viewed: Writings on Twentieth-Century Photography*, New York: Dutton.

Marien, M. (1986) "What Shall We Tell the Children? Photography and its Text (Books)," *Afterimage* 13: 4–7.

Maynard, P. (1997) *The Engine of Visualization: Thinking Through Photography*, Ithaca: Cornell University Press.

Michaud, Y. (1998) "Forms of Looking: Philosophy and Photography," in M. Frizot (ed.), *A New History of Photography*, Koln: Konemann.

Mitchell, W. J. T. (1992) *The Reconfigured Eye: Visual Truth in the Post-Photographic Era*, Cambridge, Mass.: MIT Press.

Moholy-Nagy, L. (1980) "The Future of the Photographic Process," in B. Newhall (ed.), *Photography: Essays and Images*, New York: Museum of Modern Art.

Newhall, B. (1982) *The History of Photography from 1839 to the Present*, 5th edn, New York: Museum of Modern Art.

Phillips, C. (1989) "The Judgment Seat of Photography," in R. Bolton (ed.), *The Contest of Meaning: Critical Histories of Photography*, Cambridge, Mass.: MIT Press.

Rosenblum, N. (1997) *A World History of Photography*, 3rd edn, New York: Abbeville.

Savedoff, B. (1997) "Escaping Reality: Digital Imagery and the Resources of Photography," *Journal of Aesthetics and Art Criticism* 55: 201–14.

Scruton, R. (1990) "The Photographic Surrogate," in *The Philosopher on Dover Beach*, Manchester: Carcanet.

Sekula, A. (1981) "On the Invention of Photographic Meaning," in V. Goldberg (ed.), *Photography in Print: Writings from 1816 to the Present*, Albuquerque: University of New Mexico Press.

Snyder, J. (1989) "Inventing Photography," in S. Greenough, J. Snyder, D. Travis and C. Westerbeck (eds), *On the Art of Fixing a Shadow*, Washington: National Gallery of Art.

Snyder, J. and Allen, N. W. (1975) "Photography, Vision, and Representation," *Critical Inquiry* 2: 143–69.

Solomon-Godeau, A. (1991) *Photography at the Dock*, Minneapolis: University of Minnesota Press.

Sontag, S. (1977) *On Photography*, London: Penguin.

Stieglitz, A. (1980) "Pictorial Photography," in B. Newhall (ed.), *Photography: Essays and Images,* New York: Museum of Modern Art.

Strand, P. (1980) "Photography," in B. Newhall (ed.), *Photography: Essays and Images*, New York: Museum of Modern Art.

—— (1981) "The Art Motive in Photography," in V. Goldberg (ed.), *Photography in Print: Writings from 1816 to the Present*, Albuquerque: University of New Mexico Press.

Szarkowski, J. (1966) *The Photographer's Eye*, New York: Museum of Modern Art.

Taft, R. (1938) *Photography and the American Scene*, New York: Dover.

Talbot, W. H. F. (1980) "The Art of Photogenic Drawing," in B. Newhall (ed.), *Photography: Essays and Images,* New York: Museum of Modern Art.

Trachtenberg, A. (1989) *Reading American Photographs*, New York: Hill and Wang.

—— (1998) "Daguerreotype," in M. Kelly (ed.), *Encyclopedia of Aesthetics*, New York: Oxford University Press.

Uelsmann, J. (1981) "Some Humanistic Considerations of Photography," in V. Goldberg (ed.), *Photography in Print: Writings from 1816 to the Present*, Albuquerque: University of New Mexico Press.

Walton, K. (1984) "Transparent Pictures," *Critical Inquiry* 11: 246–77.

Weston, E. (1980a) "Random Notes on Photography," in B. Newhall (ed.), *Photography: Essays and Images,* New York: Museum of Modern Art.

—— (1980b) "Seeing Photographically," in A. Trachtenberg (ed.), *Classic Essays on Photography*, New Haven: Leete's Island Books.

—— (1981) "Daybooks and Leaflet Written for the Los Angeles Museum," in V. Goldberg (ed.), *Photography in Print: Writings from 1816 to the Present*, Albuquerque: University of New Mexico Press.

White, M. (1980) "Found Photographs," in B. Newhall (ed.), *Photography: Essays and Images,* New York: Museum of Modern Art.

Further reading

Baatz, W. (1997) *Photography: An Illustrated Overview*, New York: Barron's. (A pocket-sized, illustrated digest.)

Binkley, T. (1997) "The Vitality of Digital Creation," *Journal of Aesthetics and Art Criticism* 55: 107–16. (A useful discussion of digital imaging.)

Daval, J-L. (1982) *Photography: History of an Art*, Geneva: Skira. (An account of photography as technology and art, in America and beyond.)

Frizot, M. (ed.) (1998) *A New History of Photography*, Cologne: Könemann. (Uneven but useful compendium of essays with a good bibliography and a thousand images.)

Lyons, N. (ed.) (1966) *Photographers on Photography*, Englewood Cliffs, N.J.: Prentice-Hall.

Malcolm, J. (1997) *Diana and Nikon*, 2nd edn, New York: Aperture. (A critical review of the traditions of photographic history.)

Scharf, A. (1974) *Art and Photography*, London: Penguin.

Szarkowski, J. (1973) *Looking at Photographs*, New York: Museum of Modern Art.

41
PAINTING

Dominic McIver Lopes

Suppose that, due to an episode of virulent iconoclasm, every painting, print and drawing were destroyed. Will we have lost something whose aesthetic value nothing can replace? The answer is not as straightforward as may first appear. We value paintings for several reasons: they describe scenes, delight the senses, express emotions, communicate ideas and allude either to other art works or to common experience. But we may value a work of poetry, film, dance or music for all the same reasons. Indeed, a film may describe a scene better than any painting, an aria express emotions more powerfully, a dance delight the senses more exquisitely, or a poem convey ideas more clearly. This suggests that if painting is to have a value, or values, of its own, then it must do at least some of these things in a distinctive manner, and as we shall see, this distinctiveness is difficult to characterize. It will help if we keep two questions in mind. The first concerns how to characterize painting's distinctive character. An answer to this question is necessary if we also want to know what particular value or values accrues to paintings and not to other art works. Answers to both questions together amount to an aesthetics of painting.

An aesthetics of painting may, but need not, explain why some paintings count as works of art. According to traditional definitions of art, something is a work of art in virtue of its having some intrinsic art-making property or cluster of properties, such as expressiveness or 'significant form.' Whatever these properties may be, we would expect them to be ones conferring aesthetic value on the work. The distinctive manner in which they are realized in painting will form part of an account of painting as an art apart from the other arts. However, some philosophers have proposed that something is not a work of art because of any intrinsic feature, but because it is appropriately related to a larger historical, institutional or theoretical context. This explains why certain works, such as Andy Warhol's *Brillo Boxes*, which are indistinguishable from ordinary objects, are nonetheless works of art. Presumably, we can judge the aesthetic value of a painting just by looking at it, but, as *Brillo Boxes* shows, we may not be able to distinguish art from non-art just by looking. If this is so, the concepts of art and the aesthetic come apart: not all paintings with aesthetic value need be works of art, and not all art paintings need have aesthetic value. The lesson is that whether or not one takes an aesthetics of painting to be the basis of an account of art painting depends on one's definition of art.

Before turning to some accounts of the aesthetics of painting, let us settle upon a definition of 'painting.' I shall use the term to refer to any picture whose surface is made up of a pattern of marks inscribed by movements of the artist's body. This definition is unconventional as it includes drawing and much printmaking, and it is not completely informative, as it takes for granted that we know what a picture is (and thus why handwriting is not necessarily painting). Even so, it is a good working definition because it picks out all pictures that are made by *drawing* rather than by photographic or imaging processes. This reflects the usual division of pictures into photographic and non-photographic works. The definition also allows that a painting need not contain a recognizable image: it is a challenge facing any aesthetics of painting to account for abstract painting. Finally, the definition reminds us that appreciating a painting partly involves an appreciation of the painter's purposive marking up of the paint surface. This is something an aesthetics of painting must accommodate.

The mimetic account

Many paintings appeal to us because they enable us to see things in them that we would take pleasure in seeing face to face. This is due to a special feature of representational pictures: when one looks at a painting of a landscape, and understands it correctly, it is as if one is looking at the landscape. Thus if the landscape is worth looking at, then so is the painting of it. One might think that this fact sets painting apart and is the source of its particular value. A poem or a musical composition may represent things we would delight in seeing, but only paintings furnish us with a source of the same kind of delight as the scenes they represent, because only they enable us to see those scenes in them. Painting taps directly into the pleasures of sight. This view, which I shall call the mimetic account, has considerable intuitive appeal, and although roundly scorned by art theorists (who sometimes lampoon it as the 'pretty girl theory of painting'), there is more to it than meets the eye.

According to the mimetic account the value of a painting derives from what it represents, but talk of 'what a painting represents' is ambiguous. Let us call the real-world things a painting represents its 'subject.' The subject of Picasso's painting entitled *Gertrude Stein* is Gertrude Stein, the American modernist writer. A painting's subject should be distinguished from its content: how it represents the world as being. To begin with, a painting of a fictional scene has no subject, yet it represents the world as containing objects. More importantly, the distinction allows us to take account of the phenomenon of representation-as. The properties a painting attributes to its subject, if it has one, need not be ones its subject actually has. A portrait of Stein might (accurately) represent her as stern and stout, or it may (inaccurately) represent her as timid and delicately built. In short, pictures with different contents may represent the same subject.

The distinction between subject and content is crucial to the mimetic account, for it asserts not that a painting is worth looking at when its subject is worth looking at, but rather when its subject, *as it is represented*, is worth looking at. Paintings may, and frequently do, improve on reality, or direct our attention to aspects of the world we overlook, showing that they are worth looking at. This adds significantly to the appeal of the mimetic account, by explaining why we sometimes go to the trouble of making paintings of things we can look at face to face.

The mimetic account starts with the claim that a painting has a valuable aesthetic property only if it represents something as having that property. Of course, this cannot be the whole story: after all, a poem may also represent any object as having any property, simply by describing it as having the property ("There was a writer divine/Whose name was Gertrude Stein./Through Picasso we learn/She was stout and stern/And neither timid nor fine.") As we have already remarked, what is notable about painting is the way its content enters into visual experience. When we look at a painting and understand it correctly, we typically have a visual experience whose content is determined by the content of the painting. Paintings not only represent objects but also elicit 'object-presenting experiences.' According to the mimetic account, then, a painting has a valuable aesthetic property if and only if, by representing something as having that very property, it elicits a visual experience as of something with that property.

It is tempting, but mistaken, to take object-presenting experience to be a kind of illusion, to think that it is necessarily the kind of experience we might mistake for an experience of seeing an object face to face. Seeing things in paintings is rarely like seeing them face to face, so if the mimetic account entails that it is, then the mimetic account is wrong. But the mimetic account requires not an illusionistic experience but merely experience *as of* what a painting represents. Looking at a cubist still life or a cartoon strip one still has an experience as of a bowl of fruit or Uncle Duke, though the experience is manifestly unlike any face-to-face experience.

One might wonder how it is that paintings manage to elicit object-presenting experiences in the first place. To ask this is to seek a theory of pictorial representation, and there are several plausible candidates. I shall mention just one, the resemblance theory. Let us call the pattern of marks on a painting's surface its 'design.' According to the resemblance theory, a painting has a particular content only if its design (not its content!) looks the way its subject might look. The difficulty is that paintings' designs, being flat and static, rarely look *just* like real-world objects. We must specify which design–subject resemblances are required, and this happens to be no easy task. Arguing that the task cannot be accomplished at all, some have proposed alternatives, and the debate among partisans has grown quite involved (Goodman 1976; Schier 1986; Walton 1990; Lopes 1996; Hopkins 1998). Luckily, we need pursue the matter no further. The mimetic account of painting requires only that paintings do in fact evoke object-presenting experiences. Since any adequate theory of pictorial representation must explain this fact, the mimetic account need not choose among those theories.

Failure to register this point is one source of the mimetic account's unpopularity, since its principal defender, the eighteenth-century writer Gotthold Lessing, unnecessarily links it to the resemblance theory. In his *Laocoön*, Lessing argues that we value painting because "painting alone can represent material beauty" (Lessing 1962: sect. 20). Moreover, material beauty is defined as the harmonious arrangement of the parts of an object in space. The reason that only paintings can represent the parts of things as harmoniously arranged is that only paintings are made up of spatially contiguous parts. But this assumes, erroneously, that only a contiguous spatial design can represent anything as having spatially contiguous parts. Lessing falls into this error because he is committed to the resemblance theory of pictorial representation. In other parts of the *Laocoön*, he observes that only pictures afford object-presenting experiences of beauty, and he should have claimed no more than this.

Setting Lessing's error aside, the mimetic account still faces formidable difficulties. One is posed by paintings of scenes we would not normally enjoy looking at. We normally feel revulsion at the sight of anything violent, horrible, pitiful or grotesque, so if paintings of such things have value, it is not because what they represent is nice to observe. While this is part of a larger puzzle about representations of tragic events in any of the arts, it is particularly troubling here, since the mimetic account locates the whole value of painting in its content, and no other element of painting can redeem it.

Some early writers who have worried about how we can enjoy tragic dramas have suggested that our pleasure comes not only from the content of the drama but also from the fact that it is a representation (Aristotle 1987). Likewise, one might think that paintings are valuable not only because they depict things worth looking at but also just because they can successfully represent things

(Hutcheson 1973: sect. 4). There is something to this. We do sometimes delight in the mere fact that a flat surface before us cleverly imitates a scene, evoking an object-presenting experience of the scene. And this delight is at least sometimes independent of the painting's content. Some of the most charming *trompe-l'oeil* images represent the most banal subjects. Perhaps in paintings of unpleasant scenes this charm allays the unpleasantness. But although this suggestion may contain a grain of truth and may conceivably help solve the problem of tragedy, it has never been presented in enough detail to be evaluated properly. It is not even clear, for instance, whether the claim being made is empirical or conceptual, and thus what sorts of reasons could be given for it. Moreover, it is doubtful that the suggestion could survive our recognition that we value paintings even when they do not successfully represent their subjects (as is the case with much painting of the twentieth century). At any rate, additional difficulties face even the amended version of the mimetic account.

One concerns the nature of the object-presenting experiences elicited by paintings. Painting does not have a monopoly on such experiences: we have experiences as of dramatic characters when watching plays, and we see things in figurative sculptures. Presumably, each of these involves a different kind of object-presenting experience, but how are we to characterize the difference? We might say that an experience of a painting differs from that of a sculpture because of its design features (for example it is flat). But the mimetic account excludes this response, by locating what is distinctive of painting in our experience of its content, not our experience of its design.

More seriously, the mimetic account neglects the undeniable appeal of many paintings' designs apart from their contents: consider the jeweled surfaces of Byzantine mosaics. It also overlooks the contribution made by our awareness of the painter's touch, as in Van Gogh's paintings. Since it was the latter that distinguished painting from photography, the mimetic account fails to distinguish the aesthetics of painting from that of photography. The former leads to another worry, that the mimetic account has nothing to say about abstract painting.

Formalism

Formalism was backed in the early twentieth century by the art critics Clive Bell (1914) and Roger Fry (1927) partly as a way to accommodate the vogue for abstraction. Bell and Fry distinguish a painting's 'plastic form' from its 'illustrative content.' The former comprises in the first instance the lines, shapes, and colors (and the relations between them) of its design. For most formalists, plastic form also comprises the three-dimensional shapes and planes represented in a painting (and relations among them). Thus plastic form traverses the design–content distinction drawn above. Form is to be distinguished from a portion of a painting's content: what scenes and actions it represents, what they allude to or express, and what, if any, larger ideas are communicated. It is handy to think of this 'illustrative' content as just what is left out of abstract painting.

The formal properties of painting are, if described in the right way, distinctive of painting. The lines and colors and textures (and relations among them) that comprise the image are, after all, the visible traces of the painter's movements. It is these that distinguish painting from its sister art of photography; it is by means of them that we can tell photographs from paintings. Thus while every artform has formal properties, the value of painting lies in its distinctively painterly formal properties. Formalism answers the first question we must ask of an aesthetics of painting.

However, it is less clear how value accrues to painting in virtue of its form. According to Bell, a painting's plastic form has value when it is 'significant,' causing viewers to experience an 'aesthetic emotion' (Bell 1914). Since, as Bell admits, the nature of this aesthetic emotion is a mystery, it is hard to see what evidence might be marshaled in favor of its being caused by formal properties. Nevertheless we may set this worry aside, for whether the value of painting lies in its capacity to cause an aesthetic emotion or in something else entirely, there are difficulties with the claim that painting can be appreciated, or appreciated fully, only through its plastic form.

Here we may distinguish between strong and weak versions of formalism. According Bell's brand of formalism, the illustrative content of a painting is irrelevant to its value as a painting. According to a weaker formalism favored by Fry, there are two arts of painting, that of illustration and that of plastic form, each having a separate value (Fry 1927). Since strong formalism is tenable only if weak formalism is tenable, we may concentrate on the latter. Three main reasons have been given in its support. First, plastic form and illustrative content may vary independently of one another, so that one form can illustrate many things or many forms illustrate one thing. Second, we can experience what a painting represents or its formal properties, but not both at once. To experience both we must "constantly shift attention backwards and forwards from one to the other" (ibid.: 23). Finally, the aims of illustration and formal design are different and competing.

The first two reasons must be taken in conjunction with the third. Neither the claim that form and illustrative content may vary independently, nor the claim that they cannot be perceived simultaneously, shows that their values are independent, unless these claims are taken together with the claim that the two arts have separate aims. And this claim is overstated. While it is true that one aim may be pursued to the neglect of the other, it is an abiding aim of painters to achieve a coherence of form and illustrative content, in which recognition of the content stabilizes and amplifies the composition, and in which the composition clarifies and adds expressive force to what is represented. There is as much reason to think this coherence a particular value at which some painting aims as there is to think formal properties have independent value. Some paintings are appreciated only insofar as they achieve such a coherence. Moreover, seeing every form may require seeing what is illustrated. One may have to recognize the depicted gestures and movements of a group of figures in order to see their formal composition. A person suffering from a kind of visual agnosia depriving him of the ability to recognize objects but leaving intact the ability to see colors, lines and shapes, could not see all the formal properties of some paintings.

Double aspect accounts

Rejecting the formalist claim that the arts of plastic form and illustration inevitably conflict gives us no reason to reject Fry's assertion that we can experience a painting's form or its illustrative content but not both at once, and this hints at a third approach to the aesthetics of painting. Experiences of paintings have two aspects: we experience a painting's design and we experience what it represents. Perhaps where we have gone wrong so far is in focusing on one aspect at the expense of the other: design (plus selected elements of content) in the case of formalism, and object-presenting experience in the mimetic account. The middle path is to locate the distinctiveness and value of painting in our experience of the relationship between both aspects. This relationship can be understood in two ways.

Parallelism

The first is that endorsed by Fry (substituting 'design' for 'form'), though its chief proponent is the art historian E. H. Gombrich (1969). On this view, which I call 'parallelism,' it is possible to experience a painting's design (its flat surface composed of brush strokes, marks and lines) or its content (the three-dimensional scene it represents) but never both at one and the same time. This is analogous to the way we can see a duck or a rabbit consecutively in the famous drawing (Figure 41.1). Wittgenstein called this kind of seeing, which involves switching between two aspects, 'seeing-as' (Wittgenstein 1967: II.xi). What is characteristic of seeing-as is that experience of one aspect precludes awareness of the other. Likewise, what is characteristic of painting, according to parallelism, is its double-aspect phenomenology.

Unlike Fry, Gombrich does not hold that painting's value lies in one aspect

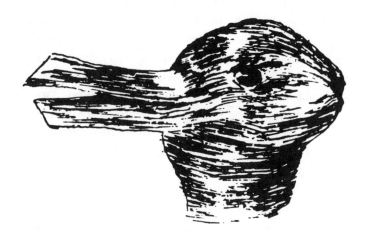

Figure 41.1 The duck–rabbit illustration

alone, or that their values necessarily collide. Rather, it may lie in what can be gained by switching between aspects. Gombrich is not very clear about what this value might be, but two possibilities come easily to mind. First, the value of painting may be the sum of the value of each aspect: the value of the formal properties of its design plus the value of seeing its content. Second, each aspect may enhance the other. The value of the object-presenting experience is sometimes amplified by seeing that it is caused by a designed surface – we see how good the trick is – and the value of the design is sometimes amplified by seeing how it sustains an object-presenting experience.

The objection to parallelism is that it entails that object-presenting experience is illusionistic: it is experience of a kind the object itself might cause. According to parallelism, awareness of a designed surface is no part of the object-presenting experience a painting elicits. But this awareness is just what alerts us to the fact that we are looking at a painting of a scene rather than the scene itself. If parallelism is true, then it follows that when we attend to the represented scene, our experience is illusionistic: we have an experience of the scene like one the scene itself might cause. Attending to the representational aspect obscures awareness of just what would alert us to the fact that the aspect is, after all, just a representation. Except in rare cases, however, object-presenting experiences of paintings are not illusionistic. Looking at a drawing and seeing in it what it represents is not like seeing its subject face to face. The objection is not simply that looking at a painting does not cause illusionistic experience, for parallelism admits we experience paintings' designs. The objection is that experiences of paintings are not necessarily illusionistic *even insofar as we attend just to their contents*.

Twofoldness

The alternative is that the two aspects of painting are simultaneous aspects of the same experience. This kind of seeing is what Richard Wollheim calls 'seeing-in' (Wollheim 1980, 1987: 46–62; see also Budd 1993). We sometimes see figures in clouds or water stains or ink blots, and when we do, our experience amalgamates features of the 'design' with features of the presented object. Awareness of one does not annihilate awareness of the other; rather, the two aspects blend into one 'twofold' experience. The contrast between seeing-in and seeing-as can be brought out by a second look at the duck–rabbit figure. Gombrich observed that the figure can be seen as a duck or a rabbit but not both at once. This is true, but it is also true that we see both the duck and the design simultaneously, or both the rabbit and the design simultaneously. The relationship between two the aspects of paintings is like that between duck (or rabbit) and design, not like that between duck and rabbit.

Although Wollheim describes it as a theory of pictorial representation, the twofoldness account is in fact a characterization of our experiences of paintings. Wollheim notes that seeing-in is triggered by certain differentiated designs, but declines to say what principles underlie what can be seen in what designs. This is the task of a theory of pictorial representation, and several quite radically different theories of pictorial representation accommodate twofoldness. We need not choose among these theories.

Unlike parallelism, this account does not construe object-presenting experience as illusionistic. Seeing a rabbit in a painting is not like looking at a rabbit face to face, for it is shot through with awareness of the design. Some have pointed out that this extends painting's content (Lopes 1996, Podro 1998). If recognizing an object in a painting is permeated by awareness of the design, so that the object need not look the way it might look when seen face to face, then the design may complicate and elaborate the recognition in new structures. The interplay of form and content in cubist paintings seems to work this way. At the same time (and contrary to formalism), awareness of content impacts awareness of design. What features of the duck–rabbit design one notices depends on which animal one sees in it. For instance, we hardly notice the bump that forms the rabbit's mouth when we view the image as a duck. In these cases, twofoldness is the source of a particular value in painting. We may appreciate a painting's formal properties or properties of the scene it enables us to see, but we may also appreciate the way in which the two complicate and transform each other in a single experience.

An additional virtue of the account is that it copes in a natural way with abstraction. Abstract paintings typically consist of designs in which we may see three-dimensional spaces and sometimes movement as well. Experiencing both simultaneously makes us aware of interplays between design space and represented space that appear to be what many abstract artists strive to achieve (Wollheim 1987: 62).

But are experiences of paintings inevitably twofold? Wollheim argues that twofoldness is essential to our experience of art painting. The reason is that twofoldness is the best explanation of the constancy of object-presenting experiences (Wollheim 1980: 215–6). When a painting is viewed from an oblique angle, the shapes we see in it are not distorted, as the laws of optics predict. An image of a cube looks cubical even when viewed from an angle from which it projects an irregular shape on to the retina. It appears that the brain corrects for shape using information about the painting's orientation relative to the viewer. Thus what is seen in the painting depends upon the appearance of its designed surface. We must experience both simultaneously.

This argument is invalid for two reasons. That the brain uses information about the surfaces of paintings does not show that design information enters into *conscious* experience. The information may remain at the sub-personal level, where it allows the brain to correct for viewing position, but never entering awareness. Moreover, in some cases, such as *trompe-l'oeil* ceiling painting, we cannot see the design at all. It is true that when not viewed from the expected viewpoint, these paintings do look distorted. But this shows only that design information is necessary for constancy, not that it is essential to object-presenting experience.

Illusionistic or *trompe-l'oeil* paintings are one kind of counterexample to the twofoldness account, for their success generally depends on our not noticing their design properties, or not noticing them when we attend to what they represent. In another kind of counterexample, the representational aspect is suppressed or absent. For example, 'minimalist' abstract paintings which do not project movement or three-dimensional space may accurately be described as 'pure design.' And not all counterexamples in this category are abstract. Consider a Jasper Johns-like painting of an array of numerals. Painted numerals are not represented numerals; they just are numerals. We no more see the numeral 2 in that numeral than we see Tony Blair's face in Tony Blair. Thus we may attend to the designs of these paintings and to what they are (numerals) but we cannot attend to what they represent, for there is nothing they represent.

Non-essentialist accounts

We have sought the value of painting in some essential feature that sets it apart, but as we have seen, however, it is not easy to isolate this feature. One might locate it in paintings' designs, or in the way they make scenes visible to us, or in some relation between the two. But none of four attempts to flesh out these ideas was able to account for all paintings. The mimetic account cannot cope with abstraction, paintings whose designed surfaces we admire, or, perhaps, paintings of disturbing scenes. Formalism leaves out paintings which strive for a unity of plastic form and illustrative content. Parallelism reckons only with illusionistic painting, while twofoldness overlooks illusionism, some abstraction and some representational painting. Moreover, some of these accounts failed to pick out a value unique to painting: painting, for example, is obviously not the only mimetic art.

Even if we have considered and rejected every possible option, however, we need not conclude that painting has no value, or, rather, values. There may be no single aesthetics of painting, if paintings belong to different, sometimes overlapping genres. The value of a painting may sometimes lie in the object-presenting experience it elicits, or in its formal properties, or in the interplay between its formal order and the illusion it projects, or in its twofoldness.

If this is correct, then it follows that we can properly judge a painting's value only when we interpret it as falling within the appropriate genre. We miss as much judging a cubist work by mimetic criteria or a *trompe-l'oeil* painting by formalist criteria as we miss by judging hiphop as jazz. If this is correct, then an assumption with which we began, that we can assess the value of paintings just by looking, is false. We must bring to our judgement of paintings knowledge of the genres into which they fall (Walton 1970).

This proposal offers a way to accommodate a surprising recent discovery. Empirical studies have shown that congenitally blind people are able to interpret and draw pictures made of raised lines (see Lopes 1997). These pictures fall within our definition of painting, and they share important features in common with visual paintings, including the use of vanishing-point perspective. Moreover, blind people may attend either to their design properties or enjoy object-presenting experiences. Yet each account of the aesthetics of painting we have considered is couched in terms of visual experience, and visual experience differs from tactile experience in content and phenomenology. If we wish nevertheless to accommodate an aesthetics of tactile painting, we need only allow that tactile paintings form a separate set of genres, overlapping the genres of visual painting.

Paintings describe scenes, delight the senses, express emotions, communicate ideas, and allude either to other art works or to common experience. There is no single reason for which we value all paintings and only paintings as aesthetic objects. A reason to value one painting may not be a reason to value all, and it may be a reason to value something that is not a painting at all. This need not disappoint us. An outbreak of iconoclasm would deprive us not of something of unique value but of many things with a variety of values.

See also Pictorial representation, Fakes and forgeries, Photography, Sculpture, Aristotle, Formalism.

References

Aristotle (1987) *The Poetics of Aristotle*, trans. S. Halliwell, Chapel Hill: University of North Carolina Press.

Bell, C. (1914) *Art*, London: Chatto and Windus.

Budd, M. (1993) "How Pictures Look," in D. Knowles and J. Skorupski (eds), *Virtue and Taste*, Oxford: Blackwell.

Fry, R. (1927) "Some Questions in Esthetics," in *Transformations*, London: Chatto and Windus.

Gombrich, E. H. (1969) *Art and Illusion*, 2nd edn, Princeton: Princeton University Press.

Goodman, N. (1976) *Languages of Art*, 2nd edn, Indianapolis: Hackett.

Hopkins, R. D. (1998) *Picture, Image and Experience*, Cambridge: Cambridge University Press.

Hutcheson, F. (1973) *An Inquiry Concerning Beauty, Order, Harmony and Design*, ed. P. Kivy, The Hague: Martinus Nijhoff.

Lessing, G. (1962) *Laocoon*, trans. E. A. McCormick, Indianapolis: Bobbs Merrill.

Lopes, D. (1996) *Understanding Pictures*, Oxford: Oxford University Press.

—— (1997) "Art Media and the Sense Modalities: Tactile Pictures," *Philosophical Quarterly* 47: 425–40.

Podro, M. (1998) *Depiction*, New Haven: Yale University Press.

Schier, F. (1986) *Deeper into Pictures*, Cambridge: Cambridge University Press.

Walton, K. (1970) "Categories of Art," *Philosophical Review* 79: 334–67.

—— (1990) *Mimesis as Make-Believe*, Cambridge, Mass.: Harvard University Press.

Wittgenstein, L. (1967) *Philosophical Investigations*, trans. G. E. M. Anscombe, Oxford: Blackwell.

Wollheim, R. (1980) "Seeing-in, Seeing-as and Pictorial Representation," in *Art and Its Objects*, 2nd edn, Cambridge: Cambridge University Press.

—— (1987) *Painting as an Art*, London and New York: Thames and Hudson.

Further reading

Alperson, P. (ed.) (1992) *The Philosophy of the Visual Arts*, New York: Oxford University Press. (An anthology promoting diverse approaches to the subject.)

Baxandall, M. (1985) *Patterns of Intention*, New Haven: Yale University Press. (A philosophically informed account of art-historical explanation.)

Budd, M. (1995) *Values of Art*, London: Penguin. (Contains a chapter on pictures.)

Danto, A. (1981) *Transfiguration of the Commonplace*, Cambridge, Mass.: Harvard University Press. (A now-classic account of painting as an artform.)

Feagin, S. (1997) "Paintings and Their Places," in S. Davies (ed.), *Art and Its Messages*, University Park: Pennsylvania State University Press. (An interesting discussion of how paintings can convey knowledge.)

—— (1998) "Presentation and Representation," *Journal of Aesthetics and Art Criticism* 56: 234–40. (A defense of twofoldness.)

Hopkins, R. (1997) "Pictures and Beauty," *Proceedings of the Aristotelian Society* 42: 177–94. (A defense of the mimetic account.)

Savile, A. (1987) *Aesthetic Reconstructions*, Oxford: Blackwell. (Features a detailed discussion of Lessing.)

Schier, F. (1986) "Van Gogh's Boots: The Claims of Representation," in D. Knowles and J. Skorupski (eds), *Virtue and Taste*, Oxford: Blackwell. (A subtle discussion of the aesthetic and cognitive value of painting.)

Tilghman, B. (1988) "Picture Space and Moral Space," *British Journal of Aesthetics* 28: 317–26. (A discussion of the moral content of pictures.)

42
SCULPTURE
Curtis L. Carter

Notwithstanding the fact that sculpture is entrusted with the representation of gods, heroes, heads of state and athlete-heroes, and that works of sculpture occupy prominent spaces in virtually every community, Western philosophical aesthetics has given the art relatively little attention. Few philosophers have discussed it, and such efforts as there have been seem incommensurate with the important roles accorded the art by religion, the state and other arts.

This essay will, in a preliminary way, consider two possible paths to the development of a philosophy of sculpture. The first is that offered by philosophy itself, and the thoughts of philosophers from Lessing to Goodman will be reviewed. The other is that offered by the history and practice of sculpture itself, where problems of philosophical interest arise, as sculpture is seen in its cultural context. My aim, beyond drawing attention to philosophical questions, is to make some broad suggestions as to how to address them.

Sculpture is characterized in the *Encyclopedia Britannica* as "the art of representing observed or imagined objects in solid materials and in three dimensions." Representation in this context refers to the interpretive re-creation in a medium such as stone of the natural appearance or ideal features of objects, or of ideas in the mind corresponding to these features. Understood in this traditional sense, sculpture is one of the oldest artforms, clearly embracing artifacts found in the caves of prehistoric groups as well as objects produced in all subsequent cultures. At the same time, suggestive evidence of the power of sculpture is its use, or prohibition, by various religions. While several animistic religions accord sculpture a central role in religious practices, the major monotheistic religions, including Judaism, Islam, and some groupings within Christianity, ban as idolatry the making of sculptures based on the human body or other living creatures.

Philosophical questions

Neglect of sculpture

Why has sculpture been neglected by philosophers? Many reasons might be offered to account for this neglect. It is perhaps not accidental that both sculpture and dance, the two arts most neglected by philosophers, happen to be those most closely linked to the human body. Francis Sparshott's analysis of the reasons for the neglect of dance in aesthetics may provide some insight into the corresponding neglect of sculpture, although not all of the circumstances are parallel. Among the possible reasons given for neglect of dance are its lack of a repertory of stock problems and themes, the lack of a secure place for dance in the systems of the fine arts, and Puritanism with respects to arts based on the body (Sparshott 1988: 3–82).

The situation with sculpture is somewhat different with respect to the first two issues. There are certain themes that appear early and regularly in writings on sculpture: for example sculpture as a representational art, the identification of sculpture with three-dimensional arts and solid materials, its relation to painting and architecture, and public uses of sculpture. Also, sculpture does appear in the most important classifications of the arts (Hegel 1975, Kristeller 1965) but is often in the shadow of architecture and painting. The influence of Puritanism is another matter. One crucial difference is that the actual physical sensuous body which appears centrally in the performance of dance appears only as a representation in sculpture, and is less likely than nude dancing to evoke puritanical concerns over public displays of sexuality. In any event, the puritanical issue in itself would not be sufficient to account for the low profile of sculpture in philosophy, but when coupled with the low priority of the physical body, in comparison with the spiritual soul and the rational mind in classical and modern philosophy, this factor cannot be entirely discounted.

Martin cites three reasons for neglect of sculpture: doubts about the autonomy of sculpture, the vast range and complexity of sculpture (relief versus in the round, figure versus machine, space versus light and so on), and the influence of perceptual theories that favor visual properties of paintings over the tactile properties of sculpture (Martin 1966: 5–12). It is true that doubts about the autonomy of sculpture may have contributed to its neglect. However, Martin's argument concerning the range and complexity of sculpture is less compelling, for the same argument could be applied to music, painting, and other arts whose developments are scarcely less complex. Similarly the perceptual argument is lacking in force, as it assumes that the primary perceptual issue with the apprehension of sculpture is its tactile dimension. I would contend, however, that sculpture is both visual art and tactile art, and that sculpture is experienced primarily though the visual sense, as are the other visual arts. This is not to say that there are no important differences in the way we perceive sculpture with three-dimensional and kinetic properties as opposed to paintings consisting of figures and color markings on a plane. Rather, it is only to argue that visual perception is the main access to sculpture, except in the unusual cases where touch is permitted or when it is required for the visually impaired.

Perhaps the strongest explanation for the neglect of sculpture in recent times is the claim that sculpture is not regarded as a stable concept with fixed boundaries. The variety of forms and materials found in sculpture, especially in the twentieth century, and the openness of sculpture to interaction with other arts, support this claim. But although these factors might contribute to the neglect of sculpture in the second half of the twentieth century, they do not fully account for philosophy's neglect of sculpture. Moreover this argument over the instability of the concept of sculpture suggests an opportunity for analytic philosophical work on the concept sculpture, rather than a reason for its continued neglect.

Finally, it may be that an artform so accessible in public spaces and everyday life does not initially appear to warrant extensive analysis by philosophers. In most urban environments, as well as in smaller cities and towns, people regularly encounter sculptures. In many instances the sculptures are associated not with the fine arts but with utilitarian purposes in civic and religious life. Similarly, souvenir replicas of sculptures, which are common in everyday experience, are not typically considered fine art, and certain everyday manufactured objects appear not to differ from machine-inspired and minimalist sculptures. All of these considerations direct attention away from sculpture as a fine art, and may thus contribute to the neglect of sculpture by philosophers. In any event, the neglect of sculpture warrants further reflection.

Definition of sculpture

The definition used here refers to the general properties of sculpture that enable one to identify, classify and establish sculpture as different and separate from natural objects, craft items, and the products of other conceptual enterprises, such as science. Our initial definition of sculpture (as the art of representing observed or imagined objects in solid materials and in three dimensions) already represents a condensed definition. At once it gives an account of sculptures as a particular type of object and distinguishes sculpture from non-art objects. For example, as an art, sculpture represents a practice in which the treatment of materials differs from their use in non-art contexts. In sculpture, natural or fabricated materials are acted upon by an artist who physically or conceptually alters them, producing aesthetic or conceptual changes that are reflected in our experiences and uses of them. This transformation of the raw material into a particular type of cultural object endows it with symbolic meaning and locates it in the art world, where a network of practices and institutions exists to make and interpret the work and make it available to a wider public. The meaning of sculpture thus derives from its being altered by an art practice with a history and context of interpretation, within which individuals may engage the work for purposes of enjoyment and understanding as well as for its utility. This is what distinguishes sculpture from non-art. Apart from its connection to an art practice, none of the other features of the definition apply uniquely to sculpture. For instance, mirror images are representational without being art works and, similarly, tree trunks are composed of solid materials and are also three-dimensional objects but are not considered sculptures.

The next stage in the theory of sculpture is to classify it in relation to the other fine arts. Again, the features named in our initial definition tell us some things about the common features sculpture shares with other arts as well as their relative differences. As a representational art, at least in important stages of its development, sculpture is in the company of painting, print making, poetry and, to a lesser degree, music and dance which are sometimes representational. However, none of these other arts are at once representational, in solid materials, and three dimensional, or at least not in the same way as sculpture. And they may differ in their means of representation, as we shall see. Hence our initial definition provides a useful beginning with respect to a theory of sculpture. This initial definition will require modification as the purposes of sculpture change and as the medium expands to include kinetic and light sculptures and to fabrication techniques that go beyond casting and carving.

Early writers

In order to pursue the discussion of a theory of sculpture in relation to the other arts, it will be necessary to survey briefly the efforts of philosophers to address this subject. Few philosophers have set out directly to provide a theory, but their fragmentary discussions of sculpture do point in this direction. According to Kristeller, sculpture was first recognized in the eighteenth century (from the perspective of Western aesthetics) as one of the five major arts that most writers and thinkers, as well as other knowledgeable members of the general public, agreed constituted the "irreducible nucleus of the modern system of the arts" (Kristeller 1965: 165–227).

Among the nineteenth-century philosophers to consider sculpture were Gotthold Lessing, G. W. F. Hegel, and Arthur Schopenhauer. Their main concerns were the delineation of sculpture's own characteristics and functions and the comparison of sculpture to the other arts, especially to architecture and painting. Thus, the eighteenth-century writer Lessing in his *Laocoön* (1957) asserted that the essence of sculpture is its concern with static bodies comprising an inert mass in space. It follows that sculpture consists of a free-standing mass surrounded by or placed in space. According to Lessing, sculpture can be identified as spatial art distinct from such temporal arts as poetry and drama, which represent action and passion. However, this does not mean that time is irrelevant to sculpture, for minimally time applies, in the sense that time was invested by the sculptor in making the work, and in the fact that it endures through time. Rather, Lessing's view is that time is not essential to sculpture, and that sculpture is not capable of representing the duration of actions, but only a single frozen moment.

Hegel, writing in the first half of the nineteenth century, also included sculpture in his classification of the major arts (Hegel 1975: II, 701–91). For Hegel, sculpture, like painting, music, and poetry, had as its function the expression of spirit or mind. In particular, Hegel found in sculpture the ideal medium for what he described as the classical stage, one of the three (symbolic, classical, romantic) metaphysical and historical stages that he discerned in the unfolding of art in all cultures. For Hegel, the classical stage of art is marked by a harmonious fusion of idea and material, and he found sculpture especially suited to expressing the form of the human figure. However, he found sculpture less able than painting, music, and poetry to express the subtle particularities of thought and feeling that give meaning to art. Sculpture is thus placed near the bottom of Hegel's hierarchical classification of the fine arts, just above architecture, but below painting, music, and poetry.

Schopenhauer (1977: III, 193–9) views Greek sculpture as the norm for representing the human form. He identifies beauty and grace as its main features, in contrast to the art of painting where expression, passion, and character are the chief concerns. Exposure to nude forms provides the artist experience necessary to objectify ideal form in sculpture. Perfect beauty and grace demanded of sculpture are a product of an a priori notion of beauty that exists latent in the mind and is activated through the artist's perception and judgement of the details of actual nude bodies. Schopenhauer identifies sculpture with the affirmation of the will to live, whereas he views painting as its negation. The result is that ugly faces and emaciated bodies are deemed suitable subjects for paintings, but not for sculpture, where beauty is demanded.

Lessing, Hegel, and Schopenhauer each contributed to our understanding of sculpture and its place in aesthetics. Lessing drew attention to space as a key element in understanding sculpture. The main difficulty with Lessing's view is that it excludes mobiles and other forms of kinetic sculpture. Hegel found in the human body the highest form provided by nature as well as the *natural* form most suited to the expression of inner thoughts and feelings. He thus helped to explain why the human body was a primary subject for sculpture. His views offer a link between the prominence of the body in classical Greek sculpture and in the work of Auguste Rodin. By shifting the emphasis from representation, or imitation of nature, to expression of inner states, Hegel prepared the way for Rodin's revolutionary approach to the human figure. Schopenhauer drew attention to certain aesthetic properties of sculpture (beauty and grace). His attempt to impose seemingly arbitrary differences between the subject matters appropriate to sculpture and painting respectively, however, would lead to needless downgrading of sculpture as a medium suitable for depicting the ugly sides of life.

Twentieth-century writers

Except for the occasional mention, mostly in discussions focusing on painting or architecture, sculpture has received little attention from philosophers in the twentieth century (Dewey 1987: 232–4, Greene 1940: 82–96, Read 1956, Weiss 1961: 85–91, Martin 1966, Goodman 1967: 19, 20, 120). Two of these writers, Dewey and Goodman, suggest possible questions for developing a philosophy of sculpture today.

Dewey

Dewey does not treat sculpture as a separate subject; however, it is possible to sketch a partial view of a philosophy of sculpture by drawing upon isolated passages from *Art As Experience* (1987). It is important to note that Dewey departs from the view of Lessing, Hegel and Schopenhauer that ancient Greek sculpture is the sole or primary model for the aesthetics of sculpture. The use of flattened or rounded planes in Greek sculpture as a means of expressing the human figure, admirable in itself, may obscure the perception of the best in Egyptian sculpture, which is based on the relation of larger masses, or of African sculpture with its sharp angularities, or of modern sculpture, which is based upon rhythms of light generated from continually broken surfaces (Dewey 1987: 170). Reliance on one model, he says, tends to create insensitivity to the broad range of possible forms and rhythms found in other types of sculpture. Dewey's important observation is especially welcome in an era of increasing sensitivity to cultural differences in artistic expression.

Dewey's main contributions to the theory of sculpture are to question the past efforts to define the arts as separate classes, and to replace the idea of representation with that of expression. He cautions us that any hard and fast definition aimed at rigid classification runs counter to historical developments, insofar as sculpture was for a part of its history an organic component of architecture. Thus he argues that the division of the arts as either space or time arts ignores the fact that space and time affect each other reciprocally in the experience of art. If sculpture were characterized merely as an art of space, this would, Dewey argues, deny to sculpture rhythm, which he regards as a fundamental element in aesthetic experience.

For Dewey, a sculpture is not complete until it is perceived as an aesthetic object into which temporal as well as spatial properties enter. This does not provide a basis for classifying sculpture in relation to the other arts. Yet Dewey recognized that sculptors, like artists in all fields, have tended to develop their medium so as to differentiate it from others, resulting in the production of free standing sculptures (Dewey 1987: 222). He agrees that each medium has its own efficacy and value. Nevertheless Dewey argues that, instead of forming discrete entities, art media, including sculpture, represent a continuum that allows us to distinguish one from another without saying precisely where one begins and the other ends. As one way to understand the differences, Dewey divided media loosely into a spectrum of automatic arts and shaping arts. Automatic arts, such as dancing and singing, rely directly and to a greater extent on the human body–mind and are associated with spontaneity. Shaping arts also rely on bodily movements, but these are used in sculpture to manipulate instruments of technology necessary to express imaginative and emotional values through external materials. The shaping arts must also absorb the life-giving energies of the automatic in the process. These broad categories allow for intermediate forms such as relief sculptures, and for transitions and mutual influences, such as architecture and sculpture. Thus Dewey avoids both a compartmentalization of the arts and running the arts all together.

Dewey's comparison of sculpture and architecture concentrates on the expressive and social values of each. He doubts that sculpture apart from architecture will achieve great aesthetic heights, despite the tendency of sculpture in the modern age to develop independently. Both rely on unity of expressiveness and purpose to achieve complementary aims. Yet he assigns to each a characteristic effect. Architecture draws upon a wide range of materials from nearly natural ones such as bricks and steel to entirely man-made materials, and expresses most completely the stability and endurance of existence. Sculpture's effect is grounded in the memorial. Whereas "buildings enter into and shape life directly, sculpture specializes in reminding us of heroism, devotion, and achievements of the past" (Dewey 1987: 232). Architecture, he says, draws its meanings from the collective human life, while "sculpture expresses life in its individualized forms" (ibid.: 233).

Dewey replaces representation with expression as the preferred mode of characterizing sculpture. He finds representation tied to fixed and unchanging ideal forms harking back to Plato and Aristotle unsuitable to deal with the novelty and individualized forms of sculpture in modern times. For Dewey sculpture is expressive when the material is employed in a process that fuses inner experience with objective conditions, giving both a form that they did not previously possess. He does not deny that some sculptures are able to function as representations, but argues rather that expression more adequately characterizes the process and experience involved in making and interpreting sculptures. Moreover, by dislodging the ancient Greek ideal of representational sculpture and extending it to include expressive Egyptian, African and modern sculpture, Dewey must expand sculpture's aesthetic base from representation to expression.

Goodman

In his *Languages of Art* (1967) Goodman proposes a fresh approach to the classification of the art media, based in part on his analysis of the arts as representational and expressive symbol systems and his distinction between autographic and allographic arts. Applying his critique of the copy theory of pictorial representation to sculpture, Goodman argues that the sculptor undertakes a subtle translation of the subject based on its orientation, distance, and lighting as well as the artist's knowledge, training, habits and concerns. The result is not duplication or realism (Goodman 1967: 19–20).

Representation is a matter of classifying or characterizing objects rather than creating an illusion. It is a creative process of inventing symbols rather than copying. Viewed in this light, sculptural representation depends upon the application of labels according to the symbol system in which the sculpture is being interpreted. As analyzed by Goodman, representation and expression are not necessarily incompatible; rather they are simply different, possibly complementary types of symbolism. If the principal feature of a representation is to denote what it refers to by moving from the symbol to its referent, the main requirement of expression is literally or metaphorically to possess the features it symbolizes. Hence, a sculpture of Napoleon may refer to Napoleon or to any number of things, depending on the symbol system. On the other hand, a sculpture can only express a feeling when the feeling is an actual or metaphorical property of the symbol, as the attitude of arrogant, self-confidence is expressed in Rodin's bronze *Study for Balzac Monument* (1893). If it is metaphorical, the feeling is transferred from an exterior source. Hence one advantage of Goodman's characterization of representation and expression in sculpture is that it embraces a greater diversity of sculpture, including works from virtually all cultures and styles, figurative or abstract.

Thus far, Goodman's theory of symbols, properly fleshed out, would identify sculpture as a type of symbolism within the arts. It might also aid in differentiating sculpture from architecture or painting, by inviting a close scrutiny of the types of symbolic properties and relationships that occur in representative works proposed for inclusion in the respective media. Goodman's distinction between autographic and allographic arts offers additional clarification. An art medium is autographic "if and only if the distinction between original and forgery is significant" (Goodman 1976: 113), or when its symbol system lacks a notational system. Conversely, an art medium is allographic when the difference between originals and forgeries does not matter, or when the artform allows for a notational system. None of the properties of autographic works can be dismissed as contingent or insignificant; thus, variations in an autographic work would result in significant differences in the experience of a knowledgeable viewer.

Seen in this light, sculpture both carved and cast is deemed autographic, along with paintings and artists' prints. With cast sculptures, multiples from the same mold, when created under conditions specified by the artist, are accepted as originals capable of being forged. Multiple casts from the same mold, similarly to multiples in a set of prints from the same plate, are thus multi-stage arts where the multiple copies are all deemed original works. Thus Goodman argues that variations in an autographic work would result in significant differences in the experience of a knowledgeable viewer, placing sculpture and painting in the same category as the autographic arts.

The relation between sculpture and architecture is more complex, however, as architecture is assigned to the allographic arts because buildings conform to the architect's plans and specifications much as a musical performance complies to a score. According to Goodman, the distinction between sculpture and architecture is that sculpture belongs to the autographic arts, whereas architecture is an allographic art.

A further implication of Goodman's views for the ontology of sculpture is that the identity of a sculpture consists of its symbolic properties. Goodman would likely acknowledge that symbols have physical as well as conceptual dimensions, and he does not deny the physical properties of sculpture. Nevertheless, his view of sculpture represents a major shift from those who would define the essence of sculpture as three-dimensional solid materials whose main features are physical mass, volume, or light.

Sculpture as an independent art

This brief analysis of philosophers' views on sculpture allows for some tentative conclusions concerning the autonomy of sculpture as an art in its own right, independent of its connections to architecture and painting. By locating sculpture in the eighteenth-century classification of the five major arts, Kristeller advanced the case for its independence. The fact that architecture does not appear in the list would raise doubts about any thoughts of sculpture's being dependent for its identity on architecture. Hegel is ambivalent on this point. He also lists sculpture as one of the major fine arts in his classification system, and locates sculpture above architecture in his hierarchical classification of the arts. However, he also states that sculpture can never actually exist apart from architecture. Perhaps he has in mind the model of classical Greek sculpture, where statues functioned primarily in the contexts provided by temples or other public buildings and theaters. It may be simply that Hegel's remarks here apply to placement within architectural environments, but not to sculpture's standing as an independent art. Hence, Hegel's remarks on the subordination of sculpture to architecture cannot be taken literally. Dewey's doubts about the future of sculpture apart from architecture appear to be unfounded given the continued vitality of free sculpture that continues to be produced. His arguments point to the possibilities of collaboration between sculpture and architecture rather than to the denial of successful independent sculpture.

With respect to painting, there is hardly a question of sculpture's being subsumed under painting. The focus is mainly on features that distinguish sculpture and painting and the question of rank in the respective systems of the arts, where painting is generally ranked above sculpture by Hegel and others. Key differences are two-dimensional plane surfaces of paintings versus three-dimensional aspects of sculpture, the greater capacity of painting to represent actions, and differences in materials and in compositional elements (for example line, color, and shape in painting versus mass, volume, and light in sculpture).

The arguments for sculpture as an independent art begin with the fact that the sculpture is nearly always made by an artist working in a different artistic practice from the architect's practice. Goodman's classification of sculpture as an autographic art and architecture as allographic helps to make clear the independence of sculpture by highlighting significant differences between the two. One interesting point to note is that the status of sculpture has never been called into question by advances in technology, or by the invention of new media such as photography, which led many to pronounce the death of painting. Sculpture is an independent artform even while it has frequently functioned in collaboration with these other artforms.

Sculpture as a public art

One of sculpture's most important characteristics is its public nature. It is not necessary to argue in support of this point that all sculpture is public, as there are at least some clear-cut instances, such as personal portraits, that qualify as belonging to the private sphere. However, it may well be true that, more so than other artforms, with the exception of architecture, sculpture exists as a type of public art in the public sphere. Sculpture, however, differs from architecture in its public function, as it is not intended to provide shelter or to compartmentalize space for functional needs, as does architecture. Unlike music, poetry, theater or painting, where the audience has a choice to turn off the source, public sculpture persists in a fixed and determined space that does not permit its audience a choice of whether or not to experience it when visiting the space. For instance, when attached to the architecture of public buildings or located in major plazas or parts, sculpture is accessible to all people using the environment.

The concept of public space implies a public sphere. Both notions are in need of clarification. One problem with the terms 'public' and 'public sphere' is that they have a history of considerable fluidity and diversity in meaning, depending on political and local settings. For instance, the public sphere in a monarchy might refer to property ownership and control of the reigning monarch, whereas in a democracy ownership and access reside in the hands of the people, or a representative government acting on their behalf. Within such entities there exist different segments of society characterized variously as the bourgeoisie and the proletariat or the ruling class and the working class, each with differing interests and some shared interests. Add to these broad categories the media, interest groups, political parties, government bureaucracies and the legal system, all of which help define the public sphere. Moreover, differing and perhaps competing interests in the public sphere can lead to very different requirements for public sculpture. One only had to visit Moscow or Saint Petersburg and view the massive piles of discarded sculptures of former party heroes just after the Communist government was toppled to appreciate this point. From the list of various interests that might comprise or influence the public sphere, it can be anticipated that public art from time to time will be called upon to serve various publics which comprise the public sphere.

Given these complexities, how might a philosopher begin to address the issue of public sculpture? The first task might be to investigate the distinction between public and private spheres as this distinction applies to sculpture. Ultimately, it may turn out that whatever is private is dependent on the public sphere and vice versa; however, it is useful for our purposes to assume that these notions indicate some important differences. In general, 'private' refers to the sphere of individuals and families, whereas 'public' refers to the sphere in which all stakeholders in a community have an interest and are entitled to some say, either directly or by proxy. Hence commissioning a portrait for the enjoyment of one's self and family or friends does not as such count as public art. A decision of the United States Congress or an agency of the government to commission a sculpture to honor the soldiers lost in the Vietnam War would result in a case of public sculpture.

The next consideration is to look at the particular role of the artist in public sculpture. First, the sculptor who is charged with making a public sculpture is acting in the name of the community. One important role of public sculpture has been to create images that mythologize history. Operating in a utopian mode, public sculpture might aim at fostering unity among people by idealizing the sentiments of the community or focusing on areas of common agreement. In the past, heroic sculptures featuring beloved national figures were used to instill feelings of patriotism and national unity. However, in an age of anti-heroism a different approach is called for. One of the most successful anti-heroic sculptures is the Vietnam Veterans' Memorial designed by Maya Linn and located on the mall in Washington, D.C. Here it was necessary to address conflicting sentiments including the feelings of unappreciated soldiers and the public's divided views over an unpopular war. Despite an initial public outcry, the Memorial has become an embracing symbol of "national mourning and reconciliation" as well as a "critical parody, reversing the usual role of war monuments" (Mitchell 1992: 3). It has managed to satisfy the needs of many diverse groups, resulting in a stream of visitors who often participate in the memorial by leaving gifts honoring the soldiers named on the wall.

As the contemporary mood has changed, there is increasing interest in the critical function of public sculpture. Public sculpture is a type of symbolic intervention and it often confronts history, politics and society, forcing a reexamination of painful moments in history. In 1988, Hans Haacke contributed the work, *Und ihr habt gesiegt (And You Were Victorious After All)*, to an exhibition initiated by the citizens of Graz, Austria. The exhibition was intended to challenge artists to "confront history, politics and society" and to remind the citizens of Nazi atrocities fifty years earlier. Haacke's sculpture re-created the Nazi draping of the *Column of the Virgin Mary*, located in Graz, and carried the inscription, "And You were Victorious After All." Haacke's commissioned work was destroyed by a Neo-Nazi fire bomber shortly after it was installed. The sculptor's work generated an extreme reaction, suggesting that it evoked powerful and unresolved feelings carried forth from the Nazi era concerning which there was no consensus (Causey 1998: 219).

Such incidents raise broader questions concerning the sculptor's role in creating public sculpture. The artist may be placed in a unique and problematic role in creating public sculpture. Should the artist simply absorb and represent the views of the community through non-controversial images? Or is the role of the sculptor to assume the position of social critic and proceed accordingly? Forcing the sculptor to become a spokesperson or a commentator for the community on significant and sensitive aesthetic, political and social issues has become increasingly problematic in culturally diverse, ideologically driven, advanced technological societies. This is notably the case in an environment where substantial doubt exists whether artists have the necessary knowledge or wisdom to dispense truth, and where interpretations of history shift rapidly with changes in ideology. From the artist's perspective there is the risk of becoming an instrument of propaganda for the state or one of the many interest groups comprising the community.

This calls for a rethinking of the processes guiding the creation of public sculpture to allow greater community participation. It suggests that public sculpture is not about artists working in isolation to make beautiful sculpture according to a personal aesthetic, or about artists and the state collaborating to impose certain aesthetic or political views on the people. Richard Serra's *Titled Arc* (1981), created for the Federal Plaza in New York, was a failed attempt to impose an aesthetic statement in conflict with aesthetic interests of the community (Weyersgraf-Serra and Buskirk 1988). After a lengthy court battle, the twelve-foot steel wall was removed in 1989. The artist's arguments that the site-specific sculpture was a critical work in his career and that it gave shape to the featureless space of the plaza did not prevail over citizens' objections to its intrusiveness. Ironically, despite its removal, the public debate surrounding the *Titled Arc* incident heightened public involvement in the process of creating public sculpture in significant ways. It initiated thoughtful and passionate dialogue involving artists, representatives of the government, the legal system and the public, and forced them to confront how public sculpture can accommodate the competing interests of the artist, the community and the state.

One approach intended to address the need for community participation in public sculpture is Joseph Beuys's social sculpture. A major shift in thinking about public sculpture was required when Beuys advanced his concept of social sculpture with *7000 Oaks* at Documenta in Kassel, Germany in 1982. The work began with "seven thousand large basalt stones arranged in a triangular pile pointing to a single oak tree" (North 1992: 11). Beuys then called for individuals or organizations to purchase the stones, replacing each stone with a person, to enable planting of seven thousand trees in Kassel. This process resulted in extending the sculptural object into a process action, or perhaps in replacing the sculptural object by the audience. The radical shift toward community involvement in Beuys's work and that of other late twentieth-century sculptors transfers the focus of public sculpture from the objects generated and the inner resources of the sculptor's mind to the audience's experience and actions. The audience through its experience and participation in effect *becomes* the sculpture.

There is one more question that might interest philosophers today: what is the relation of public sculpture to mass art? Public sculpture has some features of mass art as defined by Noël Carroll (1998): it is produced for, and consumed by, many people and brings aesthetic experience to a mass audience; it is class indifferent; is readily accessible with minimum effort to large numbers of people. Moreover, public sculpture, in its most successful forms at least, shares with mass art a distrust of the avant-garde. Historically, public sculpture encounters problems with its audience when it veers toward the avant-garde. This depends on the context and may not be so in every case, as the Beuys work would indicate. Public sculpture differs from other types of mass art such as movies, television, and rock and roll music which exist as multiple instances deriving from mass technologies of production and distribution (Carroll 1998: 185–211). I conclude that public sculpture shares with mass art important features, but it fails to satisfy Carroll's requirements of being a multiple instance or type art work produced and distributed by a mass technology.

What, then, has become of our initial definition of sculpture as the art of representing observed or imagined objects in solid material and in three dimensions? It would appear that the definition remains useful for traditional sculpture through most of history. However, it is necessary to modify the definition to include recent developments where expression supersedes representation, and new concepts and materials emerge. Social sculpture requires a new look at representation. For instance, is there a sense in which social sculpture can be representational? It does not resemble or copy, but it can refer to ideas in a broad sense. Social sculpture does not preclude the use of solid materials, but the main focus has shifted from these materials to social and political actions. To the extent that social action is three-dimensional, this feature still applies to contemporary practices in sculpture, but three-dimensional art now embraces actions in social space as well as physical space. The temporal dimension is of particular significance in public sculpture, as it can involve history as well as thought and actions in real time. Philosophers may wish to ponder the implications of these changes for the theory of sculpture.

See also Pragmatism, Pictorial representation, Art and emotion, Architecture, Painting, High versus low art.

References

Carroll, N. (1998) *A Philosophy of Mass Art,* Oxford: Oxford University Press.
Causey, A. (1998) *Sculpture Since 1945,* Oxford: Oxford University Press.
Dewey, J. (1987) *Art as Experience,* Carbondale: Southern Illinois University Press.
Goodman, N. (1976) *Languages of Art,* 2nd edn, Indianapolis: Bobbs Merrill.
Greene, T. M. (1940) *The Arts and the Art of Criticism,* Princeton: Princeton University Press.
Hegel, G. W. F. (1975) *Aesthetics,* Oxford: Oxford University Press.
Kristeller, P. O. (1965) "The Modern System of the Arts," in *Renaissance Thought and the Arts,* New York: Harper and Row.

Lessing, G. (1957) *Laocoön*, trans. E. Frothingham, New York: Noonday.

Martin, F. D. (1966) *Sculpture and Enlivened Space*, Lexington: University Press of Kentucky.

Mitchell, W. J. T. (ed.) (1992) *Art and the Public Sphere*, Chicago: University of Chicago Press.

North, M. (1992) "The Public as Sculpture: From Heavenly City to Mass Ornament," in W. J. T. Mitchell (ed.), *Art and the Public Sphere*, Chicago: University of Chicago Press.

Read, H. (1956) *The Art of Sculpture*, New York: Bollingen.

Schopenhauer, A. (1977) *The World As Will and Idea*, New York: AMS Press.

Sparshott, F. (1988) *Off the Ground*, Princeton: Princeton University Press.

Weiss, P. (1961) *Nine Basic Arts*, Carbondale: Southern Illinois University Press.

Weyergraf-Serra, C. and Buskirk, M. (1988) *Richard Serra's Titled Arc*, Eindhoven: Van Abbemuseum.

Further reading

Hughs, A. and Ranfft, E. (eds) (1997) *Sculpture and its Reproductions,* New York: Reaktion. (An analysis of problems of reproduction in sculpture from classical to contemporary times.)

Krauss, R. (1977) *Passages in Modern Sculpture*, New York: Viking. (An analysis of critical and philosophical issues in modern sculpture.)

Noguchi, I. (1994) *Noguchi: Essays and Conversations*, New York: Abrams. (Artist's reflections on the meaning of sculpture, sculpture gardens and sculpture in theater.)

43
ARCHITECTURE
Edward Winters

What is architecture? And in what way, peculiar to architecture, does it engender aesthetic understanding? Attempts to answer the first of these questions generally begin from the position that architecture is built form (or inhabitable space), and then add some further quality which a work must have to provide it with a status which is above and beyond mere building. So, for instance, it might be thought that symbolism is a candidate for the additional feature. Thus, 'Architecture is *symbolic* building,' would provide a definition of architecture whereby the presence of symbolism is thought to lift architecture out of the realm of meager utility. The second question then arises concerning the nature of the defining addendum and the role it plays in our aesthetic appreciation.

Attempts to answer this second question impinge upon (and are complicated by) attempts to answer the first. In what way would we understand architecture, given that its works are not only symbolic, for instance, but are intrinsically part of the built environment? That is, once we stress the second part of the *definiendum*, we are obliged to make sense of the claim that 'Architecture is symbolic *building*.' How are we to take account of the fact that utilitarian considerations enter into our conception of its works? Architecture is not sculpture. That its works are *designed* to serve our purposes – designed to accommodate our practices of worship, work, rest and recreation – is not some accidental feature of them. Architecture, that is, requires a conception of its works which contains utility as a substratum of the aesthetic appreciation of them.

The theory of architecture anticipates the philosophy of architecture and Vitruvius (1960) writes that architecture must contain *firmitas, utilitas et venustas* (firmness, utility and delight). However, no systematic account of how each contributes to each is forthcoming, and this leaves the constituent parts of architecture like the list of ingredients of a recipe. These are considerations that the builder must keep in mind when designing a work, but until we better understand the part each plays in combining to make a significant whole, we will be at a loss

519

as to how to explain our grasp of architecture. Moreover, the theory of architecture has tended to propose methods of building and, while it may provide indirect principles of architectural appreciation, it has not systematically addressed the kinds of concern on which the philosophy of architecture has focused.

Vitruvius, however, did think that architecture had meaning, and so he did have something to say upon how we might gain an understanding of its works. And one version of architectural understanding can be traced back to his work. For we are told that the origin of the classical orders is to be found in classicism's stylization of the built form of primitive construction. Others have followed this line of thought, but it remains unclear as to how meaning alone can provide a basis for *aesthetic* understanding. It is important, however, to see how it is that in answering our first question, a number of thinkers have attempted to provide architecture with some sort of symbolic meaning or content. It is to two prominent theories within this area that we now turn.

Architectural content

The representational theory

Architectural theorists have provided a view which is often given in defense of classicism. I shall call this view the *representational* theory. This account has a forceful proponent of its merits in Vitruvius. The line of inheritance can be traced through Alberti (1955), William Chambers (1757) and more lately to Demitri Porphyrios (1982). This view has it that the classical building and its elements refer to the primitive building and its elements. Each one is 'formalized' and is thereby referred to or represented. The column refers to, or represents, the cut down tree; the capital refers to a pad that sits the wooden beam atop it. In its formalization, the classical building refers beyond itself to the elements of primitive building: to its primitive materials and to its methods of construction. But it does so in enduring materials: in stone and marble. In formalizing the primitive, the classical building recreates or represents the building which is its referent. Moreover, this view enjoys the generality at which a philosophy of architecture should aim. The argument is that whereas other styles of architecture are merely fashionable dressing, merely a way of stylistic decoration, classicism gives architecture a content which can be apprehended by the intellect. Classicism, accordingly, is not a style. It is, supposedly, the only intelligible form of architecture.

The semantic theory

A very general view of architectural meaning is proposed by Nelson Goodman (1988). I shall call this version of the content theory the *semantic theory*. In his efforts to give a unified and systematic account of everything cultural, Goodman sets out to show the variety of routes that a spectator might take from building to referent. A building can denote its referent. Denotation is a simple relation and needs no further explanation. The words 'city' and 'Berlin' both denote Berlin, but so too, according to Goodman, does a picture postcard of that city (or some distinctive part of the city, a famous landmark for instance). The Sydney Opera House, we are told, denotes sailing boats. Understanding what the Sydney Opera House means is to apprehend the reference to sailing boats given by the building. (Of course, in other contexts, the opera house might denote Sydney or even Australia. But *as a work of architecture* it denotes sailing boats).

Not all buildings denote. Buildings can have other sorts of meaning. A building can exemplify the properties to which it refers. The explanation of exemplification is given in greater depth in *Languages of Art* (Goodman 1968). Reference in exemplification runs counter to the direction of reference in denotation. The direction of denotation is language –> world, whereas in exemplification the direction is world –> language. A tailor's swatch exemplifies some (but not all) of the properties of the squares of material to be found in its contents. The coarseness of weave, the pattern, the relative weight of the cloth, the color, and so on, are all properties that the samples of material exemplify. The shape of the cloth, with its pinking-sheared edge, and its size are not so exemplified, and in consequence they are not referred to by the tailor's swatch. In other words, the context prescribes those properties which are, and those properties which are not, referred to by means of exemplification. A modernist building of a certain sort – a building which results from the architect's concern to construct the building in such a way that every construction detail should be part of its appearance – might be said to exemplify its means of construction. In Goodman's terms, the building thereby refers to its means of construction. A building by the Dutch architect Rietveld, for instance, might be thought to separate elements into beams, columns, frames and openings in order that the elemental 'putting-together-of-the-building' becomes exemplified. Goodman writes: "In other buildings made of columns, beams, frames, and walls, the structure is not exemplified at all, serving only practical and perhaps also other symbolic functions" (Goodman 1988: 38), and continues:

> A purely formal building that neither depicts anything nor expresses any feelings or ideas is sometimes held not to function as a symbol at all. Actually, it exemplifies certain of its properties, and only so distinguishes itself from buildings that are not works of art at all.
>
> (Goodman 1988: 41)

The phenomenon sketched out here is what Goodman calls literal exemplification. The building literally possesses the properties which it exemplifies. But some of the properties that a building exemplifies could not be attributed to a pile of stones or glass and steel or whatever. No building could literally exemplify 'soaring and singing'; but a number of Gothic cathedrals might metaphorically exemplify these properties. This form of reference is expression. A building can express properties which it does not literally have. A building, that is, might refer to properties that it could not literally possess.

Content and the aesthetics of architecture

Common to both content views sketched out here is the idea that when we are confronted with a building and we ask ourselves what it means, or how are we to understand it, an answer is to hand. And in both cases the answer is given in terms of some specified architectural content. But while both accounts answer the questions asked earlier, neither affords an account of the content of architectural *experience*.

This provides a challenge to the content theories, if we think that it is in the understanding of the work of architecture that my pleasure resides, and that it is in my understanding that I can justify the experience that I have. For we can make evaluative judgements of buildings. What places constraints upon both the architect and his critic is the context which guides or limits the occasion of the architect's work within the institution which is architecture. That context is to be described in terms of the tradition within which the architect is working. It is with reference to the tradition that I can come to understand and to criticize the work that is put before me; and which places upon my description of the work, the pressure to see it this way rather than that. It may be true that in appreciating classical buildings I see the building as connected with primitive forms of construction, but even if we concede this, it remains difficult to see how the building is 'of' the primitive hut in any way comparable to ways in which portraits are of their sitters or novels are about political skulduggery. It may be part of the *content of my experience* that I connect the classical building with primitive construction, but that does not entail that primitive construction forms part of the *representational* content of the classical building. Our appreciation of a classical building can constitute an aesthetic appreciation without any recognition of the ancient origins of its form. (This is not to deny that once we do so recognize those origins, we can have our aesthetic appreciation enriched.) But would it make sense to say that we could have (even a partial) aesthetic appreciation of a portrait or a novel if we failed to grasp its representational content?

What the representational theorist takes for the representational relation is, perhaps, better conceived as a connection between works of art generally, so that in experiencing one work, the spectator's experience of other works impinges upon his present experience. So, when I am standing in the cloister of *San Carlo alle Quattrofontane*, for instance, my experience of that building will be more or less rich depending on my familiarity with the history of art pertinent to the building in which I stand. Provided that I am acquainted with the classical orders and the strictness demanded in their application, I shall see Borromini's cloister as impertinent, audacious, or even outrageous. These descriptions will capture my experience, given that the experience is so colored by my other experiences. They will explain my amusement at the building, or my sneaking admiration, or my utter disgust. And in explaining why I so see the building I will call upon another to share the experience I have and to share my response to it. But my response to the building is contained in my experience of it, and so I have not ventured beyond the experience in accounting for my appreciative understanding.

We can now begin to see how an understanding of a work of architecture brings with it the evaluation that is characteristic of our appreciation of works of art generally. To understand a building is to see it in a certain way. It is to be disposed to give such and such descriptions which articulate the experiences that we have in its presence. Such understanding can be clumsy, rudimentary, deep or subtle. And it can vary in degrees according to how much attention we pay to the building under scrutiny. But this admission of degrees of understanding can easily be accommodated within the context of a wider aesthetic theory which places emphasis on the experience of the spectator. The semantic theory, in contrast, seems to make it an all-or-nothing grasping of the building's meaning. Moreover the semantic theory seems incapable of uniting meaning and evaluation.

A further point regarding evaluation escapes Goodman's analysis. For if a building is weak in some respect or if it is an example of a type, but only a mediocre example, or if it is clumsy or drab, then these descriptions are relevant to our aesthetic estimation of it. That is, these features are part of the 'meaning-for-us' of the building. But the semantic theory cannot bring this out. It cannot bring this out because these descriptions belong to our experience of the building. Reference, in Goodman's terms, is a relation between a building and what it means. Accordingly, to understand a building is to trace the path of building to referent. But the description of the experience of the building throws the weight from the object in the world (the building) to the object of our experience (the building as seen). We value architecture because of the way that we have come to experience it; and we have come to experience it as we do because of the ways in which we inhabit it. Nothing to do with *reference* is required to give an account of architectural understanding. Architecture is not concerned with meanings so much as it is with significance.

Functionalism

Functionalism takes seriously the second of the questions asked in the introduction. It provides an account of what is peculiar to architecture in the way in which it engenders our understanding, but it has two ideals of what that understanding is. The first of these regards functionalism as the grounds for our aesthetic understanding, while the second simply rejects *aesthetic* understanding in favor of social science. Architectural theorists often vacillate between the two standpoints, and it is difficult to see clearly where the lines are drawn. Moreover, the claims of the functionalists are often, if not always, inconsistent. Nevertheless, functionalism in one form or another has exerted an enormous influence over architectural practice, its history and its theory.

Functionalism, in both its strands, can be seen to have developed from the structural rationalism to be found in the theoretical writings of Viollet-le-Duc:

> There are in architecture . . . two indispensable ways in which truth must be adhered to. We must be true in respect of programme, and true in respect of the constructive processes. To be true in respect of the programme is to fulfil exactly, scrupulously, the conditions imposed by the requirements of the case. To be true in respect of the constructive processes is to employ the materials according to their qualities and properties.
>
> (Viollet-le-Duc 1959: 448)

He goes on to recommend that 'artistic' considerations of symmetry and apparent form are only secondary in the presence of these two dominant principles. What emerged from Viollet-le-Duc's *Discourses* was a commitment to architecture which 'expressed' the programme and the structure of the building. Nevertheless, such expression is to be *seen* in the building under review, and it is a mark of a work's success that we come to regard it as true to these principles. But such a regard is only really coherent if the 'truth' of the building shows up in our experience. Viollet-le-Duc's conception of architecture was, therefore, an aesthetic conception, since it makes claims about how a building can be properly conceived and appreciated in accordance with recommendations of appropriateness.

Aesthetic functionalism

One strand of modernism arising from this background regards the function of a building as determining its form, so that the form of the building is aesthetically conceived as being appropriate to the utility for which the building was designed. According to this view, the beauty of a building is to be assessed in terms of its form in relation to its function. That is, we must consider the utility of a building when considering the aptness of its form. So a building can have this further value added to its utility, and this further value is, in some specifiable way, to be determined by the building's utility. This way of putting the matter immediately demonstrates its appeal. For we can now, at a stroke, answer both questions with which we began this chapter. Architecture is the *art* of building. Further, it peculiarly engenders our aesthetic understanding by its functional aspect prescribing its form. And this functional prescription just is what provides architecture with its status as an art. Our responses to works of architecture constrain us to see how the built form is appropriate to the purpose of the building. Rather than reducing 'artistic' concerns to secondary status, the expression of function becomes the peculiar aesthetic consideration intrinsic to works of architecture.

Austere functionalism

The second strand of functionalism deriving from structural rationalism is really a dismissal of aesthetic considerations altogether. According to the conception of function as socially determined, we need pay no attention to how the building is seen. Hence the building is a product of its function if it best facilitates the activity for which it is designed. (For instance, I am unconcerned with the 'look' of my car brakes, my interest is in their capacity to bring my car to a stop when pressure is applied to the foot pedal.) The concept of function here is akin to that used in engineering. As such, it is not an aesthetic theory at all, but rather regards aesthetics as a separate matter, an accidental bonus at best, entirely irrelevant or even 'false consciousness' at worst. That this is an ideal to which modern architects have been inclined can be gleaned from *La Sarraz Declaration* 1928 of CIAM (*Congrès Internationaux d'Architecture Moderne*) (CIAM 1979). The declaration emphasized building rather than architecture. It sought to place architecture, not in the context of the broader arts, but in the context of economics, politics and social science. It aimed to replace the work of the craftsman with industrial processes, and sought "the universal adoption of rationalized production methods" (Frampton 1985a: 269) in its efforts to increase housing and supersede the methods of a craft era.

Regarded by many as the home of modernist functionalism, the Bauhaus formed a department of architecture in 1927 under the leadership of the Swiss architect Hannes Meyer. One year later, upon the resignation of Walter Gropius as Director, Meyer succeeded him.

Meyer organized the Bauhaus into four major departments: architecture (now called 'building' for polemical reasons), advertising, wood and metal production, and textiles. Supplementary scientific courses, such as industrial organization and psychology, were introduced into all departments, while the building section shifted its emphasis to the economic optimization of plan arrangements and to methods for the precise calculation of light, sunlight, heat loss/gain, and acoustics.

(Frampton 1985a: 129)

Both in the ideological parlance and in the tone of the Declaration, together with the shift in focus of Meyer's Bauhaus, it is clear that aesthetic considerations do not intrude upon the central task of the architect as conceived by this austere strand of functionalism.

However, even if such a view were sustainable, it would not fall within the aesthetics of architecture, except as a challenge to provide a positive account that would persuade the spectator that architecture is worth looking at, and that architects can thereby provide works which are valuable in and of themselves. Rather than solving the problem with which we started, austere functionalism dissolves the problem by retreating from architecture to mere building, and thereby provides a criterion by which we measure the successful work: efficiency.

Nevertheless, it is worth noting that the buildings, furniture and fittings designed by austere functionalists *are worth looking at*. That is, whatever the claims of the designers and their supportive theorists, the look of the works is aesthetically estimable and it seems incredible that this is mere caprice. Austere functionalism is a prime example of a critically engaged theory which immunizes its works from *aesthetic* criticism (by removing them from its orbit) and thereby promotes and protects its adherents in their artistic practice. (Much of this is true of all the modern arts, together with the various polemical arguments developed to sustain them; a great deal of which, when *looked* at, turn out to be pleasantly decorative.)

Functionalism, under both its aspects we might feel, is inadequate as an account of our aesthetic responses to architecture. For the notion of function, in the context of architecture, remains irredeemably vague. Consider, for instance, the urban design of the square. Take the Plaza Major in Madrid. What is its function? On Tuesdays it is a market, on Saints' days it is a fairground, on Sundays townspeople gather to parade in their finery. In the evenings families meet up for drinks, and on Saturday mornings it becomes a center for the exchange of rare stamps. When built, it was the palace of the King and was overlooked by courtiers' balconies. It was, at one time, the *plaza de torres*. During the Inquisition it was used for show trials and ritual executions. It now houses offices and a range of cheap to expensive hotel accommodation, bars and restaurants. That is, the life of its design – the range of activities made available by it – has outstripped any restrictive conception of 'the function' for which it was designed. It seems merely stipulative to deem any of its varied historical uses illegitimate. Moreover, since the business of aesthetics is born of a conception of ourselves as free, we might think it is of the essence of our conception of architectural utility that it should remain irredeemably vague, so that any morally permissible human purpose might be pursued within the designed environment. It remains true that while the fact that a building has utility enters into our conception of the nature of architecture, we cannot be required to specify in detail what particular use a building must have. As Scruton has put it, it is unclear "how any particular 'function' is to be translated into architectural 'form.' All we can say . . . is that buildings have uses, and should not be understood as though they did not" (Scruton 1979: 40)

Scruton's account

The aesthetics of architecture, as a distinct area within the analytical philosophy of art, might reasonably be said to have been inaugurated with the publication in 1979 of Scruton's *The Aesthetics of Architecture*. Here, for the first time a philosopher has considered the issues raised previously in the theory of architecture, and has sustained a position which calls upon the philosophy of mind and action and the theory of meaning: resources unavailable to the non-philosopher. Moreover, this work is resolutely focused on the conditions of our appreciation and understanding of architecture. And so matters of how best to build, those which exercised much of architectural theory written by practicing architects, are rightly marginalized. Much of the power of Scruton's work comes from his Wittgensteinian conception of mind and the account of experience to be found therein. (Indeed, in raising difficulties for the accounts sketched earlier we have already had recourse to such a conception of architectural *experience* as developed in the work of Scruton.) Added to this account is a political conception of community as a defining feature of the self, which draws on both Wittgenstein and Hegel, and has much in common with communitarianism as a political philosophy designed to counter modern liberalism.

As such, Scruton's architectural aesthetics has two aspects. His most positive contributions are to provide an account of what it is to experience and to judge works of architecture, and to give an account of the depth and flexibility of aesthetic experience as that shows up in our appreciation of architectural works. His political philosophy, with its attendant conception of the self, then provides a defense of classicism when coupled with this conception of aesthetics. While it is not easy to unpick these two strands in his thought (indeed his position claims that each has to be developed in tandem with the other), much of the former can be grasped and applied to architecture more broadly than his conservative position might initially suggest. Further, even if we grant the interdependence of these two strands, his communitarian commitments might still be used in defense of the kinds of architecture to which he feels most hostile.

Experiencing and judging architecture

Appreciation pulls together two requirements that any adequate account of the aesthetics of architecture must address. We both enjoy works of architecture and feel that we can come to understand them. At the heart of our appreciation of the visual arts is a certain kind of experience which requires imaginative attention to its object. I do not merely perceive a building in front of me in the manner of any sighted creature. I can come to see the building in terms of a descriptive content which pulls together the various fragmentary perceptions I have when moving in and around it. I can see, for instance, that a colonnade develops a rhythm which provides direction, and grounds my expectation of other aspects of the building yet to be seen; or which satisfies my expectation or pleasantly surprises me, given other aspects of the building already seen. I can see elements of the building grouped in certain ways which make a visual sense of the composition at which I look. Moreover, this descriptive content, being aspectual, is based upon, but irreducible to, the material building at which I stare. That is to say that the *experience*, so described, is imaginative. Two important points immediately follow from this. My experience of the building is subject to the will. It is a way of seeing the building for which I am responsible. (I cannot be wrong about how I see the building.) And secondly, my seeing the building under some description provides my imaginative experience with a content that is accessible, at least in principle, to any other suitably sensitive spectator.

Now when we come to judge works of architecture, we are in the position to try out 'interpretive' visualizations in order to arrive at a construal which best fits the work under consideration. And the nature of my judgement is such that I can argue with others to try and persuade them of its force. As such, the critical nature of the judgement calls for justification. Moreover, the nature of the imaginative experience requires a unified description of the work under view. And so I shall feel called upon to organize the disconnected pieces of my perceptual world into a single continuous imaginative experience of a unified whole. (Thus we think of a work of art as having a definite sense.) This activity, in which I find myself engaged, is by its very nature judgemental, for it seeks this unity in the work conceived as imaginative, harmonious, agreeable and sensible.

Architectural aesthetics and our place in the world

Scruton places much emphasis on the fact that we are active in our appreciation of architecture; that it is not merely a passive contemplation in which we indulge ourselves. It is within the 'aesthetics of the everyday' that this conception of the importance of aesthetics comes to the fore. We inhabit a world in which there are social structures that predate our individual existence and that will survive our demise. Our 'selves' are created in that world, and they are dependent for their nature upon the institutions which bind us to our forebears, our fellows and to those that are yet to be. Over and above the vicissitudes of our natural lives, with their immediate drives and appetites, there appears to be a cultivated world of ceremony and decorum in which we find our home. The arts in general, but architecture in particular, provide focus for our attention to our selves as moral agents, able to step aside from the burden of our natural state and to regard ourselves as free. It is in this conception of architecture as a ground for such lives that we can best see the contrast with austere functionalism. Appreciation of architecture and the kind of understanding thus engendered lie at the heart of our conception of ourselves.

> In so far as there is . . . an aesthetics of everyday life, all men must to some extent engage in it, or, if they fail to do so, have a defective understanding of the world. In every task, however functional, there are infinite ways of proceeding. All our choices are extracted from a chaos of functionally equivalent alternatives, and in all choices which affect, not just present purposes, but also distant (and perhaps unstateable) aspirations, it is the non-utilitarian residue that is paramount. To build well is to find the appropriate form, and that means the form which answers to what endures, not what expires. The appropriate form ministers . . . not just to present purposes, but to a sense of ourselves as creatures with identities transcending the sum of present purpose and desire.
>
> (Scruton 1979: 239–40)

We might now regard the experience of architecture with the solemnity and seriousness which Scruton has attributed to it. It remains, however, a moot point as to whether we should choose the kinds of life that Scruton recommends. Even if we agree with him that architecture is a primary locus for our thoughts and feelings when considering where and with whom we should make our homes, we might still feel that cultural diversity, invention, novelty and convenience may play their part in forming that home. Quite apart from the modernity he so loathes, there are other traditions from which we might develop and enjoy the making of such a home. Accepting Scruton's eloquent espousal of the experiential in our appreciation of architecture, we might still feel that there is a need for *critical* invention and the incorporation of other cultural influences as the postmodern world develops. In this respect it is important to mention Kenneth Frampton's enormously influential paper, "Critical Regionalism" (Frampton 1985b), which advocates a return to regional vernacular architecture with the addition of a genuinely critical stance toward the works which issue from it. Here, if we take serious heed of Scruton's well defined circumscription of what the aesthetic experience of architecture is, we might find the best picture of a global understanding of the importance of architecture as a kind of visual art.

See also Sculpture, Environmental aesthetics.

References

Alberti (1955) *Ten Books on Architecture*, trans. J. Leoni, London: Tiranti.

Chambers, W. (1757) *A Treatise on Civil Architecture*, London.

CIAM (1979) *CIAM Dokumente 1928–1939*, Basel and Stuttgart: ETH/GTA for Congrès Internationaux d'Architecture Moderne..

Frampton, K. (1985a) *Modern Architecture: A Critical History*, London: Thames and Hudson.

—— (1985b) "Critical Regionalism," in H. Foster (ed.), *Post Modern Culture*, London: Pluto.

Goodman, N. (1968) *Languages of Art*, Indianapolis: Bobbs-Merrill.

—— (1988) "How Buildings Mean," in *Reconceptions in Philosophy and Other Arts and Sciences*, London: Routledge.

Porphyrios, D. (1982) "Classicism is Not a Style," *Architectural Design* 5/6: 50–7.

Scruton, R. (1979) *The Aesthetics of Architecture*, London: Methuen.

Viollet-le-Duc, E-E. (1959) *Discourses on Architecture*, trans. B. Bucknall, London: Allen and Unwin.

Vitruvius (1960) *Vitruvius: The Ten Books on Architecture*, trans. M. Morgan, New York: Dover.

Further reading

Haldane, J. (1999) "Form and Meaning in Architecture," *Architect's Journal* 4: 9–20. (A survey of the ways in which built form has been imbued with meaning.)

Hill, R. (1999) *Designs and Their Consequences*, New Haven: Yale University Press. (Written by an architect, this book draws upon analytical philosophy, psychology and cultural theory in its attempt to give a broad account of our interpretation of architecture.)

Scruton, R. (1994) *The Classical Vernacular: Architectural Principles in an Age of Nihilism*, Manchester: Carcanet. (In a collection of essays spanning twenty years, Scruton develops a range of philosophical arguments in defense of classicism and against modernism.)

Van Eck, C. (1994) *Organicism in Nineteenth Century Architecture*, Amsterdam: Architectura and Natura Press. (This work studies the history and philosophy of organicism from antiquity to the eighteenth century, and provides an interpretive account of this important strand of architecture and its theory.)

44

MUSIC

Mark DeBellis

What is music's power over us? What is at the root of its capacity to animate and enrich our lives? One line of response – perhaps the immediate, intuitive answer most people would give – is that we value music for how it makes us *feel*, for its ability to evoke emotion in us. A conception of the nature and purposes of music that stresses the arousal of emotion is called *expressionist* (Meyer 1956).

A second view – which may or may not be held in conjunction with the first – is that music is essentially *iconic*: that it is an imitation or representation of, and thereby refers to, some aspect of the extramusical, 'human' world of emotions, character, and ideas. This is a *referentialist* view. (The thought here is that music derives its human relevance through signifying something in the human world.) Referentialism is not the same as expressionism, because saying that a piece of music makes us sad need not be taken to imply, or to be implied by, saying that the music is an *imitation* of, or is *about*, sadness. However, someone may be drawn to hold both referentialist and expressionist views if he or she thinks, say, that music imitative of sadness does in fact typically make listeners sad, or that what it *is* for something to be an imitation or representation of sadness is, at least in part, for it to evoke that emotion.

A third line of approach to these questions focuses on the cognitive grasp of musical properties and relationships such as repetition and contrast, formal structure (sonata, rondo, ABA form), motivic relationships, harmonic structure, and so on, where such properties are understood to be non-referential. This approach is termed *formalism*. Formalism, like other views, comes in both exclusionary and non-exclusionary versions: in the exclusionary version, one argues that the formalistic is all there is in some sense, denying the existence or importance of the referential element (Hanslick 1986); in the latter, one merely concentrates on what is intrinsic to the music while acknowledging that there may be a referential aspect as well (Meyer 1956). Formalism as stated here is not inconsistent with expressionism, since one can argue that the cognition of tonal patterns characteristically leads to emotive responses.

But what are the reasons why someone would hold one conception of music instead of another? In order to see our way through the issues, let us focus on the following topics: expressive character and the emotions; representation; reference and signification; and musical understanding. As we proceed, we will find it necessary, from time to time, to refine the taxonomy of conceptions of music just given, in our attempt to see just what is at stake.

Expressive character and the emotions

'The music is sad.' Sometimes this is said of pure instrumental music, sometimes of music that accompanies, and suits (or fails to suit) a text or dramatic situation. In either case, the music itself cannot be sad in the way people are. So what do we mean?

This is the issue of expressive character: what we ascribe to music using terms for 'human' qualities, such as emotive characteristics ('happy,' 'sad'), or traits of mind or character ('decisive,' 'heroic'). (It need not be assumed, however, that expressive character can always be specified adequately in words.) Kivy (1989) provides one of the most trenchant treatments of the topic; let us consider his views.

It is helpful, first of all, to understand Kivy's theory in opposition to the (initially attractive) expressionist conception, on which an expressive character is a propensity to evoke emotions or feelings in a listener. In its simplest form this would be the view that sad music is music that makes us sad. Let us call this simple arousalism. ('Simple,' because it assumes that the emotion evoked is just the *same* as that which figures in the specification of expressive character. A more complicated form of the theory might hold, instead, that sad music is music that inspires not sadness but pity, that is, a characteristic human reaction to the sadness of others.)

Kivy rejects simple arousalism (as well as all expressionist views of expressive character). "It is quite compatible with my perceiving the most intense and disquieting emotions in a work of art," he writes, "that I not myself be moved in the least" (Kivy 1989: 23). The listener's response to expressive character is, on his view, one of recognition: it is a cognitive rather than affective response. According to Kivy, the recognition of expressiveness is to be explained, in large part, via recognition of music's resemblance to the human behavioral expression of emotion. Because we perceive a structural similarity between sad music and the behavioral expression of sadness, he says, we hear such music as appropriate to the expression of sadness, and hence as expressive of sadness (ibid.: 50).

Figure 44.1 Short passage from Handel's *Messiah*
Source: Kivy, *Sound Sentiment* (1989), p. 51

What kinds of behavioral expression does Kivy have in mind? The first is impassioned speech, illustrated by a passage from Handel's *Messiah* ("Rejoice Greatly, O Daughter of Zion!"; see Figure 44.1). This, he says, "resembles the voice rising in joy" (ibid.: 51).

Second, expressive music may bear a resemblance to motion of the human body, to "gesture [or] carriage" (Kivy 1989: 53). Kivy contrasts the "Pleni sunt coeli" of Bach's *Mass in B Minor* with "I know that my Redeemer liveth" from *Messiah*: the former is a "sound map" of leaping, vigorous joy, the latter dignified strides and gesture (ibid.: 53–4). Resemblance either to utterance or bodily movement forms the basis of one component of Kivy's theory, which he terms the 'contour' thesis (the second component being 'convention').

Insofar as he accounts for expressiveness via speech, Kivy taps into one of the most venerable, time-honored philosophical ideas about the nature of music (as he acknowledges), one that has persisted and shaped musical thought in many eras and places. In Book III of the *Republic*, Plato singles out the musical modes that imitate the "utterances and accents" (or "tone and rhythm") of the brave person, on the one hand, and one who seeks to bring about peace, on the other (*Republic* 398c–399c). Plato conceives of music as imitation, where what it imitates is speech. A 'speech theory' is at work in the speculations of late-sixteenth-century Florentine scholars and musicians such as Girolamo Mei and Vincenzo Galilei, who extolled the expressive power of ancient Greek music compared with the contrapuntal practice of their own day (see Strunk 1998, Lippman 1986–90, le Huray and Day 1981). These ideas, discussed in informal gatherings by a group that came to be known as the Camerata, influenced early opera, which employed a musical style known as the *stile rappresentativo* (representational style), or recitative, intermediate between song and speech. The 'speech theory,' in various forms, held sway through much of the eighteenth century, though it was increasingly called into question by the proponents of 'expression' over 'imitation.' Expression consisted in 'raising the passions' or 'affections'; such a view of music was, essentially, a form of arousalism. (The debate over imitation and expression was linked to changing attitudes toward vocal and instrumental music, though the two oppositions do not coincide.)

There is more to the contour model than speech. Kivy invokes, as well, resemblance to "bodily gesture and posture" as a basis of musical expressiveness:

> the rhythmic movement of the human body in all kinds of emotive expressions is mirrored by and recognized in music . . . funeral marches are slow and measured, as sadness slows and measures our expression of it; . . . rapid rhythmic pulses in music are suggestive of rapid behavior under the influence of the lighter emotions.
>
> (Kivy 1989: 55)

Higher pitch, moreover, has a natural connection with higher energy levels, Kivy argues.

Kivy's contour model is, at bottom, a form of imitation theory, in that it sees music in terms of a resemblance relation to the extramusical, 'human' world. Is it an instance of referentialism, then, in the sense sketched earlier? Yes and no: for at this point it proves necessary to separate some of the strands interwoven in the account of referentialism given earlier. For while Kivy's model is imitative, it does not impute the semantic notion of *reference* to expressiveness. His model has it that sad music *resembles* sad behavior, not that it is *about* sad behavior or sadness. Hence, as far as the contour model is concerned, Kivy sides with the referentialist to the extent that they both explain music's human relevance in terms of resemblance to the human world; but they part company in that, unlike the referentialist, Kivy does not take this relation to entail reference.

In any event, Kivy recognizes that the contour model cannot account for the expressive qualities of major ('happy') and minor ('sad'). He puts forth, as well, a 'convention' theory, on which musical expressiveness is derived from the "customary association" of musical and emotive properties (Kivy 1989: 77). Together contour and convention are to account for all instances of musical expressiveness.

Kivy's account is persuasive in many ways, and surely much in it is right and important. It is a valuable insight that we tend to 'animate' non-sentient sounds with human qualities, and it can be no coincidence that high energy levels are associated with high pitch and rapid movement, both in and outside of music.

We might have some worries, though, about Kivy's account, or any form of imitation theory. The first is that some of the examples that purport to show a structural similarity – that is, some more-or-less abstract similarity between the 'shapes' of emotive behavior and expressive music – do not clearly demonstrate this. What they do clearly exhibit is a similarity in emotive content, but, after all, that is something we already knew to be there. Consider the *Messiah* example, in which, Kivy says, the rising melodic line "resembles the voice rising in joy." Is a rising pitch contour in fact one of the marks by which we ordinarily tell, from a person's speech, that he or she is joyful? Or is it just as likely to be found in the utterances of one who is desperate or frantic? (Yes, 'rejoice' tends to rise in pitch when uttered joyfully, but so it does when pronounced ironically.) It is doubtful that there is any real correlation here. But then why does the example seem so convincing at first? Because in both the joyful, rising melodic line and joyful speech, we discern joy, and so, to *that* extent, music and speech resemble one another. We then mistakenly suppose that this resemblance must be a resemblance *of contour*; but that may well be a confused projection from the similarity we do perceive. The appeal to resemblance fails to have explanatory power, since to say we hear both music and speech as joyful is merely to restate the problem of expressive character (Morellet 1986: 272, Twining 1986: 249).

A second point is that the human action expressive music is taken to resemble need not be limited to behavior *expressive* of some emotion. Consider the way a goal-directed chord progression – one containing a deceptive cadence, say – may be heard as encountering obstacles and diversions, eventually overcoming them with a sense of satisfaction. We should say here that the music resembles (not the *expression* of satisfaction, but) what *causes* satisfaction, namely, the achievement of a goal in the face of difficulties. What is plausibly taken to be the object of resemblance here is causally upstream from the emotion, not downstream from it as its expression would be.

Finally, we might wonder whether the convention model adequately accounts for everything that cannot be explained in terms of contour. Given that the minor mode has an expressive character more sad than cheerful, do we know that it derives that character wholly through customary association? Kivy asks us, in effect, to assume that if an expressive element is not a function of contour, then it must be a function of convention. It seems to me that, in our present state of knowledge, we have no reason to assume that.

But if the minor mode gets its expressive character neither through resemblance to expressive behavior nor through convention, what is left? From what does it derive its gloomy quality? That is indeed the mystery, and perhaps the apparent hopelessness of appealing to imitation in this and many other cases of expressiveness – especially as far as instrumental music is concerned – is what led so many eighteenth-century thinkers to turn instead to expression, to the idea that music 'raises the passions.'

This brings us to the vexed question of what role in musical experience, if any, is played by listeners' emotions (as distinguished from recognitional responses). One thesis considered already, that of simple arousalism, is that music's having a sad expressive character simply *consists* in its capacity to make the listener sad. That claim is implausible, for the reasons Kivy adduces, among others. But it might still be the case that sad music often does *in fact* make listeners sad, and that evocation of this response is an important part of why music matters to us. Davies defends the thesis that expressive music typically calls forth a "mirroring response" (Davies 1994: ch. 6). Of course, a problem for any such view is why anyone would want to seek out experiences, such as sadness, that are *prima facie* unpleasant (a problem well known in connection with Aristotle's notion of catharsis). Davies suggests that our interest in understanding art derives from a more basic sort of curiosity, and that negative emotions are not "an unpleasant extra" to be tolerated, but part and parcel of life itself (ibid.: 317; see also Levinson 1990: ch. 13).

Representation

Plato's assimilation of music to imitation, or *mimesis*, raises the question: is music a representational art? Certainly music can *enter into* representation, as it does in opera, for example. But is the music that enters into a hybrid artform such as opera itself representational; is music without text ever representational? And where music bears an emotional character, need it be regarded as *representing* that emotion? To make headway with these questions, one needs to spell out just what is meant by representation – which, to some extent, amounts to saying what parallels with painting and stories are to be preserved – and various theorists do so in different ways.

Hanslick, in his classic formalist polemic, argues that music cannot represent 'definite' feelings because it is incapable of conveying the conceptual content that individuates a *specific* emotional state (Hanslick 1986: 9). The feeling of hope, for example, essentially involves "the representation of a future happy state which we compare with the present." Hanslick is quite forward-looking in his appreciation of the cognitive element in emotion, and his argument is valuable for showing us what music *cannot* do; but perhaps he fails to consider broadly enough the things music *can* do that evade his narrow definition of representation. It is not clear, for example, why a represented emotion has to be as determinate as Hanslick implies. It may be that any feeling of joy must be accompanied by, or incorporate, a representation of some object about which one has the relevant attitudes; but it does not follow that a representation of joy must pin down some particular object or the relevant attitudes, any more than a (grainy) photograph of a speckled hen must represent it as having a precise number of speckles.

Scruton, another foe of musical representation, states that representation requires that the listener distinguish between subject and medium, that there be awareness of and interest in the subject, and that the work express *thoughts* about the subject which the listener must understand (Scruton 1983: ch. 7; see also Scruton 1997: ch. 5). Scruton argues that music fails to be representational by these criteria among others. He grants that we can hear music "*as* the drifting of sails," for example, but claims that someone deaf to this aspect can still fully understand the music (Scruton 1983: 68–9). Understanding music, on Scruton's view, never requires apprehending thoughts about a subject, and therefore, he concludes, music is not a representational art. (Scruton on musical understanding is discussed in more depth later.) In this writer's view, Scruton's argument begs the question. Kuhns argues *contra* Scruton, moreover, that music is representational because tones or passages may refer to one another: music quotes music, and themes and variations establish patterns of reference. "Because music expresses thoughts about music it is the representational art *par excellence*" (Kuhns 1978: 123). Kuhns' argument, interestingly, renders problematic the very distinction between formalism and referentialism; his view has affinities with (and in some ways anticipates) that of Goodman, discussed later.

The issues of expressiveness, representation, and the listener's response are tied together in an original and stimulating way by Walton (1994). Walton construes 'represent' sufficiently widely for most music to count as representational by his lights; yet he is concerned to articulate the differences between music on the one hand, and paintings and novels on the other. Central to Walton's account is the idea that representational art works call for acts of imagination: in reading a story or looking at a painting one imagines people and situations that comprise a fictional world. Music, too, Walton tells us, stimulates imaginative experience on the listener's part. One imagines conflict and resolution, motion and rest. But the fictional worlds induced by music are far less determinate than those of pictures and stories: we do not imagine particular agents moving through tonal space or engaging in conflict. And whereas pictures generally call for the viewer to imagine that he *sees* an object of a certain kind, music typically does not require the listener to imagine *hearing* the subject of representation (for example, the ascension of a saint into heaven). But the effect of both of these factors is, paradoxically, not to distance the listener from the world of the music: "it is though I am inside the music, or it is inside me" (Walton 1994: 54). Walton's explanation for this intimacy is that the listener's imaginative participation consists in imagining that he or she *experiences* a certain emotion; and this takes place via his or her imagining the experience of musical sounds *to be* an experiencing of emotion. This, Walton points out, is importantly different from what goes on with stories or pictures, where one empathizes with a character who (fictionally) expresses emotion; in music, one imagines neither character nor (fictive) expression. Walton's discussion is sensitive to many subtleties in the experience of art.

Reference and signification

Probably the most elaborately worked out and far-reaching contemporary theory of musical reference is that of Goodman (Goodman 1976; Goodman and Elgin 1988). Goodman includes music in his considerably more general account of symbol systems, which relates and contrasts several different modes of reference with one another. Probably the most familiar kind of reference is what Goodman calls *denotation*, which is a relation between a symbol and the thing(s) it applies to: for example, the name 'Caesar' denotes the man Caesar and the word 'red' denotes red things. But Goodman is concerned to limn other, contrasting notions of reference, of which the most important for our purposes is *exemplification*. If denotation is thought of as running 'downward' from a term to a thing, exemplification runs in the opposite direction, 'upward' from a thing back to a term. To illustrate: say you go to a tailor and ask what the color of a certain garment will be. The tailor shows you a sample of red cloth, which tells you the color. Now, ordinarily, the sort of thing that refers to something else is a *word*: for example, the word 'red' refers to (here, denotes) the swatch of red cloth (among other things). But in the case of the tailor's demonstration, what is doing the referring? The swatch itself. And what is being picked out or referred to? The property *red*. We say that the swatch of cloth *exemplifies* the property red. (Actually, on Goodman's official theory, it is the word, or predicate, 'red', rather than the property, that is exemplified, but this distinction is not important for our purposes. It is on the official theory that exemplification runs backwards from a thing to a *term*.)

In relation to what we earlier called referentialism, Goodman's view is in a way the mirror image of Kivy's. Where Kivy embraces resemblance but (as it were) drops reference, Goodman keeps reference but eschews resemblance. Goodman sees no mileage whatever in imitation theories, but reckons semantic relations to be at the core of what art does.

The example of the red swatch is a case of what Goodman calls *literal* exemplification, since the swatch is literally red. But on Goodman's view exemplification comes in both literal and metaphorical varieties. A sad piece of music, according to Goodman, metaphorically possesses the property of sadness, and, moreover, exemplifies that (metaphorically possessed) property. This is an instance of metaphorical exemplification. (Again, I am translating from the official theory, which puts everything in terms of predicates.) Hence what we earlier called expressive character is, on his view, to be understood as metaphorical exemplification. Goodman's point (and here his view contrasts most sharply with that of Kivy or Davies) is that expressive character is not just a property an art work *has*, but something to which it bears a symbolic relation.

Goodman's notion of exemplification is, moreover, illuminating for music in many ways that go beyond the issue of expressive character. Exemplification, both metaphorical and literal, is arguably a central kind of musical signification, figuring importantly in intramusical reference: music's referring to music, either to some type or genre (of which the referring work may or may not be an instance), or to some specific work or part of a work (either itself or another).

There is an interesting disciplinary contrast to be noted between the relatively parsimonious attitude of some philosophers (Goodman excepted) and the relative liberality of many musicologists toward extending semantic notions to music. The philosophers' objection is, typically, that reference can have no point without assertion: "in order for aboutness to matter in music, the music must say something interesting or useful or in some other way valuable *about* what it is about. Naked aboutness is nothing at all" (Kivy 1997: 175). But music does not assert anything, those philosophers argue, so semantic notions are largely irrelevant to it. Rather striking, by contrast, is the prevalence with which musicologists and music critics invoke reference, allusion, and other semantic notions for purposes of musical explication. The musicians are on to something. *Prima facie* cases of intramusical reference include the following. Brahms, in the last movement of his First Symphony, alludes to the famous theme of Beethoven's Ninth; more generally, Brahms's music is replete with stylistic allusions. Bach's *Air* from the *Orchestral Suite no. 3 in D*, though it is not an aria or an instance of vocal music, *refers* to those genres: it is an orchestral piece that is, in a way, about vocal music. Twentieth-century neoclassical works, such as Stravinsky's *The Soldier's Tale*, refer to tonal music and its cadences, harmonies, formulas, and other techniques, from, as it were, a distance: they do not employ those techniques so much as allude to them. Semantic notions are essential here: simply to construe *The Soldier's Tale* as imperfectly *resembling* tonal music, or as imperfectly utilizing its procedures, would leave out something artistically important – it would constitute an impoverishment of our understanding of the work.

Goodman's framework has the potential to illuminate the character of musical signification in these and many other connections. Stylistic reference, allusion, and parody all may be argued to depend upon exemplification: in some cases, *contrastive* exemplification, as when a piece in one genre refers to another. Goodman construes theme-and-variation in terms of a complex network of reference, in which a variation refers to the theme by exemplifying predicates that refer to the latter (including contrastive exemplification, such as slow tempo where the theme is fast) (Goodman and Elgin 1988). An important lacuna in Goodman's theory, however, is the absence of a clear criterion for when a predicate is exemplified (Beardsley 1981).

No discussion of musical signification can fail to mention the important works of Langer (1942, 1953) and Meyer (1956). On Langer's view, music is a symbol of the 'inner life' of feeling. This is, essentially, an imitation theory. But music is only an 'unconsummated symbol' of feeling because it represents only the latter's formal character. Meyer, writing from the standpoint of music theory, deals with musical meaning within the work: with how, for example, a musical event can point to another by causing the listener to expect the latter. The writings of Langer and Meyer are richly insightful and repay careful study.

Understanding music

Thus far, we have considered the matter of the listener's response to music only piecemeal. The expressionist conceives of it as an emotional reaction; Kivy thinks of it, in connection with expressive qualities, as the recognition of expressiveness; and Walton takes the listener's input to involve an imaginative reconstrual of emotion. We can focus the inquiry a bit more sharply now by asking whether there is such a thing as *understanding* music, and if so what it consists in.

It is here that the formalist conception of music comes into its own. This viewpoint is epitomized by much (though not all) work in music theory and analysis, and much of cognitive psychology as well. An approach that partakes from both is that of Lerdahl and Jackendoff (1983). Their approach is modeled on linguistic theory and outlines several levels of musical cognition, including grouping, meter, and hierarchical structure based on tension and resolution. One of the theory's main tenets is that passages of tonal music are heard as elaborations – more complicated versions – of simpler passages. This idea is derived in part from the music theorist Schenker (see Forte 1959 for an introduction).

Music theory raises many interesting questions for aesthetics. What are the scope and limits of formalistic understanding? What is the value of articulation, that is, describing the organization one hears in a piece? And in so far as music theory characterizes not only what we hear, but also the technical means by which music works on us, two distinct kinds of musical understanding may be seen to come into play: the listener's appreciation of the art work, and the theorist's technical understanding of how music works. Now is it legitimate to think that the latter kind of understanding can, and even should, feed into and refine the former? Or is that 'undemocratic' and 'elitist'? Do we, or should we, think of music differently from the other arts in this regard? Kuhns (in a slightly different context) argues forcefully for the integration of mind and ear:

> The difficulty with music is that to understand it requires something of a special undertaking; we need to be trained. There is . . . in artistic matters a widespread belief that the 'common reader' ought to be honoured, and is a good measure of what is going on. In fact we know this is a poor standard for evaluation . . . Oddly, music may be the art most immediately pleasurable and the most difficult to learn to respond to adequately; while painting and poetry may require more exposure for pleasure and yet lie closer to sensitivities cultivated in common education.
>
> (Kuhns 1978: 121)

The distinction and relationship between listener's and theorist's understanding are elucidated by Tanner (1985), Budd (1985), Walton (1993), and Kivy (1990). DeBellis (1995) attempts to bridge the gap between the theorist's demand for explanation and the goal of appreciation.

In Roger Scruton's (1997) comprehensive study of musical aesthetics, the concept of musical understanding takes center stage. On Scruton's view, understanding music is a kind of 'intentional understanding' as distinguished from scientific explanation. Unlike ordinary perception, which seeks to find out what the material world is like, in musical experience the focus is on perceptions endowed with an intrinsic meaning apart from the world: musical experience "is not a window but a picture" (Scruton 1997: 220–1). Hearing music with understanding, moreover, involves 'indispensable' metaphors of space, movement, and animation. For example, to hear a melodic line as *moving* is metaphorical, for nothing, after all, *moves*: it is a species of imaginative perception (see Zuckerkandl 1956: ch. 7).

A quietly devastating critique of the whole notion of large-scale musical form, as it relates to the listener, is made by Levinson (1997). He argues that – though nothing prevents us from noticing that a piece is in ABA form, and, to be sure, there is value to be gained from noticing that – basic musical understanding works on a rather different level, consisting for the most part in awareness of moment-to-moment connections (See also Gurney 1966, Cook 1990: ch. 1). Levinson acknowledges, of course, that we hear the return of the main theme *as* a return, or the bridge material *as leading* from one area to another; but

Levinson's point is that none of this requires a synoptic, architectonic grasp of the piece as a whole, present to us all at once in the manner of 'listening diagrams' in music appreciation texts. Levinson's argument is supremely important for how we understand musical understanding, for he calls into question a crucial, yet rarely-questioned assumption of music theory, programs of music appreciation, and other formalistic approaches: that an awareness of large-scale form is essential for appreciation.

Each of the three conceptions of music – expressionist, referentialist, and formalist – plausibly captures part of the puzzle; at the same time, the boundaries between them have proven to be more elusive than perhaps at first they appeared. The expressionist is surely right in thinking that musical understanding demands a certain kind of emotional involvement, albeit one whose exact nature and relation to non-musical emotive experience must be elucidated with subtlety and care. Talk of music as representational, on the other hand, requires a rich conception of the listener's imaginative participation and an understanding of the differences between 'fictional worlds' in music and those in paintings and stories. As we have seen, moreover, reference and the extramusical can come apart, as in Goodman's account, on which music refers through such devices as variation, stylistic allusion, and parody.

With formalism the question is not so much whether there is a cognitive dimension to musical understanding (for surely there is). The question is rather what role the explicit awareness and description of formal relationships has to play, alongside the emotive and the referential, in how we talk and learn about music, and engage in criticism of it. Kuhns argues eloquently for the importance of training for the listener, and hence conscious reflection on musical structure. But Levinson's central claim is that awareness of the sorts of structure most often talked about by musicologists and theorists is not necessary for musical understanding. In this he brings out the important distinction between a theory of musical form, and a theory of musical understanding.

See also Plato, Expression in art, Imagination and make-believe, Representation in art, Art, Expression and emotion, Authenticity in performance.

References

Beardsley, M. C. (1981) "On Understanding Music," in K. Price (ed.), *On Criticizing Music: Five Philosophical Perspectives*, Baltimore: Johns Hopkins University Press.

Budd, M. (1985) "Understanding Music," *Aristotelian Society Supplementary Volume 59*, 233–48.

Cook, N. (1990) *Music, Imagination, and Culture*, Oxford: Oxford University Press.

Davies, S. (1994) *Musical Meaning and Expression*, Ithaca: Cornell University Press.

DeBellis, M. (1995) *Music and Conceptualization*, Cambridge: Cambridge University Press.

Forte, A. (1959) "Schenker's Conception of Musical Structure," *Journal of Music Theory* 3, 1–30.

Goodman, N. (1976) *Languages of Art*, 2nd edn, Indianapolis: Hackett.

Goodman, N. and. Elgin, C. Z. (1988) *Reconceptions in Philosophy and Other Arts and Sciences*, Indianapolis: Hackett.

Gurney, E. (1966) *The Power of Sound*, New York: Basic Books.

Hanslick, E. (1986) *On the Musically Beautiful*, trans. G. Payzant, Indianapolis: Hackett.

Kivy, P. (1989) *Sound Sentiment*, Philadelphia: Temple University Press.

—— (1990) *Music Alone: Philosophical Reflections on the Purely Musical Experience*, Ithaca: Cornell University Press.

—— (1997) *Philosophies of Arts: An Essay in Differences*, Cambridge: Cambridge University Press.

Kuhns, R. (1978) "Music as a Representational Art," *British Journal of Aesthetics* 18, 120–5.

Langer, S. K. (1942) *Philosophy in a New Key*, Cambridge, Mass.: Harvard University Press.

—— (1953) *Feeling and Form*, New York: Scribner's.

Le Huray, P. and J. Day (eds) (1981) *Music and Aesthetics in the Eighteenth and Early-Nineteenth Centuries*, Cambridge: Cambridge University Press.

Lerdahl, F. and R. Jackendoff (1983) *A Generative Theory of Tonal Music*, Cambridge, Mass.: MIT Press.

Levinson, J. (1990) *Music, Art, and Metaphysics*. Ithaca: Cornell University Press.

—— (1997) *Music in the Moment*, Ithaca: Cornell University Press.

Lippman, E. (ed.), *Musical Aesthetics: A Historical Reader*, New York: Pendragon Press.

Meyer, L. B. (1956) *Emotion and Meaning in Music*, Chicago: University of Chicago Press.

Morellet, A. (1986) "De l'Expression en musique et de l'imitation dans les arts," trans. E. Lippman, in E. Lippman (ed.), *Musical Aesthetics: A Historical Reader*, New York: Pendragon Press.

Plato (1963) *Republic*, trans. Paul Shorey, in E. Hamilton and H. Cairns (eds), *The Collected Dialogues of Plato*, Princeton: Princeton University Press.

Scruton, R. (1983) *The Aesthetic Understanding*, London: Methuen.

—— (1997) *The Aesthetics of Music*, Oxford: Oxford University Press.

Strunk, O. (ed.) (1998) *Source Readings in Music History*, rev. edn, New York: Norton.

Tanner, M. (1985) "Understanding Music," *Aristotelian Society Supplementary Volume* 59, 215–32.

Twining, T. (1986) "Two Dissertations on Poetical and Musical Imitation," in E. Lippman (ed.), *Musical Aesthetics: A Historical Reader*, New York: Pendragon Press.

Walton, K. (1993) "Understanding Humour and Understanding Music," in M. Krausz (ed.), *The Interpretation of Music*, Oxford: Oxford University Press.

—— (1994) "Listening with Imagination," *Journal of Aesthetics and Art Criticism* 52, 47–61.

Zuckerkandl, V. (1956) *Sound and Symbol: Music and the External World*, trans. W. R. Trask, Princeton: Princeton University Press.

Further reading

Addis, L. (1999) *Of Mind and Music*, Ithaca: Cornell University Press. (An insightful recent essay on music and its power, which takes Langer's theory as its point of departure.)

Adorno, T. (1989) *Introduction to the Sociology of Music*, trans. E. B. Ashton, New York: Continuum. (A Marxist view of the sociology of music.)

Alperson, P. (ed.) (1998) *Musical Worlds: New Directions in the Philosophy of Music*,

University Park: Pennsylvania State University Press.

Bent, I. (1987) *Analysis*, New York: Norton. (A survey of musical analysis.)

Bowman, W. D. (1998) *Philosophical Perspectives on Music*, Oxford: Oxford University Press. (A useful recent text.)

Budd, M. (1985) *Music and the Emotions*, London: Routledge and Kegan Paul. (Philosophically acute though unsympathetic to the slightest flaw.)

—— (1995) *Values of Art*, London: Penguin. (Contains a chapter on music as an abstract art.)

Bujic, B. (ed.) (1988) *Music in European Thought, 1851–1912*, Cambridge: Cambridge University Press. (A historical reader.)

Cavell, S. (1969) "Music Discomposed," in *Must We Mean What We Say?* New York: Scribner. (Discusses the problems of modernism.)

Cone, E. T. (1974) *The Composer's Voice*, Berkeley: University of California Press. (Discusses musical agents or "personae.")

Krausz, M. (ed.) (1993) *The Interpretation of Music*, Oxford: Oxford University Press.

Levinson, J. (1996) *The Pleasures of Aesthetics*, Ithaca: Cornell University Press. (See especially the chapter on expressiveness and meaning.)

Lippman, E. (1992) *A History of Western Musical Aesthetics*, Lincoln: University of Nebraska Press. (A comprehensive historical survey.)

Raffman, D. (1993) *Language, Music, and Mind*, Cambridge, Mass.: MIT Press. (Cognitive science brought to bear on the problem of musical ineffability.)

Robinson, J. (ed.) (1997) *Music and Meaning*, Ithaca: Cornell University Press. (Recent philosophical essays.)

Schenker, H. (1979) *Free Composition*, 2 vols, trans. and ed. E. Oster, New York: Longman. (The dominant paradigm in theory and analysis of tonal music.)

45
DANCE
Graham McFee

The philosophical aesthetics of dance may be roughly characterized in three parts, each concerned centrally with dance as an artform, or with dances that are art works. First, it shares many issues with philosophical aesthetics in general: for instance, concern over the role of the intentions of the artist for understanding his/her art works recurs *vis-à-vis* choreographers, even if with a characteristic dance 'twist'. Equally, commitments in general aesthetics will typically be replicated in the aesthetics of dance: for example, if one asserted the historical character of art (McFee 1992b), a similar assertion for dance would be expected. Issues of this sort will not be the focus here.

However, our attention to dance *as an art* imports a contrast between the interest, appreciation, judgement, and so on appropriate to art, and the interest, appreciation, judgement, and so on appropriate to all the other things in which aesthetic interest is taken (natural beauty, fountains and firework displays, wallpaper, gymnastics): sometimes called a contrast between *the artistic* and *the aesthetic* (Best 1992: 166–72; McFee 1992a: 38–44). Then art works are appropriately perceived under artistic concepts, and misperceived if regarded as (merely) aesthetic, such that a term (say, 'gaudy') applying on both sides of this contrast amounts to something different in the two cases. The importance of this contrast should be clear in what follows.

As a second part of dance aesthetics, some issues are shared with other performing arts (Thom 1993), whatever nuances dance introduces. The elaborated discussion of music provides the most fully articulated model in the literature, for dance is a 'Jenny-come-lately' to the aesthetic feast, trying to find its own elbow room (Sparshott 1988: 7–8).

Third, dance aesthetics has characteristic issues of its own; although (as noted) understanding them will typically draw on discussions elsewhere in aesthetics, perhaps elsewhere in philosophy. The aesthetics of music is a prime source here, illustrating connections between the second and third aspects of the aesthetics of dance, the aspects discussed here.

In elaborating these aspects, many concerns derive from the nature of dance, or from what dances are. Like music, dance typically exists "at a perpetual vanishing point" (Siegel 1972: 1): one encounters the art works in the evanescence of performances. But, unlike music, dance is essentially physical: to confront a dance is, minimally, to confront an assemblage of moving bodies, at least in typical cases. So (typically) the relationship between the dance itself and particular performances will both resemble and differ from that between a musical work and its performances. Dance notation (for most philosophers, first seen in Goodman 1968: 125) unites these concerns. Here, again, the discussion of dance assumes positions in general aesthetics: say, the plausibility of Goodman's constraints on notationality (ibid.: 129–54). Further, acknowledging the essentially interpretative nature of such dance notation reintroduces a contrast fundamental to any discussion of performing art: that between critics' interpretation and performers' interpretation (McFee 1992a: 103–4).

Since the concern here is centrally with the discussion of dance works that are art, the (possible?) connection of artistic value to educational value (as well as the history of dance studies within aesthetics) prompts an interest in the place or role of dance in education.

The sections of this treatment reflect these concerns.

Dance identity

Dance as multiple art and performing art

With dance, as with music, there are at least two 'objects of appreciation': the work itself and tonight's performance of it. These might be treated differently for critical purposes: thus, the dance seen last night might have been a wonderful performance of a mediocre work or (more likely) the opposite. Further, dance (again like music) is typically a multiple art: the same dance can be performed both on different occasions in the same place and on the same occasion in different places. Of course, the limits on such examples of 'the same work' are a topic for discussion, to which we will return. To provide a conceptual structure for discussion of such multiples, some writers (Wollheim 1980: sections 35–6; McFee 1992a: 90–4) have employed a type/token framework, such that dance performances are *tokens* of an (abstract) *type*.

Types and tokens

To understand this type/token contrast, consider national flags. Here, we recognize both the *type* (for example, the Union Jack) and *tokens of the type* (a large Union Jack flying on Eastbourne Town Hall, small flags waved for the

Queen on state visits). Thus, if ten people were each given a national flag, there might be (a) ten token-flags but three type-flags (Union Jack, Stars and Stripes, Tricolor), or (b) ten token-flags and only one type-flag (all the Union Jack), and so on. Also, we acknowledge that destroying all the big and little pieces of cloth, paper and plastic would not destroy the Union Jack *itself*. The flag itself (the type) is an abstract object, to be differentiated from any of its instantiations (the tokens).

So the type/token contrast offers a way to treat multiple objects (like flags): the concrete object (the token) can be contrasted with the abstract object (the type). And, as above, such a contrast treats dance performances as tokens of a dance-type: Tuesday's performance as one token of *Swan Lake*, Wednesday's as another.

But there seem more than two 'objects of analysis' here (although the type/token contrast only has, as it were, two 'slots'): a *performer's interpretation* of a role or a dance is contrasted with the particular (his performance *tonight* of that work/interpretation) or with the general (the dance itself). So this sort of type/token account may need modification or clarification (Sharpe 1979, McFee 1994b, Meskin 1999: 46–7).

Further, one feature of the identity of art works fits at best awkwardly with the type/token treatment: namely, that each performance is *the very same art work*, not merely one of the same kind. There is numerical identity here. In contrast, examples typically used to illustrate the type/token contrast (say, national flags or words) are not cases where *numerical* identity (in contrast to qualitative identity) makes sense. For example, the five-word sentence 'My cat ate your cat' employs five token-words and only four type-words, because the word 'cat' occurs twice. If we imagine someone speaking this sentence (utterance) or writing it (inscription), there are accordingly either two utterances or two inscriptions of the word 'cat.' But it seems odd to puzzle further if there are one or two *words*, since we know that both utterances/inscriptions of 'cat' are tokens of the type-word. It makes no sense to ask if the first and second occurrences of the word 'cat' are occurrences of *numerically identical* or *numerically distinct* words, although they are clearly different utterances or inscriptions. Yet just this contrast must make sense for dance performances: if there is only one dance work (say, *Swan Lake*) 'in the offing', its status as *the art work* guarantees that any performances of it instantiate *that very* art work, despite differences between performances (see later). But the type/token language – well-suited to the discussion of words and flags – has no obvious way to accommodate this.

Performer's versus critic's interpretation

The idea of performer's interpretation (introduced earlier) should be contrasted firmly with critic's interpretation: the former refers to a distinctiveness of *how* this dancer performs, and is constituted simply by his/her performing in that way (even if the dancer also chooses to talk about it). Such interpretation is unique to the performing arts: given that it is constituted by actions, stressing its role as *interpretation* can mislead, for *of what* exactly is it an interpretation? Rather, the performer's interpretation brings the art work (the performance) into being: at least, into public being. Critics' interpretations, by contrast, amount roughly to strings of words said about art works; and are a feature of all arts.

But the very idea of a performer's interpretation highlights two fundamental features of the performing arts, both of which will be important in what follows. First, the art work is only encountered when one encounters a *performance* of it, which will always be some performer's interpretation or other. This is important for recognizing the concreteness or specificity of dance. (One might quibble about the status of, say, video recordings, but the moral is straightforward: if watching the video recording counts as watching the dance, it is a *performance*, albeit an indirect or recorded one. If, by contrast, watching the video recording does not count as watching *the dance*, we can regard it as slightly less than a performance (Sparshott 1995: 448–51)).

Second, the dance work itself is always underdetermined, relative to any particular performance of it, since each performance makes concrete in particular ways features of the dance which might have been concretized in other ways, indeed, which might be made concrete in those other ways in another performance of that dance, even one by the same company. This feature of dances is also reflected in dance notation (see later). For we might conceptualize the dancers making concrete the dance, instantiating it, as giving substance to the notation for that dance. In doing so, they implicitly emphasize some of the features of the dance, at the expense of others. This is, of course, to produce a *performer's interpretation*.

Dancers' actions, which (along with, say, music, costume and the like, where appropriate) bring the dance into being, we might regard as the following of a recipe, as "produc[ing] . . . those things . . . of which the witnessable work consists" (Urmson 1976: 243). Similar things might be said of any performing art.

Yet this similarity conceals diversities, with dance differing crucially from music. Musicians *produce* the sound: but dance movements *comprise* the dance (although in a context of music). Those movements on that occasion really do comprise the dance; really do instantiate it. And nothing else would.

Dance as corporeal

Here, the bodily or corporeal nature of dance might be stressed. Although it is a valuable counterbalance to undue emphasis (in the writing of some aestheticians) on insufficiently physical virtues of art works, the point can be over-stressed; also, it can be poorly understood or poorly explained. For instance, explaining the importance of the body for dance, Judith Hanna writes: " the instrument of dance and of sexuality is one – the human body" (Hanna 1988: 13) . Her thought is clearly that some of the value of the sexual would *thereby* accrue to dance. But we 'use' the same body for many activities, some meaning-bearing, others not: this fact alone takes us nowhere. However, it highlights two key facets of the transformation of 'ordinary' movements into dance. For example, the graceful sweeping movement of a road-sweeper might be incorporated into a dance, with a literal choreographer even retaining the broom (McFee 1992a: 51; 1994a: 106). But the sequence of movement is no longer *mere* sweeping (however much it resembles it): it has become dance. Following Danto (1981: 208), this could be called "the transfiguration of the 'ordinary' activity" into dance. In such cases, what is transfigured is (typically) *already* action, rather than mere movement (Carr 1987: 352). So, to insist that dance is 'just movement' is a polemical answer (for a parallel with music, see Cavell 1969: 221). Moreover, the transfiguration makes the dance not just action that makes sense as *intended* (Best 1978: 138–41; McFee 1992a: 243–4), but also renders it more strongly meaning-bearing: as intentionally *art*, with whatever character follows from that.

Dance, value and understanding

The 'transfiguration' of movement patterns into works in the artform of dance has crucial implications, reflected in our dance-aesthetics. First, different sets of qualities (or properties) are truthfully ascribed to the movement (and so on). In our example of 'sweeping', the dance might be (for instance) witty in a way the mere sweeping could not be. Recognizing the dance work *as art* brings with it a vocabulary of the art-critical, ascribing artistic properties to that movement sequence. These are arguably then real properties of the dances, despite requiring the suitably sensitive 'recognizer' (Dancy 1993: 418). As noted initially, even if the same term is used to ascribe properties to both art work and 'ordinary' movement (say, the term 'graceful'), it amounts to something different in each case: roughly, one is the grace of dance works, in such-and-such a genre, and so on. Thus, recognition of the grace of the art work appeals implicitly to the history and traditions of dance, in that genre (even when rejecting aspects of those traditions: Sparshott 1998: 94).

Second, this transfiguration brings with it kinds of *understanding* not available for the mere sweeping: in both cases, we can (perhaps) understand the causal mechanisms, but the dance involves something different to understand, a 'something' picked-out in speaking of the arts in terms of communication. For the dance is created or intended to be understood (when it attracts a suitably knowledgeable audience): this recognition is integral to recognizing the dance as art (or the movement sequence as dance). Disputes about cognitivism in dance (the idea that dances are fit objects of understanding) will parallel discussions for *music alone* (Kivy 1993: 360–73; McFee 1997). At the least (as before), whatever follows about understandability from art-status (if anything does) will apply to dances also. For the special case of music, as Stephen Davies puts it, "I am not embarrassed to use the term 'meaning' here because I think both that music can and should be understood to be appreciated and that it is created to be so" (Davies 1994: ix). Something similar might be said for dance. Whatever one's reservations about the term 'meaning' here (Carr 1997), this dimension is precisely how 'real things' – and especially aesthetically pleasing 'real things' – differ from art works: thinking otherwise *reduces* art, treating art works as merely aesthetically-pleasing (or perhaps aesthetically-relevant) 'real things'. In our case, it would dissolve the conceptual difference between the dance and the (mere) sweeping.

A third implication relates that movement sequence's art-status (associated with its meaning-bearing character) with the dance's *value*. So, the transfiguration into dance brings not merely a critical vocabulary, reflecting what (following Davies) we call 'meaning,' but also value (of a non-monetary sort). For any argument for that movement sequence's art-status is simultaneously an argument for its value; and such an argument refers (perhaps implicitly) to the past of the art of dance. Of course, this simply applies features recognized for other arts to the art of dance: art-status involves locating this dance work both in the history of dance (of this kind) and in "the lay of the art world" (Carroll 1994: 25). Doing so treats this work too as valuable *because* it is dance, which means regarding it in ways one (appropriately) regards other dance works. In addition to its general relevance, the value that attaches to dance as art may also be crucial in justifying dance's educational role (McFee 1994a: 55–6).

Should one be able to justify (or explain) such artistic value to those who do not understand it? This seems a tall order. As with most artforms, the fact and the nature of the value of dance is taken for granted by most who discuss such matters: as Roger Scruton writes (of literary discussions, but the point holds): "in the nature of things, the arguments of a critic are addressed only to those who have sufficient reverence for literature; for only they will see the point of detailed study and moral investigation" (Scruton 1998: 20). And this is true of the writing of the aesthetician too. So the value of art is sometimes not a live issue.

Dance notation and understanding

Dance notation is essentially movement notation: at best, it can be used to accurately record movements of the body (and, by combination, of more than one body). Some notation systems lend themselves to the characteristics of dance styles (the 'flatness' and assumed position of the viewer in Benesh notation makes it especially suitable for classical ballet, performed in a proscenium arch). But nothing in the movements themselves *guarantees* that a dance is recorded, although the (un-)likelihood of a line of people on pointe being anything *other than* dance might overcome this constraint in practice. Still, the theoretical point is that notation cannot guarantee that the movement sequence notated is dance (and not some other activity). Yet, for (say) anthropologists interested in movement patterns, this is a strength of such notated scores. Whether or not such-and-such is dance will be beside the point for them, if their interest is restricted to the movement patterns employed.

So, recognizing that such-and-such is dance is already a kind of interpretation of it. As Suzanne Youngerman puts it, "notation systems are more than tools for documentation; they are systems of analysis that can be used to illuminate many aspects of the phenomenon of movement. Notation scores embody perceptions of movement" (Youngerman 1984: 101). Thus, notation systems instantiate methods of analysis or conceptualization, rather than neutrally describing movements which might *then* be analyzed. In part, this follows from conceptualizing four-dimensional human activity in the two dimensions of a notated score, with different notation systems finding different resolutions. That a notator divides the movement up in this way, rather than that, follows from using (say) Labanotation – where the temporal dimension is one of those on the page – rather than Benesh notation, which treats time symbolically. Further, notations are interpretative in embodying choices: to notate the movement of a person's arm, one could inscribe the motion-pattern of hand, forearm, elbow, upper-arm, etc. But, given the connections ('the forearm-bone connected to the elbow bone'), it may be sufficient to notate the movement of the elbow. Yet this is a decision which another notator might make differently.

Suppose that the notation were used as a 'marker' of authenticity: that a dance conforming to this notation is indeed such-and-such a dance (say, *Swan Lake*). Then someone wishing to stage that dance must pay attention to precisely what is notated (and, by implication, less attention to what is not): so, to the elbow movements in the case above. In this sense, the notator is required to recognize what is central, what peripheral, to this sequence.

Judgement might be required in other ways too. The renowned notator Ann Hutchinson-Guest reported being asked to notate a segment of a dance which the choreographer demonstrated by shuffling across the stage. The dancers, reflecting years of ballet training, could not bring themselves to shuffle: so they actually performed a sequence of classic ballet steps (*chassé, chassé, pas be bourrée*). Now, should Guest notate what this group of dancers (and, predictably, future generations of ballet dancers) *did* perform, or what they *should* perform (to 'obey' the choreographer)? In such a case, no answer avoids dependence on the informed judgement of the notator.

Equally, faced with a score in dance notation he/she understands, what characteristics will a dancer take to be central, such that movements (and so on) failing to satisfy them preclude having instantiated that dance? Or what notated features might reflect *typical* if inessential aspects of the dance? Perfect compliance with any score cannot be expected as a dancer's goal, much less as a realistic expectation of typical performances. (Although this 'full compliance' is just what Goodman (1968: 187) does expect: indeed, he urges that a musical performance where one note is played that is not reflected in the score fails as a performance of that work.) But a poor performance of a work is still a performance of that work – perhaps, until it gets just too bad (when whether it is a performance of such-and-such a work will be a matter for dispute, with the answer not obvious) – and not all performances of less than full compliance are poor. To give a music example, the pianist Glen Gould produced powerful, expressive performances of Schoenberg's piano music (some of which are 'captured' in recordings), but his performances are often further from the score than less powerful renditions.

In this climate, both stager and dancer have roles in turning score into performance, and in arguing (implicitly or explicitly) that the performance in question is indeed of the work; that it satisfies the notated score sufficiently closely to constitute that dance work.

Dance notation and dance identity

So a notated score might be conceptualized as having a role in arguments about work-identity. As with most performing arts, one can create an art work in dance either by making an initial performance or by creating a score: just as a composer could create a work for solo piano either at the keyboard or through writing a score. Of course, most dances are created by arranging the initial performance; further, at least today, most dances are never notated. Still, the possibility of notation (the notationality) can be a revealing conceptual possibility.

With a dance composed by writing a score, any dance performance which conforms to the score, and is appropriately seen as dance, will instantiate that art work: in creating a recipe, one implicitly specifies *which* of its features are crucial. By contrast, creating the dance work (the abstract object) by creating a 'first performance' leaves open which of this particular dance-performance's features are crucial for other dances if they are to instantiate that dance work. Thus, sorting out identity-matters for performing arts will be facilitated if art works within those arts are (or anyway can be) created by making recipes or mechanisms: that is, scores. This conclusion cannot be any more threatening for dance than its parallel would be for music, where it is a commonplace.

So dance's notationality remains important despite some dances presently lacking notated scores: some just *are* not notated, some (perhaps) could not be. But notationality still suggests one conceptualization of a relationship between the dance work and its performances, exploiting the possibilities of creating dances by creating notated scores. Consider a time when there was no established system of notation, and hence no 'texts' recognized as authoritative by those knowledgeable about dance. Since dances were (still) abstract objects, they were still in principle notatable even if there were not appropriate notation systems. Today, having such systems, we can readily imagine dances as *in principle* notatable. In thus emphasizing notationality, one emphasizes the connection between the nature of dances and the character of scores.

Suppose that some contemporary dancework (say, Christopher Bruce's *Swan Song* of 1987) had disappeared from the dance repertoire. In a hundred years' time, a complete Labanotation score (including Effort notation) for it is found. Now *Swan Song* can be performed, as had been impossible (in practice) for the previous one hundred years. But, of course, a whole background of dance understanding – what Wittgenstein (1969: section 165) calls a "special conceptual world" – must already be in place: one could not reconstitute *dance* from this score alone, nor even (perhaps) the dance-manner appropriate to dance of Christopher Bruce. My example is only of *this particular* dance as lost and then, as it were, found. Now, has this dance existed all that time (as the language of 'lost' and 'found' suggests) or not? Neither answer seems satisfactory: but why must we decide? No substantial question remains unanswerable. The score has returned (the possibility of) the dance itself to us. Therefore, the impact of notationality, although slight, can advance our appreciation the dancework itself as well as 'constraining' its performances. We need not be misled in referring to 'the dance itself,' the *abstract dance work*, here.

In this case, the appeal is to something like Goodman's principle: that two dance performances both satisfying a particular notation are performances of the same work; and performances failing to instantiate that notated score are not of the same work (subject to the qualifications made), with the greater weight given to the negative judgement. Such a conclusion places an importance on both the particular notation used (when, if ever, are two scores equivalent?) and the competence of the judges.

Two differences between dance and music, in typical cases, are highlighted by thus emphasizing the particular notation: there is more than one dance (movement) notation, in ways there is not for music; and, to date, dance notation lacks the prominence within the dance world that musical notation has in its world. Musicians will typically understand notation; indeed, in some spheres, only someone who could read musical scores would be taken seriously as a musician (for jazz, this is not a strict requirement). But there is nothing like as strong a requirement that dancers or choreographers understand dance scores. As was recognized earlier, even a choreographer who was master of one notation system could not reliably read or perform another.

As Goodman (1968: 129–54, 211–18) notes, a relevant consideration will be practicality: ideally, scores should be easily 'read' and easily (and clearly) 'written'. So that asking 'Who can read what?' is partly a conceptual, partly a practical, matter. The potential usefulness for dance of notated scores, for purposes of both authenticity and preservation, requires notations both readable and reliable. (And, of course, dancers trained to instantiate those scores: Challis 1999: 148–50.)

Dance, value, and the educational

The educational role of dance (especially its role in formal education) has been an abiding concern in writing in the UK since the work of early twentieth-century theorists (such as Rudolf Laban) was appropriated by the UK's educational establishment. (The same has not been true in the USA, for example.) But, since key topics for education concern the value of dance, some of the questions posed are fundamental: and they are insistent questions, given pressure on curriculum time and the possibility of aesthetically-motivated physical activities other than dance (such as gymnastics or diving: see Best 1978: 104–7 on 'aesthetic sports'). If dance were no more than physical conditioning with an aesthetic dimension and a social benefit, no justification offered for it could supersede, say, a justification for gymnastics. So some more fundamental contrast must be sought, and it must sustain an educational role for dance.

A feature of dance not shared with these other physical activities is its art status. Could this explain its educational value? As suggested earlier, a general account of the value of the arts might stress conceptual changes which art appreciation might bring about, understanding this as a kind of emotional education (McFee 1994a: 40–1, 1992a: 168–70). But how do the conceptual changes thus initiated bear on human concerns? 'Education' here is more than simply an induction into knowledge *about* the artform: in this case, more than dance history, dance anthropology, dance sociology, or whatever. What is required, instead, is genuine artistic knowledge.

Such knowledge or understanding is essentially practical, embedded in performances and their appreciation. So, if such a conception can be sustained, its recognition will have general implications, at least for the epistemology of aesthetics and of education (McFee 1998). But it will also bear on how artistic value is understood: the obviously recognitional character of such value (if it were granted) might suggest a conception compatible with a view of value as open to perception, such that there are reasons recognized in the exercise of artistic judgement (see Dancy 1993: 418–19). Granting artistic value here may lead to a reconceptualization (or reassessment) of valuing in general.

The distinctiveness of the aesthetics of dance, which supports the need to treat dance examples case-by-case, does not preclude importing insights from other aspects of philosophical aesthetics; and this follows from the relation of the aesthetics of dance to aesthetics more generally. Again, in this way, topics distinctive of the aesthetics of dance – some of which are introduced here – suggest both characteristic issues for the aesthetician and questions that might shed light on other matters.

See also Value of art, Interpretation, Theater.

References

Best, D. (1978) *Philosophy and Human Movement*, London: Allen and Unwin.
—— (1992) *The Rationality of Feeling*, London: Falmer.
Carr, D. (1987) "Thought and Action in the Art of Dance," *British Journal of Aesthetics* 27: 345–57.
—— (1997) "Meaning in Dance," *British Journal of Aesthetics* 37: 349–66.
Carroll, N. (1994) "Identifying Art," in R. J. Yanal (ed.), *Institutions of Art: Reconsiderations of George Dickie's Philosophy*, University Park: Pennsylvania State University Press.
Cavell, S. (1969) *Must We Mean What We Say?* New York: Scribners.
Challis, C. (1999) "Dancing Bodies: Can the Art of Dance Be Restored to Dance Studies?" in G. McFee (ed.), *Dance, Education and Philosophy*, Meyer and Meyer.
Dancy, J. (1993) "Intuitionism," in P. Singer (ed.), *A Companion to Ethics*, Oxford: Blackwell.
Danto, A. (1981) *The Transfiguration of the Commonplace*, Cambridge, Mass.: Harvard University Press.
Davies, S. (1994) *Musical Meaning and Expression*, Ithaca: Cornell University Press.
Goodman, N. (1968) *Languages of Art*, Indianapolis: Bobbs-Merrill.
Hanna, J. L. (1988) *Dance, Sex and Gender*, Chicago: University of Chicago Press.
Kivy, P. (1993) *The Fine Art of Repetition*, Cambridge: Cambridge University Press.
McFee, G. (1992a) *Understanding Dance*, London: Routledge.
—— (1992b) "The Historical Character of Art: A Re-Appraisal," *British Journal of Aesthetics* 32: 307–19.
—— (1994a) *The Concept of Dance Education*, London: Routledge.
—— (1994b) "Was That *Swan Lake* I Saw You at Last Night?: Dance-Identity and Understanding," *Dance Research* 12: 20–40.
—— (1997) "Meaning and the Art-Status of *Music Alone*," *British Journal of Aesthetics* 37: 31–46.
—— (1998) "Truth, Arts Education and the 'Postmodern Condition'," in D. Carr (ed.), *Education, Knowledge and Truth: Beyond the Postmodern Impasse*, London: Routledge.
Meskin, A. (1999) "Productions, Performances and their Evaluation," in G. McFee (ed.), *Dance, Education and Philosophy*, Aachen: Meyer and Meyer.

Scruton, R. (1998) *An Intelligent Person's Guide to Modern Culture*, London: Duckworth.

Sharpe, R. A. (1979) "Type, Token, Interpretation, and Performance," *Mind* 86: 437–40.

Siegel, M. (1972) *At the Vanishing Point*, New York: Saturday Review Press.

Sparshott, F. (1988) *Off The Ground: First Steps to a Philosophical Consideration of the Dance*, Princeton: Princeton University Press.

—— (1995) *A Measured Pace: Towards a Philosophical Understanding of the Arts of Dance*, Toronto: University of Toronto Press.

—— (1998) *The Future of Aesthetics*, Toronto: University of Toronto Press.

Thom, P. (1993) *For an Audience: A Philosophy of the Performing Arts*, Philadelphia: Temple University Press.

Urmson, J. O. (1976) "The Performing Arts," in H. D. Lewis (ed.), *Contemporary British Philosophy*, 4th Series, London: Allen and Unwin.

Wittgenstein, L. (1969) *Zettel*, Oxford: Blackwell.

Wollheim, R. (1980) *Art and Its Objects*, 2nd edn, Cambridge: Cambridge University Press.

Youngerman, S. (1984) "Movement Notation Systems as Conceptual Frameworks: The Laban System," in M. Sheets-Johnstone (ed.), *Illuminating Dance: Philosophical Explorations*, London: Associated University Presses.

Further reading

Banes, S. (1987) *Terpsichore in Sneakers: Post Modern Dance*, 2nd edn, Boston: Houghton-Mifflin. (A book-length treatment of key themes in the history of dance.)

—— (1994) *Writing Dancing in the Age of Postmodernism*, Hanover, N.H.: University Press of New England. (A vigorous and theoretically acute discussion of issues from the dance perspective.)

Fancher, G. and Myers, G. (eds) (1981) *Philosophical Essays on Dance*, Brooklyn: American Dance Theater. (An anthology bringing together dancers, critics and philosophers, with responses including some from choreographers.)

Williams, D. (1991) *Ten Lectures on Theories of the Dance*, Metuchen, N.J.: Scarecrow Press. (A difficult, but philosophically-informed, treatment from an anthropological point of view.)

46
THEATER

James R. Hamilton

In a now familiar history of the rise of the concept of the 'fine arts' in the sixteenth through the eighteenth centuries (Kristeller 1951, 1952), theater as an artform was almost always discussed as a form of dramatic poetry or literature. Simply put, any values of the theatrical performance worth talking about were taken to be those of dramatic literature. If there were features of the performance that merited comment, such as the delivery or the persona of the actress, these were evaluated primarily in terms of their contribution to the audience's grasp or appreciation of the literary work being presented. The few exceptions to this general practice were more nearly cases of social commentary, even mere items of gossip about actresses (usually), than contributions to the understanding of whatever values might actually attach to theatrical performance itself.

This comes as no surprise. The concept of the 'fine arts' is shaped in the Western European tradition by the viewpoint of the amateur audience for the arts (Kristeller 1952: 17–18). And it is plausible to think that what the audience in the Western European theater tradition grasps, in auditing a play, just is the story told or presented in the performance.

This traditional view of theater is still with us. When asked what they saw in the previous evening's performance, most people will respond by telling some part of a story. This view of theater has remained firmly in place even beyond the beginning of the twentieth century, despite the fact that the relatively stable set of theatrical practices on which the view rested began to change. There are some notable examples of novel theater practices beginning around the end of the nineteenth century. The Symbolists introduced non-dramatic forms of writing for the theater. The Dadaists and Futurists presented not only non-dramatic theater pieces but provocations to the audience that seemed entirely non-theatrical as well as nonsensical. The turn of the last century also saw gradually increasing awareness on the part of theater practitioners of forms of theater outside their familiar European mainstream. As a result, people within theater itself began only at the beginning of that century to rethink the values of theatrical performance, looking to see if there are values of theatrical performance independent of the dramatic text being illustrated. A further consequence is that only very lately has the philosophical discipline of aesthetics begun to undertake a similar reconception of theatrical practice.

Thus, despite its ancient history as a set of practices, theatrical performance is a relatively new subject for philosophical examination in its own right. Nor has much work been done concerning it, and what has been done is fragmentary and dispersed (Saltz 1998: 375). So it seems profitable now to ask what precisely makes theater different from, and how it is related to, the other arts, especially the other performing arts.

I will center the discussion that follows around various features of the fact that theatrical performances are presented to audiences in public. By focusing on this 'social dimension' of theater, I will examine what can be done to provide a satisfactory philosophical account of theater as a distinctive set of social practices or activities. An important caveat to be stated here is that some of what at first sight seem straightforward philosophical, or conceptual, questions could turn out to be historical questions, best answered by reference to art historical traditions of theatrical practice.

An obvious feature of theater, when considered as a social activity, is that it has similarities to and differences from other public activities. Those other activities also involve a division between some people who are the central participants and others who are not the central participants. Spectator sports, certain kinds of company picnics, as well as some religious and political rituals bear important similarities to theatrical events. As is well known, Aristotle asserted that Greek theater arose out of Greek religious festivals (Aristotle 1941: 1458–9). Whether he was right about the actual historical origins of theater, the distinction between theater and ritual is still important. What developed, if it did, out of Dionysian ritual was something else, something no longer a religious ritual. This may seem obvious; but not everyone sees the point (Schechner 1993, Turner 1982). Moreover, even if it is obvious, laying out the precise nature of the distinction poses a difficult challenge.

Actually three challenging questions are posed here. Moving from the most general to the most particular, we can express them this way. First, what distinguishes activities in which there are performances for audiences from other public gatherings where there are no such performances? Second, what distinguishes activities in which there are artistic performances from performances that are not for arts audiences? And third, what distinguishes activities in which there are theatrical performances from other artistic performances?

In this part of the essay, I consider four strategies for responding to the first question. I adopt two criteria for counting a strategy successful. First, it should allow us to account for differences and similarities among performances, spectator sports, company picnics, and religious rituals, cutting up the pie, so to speak, in more or less the intuitively correct ways. And second, a strategy for responding to the first question should not preclude a further distinction between artistic and non-artistic performances (Thom 1993: 4–6) nor exclude from performances in general, features we already know to hold true of more specific kinds of performance types. In addition to these criteria for a successful strategy, I also adopt a method for bringing out sharply both the strengths and weaknesses of each strategy, namely the conceit of looking for some activity bearing a feature such that an activity bearing that feature would actually bring it about that a performance begins to take place where none had been taking place before. I call this a 'conceit' because, in any culture that has any kinds of performances for audiences, occasions for such events will be so institutionalized that only rarely will those events be brought about by such an activity or feature as I am imagining.

The first general strategy for responding to the first question would have us seek to determine how some kinds of public activities done by some people characteristically render some other people into an audience for those activities. The second general strategy would have us focus on different kinds of roles people can play in public gatherings, and seek to determine what features are characteristic of that particular set of roles we call 'being an audience.'

Following out the first strategy, we might venture that what makes a group of people into an audience is that they are the ones in the gathering for whom something is being done by others in the gathering. This suggestion picks out a feature of some actions done in public that would explain how those activities generate audiences while other activities do not. The feature picked out here would seem to do that job because, if an activity is done for others, there will be some sense in which those doing it and those for whom the doing is done would seem to be at least functionally separable and in roughly the right ways.

One difficulty with this approach has to do with whether we can specify a sense of 'doing something for' that turns some part of the public gathering into exactly an audience, as opposed to turning them into some other kind of separable group kind. For example, the feature we have specified so far fits elements of religious rites pretty well. But those who believe the rites are efficacious are unlikely to agree that what is going on just is a performance nor, more generally, that they are correctly characterized as the 'audience' to the rite. To think otherwise seems to mistake what is meant when a religious rite is said to be 'done for' its participants. It seems more appropriate to call them something like the 'recipients' or 'beneficiaries' of the rite rather than its 'audience.' In another and perhaps related sense of 'doing something for,' the annual company picnic is clearly set forth by some in the public gathering for others in the same gathering. But this way of doing something for another, even as it has its home in reference to a public gathering, does not bring about anything like the transformation we seek to pick out and explain. So, the problem with this approach is that it is not clear that there exists a specific sense of some people 'doing something for' other members of a gathering that generates precisely an 'audience' group kind out of those others.

One may also wonder if any action done for another, by itself, can have an audience-generating effect. It seems we could know we had specified a sense of 'doing something for' that generates audiences only if such activities generated a characteristic kind of response, an 'audience response.' In the absence of such a response, no action can have had the desired generating effect. But then, it is reasonable to think, for the first strategy to work, something like the second must also have been in play.

Be that as it may, it is worth noting that the first strategy in no way precludes features of more specific kinds of performance. It still leaves open the distinction between artistic and non-artistic performances; and it is sufficiently general to allow for any of the more specific features of art-performance kinds such as theater, dance, and music.

The second general strategy for responding to the first question proposes that we ask what is different in the kind of public role people are playing when they are audiences and the kinds of public roles they are playing in other kinds of public gatherings. Following out this strategy, we might venture that at least part of what is different is that audiences observe something they are not necessarily participating in themselves. This feature of some members of a gathering seems to pick out what it is about some people in gatherings that separates them from others, and in the relevant ways. If someone is observing, but not participating in what is observed, he or she is at least functionally separated from those others. And it will follow that anyone who plays that role, who observes in this way, is thereby being an audience. So, at least as far as we have gotten, the feature picked out seems to sort group kinds in more or less the right ways: the public role audiences play is, on this view, very much like the public role of being spectators of sporting events, but in crucial respects very different from those public roles played by recipients of religious rites and party goers at the company picnic.

This strategy aims at focusing on what audiences and the other group kinds mentioned do, rather than on what others do for them that turns them into an audience. But in fact, it fails to specify any particular kind of action or feature of actions groups do, the doing of which has the relevant audience-generating effect. This is because the feature specified – being an observer – is a feature of a response of a given kind. It is not strictly true that the group does not take part in what is being done; for they take part just insofar as they observe and react to what they observe in the appropriate way. But this just means they have been turned into an audience by some prior action of some kind. And now we are back to the first general strategy, namely that of indicating some particular sort of triggering action that prompts just this kind of response.

Neither strategy for distinguishing activities that involve performances for audiences from other similar public gatherings is fully satisfactory, because each seems to need something like the other to make it work. This suggests some sort of combined strategy is needed, one in which the specified feature of the activities of those who become performers is rationally connected to the specified feature of the responses of those who become audiences. Two competitor strategies of a combined sort come readily to mind. The first derives from a philosophical story, originated by Grice, about communication. On this story, performing requires not only that someone do something, A, with the intention of communicating P but also that someone else, in order to receive this performance (to understand that P is meant by A), must recognize that the first person intends that A means P (Grice 1957). The last clause specifies a 'common knowledge' aspect in Grice's story about communication. A second combined strategy is a story about the creation of observation spaces. On this view, what gets created in public performances (by either the potential performer or the potential audience) is a kind of space in which the performing and observing are done. Varieties of this view have been proposed by some theater theorists and practitioners (Boal 1990, Brook 1995).

An advantage of the Grice-style strategy has to do precisely with the requirement of knowledge of communicator's intentions on the part of the communicatee. This seems to be exactly the kind of knowledge on the part of those who will function as audience that was required to make the 'doing something for' strategy work, to generate an 'audience response.'

The main problem with the Grice-style strategy, oddly enough, has to do with the very same feature. Remember that the account we give in response to the first question must not end up precluding features we already know to hold true of more specific kinds of performance types. But many interesting effects on audiences for theater and dance, even effects that contribute ultimately to the audience's grasp of meanings, happen without cognitive recognition on the part of audiences that are intended to have those responses.

Consider two general types of theatrical effects. First, an audience's sense of the power of a performance or of the intimacy in the performance is created by effects of which many audiences are completely unaware. Such effects are induced by means of the ways actors are grouped, their relative proximity to the audience, their elevation in the audience's visual plane, their postures, the specific lighting, the specific sounds used as background or even the absence of other sounds.

Second, an audience's sense of the meaning of the lines spoken by actors can vary according to effects of which they may be unaware. The same line said in the same way may be understood by an audience in different ways if it is delivered while the actor is walking towards the audience, across the stage in front of them, or while backing or walking away from them. The feel of a line can be altered by such factors as whether the piece is presented in proscenium, thrust, or round (three traditional theater arrangements).

Insofar as these kinds of effects take place without cognitive recognition on the part of audiences that are intended to have those responses, requiring that audience uptake involve recognition of the performer's intentions is simply too strong a requirement in an account of theatrical performance. So, since it excludes this feature of theatrical performances, we should reject the Grice-style account of the more general phenomenon of that kind of public gathering that constitutes a performance.

Finally, let us examine the creation-of-observation-spaces strategy. This view holds that a performance is created by any action having the feature of creating a public and presently active observation space where none had been before. This strategy is also a combined strategy, for it specifies a feature of an action, creating an observation space, that can be done by potential performers or potential audiences or both, and has the desired role-generating effect on each. Specifically, no matter who actually does the action, this feature is thought to be of a kind that could trigger a distinctively audience-like reaction having the effect of generating a functionally distinct group that plays the role of audience.

This is a promising strategy. Like our first strategy, this one does not preclude further distinctions between artistic and non-artistic performances, nor does it preclude from performances in general, features we already know to hold true of more specific kinds of performance type. Like our second strategy, this one seems to pick out what it is about some people in gatherings that separates them from others, and in the relevant ways. And, at least as far as we have gotten with the strategy, the feature specified seems to sort group kinds in more or less the right ways: if a public and active observation space is created, some people are functioning in it as an audience, and they are acting very much like spectators of sporting events, but in crucial respects very differently from recipients of religious rites and party goers at the company picnic. Moreover, like our third strategy, this one would seem to require some level of common knowledge, for, just insofar as an individual is still part of the group in which an observation space is created, the individual could hardly be unaware an observation space had been created. But this strategy avoids the pitfall of the third strategy; for an observation space to be created, those in the role of audience do not have to know all the communication intentions of those playing the role of performers.

Of course, actually playing out the strategy is another matter, and one for which there is no room in the present essay. But, within the kind of strategy we have developed so far, we can examine other aspects of theater as a social phenomenon to see how they might be brought to bear on our second and third questions. In the remainder of the essay, I will first argue that theater is an inherently social activity, and I will examine what bearing that fact could have on the distinctions between theater, dance and musical performance. Second, I will point out some kinds of relationship that exist between specifically theatrical performers and their audiences, and I will examine what bearing they could have on the distinctions between theater, dance, and musical performance.

Theater involves public gatherings. It takes place in public spaces, spaces that are socially and often legally set aside for its performances. The word 'audience,' as it is used in the familiar formulation 'audience for art,' does not necessarily mean actual gatherings of people. But as the word 'audience' is used with respect to theater it does. Theater is an inherently social activity.

The thesis that theater inherently involves gatherings of people is compatible with the claim that a theatrical performance may take place with only a few audience members, only one, or even none at all. For that thesis has to do with the nature of a contrast between the practice of theater and the activities involved in the practices of the other performing arts.

This point can be understood most clearly by observing a distinction between what we may call 'audience practices' and 'non-audience practices.' An 'audience practice' is the conduct of some activity requiring some level of skill for its execution, with a view to presenting the activity, some of its features, or its products to an audience. A 'non-audience practice' is the conduct of some activity requiring some level of skill for its execution with a view to realizing the activity, some of its features, or its products by the persons engaged in the activity.

Of course, a non-audience practice of playing music might be observed. A group of musicians playing by themselves might be overheard by passers-by. And that music may be listened to by those passers-by with just the same kind of attention and pleasure as they would have had were they to have gone to a concert hall to hear this music performed (Walton 1979). This does not, by itself, transform our musicians' non-audience practice into an audience practice of playing music. Similarly, if a group of musicians, playing on-stage in front of an audience in the concert hall where they have been hired to play, nevertheless feel they are playing among themselves, this does not transform their activity into a non-audience practice of playing music.

The point is that, whereas playing music and dancing are activities that commonly can have both audience and non-audience forms of practice, there seems to be no activity of theatrical playing that has a common non-audience practice form. The thesis that theater inherently involves gatherings of people just comes to the claim there are no common non-audience practices that are recognizably the making of theater.

One might think that games of make-believe should be counted as the common non-audience practice of theater. The proponent of this view would be right to point out that make-believe or the propensity to engage in make-believe is among the raw ingredients in human nature utilized in theatrical craft. But, whereas we do not hesitate to think of people at a party, for example, as dancing or singing, when children engage in games of make-believe we do not think they are making theater, but only by or for themselves.

What are we to make of this contrast between theater, dance, and music? Not much, I think. The fact that theater has no non-audience practice marks out no feature that can be used to distinguish theater from the others, when all are considered under the aspect of audience practices.

Let us then examine several of the particular relationships that exist between theatrical performers and theater audiences. There are three kinds of relationships that might seem to distinguish theater from the other performing arts.

First, spatio-temporal relationships characteristic of theatrical performance can be illustrated by a fact about any more or less familiarly standard performance of *Hamlet*. In a standard performance it will be true that 'Hamlet leaves the room if and only if the actor playing Hamlet leaves the stage room.' Of course there will be non-standard performances in which one or both of these conditionals will not be true. Still, generally, it is the case that whenever references are made in performances to times and places other than those of the performance event, performers and audiences remain, and remain aware they are present to each other.

The fact that audiences and performers are mutually present may become a theme of a performance. This may have some philosophical importance for the task of distinguishing theater from dance and musical performance. After all, in neither dance nor musical performance (at least standardly) do performances involve references to other times and places. However, whether we have a handle on what we need here requires a much longer discussion, concerning the nature of theatrical presentation and representation. And it is not yet clear we can just help ourselves to this feature in carrying out our task. For one thing, it is not obvious what exactly it means to say that in theater there are 'references' to other times and places.

That there are variations as to how audiences and performers are present to each other is another matter. For the relationships between any given variation and the content of a performance is a matter for aesthetic analysis in a way that may be distinctive of theater. Several more or less standard variations of spatial arrangements exist, each of which has associations with different kinds of access to the content of a performance (Hilton 1987, Carlson 1996). A simple pair of examples will help us here. In an arena arrangement for a fairly standard performance, there usually will be no large vertical objects, because that would prevent some members of the audience from seeing some of the stage action most of the time; and, without such objects in the set, many effects creating a sense of grandeur will be impossible. On the other hand, arena arrangements are usually much more intimate than are most proscenium arrangements. These arrangements in theater have effects on reception, both as to mode and to content, that do not seem to have analogs in dance and musical performances, even when the cues for reception are similar (that is movements and sounds). So, here we might think to locate some distinguishing features among the activities of dance, musical performance, and theater.

A caveat is in order. Showing that a set of features is distinctive to a practice is not enough to show it is the set of features that distinguishes the practice from some others. It may be nothing more than a generalization true of the practice but having no criteriological role to play (Tilghman 1984: 13). Nevertheless this line of inquiry does look promising.

A second kind of relationship has to do with the connections between the intentions of performers and the expectations of audiences. Performers have intentions with respect to what audiences are to be aware of in their perform- ance, and perhaps with respect to how audiences are to react to their performance. Audiences in turn have expectations of performers that can impose restrictions on what performers can intend. Some of these intentions and expectations are fully conscious in the moment of performance and can have immediate effects on the event itself. Perhaps this accounts for our sense of the liveness in theatrical performance. But other intentions and expectations are shaped before, and independently of the moment of performance.

Of these, some are consciously chosen and others are accepted as part of the cultural environment by both performers and audiences. Typically, an actor's decision as to how to deliver a line is a conscious choice. Equally typically, the choice to deliver most of the lines either standing, walking, or sitting in front of the audience, and the audience's expectation that this is how it shall be done, are more nearly shaped by the cultural environment the performer and audience share. This can be brought out by imagining what would have to change for it to be common and commonly expected practice for actors to deliver their lines while walking upside down on their hands out among the audience.

One issue that needs analysis here is how these intentions and expectations, occurrent and dispositional, play a role in enabling the performers to activate desired audience responses and contribute to audience uptake of the material content being presented to them. Another important feature of this set of relationships has to do with the fact that out of them comes most of what we recognize as what counts as style, movement, and tradition in theater. But exactly how styles, movements, and traditions are embedded in, and effectively expressed by, the intentions and expectations of performers and audiences is not yet analyzed.

Whatever the analysis we give here, however, it seems unlikely we will find much to say about theater that is different on these issues from what we might say about musical performance and dance. In all three cases, details of content aside, there are questions about intentions and expectations that affect the relationships between performer and audience in much the same sorts of ways.

Third, in some manner, performers engage in shared cooperative activities with each other (Gilbert 1990, Bratman 1992) and with audiences. These phenomena are intricately bound up with both the creation and the reception of theatrical performance. But they are involved in different ways in the creation, as opposed to the reception, of a theatrical performance. Members of the performing ensemble engage in activities requiring mutual responsiveness, engaging sets of intentions, and relying upon some degree of shared knowledge. Of course, the same things can be said for some of the relations between the ensemble and the audience. But surely the contents of the responses, intentions, and beliefs will be different in the two relationships. Three examples suffice to show this. We would not expect an audience member to start saying a character's lines in response to a cue from one of the performers; ordinarily that is the wrong kind of response on the part of an audience member. Members of an ensemble may intend a specific moment in the performance to evoke astonishment in the audience; but audiences do not share an intention with each other to become astonished at such moments, nor do they share an intention with the performers that they will respond with astonishment at such moments. And finally, the ensemble usually knows how the scene is about to be played in a way that even the most perceptive audience can only be said to guess, at least on first audition; that kind of knowledge is usually not shared between ensemble and audience.

The phenomenon of 'shared cooperative activities' plays significant roles in dance and music. I do not see any obvious differences in the ways in which the phenomenon works in the three performing arts. I think it unlikely then that any further analysis of this phenomenon will yield much by way of a distinction among theater, dance, and musical performance.

In sum, I have suggested that a promising account of what makes a public gathering a public performance is that it is created by some action having the feature of generating a public and presently active observation space. I have said nothing about what then makes a performance into an artistic performance. Although I have not argued for it, I think it worth considering that this may turn out to be a matter to be determined more by appeal to historical conditions and traditions than by resort to philosophical argumentation. But there are some promising lines of philosophical inquiry, having to do with spatio-temporal relationships in particular, concerning the articulation of some distinct, if not distinguishing, features among the various performing arts.

See also Aristotle, Nietzsche, Tragedy, Music, Literature, Dance.

References

Aristotle (1941) *Poetics*, in R. McKeon (ed.), *Basic Works of Aristotle*, New York: Random House.

Boal, A. (1990) *Theatre of the Oppressed*, New York: Theatre Communications Group.

Bratman, M. (1992) "Shared Cooperative Activity," *Philosophical Review* 101: 327–41.

Brook, P. (1995) *The Empty Space*, New York: Simon and Schuster.

Carlson, M. (1996) *Performance*, London: Routledge.

Gilbert, M. (1990) "Walking Together: A Paradigmatic Social Phenomenon," *Midwest Studies in Philosophy* 15: 1–14.

Grice, H. P. (1957) "Meaning," *Philosophical Review* 66: 377–88.

Hilton, J. (1987) *Performance*, London: Macmillan.

Kristeller, P. (1951) "The Modern System of the Arts (I)," *Journal of the History of Ideas* 12: 496–527.

Kristeller, P. (1952) "The Modern System of the Arts (II)," *Journal of the History of Ideas* 13: 17–46.

Saltz, D. (1998) "Theater," in M. Kelly (ed.), *Encyclopedia of Aesthetics*, New York: Oxford University Press.

Schechner, R. (1993) *The Future of Ritual*, London: Routledge.

Thom, P. (1993) *For an Audience*, Philadelphia: Temple University Press.

Tilghman, B. (1984) *But Is it Art?* Oxford: Blackwell.

Turner, V. (1982) *From Ritual to Theater Performance*, New York: PAJ.

Walton, K. (1979) "Style and the Products and Processes of Art," in B. Lang (ed.), *The Concept of Style*, Ithaca: Cornell University Press.

Further reading

Blau, H. (1990) *The Audience*, Baltimore: Johns Hopkins University Press. (The first serious study, largely influenced by deconstructive philosophy, of the performer–audience relationship, especially as it obtains in theater.)

Borges. J. "Averroe's Search," in D. Yates and J. Irby (eds), *Labyrinths*, New York: New Directions. (This story provides an exceptionally clear thought experiment about a culture in which no theater exists.)

Fischer-Lichte, E. (1992) *The Semiotics of Theatre*, Bloomington: Indiana University Press. (A classic semiological analysis of theater.)

Hamilton, J. (1982) "Illusion and the Distrust of Theater," *Journal of Aesthetics and Art Criticism* 41: 39–50. (A criticism of the idea that there is anything that is essentially theater, let alone that it could be essentially the creation of illusion.)

Saltz, D. (1991) "How to Do Things On Stage," *Journal of Aesthetics and Art Criticism* 49: 32–45. (A very clear analysis of the ontology of theater relying on a suitably and substantially modified speech act analysis of the theatrical event.)

States, B. (1985) *Great Reckonings in Little Rooms: On the Phenomenology of Theater*, Berkeley: University of California Press. (A classic study of theater from a phenomenological point of view.)

Velleman, D. (1997) "How To Share An Intention," *Philosophy and Phenomenological Research*, 57: 29–50. (A critical examination of the phenomenon of shared intentions, especially as they figure in discussions of cooperative activities.)

INDEX